For Jenny Christmas (...)

CZECHOSL

THE ROUGH

*Kathryn, Joan &
David.*

ROUGH GUIDE CREDITS

Series Editor: Mark Ellingham
Editorial: Martin Dunford, John Fisher, Jack Holland, Jonathan Buckley, Greg Ward,
   Richard Trillo, Jules Brown
Production: Susanne Hillen, Kate Berens, Gail Jammy
Typesetting: Andy Hilliard

Thanks to everyone at Kennington Lane for help and support: to **Herr Holland** who edited it (with help from Dan Richardson and Jules Brown); Kate Berens for patient proofreading; and Andy Hilliard for typesetting.

Thanks too to all at Middleton Road, particularly the out-laws; to Kate, Nat, Al and Adam (and the 400/Four) for getting up as early as the Czechs and Slovaks, the Brabec boys from Nižkov, Pavla Kloudová and her glass tea-pot, Viera Langerová for a place to stay on Petržalka, the old folks back in Wetherby, Don Sparling for some serious grounding, Jim Bittner, Simon Broughton, Ivan Plicka, Christine Minářová, Miroslav Hrubý aka Louis, Norman Lebrecht, Mr Peter Biely at ČEDOK in London, Robert Pynsent, David Gill for help with the margarine, Morven McLean at Keston College, Jan Kavan and of course our comrades downstairs on the *Rough Guide* to Poland. And, right at the last moment, a big hello to Stan.

The publishers and authors have done their best to ensure the accuracy and currency of all the information in
Czechoslovakia: The Rough Guide; however, they can accept no responsibility for any loss, injury or
inconvenience sustained by any traveller as a result of information or advice contained in the guide.

This reprint published by Rough Guides Ltd, 149 Kennington Lane, London SE11 4EZ
Distributed by Penguin Books, 27 Wrights Lane, London W8 5TZ
Prevously published by Harrap Columbus.

Typeset in Linotron Univers and Century Old Style to an original design by Andrew Oliver
Printed by Cox & Wyman, Reading, Berks
Reprinted 1991 and 1992

Illustrations in Part One and Part Three by Ed Briant.
Basics illustration by Tommy Yamaha. Contexts illustration by Sally Davies.

432pp. includes index

British Library Cataloguing in Publication Data:

A catalogue record for this book is available from the British Library.

ISBN 1-85828-009-5
(previously published by Harrap Columbus Ltd under ISBN 0-7471-0260-0

CZECHOSLOVAKIA

THE ROUGH GUIDE

Written and researched by

ROB HUMPHREYS

with additional contributions by

Gerard Davies, Jonathan Bousfield, Andrew Tickle

Edited by
Jack Holland
with Jules Brown and Dan Richardson

THE ROUGH GUIDES

CONTENTS

Introduction xiii

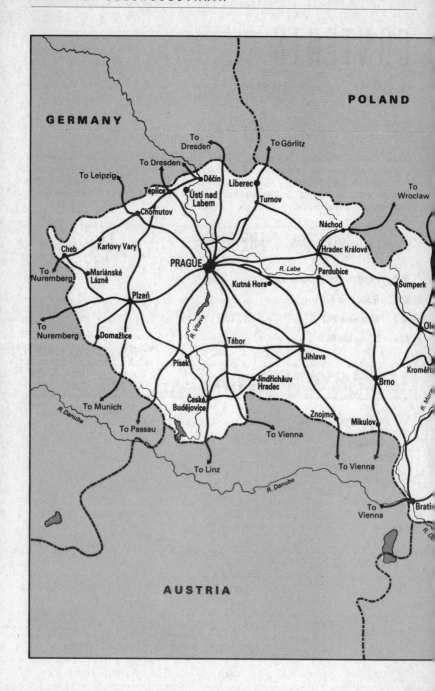

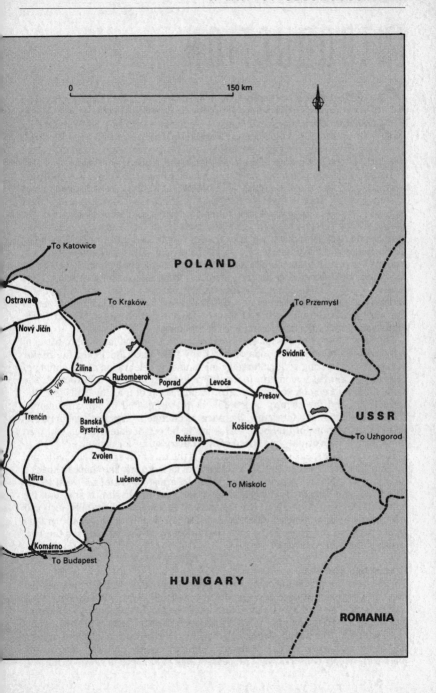

INTRODUCTION

Czechoslovakia has rarely been in full control of its historical destiny. The Nazis carved up the country in 1938, only twenty years after its foundation; the Iron Curtain descended just ten years later; and in 1968, Warsaw Pact tanks trampled on the country's dreams of "socialism with a human face". Even now, Czechoslovakia's future success will be determined more in the corporate and banking institutions of the West than in the ministries of Prague.

Yet the events of November 1989 in Czechoslovakia – the **Velvet Revolution** – were probably the most unequivocally positive of all the recent happenings in Eastern Europe. True to their pacifist past, the Czechs and Slovaks shrugged off forty-one years of Communist rule without so much as a shot being fired. "In Poland it took ten years, in Hungary ten months, in East Germany ten weeks, perhaps in Czechoslovakia it will take ten days" enthused Tim Garton Ash, arriving in Prague on "Day Seven". He wasn't far wrong. The rapid emergence of a leader of impeccably democratic intellectual and moral credentials helped boost the people's exhilaration in the face of an uncertain future. But as Václav Havel himself was the first to admit, his presence alone has not been – and will not be – enough to overcome the enormous difficulties involved in transforming one of the most orthodox and stable of state-socialist societies into a Western-style democracy with a fully functioning market economy.

For the visitor, all of this makes Czechoslovakia a fascinating place to travel in right now. More accessible today than at any time since the 1930s, the **major cities** are still buzzing with cultural life in continuing celebration at the ending of censorship, and fail to conform to most people's idea of Eastern Europe. At the same time, the remoter regions are more reminiscent of the late 1940s than the early 1990s, and the country as a whole is not yet geared up for consumptive Western-style tourism. Inevitably, the **pace of change** in Czechoslovakia means that certain sections of this book are going to be out of date even as you read them, such is the volatility and speed of the country's transformation.

Geographically speaking, Czechoslovakia is the **most diverse** of all the former Eastern Bloc countries. In the 900 kilometres of its long, fish-like shape, it spans a full range of cultural influences, from the old German towns of the west to the Hungarian and Ukrainian villages in East Slovakia. In physical terms, too, it's impossible to generalise about Czechoslovakia: Bohemia's rolling hills, lush and relentless, couldn't be more different from the flat Danube basin, or the granite alpine peaks of the High Tatras, the beech forests of the far east, or the coal basins of the Moravian north.

Czechs and Slovaks

The sharpest division in the country now is no longer between Party member and non-Party member, or even between the new Left and Right, but between **Czech and Slovak**. The Czechs who inhabit the western half of the country – Bohemia and Moravia – are among the most Westernised Slavs in Europe: urbane, agnostic, liberal and traditionally fairly well-off. The Slovaks who inhabit the eastern half of the country – Slovakia – are by contrast fervently Catholic, and, for the most part, deeply conservative. The peasant way of life here is slowly dying out, but the traditional codes of conduct which accompany such an agrarian society remain embedded in Slovak cultural life.

This Czech-Slovak divide is something you'll come across again and again. Czechs and Slovaks rarely mix socially, they visit one another's republics only as tourists and know little about each other's ways, relying instead on hearsay and prejudice. To the older generation of Czechs, the Slovak language is a rather peculiar peasant dialect, and the Slovaks themselves tainted either with their wartime collaboration, or more recently with Communist collaboration – Husák, Bilak and Indra, the three greatest exponents of the post-1968 "normalisation" policy, were all from Slovakia.

Talk of the imminent **break-up of Czechoslovakia** is alarmist: few people, Slovak or Czech, support such drastic measures. The country's ethnic divide is more manifest in their mutual ingrained bigotry, a problem exacerbated by the last forty years of neglect. Even the much-vaunted economic imbalance between the advanced Czech republic and the backward Slovak one counts for little compared with the country's overall dire straits vis-à-vis Western Europe. In any case, with its enormous emigré backing (there are estimated to be over one and a half million ethnic Slovaks in the United States), Slovakia may soon be in a better economic position than the Czech Lands.

Where to go and when

Almost entirely untouched by the wars of this century, Czechoslovakia's capital, **Prague**, is justifiably the most popular destination in the country, and many visitors never leave its environs. Yet, being at the centre of the westernmost province, **Bohemia**, Prague is perfectly poised for launching off into the countryside. Both the gentle hills and forests of **South Bohemia**, one of central Europe's least-populated regions, and the **spa towns of West Bohemia** – Karlovy Vary, Mariánské Lázně and Františkovy Lázně – are only a couple of hours' drive from Prague. **Mountains** form Bohemia's natural borders, and the weird **sandstone "rock cities"** in the north and east of the region are some of its most memorable landscapes.

Moravia, the country's most central province, is every bit as beautiful as Bohemia, though the crowds thin out significantly. The largest city, **Brno**, has its own peculiar pleasures – not least its inter-war functionalist architecture – and gives access not only to the popular Moravian karst region, but also a host of other nearby castles and chateaux. The north of the region is often written off as an industrial wasteland, but **Olomouc** is a charming city, more immediately appealing than Brno, and a short step away from the region's highest mountains, the **Jeseníky**.

By no means a Slovak Prague, **Bratislava** nevertheless has its virtues, and its compact old town is lively day and night. Slovakia has some of Europe's highest mountains outside the Alps: they have long formed barriers to industrialisation and modernisation, preserving and strengthening regional differences in the face of Prague's centralising efforts. Medieval mining towns like **Banská Štiavnica** and **Kremnica** still smack of their German origins, and the cathedral capital of the east, **Košice**, was for centuries predominantly Hungarian. In the **Orava** and **Liptov** regions, many of the wooden-built villages, which have traditionally been the focus of Slovak life, survive to this day. In the far east, bordering Poland and the Soviet Union, **Carpatho-Ruthenia** has a timeless, impoverished feel to it, and is dotted with wooden Uniate churches and monuments which bear witness to the heavy price paid by the region during the liberation of World War II.

Generally the **climate** is decidedly continental with short, hot summers and bitterly cold winters. Spring and autumn are often both pleasantly hot and miserably wet, all in the same week. Winter can be a good time to come to Prague: the city looks beautiful under snow and there are fewer tourists to compete with. Other parts of the country have little to offer during winter (aside from skiing), and most sights stay firmly closed between November and March.

Taking all this into account, the **best months to come** are May, June and September, thereby avoiding the congestion which plagues the major cities and resorts in July and August. Prague in particular suffers from crowds all year round, though steering clear of this high season will make a big difference. In other areas, you may find yourself the only visitor whatever time of year you choose to go, such is the continuing isolation of the former Eastern Bloc countries.

AVERAGE TEMPERATURES (°F)												
	Jan	Feb	March	April	May	June	July	Aug	Sept	Oct	Nov	Dec
Prague	-1	0	4	9	14	17	19	18	14	9	4	0
Brno	-2	-1	3	8	13	16	18	17	14	8	3	-1
Bratislava	-1	0	5	10	15	18	20	19	16	10	4	0
Banská Štiavnica	-3	-2	2	7	12	15	18	17	13	8	2	-1
Košice	-3	-2	3	9	14	17	19	18	14	9	3	-1

Note that these are **average daily temperatures**. At midday in summer, Bratislava can be blisteringly hot. Equally, in most mountainous regions it can get extremely cold and wet at any time of year.

PART ONE

THE
BASICS

GETTING THERE

By far the most convenient way to get to Czechoslovakia is by plane, with flights from London twice daily throughout the year. Rail tickets work out only slightly less expensive, though they provide the option of breaking your journey along the way.

FLIGHTS

The easiest way to get to Czechoslovakia is to **fly to Prague**. Since the events of 1989, *ČSA* (Czechoslovak Airlines) and *BA* (British Airways) have both increased the number of **scheduled flights** to the country. *BA* offer daily flights all year round, while *ČSA* fly daily except Wednesdays and Sundays. The cheapest ticket you'll find from either airline is an Apex return fare of around £220 between April and September; about £20 cheaper over the winter period. The usual Apex fare restrictions apply: reservations must be booked at least 14 days in advance, you must stay over for one Saturday night and there's a refund of 50 percent on tickets cancelled before the 14-day deadline. Tickets are valid for three months and can be booked direct from either airline or from most high-street travel agents.

Both airlines offer **under 24** youth fares of £180 return or £100 one-way, which can only be booked the day before departure, and are subject to availability. Those **over 60** can get a special summer return fare of around £175 with the same restrictions as an Apex ticket, and you can take a friend over 55 with you for the same price.

Charter flights to Prague are thin on the ground, only occasionally making it into the "bucket shop" adverts of the various London freebie magazines, *Time Out*, *The Evening Standard* and the quality Sunday papers. If there are any bargains going, specialist discount flight agents like *STA* and *Campus Travel* should be able to help you. Even so, you'll be pushed to find a return fare of less than £150, and in peak seasons flights are booked up weeks in advance. It might be worth considering flying to a neighbouring European capital like Berlin or Vienna, from which the return fares can cost as little as £100, though of course you'll have to add on the cost of travel from these places into Czechoslovakia.

FLIGHTS FROM EIRE

There are no direct flights from Ireland to Czechoslovakia, so the easiest option is to get to London and make your bookings from there. Independent travel experts *USIT* (O'Connell Bridge, 19/21 Austin Quay, Dublin 2; ☎001-778117) are the best people to consult.

FLIGHTS FROM DOWN UNDER

There are currently no direct flights from Australia or New Zealand to Prague; it's cheaper to fly to London or any other major European city and pick up a discount flight from there. *ČSA* run flights from Prague to Singapore and vice versa, with bucket shops in Singapore offering much better deals than the official Apex price of over £1800 return. It's worth contacting **STA**, 1a Lee St, Railway Square, Sydney 2000 (☎2/212 1255), and in New Zealand, **STS**, 10 High St, PO Box 4156, Auckland (☎9/399 723), who have their finger on most of the cost-cutting exercises possible in air travel – see the phone book for other branches in other cities.

> Prices for all tickets to the West bought inside the country are likely to remain artificially high and payable in Western currency only. Make sure you buy a return ticket before you get there.

TRAINS

Taking the **train** to Czechoslovakia is arguably the most pleasurable way of getting there, allowing you stopoffs in other European cities en route, but it won't save you much money on the flights, especially if you're over 26. An ordinary **return fare** to Prague will set you back £211 and take 24 hours on the fastest route (via Ostend) with a change at Cologne. The more circuitous route (via Paris) is not only more pleasant (it's a through-train from Paris) but cheaper, with special discount return fares at around £188. **Tickets** (which can be bought from any *BR* ticket office and most high-street travel agents) are valid for two months and allow one stopoff en route. Bicycles go free of charge, though take a couple days extra to get there.

If you're **under 26**, *Eurotrain* offer a return fare of £135 either via the Hook of Holland or Ostend (but not Paris) and then Cologne, Stuttgart, Nuremberg and Plzeň. If you travel overnight on the Hook of Holland ferry you'll be charged an extra £12 each way and get some lousy connections. Tickets are valid for two months with unlimited stops en route. If you're under 26 and travelling for less than a month, the best option is an **InterRail** pass, which costs £175 and entitles you to free travel for a calendar month across all European railways including Turkey and Morocco, as well as half-price on

British Rail and reductions on certain ferry services including *Sealink*. Inside Czechoslovakia it allows free travel on a railway system which connects almost every town and village in the country (albeit slowly). If you're intending Czechoslovakia to form a stopover on your European travels, this is the ticket to go for. A variation on the standard card is the **InterRail Flexicard** (£145), which provides the same benefits as the InterRail pass but is valid for any ten days within a month.

RAIL ENQUIRIES

British Rail European Travel Centre, Victoria Station, London SW1 (☎071-834 2345).

Eurotrain 52 Grosvenor Gardens, London SW1 (☎071-730 3402)

COACHES

It would be difficult to argue that travelling by coach is anything but a last resort. There is just one direct coach service to Prague, which runs every Saturday from the Czechoslovak embassy in London. Operated by *Kingscourt Express* (☎0860-791754), tickets cost around £85 return, and the journey time is about 24 hours. *Eurolines* (52 Grosvenor Gardens, London SW1; ☎071-730 8235) run coaches to Munich every Thursday, Friday and Saturday leaving at 9.20am; tickets cost £55 single and £94 return, but remember it'll cost you about half as much again to reach Prague from Munich.

DRIVING AND HITCHING

Driving to Czechoslovakia can hardly be considered the most relaxing option, but with two or more passengers it can work out relatively cheap. From Calais or Ostend the most direct route is via Brussels, Cologne, Frankfurt and Nuremberg, entering the country at the Waidhaus–Rozvadov border crossing; a distance of around 1200km. Some people prefer to head further north to Bayreuth and cross at the Schirnding–Pomezí border post, especially if aiming for the spa region of West Bohemia. Although it's perfectly possible to do either route in under 24 hours, it makes more sense to allow a couple of days and break the journey somewhere in the hills of southern Belgium or the northern Rhineland. An alternative route which halves the distance driven is to catch a ferry from Harwich to Hamburg (20hr) and drive down via Berlin and Dresden, but bear in mind that you must book a couchette on the ferry which makes the single adult fare plus medium-sized vehicle over £110. Contact *Scandinavian Seaways* at Parkeston Quay, Harwich, Essex CO2 4QG (☎0255-241234) or 15 Hanover St, London W1 (☎071-493 6696).

If you're **hitching** to Czechoslovakia your best bet is to follow the Ostend–Nuremburg route. Buying a train/ferry ticket to Ostend or Calais will save you the hassle of hitching out of London and on to the Belgian autoroutes. Hitching in Belgium, Germany and Czechoslovakia will seem like a doddle compared to anywhere in Britain, but again don't bank on getting there in less than two days. For all trips overland you should take a few Belgian francs and some Deutschmarks for the journey.

Another possibility is to take advantage of the German *Mitfahrzentralen* organisation who link up drivers and hitchers for a small fee plus a bit towards petrol. It won't get you to Prague, but for £35 you can get to Berlin. There's a *Mifahrzentralen* office at 50–60 Grant Place, Croydon CRO 6PJ (☎081-654 3210).

ORGANISED TOURS

As the red tape involved in travelling to Czechoslovakia begins to dissolve, the attractions of the **package deal** start to diminish. The only tour operator which actually specialises exclusively in Czechoslovakia is **ČEDOK** (see box below for address, and also "Information and Maps" for more on what *ČEDOK* have to offer),

who charge fairly exorbitant rates for what you get. *ČEDOK's* cheapest tour is the City Break in Prague, with a return flight from London and three nights' accommodation for around £270; better value are the seven-night deals at around £370 per person. With the City Breaks, there's no compulsion to go on any organised tours once you're there, but should you wish to, each activity will cost extra.

All the other tours *ČEDOK* offer involve being chaperoned around to a greater or lesser extent. You can take in three nights in Prague, one in Bratislava and another three in Budapest (around £470); the same tour with two nights in Warsaw instead of one in Bratislava (around £590), or three nights each in Vienna and Budapest and four in Prague (around £690). *ČEDOK* run a variety of eight-day coach tours around the country which all cost around £300. The agenda can vary enormously. The trip to the High Tatras, for example (around £300), allows you a full five days to explore the mountains at your own leisure, while the fourteen-day Grand Tour of Czechoslovakia (around £410) leaves you very little time to yourself. A six-night beer tour takes in two nights at the Munich Oktoberfest, a tour round the brewery at Plzeň (Pilsen) and two nights in Prague, all for around £440.

As well as the above tours, a number of operators (including *ČEDOK*) also offer more specialist holidays – mountain/spa vacations, music tours, hunting parties, art history packages and plenty more. Some companies, like *Daysaway*, will sort out an itinerary to suit your requirements, though they deal only with group bookings. *ČEDOK* are the best people to approach for skiing packages.

SPECIALIST TOUR OPERATORS

Bike Events PO Box 75, Bath BA1 1BX (☎0225-480 130). Cycling tours.

Blair Travel and Leisure 117 Regent's Pk Rd, London NW1 (☎071-483 2297). Performing arts.

ČEDOK 17–18 Old Bond Street, London W1 (☎071-629 6058). General tours plus ski and spa holidays.

Daysaway 118 Cromwell Rd, London SW7 (071-370 0657). Open to suggestions for group tours.

Euroexpress (☎0293-511125) Offer day trips to Prague from Gatwick for £156 each.

Explore Worldwide 1 Frederick St, Aldershot GU11 1LQ (☎0252-344161). Summer hiking tours.

Prospect Art Tours 10 Barley Mow Pass, London W4 (☎081-995 2151). Art history.

Regent Holidays 13 Small St. Bristol BS1 1DE (☎0272-211 711). General and specialist tours.

Specialtours 81a Elizabeth St, London SW1 (☎071-730 2297). High-brow "theme" arts tours.

Travelscene 11–15 St Ann's Rd, Harrow, Middlesex HA1 (☎081-427 4445). Three- and five-night holidays in Prague.

RED TAPE AND VISAS

British, Irish, US and Canadian nationals need only a full passport to enter Czechoslovakia. British subjects can stay for up to six months; all other nationals are allowed three months. If you hold a New Zealand or Australian passport you'll need a visa (valid for 30 days), available from a Czechoslovak embassy or consulate – usually on the day – for £20.

Visas cannot be obtained at the border except at the four German and Austrian road crossings, and are not valid until you've exchanged a minimum of DM30 for each day of your intended stay. If you need an **extension**, the local police office will issue one without too much fuss for around 100kčs. If you need to stay longer than three months (or six if you're British), you'll have to fill in the application form *Žádostface o povolení dlouhodobého pobytu na území ČSFR*, attach six photos and pay a fee of 100kčs. It's best to try this at the head passport office at Olšanská 2, Žižkov, Prague.

CUSTOMS

Since the Velvet Revolution in 1989, **border controls** have relaxed considerably. When entering by road or rail (and occasionally by plane) you may be asked to declare any cameras, tape recorders or any other Western consumer goods as well as the amount of Western currency you are importing. On leaving the country your baggage may be checked to make sure you haven't sold any of the stuff on the black market, and that you've changed your money at the official exchange rate. Export controls are notoriously restrictive (officially you're only allowed to export 600kčs worth of goods, and the export of almost everything from spare parts for cars to children's clothes is forbidden), but in practice they're only interested in people trying to smuggle large amounts of high-quality Bohemian crystal and glassware over the border.

Duty-free allowances when travelling in to Czechoslovakia include 250 cigarettes, one litre of spirits and two litres of wine.

CZECHOSLOVAK EMBASSIES AND CONSULATES

UK and Eire 28 Kensington Palace Gardens, London W8 4QX (Mon–Fri 10am–1pm; ☎071-727 3966).

Australia 169 Military Road, Dover Heights, Sydney, NSW 2030 (☎02-371 8878).

Austria Penzinger Strasse 11–13, 1140 Vienna (☎1-894 3741).

Belgium 152 Avenue A. Buyl, 1050 Brussels (☎02-647 5898).

Canada 50 Rideau Terrace, Ottawa, Ontario K1M 2A1 (☎514-849 4495).

France 15 Avenue Charles Floquet, 75 007 Paris (☎47 34 29 10).

New Zealand 12 Anne St, Wadesdown, PO Box 2843, Wellington (☎04-723 142).

USA 3900 Linnean Ave N.W., Washington DC 20008 (☎202-363 6315).

HEALTH AND INSURANCE

However small or large the medical problem, on production of a passport all foreign nationals can get free medical care, with a nominal charge for certain drugs or medicines which have to be imported from the West. There are no inoculations required for Czechoslovakia but health standards are coming under increasing criticism.

HEALTH CARE AND HOSPITALS

Minor ailments can be easily dealt with by the **chemist** or *lekárna* (in Slovak *lekáreň*), but language is likely to be a major problem outside the capital. If it's a repeat prescription you want, take any empty bottles or remaining pills/capsules you have with you. If the chemist can't

help you they'll direct you to a **hospital** or *nemocnice* (in Slovak *nemocnica*). As in the West, doctors are over-worked but unlike their Western colleagues they're also underpaid. Again, outside Prague language will be the biggest problem, although technical terms in Czech/Slovak and English often have a common Latin or Greek root. If you do have to pay for any medication, keep the receipts for claiming on your insurance once you're home.

Tap water is officially safe but few Czechs or Slovaks drink it after recent statistics here revealed that over 70 percent of the country's waterways are seriously polluted. Luckily there are hundreds of natural springs which pump out gallons of sparkling mineral water, though it's an acquired taste for those used to Western brands.

INSURANCE

Since health care is practically free, it's not absolutely essential to take out any **insurance**. However, most travel insurance policies cover many other eventualities like permanent injury and theft, so it's a very wise investment. Ask about policies at any bank or travel agency, or use a specialist low-priced firm like *Endsleigh Insurance* (97 Southampton Row, London WC1; ☎071-436 4451), who offer a month's basic cover for around £20. If you do have anything stolen (including money), register the loss immediately with the police, as without a report you won't be able to claim.

COSTS, MONEY AND BANKS

Compared to other Eastern Bloc countries, Czechoslovakia has always been well-off. Right now though, the standard of living is likely to take a temporary tumble, as the transition to a market economy, favoured by the present government, is made.

Until January 1991 the Czechoslovak crown was a non-convertible currency: it could not be bought or sold on the foreign exchange markets, but was nominally linked in value to the Deutschmark. Now the crown is **fully convertible** and no longer protected from the uncertainties of market forces, its value is likely to plummet drastically – at least until the economy stabilises. For years the crown was fixed at 5kčs to 1DM, making it roughly 15kčs to the pound. An indication of the real value of the crown came in early 1989 when there was an auction of hard currency by various state industries which had a surplus of the stuff – one US dollar went for over 100kčs. Now it's anybody's guess.

Nevertheless, for the Western tourist Czechoslovakia is likely to remain a **very inexpensive** place to visit. Prague, Bratislava and the High Tatras have always been slightly more expensive than the rest of the country, and if anything these differences will become more marked as time goes on. But your main problem will be keeping up with the unexpected price-rises and devaluations which are certain to accompany the country's moves towards a market economy. Confusion is the worst of this, since your hard currency will retain (or increase) its value as the crown nose-dives. Already for many transactions the **US dollar** and the **Deutschmark** rule supreme; it's virtually impossible to rent a flat in Prague, for example, unless you pay in hard currency. With the currency now fully convertible, and most state subsidies being withdrawn, inflation is likely to rocket in the near future. For this reason we've refrained from quoting exact figures either in crowns or hard currency in the main body of the book, using relative terms (cheap/moderate/expensive) as a guide instead. The following points give some indication of what these terms mean.

COSTS

Even with the recent price rises (100 percent and more in many cases) you can easily get by on a **daily budget** of £10–15 or less. In fact, you'd be hard pushed to spend over £20 a day outside Prague, even if you tried.

Accommodation is the largest daily expense, with hostels and private accommodation still relatively scarce and hotel prices artificially inflated for foreigners. All this will no doubt change under the new government, but at the time of going to press a double in an average hotel costs between £5–8, private rooms £4–7 per person and hostels as little as £1–2 a night. In Prague, however, where demand still far outstrips supply, you can expect to pay anything from £10 to over £200 for a double hotel room.

All other **basic costs** like food, drink and transport continue to rise as the ending of all subsidies takes its toll and increased taxes are placed on items such as alcohol and tobacco. Even so, a good meal washed down with a couple of beers in a provincial restaurant will set you back as little as £2–3 a head, and even in the top-class city establishments, prices rarely go much over £10–15 a head. Only if you have your own vehicle will you find money slipping through your fingers – in this case hard currency – as you are charged almost £3 a gallon for high-octane fuel.

MONEY

The currency in Czechoslovakia is the crown or *koruna* which is divided into one hundred *heller*. There are **notes** of 10kčs, 20kčs, 50kčs, 100kčs, 500kčs and 1000kčs; and **coins** of 5h, 10h, 20h, 50h, 1kčs, 2kčs and 5kčs. A whole new series of notes replacing the old workerist ones is being gradually introduced so that any 1000kčs notes issued before 1985 are now invalid. Production has also stopped on the new bile-green 100kčs note introduced only months before the Velvet Revolution and sporting a picture of Klement Gottwald, Czechoslovakia's first Communist President.

CHANGING MONEY

At the time of writing, regulations on buying Czechoslovak crowns at British banks were uncertain: it's likely that they will be available, in limited quantities, at a few days' notice. In the meantime, **travellers' cheques** in US dollars or Deutschmarks are undoubtedly the safest way of carrying your money, but you'll have to go to a bank or a five-star hotel to exchange them, and in the more remote regions anything except *American Express* will get a close inspection (and even rejection). Border-post exchange offices almost certainly won't accept anything except cash, worth remembering if you're arriving outside banking hours. **Eurocheques** are unknown outside the three big cities.

Credit cards like *Visa* and *Master Card* (*Access*) are accepted in most hotels, upmarket restaurants and some of the flashier shops. You can also get cash on your plastic at banks and five-star hotels, subject to withdrawing a minimum of the equivalent of £50. It's a good idea to keep at least some hard currency in **cash** for emergencies because it will be accepted almost anywhere. With the banks offering virtually the same rates as the streets, the attraction of resorting to the **black market** is pretty slim for Westerners. Before the currency reform, it was a universal and fairly harmless pursuit, occasionally interrupted by a plainclothes policeman, but nowadays, it really doesn't seem worth the risk – you'll have to change a large amount to make any great profit out of the deal.

INFORMATION AND MAPS

Before you leave, it's worth dropping in at the Czechoslovak Travel Bureau (ČEDOK) to pick up a stock of their copious supply of leaflets and bumph. As well as the usual glossy brochures, they have useful rough maps of the country, showing the major campsites, spas and rural attractions, along with details of the latest regulations and changes likely to affect the traveller.

TOURIST OFFICES

Prague and Bratislava both have tourist offices (*PIS* in Prague and *BIPS* in Bratislava) specifically set up to give information to foreign visitors. Otherwise **ČEDOK**, the state-controlled travel agency, has branches in most Czechoslovak towns, generally open Monday to Friday 9am to noon & 1 to 5pm, plus Saturday mornings in larger places. Originally conceived as a travel agency for Czechs and Slovaks to book their organised tours round the Eastern Bloc, *ČEDOK* offices rarely have any maps, brochures or information about the town you're actually in, and in addition, their staff are notoriously underpaid, unmotivated and unhelpful. In larger cities there should be at least one person who speaks faltering English, and in the smaller towns someone may speak German. Really, the only reason for going to *ČEDOK* is to book a hotel room – but they only deal with the more expensive ones, and, at the moment, won't touch private rooms. A nominal fee is charged for this service.

The lack of basic tourist information in almost every town in Czechoslovakia is one of the most glaring (and deliberate) omissions of the previous regime as regards tourism. Foreigners were effectively discouraged from embarking on individual travel in the country and rounded up into organised tours. Hopefully, this will change in the near future as locally organised tourist offices start to emerge, and Czechoslovakia wakes up to the income to be derived from tourism. . .and tourists.

MAPS

The regional and city maps in this guide should be fine for most purposes, but if you crave a bit more detail, all kinds of maps are available **in Czechoslovakia** itself, (though subject to the usual shortages). You can buy them, often very cheaply, from bookshops (*knihkupectví*) and some hotels – just ask for a *plán města* (town plan) or *mapa okoli* (regional map) followed by the name of the town or region. Gazeteered **town maps** with local bus, tram and trolleybus routes marked on, are available for most towns and cities.

For **road maps**, the 1:400,000 *Auto atlas ČSSR* (the country's old acronym) is cheap, written in four languages including English, and marks all campsites and petrol stations. A more detailed set of 17 1:200,000 maps covering the country is the *Poznávame československo* series which mark all castles, museums and other sights (though not campsites) as well as giving a brief dry English account of the major towns and villages. The same 1:200,000 maps under the title *automapa* list hotels, campsites (including diagrams helping you find them) and so forth, instead of the sight-seeing information, and are well worth considering if you're intending to camp in out-of-the-way places.

For **hiking**, the 1:100,000 *turistická mapa* series marks the complex network of coloured footpaths which weave their way across the country. Certain very popular regions are treated to 1:50,000 maps, but whichever one you get, make sure you make the right choice between the *letná mapa* (summer map) and the *zimní mapa* (winter map) which concentrates on pistes, ski-lifts and other such matters. Czech maps have their keys in four languages including English, but the Slovak ones present a few problems with the key in five languages – Slovak, Hungarian, Polish, Russian and German – but not English.

If you need to buy maps before you go, *Stanfords*, 12–14 Long Acre, London WC2 (☎071-836 1321) have the best selection, though you pay considerably more than you would in Czechoslovakia. Few of the big foreign cartographers cover the country, and those that do tend to be short on accuracy. One exception is the Austrian company *Freytag & Berndt* who produce a reasonable 1:600,000 fold-out road map of Czechoslovakia (£5.50). *Falk*'s origami map of Prague (£4.50) is the most useful to the city.

GETTING AROUND

The most pleasant way of travelling around Czechoslovakia is by train. The system, which has changed little since it was bequeathed to the country by the Austro-Hungarian Empire in 1918, is comprehensive, often breathtakingly beautiful but also rather slow. If you're in a hurry, buses are always quicker, more frequent and only slightly more expensive. Bus and train timetables can be found in the "Travel Details" section at the end of each chapter.

TRAINS

Trains go just about everywhere, and the antiquated rolling stock is a pleasure to travel in. The restaurant cars are still relatively cheap, and are run with a kind of shabby semblance of Austrian formality. Many of the stations in the Czech Lands recall the nineteenth-century civic pride which accompanied the building of the original tracks. In Slovakia, where the system is less developed, a lot of the journeys are worth making simply for the wonderful scenery. Try the Banská Bystrica–Diviaky line or the Brezno–Margecany trip in the Low Tatras. As state subsidies are reduced, costs will rise: a second-class single from Prague to Košice (perhaps the longest journey you'd ever have to make) currently costs about £2.50; expect it to rise.

TRAINS AND RESERVATIONS

The Czechoslovak State Railways, *Československé státní dráhy (ČSD)*, run two main **types of train**. *Rychlík* trains are the faster ones which stop only at major towns, costing very little per kilometre, though almost double the price of an *osobnývlak* or local train which stops at every single station on the line and averages about 30km an hour. Other fast trains go by the name of *expres* or *spěšný*. It's actually better to avoid the international expresses which, although theoreti-

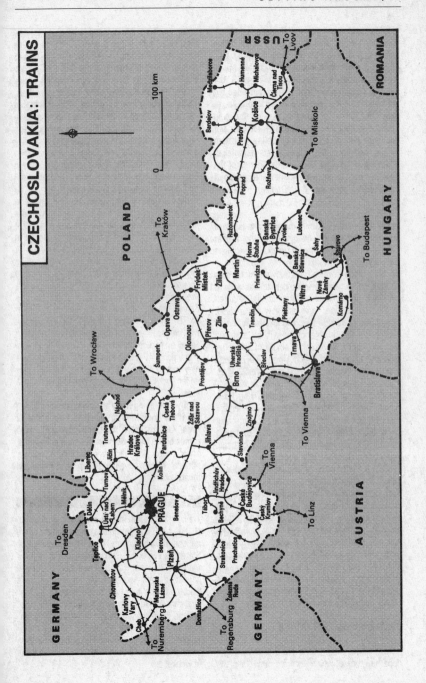

CZECHOSLOVAKIA: TRAINS

cally fast, often get delayed at border crossings. All international through-trains and any other services marked with an "R" surrounded by a box, require a **seat reservation** or *místenka* (*miestenka* in Slovak). For those marked with an "R" but without a box, reservations are recommended but not obligatory: it's advisable to get one if you're travelling at the weekend on one of the main routes. The *místenka* only costs a few crowns, but you must get it at least an hour before your train leaves, and after you've purchased your ticket. Write down the time, date and destination of the train you want to catch and join the long queue at the special window marked *místenka*.

TICKETS

A ticket (*jízdenka* in Czech *lístok* in Slovak) for a domestic journey can be bought at the station (*nádraží* in Czech *stanica* in Slovak) before or on the day of departure. If you're buying it in advance, write down all the relevant information on a piece of paper and hand it to the clerk to avoid any linguistic misunderstanding. Compared to Western Europe, fares are very low indeed, though not so for the Czechs and Slovaks: if you simply say the destination, it will be assumed that you want a second-class single on an *osobný vlak* (the ticket most Czechoslovaks buy). If you want a return ticket, you must say *zpáteční*. First-class carriages exist on all fast trains: say *první třída* (in Slovak *prvá trieda*) when asking for a ticket. These first-class tickets are 50 percent more expensive but should guarantee you a seat on a busy train if you've forgotten to buy a *místenka*. If you end up in the wrong carriage, you'll be fined 100kčs on the spot.

ČSD run **sleepers** to and from a number of cities, and the couchettes are reasonably priced. You must, however, book as far in advance as possible and in any case no later than 6 hours before departure. There are 50 percent reductions on fares for those over sixty or under twelve, and you can take two children under five for free (providing they don't take up more than one seat). There are even some "creche carriages" on the slower trains, for the exclusive use of mothers and children under five. Smoking is not allowed on any domestic service in Czechoslovakia.

STATIONS AND TIMETABLES

Under the heading *zpoždění*, the larger stations have a simple airport style flip-over arrivals and departure board which includes how late the

train is running Many stations have poster-style displays of arrivals and departures, the former on white paper, the latter on yellow, with fast trains printed in red. In addition to the above, all but the smallest stations have a comprehensive display of **timings and route information** on rollers. These timetables may seem daunting at first, but with a little Czech or Slovak they should become increasingly decipherable. First find the route you need to take on the diagrammatic map and make a note of the number printed beside it in red; then follow the timetable rollers through until you come to the appropriate number. The only problem now is language since everything will be written in Czech or Slovak, and few railway workers speak English or even German. Arrivals are *příjezd* or *príchod* in Slovak (*příj./prích.* in short form) and departures are *odjezd* or *odchod* in Slovak (*odj./odch.* in short form). A platform or *nástupiště* is usually divided into two *kolej* (in Slovak *kolaj*) on either side. Some of the more common notes at the side of the timetable are *jezdí jen v* (only running on) or *chodí len v* in Slovak, followed by a date or a symbol: a cross or an "N" for a Sunday; a big "S" for a Saturday; two crossed hammers for a workday; "A" for a Friday and so on. Alternatively it could be *nejezdí v* or *nechodí v* (not runnning on). Small stations may simply have a board with a list of times under the title *směr* (direction) followed by a town.

If you're going to be travelling on the trains a lot, it's a good idea to invest in a timetable or *jízdní řád* (in Slovak *cestovný poriadok*) which comes out in May and sells out soon afterwards. There's one for each region and a bumper national edition, available from bookshops and tobacconists.

BUSES

Trains will take you most places but if you have to change a lot, it might be easier to take one of the regional **buses** (*autobus*) run by the Czechoslovak State bus company, *Československá státní automobilová doprava* (*ČSAD*). From city to isolated hamlet, there's always a bus service of some kind, and from town to town it's usually faster (and consequently more expensive) than the train. Bear in mind though that in rural areas, timetables are often designed with the working and/or school day in mind. That means up and out at 6am and back at around 3pm, with few or no services at weekends.

Bus stations are usually next to the train station and if there's no separate terminal, you'll have to buy your ticket from the driver. The bigger terminals are run with train-like efficiency, and it's absolutely essential to book your ticket in advance if you're travelling at the weekend or early in the morning on one of the main routes. Bus **timetables** are even more difficult than train ones, due to the lack of a map at any of the stations. Just scour the services until you spot your destination (see "Stations and Timetables" for key phrases). Minor bus stops are marked with a rusty metal sign saying *zastávka*. If you want to get off, ask *můžu vystoupit?* (in Slovak *môžem vystúpiť*); "the next stop" is *příští zastávka* (in Slovak *ďalšia zastávka*). It's probably not worth buying any of the ten bulky timetables which cover the country, but you might feel the urge to buy at least volume 11 which details the *medzinárodné a diaľkové linky* (international and long-distance services).

URBAN PUBLIC TRANSPORT

Urban public transport is generally excellent, with buses (*autobus*), trolleybuses (*trolejbus*) and even the occasional tram (*tramvaj* or *električka* in Slovak) runnning from dawn until around midnight (and all night in the three big cities of Prague, Brno and Bratislava), each journey costing just one or two crowns. With a few exceptions, such as in Olomouc, you must buy your ticket before getting on board. Tickets are available from newsagents, tobacconists, hotel receptions or one of the yellow machines at the stop, and are validated in the punching machines once you're on board. There are no conductors but if you're discovered without a valid ticket you'll be fined 100kčs on the spot. **Inspectors** travel around checking tickets at the most unlikely times of the day, wearing the most unlikely gear; so be warned. If you're a tram freak, you might like to know that the following cities still have trams: Prague, Plzeň, Most, Liberec, Brno, Olomouc, Ostrava, Bratislava and Košice. The rolling stock is mostly circa 1950, with only Prague having more recent models. Certain cities, each listed in *The Guide*, run all their old trams on one day in the year, right down to the horse-driven carriages.

TAXIS

With such a good public transport system, you should have little need to use **taxis**, which are considerably more expensive though still rela-tively cheap by Western European standards. The easiest way to get one is to go to a taxi rank: hailing them can be a fruitless business. Make sure the meter is switched on as soon as you set off and (even better) ask the driver how much he or she reckons the journey will cost. Fares go up by 50 percent after 10pm.

CARS, MOTORBIKES AND HITCHING

With fewer than one in ten people owning a vehicle and most of those only used at the weekend, travelling by **car** in Czechoslovakia is a very relaxing way of seeing the country. Road conditions are generally not bad, but, apart from a few stretches of dual carriageway built by the occupying Germans during the war, there's just one fully fledged motorway to speak of. The only place where you might encounter any problems is in the bigger cities, where the lane system is confusing, tramlines hazardous and parking a nightmare.

PAPERWORK

As far as **paperwork** goes, you'll need to carry the vehicle's registration document. If it's not in your name, you must have a letter of permission signed by the owner and authorised by the *AA*, *RAC* or other official body (this does not apply if you're hiring a car). You'll also need your **driving licence** (international driving licences aren't officially required) and although it's not compulsory it's a good idea to carry an international **green card**, which costs around £20 for a month's third party, fire and theft cover and is available from any *AA* or *RAC* insurance office. You're also required to carry a red warning triangle, a first-aid kit, a set of replacement bulbs and display a national identification sticker.

RULES AND REGULATIONS

Rules and regulations are pretty stringent – a legacy of the old police-state – and on-the-spot fines are regularly handed out, ranging from a pathetic 20kčs to over 200kčs. The basic rules are driving on the right; compulsory wearing of seatbelts outside built-up areas; children under 12 travel in the back. **Speed limits** are 110kph on motorways (and if you travel any faster you *will* be fined), 90kph on other roads and 60kph in all cities, towns and villages between 5am and 11pm. In addition, there's a special speed limit of 30kph for level crossings (you'll soon realise why if you try ignoring it). It's against the law to have any alcohol in your blood when you're driving and in the bigger towns if you're driving after 11pm there's a strong chance of being stopped and breathalised. Other petty rules include no changing lanes just before a junction; no U-turns in the road; no crossing over the white lines in the middle of the road (broken or unbroken) unless it's to overtake etc, etc. The driving offence which most commonly catches foreigners unawares is the one about **parking and waiting**. You're likely to get into trouble if you stop – or even pause – in any of the following places: on the ridge of a hill, within fifteen metres of a pedestrian crossing, intersection, bridge or level crossing. Also, don't overtake a tram when passengers are getting on and off, if there's no safety island for them.

As a driver, one of the most unnerving aspects of Czechoslovak roads is the lack of road markings at junctions, so look out for a signpost showing a yellow diamond; this indicates that you have right of way.

PETROL

For the moment at least, foreigners must buy special *Tuzex* coupons from any bank for all types of **fuel**, and with the price of petrol hovering around 60p a litre (and likely to rise*), it's an expensive proposition. If you're arriving in the country at a weekend, make sure you buy some in advance (from your national branch of *ČEDOK*: addresses on p.9) or you'll be left stranded until the banks open on Monday morning.

Petrol or *benzín* comes in two types: *super* (96 octane) and *special* (90 octane); diesel or *nafta* is also available but two-stroke petrol or *mix* which powers the old East German Trabants and Wartburgs is being phased out. Remember that petrol stations aren't as frequent as in Western Europe and most are closed at lunchtimes and after 6pm (though 24-hour ones can be found in all major cities). **Lead-free** petrol, known as *natural* or *bezolovnatý* is available from a handful of garages in the Czech Lands, (*ČEDOK* publish a list of them) but seldom so once you get east of Bratislava.

---

* At the time of going to press, the country was experiencing a major energy crisis, caused by the sudden switch to hard currency trade by the country's main oil supplier, the Soviet Union, and compounded by the Gulf Crisis. This has caused mile-long queues and severe petrol shortages.

BREAKDOWNS AND SPARES

If you **break down**, dial ☎154 at the nearest phone and wait for assistance. For peace of mind it might be worth taking out an insurance policy like the *AA* Five-Star scheme, which will pay for any on-the-spot repairs and, in the case of emergencies, ship you and all your passengers back home free of charge. Every other car in Czechoslovakia is a Škoda and the rest are Ladas and Trabants, so obtaining **spare parts** for any other vehicles can be a lengthy and costly process. Small (Polish) Fiats, Renault 12s and VW Golfs are probably slightly better catered for than most, but there are few Western-marque garages other than in Prague and Bratislava (see the "Listings" sections for details). If it's simply a case of a flat tyre, go to the nearest *pneuservis*.

CAR HIRE

Car hire in Czechoslovakia is fairly dear – currently around £185 per week for a Škoda with unlimited mileage. Cars can be booked through the usual agents in Britain (see box). In Czechoslovakia there are two state firms with branches in most major cities: *Pragocar*, whose head office is at Praha 1, Štěpánská 42 (☎02-352 825) and *Brnocar*, Solniční 6, Brno (☎05-24039) (in Bratislava *ČEDOK* deal with car hire), both of which charge much the same rates as the major Western firms, with payment acceptable only in hard currency. Another possibility is to hire a car in Germany or Austria where rates are much cheaper (around £125 for the equivalent machine) and drive it over the border.

INTERNATIONAL CAR HIRE RESERVATIONS

Avis ☎081-848 8733
Budget ☎0800-181 181
Europcar ☎081-950 5050
Hertz ☎081-679 1799

MOTORCYCLES

Czechoslovakia is a great country for **motorcycling** – except for the speed limit, which was designed for domestic bikes, the biggest of which are the Jawa 350s which the police ride. In towns and villages the limit is 60kph but out on the open roads and even on motorways the limit is 80kph. Unless you ride a Jawa, or the other domestic machine, an MZ, be prepared for crowds of curious onlookers to surround your bike in every town and village. Helmets are compulsory as is some form of eye protection (goggles or visor) for the driver. Pillion passengers must wear helmets outside built-up areas. It is not possible to hire motorbikes or mopeds in Czechoslovakia.

HITCHING

Hitching throughout Czechoslovakia is fairly good. Despite the low cost of public transport, it's still too much for many young people and there's usually a long line of hitchers on the roads out of town. The main problem is the lack of vehicles, so to hit what rush hour there is, you'll have to set out early – and that means 6–8am. Although many Czech and Slovak women hitch, usually in pairs, women travelling alone should still exercise the usual caution about which lifts to accept. "Where are you heading?" is *gde jdete?* and if you want to get out of the car, just say *můžu vstoupit* ("I want to get out").

PLANES AND BOATS

Domestic flights run by *ČSA* and the Slovak airline, *Slov-Air*, link all major cities in Czechoslovakia. Though not exactly cheap, particularly when compared with the train or bus, they can prove useful if time is short and you want to get to the east of the country quickly. Prague to Košice (via Bratislava), for example, works out at about £40 single fare (you can pay in crowns), nearly three times the train, but reduces the journey time from twelve hours to two. If you do decide to fly, make sure you book well in advance – demand is high, and flights to places like Poprad in the High Tatras are booked solid in the high season. Further details can be had from *ČSA* offices in most large towns.

The opportunity for travelling by **boat** is pretty limited in a land-locked country like Czechoslovakia, but there are a few services worth mentioning. From Prague, boats run by *ČSAD* (the state bus company) sail all the way down to Zvíkov, with a change of vessel at each of the dams on the way. There's also a summer service on Lake Lipno in South Bohemia. German boats chug down the Labe (Elbe) between Děčín and Dresden, although information and tickets can be difficult to obtain from the Czech end. Finally *Czechoslovak Danube Navigation* operate a service between May and September from Bratislava to Vienna or Budapest. **Tickets** cost roughly £15 return and must be paid for in hard currency. Tickets to Vienna tend to be heavily booked up in advance by tour groups, and if you're heading for Budapest you'll need to get a Hungarian visa before you set off. It might be easier to settle for the domestic service between Bratislava and Komárno which operates daily from April to September and costs very little.

CYCLING, WALKING AND ROCK CLIMBING

Cycling is, of course, the perfect way to see a small-town country like Czechoslovakia. You'll have to bring your own machine (and plenty of spare parts), since, as yet, very few places hire out bikes. The surfaces are pretty tough on the backside and even the rolling hills of Bohemia are hard work. A mountain bike is the ideal choice, particularly if you're thinking of checking out any of the backroads over the mountains. Taking a bike on the train is not usual behaviour in Czechoslovakia, but it's easy enough to persuade the guard on a local train to let you on, perhaps for a small fee.

Walking is a very popular pastime in Czechoslovakia. Young, old or indolent, they all spend their weekends following the dense network of paths which cover not just the hills and mountains but the whole countryside. All the trails are colour-coded with clear markers every 200m or so, and signs which tell how long it'll take you to reach your destination. The walks are usually fairly easy-going, but it can be wet under foot even in summer and, particularly if you venture into the mountains proper, you'll need some fairly sturdy boots. There are no hiking guides in English, but it's a good idea to get hold of a *turistická mapa* of the region, which details all the paths in the area, as well as any campsites, hostels and hotels (see "Information and Maps").

There are some great opportunities for **rock climbing** in Bohemia and Slovakia. North and east of Prague are concentrated areas of limestone and basalt rocks: the most popular is the Český ráj, just 80km northeast of the capital; equally good is the Český Švýcarsko region which borders with Saxony, or the Adršpach rocks near the Silesian border. In Slovakia, the Slovenský raj offers smaller-scale sandstone opportunities, whereas the Malá Fatra and the Tatras themselves are in a different league – higher altitudes and longer, more arduous climbs. You'll need to take your own equipment wherever you go, and take the usual precautions on all climbs.

FINDING A PLACE TO STAY

For the moment at least, finding a place to spend the night can be the most difficult part of travelling in Czechoslovakia. Visitors from abroad have traditionally been shepherded into the state hotels where prices for foreigners (*cizinci* or *cudzinci*) are nearly three times those for Czechoslovaks. Unfortunately this attitude still prevails, and there are very few ways to escape from it; the country has only a handful of youth hostels (and they're nearly always full) and the private room network is still in its infancy. When the new laws on private enterprise take effect, and the currency finally becomes fully convertible, many of the problems outlined below will – hopefully – be somewhat alleviated.

If you're going to one of the big cities at a time when demand for beds will be great (from late spring to late summer, and over the Christmas holidays), it's sensible to arrange accommodation before you arrive; the accommodation situation in Prague is particulary difficult, with visitors shunted out to dingy hotels miles from the centre. Most people book their accommodation through *ČEDOK* in London, who'll arrange as many nights as you like in as many different towns as you like. The snag is that they only book the more expensive hotels (£40 a night and upwards in Prague). Cheaper outfits – like *TK Travel* (14 Buckstone Close; ☎081-699 8065) and *Czechbook Agency* (52 St John's Park; ☎081-853 1168) who offer private and self-catering accommodation throughout Bohemia and Moravia ($12–

15 per person/per night), and *Travel 2000* (Hlavní 74, 62 400 Brno; ☎05-74 61 88/62 15 41) who arrange private accommodation with families who speak some English – are beginning to emerge. Another alternative, if you speak at least some German, is to use the listings in *The Guide* to ring and book a hotel yourself.

HOTELS

Czechoslovakia's **hotels** are classified from A to C, according to the facilities they provide and the price they charge. The flashier hotels use the star system, but whatever scale is used, letters or stars, it should be taken as only the roughest of guides – conditions and prices vary greatly from one part of the country to another. Generally though, you'll pay a great deal more in Prague (£10 and upwards for a double room) than in any of the other cities, and considerably less in the countryside (£3 a double is rock-bottom) – and remember, too, that singles are sometimes difficult to find. The biggest problem is that, even in the most unlikely out-of-the-way places, hotels are often booked up with tour groups. Try some pleading and/or bribing, and at the very least, the receptionist might ring round other hotels in the area to check vacancies for you.

Hotels themselves tend to be drab, concrete affairs, often a glorified high-rise on the outskirts of town. There are, of course, exceptions, particularly in the spas, although the interiors of even the older buildings have been routinely modernised. Most hotel rooms are sparsely furnished, with just a wash-basin and the obligatory *Tesla* radio permanently tuned to the state radio station. Facilities are often mere gestures; hot water can be a real find (as can clean toilets) and even heating is erratic – it's either boiling and you can't turn the thing off, or else it's unremittingly cold. In the top hotels, of course, you can be fairly certain of pristine service and overheated rooms. **Breakfast** is normally not included, unless you're paying a lot for your room. If it is, you'll be given a voucher which covers a specific amount of money, which you hand in to the waiter as payment. Without fail, hotels also have a restaurant and/or a bar and often double as the town's nightclub.

It seems unlikely that any Czechs or Slovaks are going to be able to buy out any of the state hotels, or even set up their own in the near future. Those hotels that have been sold off (usually the expensive ones), are frequently joint ventures with the Western partner having no more than a 49 percent stake – room prices tend to be high in these places.

PRIVATE ROOMS AND HOSTELS

Private rooms exist in most major cities and resorts, but until recently Westerners were only allowed to stay in them in Prague, Brno and Bratislava, with a minimum stay of three nights. With the new law on private businesses passed in 1990, and most Czechs and Slovaks desperate to supplement their income, there should be a huge increase in the number of private rooms available. Just keep your eyes peeled for signs saying *pokoj* or more likely *Zimmer Frei*. Prices used to be fixed at 50kčs per person per night, but expect to pay more than this now – or the equivalent in hard currency.

A handful of Czechoslovak **youth hostels** called *Juniorhotels*, run by *Cestovní kancelář mládeže (CKM)*, charge as little as 50kčs per person to IYHF members (considerably more to non-members). The problem is they're booked up long in advance by youth groups. If you book them from abroad, the price leaps up to around £7–8 a night. These anomalies may be ironed out now that the crown is convertible: if not, you'll just have to hope for vacancies.

In the mountains of the Krkonoše and the High Tatras, there are a fair number of **mountain huts** (*bouda* or *chata*) scattered about the hillsides. Some are little less than hotels and cost over £5 a double, but the more isolated ones are simple wooden shelters costing as little as £1 per person. None are accessible by road, but many are only a few miles from civilisation. Ideally, these should be booked in advance (through *ČEDOK* in Vrchlabí for the Krkonoše, or *Slovakoturist* in Nový Smokovec for the High Tatras) but this can only be done at the moment from inside the country – a lengthy and bureaucratic process. If you turn up before 6pm at the more isolated ones, you may strike lucky but don't bank on it – best to take a tent with you just in case.

A more reliable alternative to the youth hostels in the big university towns is **student accommodation**, which is let out cheap to travellers in July and August. The beds, usually in dormitories, cost about 50kčs per person for students, double that for non-students. Again,

they're heavily booked up in advance by groups, but they'll try their best to squeeze you in. Curfews operate in many hostels and they tend to be pretty early (around 10–11pm). Addresses change each year, so to find out the current address, go straight to *CKM*, which has offices in most major towns (listed in *The Guide*), or drop in at the head office in Prague (Žitná 12, Nové Město, Praha 2; ☎02-294 587).

Rock-bottom accommodation comes in the form of *turistická ubytovna*, ridiculously cheap and basic **dormitory hostels** with few facilities beyond a bunk bed, toilet and cold shower. Normally, there are one or two in every town and village, but they're often owned by one of the big state corporations to house immigrant workers or for Czechoslovak workers' vacations. If they're open, it's usually because there's a group booked in; if there's no group booked in, they're generally closed. This Catch 22 situation is a regular feature of *turistická ubytovna*, but there are exceptions (most of which are listed in the text) and it's worth enquiring about them at the local *ČEDOK*.

CAMPING AND OTHER OPTIONS

Campsites, known as *autokempink*, are plentiful all over Czechoslovakia. Although some are huge, ostentatious affairs with shops, swimming pools, draught beer and so on, most are just a simple stretch of grass with loos and cold showers. Many sites feature **bungalows** (*chata*), sometimes reserved for certain organisations, but often out for hire for anything upwards of £5 for two people. The flashiest bungalows are really small chalets, while the most primitive are little more than rabbit hutches. *ČEDOK* produces a booklet listing most of the bigger sites.

The more basic campsites, called *tábořiště* (in Slovak *táborisko*), are only marked on the 1:100,000 tourist map. They open in the height of summer only, providing just *ad hoc* toilets and a little running water. Very few sites are open all year round, and most don't open until May at the earliest, closing mid- to late September. Even though prices are inflated for foreigners, costs are still reasonable; two people plus car and tent weigh in at around £1–2. The nicest thing about camping in Czechoslovakia is that camp-fires are allowed on almost all campsites, and guitar-playing sessions go on until well into the night.

Before the Velvet Revolution **camping rough** was strictly illegal, although most young Czechoslovaks and East Germans paid little or no attention to that. The problem for foreigners was that they had to register with the police for every night in the country. With the lifting of visa restrictions, it may become easier to camp rough. Obviously if you're in a camper van, you're very unlikely to get hassled.

FOOD AND DRINK

No doubt the regional differences in food were once as great as they are in folk costumes and dialect, but outside the home, forty years of intensive centralisation has produced a nationwide cuisine, mostly derived from the Germanic-influenced Bohemian cuisine, with a predilection for big slabs of meat served with lashings of gravy, dumplings and pickled gherkins, not to mention a good helping of sauerkraut.

Don't, however, judge Czechoslovak food by the mediocre fare served up in most restaurants. At home Czechs and Slovaks prepare the same dishes with a flair and imagination unknown to most state-trained chefs. If you don't get the opportunity to eat in someone's house, be prepared for some pretty stodgy servings of meat and one veg. On the plus scale, Prague ham is justly famous and Czech beer is among the best in the world*. Slovak food is traditionally spicier and more varied – a hangover from Hungarian rule. It's also possible to eat the real thing amongst the half-million strong Hungarian-speaking community of Bratislava and southern Slovakia.

---

* Even Hitler was tempted enough to break his life-long vow of vegetarianism and teetotalism and tuck into some Prague ham and Pilsen beer when he and his troops marched into the capital in March 1939.

Czechoslovakia is no place for **vegetarians** or health freaks; its meat consumption is one of the highest in the world, around half a kilo a day per head of the population. On top of that, most of the animals are factory farmed – you'll rarely see a field of cattle – and often seriously ill by the time they're slaughtered, rendering large parts of the carcass unfit for human consumption. Inefficiencies of agricultural production mean that even in this rich and plump land, you'll be offered very few fresh vegetables as a compensation. A direct consequence of this has been the lasting popularity of wild mushroom picking as a national pastime.

BREAKFAST AND TAKE-AWAY SNACKS

Most Czechs and Slovaks get up so early in the morning (around 5 or 6am) that they seldom start the day with anything other than a quick cup of coffee. The usual mid-morning snack is *párek* (in Slovak *párok*), perhaps the most ubiquitous **take-away food** in the country, a dubious-looking frankfurter (traditionally two – *párek* means a pair), dipped in mustard and served with a white roll (*v rohlíku*). In most towns, some wizened character will be selling *slané tyčinky* (a salted stringy cheese) on the street, a snack which the Czechoslovaks eat with the same gusto as we do crisps. In the autumn you'll find freshly cooked corn-on-the-cob (*kukuřice* or *kukurica*) sold on the streets. A Czech speciality all year round is *smažený sýr* (in Slovak *vyprážený syr*) – a slab of melted cheese (and, more often than not, ham) fried in breadcrumbs and served with a roll (*v housce*). If it's *plněný* or *se šunkou*, then you can be certain it's got ham in it, and it generally comes with a little tartare sauce. The greasiest option of the lot is *bramborák*, a thin potato pancake with little flecks of bacon or salami in it. Finally, there's *langoše*, though particularly prevalent in Slovakia, it's actually a Hungarian invention – a deep-fried doughy base smothered in garlic.

Western-style fast food has yet to hit Czechoslovakia, but judging from the popularity of the one and only "real" hamburger outlet in Prague, there's a big market for it. International street snacks that do exist include *hranolky* (chips) or *krokety* (croquettes), served with the domestic version of tartare sauce, a lot less piquant than its western counterpart. Czechoslovak crisps (called *chips*) are lightly salted, greasy and generally stale.

About mid-morning, most Czechoslovak workers head for the local **bufet**, a stand-up canteen, usually self-service (*samoobsluha*), serving slightly more substantial cheap food all day from as early as 6am until late afternoon, with a lunchtime rush between noon and 2pm. There's usually a lot of tired-looking meat sausages on offer, the cheapest of which is *sekaná*, bits of old meat and bread squashed together to form a meat loaf. For connoisseurs only. *Guláš* is popular – though most Hungarians would balk at it – usually *Szegedinský* (pork with sauerkraut) but sometimes *special* (with better meat and a creamier sauce). If you're feeling up to it, you could take a chance with some chicken roast on a spit.

Less substantial fare boils down to *chlebíčky* – artistically presented open sandwiches with differing combinations of gherkins, cheese, salami, ham and aspic – and great mountains of salad, bought by weight (200 grammes is a medium-sized portion) – *feferonkovýsalát* is a mildly hot pepper and pea salad, while *vajíčkový salát* is a rich egg and mayonnaise dish. Others, like *vlašský* or *talianský* (Italian) and *francouský* (French) *salát* are in reality Czechoslovak affairs with plenty of salami, ham, potato and mayonnaise.

BAKERIES

If the country's *bufet*s turn your stomach, it might be easier to gather your own provisions from a **bakery** (*pečivo*) – Czechoslovak bread is some of the tastiest around when fresh. The bread which creates the queues is *domáci*, meaning homemade (though it rarely is), a special version of the usual *kmínový chléb*, a brown rye-flavoured bread with a sprinkling of caraway seeds. Real rye-bread is *žitný chléb*, while *graham chléb* is a much lighter, whiter loaf, topped with an egg glaze. Despite the name, *Moskva* is a national favourite, a moist, heavy, bitter-sweet loaf which lasts for days. Rolls come in two varieties: *rohlík*, a plain white finger roll, and *houska*, a rougher, tastier round bun.

Czechoslovak bakeries also sell sweeter fare, though nothing like the cream cakes and pastries found in an English bakery. The pastry (*koláč*) is more like sweet bread, quite dry and fairly dense with only a little condiment to flavour it, such as almonds (*oříškový*), poppy seed jam (*mákový*), plum jam (*povidlový*) or a kind of sour-sweet Slovak curd cheese (*tvarohový*). Most bakers stock a hefty supply of biscuits (*sušenky*), as well as another national favourite *oplatky*, paper-thin wafers stuffed with chocolate or sugar.

COFFEE, CAKES AND ICE CREAM

Like the Austrians and Hungarians who once ruled over them, the Czechs and Slovaks have a grotesquely sweet tooth, and the coffee and cake hit is part of the daily ritual. **Coffee** is drunk black and described rather hopefully as "Turkish" or *turecká*. Downmarket *bufet*s sell *ledová káva*, a weak cold black coffee, but the king of the lot is *Viděnská káva* (Vienna coffee), a favourite with the old folks, not quite as refined as the Austrian original, but still served with an adequate dollop of whipped cream. Espresso coffee (*presso*) is becoming trendy in the big cities, though it rarely matches up to the Italian drink. Whatever you do, avoid *kapucín* which is nothing like the cappuccino it purports to be. **Tea** is drunk without milk and weak, although you'll usually be given a glass of boiling water and a tea-bag so you can do your own thing. **Milk** itself is rarely drunk on its own, though it can be bought in supermarkets – but bearing in mind that some 70 percent of it has recently been deemed unfit for human consumption due to pollution, it might be wiser to buy UHT milk. There's a wide selection of yoghurts and sour milks which you can buy in most supermarkets; *bílý jogurt* is natural yoghurt, but look out for *kefír* or *biokys*, the thick and thin respectively of the sour milks.

The *cukrárna* (in Slovak *cukráreň*) or cake shop is an important part of the country's social life, particularly on Sunday mornings when it's often the only place that's open in town. People scurry through the streets with piles of boxes under their arms, containing two main types of **cake**; *dort*, like the German *tort*, consist of a series of custard cream, chocolate and sponge layers, while *řez* are lighter square cakes, usually containing a bit of fruit. A *věneček*, filled with "cream", is the nearest you'll get to an eclair; a *větrník* is simply a larger version with a bit of added fresh cream.

Whatever the season, Czechs and Slovaks have to have their daily fix of **ice cream** (*zmrzlina*), dispensed from little window kiosks in the sides of buildings. In the *cukrárna* there's generally more choice, but it's at the outlets advertising *italská zmrzlina* (actually nothing like Italian ice cream) that the longest queues form.

MAIN MEALS

Sit-down *bufet*s do exist, but for a better class of food, it's best to head for a fully fledged restaurant (*restaurace* or *reštaurácia*) which serves hot meals non-stop from about 11.30am until 9pm: come any later and chances are you'll go away hungry. Wine cellars (*vinárna* or *vináreň*) – though not necessarily their kitchens – sometimes stay open after 11pm. Lunch (between noon and 2pm) is the main meal of the day and generally the best time to go to a restaurant when the choice of food is at its widest. Menus and prices are nearly always displayed outside, as well as the category of the establishment, from *sk. IV* (the lowest group) to *sk. I + 20%* (top-class outfits). Whether this system will be retained once private restaurants take off remains to be seen.

Away from the big hotels, the menu (*jídelní lístek* or *jedálny lístok* in Slovak) is usually in Czech or Slovak only and deciphering it without a grounding in the language can be quite a feat. Just bear in mind that the right-hand column lists the prices, while the far left column gives you the estimated weight of every dish in grammes; if what you get weighs more or less, the price will alter accordingly. A modest form of tipping exists, generally done by rounding up the bill to the nearest five or ten crowns.

Most menus start with the **soups**, one of the country's culinary strong points and mainly served at lunchtimes. Posher joints will have a serious selection of starters such as *uzený jazyk* (smoked tongue), *tresčí játra* (cod's liver) or perhaps *kaviárové vejce* (a hard-boiled egg with caviar on top). *Šunková rolka* is another favourite, consisting of ham topped with whipped cream and horseradish, but you're more likely to find yourself with less sophisticated fare such as cold meats.

Main courses are overwhelmingly based on pork or beef. The Czechs and Slovaks are experts on these meats, and although the quality could be better, the variety of sauces and preparative techniques beats traditional English cooking

hands down. The difficulty lies in uncoding names such as *klašterny tajemství* (mystery of the monastery) or even a common dish like *Moravský vrabec* (literally "Moravian sparrow", but actually just roast pork). Fish, chicken and other fowl like duck are listed under a separate heading. One luxury worth taking advantage of is that carp (the traditional dish at Christmas), a rare treat in Britain, is cheaply and widely offered just about everywhere in Czechoslovakia.

Most main courses are served with dumplings or **vegetables**, most commonly potatoes or sauerkraut, and less frequently peas or beans. **Dumplings**, though German in origin and in name, are now the mainstay of Bohemian and Moravian cooking. The term itself is misleading for English-speakers since they resemble nothing like an English dumpling – more like a heavy white bread. *Houskové knedlíky* come in large flour-based slices (four or five to a dish), while *bramborové knedlíky* are smaller and made out of potato and flour. In people's houses, you may be treated to *ovocné knedlíky* (fruit dumplings). Fresh salads are few and far between – beyond a bit of lettuce, tomato or cucumber in season – and arrive in a slightly sweet watery dressing.

With the exception of *palačinky* (pancakes) filled with chocolate or fruit and cream, **desserts**, where they exist at all, will be pretty unexciting. Even the ice cream isn't up to the standards of the street, so go to a *cukrárna* if you want a dose of sugar.

VEGETARIAN FOOD

Vegetarians in Czechoslovakia are going to have a pretty hard time, especially those who don't eat fish. As a serious meat-eating nation, denied access to much of the outside world for the last forty odd years, most Czechs and Slovaks simply can't conceive of anybody going through even a small portion of their life without eating meat (unless they're critically ill or clinically insane). So simply saying you're a vegetarian (*jsem vegeterián* for men, *vegeteriánka* for women) or that you don't eat meat or fish (*nejím maso nebo ryby*), may instil panic and/or confusion in the waiter – it's better to ask what's in the dish. Most menus have a section called *bezmasa* (literally "without meat") but this just means the dish is not entirely based around a slab of burnt flesh, for example *omeleta se šunkou* (ham omelette). The best you can hope for is *knedlíky s vejce* (dumplings and egg) or *omeleta s hrášem* (pea omelette), both of which most chefs will knock up for you without too much fuss. Another possibility is **pizza**, an approximation of which became popular in larger urban centres during the last years of state socialism. **Vegans** have little choice in restaurants, aside from certain pizzas; even dishes like beans or lentils regularly turn up with an egg plonked in the middle.

A FOOD AND DRINK GLOSSARY (IN CZECH/SLOVAK)

Basics

Snídaně/raňajky	Breakfast	Chléb/chlieb	Bread	Ovoce/ovocie	Fruit
Oběd/obed	Lunch	Maslo	Butter	Cukr/cukor	Sugar
Večeře/večera	Supper/	Houska	Round roll	Sůl/soľ	Salt
	dinner	Rohlík	Finger roll	Pepř/čierne	Pepper
Nůž/nôž	Knife	Chlebíček	Open	korenie	
Vidlička	Fork		sandwich	Ocet/ocot	Vinegar
lžíce/lyžica	Spoon	Med	Honey	Hořčice/horčica	Mustard
Deska/doska	Plate	Mléko/mlieko	Milk	Tartarská omáčka	Tartare sauce
Šálek/šálka	Cup	Vejce/vajcia	Eggs	Křen/chren	Horseradish
Pohár	Glass	Pečivo	Pastry	Rýže/ryža	Rice
Předkrmy/predkrmy	Starters	Maso/mäso	Meat	Knedlíky/knedle	Dumplings
Polévka/polievka	Soup	Ryby	Fish	Jidla na	Main dishes
Zákusky/Múčnik	Dessert	Zeleniny	Vegetables	objednávku	to order

Soups, fish and poultry

Boršč	Beetroot soup	Hrachová	Pea soup	Pstruh	Trout
Bramborová/	Potato soup	Kachna/kačica	Duck	Rajská/	Tomato soup
zemiaková		Kapr/kapor	Carp	paradajková	
Čočková/	Lentil soup	Kuře/kurča	Chicken	Sardinka	Sardine
šošovicová		Kuřecí/kuracia	Thin chicken	Zavináč	Herring/rollmop
Fazolová/fazuľová	Bean soup		soup	Zeleninová	Vegetable soup
Hovězí/hovädzia	Beef soup	Makrela	Mackerel		

Meat dishes

Dršťky/držky	Tripe	Kýta/stehno	Thigh	Šunka	Ham
Čevapčiči	Spicy meat	Ledvinky/obličky	Kidneys	Telecí/teľacie	Veal
	balls	Salám/saláma	Salami	Vepřové/bravčové	Pork
Hovězí/hovädzie	Beef	Sekaná	Meat loaf	Vepřové řízek/	Breaded pork
Játra/pečeň	Liver	Skopové/baranina	Mutton	bravčový rezeň	cutlet or
Jazyk	Tongue	Slanina	Bacon		schnitzel
Klobásy	Sausages	Svíčková/		Žebírko/rebierko	Ribs
Kotleta	Cutlet	sviečkovica	Sirloin		

Vegetables

Brambory/zemiaky	Potatoes	Květák/karfiol	Cauliflower	Ředkev/reďkovka	Radish
Cibule/cibuľa	Onion	Kyselá okurka	Pickled gherkin	Řepná bulva/	Beetroot
Česnek/cesnak	Garlic	Kyselé zelí/	Sauerkraut	cukrová repa	
Čočka/šošovica	Lentils	kyslá kapusta		Hranolky	Chips
Fazole/fazuľa	Beans	Lečo/liečo	Ratatouille	Špenát	Spinach
Houby/huby	Mushrooms	Mrkev/mrkva	Carrot	Zelí/kapusta	Cabbage
Hrášky	Peas	Okurka/uhorka	Cucumber	Žampiony/	Mushrooms
Chřest/špargľa	Asparagus	Rajče/rajčina	Tomato	šampiony	

Fruit and cheese

Banán	Banana	Oříšky/oriešky	Peanuts
Borůvky/borievky	Bilberries	Ostružiny/černica	Blackberries
Broskev/broskyňa	Peach	Oštěpek	Heavily smoked curd cheese
Bryndza	Goat's cheese in brine		
		Parenyica	Rolled strips of lightly smoked curd cheese
Citrón	Lemon		
Druh citrusu	Grapefruit	Pomeranč/pomoranč	Orange
Hrozni/hrozno	Grapes	Pivny sýr	Cheese flavoured with beer
Hruška	Pear		
Jablko	Apple	Rozinky/hrozienky	Raisins
Kompot	Stewed fruit	Švestky/slivky	Plums
Jahody	Strawberries	Třešeň/čerešňa	Cherry
Maliny	Raspberries	Tvaroh	Fresh curd cheese
Mandle	Almonds	Urda	Soft, fresh whey cheese
Meruňka/marhuľa	Apricot		
Niva	Semi-soft crumbly blue cheese	Vlašské ořechy/ orechy	Walnuts

Common terms

Čerstvý	Fresh	Nakládaný	Pickled
Domáci	Home-made	(Za)pečený	Baked/roast
Dušený/dusený	Stew/casserole	Plněný/plnený	Stuffed
Grilovaný	Roast on the spit	Slatký	Sweet
Kyselý/kyslý	Sour	Smažený/vyprážený	Fried in breadcrumbs
M.m.	With butter	Syrový/surový	Raw
Na kmíně/na ražni	With caraway seeds	Udený/údený	Smoked
Na roštu/na rasci	Grilled	Vařený/varený	Boiled
Nadiváný	Stuffed	Znojmský	Served with gherkins

Drinks

Čaj	Tea	Mléko/mlieko	Milk
Destiláty	Spirits	Pivo	Beer
Káva	Coffee	Suché víno	Dry Wine
Koňak	Brandy	Svařené víno	Mulled Wine
Láhev/fľaša	Bottle	Vinný střik	White wine with soda
Led	Ice	Víno	Wine
Minerální (voda)	Mineral (water)	Na zdraví/nazdravie	Cheers!

DRINKING

Alcohol consumption in Czechoslovakia has always been fairly high, and in the ten years following the events of 1968, it doubled. A whole generation found solace in drinking; in Bohemia and Moravia, beer and wine are the refuge, while in Slovakia they make up for it in spirits. It's a problem which seldom spills out onto the streets; violence in pubs is uncommon and you won't see that many drunks in public, but it's not unusual to see someone legless in the afternoon, on their way home from work.

WHERE TO DRINK

Even the most simple *bufet* in the Czech Lands almost invariably has draught beer, but the **pivnice** (which close around 10 or 11pm) is the place where most heavy drinking goes on. It's common practice to share a table with other drinkers and anyone with just a little German will inevitably be called upon to make conversation once English-speaking voices are heard. Such encounters can be fun, but *pivnice* (and the more local *hospoda* or *hostinec*) are traditionally male preserves, so outside of the big cities, women tend to head instead for the more mixed atmosphere of the country's restaurants or **vinárna** (in Slovak *vináreň*). The latter are the traditional places in which to drink wine, have slightly later opening hours and often double as an upmarket restaurant or some sort of nightclub. The younger generation hang out more in the **kavárna** (in Slovak *kaviáreň*) or *video-kavárna*, the latter usually charging a cover for the privilege of watching MTV.

SOFT DRINKS

Unfortunately, aside from the country's plentiful mineral water, the **soft drinks** in Czechoslovakia are pretty nasty. Apart from the ubiquitous *Coke* and *Pepsi*, always in their unadulterated "original" sugar-sweet formulae, there's little to choose between *Perla*, a sugary lemon drink and *Topic*, reputedly made with grapes and herbs but too sugary to taste of either; *Vinea* is a slightly subtler version. If you ask for a lemonade (*límonáda*), you're just as likely to get orangeade, and vice versa if you ask for *oranž*. Unless you long for a cross between cherryade and dandelion and burdock, avoid the variety of vivid fizzy drinks which go under the promising name of *d žus* (pronounced "juice"). Fresh fruit juice is, as yet, absolutely unobtainable. However, occasionally you may come across bottles of Cuban grapefruit juice or tins of Vietnamese pineapple juice. The safest bet for those without a sweet tooth is to ask for *soda*, which is just that, or *tonic* which is still slightly sweeter than most. *Minerální voda* (mineral water) is everywhere, always carbonated, and a lot more tasty than western brands. Try *Mattoni* for a milder option.

BEER

Czechoslovakia lies third in the world league table of beer consumption, and although it's fallen far behind in the production tables with only three export brands, its beer ranks among the best in the world. It may not boast the variety of neighbouring Germany, but it remains the true home of most of the lager drunk around the world today.

It was in the Bohemian city of Plzeň (Pilsen) that the first **bottom-fermented** beer was introduced in 1842, after complaints from the citizens about the quality of the top-fermented predecessor. The new brewing style quickly spread to Germany, and is now blamed for the bland rubbish that is served up in the English-speaking world as lager or *Pils*. But whether due to lack of

technological know-how or through positive choice, brewing methods in Czechoslovakia have remained stuck in the old ways, eschewing chemical substitutes. Nationalisation and centralisation have seriously affected the variety on offer, but since so little is exported it's easy to make personal discoveries. The distinctive flavour of Czech beer comes from the famous Bohemian hop, the Žatec (Saaz) Red, still hand-picked and then combined with the soft local water and served with a high content of absorbed carbon dioxide – hence the thick, creamy head. Even if you don't think you like lager at all, you must try at least a *malé pivo* (0.3 litre). The average jar is pretty strong stuff, usually about 1050 specific gravity (12° to the Czechs and Slovaks who use their own peculiar Balling scale).

The most natural starting point for any beer tour of Czechoslovakia is **Plzeň** (Pilsen) in West Bohemia, whose bottom-fermented local beer, *Plzeňský Prazdroj 12°* (*Pilsen Urquell*), is the original *Pils*. Plzeň also boasts the *Gambrinus* brewery, thus producing two out of the three Czech export beers. The other big brewing town is **České Budějovice** (Budweis), home to *Budvar*, a mild beer for Bohemia but still leagues ahead of *Budweiser* beer, the German name for *Budvar* that was adopted by an American brewer in 1876 and is now exported all over the world. The biggest brewery in the country is in the Smíchov district of **Prague** where *Staropramen 12°* is produced, a typical Bohemian brew with a mild hoppy flavour. Prague also produces some of the country's best special beer; *Flek 13°*, a dark caramel beer brewed and served exclusively at a pub called *U Fleků* in Prague's Nové Město since 1399, and *Braník 14°*, a light malty beer from south Prague, creamy even by smooth Bohemian standards. In Moravia, the love of beer is somewhat tempered by the south and east Moravians partiality for wine, but the breweries of Brno and Ostrava have some good light and dark beers of their own. The Slovaks, by contrast, have no great tradition of beer drinking, but union with the Czech Lands in 1918 has gradually changed things. Since 1945 their beer consumption has increased tenfold, and the strongest brew of the lot, *Martinský Porter 20°* – sensibly difficult to get hold of – hails from Martin, deep in the Slovak mountains.

WINE AND SPIRITS

Czechoslovakia's **wine** will never win over as many people as its beer, but since the import of

French and German vines in the fourteenth century, the country has produced a modest selection of medium quality wines. Since none are exported, and the labelling is notoriously imprecise – most wines are made by large farm co-ops and sold under brand names – it's difficult to give a very clear picture. Suffice to say that most domestic wine is pretty drinkable and rarely more than about £1–2 a bottle, while the best stuff can only be had from the private wine cellars, hundreds of which still exist.

The biggest producers and consumers by far are the Slovaks, whose two main wine regions are along the hot southern edge of the republic. The vineyards of the Small Carpathians stretch right down to the suburbs of Bratislava, while those of the Slovak Tokaj are bang next to the main Hungarian wine-producing region of the same name, and produce a passable dry white known as *Furmint*. South Moravia boasts some fine white wines, grown under identical conditions as those of the Austrian Weinviertel. Bohemia's wine-growing region consists of only 1000 acres around the town of Mělník, but it produces at least one good red, *Ludmila*, and a couple of whites. *Burčak*, a misty wine that contains little or no alcohol, is drunk in the autumn soon after the harvest.

All the usual **spirits** are on sale and known by their generic names, with rum and vodka leading the sales. Domestic brands originate mostly from Slovakia and east Moravia, like *hanácká*, a vodka from the Haná region around Olomouc. The home-production of brandies is a national pastime, resulting sometimes in almost terminally strong brews. The most famous of the lot is *slivovice*, the plum brandy, originally from the border hills between Moravia and Slovakia but now available just about everywhere, though the home-made stuff is best. You'll probably come across *borovička* at some point, a popular firewater from the Slovak Spiš region, made from pine trees; *myslivec* is a rough brandy with an ardent following. There's also a fair selection of intoxicating **herbal concoctions**. *Fernet* is a dark-brown bitter drink, known as *bavorák* (meaning Bavarian beer) when it's mixed with tonic, while *becherovka* is an unusual herbal spirit quite unlike most other spirits.

COMMUNICATIONS AND MEDIA

Poste restante (pronounced as five syllables in Czech and Slovak) services are available in major towns, but remember to write *Pošta 1* (the main office), followed by the name of the town. Get the sender to write their name and address on the back so that it can at least be returned if something goes wrong. If you're passing through the capital at some point, it might be safer to have mail sent to your embassy, but write and tell them beforehand that you intend to do this. Bear in mind that letters take five days or more to reach the UK from Czechoslovakia.

TELEPHONES

Cheap local **phone calls** can be made from any phone box in Czechoslovakia. There are usually instructions in English, but despite the graphic description, you may still encounter problems. Theoretically you simply pick up the receiver and dial the number with your 1kč poised in the slot. The old orange phones are reputedly less reliable than the new yellow ones, though both only take 1kč coins. To call outside the local area code, you must find one of the elusive grey phone boxes which take 1, 2 and 5 kčs. If you have any prob-

POST OFFICES

Most post offices (*pošta*) are open from 7 or 8am to 5 or 6pm daily except Sundays. They're pretty baffling institutions with separate windows for just about every service. Look out for the right sign to avoid queueing unnecessarily; *známky* (stamps), *dopisy* (letters) or *balky* (parcels). You can also buy stamps from *PNS* newsagents and kiosks, though usually only for domestic mail.

lems, ring 0149 and ask for an English-speaking operator.

It's also theoretically possible to make international calls from the grey phone boxes, but few people do. It's a lot less hassle and exactly the same price (which is expensive) to go to the telephone exchanges situated in most major post offices. Write down the town and number you want, leave a deposit of around 200kčs and wait for your name to be called out. Keep a close watch on the time since international calls cost about £1 for two minutes at whatever time you call. You can also make calls from most hotels, although their surcharge is usually pretty hefty. It might be easier in the long run to ask for a collect call – which will cost the recipient less than it would cost you. Ask for a *hovor na účet volaného*.

Telegrams can be sent from any post office or by phone (though not from phone boxes) by dialling 127. **Telex** and **Fax** machines are gradually arriving in many big hotels (charges are expensive as in the West), and if you want a **photocopy** (*xerox*), ask at a hotel before joining the long queue in town.

DIALLING CODES FROM CZECHOSLOVAKIA

UK ☎0044
EIRE ☎00353
AUSTRALIA ☎0061
NEW ZEALAND ☎0064
US & CANADA ☎001

NEWSPAPERS AND MAGAZINES

Following the death of censorship, the press in Czechoslovakia is thriving. A regular batch of new titles starts up every month and even the old Communist press is changing its old ways. With demand outstripping supply, there's still plenty of room for more magazines and newspapers, but it remains to be seen what will happen when the subsidies for paper are withdrawn in the coming months causing prices to rocket as they have done in Poland.

By far the most popular **daily newspaper** is *Lidové noviny*, originally a monthly *samizdat*, now a respected independent national newspaper, many of whose contributors were involved in the human rights organisiation Charter 77. *Rudé právo*, once the mouthpiece of the Communist

Party, guaranteed a readership of around one million, has seen its sales plummet since November 1989. The same goes for *Pravda*, its Slovak counterpart, and *Újszó*, the Hungarian-language edition. *Práce* (*Práca* in Slovak), once the widely read organ of the impotent official Trade Union organisation *ROH*, is seeking new backers and a new identity. The weekly *Fórum*, as its name suggests, is produced by Civic Forum (*OF*) and its Slovak partner People Against Violence (*VPM*), who together led the Velvet Revolution and romped home in the general elections of June 1990. The paper (with a corresponding daily called *Občánský denník*) is not as popular as the movement it supports, but it forms a welcome voice in the new climate of dialogue and tolerance. Other titles like *Svobodné slovo* and *Právo lidu* are backed by parties which became puppet partners in the Communist-dominated *Národní fronta*, the organisation that led the country for the last forty-two years: understandably, these papers are today deeply unfashionable. The right-wing press has yet to find its feet: *Lidová democracie*, the Czech Catholic centre-right daily has the usual problems of shaking off the mantle of collaboration common to all pre-1989 publications; a predicament its newly founded Slovak counterpart *Slovenskýdenník* doesn't share.

Czechoslovakia's **youth press** was one of the first to speak out against the regime in the run-up to its downfall at the end of 1989. The most vociferous newspaper, and one of the first to condemn the November 17 *masakr* (see p.86) was *Mladá fronta* (Youth Front), the paper of the now defunct Communist youth organisation *SSM*. These days it's busy trying to transform itself into an independent daily, and as such it's somewhat less tainted than most "official" publications; *Smena* (Shift) is its Slovak equivalent. *Mladý svět* (Youth World) is a slightly more populist youth weekly, with an agony aunt and a lonely hearts column. *Zelezní* (Green), the paper of the newly formed Green Party, proclaims its message of doom and gloom on a bi-weekly basis. *Polarita* is the newspaper of the new but weak independent socialist movement *Levá alternativa* (Left Alternative), whose most notable contributors include Petr Uhl and Egon Bondy of *The Plastic People of the Universe* (see *Contexts*).

In the three big cities of Prague, Brno and Bratislava, commuters hide London-style behind the entirely forgettable local **evening papers**, usually called *Večerník* ("Evening") or something similar. Regional and single-issue papers are generally enjoying a renaissance as long-supressed grievances get aired. Cheap back-issues of German and Austrian glossies grab the attention of most of the nation more effectively than domestic **magazines**, and it'll be interesting to see what happens to *Vlasta* (*Slovenka* in Slovak, *Nö* in Hungarian), the nation's weekly women's magazine sponsored by the Union of Women. Porn has yet to arrive wholesale in the country, but judging by the popularity of the now ubiquitous *strip-týz* shows, there's an eager male public out there waiting.

For years, **foreign-language newspapers** were restricted to old copies of the *Morning Star* and *L'Humanité*, and by and large, it's still pretty difficult to get hold of any of the Western press. If you're very lucky, you might pick up a copy of *The Guardian*, printed in Frankfurt that morning. The only English-language publication produced domestically is *Czechoslovak Life*, a glossy monthly aimed at the tourist market. *Prager Press* is the weekly German equivalent, though somewhat more practical, since it lists the week's major cultural events and contains some handy listings. Along with the *Prager Volkszeitung*, it's all that remains of the country's once thriving (pre-1945) German-language press.

TELEVISION AND RADIO

Until recently, the only good thing to be said about Czechoslovakia's state television and radio network was that, since federalisation in 1969, it had consistently broadcast in Czech *and* Slovak. The commitment to **bi-lingual broadcasting** has been so strictly adhered to, that in the course of an ice hockey match, the first half will be commentated in Czech, the second in Slovak. For the last twenty years this, more than anything else, has helped nurture a generation for whom the differences between the two nations, at least linguistically, are an irrelevance.

The struggle for control of the state's two **television** channels was one of the hardest fought battles of the first week of the revolution. When finally, footage of the *masakr* was shown on prime-time TV, the students and actors on strike knew they were on their way to winning over public opinion. Most of the time, however, Czechoslovak TV is pretty bland stuff with keep-fit classes and classical concerts taking up most peak-time viewing. All foreign films and serials are dubbed and everything shuts down well before midnight. You'd be much better off tuning in to Soviet TV, available in most areas, bringing you plenum meetings, army manoeuvres and lavish operas until the early hours, thanks to the time difference.

The state **radio** channel, to which all hotel wireless sets are tuned, gives out news, interspersed with patriotic classical ditties. Most cafés and bars tune into Austrian, German or even French stations for their daily dose of musak. The *BBC World Service* is best picked up on short wave (frequencies change monthly), since finding it (and keeping it) on medium wave can be a frustrating game. *Voice of America* is unfortunately much easier to get hold of.

OPENING HOURS AND OFFICIAL HOLIDAYS

Shops in Czechoslovakia are open Monday to Friday from 9am to 5pm, with some shops and most supermarkets staying open till 6pm or later. Smaller shops close for lunch for an hour sometime between noon and 2pm, while others stay open late on Thursdays. Shops that open on Saturday close at noon or 1pm. Count on all shops being closed on Sunday. Pubs and restaurants tend to close between 10 and 11pm, with food often unobtainable past 9pm. Over the weekend, they close for one or two days out of Saturday, Sunday or Monday.

Official holidays were always a potential source of contention with the old regime. Even the final big **May Day** celebrations which took place in 1989, were marred by "anti-socialist elements" who unrolled banners calling for democracy and *glasnost*. The low-key May Day festivities of 1990, which went by the name of *Májales*, stressed the 100-year tradition of the event, and the public holiday, at least, looks set to stay for the moment, as do the other *slavné májové dny* (Glorious May Days): **May 5**, the day of the Prague Uprising in 1945, and **May 9**, the day of Liberation from the Nazis. Previously, those who attempted to celebrate the Foundation of the Republic on October 28 were prevented from doing so by the police: now it's been reinstated as a national holiday. Apart from **Easter Monday**, the other national holidays – the Great October Revolution, Victorious February (the 1948 coup) – were associated with the Communist regime, so it's not yet clear when and what the new public holidays will be. Religious differences have caused problems over the decision to celebrate **July 5**, the day Saints Cyril and Methodius introduced Christianity into Czechoslovakia, instead of July 6, the anniversary of Hus's death – something most Catholics would prefer to forget.

FESTIVALS AND OTHER ENTERTAINMENTS

Czechoslovakia has few national annual events, and aside from the usual religious-orientated celebrations and mass pilgrimages, most annual shindigs are arts and music-based festivals, confined to a particular town or city. In addition, there are also folkloric events in the nether regions which take place in the summer only, the Strážnice folk festival being by far the most famous.

FESTIVALS AND OTHER ANNUAL EVENTS

The *Strážnice Folk Festival* is the biggest and most prestigious of the many annual **folk festivals**, with groups from all over Czechoslovakia striving to perform here. Other ones worth look-

FESTIVALS DIARY

APRIL

Mid-April Kroměříž: home-grown Jazz Festival.

Late April–early May Brno: International Trade Fair.

MAY

May 12–June 2 Prague: International Music Festival with concerts all over the city.

Mid-May Zlín: International Childrens' Film Festival.

JUNE

Mid-June Mariánské Lázně: International Festival of Mime.

End June–early July Strážnice: International Folk Festival.

Mid-June Litomyšl: National Opera Festival.

June Gombasek: Hungarian Folk Festival.

June Svidník: Ukrainian (Rusyn) Folk Festival.

JULY

Early July Chrudim: Puppet Festival.

First weekend in July Levoča: Marian Pilgrimage.

July Karlovy Vary: biennial International Film Festival.

July Východná: International Folk Festival.

AUGUST

Mid-Aug Domažlice: Chod Folk Festival.

Mid-Aug Valtice: Baroque Music Festival.

End Aug Strakonice: International Bagpipers' Festival.

End Aug Brno: International Grand Prix motorcycling event.

SEPTEMBER

Early Sept Kroměříž: Chamber Music Festival.

Early Sept Žatec: Hop (and beer) Festival.

Late Sept–early Oct Teplice: Beethoven Music Festival.

Late Sept–early Oct Brno: International Music Festival.

Sept Bratislava: International Jazz Festival.

OCTOBER

Early Oct Pardubice: Grand steeple-chase event.

Early Oct Košice Marathon.

Oct Prague: International Jazz Festival

ing out for are the *Chod Festival* in Domažlice every August and the *Folk Dance Festival* held in July in Východná in Slovakia.

The 1980s witnessed a revival of **pilgrimages** (*pouť* or *púť*), usually centred around the cult of the Virgin Mary. The biggest gatherings are on the first weekend in July at Levoča, in the Spiš region of East Slovakia, when up to 250,000 people descend on the small pilgrimage church above the town. Lesser celebrations go on in the region over the following two months.

For the Orthodox and Uniate churches, which predominate in the east of the country, **Easter** (in Czech *velikonoce*, in Slovak *Veľká noc*) is much more important than Christmas, and the processions and services can be elaborate and lengthy affairs that are well worth catching. For the rest of the country, it's a good excuse for a party, and also the age-old sexist ritual of whipping girls' calves with braided birch twigs, tied with ribbons (*pomlazka*) – objects which you'll see being furiously bought and sold from markets in the run-up to Easter Sunday. To prevent such a fate, the girls are supposed to offer the boys a coloured easter egg. What may once have been an innocent bucolic frolic has now become another excuse for Czech and Slovak blokes to harass any woman who dares to venture onto the street during this period.

As in the West, **Christmas** (*Vánoce/Vianoce*) is a time for over-consumption and family gatherings and, therefore, a fairly private occasion. On December 4, the feast day of St Barbara, cherry tree branches are bought as decorations, the aim being to get them to blossom before Christmas. On December 6 the "Good Bishop", the Czechoslovak equivalent of Father Christmas, tours around the neighbourhood accompanied by an angel, handing out sweets and fruit to children who've been good and coal and potatoes to those who've been naughty. With a week to go, large barrels are set up in the streets from which huge quantities of *kapr* (carp), the traditional Christmas dish, are sold. Christmas Eve (*Štědrý večer*) is traditionally a day of fasting, broken only when the evening star appears, signalling the beginning of the Christmas feast of carp, potato salad, schnitzel and sweet breads. Only after the meal are the children allowed to open their presents.

OTHER FAIRS AND CELEBRATIONS

The ritual slaughter of the pig, known as **zabíjačka**, still takes place in parts of Bohemia and Moravia (as in Bavaria) towards the end of January, traditionally a time when all other winter provisions are exhausted. Every single bit of the animal is prepared as food for the feast which accompanies the event.

Birthdays are not half as important in Czechoslovakia as **saint name days** which fall on the same day each year. Thus popular names like Jan or Anna are practically national celebrations, and an excuse for everyone to get pissed since most people know at least somebody with those names.

The spectre haunting Czechoslovakia at the moment is **burza** (which literally means "exchange"), something like a cross between a car-boot sale and a flea market. They vary in size from the huge events which take place in football stadiums to sad, provincial affairs in the local car park. Natural East European curiosity and the drop in living standards usually ensures a big turn-out, but don't expect to pick up too many bargains, since the stuff consists mostly of bad quality quartz watches and video cassettes.

Not much of the festive spirit about it, but the **International Trade Fair** held in Brno every April/May is more interesting than it sounds, as well as being set in a virtual museum of pre-war avant-garde architecture. After 1948, it became a showcase for shoddy COMECON goods, but the 1990s should see it shake off its reputation for Cuban cigars and cheap Romanian stereos.

MUSIC

Folk songs lie at the heart of all Czech and Slovak music: people strike up traditional songs and contemporary folk tunes at the slightest excuse, especially in the countryside. A living tradition still exists in some of the more remote mountain regions of Slovakia: elsewhere professional and amateur groups keep the music alive. Styles of music vary from the more familiar Bohemian dances to the Carpathian shepherd songs of Slovakia, but the richest tradition is in Moravia, which bridges the gap between the two styles. *Dudy* (bagpipes), or *gajdy* in the Moravian dialect, are still used in the western part of the country, while the *cimbalom* (a kind of zither), and *fujara* (half flute, half bassoon), the traditional instrument of the shepherd, begin to appear further east.

The nation's great wealth of folk tunes have found their way into much of the country's **classical music**, of which the Czechs are justifiably proud, having produced four composers of considerable stature – Smetana, Dvořák, Janáček and Martinů – and the more liberal can even claim Mahler as a fifth. The Slovaks, too, can boast some impressive musical connections; Komárno is the birthplace of Franz Lehár, the Hungarian composer, while Bratislava is the home town of Johann Nepomuk Hummel. The country has also produced a host of singers, like the late Ema Destinnová, and virtuoso violinists, the latest of whom play with the prestigious Suk Quartet who regularly perform outside the country.

All three big cities have **music festivals**, which give most of their space over to national composers. Smaller towns have annual festivals often dedicated to composers: Smetana (Litomyšl), Beethoven (Teplice), Chopin (Mariánské Lázně). Throughout the year, it's easy to catch works by Czech or Slovak composers since the repertoires of most regional companies are ardently nationalistic. Most opera houses and concert halls are closed in July and Aug): as compensation, watch out for the summer concerts held in many of the country's countless castles.

Jazz (or *džez* as it is sometimes written) has an established tradition in Czechoslovakia, despite the best efforts of the Nazis and the Communists to suppress it, though venues are almost entirely confined to Prague, except for occasional one-off gigs in the other big cities. The *Bratislava Jazz Days* are held annually in September, followed closely by Prague's *International Jazz Festival* in October, one of the best Eastern Europe has to offer.

Turn on your radio anywhere in Czechoslovakia and you won't be inundated by **rock and pop music** The majority of the indigenous product is divided evenly between Western musak and heavy metal, but these two trends ignore the more interesting side of Czechoslovak music, the protest songs which grew out of the 1960s and the punk-influenced sound of *The Plastic People of the Universe* and their various imitators. As yet, very little of this type of music is on disc, but check out the fly-posters for up-and-coming gigs, which cover the whole spectrum from highly accomplished folk/jazz performers to crass derivations of *Motorhead*.

CINEMA

Cinemas (*kino*) are cheap and rudimentary, and can be found in almost every town and village in Czechoslovakia, showing all the major international films as well as the home-produced ones. The majority of foreign films are dubbed into Czech (indicated by a small white square on the poster), but a few foreign films are shown with subtitles. This month's film listings are usually fly-posted up around town or outside each cinema. Titles are always translated into Czech or Slovak, so you'll need to have your wits about you to identify films like *Umělcova smlouva* as *The Draughtsman's Contract* (the film's country of origin is always shown – *VB* means it's British, *USA*, American).

Prague's Barrandov Studios produced a string of innovative films in the 1960s, known collectively as the Czech New Wave, which included **Miloš Forman**, perhaps the country's best-known director. The industry's strength has always been in comedy, satire and history as farce as in *Obchod na korce* (*The Shop on the High Street*) by Ján Kadár, set in the Slovak Nazi puppet state in World War II. **Jiří Menzel** made his name in similar vein with the film *Ostře sledované vlaky* (*Closely Observed Trains*), set in the final stages of the last war, an antidote to the endless overblown stories of heroism.

One of the fields in which the Czechs and Slovaks excel is in animation, with **Jan Švankmajer** having established a considerable international following with his disturbing version of *Alice in Wonderland* and most recently with his bitter statement on *The Death of Stalinism in Bohemia*, commissioned by the BBC. Sadly, it's well-nigh impossible to catch a showing, though should you be fortunate enough, language is unlikely to be a problem. The only **film festival** of note is the biennial held in Karlovy Vary in July, though up until now it has attracted very little international attention. Tickets are, nevertheless, hard to come by.

THEATRE

Theatre is cheap and popular in Czechoslovakia, and most towns with a population of over 20,000 have at least one permanent venue with the month's programme pinned up outside and elsewhere around town. The serious stuff goes on in the *kamenná divadla* or "stone theatres", mostly opulent opera houses built by the Habsburgs in the late-nineteenth century. Aside from the odd British or American touring company, there's precious little in English, although the ticket prices are cheap, and the venues often interesting enough in themselves – the Czechs and Slovaks go as much for the interval promenade as for the show itself. Of the smaller fringe companies, Brno's *Divadlo na procházku* (Theatre on a Shoestring) leads the way, but only Prague's *Laterna magika* deliberately gears its programme towards tourists. In Prague, there's a strong tradition of mime, from the classical variety put on by Ladislav Fialka and his troop, to more experimental stuff from international stars like Boris Polívka.

With over fifteen permanent **puppet theatres**, Czechoslovak puppetry is big business. Of the traditional forms of puppetry, only the Spejbl & Hurvínek Theatre in Prague survives; the rest have introduced live actors into their repetoire, making the shows less accessible if you don't speak the language. However, this trend has thrown up innovative and highly professional companies like Hradec Králové's *Drak* who specialise in shows for adults and have toured extensively throughout Europe. To see a show, look out for the words *loutkové divadlo*, or in Slovak the *babkové divadlo*.

CASTLES, CHURCHES AND MUSEUMS

Czechoslovakia has something like two thousand castles ranging from the piles of thirteenth-century rubble to the last vain attempts produced earlier this century by a now extinct aristocracy. Many have been converted for modern use, such as old people's homes, trade union holiday retreats and even training centres for the secret police; many more, due to lack of funds, are struggling to survive into the next century. The country's churches and monasteries are similarly blighted by years of structural neglect and more frusratingly have adopted a policy of locking their doors outside worshipping hours. Museums and galleries, by contrast, thrived under the Communists, having been set up mostly for propaganda purposes, but often containing the odd surprise to make a visit there worthwhile.

OPENING HOURS AND TICKETS

The basic **opening hours** for castles and monasteries are Tuesday to Sunday 8am/9am to noon/1pm, and 2pm to 4pm/5pm. In Prague the main museums open 10am to 6pm. From the end of October to the beginning of April, most castles are closed. In April and October, opening hours are often restricted to weekends and holidays only. Whatever the time of year, if you want to see the interior of the building, nine times out of ten you'll be forced to go on a guided tour (nearly always in Czech or Slovak, occasionally German) that will last at least 45 minutes. Ask for an *anglický text*, an often unintentionally hilarious English resumé of the castle's history. More than likely you'll be asked to wear special furry overshoes which protect and polish the floors at the same time. Tours almost invariably set off on the hour, and the last one leaves an hour before the final closing time. Entrance tickets cost very little – hence no prices are quoted in the text – and no proof is needed to claim student status, which chops the price in half.

CHURCHES AND MONASTERIES

Czechoslovakia's Jesuits and Franciscans, Dominicans and Cistercians have long since gone, their **monasteries** turned into schools, factories and prisons. Only a few remain open to the public, keeping similar hours to the country's castles. Way back in the fifteenth century, the vast majority of the population of Bohemia and Moravia were Protestant or Hussite, and the Slovaks converted to the Lutheran doctrine a century later. But the ferocity of the Counter-Reformation was unequalled in both the Czech Lands and Slovakia, and nowadays the country is predominantly **Roman Catholic**, with its most ardent followers in Slovakia, and its least committed in Bohemia. Hundreds of Baroque churches litter the countryside, but their opening hours are brief and erratic. The only time you can guarantee their being open is just before and after a service (times are posted outside the main doors). At other times, it's worth asking around for the local *kňaz* (priest) or *kaplan*, who's usually only too happy to oblige with the key (*klíč*). In the Czech Lands, widespread agnosticism and the punitive policies of the last regime (self-confessed believers were not allowed to join the Party or take up teaching posts) have left many churches in a terrible state of disrepair. Not so in Slovakia, not because the activities of the state were any less harsh, but because the church-going population was more determined to maintain its religious tradition.

CZECHOSLOVAKIA'S CASTLES AND CHATEAUX – THE TOP FIFTEEN

Čachtice (p.290). More impressive for its legends than the ruins themselves, Čachtice was the home and ultimately prison of Elizabeth Báthori, the Blood Countess.

Český Krumlov (p.140). The country's largest complex after Prague Castle. Highlights include an eighteenth-century Rococo theatre with all the original trappings.

Chlumec nad Cidlinou (p.199). A miniature masterpiece by the country's most original eighteenth-century architect, Santini-Aichl, containing sculptures by Matthias Braun.

Jaroměřice nad Rokytnou (p.228). Not exactly the *chef d'oeuvre* of Viennese master Johann Lukas von Hildebrandt, but easily the largest eighteenth-century château in the land.

Jindřichův Hradec (p.134). Few examples of Bohemian Renaissance architecture exist: this is one of the best.

Karlštejn (p.120). Country castle of Charles IV, beautifully situated in the hills to the southeast of Prague. The fourteenth-century frescoes and the rich Holy Rood chapel are a more than adequate recompense for the castle's lack of furnishings.

Lednice (p.226). The country's most frequently visited castle and its best example of nineteenth-century neo-Gothic.

Litomyšl (p.201). Birthplace of the composer Smetana and now a museum of musical instru-ments. Architecturally, it's a Bohemian interpreta-tion of the Italian Renaissance.

Nové Město nad Metují (p.194). Contains wonderful and varied furnishings ranging from the original sixteenth-century decor to Cubist leather wallpaper and Art Nouveau ceramics.

Pernštejn (p.221). The best of a great cluster of châteaux within easy reach of Brno. It's the most perfectly positioned medieval castle you could imagine, power-base of the Moravian Pernštejn family.

Prague Castle (p.50). A puzzling and varied complex of buildings stretching across the centu-ries from the austere Romanesque basilica of St George to the late Renaissance fantasia played out on the walls and ceiling of the Rudolf Gallery.

Spišský hrad (p.331). A vast sprawling hilltop ruin and undoubtedly the most spectacular pile of rubble in Slovakia.

Telč (p.232). A late sixteenth-century château built by the lords of Hradec forms the perfect accompa-niment to this dazzling Renaissance town.

Vranov (p.227). An impressive complex of Baroque buildings, high up on a ridge by the Austrian border and designed by the great Fischer von Erlach, whose giant oval hall is the château's showpiece.

Zvíkov (p.128). Quiet fouteenth-century retreat, stunningly located at the confluence of the Otava and the Vltava.

In the north and east of Slovakia, there's a small number of Orthodox (*Pravoslavný*) believers and a much larger contingent who belong to the **Uniate Church** (*Grecko-katolický*), an obscure branch of Roman Catholicism whose small wooden churches, packed with icons and Byzantine paraphenalia, appear just like Russian Orthodox churches to the uninitiated. You'll find a much more thorough account of the Uniates and their churches in the section on Carpatho-Ruthenia in Chapter Four, *Slovakia*. Suffice to say that the buildings are fascinating, especially their dark and poky interiors, but they are kept firmly locked with little indication of what time the next service will be held.

Czechoslovakia's once considerable Jewish population has been whittled down to around 2000, over half of whom live in Prague, the only place where regular worship still takes place.

Very few of the now disused **synagogues** have been saved from collapse, though there are some notable exceptions like Mikulov in South Moravia and Trenčín in West Slovakia.

MUSEUMS AND GALLERIES

Czechoslovakia's **museums** are often stronger on quantity than quality, and exclusively Czech or Slovak labelling only makes matters worse. Occasionally you'll come across a real gem – the local museums in Slovakia often boast amazing collections of folk art – sometimes even with an *anglický text* provided, but, generally speaking, most museums are far from riveting – school groups are often the only visitors. There are three main types, plus one other now extinct: a **národní muzeum** or national museum, which exists only in the two federal capitals, Prague and Bratislava, and is normally an unremarkable archaeological and art collection gathered from the region, often accompanied by a liberal sprinkling of stuffed animals from round the globe. A **krajské muzeum** or regional museum traces the local history through arts, crafts and old photos, while a **městské muzeum** or town museum is more provincial still. Finally, every town was obliged to have a museum of "working-class history" – either as a separate entity or tacked on to the end of the regional or town museum – which amounted to little more than a lengthy eulogy of the Communist Party and a quasi-historical justification for the status quo. Now undergoing a major identity crisis, it remains to be seen in what form these latter museums will continue – if at all.

The big cities boast the best **art galleries**, though even Prague's Národní galérie (National Gallery) collections pale in comparison with those of most major Western European cities. The impact of Socialist Realism was as heavy here as elsewhere in the Soviet Empire, and the results can still be seen in the country's provincial art galleries. Before the war, Czechoslovakia was at the forefront of the European avant-garde, but up to now only a few works from this period have been put on show, except during the occasional one-off exhibition. Many of the country's best artists – people like Kupka and Mucha – worked abroad, and little attempt was made by the last regime to buy back the works of such "degenerates", which, as a result, now grace the galleries of Paris and New York. Nevertheless, exhibitions of new artists are constantly doing the rounds, and, with the lifting of censorship, some of the country's better artists, who were previously banned, will once more be able to put on shows.

Opening hours for museums and galleries tend to be between 9am and 4pm, usually without a break at lunch. Many stay open all year round or switch from a Tuesday to Sunday summer routine to Monday to Friday during the winter. Full opening hours are detailed in *The Guide* and again, ticket costs are negligible – and claiming you're a student will cut costs in half.

SPORT

Czechoslovakia is probably most famous for its world-class tennis players and for its national ice hockey team. But the sport which actually pulls the biggest crowds is football. Getting tickets to watch a particular sport is easy (and cheap) enough on the day – only the really big matches sell out. Actually taking part is more difficult – Czechs and Slovaks belong to local clubs and there are very few hire facilities for the general public.

FOOTBALL

Football's *první liga* or national league and the *Československý pohár* (the "knock-out competition") are dominated by the country's number one team *Sparta Praha* who supplied a large proportion of the national squad for the 1990 World Cup Finals in Italy, including the competition's top-goal scorer Tomáš Skuhravý. Games are played on a Sunday afternoon; tickets for a major domestic or international match cost less than a £1. The Czechoslovak **style of play** is difficult to pinpoint, but a battle of wits is definitely preferred to the English style of direct attacking or the Latin preference for individual flair. Working-class towns like the mining town of Ostrava produce some of the country's better sides like *Baník Ostrava* and *Vítkovice*. Clubs are still organised in the traditional "socialist" manner: sides sporting the prefix *Dukla* are picked from the army, those with the initials *RH* (*Rudá hvězda* – Red Star) are made up of full-time policemen (probably the most unpopular clubs in the country), and other initials are derived from various state industries. Although some sides like *Dukla Praha* are among the best in the country, it's difficult to imagine how any of these teams are going to transform themselves into commercially viable clubs when their home gates rarely reach four figures.

ICE HOCKEY

Ice hockey runs football a close second for the nation's most popular sport. It's not uncommon to see kids playing their own form of the game in the street, rather than kicking a football around. The national league is dominated by *Sparta Praha* but the Moravian army team *Dukla Jihlava* and *VSŽ Košice*, the East Slovak steelworkers' side, are both equally well respected. Games are fast and physical, cold but compelling viewing, taking place on Tuesday and Friday at around 6pm. The season starts at the end of September and culminates in the annual World Championships, when the fortunes of the national side are subject to close scrutiny, especially if pitched against the Soviets. A double victory against them in 1969 precipitated riots in towns across the country, culminating in the torching of the *Aeroflot* (Soviet Airlines) offices in Prague.

TENNIS AND OTHER SPORTS

Tennis has been one of Czechoslovakia's most successful exports of the 1980s, although the country holds no major international events and its national Davis Cup team rarely gets anywhere. Martina Navrátilová, now nearing the end of her magnificent career, has been the most consistent Czech player on the circuit, although she became a naturalised American some years ago. On the men's side Ivan Lendl has been a towering figure in world tennis throughout the 1980s, even though a Wimbledon title has consistently eluded him. He too has had his day, and the country badly lacks a young generation of players to take

their place in the world ranking. Any home-grown talent there is will be on display in the Czechoslovak Open, held every August in Prague.

Table-tennis is taken very seriously in Czechoslovakia, although the last time the country won the European Championships was back in the 1970s. **Motor sports** are also popular, particularly motocross and speedway, for which the country's two-stroke Jawas are justifiably famous. The Brno Motorcycle Grand Prix is on the world circuit and takes place every August, attracting thousands of leather-clad bikers from all over Europe.

The Czechoslovaks may not produce any world-class skiers but with much of the country covered in a thick blanket of snow for three months of the year, **skiing** is a popular and necessary skill which most people learn at school. The main ski resorts are in Slovakia but there are also facilities in parts of Bohemia and Moravia. *ČEDOK* are the major agents for skiing holidays – see p.5 for more details. If you go independently, you'll need to take your own equipment with you as hiring stuff is difficult. Prices for the lifts are very low compared to Western standards, but then poor facilities and long queues make up for it.

POLICE, TROUBLE AND SEXUAL HARASSMENT

The Police (Veřejná bezpečnost or VB) are almost as unpopular as the secret police (Státní bezpečnost or StB), certainly among the younger generation – and they know it. Their participation in the November 17 *masakr* destroyed what little credibility they had managed to hold on to over the last forty years of Communist control.

Public confidence in their competence has also suffered a severe blow due to the level of **crime** in the country which has risen rapidly since the revolution. A spate of murders early in 1990 shocked this generally quite peaceable country, and prostitution is rife in the big cities. Some blame Havel's New Year amnesty which relieved Czechoslovakia's over-crowded prisons, but most blame the VB for not reporting and not preventing crime in the past. As a Westerner, petty theft from cars and hotel rooms are the biggest worries. Try not to look too obviously affluent and keep your valuables on you at all times. The best way to protect yourself, of course, is to take out **travel**

insurance (see p.7). If you are unlucky enough to have something stolen, report it immediately to the nearest police station. It's unlikely that there'll be anyone there who speaks English, and even less that your belongings will be retrieved, but at the very least, you should get a statement detailing what you've lost for your insurance claim. Try the phrase *pravě mi ukradl někdo* – "I have just been robbed".

Everyone is obliged to carry some form of ID and you should carry your **passport** with you at all times, though realistically you're extremely unlikely to get stopped (unless you're driving), since the VB are now so deferential that they confine themselves to socially acceptable policing activities like traffic control and harassing gypsies.

As far as **sexual harassment** is concerned, things are, if anything, marginally less intimidating than in the West, although without the familiar linguistic and cultural signs, it's easier to misinterpret situations. Most of rural

Czechoslovakia is still very conservative, especially the further east you go, and women travelling alone can expect to encounter stares, comments and occasionally worse. In the big cities, attitudes are much more liberal, though single women should avoid going to top hotel nightclubs, where it will be assumed by many men that you are a prostitute. Hitch-hiking is a risk, as it is anywhere, and although it's quite common to see Czech and Slovak women hitching, they at least have the advantage of a common language.

In Czechoslovak society, despite the sloganeering of the Communist regime, women are still treated as second-class citizens for the most part, and a feminist **women's movement** is virtually non-existent. Ironically, part of the reason for this is the adverse effect of the official campaigns for women's equality which forced women to take jobs, usually at the bottom end of the pay ladder. What women's organisations there are tend to focus on environmental themes, such as Prague Mothers Fighting for Ecology (c/o Ruth Kolinska, Široká 15, Prague 1, 110 00).

DIRECTORY

ADDRESSES The street name is always written before the number. The word for street (*ulice* or *ulica*, occasionally abbreviated to *ul.*) is usually missed out, for example Celetná ulice is simply known as Celetná. Other terms are often abbreviated: *náměstí* (square in Czech) becomes *nám.*, *trieda* (avenue in Slovak) becomes *tr.* and *nábřeží* (embankment in Czech), *nábř.*

BOTTLES Czechoslovakia has yet to join the throw-away culture and all drinks come in bottles which have a deposit on them. Shops will accept bottles from other outfits providing they stock the type you're trying to fob off on them.

CIGARETTES Loosely packed and lethal, their only virtue is their cheapness. The poseurs smoke the top of the domestic range, *sparta* – paradoxically named after the country's leading football team. President Havel smokes *petra* and the workers smoke *mars* or the filterless *start*. Other

brands to avoid are easy to spot by their ridiculous names – *disco, hi-fi* and *dalila*. *Marlboro* lead the Western packs, with *Peter Stuyvesant* running a close second. Matches are *círky* or *zápalky*.

CONTRACEPTIVES Condoms (*preservativ*) are only on sale from chemists and still subject to periodic shortages. Their sturdiness can't be guaranteed; bring your own.

DISABLED TRAVELLERS Very little attention is paid to the needs of the disabled in Czechoslovakia. *ČEDOK* claims to be able to book holidays which cater for the disabled, but most people's experiences prove otherwise. There is however an official national organisation with its headquarters on Karlínské náměstí. 12, Prague 8.

ELECTRICITY is the standard continental 220 volts. Round two-pin plugs are used so you'll need to bring an adaptor.

EMBASSIES AND CONSULATES All foreign embassies are in Prague, mostly in the Malá Strana. So far, only the Austrians have a consulate in Bratislava, although others are likely to follow suit in the near future (for addresses see p.6).

EMERGENCIES Police ☎150, Ambulance ☎155, Fire ☎158.

FILM Domestic colour films are poor quality and imported ones aren't widely available yet. You may also have problems getting the East European variety processed back home. Best bring your own supply.

GAY LIFE There is no great "scene" as such, but homosexuality is not illegal. Attitudes begin to harden as you move east into the more devoutly

Catholic territory of Slovakia. There's a monthly paper called *Lambda* and a helpline (evenings only; ☎02-57 73 88) usually with at least one English-speaker on call.

JAYWALKING is illegal in Czechoslovakia and only really rebellious citizens do it, even if there isn't a car in sight. If caught, you'll be fined on the spot.

LANGUAGE A number of month-long beginners' courses are held regularly in Prague, Karlovy Vary, Brno, Olomouc and Bratislava. Average cost is £300 for the month, which includes half-board and accommodation. For further details (and possible financial assistance) contact the British Council.

LAUNDRY Self-service launderettes don't exist, so you're on your own. You can get things service-washed or dry-cleaned in a couple of days at a *čistírna*, a sort of cheap version of a dry-cleaners.

LEFT LUGGAGE Every tram and bus station bar the most isolated hamlet has lockers and/or a 24-hour left luggage office, which will only take bags of 15kg and under. If it's very heavy, say *promiňte, je těšký* and offer to carry it yourself – *já to vezmo*. The instructions for the lockers are in Czech/Slovak, Russian and German only. Basically, you need to find an open one, put a crown in the slot on the inside of the door and set the code (choose a number you can easily remember and make a note of it), then shut the door and make a note of the locker number.

RACISM It is a sad fact that racism in Czechoslovakia is a casual and common phenomenon. The country's half million gypsies bear the brunt of the nation's ignorance and prejudice, and a vicious spate of attacks on gypsies set the new

decade off to an ominous start. Consequently, anyone even remotely dark-skinned can expect to arouse, at the very least, a great deal of curiosity.

STREET NAMES In towns and villages across the country, streets named after the stars of international communism were torn down in the aftermath of the Velvet Revolution. This process is still continuing, and while confusing, it will be interesting to see who survives the purge, and where.

TAMPONS Sanitary towels (*vložky*) are cheap and easy to get hold of, though rather crudely constructed. Tampons (*tampóny*) suffer from acute supply problems – it's best to bring your own.

TIME Czechoslovakia is generally one hour ahead of GMT and BST, with the clocks going forward as late as May and back again some time in September – the exact date changes from year to year.

TOILETS Public toilets (*záchod* or *WC*) are few and far between. In addition, they're often closed late at night and at weekends, and, once you get inside, are anything but beautiful. You can buy toilet paper (by the sheet) from the attendant, whom you will usually have to pay as you enter, depending on the purpose of your visit. It's generally acceptable to use the toilets in state-run restaurants and hotels.

TOWN NAMES In certain areas of Czechoslovakia where there was a significant German-speaking population until 1945, the German name for the town is given in brackets after the Czech or Slovak name; the same rule also applies to Hungarian speaking towns. Eg: Liberec (Reichenberg) and Rimavská Sobota (Rimaszombat).

PRAGUE AND AROUND

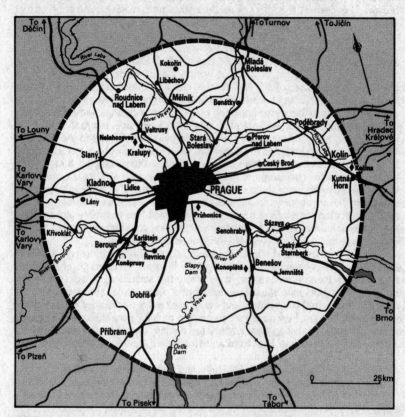

For most outsiders, **Prague** *is* Czechoslovakia. Few people can name even one other city, and a staggering ninety percent of Western visitors spend all their time in and around the capital. Domestically, too, Prague is pre-eminent: all the big decisions are made here, despite the occasional rumblings of discontent from the regions since federalisation in 1969. The result has been to draw an economic and cultural line between the city and the rest of the country, with Prague seeing itself as the centre of all things Czech. Certainly, Praguers exude an air of confidence about their city, which is – after all – easily the country's largest, with a population of around 1,250,000. On the whole, it's a confidence that's well founded, primarily since there are few other cities in Europe that look so good – and no other capital where six hundred years of archi-tecture are presented so completely untouched by natural disaster or war.

Indeed, Prague is one of the least *Eastern* European cities you could imagine, closer in many ways to Paris than Moscow, and keen to capitalise on its position as the political and cultural centre of the newly emerging *Mitteleuropa*.

Although there's no shortage of city sights, many visitors stick to just a few tried and tested areas, happy with the constantly changing facades and endlessly picturesque streets of **Hradčany**, the castle area, and the old town of **Staré Město**. Dig deeper, though, into eighteenth-century **Malá Strana**, or further afield into the outlying district of **Vyšehrad** or even the city's extensive **suburbs**, and you'll find plenty of offbeat interest. If you're curious, you could while away a week here without any difficulty whatsoever. The only problem is likely to be access. As long ago as the 1920s, one visitor – E. I. Robson – warned "You must not be deterred by piles of fallen masonry, clouds of dust and impenetrable forests of scaffolding poles", and there's still some truth in this observation. Partly, it's because Prague has been too successful in preserving its architecture over the centuries: there are simply too many ancient buildings to maintain, while the photogenic houses with painted plasterwork require constant repainting. However, the major contemporary problem is pollution. Thanks to the coal-fired boilers which provide the city with most of its energy, it has been estimated that Prague now receives one hour's sunshine a day less than it should. None of this, though, deters the thousands of tourists, mainly German and Italian, who have flooded into the city since the country's "Velvet Revolution". This relatively recent influx can be an obstacle to appreciating the city – Prague's restaurants and hotels particularly are failing miserably to cope with the crowds – and the best solution is to follow the Czech routine: rise early, eat your biggest meal of the day at lunchtime and drink yourself into the ground in the evening.

The city's outer suburbs look like every other in Eastern Europe – half-built high-rise estates swimming in a sea of mud – but once you're clear of them, the area **around Prague** shifts gear straight into the somnolent villages and softly rolling hills of Bohemia. Most Praguers own a *chata*, or country cottage, somewhere in these rural backwaters, and every weekend the roads out of the city are packed with Škodas. Few places are more than an hour from the centre by public transport, making most an easy day trip for visitors, too. The most popular destinations are the castles of **Karlštejn** and **Konopiště**, neither of which are particularly appealing, given the daily swarm of coach parties. You're better rewarded by heading north, away from the hills and the crowds, to the chateaux of **Veltrusy** and **Nelahozeves** (Dvořák's birthplace), or to the wine-town of **Mělník**.

The wooded hills around **Křivoklát** in the northeast, or **Kokořín** in the southwest, both around 40km from Prague, are too far for most day-trippers. Even further afield, the undisputed gem of the region is the medieval silver-mining town of **Kutná Hora**, 60km east of Prague. But if you want a view of Bohemia that's quite distinct from the urban attractions of Prague, all of these places are worth considering as an overnight stop.

An historical background

The Czechs have a legend for every occasion and the founding of their capital **Prague** (Praha) is no exception. Some time in the seventh or eighth century AD the Czech prince, Krok, moved his people south from the plains of the river Labe (Elbe) to the rocky knoll that is now Vyšehrad (literally "high castle"). His youngest daughter, Libuše, a woman endowed with the gift of prophecy, fell into a trance one day and pronounced that they should build a city "whose glory will

touch the stars", at the point in the forest where they found an old man construct-
ing the threshold of his house. He was duly discovered on the Hradčany hill,
overlooking the Vltava, and the city was named *Praha,* or threshold.
Subsequently, Libuše was compelled to take a husband, a man called Přemysl
(Shepherd), allegedly the founder of the Přemyslid dynasty which ruled Bohemia
until the fourteenth century.

So much for the legend. Historically, though, Hradčany and not Vyšehrad was
where the first Slav settlers established themselves. The Vltava was relatively
shallow at this point, and it probably seemed a safer bet than the plains of the
Labe. The earliest recorded **Přemyslid** was Prince Bořivoj, the first Christian
ruler of Prague, baptised in the ninth century by the Slav apostles Cyril and
Methodius. It was his grandson, Prince Václav, who was to become the dynasty's
most famous member – the Good "King" Wenceslas of the Christmas carol and
the modern country's patron saint.

Under the Přemyslids the city prospered, benefiting from its position on the
central European trade routes. Merchants from all over Europe came to settle
here, and in 1234 the first of Prague's historic **five towns**, the Staré Město, was
founded. In 1257, King Otakar II founded the Malá Strana on the slopes of the
castle, as a separate quarter for Prague's German merchants, but he failed in his
attempt to become Holy Roman Emperor and the Přemyslid dynasty died out in
1306. The crown was handed over by the Czech nobles to the Luxembourgs, and
it was under Charles IV of Luxembourg, who did succeed in being elected
Emperor, that Prague enjoyed its **golden age**. In just thirty years Charles transformed Prague into one of the most important cities in fourteenth-century
Europe, establishing institutions and buildings that still survive today – a university, a cathedral, a host of monasteries and churches – and founding an entire
new town, Nové Město, to accommodate the influx of students.

His son, Václav IV, was no match for such an inheritance, and the city was
soon in crisis. Following the execution of the radical reformist preacher Jan Hus
in 1415, the whole country became engulfed in **religious wars**, with Prague
experiencing some of the most bitter struggles. Not until the Polish Jagiello
dynasty succeeded to the throne later that century was a degree of prosperity and
religious tolerance restored. However, trouble broke out again between the
Protestant nobles and the Catholic Habsburgs in 1618, this time culminating in a
decisive defeat for the Protestants at the Battle of Bílá hora (White Mountain), on
the outskirts of the city. Then followed the period the Czechs refer to as the **dark
ages**, when the full force of the Counter-Reformation was brought to bear on the
city's people: Czechs were forced to conduct their affairs in German, and were
persecuted for their religious beliefs. Paradoxically, though, the spurt of Baroque
rebuilding during the Counter-Reformation lent Prague its most striking architectural aspect, and from this period date the majority of the city's impressive
palaces.

The next two centuries saw Prague's importance gradually whittled away until
it became little more than a provincial town in the greater Austrian Empire. Two
things dragged it out of the doldrums. The first was the **industrial revolution** of
the mid-nineteenth century, which brought large numbers of Czechs in from the
countryside to work in the factories, and led the city to expand beyond its medieval boundaries for the first time. The second was the Czech **národní obrození**,
the contemporary national revival movement, which gave Prague a number of
symbolically significant monuments, like its proud National Theatre. More impor-

tantly, the národní obrození led to the foundation of the **First Republic** in 1918, once again putting Prague at the centre of the country's political events. Architecturally, the city's position was consolidated too, as the inter-war period embellished Prague with a rich mantle of Bauhaus-style buildings.

After World War II, which it survived remarkably unscathed and industrially intact, Prague disappeared completely behind the Iron Curtain. Internal centralisation only increased the city's importance – it hosted the country's show trials, and at one time boasted the largest statue of Stalin in the world. The city briefly re-emerged on to the world stage during the cultural blossoming of the **Prague Spring** in 1968, but following the Soviet invasion, Prague vanished from view for another twenty-one years. However, there was one more upheaval to come. In November 1989, a peaceful student demonstration in Prague, brutally broken up by the police, triggered off the **Velvet Revolution** which eventually toppled the government. Today, the mood of optimism which followed the revolution is gradually beginning to evaporate, as the price of the last forty years' economic mismanagement makes itself felt, but there is still a great sense of release in the capital. Paranoia and fear, at least, are things of the past and there's a sense of openness here which makes any visit rewarding.

ARRIVING: THE PRACTICAL DETAILS

As capital cities go, Prague is relatively easy to get to grips with. Other than the airport, **points of arrival** are all fairly central, and the **public transport system** is excellent. Unless you've booked in advance, the only thing likely to take up much of your time on arrival is securing a **bed** for the night, though that should become easier once Praguers become used to the large number of tourists making for their city.

> The telephone code for Prague is ☎02

Points of arrival and information

Prague's **airport**, Ruzyně* (☎36 77 60/36 78 14), 15km northwest of the city, is pretty unimpressive, with few of the hi-tech facilities you'd expect from the capital city's main point of entry. For years, taxis from the airport into the centre cost 100kčs, expensive for Czechs but not for Westerners who could also usually avail themselves of the taxi drivers' long-established black-market services. But with fuel costs rising, taxis may soon become a less attractive option. There should be a sign at the airport's exit doors displaying the average fare to the major hotels; if in doubt, agree on a price before getting in. Otherwise, the simplest and cheapest way of getting into the centre is to take city bus #119 (every 20min), which stops

---

* Ruzyně is also the name of one of Prague's most notorious prisons, situated near the airport, in which Havel and many of the present government spent a fair few months at various times under the Communist regime.

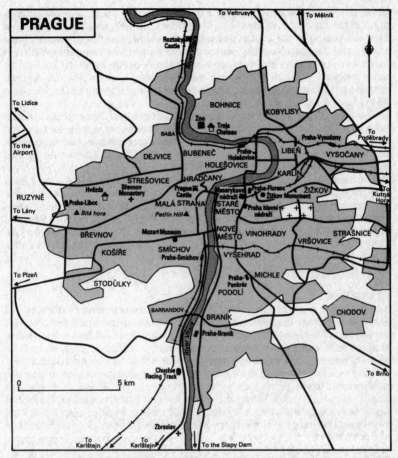

across the road from the main exit doors, staying on until the last stop, outside the Dejvická Metro station in Dejvice, at the end of Metro line A. Alternatively, take the more expensive *ČSA* bus, which drops you at the *ČSA* offices, not far from náměstí Republiky in Nové Město.

If you're heading out **to the airport**, don't get off the city bus until the last stop – the building saying *Praha letiště* (Prague Airport) is a good 2km from the international terminal. Once at the airport, it's not unusual for just one checking-in desk to be open, so get there with plenty of time to spare. The bus journey takes half an hour and there's a restaurant in which to fritter away your surplus crowns.

Arriving by train and bus

Arriving by **train** from the West, you're most likely to end up at the post-modern **Praha hlavní nádraží**, on the edge of Nové Město and Vinohrady. It's only a short walk into the centre from here, but there's also a Metro station inside the railway station. International expresses, passing through from Berlin/Warsaw to

Budapest/Vienna often stop only at **Praha-Holešovice**, in an industrial suburb north of the city centre, at the end of Metro line C. Some trains from Moravia and Slovakia wind up at the central **Masarykovo nádraží** (previously named Praha střed), near náměstí Republiky; and provincial trains from the south usually get no further than **Praha-Smíchov**, connected to the centre by Metro line B. The most awkward point of arrival is **Praha-Vysočany**, where slow trains from certain parts of East Bohemia terminate; to reach the centre from here, take tram #3 to Masarykovo nádraží.

There are secure lockers and **left luggage** offices (open 24hr except for a half-hour break in the middle of the night) at all the stations, though the lockers tend to be full during the day. If you're catching an **express train out of Prague**, don't leave buying your ticket (and seat reservation if necessary) until the last minute as the queues can be long and slow.

The main **bus station** is Praha-Florenc, on the eastern edge of Nové Město (on Metro line B), where virtually all long-distance international or domestic services terminate. Buses to most places in Czechoslovakia are fairly frequent and efficient, but remember to book your seat at least a day or so in advance, especially if you're leaving early in the morning or at the weekend. For destinations around Prague, you'll be directed to a variety of obscure bus termini, most of which are easy to reach by Metro. Ask at *PIS* on Na příkopé (see below) or check the timetables at Praha-Florenc for details.

Information

The best place to go for information is the **Prague Information Service**, or *PIS* (*Pražská informační služba*), at Na příkopě 20, Nové Město (April–Oct Mon–Fri 8am–8pm, Sat 8am–noon; Nov–March Mon–Fri 8am–7pm, Sat 8am–noon), whose staff speak at least four languages between them, including English, and will be able to answer most enquiries, except on the subject of accommodation (for which see "Finding a place to stay" below). *PIS* also distributes some useful free publications, worth picking up while you're there: *The Month in Prague*, an English-language leaflet listing the major events, concerts and exhibitions; a separate broadsheet of cinema listings; a fairly basic orientation map. If you want a more detailed **map**, go to the nearest *knihkupectví* (bookshop) or *tabák* and buy a *plán města,* which costs very little and has all the tram, bus and Metro routes superimposed upon it.

Getting around

Prague is reasonably small and most of its sights are concentrated in the five old towns, all of them easily covered **on foot**. At some point, however, in order to cross the city quickly or reach some of the more widely dispersed atttractions, you'll need to use the city's public transport system.

Public transport

Public transport subsidies look like being one of the first casualities in the move towards a market economy, so it's difficult to predict what will happen to what has always been a very cheap and efficient system. Meanwhile, **tickets** for all the transport options – the Metro, trams and buses – are interchangeable: you use a separate ticket each time you ride (apart from changing lines on the Metro, when you retain your ticket), punching it in one of the archaic little devices at hand. Instead of hoarding change for the yellow ticket machines, found inside Metro stations and at some bus and tram stops, it's easier to buy as many tickets as you think you'll need in advance from a newsagent, *tabák*, street kiosk or hotel reception desk. If you're zooming about the city, and changing frequently, it might be worth buying a **day pass** (which costs roughly the equivalent of eight rides), available from the red machines in Metro stations.

The futuristic Soviet-built **Metro** (daily 5am–midnight) is the most useful form of city transport; fast, smooth and ultra-clean. Its three lines (with a fourth planned) intersect at various points in the centre and the route plans are easy to follow – we've provided one below. The stations are fairly discreetly signposted above ground (and are not always exactly where they appear to be on the map); *výstup* means exit, and *nástup* means connection. Each ticket is valid for an hour, and should be punched at the guardless barriers before the commencement of the journey.

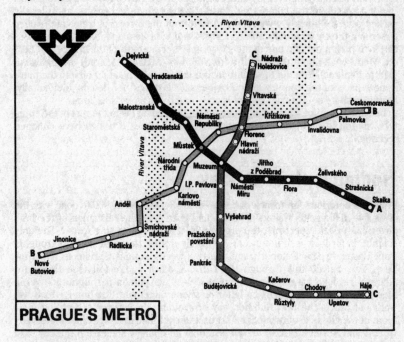

PRAGUE'S METRO

The **tram** system, in operation since 1891, navigates Prague's hills and cobbles with remarkable dexterity – the present Škoda ones are approaching their fiftieth year of service, but are slowly being replaced. After the Metro, trams are the fastest and most efficient way of moving around, running every 10–20 minutes throughout the day – check the timetables posted at every stop. Some operate specifically to transport workers in and out of town (Mon–Fri 5–8am & 1–3pm), while others run seven days a week and hourly throughout the night. Tram #22, which runs from Vinohrady to Hradčany, is a good way to get to grips with the lie of the land, and is a cheap method of sightseeing.

You'll rarely need to use Prague's **buses** and **trolley buses,** which for the most part keep well out of the centre of town. If you're intent upon visiting some of the more obscure suburbs, though, you may have to rely on them: their hours of operation are similar to those of the trams, and route numbers are given in the text where appropriate.

Taxis, cars and bikes

The easiest way to pick up a **taxi** is at one of the city's many ranks – notably on Václavské náměstí, Národní and outside the Obecní dům – although it works out cheaper if you flag one down on the street. Fares are rapidly approaching Western European prices due to the country's current energy crisis, so it's not a particularly cheap way to get around. If you can't find a taxi, phone ☎20 39 41 or ☎20 29 51.

Although traffic in Prague is relatively light, there's little point in **driving** around since much of the city centre is pedestrianised and the fines for driving in restricted streets, while hardly exorbitant, are frequently imposed by the police. Parking spaces in the centre, few and far between, are expensive, and illegally parked cars are quickly towed away. Add to that the careering trams and trolley buses and the treacherous cobbled streets, and your best option, if you do have a car, is to park it outside one of the skyscraper hotels south of the centre and take the Metro back into town – try the *Hotel Forum* (Metro Vyšehrad) or *Panorama* (Metro Pankrác). You might want to **hire a car** if you're heading off into the more remote parts of the country after Prague: see "Listings" for details. Incidentally, Prague rush-hour – insofar as there is one – can begin as early as 2pm.

Facilities for **bike hire** are non-existent in the capital (as in the rest of the country), though it might be worth enquiring at *PIS* to see if things have changed recently.

Finding a place to stay

Prague is notorious for its lack of beds – officially, around 10,000 to cope with the city's five-million-plus visitors a year – and even with the relaxation of the laws governing private operators, the problem is, if anything, getting worse. The only solution is to book well in advance, certainly during the **high season** (roughly from Easter to late October), and the two weeks around Christmas and New Year. You can do this through the *ČEDOK* office in London (see *Basics* for address), which charges a minimum of £30–50 per person per night, or (with a little knowledge of German) by letter or phone direct with the hotel, which will work out much cheaper. Another way of avoiding the hassles of fighting for a room in the city is to stay outside Prague and commute in. Places like Poděbrady (p.114) and Řevnice (p.120) are all less than an hour by train from the city, and their hotels and campsites are only very rarely full.

Booking offices

If you do arrive without a room reservation, currently the only thing to do is head for one of the two main **booking offices** for foreigners, *ČEDOK* or *Pragotur*. However, the alternative private agencies, like *Toptour*, that are beginning to emerge, should eventually relieve the queues. In the meantime, get there at least half an hour before the offices open, or if you've just arrived by plane, as soon as possible.

ČEDOK, Panská 5 (☎212 71 11; April–Nov Mon–Fri 9am–10pm, Sat 8.30am–6pm, Sun 8.30am–4.30pm; Dec–March Mon–Fri 9am–8pm, Sat & Sun 8.30am–2pm). Deals with the top end of the hotel market only.

Pragotur, U Obecního domu 2 (Mon–Fri 8am–9.30pm, Sat 8am–8pm, Sun 8am–3.15pm). Deals with the lower end of the hotel market and will also book private rooms for a minimum of three nights (no advance booking possible).

Toptour, Rybná 1. At the time of writing, the only private accommodation agency in Prague, dealing with private rooms only.

Hotels

If you do book in advance, or – less likely – have a choice on arrival, the following list gives a sample range of hotels, from the very cheapest to the most expensive. The price bands are given in the current sterling equivalent due to the uncertainty about the future movement of the Czech crown, and are for a double room.

Cheap (under £15)

Balkán, Svornosti 28, Smíchov (☎54 07 77). Bottom of the range in every respect; inexpensive but run-down. Metro Anděl.

Moravan, U Uránie 22, Holešovice (☎80 29 05). One of the few really cheap hotels in Prague, with doubles and trebles only. Metro Nádraží Holešovice.

Národní dům, Bořivojova 53, Žižkov (☎27 53 65). Reputedly the cheapest hotel in town, which makes it difficult to get a room. Tram #9, #10, #13 or #26.

Ostaš, Orebitská 8, Žižkov (☎27 28 60). Cheap and cheerful, and within walking distance of Praha-Florenc bus station.

Tichý, Seifertova 65, (☎27 30 79). *Tichý* means "silent", but don't believe it as this hotel is right on the main road. Tram #9, #10, #13, #26.

Middle of the range (£15–30)

Axa, Na poříčí 40, Nové Město (232 72 34). A tatty hotel, just five minutes' walk from náměstí Republiky.

Botel Albatross, nábřeží L Svobody, Nové Město (☎231 36 34). Beds for hire on a moored boat. Not quite as romantic or cheap as you'd expect, but the best of the city's three floating hotels.

Expensive (£30–100)

Alcron, Štěpánská 40, Nové Město (☎235 92 16). Top-notch 1930s' hotel, just off Václavské náměstí. A favourite haunt of Western journalists during the 1968 Prague Spring.

Evropa, Václavské náměstí 25, Nové Město (☎236 52 74). Without doubt, the most beautiful hotel in Prague but, surprisingly, not the most expensive. Built at the beginning of the century, it retains many of its period fittings – book well in advance.

Palace, Panská 12, Nové Město (☎26 83 41). Originally built in the 1900s; tastelessly modernised and thoroughly snooty.

Paříž, U Obecního domu 1, Staré Město (☎232 20 51). A modernised, turn-of-the-century hotel, superbly located off náměstí Republiky. Not as pricey as you might think.

Private rooms and hostels

Private rooms for rent are appearing all over Prague, but as yet there's no established line of communication between operators and customers (other than through *Pragotur* and *Toptour*). If you've got your own transport, you could try simply driving around and looking for *Zimmer Frei* (Rooms to Let) signs on houses in the outskirts.

Prague has very few **hostels**, and the ones that do exist are usually full of impoverished young Czechs and Slovaks. Still, they're worth a try if you're sticking to any kind of budget, and if the city is otherwise full, a hostel is more likely to find you a space than anyone else. In July and August, *CKM* lets out rooms in **student hostels**; to check on the latest addresses, go to the *CKM* office opposite the *Juniorhotel* on Žitná (Mon–Fri 10–11.30am & 12.30–5pm).

Dukla Karlín, Malého, Karlín (☎22 20 09). Prague's most central hostel, situated behind the Praha-Florenc bus station. Reception opens at 6pm and you'll be turfed out at 8am the next morning. If they're full, ask for floor space.

Juniorhotel Praha, Žitná 12, Nové Město (☎29 99 41). Very cheap for *IYHA* members, but invariably full. There are plans to open a new, related hostel, called the *Juniorhotel Vltava*, in the near future; ask at the *CKM* office for the latest information.

Strahov, Spartakiádní 5, Strahov. Permanent student hostel which may have room; five minutes' walk from the Strahov Monastery.

Větrník, Na Větrníku, Břevnov. If *Strahov* is full, this hostel is further out but worth trying. Metro Hradčanská, then tram #1 or #18 west.

Campsites

The only guaranteed way of finding somewhere to stay is to bring your own tent. Prague abounds in **campsites** and no matter how crowded they get, you'll rarely be refused a patch of grass. Facilities, on the whole, are rudimentary and badly maintained, but for the price they're hard to beat. *Pragotur* will help with information about campsites.

Caravancamp Vysoké školy, Plzeňská, Motol. 5km southwest of the centre. Open April–Oct. Tram #4 or #9 from Metro Anděl.

Džbán, Nad lávkou 3, Vokovice. Tent camping only. Tram #20 or #26 from Metro Dejvická; the site is 4km west, down Benešova.

Kotva Braník, U ledáren 55, Braník. 6km south of the city. Open April–Sept. Tram #3, #17 or #21 along the right bank.

Troja, Trojská 171, Troja. 3km north of the centre, by the chateau. Tram #5, #17 or #25 from Metro Holešovice, then a short walk. Open June to mid-Sept.

THE CITY

The city's most obvious orientational axis is the **river Vltava** (Moldau), which divides the capital into two unequal halves; the steeply inclined left bank, which accommodates the quarters of Hradčany and Malá Strana; and the more gentle, sprawling right bank, which includes Staré Město, Josefov and Nové Město. These central areas correspond exactly with Prague's original five historical towns. **Hradčany**, on the hill, contains the most obvious sights – the castle itself, the cathedral and the former palaces of the aristocracy. Below Hradčany, **Malá Strana**, with its narrow eighteenth-century streets, does most duty these days as the city's ministerial and diplomatic quarter, though its Baroque gardens are there for all to enjoy. Over the river, on the right bank, **Staré Město** (old town) is a web of alleys and passageways centred on the city's most beautiful square, Staroměstské náměsti. Enclosed within the boundaries of Staré Město is **Josefov**, the old Jewish quarter, now down to just a handful of synagogues and a cemetery.

HOUSE SIGNS

As well as preserving their Gothic or Romanesque foundations, many houses throughout Prague retain their ancient **house signs**, which you'll see carved into the gables, on hanging wooden signs, or inscribed on the facade. It's a system which originated in the fourteenth century, and still survives today, though now it's predominantly used by *pivnice* and restaurants. Some signs were deliberately chosen to draw custom to the business of the house, like *U zeleného hroznu* (At the Green Bunch of Grapes), a wine shop in the Malá Strana; others, like *U železných dveří* (At the Iron Door), simply referred to some distinguishing feature of the house, now usually long gone. The obsessive use of *zlatý* (gold) in the house names derives from *Zlatá Praha* or "Golden Prague" – either the halcyon days of Charles IV, when the new Gothic copper roofing shone like gold, or the period of alchemy under Rudolf II, depending on your viewpoint. Religious names, like *U černé Matky boží* (At the Black Madonna), became popular, too, especially during the Counter-Reformation. In the 1770s, the Habsburgs introduced a numerical system, with each house entered onto a register in chronological order, and later, the conventional system of progressive street numbering was introduced, so don't be surprised if seventeenth-century pubs like *U medvídků* (At the Little Bears) have two numbers attached to the house: 7 and 345, the former, Habsburg number written on a blue background, the latter, modern number on red.

Nové Město (new town), the focus of the modern city, covers the largest area, laid out in long wide boulevards – most famously Wenceslas Square – stretching south and east of the old town. Out of the centre proper, to the south, lies the castle of **Vyšehrad**, with Prague's **suburbs** spread out beyond, completely encircling the city.

Hradčany

HRADČANY's *raison d'être* is its castle, or hrad, built on the site of one of the original hill settlements of the Slav tribes who migrated here in the seventh or eighth century. The Přemyslid prince, Bořivoj, erected the first castle here, and, since then, whoever has occupied the hrad has exercised authority over the Czech Lands. However, unlike the city's other districts, Hradčany has never had an identity of its own. By around 1320, a town had grown up around the castle, but it existed as a mere appendage, its inhabitants serving and working for their masters in the hrad. Later, in 1541, all traces of the serfs, tradesmen, clergy and masons who had settled here in the Middle Ages were swept away by fire. It was the newly ensconced Catholic nobility who transformed Hradčany: with the Turks at the gates of Vienna, they were forced to pursue their building projects in Prague instead, turning the castle area into a grand architectural showpiece. But when the political centre of the Empire shifted back to Vienna, Hradčany's palaces were neglected as mere provincial buildings – although two world wars on, they have survived better than those of Vienna. Political power has returned, too, spreading its departmental tentacles across Hradčany, and though there is the odd café or *pivnice* in among the palaces, there's very little real life here beyond the stream of tourists who trek through the castle and the civil servants who work in the multifarious ministries.

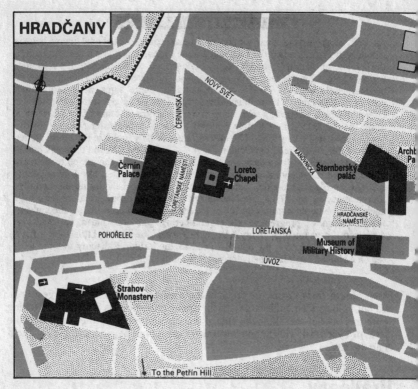

HRADČANY

CERNINSKA

NOVY SVĚT

KANOVNICKÁ

Černín Palace

LORETÁNSKÉ NÁMĚSTÍ

Loreto Chapel

Šternberský palác

Archb Pa

HRADČANSKÉ NÁMĚSTÍ

POHOŘELEC

LORETÁNSKÁ

Museum of Military History

ÚVOZ

Strahov Monastery

↓ To the Petřín Hill

Stretched out along a high spur above the Vltava, Hradčany shows a suitable disdain for the public transport system. There's a choice of **approaches** from Malá Strana, all of which involve walking. Most people take the steep short-cut up the Staré zámecky schody, but there are more opportunities for stopping and admiring the view by following the stately Zámecké schody, which leave you gasping at the castle gates. The alternative to all this climbing is to take tram #18 or #22 from Metro Malostranská, which tackles the hairpin bends of Chotkova with ease, and get off outside the Royal Gardens to the north of the hrad.

Prague Castle (Pražský hrad)

The opening hours are the same for all the sights within Prague Castle *(April–Oct Tues–Sun 9am–5pm; Nov–March Tues–Sun 9am–4pm), but you have to buy a separate entry ticket for each one, which costs just a few crowns. Entry to St Vitus Cathedral is free.*

Viewed from the Charles Bridge, **Prague Castle** stands aloof from the rest of the city, protected not by bastions and castellated towers but by an "immense unbroken sheer blank wall", as Hilaire Belloc put it, breached only by the great mass of St Vitus Cathedral. It's *the* picture-postcard image of Prague, though for the Czechs the castle has been an object of disdain as much as admiration, its alternating fortunes mirroring the shifts in the nation's history. The golden age

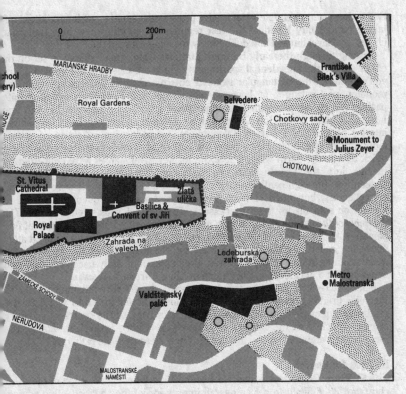

and the dark ages, Masaryk's liberalism and Gottwald's terror – all emanated from the hrad. When the first posters appeared in December 1989 demanding "*HAVEL NA HRAD*" (Havel to the Castle), they weren't asking for his reincarceration. Havel's occupancy of the hrad was the sign that the reins of government had finally been wrested from the Communists.

Two **architects** bear responsibility for the look of the castle. The first is **Nicolo Pacassi**, court architect to the Empress Maria-Theresa, whose austere restorations went hand in hand with the deliberate run-down of the hrad until it was little more than an administrative barracks. For the Czechs, his grey-green eighteenth-century cover-up, which hides a variety of much older buildings, is unforgivable. Less apparent is the hand of **Jože Plečnik**, a Slovene architect from Ljubljana, hailed as the first post-modernist, who was commissioned by the new Czechoslovak Republic to restore and modernise the castle in the 1920s – a strange choice, given Plečnik's widespread unpopularity with the architectural establishment of the time.

The courtyards

The **first courtyard**, which opens on to Hradčanské náměstí, is guarded by Ignaz Platzer's *Battling Titans* – two gargantuan figures, one on either side, wielding club and dagger and about to inflict fatal blows on their respective victims.

Below them stand a couple of impassive presidential sentries, no longer kitted out in the paramilitary khaki of the last regime, but sporting new blue uniforms, chosen by Havel himself and deliberately recalling those of the First Republic.

Passing through the early Baroque Matthias Gate, grand stairways set off on either side to the presidential apartments (which are closed to the public). Once you've entered the rectangular **second courtyard**, there's no escape from the monotonous onslaught of Pacassi's plastering and Plečnik's smooth granite paving. It's an unwelcoming and impersonal space, only relieved by Anselmo Lurago's Chapel of the Holy Cross, which cowers in one corner. Its richly painted interior houses the **Treasury** (klenotnice) – a pedestrian collection of, admittedly, priceless exhibits taken from the cathedral. Time's better spent taking a quick turn in the north wing, where the former royal stables were converted by Plečnik into the **Castle Gallery**, containing European paintings from the sixteenth to the eighteenth centuries. Rudolf II and Ferdinand II were both avid art collectors, but much of what they amassed was subsequently removed to Vienna or sold off by their successors. The best of what's left includes *The Assembly of the Olympic Gods*, a vast, crowded canvas by Rubens, a couple of fine paintings by Veronese, and *The Flogging of Christ* by Tintoretto. Immediately above the gallery are the **Spanish Hall** and the **Rudolf Gallery**, reputedly the most stunning rooms in the entire hrad complex, but sadly used only for state occasions (and, incidentally, the filming of Miloš Forman's *Amadeus*).

Once you're through to the **third courtyard**, there's very little time to take in Plečnik's granite obelisk, a monument to those who fell in World War I, or the miniscule equestrian statue of Saint George, a copy of the fourteenth-century original which is in the Basilica of sv Jiří (see below). Instead, inevitably, the focus of your attention will be the castle's finest treasure – the cathedral.

St Vitus Cathedral

The **St Vitus Cathedral** (katedrála svatého Víta) takes up so much of the third courtyard it's difficult to get an overall impression of the chaotic Gothic edifice. Its asymmetrical appearance is the product of its long and chequered history, for although the foundation stone was laid in 1344, the cathedral was not completed until 1929 – exactly 1000 years after the death of Prince Václav (Saint Wenceslas), who was the first Czech to build a church within the hrad. The cathedral enjoyed two great periods of building activity, separated by three centuries, reflecting the oscillating fortunes of the Czechs themselves.

First inspiration came from Charles IV, who had wangled an archbishopric for Prague, independent of Mainz, in 1344. Inspired by the cathedral at Narbonne, he invited a Frenchman, **Matthias of Arras**, to start work on a similar structure. Matthias, though, died in 1352, with the cathedral barely started, by which time Charles had been elected Holy Roman Emperor. Determined to make Prague the new capital of his empire, he summoned **Peter Parler**, a precocious 23 year old from a family of great German masons, to continue the work. For the next 46 years, Parler imprinted his slightly flashier, more inventive, *SonderGotik* style on buildings all over the city, but the cathedral got no further than the construction of the choir and the south transept before his death in 1399. Not until the Czechs themselves began to emerge as a nation in the nineteenth century, did building begin again in earnest. The burgeoning Romantic movement led to the foundation, in 1861, of the Union for the Completion of the Cathedral. Josef Mocker and Kamil

Hilbert completed the entire west end and, with the help of numerous Czech artists and sculptors, transformed the cathedral into a treasure-house for the emerging Czechoslovak nation.

The sooty Prague air has made it hard now to differentiate between the two building periods. Closer inspection, however, shows that the western facade, including its twin spires, is typically overrun with fussy neo-Gothic finishing, while the eastern section – best viewed from the Royal Gardens – recalls the building's authentic Gothic roots. The south door, or **Zlatá brána** (Golden Gate), is also pure Parler in style, decorated with a heavily restored fourteenth-century mosaic of the *Last Judgement*. Oddly then, it's above the south door that the cathedral's tallest steeple reveals the most conspicuous stylistic join; Pacassi's Baroque topping resting absurdly on a Renaissance parapet of light stone, which is itself glued onto the blackened body of the original Gothic tower.

THE INTERIOR

The cathedral is the country's largest church and once inside, it's difficult not to be impressed by its sheer height . Of the 22 side chapels the grand chapel of **sv Václav** (St Wenceslas), by the south door, is easily the main attraction. Built by Parler, its rich decoration resembles the inside of a jewel casket: the gilded chapel walls are inlaid with over 1300 Bohemian semi-precious stones, set around ethereal fourteenth-century Biblical frescoes, while above, the tragedy of Wenceslas unfolds in the later paintings of the Litoměřice school – a dazzling testament to the city's golden age, during the reign of Charles IV. But it's not simply the chapel's artistic merit which draws visitors. Officially dedicated to Saint Vitus, spiritually the cathedral belongs instead to Prince Václav, later Saint Wenceslas, whose remains allegedly were brought here after his death in 929 (or possibly 935, depending on which source you believe). An early Christian leader, intent on conciliation towards his German neighbours, he was only 22 when he died, killed at a church just outside Prague by his pagan brother, Boleslav the Cruel. The lion's head door-ring set into the chapel's north door is said to be the one to which Václav clung before being killed, and was transferred to the cathedral in late medieval times. A door in the south wall gives access to a staircase leading to the coronation chamber (only rarely open to the public) which houses the Bohemian crown jewels. These include the gold crown of Saint Wenceslas, containing some of the largest sapphires in the world.

The perfect Baroque counterpart to the sv Václav chapel is the **Tomb of Saint John of Nepomuk**, sited in the middle of the ambulatory, a work of grotesque excess, sculpted entirely in silver with free-flying angels holding up the heavy drapery of the baldachin. Where Charles sought to promote Wenceslas as the nation's patron saint, the Jesuits, egged on by the Habsburgs, replaced him with the Catholic martyr John of Nepomuk, who had been arrested and thrown bound

GOOD KING WENCESLAS

It's interesting to note that the nineteenth-century **Christmas carol**, *Good King Wenceslas*, is about as inaccurate as it could possibly be. For a start, Václav was only a prince, and never a king; he was "good" only in comparison to his fairly unpleasant brother, who had him killed; and the episode of the wood-gathering poor man was the invention of the carol's author, J. M. Neale.

and gagged off the Charles Bridge in 1393 on the orders of Václav IV, allegedly for refusing to divulge the secrets of the queen's confession. Legend has it that a cluster of stars appeared over the spot where he drowned, and his statue – which graces almost every main square in the Historic Lands – is traditionally depicted with a symbolic halo of stars. On the lid of the tomb, a cherub holds the saint's severed tongue, representing his unbroken oath of confidentiality. In reality, though, he was simply caught up in a power struggle between the archbishop and the king, and backed the wrong side – a fact which the Vatican finally admitted in 1961, some 330 years after his canonisation.

At the centre of the choir, within a fine Renaissance grill, cherubs irreverently lark about on the sixteenth-century marble **Imperial Mausoleum**, commissioned by Rudolf II for his father, Ferdinand I, and grandfather, Maximilian II, the first Habsburgs to wear the Bohemian crown. Beneath them lies the royal crypt (access via the south side of the chancel), where Rudolf himself is buried in a pewter coffin. A good number of other Czech kings and queens are buried here, too, reinterred this century in incongruous, identical 1930s' sarcophagi, including the Hussite King George of Poděbrady, Charles IV and, sharing a single sarcophagus, all four of his wives.

Of the later additions to the church, František Bílek's wooden sculpture of Christ on the Cross, on the north side of the transept, is the most striking, avoiding the imitative pitfalls of other contemporary works inside. Also worth some attention are the cathedral's modern **stained-glass** windows, through which stream shafts of rainbow light. The largest works, like the high chancel windows (executed in 1946–48) and the *Last Judgement* (1937–39) over the south door, are by Max Švabinský, while František Kysela employed a more abstract approach in the rose window over the west door, which contains a kaleidoscopic *Creation of the World* (1921). But by far the most famous work is the *SS Cyril and Methodius* window by Alfons Mucha in the New Archbishops' Chapel, commissioned in 1931 by the *Banka Slavie*. Each colour melts into the next, moving irresistibly towards the deep red central figure of a young boy.

The Royal Palace

Just across the courtyard from the south door of the cathedral, the **Royal Palace** (Královský palác) was home to the princes and kings of Bohemia from the eleventh to the seventeenth century. It's a sandwich of royal apartments, built one on top of the other by successive generations, but left largely unfurnished and unused for the last three hundred years. The original Romanesque palace of Soběslav I now forms the cellars of the present building, above which Charles IV built his own Gothic chambers. Both these levels have been closed to the public for some time, and these days you enter at the third and top floor, built at the end of the fifteenth century. Immediately after the antechamber (now the ticket office) is the bare expanse of the massive **Vladislav Hall** (Vladislavský sál), the work of Benedikt Ried, the German mason appointed by Vladislav Jagiello as his court architect. It displays some remarkable, sweeping rib-vaulting which draws floral patterns on the ceiling, its petals reaching almost to the floor. Here the early Bohemian kings were elected, and since 1918, every President since Masaryk has been sworn into office in the hall – including Havel on December 29, 1989. More irreverently, the hall is so large it was also once used for jousting tournaments, which explains the ramp-like Riders' Staircase, fitted into the north wing.

From the southwest corner of the hall, you can gain access to the **Ludvík Wing**. The rooms themselves are pretty uninspiring but the furthest one, the Bohemian Chancellery, was the scene of Prague's **second defenestration** (for details of the first, see p.88). After almost two centuries of uneasy co-existence between Catholics and Protestants, matters came to a head over the succession to the throne of the Habsburg archduke Ferdinand, a notoriously intolerant Catholic. On May 23, 1618, a posse of over 100 Protestant nobles, led by Count Thurn, marched to the Chancellery for a showdown with the Catholic councillors, Jaroslav von Martinitz and Wilhelm Slavata. After a "stormy discussion", the two councillors (and, unfortunately for him, their personal secretary Fabricius) were thrown out of the window. As a contemporary historian recounted: "No mercy was granted them and they were both thrown dressed in their cloaks with their rapiers and decoration head-first out of the western window into a moat beneath the palace. They loudly screamed *"ach, ach, oweh!"* and attempted to hold on to the narrow window-ledge, but Thurn beat their knuckles with the hilt of his sword until they were both obliged to let go." There's some controversy about the exact window from which they were unceremoniously ejected, although it's agreed that they both survived to tell the tale, landing in a medieval dung heap below, and – so the story goes – precipitating the Thirty Years' War.

The Basilica and Convent of sv Jiří and the Zlatá ulička

Don't be fooled by the uninspiring red Baroque facade of the **Basilica of sv Jiří** (St George). It's Prague's most beautiful Romanesque monument and inside has been meticulously scrubbed and ruthlessly restored to recreate something like the crumble-coloured stone basilica which replaced the original tenth-century church in 1173. The double staircase to the chancel is a remarkably harmonious late Baroque addition and now provides a perfect stage for the city's chamber music concerts.

To the right of the chancel, only partially visible, is the **burial chapel of sv Ludmila**, grandmother of Saint Wenceslas and widow of the first Přemyslid prince, Bořivoj I. She became Bohemia's first Christian martyr when she was murdered in 921 by the pagan faction in the Czech nobility – which, within a few years, claimed the life of Wenceslas, too.

Next door, the **Convent of sv Jiří**, founded by Boleslav II in 973, now houses the National Gallery's **Old Bohemian Art Collection**. The exhibition is arranged chronologically, starting in the crypt with a remarkable collection of Gothic art which flourished under the patronage of Charles IV. The works have been gathered from various Bohemian churches and are almost exclusively symbolical depictions of the Madonna and Child, the artists known only by their works and locations, not by name. Here you'll find – among other things – the monumental tympanum from the church of Panna Marie Sněžna in Prague, the nine-panelled altarpiece from the Cistercian monastery at Vyšší Brod, and the original fourteenth-century bronze equestrian figure of Saint George, which stands in the castle's third courtyard. The exhibition continues on the ground floor, gradually progressing into the Renaissance period, while on the first floor there is a series of canvases by the masters of Bohemian Baroque art, whose paintings and sculptures fill chapels and churches across the Czech Lands; Karel Škréta, Petr Brandl, Jan Kupecký and Matthias Bernhard Braun. There's even a little coffee bar on the ground floor if you're flagging.

Round the corner from the convent is the **Zlatá ulička** (Golden Lane), a blind alley of miniature seventeenth-century cottages in dolly-mixture colours. They were built by the 24 members of Rudolf II's castle guard, and the lane takes its name from the notorious alchemists whom Rudolf summoned to his court (but who actually conducted their experiments in the Mihulka tower). It remained as a kind of palace slum until 1951, when the lane was finally renovated for the tourists, and converted into a line of souvenir shops. A plaque at no. 22 commemorates Franz Kafka's brief sojourn here during World War I. His youngest sister, Ottla, rented the house and during a creative period in the winter of 1916 Kafka came here in the evenings to write. The tower at the far end of the lane is dedicated to its first prisoner, the young Czech noble Dalibor, accused of supporting a peasants' revolt at the turn of the fifteenth century. He apparently learnt to play the violin while imprisoned there, the sounds of which could be heard all over the castle – a tale which provided material for Smetana's opera, *Dalibor*.

If you're intent on leaving the castle altogether at this point, take the Staré zámecké schody, which lead down to Malostranská Metro station.

Beyond the castle walls

You can avoid the steep descent back to the Malá Strana by passing through the north gate of the second courtyard to the Prašný most, or **Powder Bridge**, erected in the sixteenth century to connect the new Royal Gardens with the hrad. On the left, Jean Baptiste Mathey's plain French Baroque Jízdárna (Riding School) has been converted into an **art gallery** (Tues–Sun 10am–6pm), showing twentieth-century Czech art – currently the only such exhibition in Prague, and likely to remain so until new premises in Holešovice are ready (see p.97). In the meantime, there's only a modest selection on view here, from the early Cubist paintings of Emil Filla and Bohumil Kubišta to the later Futurism of Josef Čapek, but it's all fine, original work which reveals the surprising strengths of contemporary Czech art.

Opposite the art gallery is the entrance to the **Royal Gardens** (Královská zahrada), founded by the Habsburg Emperor Ferdinand I and still the best-kept gardens in the country, with fully functioning fountains and immaculately cropped lawns. Consequently, it's a very popular spot, though more a place for admiring the azaleas and almond trees than lounging around on the grass. It was here that tulips, taken from Turkey, were first acclimatised to Europe before being exported to the Netherlands, and every spring there's an impressive, disciplined crop. Rudolf II was responsible for the "real tennis" court, built into the south terrace and tattooed with sgraffito by his court architect Bonifaz Wolmut; from the terrace, the view across to the cathedral and castle is unbeatable. At the end of the garden is Prague's most celebrated Renaissance legacy, the **Belvedere** (Královské letohrádek), a delicately arcaded summer house designed by the Genovese architect Paolo della Stella, one of a number of Italian masons who settled in Prague in the sixteenth century. Sadly, it's likely to remain closed for reconstruction for some time to come.

The Chotkovy sady and František Bílek's Villa

To the east of the Belvedere and a short walk down leafy Mariánské hradby, is Prague's first public park, the **Chotkovy sady** (founded 1833) which suffers from none of the coach-party crush of the Royal Gardens; you can happily stretch out on the grass here and soak up the sun. At the centre of the park, there's a grotto-like memorial to the nineteenth-century poet Julius Zeyer, an elaborate monument from which life-sized characters from Zeyer's works, carved in white marble, emerge amid much drapery.

Across the road from the park, hidden behind its overgrown garden, the **František Bílek Villa,** at Mieckiewiczova 1 (Tues–Sun 9am–5pm), honours one of Czechoslovakia's most unusual sculptors. Born in 1872 in a part of South Bohemia steeped in the Hussite tradition, Bílek lived a monkish life, spending years in spiritual contemplation reading the works of Hus and other Czech reformers. The villa was built in 1911 to Bílek's own design, intended as both a "cathedral of art" and the family home. Even so, it's a strangely mute red-brick building, out of keeping with the extravagant *fin de siècle* style of Bílek's sculptures: from the outside, only the front porch, supported by giant sheaves of corn, and the sculptured figures in the garden, give a clue as to its real function. Inside, the brickwork gives way to bare stone walls, lined with Bílek's numerous religious sculptures – giving the impression of walking into a chapel rather than an artist's studio. In addition to his sculptural and relief work in wood and stone, often wildly expressive, there are also ceramics, graphics and a few momentoes of Bílek's life. His work is little known outside his native country, but his contemporary admirers included Franz Kafka, Julius Zeyer, and Otakar Březina, whose poems and novels provided the inspiration for much of Bílek's art.

Hradčanské náměstí and west to the Strahov monastery

Hradčanské náměstí fans out from the castle gates, surrounded by the oversized palaces of the old nobility. For the most part it's a lifeless space, ignored by the tour groups marching through it intent on the hrad; only the occasional bookish Praguer or tired traveller make use of its park benches. Yet until the great fire of 1541, this square was the bustling hub of Hradčany, lined with medieval shops and stalls. After the fire the developers moved in, the powerful Lobkovic family replacing seven houses on the south side of the square with an over-the-top sgraffitoed pile which now houses the **Museum of Military History** (Vojenské muzeum; Tues–Sun 9.30am–4.30pm). As you might expect, this contains endless instruments of death, including such extreme opposites as an early Colt 45 and the world's largest mortar (courtesy of Škoda). Similarly constructed, Mathey's rather cold, formal **Toscana Palace** was built on the ruins of a row of butchers' shops, which once filled the west end of the square. However, not all the development was lost to monumental pomp, as the older, more palatable facades of the Hradčanská radnice and the Martinitz Palace indicate. Both are on the north side of the square, still richly patterned with sgraffito but closer in scale to the more modest proportions of the buildings in Malá Strana below. There's no such restraint in the sumptuous Rococo **Archbishop's Palace** (Archbiskupský palác; open Maundy Thursday only 9am–5pm), bought from the Royal exchequer by Ferdinand I and handed over to the first post-Hussite archbishop in the mid-sixteenth century – marking the beginning of the Roman Catholic church's suzerainty over the Czechs. The elusive interior is presently enjoyed by Archbishop Tomášek (known affectionately as "Frantši"), who is now in his nineties.

The Šternberský palác

A passage down the side of the Archbishop's Palace leads to the early eighteenth-century **Šternberský palác**, the main building of the country's National Gallery (Tues–Sun 10am–6pm). With many of the gallery's possessions displayed in other buildings throughout the city, what's on offer here is a relatively modest **European Art Collection** – though rich enough for most tastes – which divides into three main sections. Upstairs are works from the fifteenth to the eighteenth century, the most significant of which is the *Festival of the Rosary* by Dürer, depicting the Virgin Mary, the Pope, the Holy Roman Emperor, and even Dürer himself (in the top right of the painting). There are other oustanding works, too, like the *Portrait of an Old Man*, an unusually striking, almost minimalist portrayal by the Saxon painter Cranach, though you're more likely to be drawn to Ruben's colossal *Murder of Saint Thomas*, where pink-buttocked cherubs hover over the bloody scene.

Entering the **adjacent wing** propels you straight into nineteenth- and twentieth-century European art, starting with Gustav Klimt's *Virgins*, a mass of bodies and tangled limbs, which, according to tradition, were originally painted engaging in sexually explicit acts, only to be painted out in psychedelic colours in the final version. Although none of the artists here are Czech, many had close connections with Bohemia. Egon Schiele's mother came from Český Krumlov, the subject of a tiny autumnal canvas, while *Prague from the Kramář Villa*, by Oskar Kokoschka, witnesses the painter's lengthy stay here in the 1930s, when the political temperature got too hot in Vienna. Perhaps the most influential artist on show is Edvard Munch, whose one canvas, *Dance at the Seaside*, hardly does justice to the considerable effect he had on a generation of Czech artists after his celebrated exhibition in Prague in 1905.

By far the most popular section of the gallery is the "French" art section across the courtyard, featuring anyone of note who hovered around Paris in the last hundred years. Two works by Rodin are particularly appropriate given his ecstatic reception by Czech sculptors at the beginning of this century, following his Prague exhibition in 1902. Stay long enough and you'll also find an attractive early portrait from Matisse, a whole wall of paintings by Picasso, including his pre-Cubist *Naked Woman Sitting* (1906), two wonderful pink vases by Dufy, and a *Self-Portrait* by Henri Rousseau, in which the artist appears palette in hand. If all this has whetted your appetite, you can finish off with a stroll around the French sculpture in the palace gardens.

Nový Svět to the Loreto Chapel

Behind the Toscana Palace, nestling in a shallow dip, **Nový Svět** provides a glimpse of life on a totally different scale. Similar in design to the Zlatá ulička in the hrad, this cluster of miniature cottages, which curls around the corner into Černínská, is all that is left of Hradčany's medieval slums, painted up and sanitised in the nineteenth century. Thankfully, despite all the right ingredients for mass tourist appeal, it remains remarkably undisturbed, save for a few kitsch ateliers and swish wine bars.

Up the hill from Nový Svět, Loretánské náměstí is dominated by the phenomenal 150-metre-long facade of the **Černín Palace**. It's decorated with thirty Palladian half-pillars and supported by a swathe of diamond-pointed rustication, but, for all its grandeur, it's a miserable, brutal building, commissioned in the

1660s by Count Jan Humprecht Černín, one-time ambassador to Venice and a man of monumental self-importance. After quarreling with the master of Italian Baroque, Gianlorenzo Bernini, and disagreeing with Prague's own Carlo Lurago, Černín settled on Francesco Caratti as his architect, only to have the building panned on completion as a tasteless mass of stone. The grandiose plans nearly bankrupted future generations of Černíns, who were eventually forced to sell the palace in 1851 to the Austrian state, which converted it into military barracks. Under the First Republic, the palace housed the Ministry of Foreign Affairs, and on March 10, 1948, it was the scene of Prague's third – and most tragic – defenestration. Only days after the Communist coup, **Jan Masaryk**, son of the founder of the Republic and the last non-Communist in Gottwald's cabinet, plunged forty-five feet to his death from the top-floor bathroom window of the palace. Whether it was suicide (he had been suffering from bouts of depression, partly induced by the country's political path) or murder will probably never be satisfactorily resolved, but for most people Masaryk's death cast a dark shadow over the newly established regime.

The facade of the **Loreto Chapel** (Tues–Sun 9am–noon & 1–5pm) immediately opposite was built by Kilian Ignaz Dientzenhofer in the 1740s, and is the perfect antidote to Caratti's humourless monster; all hot flourishes and twirls, topped by a tower which lights up like a Chinese lantern at night – and which by day clanks out a tuneless version of the hymn *We Greet Thee a Thousand Times* on its 27 Dutch bells. But the two-storey cloisters and chapels are just the outer casing for the focus of the complex, the *Santa Casa*, a shrine built a century earlier than the chapel with Lobkowitz money and smothered in a mantle of stucco. Legend has it that the *Santa Casa* (Mary's home in Nazareth), under threat from the heathen Turks, was transported by a host of angels to a small village in northern Yugoslavia and from there, via a number of brief stop-offs, to a small laurel grove (hence *Loreto*) in Italy. News of the miracle spread across the Catholic lands prompting a spate of copy-cat shrines, and during the Counter-Reformation, the cult was actively encouraged in an attempt to broaden the popular appeal of Catholicism. The Prague Loreto was one of fifty to be built in the Czech Lands, each one following an identical design, with pride of place given to a lime-tree wood statue of the *Black Madonna and Child*, encased in silver. You can get some idea of the shrine's popularity with the Bohemian nobility in the **treasury**, much ransacked over the years but still stuffed full of gold. The padded ceilings and low lighting create a kind of giant jewellery box for the master exhibit, a tasteless Viennese silver monstrance studded with 6222 diamonds, standing over three feet high and weighing nearly two stone. It was constructed in 1699 on the posthumous orders of one of the Kolovrat family who made the Loreto sole heir to her fortune.

The Strahov Monastery

A short way west up Pohořelec from Loretánské náměstí, the chunky remnants of the zig-zag eighteenth-century fortifications mark the edge of the old city. Close by sits the **Strahov Monastery** (Strahovský klášter), whose gates have greeted visitors arriving in Prague from the West since its foundation in the twelfth century. Remarkably, Strahov managed to escape the 1783 dissolution of the monasteries, and continued to function until the Communists closed down all religious orders (and threw most of the inmates into prison) in 1948.

Through the cobbled courtyard, past a small church and chapel, is the monastery proper, famous for its rich collection of manuscripts and its ornate libraries. It now also houses the **Museum of Czech Literature** (Památník národního písemnictvi; Tues–Sun 9am–5pm), and the exhibition in the cloisters traces the development of the language from the Hussite period, right up to the twentieth century, when Czech typography became an art form in its own right, drawing on a variety of sources from Parisian Art Nouveau to Russian constructivism. It's Strahov's two **libraries**, though, that are the real gems. The first is the low-ceilinged Teologický sál, its wedding-cake stucco framing frescoes executed by one of the monks, based on the life of Saint Norbert (founder of the Premonstratensian order), whose relics were brought here in 1627. More impressive still are the late eighteenth-century frescoes in the loftier Filosofický sál, by the Viennese painter Maulpertsch and based on the History of Mankind.

Leaving through a narrow doorway in the eastern wall, you enter the gardens and orchards of the **Strahovská zahrada**, from where you can see the whole city in perspective: from the long ledge of Hradčany, across the rooftops of Malá Strana and the dome of sv Mikuláš, to the flat expanse of the Staré Město and the Žižkov monument behind. To the right, a path contours round to the woods of Petřín Hill (see below), a five-minute walk.

Malá Strana

MALÁ STRANA, the "Little Quarter", with its narrow eighteenth-century backstreets, is much less clinically presented than Hradčany. During the day its main arteries are filled with life, while around practically every corner there's a quiet walled garden: the perfect inner-city escape. In the evening, it's pleasant to stroll its hilly, gas-lit cobbles, and some of the city's best *pivnice* and *vinárna* are to be found in the quarter. However, few visitors stray from the well-trodden paths that link the Charles Bridge with Hradčany, thus bypassing most of Malá Strana – easy enough to do, since the whole town takes up a mere 150 acres of land spread across the southern slopes of the hrad. It's worth persevering, though, since most of Malá Strana's beauties are well-concealed.

More than anywhere else, Malá Strana conforms to the image of Prague as the ultimate Baroque city. It was here that Miloš Forman chose to shoot *Amadeus*, judging that its picturesque alleyways resembled eighteenth-century Vienna more than Vienna itself. And it's true; the streets have changed very little since Mozart walked them, as he often did in his frequent visits to Prague between 1787 and 1791.

Malostranské náměstí

The main focus of Malá Strana is the sloping, cobbled **Malostranské náměstí**, across which hurtle trams and cars, as well as a procession of people, some heading up the hill, others pausing for coffee and cakes at the *Malostranská kavárna*, whose tables and chairs spill out on to the square. The square itself is torn in two by the former Jesuit seminary and church of **sv Mikuláš** (St Nicholas), easily the most magnificent Baroque building in the city, and one of the last great structures to be built on the left bank, begun in 1702. For Christoph Dientzenhofer, a German immigrant from a dynasty of Bavarian architects, this was his most prestigious commission and is, without doubt, his finest work. For the Jesuits, it was their most ambitious project yet in Bohemia, the ultimate symbol of their stranglehold on the country. When Christoph died in 1722, it was left to his son, Kilian Ignaz Dientzenhofer (along with Kilian's son-in-law, Anselmo Lurago), to finish the project, which they did with a masterful flourish, adding the giant green dome and tower – now one of the most characteristic landmarks on Prague's left bank.

Nothing about the plain west facade prepares you for the overwhelming High Baroque interior. The fresco in the nave alone covers an area of over 1500 square metres, and is the work of the Moravian painter, Jan Lukáš Kracker, portraying some of the more fanciful miraculous feats of Saint Nicholas. But it's the sheer height of the dome that really impresses here; after years under the shadow of his father, this mighty effort revealed Kilian Ignaz's true talent.

Routes to Hradčany: palaces and embassies.

Of the two streets leading up to Hradčany from Malostranské náměstí, the first, **Nerudova**, is named after the Czech journalist and writer Jan Neruda (1834–91), who lived for a while at the Dům U dvou sluncŭ (House at the Two Suns) at the top

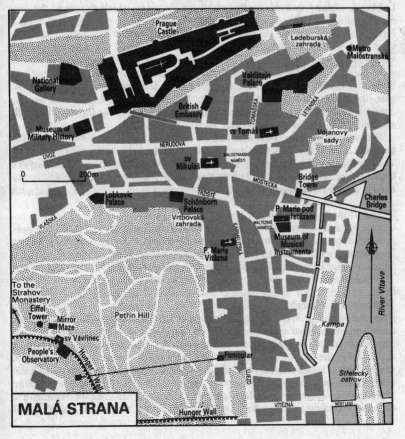

of the street. His tales of Malá Strana immortalised bohemian life on Prague's left bank, and inspired countless other writers, not least the Chilean Nobel Prize winner, Pablo Neruda, who took his pen-name from the lesser-known Czech, as a mark of respect. Traditionally, this area is Prague's artists' quarter, though apart from the son of Alfons Mucha, few of the present inhabitants are names to conjure with. The houses which line the long climb up to the hrad are typically restrained, many retaining their medieval barn doors. Past the Thun-Hohenstein Palace (now the Italian Embassy), Nerudova becomes Úvoz and leads eventually to the Strahov Monastery (see above). On the south side of the street a view opens up over red Baroque roofs, while to the north, narrow stairways squeeze between the towering buildings of Hradčany, emerging on the path to the Loreto chapel.

Another possible route up to Hradčany is by following Tržiště, which sets off from the south side of Malostranská náměstí. Halfway up on the left is the **Schönborn Palace**, now the American Embassy (whose current ambassador is Shirley Temple), its renowned gardens watched over by closed-circuit TV and machine-gun toting GIs – a far cry from the palace in which Kafka rented an apartment in March 1917. As the street swings left into Vlašská you come to the **Lobkovic Palace**, now the (united) German Embassy, which witnessed the first rumblings of the 1989 revolutions. In the summer of that year, several thousand East Germans (out of the six million or so who used to visit Czechoslovakia each year) entered the embassy compound to demand West German citizenship, which had been every German's right since partition. The neighbouring streets were jam-packed with abandoned Trabants, while the beautiful palace gardens became a muddy home to the refugees. Finally the Czechoslovak government gave in and organised special trains to take them over the Federal border, cheered on their way by thousands of Praguers and prompting the exodus which eventually brought about *Die Wende*.

The palace itself is a particularly refined building, best viewed from the gardens around the back which were laid out in the early nineteenth century by Václav Skalník, who went on to landscape the spa at Mariánské Lázně. They're usually open to the public, but given the hammering they took in 1989, they're still likely to be undergoing major botanical surgery.

North: Valdštejnské náměstí and around

Competing with the trams and cars that head down Letenská is a thankless task. A safer approach to **Valdštejnské náměstí** is to follow Tomášská, which passes Dientzenhofer's Dům U zlatého jelena, a rich Baroque building adorned with the figure of Saint Hubert, gazing adoringly into the eyes of his faithful stag (*jelen*). The **Valdštejn Palace** takes up the whole of the eastern side of the square. Fresh from his victory at the Battle of Bílá hora in 1620, Albrecht von Wallenstein (Albrecht z Valdštejna, in Czech) decided to build a palace befitting the most powerful man in central Europe. By buying or confiscating, and then destroying, twenty-one houses around the square, he succeeded in ripping apart a densely populated part of the Malá Strana to make way for the largest palace complex in the city after the hrad. The only part which is accessible to the public is the south wing, which contains a small exhibition on the history of Czech education and the teachings of Jan Amos Komenský (often anglicised to John Comenius, a man who was forced to leave his homeland after the victory of the Catholic Wallenstein, eventually settling in Protestant England). As for the rest of the palace, you'll have to make do with the view from the formal **Valdštejnská zahrada** (daily 9am–7pm), access to which is from a concealed entrance off Letenská. The occasional chamber music concert takes place in the garden's monumental *sala terrena* during the summer, while on the opposite side of the gardens, in the palace's former Riding School, there are interesting (if expensive) exhibitions of fine art and photography. Access to the Riding School is from the courtyard of the nearby Malostranská Metro station.

Along the north side of the gardens runs Valdštejnská, and tucked away down a passage here, by the Kolowrat Palace at no. 10, are four more separate palace gardens, collectively known as the **Ledeburská zahrada**. Theoretically, all of them are open to the public except the Fürstenberský zahrada, which belong to the nearby Polish Embassy, but the Černínská zahrada is the best-loved – a jumble of balustrades, terraces and (dried-up) fountains. That said, all the gardens may still be resoundingly inaccessible, as they have often been over the last few years, and if you're thwarted, try the **Vojanovy sady** instead, securely concealed behind a ring of high walls off U lužického semináře. It's a public park rather than a palace garden, with sleeping babies, weeping willows and the occasional open-air art happening.

South down Karmelitská and onto Kampa

Karmelitská runs south of Malostranské náměstí, past the **Vrtbovská zahrada**, one of the most exclusive of Malá Strana's hidden gardens; you enter from an unmarked passage at Karmelitská 25. Laid out on Tuscan-style terraces, the gardens twist their way up Petřín Hill, doling out increasingly spectacular rooftop glimpses of the city.

Further down the street, on the right, is the church of **Panna Marie Vítězná**, begun in Baroque style by German Lutherans before being handed over to the Carmelites after the Battle of Bílá hora. The church itself is dark and dingy, in a semi-permanent state of collapse, and the only reason to stop is to see the *pražské Jezulátko*, a high-kitsch wax effigy of the infant Jesus from Spain, enthroned in a glass case illuminated with strip-lights. Attributed with miraculous powers, it became an object of international pilgrimage equal in stature to the *Santa Casa* in Loreto, and, like the latter, inspiring a whole series of replicas. It continues to attract visitors (as the multilingual prayer cards attest) and boasts a personal wardrobe of no less than seventeen sets of swaddling clothes, regularly changed by the sisters in charge.

From the trams and traffic fumes of Karmelitská, it's a relief to cut across to the calm restraint of **Maltézké náměstí**, one of Malá Strana's village-like squares with a statue of John the Baptist at its centre. Its eastern end narrows to frame the church of **Panna Marie pod řetězem**, one of the oldest in Prague, founded by the Knights of Malta in 1169. All that remains is a wooden front porch and two severe towers, which once formed part of the fortified western bridgehead of the old Judith Bridge which preceeded the Charles Bridge. Just to the south, music wafts across Velkopřevorské náměstí, home to the Prague Conservatoire and the engaging **Museum of Musical Instruments** (Tues–Sun 10am–6pm), containing among other things a unique quarter-tone piano designed by the avant-garde composer Alois Hába.

From here, a few short steps past the French Embassy brings you on to the **Kampa**, Prague's largest island, separated from the left bank by a thin strip of water called the Čertovka (Devil's Stream). Unlike the rest of Malá Strana, the two or three streets that make up Kampa contain no palaces or museums; several eighteenth-century lanes and a serene riverside park offer a different diversion. The island was once the site of a wash-house for the nobility, then for centuries belonged to the Nostitz family, who were the first to develop on it. A pottery **market**, traditionally held in Na Kampě, the picturesque square connected to the Charles Bridge by some steps, has returned – albeit sporadically – with the better times.

It was in these unlikely surroundings that the Czech youth of the 1980s set up what became known as **John Lennon's mock-grave**, a seemingly innocuous wall of graffiti which still stands by the bridge over the Čertovka stream. Initially, it was somewhere to gather and pay respect to a famous pop star and lifelong pacifist, though it later developed into a forum for pouring out grievances against the totalitarian state.

Petřín Hill

Taking the first right off Újezd, a continuation of Karmelitská, brings you to the funicular (*lanovka*) which climbs up **Petřín Hill**, a bigger and better green space than most in Prague. It's good for a picnic, and topped by a scaled-down version of the Eiffel Tower, one of a number of sights set up in the park for the 1891 Prague Exhibition. The original **funicular** was powered by a simple but ingenious system, whereby two carriages, one at either end of the steep track, were fitted with large watertanks which were alternately filled at the top and emptied at the bottom. The new electric system, built in the 1960s, runs every ten minutes until around 11.30pm – tickets are the same as for the rest of the public transport system. As the carriages pass each other half-way, you can get out and visit the *Nebozízek* restaurant, where the views outstrip the food by a long chalk. At the top, it's possible to trace the southernmost perimeter wall of the old city – popularly known as the **Hunger Wall** (Hladová zeď) – as it creeps eastwards down to Újezd, and westwards to the Strahov Monastery. Instigated in the 1460s by Charles IV, it provided much needed work for the burgeoning ranks of the city's unemployed, hence its name.

Follow the wall west and you come to Petřín's aromatic rose garden, laid out before the **People's Observatory** (Mon, Tues & Thurs 2–6pm and occasional evenings), which offers a range of telescopes for use by the city's amateur astronomers. Nearby is Palliardi's twin-towered church of sv Vavřinec (St Lawrence), from where derives the German name for Petřín Hill – Laurenziberg. Further on still is the half-pint **Eiffel Tower**, an exact replica, though a mere fifth of the size of the original which had shocked Paris in 1889. Naturally, the view from the public gallery is terrific in fine weather, though you'll only be allowed up if the restoration work is complete. The conversion of one of the Gothic bastions of the tower into a **Mirror Maze** (Bludiště; April–Oct 9am–6pm) was a stroke of infantile genius by the exhibition organisers. There's a simple humour at work in the Hall of Mirrors, as well as an action-packed life-sized diorama of one of the Prague students' earlier historical victories, this time over the Swedes whom they defeated on the Charles Bridge in 1648.

From the tower, the path continues on the level, giving great views over palatial orchards and a sea of red tiles, until it ducks under the perimeter wall of the Strahov Monastery (see above). If you wander through the woods to the south of the Hunger Wall, you come to the Empire Kinský Villa, which contains an old collection of folk costumes and art, part of the original 1891 exhibition, but at present undergoing a lengthy reconstruction. Just north of the villa, hidden in the trees, is a **wooden church**, brought here, log by log, in 1929, from an Orthodox village in Ruthenia (now part of the Ukraine). Churches like this are still common in the northeastern part of Slovakia, and this a particularly ornate example from the eighteenth century, with multiple domes like piles of giant acorns.

MOZART IN PRAGUE

Towards the end of his short life, **Mozart** made several visits to Prague, staying first with his friend and patron Count Thun, in what is now the British Embassy (Thunovská 14). Later, he made successive visits to the Dušek family at the Bertramka Villa, tucked into the well-to-do hilly suburb of Smíchov. Having failed dismally to please the crowds in Vienna with *The Marriage of Figaro*, Mozart decided to premiere his next opera, *Don Giovanni*, in Prague's Nostitz Theater (now the Tyl Theatre), where *Figaro* had enjoyed great success. He wrote the finishing touches to *Don Giovanni* at the Dušeks, dedicating it to the "good people of Prague". He also gave an organ recital at the Strahov Monastery on an earlier visit, and in 1791, the year of his death, he conducted the première of *La Clemenza di Tito* in Prague. In Vienna he was buried as a little-known pauper, but in Prague 4000 people turned out for his memorial service, held in the magnificent church of sv Mikuláš, in Malá Strana, to the strains of his *Requiem Mass*.

As early as 1838 the Dušek's **Bertramka Villa** (April–Sept Tues–Fri 2–5pm, Sat & Sun 10am–noon & 2–5pm; Oct–March Tues–Fri 1–4pm, Sat & Sun 10am–noon & 1–4pm; Metro Anděl) was turned into a shrine to Mozart, but after a fire on New Year's Day 1871, very little survives of the house he once knew. None of this deters later generations of Mozart lovers, and these days what the museum lacks in memorabilia, it makes up for in Rococo ambience and the occasional recital.

Staré Město

STARÉ MĚSTO, the "old town", founded in the early thirteenth century, is Prague's most central, vital ingredient. People live, work and sleep here; most of the capital's markets, shops, restaurants and pubs are located in the area, and during the day a gaggle of shoppers and tourists fills its narrow streets. Most people unknowingly retrace the *králová cesta*, traditional route of the coronation procession established by the Přemyslids, and also the most direct route from the Charles Bridge to the old town square. However, many of the real treasures of the Staré Město lie away from the *králová cesta*, hidden in a silent, twisted matrix of streets. Apart from the Jesuits' powerhouse, the Klementinum, and the largely reconstructed Jewish Quarter, which sits within the old town, the streets remain substantially the same as the ones Jan Hus walked down in the early fifteenth century. The fire of 1541, which ripped through the quarters on the other side of the river, never reached the Staré Město, and its burghers built and destroyed fewer houses than the nobles who colonised the left bank. Nevertheless, like much of Prague, it's still overwhelmingly Baroque, built literally on top of its Gothic predecessor to guard against the floods which plagued the former town.

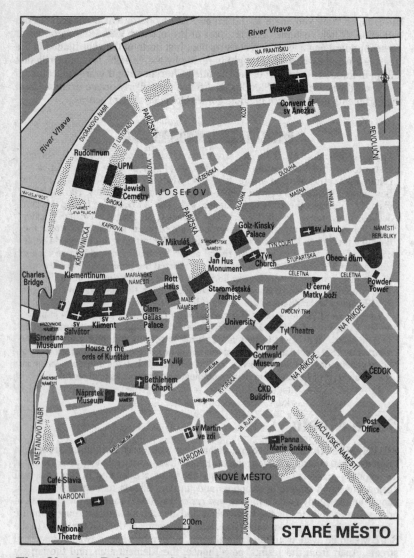

The Charles Bridge and the Křížovnické náměstí

The **Charles Bridge**, or Karlův most, is by far the city's most familiar monument. Laid out slightly skew-whiff between two mighty Gothic gateways, and punctuated by Baroque statuary, there's no better place from which to gape at the beauty of Prague or enjoy an uninterrupted view of the hrad. The bridge was begun in 1357 under the supervision of Peter Parler, and is named after his patron Charles IV (though until 1870 it was known simply as Prague or Stone Bridge). Its predecessor, the Judith Bridge, had been swept away in one of the Vltava's frequent floods, and the new bridge took a similar battering over the centuries. Due to its miraculous survival, countless apocryphal stories developed about its initial construction, including the claim that to make sure the bridge would hold together the builders mixed eggs (and, in some versions, wine) with the mortar. Having quickly depleted the city's egg supply, orders were sent out for contributions from the surrounding villages: the villagers of Velvary were worried that raw eggs wouldn't have quite he right consistency so they hard-boiled them, and from Unhošť they sent curd and cheese to bond the bricks even harder.

For all its antiquity, the bridge itself is pretty dull. It is the statues – brilliant pieces of Jesuit propaganda added during the Counter-Reformation – which have made it renowned throughout Europe. Individually, none of the works is outstanding, but taken collectively, in such a setting, the effect is breathtaking. A bronze crucifix had stood on the bridge since the fourteenth century, but the first sculpture wasn't added until the Crucifixion group was nailed to the cross in 1657. It's easily identified by the gold-leaf inscription in Hebrew above Christ's head, paid for, it is said, by a Prague Jew who was ordered to do so by the city court, having been found guilty of taking Christ's name in vain. Next to arrive was one of the Jesuits' favourite saints, John of Nepomuk, killed by being thrown off the bridge between the sixth and seventh piers and represented by the only bronze statue – it's now green with age, his gold-leaf halo of stars and palm branch gently blowing in the breeze (for the full story of John of Nepomuk's martyrdom see "St Vitus Cathedral", p.52). Most of the other thirty-odd statues of saints were erected between 1706 and 1714, carved in sandstone by the city's contemporary leading sculptors, Maximilian Brokoff and Matthias Bernhard Braun. The original sculptures have weathered badly over the years and are gradually being replaced by copies. Completely closed off to traffic, the bridge is now one of the most popular places to hang out, day and night, and apart from the steady stream of sightseers, the niches created by the bridge-piers provide a space for souvenir hawkers, buskers, punks and politicos.

Leaving Malá Strana, two unequal bridge towers, connected by a castellated arch, form the entrance to the bridge. The smaller, plainer tower was once part of the original Judith Bridge and the taller of the two is the work of Parler, crowned by one of the pinnacled wedge-spires more commonly associated with Prague's right bank. On the other side of the bridge, heading into Staré Město, is arguably the finest bridge tower of the lot, its eastern facade still encrusted in cake-like decorations from Parler's workshop. The figure of Saint Vitus is depicted centre-stage, flanked by Charles IV on the right and his son, Václav IV, on the left.

Křížovnické náměstí

Cross on to Staré Město and you're in busy **Křížovnické náměstí**, an awkward space hemmed in by its constituent buildings, and dangerous for unwary pedestrians. Hard by the bridge tower is a nineteenth-century cast-iron statue of Charles, erected on the 500th aniversary of his founding of the University, and designed by a German, Ernst Julius Hähnel, in the days before the reawakening of Czech sculpture. While you're here, you may as well pop your head around the door of Mathey's half-brick church of **sv František**, whose heavily decorated single dome nave is uncharacteristic of Prague. Over the road is the church of **sv Salvátor**, its facade prickling with saintly statues which are lit up enticingly at night. It's another over austere work by Caratti, originally commissioned as part and parcel of the Jesuits' vast Klementinum complex (see below), but worth a quick look if only for the light stucco work on its triple-naved interior.

Along Karlova: the Klementinum

Running east from bridge and square is the narrow street of **Karlova**, packed with people winding their way towards the Staroměstské náměstí, their attention firmly focused on *gofry* stalls, souvenir shops, and not losing their way. Few take in the Klementinum, the former Jesuit College, on the north side of the street, which covers an area in size second only to the hrad. In 1556 Ferdinand I summoned the Jesuits to Prague to assist in the re-Catholicisation of the Czech Lands, giving them the church of **sv Kliment** (St Clement) as their first base. Opening hours are erratic, but if you do get in you'll find a spectacular set of frescoes depicting the life of Saint Clement (whose fate was to be lashed to an anchor and hurled into the sea), and some modern additions by its new owners, the Uniate (*Grecko-katolický*) Church. The Jesuits proceeded with caution from their new church, but once the Counter-Reformation set in, they took over the whole University and provincial education system. From their secure base at sv Kliment, they began to establish space for a great Catholic seat of learning in the city by buying up the surrounding land and demolishing 25 old town houses.

The Klementinum wasn't completed until the eighteenth century, and the tables were turned soon after, in 1773, when the Jesuits were turfed out of the country and the Klementinum handed over to the university. It was turned into a library, which now houses over five million volumes, the **entrance** inconspicuously placed just past the sv Kliment church on Karlova. You're led through a couple of nondescript courtyards to the west wing, where a number of ornate eighteenth-century rooms survive intact. Officially, they're not open to the public, but if you can persuade the caretaker to let you in, you should at least be allowed to peek at the leather tomes, ancient globes and exuberant frescoes of the old Library Hall on the first floor. In the same wing there are temporary exhibitions of some of the library's prize possessions, which include the world's largest collection of works by the early English reformer John Wycliffe, whose writings had an enormous impact on the fourteenth-century Czech religious community, inspiring preachers like Hus to speak out against the social conditions of the time.

At roughly the centre of the Klementinum complex is the **observatory tower** from where seventeenth-century Prague's most illustrious visiting scientist, Johannes Kepler, did his planet-gazing. A religious exile from his native Germany, Kepler was court astronomer to Rudolf II, and lived at Karlova 4 for a number of years, during which time he drew up the first laws on the movement of the planets. He is also credited with the invention of the first astrological telescope, occasionally put on show in the Klementinum's Mathematical Hall.

Further down Karlova, the corner-house **Dům U zlaté studné** (House at the Golden Well), now a flashy wine bar, stands out like a wedge of cheese, its thick stucco reliefs of assorted saints designed to ward off the plague. Easier to miss is the **Clam-Gallas Palace**, which, despite its size – it takes up a good five or six old houses – is lost down a side street, one block further up on the left. It's a typically lavish affair by the Austrian, Fischer von Erlach, but really too big and burly for a side street in the Staré Město.

A couple of boutiques, hole-in-the-wall bars and a final twist in Karlova brings you out into the Malé náměstí, a square originally settled by French merchants in the twelfth century. It's best known for the russet-red, neo-Renaissance **Rott Haus**, previously an ironmongers' shop belonging to the German firm Rott – a building which immediately catches the eye, smothered in rich sgraffitoed agricultural scenes and motifs by the Czech artist Mikuláš Aleš. The original house sign of three white roses has been preserved on the central gable.

Staroměstské náměstí

Straight ahead is the **Staroměstské náměstí**, easily the most spectacular square in Prague, and the traditional heart of the city. From the eleventh century onwards, it was the city's main marketplace, to which all roads in Bohemia led, and was known simply as the Velké náměstí (Great Square), where merchants from all over Europe gathered. When the five towns that made up Prague were united in 1784, it was the square's town hall that was made the seat of the new council, and for the next two hundred years the náměstí was the scene of the country's most violent demonstrations and battles. More recently, the cafés have spread out their tables and the tourists have poured in to watch the town hall clock chime, and to drink in this historic showpiece.

Most of the square looks solidly eighteenth-century, but the Baroque facades hide considerably older buildings. The greatest exception is the colossal **Jan Hus Monument**, a turbulent sea of blackened bodies out of which rises the majestic moral authority of Hus himself, pointing towards the horizon. The monument bears an inscription which includes his most famous dictum, which became the motto of many a subsequent Czech revolution: *Pravda vítězí* (Truth Prevails). For the sculptor Ladislav Šaloun, a maverick who received no formal training, the monument was his life's work, commissioned in 1900 when the Viennese Secession was at its peak, but strangely old-fashioned by the time it was completed in 1915. It would be difficult to claim that it blends in with its surroundings, yet this has never mattered to the Czechs. Unveiled on the 500th anniversary of the death of Hus, accompanied by boisterous nationalist outbursts, it has always been of symbolic significance – draped in swastikas by the Nazis in March 1939, and in black by the Praguers in August 1968.

The Staroměstská radnice

When John of Luxembourg granted the town the right to have a town hall in 1338, instead of building an entirely new structure the community bought a corner house on the square, gradually incorporating neighbouring buildings to form the **Staroměstská radnice** (Old Town Hall). Over the next century, the east wing was added, with its graceful Gothic oriel and obligatory wedge-tower. On the south facade, the central powder-red building now forms the entrance to the whole complex (daily March–Oct 8am–6pm; Nov–Feb 8am–5pm). As long as at least five people turn up, a thirty-minute guided tour sets off every hour to tour the four rooms that survived the last war. Apart from a few decorated ceilings, striped with chunky beams, and a couple of Renaissance portals, you'll probably get more enjoyment from simply climbing the tower – one of the few with access for the disabled – for the panoramic sweep across Prague's spires.

On May 8, 1945, three days into the Prague Uprising, the Nazis still held on to the Staroměstské náměstí, and in a last desperate act set fire to the radnice. After the war, the south wing was rebuilt immediately, but of the neo-Gothic **east wing**, only a crumbling fragment remains; the rest of it is marked by a small stretch of grass. Set in the paving here, 27 **white crosses** commemorate the Protestant leaders who were publicly executed in the square on June 21, 1621, on the orders of the Emperor Ferdinand II, following the Battle of Bílá hora.

The greatest area of congestion is below the town hall's **Astronomical Clock**, where, every hour, tourists and Praguers gather to watch a mechanical performance by the figures of Christ and the Apostles: below, perched on their pinnacles, Death, Greed, Vanity and a Turk nod their heads until a cockerel pops out, flaps its wings and signals that the show's over. The actual clock has been here since the beginning of the fifteenth century, with the working figures added some years later by a technician who was then blinded, on the orders of the town council, to make sure he couldn't repeat the job for anyone else. In retaliation he stopped the clock, and it stayed broken until mended in the mid-sixteenth century.

Sv Mikuláš and the Týn Church

The destruction of the east wing of the town hall in 1945 rudely exposed Kilian Ignaz Dientzenhofer's church of **sv Mikuláš** (Tues, Wed & Fri 10am–1pm, Thurs 2–5pm), built in only three years between 1732 and 1735. The original church here was founded by German merchants in the thirteenth century, and served as the parish church of the Staré Město until the Týn Church (see below) was completed. Later, it was handed over to the Benedictines, who commissioned Dientzenhofer to replace it with the present building. His hand is obvious: the south front is decidedly luscious – painted in brilliant white, with Braun's blackened statuary popping up at every cornice – and it promises to surpass even its sister church of sv Mikuláš in Malá Strana, also built by Dientzenhofer. But inside, although caked in the usual mixture of stucco and fresco, the church has been stripped over the years of much of its wealth – partly because it's now owned by the Protestant Hussite church – and lacks the conviction of its namesake on the left bank.

There's no such reservation with the Staré Město's most impressive Gothic structure, the mighty **Týn Church** (Panna Marie před Týnem; open irregular hours), whose twin towers rise like giant antennae above the two arcaded houses which otherwise obscure its facade. Like the nearby Hus monument, the Týn Church is a source of Czech national pride, completed during the reign of George of Poděbrady (1436–71), the one and only Hussite King of Bohemia. In an act of proud defiance, he adorned the high stone gable with a statue of himself and a giant gilded *kalich* (chalice), the mascot of all Hussite sects. After the Protestants' crushing defeat at the Battle of Bílá hora, the chalice was melted down to provide a newly ensconced statue of the Virgin Mary with a golden halo. However, despite being one of the main landmarks of the Staré Město, it's well-nigh impossible to appreciate the church from anything but a considerable distance, since it's boxed in by – and in some cases, literally stuck to – the houses around it. To reach the entrance, take the third arch on the left, which passes under the Venetian gables of the former Týn School.

Given the church's significance, it's sad that the **interior** is mostly dingy, unwelcoming and in need of repair, with little of the feel of the original Gothic structure surviving the church's ferocious Catholicisation. One exception is the fine north portal and canopy which bears the hallmark of Peter Parler's workshop, and the fifteenth-century pulpit also stands out from the dark morass of black and gold

Baroque altarpieces, its panels enhanced by some sensitive nineteenth-century icons. The pillar on the right of the chancel steps contains the marble tomb of Tycho Brahe, the famous Danish astronomer who arrived in Czechoslovakia minus his nose, which he lost in a duel in Denmark. Brahe preceded Johannes Kepler as court astronomer to Rudolf II, and laid much of the groundwork for Kepler's later discoveries – Kepler getting his chance of employment when Brahe died of a burst bladder at one of Rudolf II's notorious binges in 1601.

The rest of the square

Until recently the **Dům U kamenného zvonu** (House at the Stone Bell) was much like any other of the burgher houses which line Staroměstské náměstí, covered in a thick icing of Baroque plasterwork and topped by a undistinguished roof gable. However, stripped down to its Gothic core in the 1970s, and displaying an unusual honey-coloured stonework and simple wedge roof, it now serves as a superb central venue for modern art exhibitions, lectures and concerts.

The Dům U kamenného zvonu is glued to the side of the largest secular building on the square, the late Baroque **Golz-Kinský Palace**, designed by Kilian Ignaz Dientzenhofer and carried out by his son-in-law Anselmo Lurago. The top floor houses specialist exhibitions of graphic art, taken from the large pool of works belonging to the National Gallery. However, for the last two generations of Czechs and Slovaks the palace is better known as the venue for the fateful speech by the Communist, Klement Gottwald, who walked out on to the grey-stone balcony one snowy February morning in 1948, flanked by his Party henchmen, to address thousands of enthusiastic supporters who packed the square below. It was the beginning of *Vitězna února* (Victorious February), the bloodless coup which brought the Communists to power and sealed the fate of the country for the next forty-one years.

Along Celetná to the Powder Tower

Celetná, a name derived from the bakers who used to bake a particular type of small loaf (*calty*) here in the Middle Ages, leads directly from the Staroměstské náměstí, east to náměstí Republiky. It's one of the oldest streets in Prague, lying on the former trade route from the old town market square, though its buildings were smartly refaced in the Baroque period, and their pastel shades are now crisply maintained. Most of Celetná's shops veer towards the chic end of the Czech market, making it a popular place for a bit of window-shopping, but the spruced-up surroundings are only skin-deep. Dive down one of the covered passages to the left and you soon enter the Staré Město's more usual, delapidated backstreets, one of which, Malá Štupartská, conceals the bubbling, stucco facade of the church of **sv Jakub**, a favoured venue for organ recitals, Mozart masses and other concerts.

Back on Celetná, at the junction with Ovocný trh, the **Dům U černé Matky boží** (House at the Black Madonna) is one of the best examples of Czech Cubist architecture, built in 1911–12 by Josef Gočár. It was a short-lived style (for more on which see "Vyšehrad", p.92), whose most surprising attribute was its ability to adapt existing Baroque motifs: Gočár's house sits much more happily amongst its eighteenth-century neighbours than the functionalist shoe-shop opposite. The original seventeenth-century Black Madonna still stands on the corner of the street behind her obligatory gold cage.

Celetná ends at the fourteenth-century **Powder Tower** (Prašná brána), the only survivor of the eight gate-towers which once guarded the Staré Město. It was used to store gun-powder – hence its name – but now looks somewhat forlorn without its accompanying fortifications. There's a small historical exhibition (April & Oct Sat, Sun & holidays 10am–5pm; May–Sept Sat, Sun & holidays 10am–6pm) in the tower, though most people climb straight up for the (quite modest) view from the top.

Beyond the tower is náměstí Republiky (see "Nové Město"), where, strictly speaking, you've left the Staré Město behind. If you're staying in the old town for the moment, either backtrack down Ovocný trh or head north to the convent of sv Anežka.

The Convent of sv Anežka

Five minutes' walk through the backstreets of the Staré Město, and a stone's throw from the Vltava river, the **Convent of sv Anežka** (St Agnes) is Prague's oldest surviving Gothic building. It was founded in 1233 as a convent for Franciscan nuns, and named after Agnes, youngest sister of King Václav I, who left her life of regal privilege to become the convent's first abbess. In 1874, she was beatified to try and combat the spread of Hussitism amongst the Czechs, and rumours circulated about the wonders that would occur when she was officially canonised, an event which finally took place on November 12, 1989, when Czech Catholics were invited to a special mass at St Peter's in Rome. Four days later the Velvet Revolution began. Even for the relatively agnostic Czechs, it was a happy coincidence.

The convent itself has been painstakingly restored over the last ten years and converted into an **art gallery** (Tues–Sun 10am–6pm). The well-preserved cloisters are now filled with unremarkable Bohemian glass, porcelain and pewter dating from the nineteenth century. Marginally more interesting is the large collection of nineteenth-century Czech art, housed in the three remaining chapels and continuing on the first floor. Much of Czech painting at this time was dominated by a depiction of historical events, and the preferred themes – on display in several works here – range from legendary figures such as Břetislav and Jitka to the real-life tragedy of the Battle of Bílá hora. Far superior in technique is the work of Josef Václav Myslbek, the grand master of Czech sculpture, whose simple statue of Saint Agnes from his *Monument to sv Václav* (see "Václavské náměstí"), is the gallery's most outstanding work. The rooms upstairs are dominated by the Romantic landscapes of Antonín Mánes, Josef Navrátil and Antonín Chittussi, which extol the virtues of the rolling hills of Bohemia. In the same vein, though more influential on successive generations of Czech artists, are the portraits and landscapes of Josef Mánes, who took an active part in the 1848 disturbances in Prague and consistently espoused the nationalist cause in his paintings.

From the Tyl Theatre to the Bethlehem Chapel

Heading south, back into the old town, a web of narrow lanes and hidden passageways unfolds, occasionally criss-crossed by busy pedestrianised streets. At the end of Ovocný trh, site of the old fruit market, is the back of the lime-green **Tyl Theatre** (Tylovo divadlo), built in the early 1780s by Prague's German community, by whom it was originally known as the Nostitz Theater. At the time, it was a daring thing to put on opera here in German as well as Italian, but the interior reflects the community's confidence – neoclassically proportioned and suitably ornate. It provided the perfect setting for the concert scenes in Miloš Forman's Oscar-laden *Amadeus*; since when the theatre has been covered in scaffolding and closed to the public.

On the north side of the Tyl is the **Charles University**, or Karolinum (named in honour of its founder Charles IV), established in 1348 as the first university in *Mitteleuropa*, open to all nationalities, and with instruction in Latin. It wasn't long before differences arose between the German-speaking students, who were in the majority, and the Czechs – with Jan Hus, the pro-Czech Rector, successfully persuading Václav IV to curtail the privileges of the Germans. In protest, the Germans upped and left, sparking off the first of many ethnic problems which continued to bubble away throughout the university's six-hundred-year history until the expulsion of the Germans after the Second World War. All that's left of Charles' original building is the Gothic oriel window which emerges from the south wall. Only a couple of small departments and the Rectorate occupy the original site, with the rest spread over the length and breadth of the Staré Město. The main entrance is a peculiarly ugly pink curtain of concrete by Jaroslav Fragner, set back from the street and inscribed with the original Latin name *Universitas Karolina*.

Rytířská, Uhelný trh and Batolomějská

Continue down **Rytířská**, and the large neo-Renaissance building at no. 29 was built to house the Prague Savings Bank, designed in the 1890s by Osvald Polívka, before he went on to erect some of Prague's most flamboyant Art Nouveau buildings. It's more than likely that the building will be closed for "reconstruction", since for over thirty years it housed the museum all Praguers loved to hate – dedicated to **Klement Gottwald**, the country's first Communist President. A joiner by trade, a notorious drunkard and womaniser by repute, he led the Party with unswerving faith from the beginnings of Stalinism in 1929, right through the show trials of the early 1950s. He died shortly after attending Stalin's funeral in 1953 (either from grief, or more likely from drink). Remarkably, he survived longer than any other East European leader from the retrospective condemnation of his own Party: while those whom he had personally sent to their deaths were rehabilitated, and the figure of Stalin denigrated, Gottwald remained sacred, his statue gracing every town in the country. Even as late as October 1989, the Czech Communists were happily issuing brand new 100kčs notes decorated with his bloated face (there are still some in circulation).

Denied the dubious privilege of a visit to the Gottwald museum, console yourself with the flourishing clothes' **markets** which line the narrow streets of V kotcích and Havelská (the latter no relation to the President, but named after the Irish monk Saint Gall, or sv Havel in Czech). **Uhelný trh**, which gets its name from the *uhlí* (coal) which was sold here from the fourteenth century onwards, now specialises in flowers, plants and vegetables, all of which should increase in volume (and price) over the next few years.

Walk down Martinská and the street miraculously opens out to make room for the twelfth-century church of **sv Martin ve zdi** (St Martin-in-the-Walls), which found itself inside the new Gothic fortifications when they were constructed in the fourteenth century, and separated from the village of sv Martin that it had originally been built to serve. It's still essentially a Romanesque structure, adapted to suit Gothic tastes a century later and thoroughly restored at the beginning of this century, when the creamy neo-Renaissance tower was added. It belongs to the Church of the Czech Brethren, to whom it has particular significance as the place where "communion in both kinds" (ie bread and wine), one of the fundamental demands of the Hussites, was first administered in 1414.

Round the corner is the gloomy lifeless street of **Bartolomějská**, dominated by a tall, grim-looking building which served as the main interrogation centre of the universally detested secret police, *Statníbezpečnost*, or StB. Although now officially disbanded, the StB remains one of the most controversial issues of the post-revolutionary period. As in the rest of Eastern Europe, the run up to the first free elections in June 1990 was marred by accusations and revelations of StB involvement, which caused the downfall of a number of leading politicians right across the political spectrum.

The Bethlehem Chapel and around

Leave the dark shadows of Bartolomějská for Betlémské náměstí, named after the **Bethlehem Chapel** (Betlémská kaple), whose high wooden gables face on to the square. The chapel is associated with the reformist teachings of Jan Hus, who preached sermons here from 1402 to 1413, not in the customary Latin, but in the language of the masses – Czech. This fact did not escape the Jesuits, who completely altered the original building once they'd got the upper hand in the religious wars, only for it to be demolished after they were expelled by the Habsburgs in 1773. What you see now (when it re-opens) is a faithful – though ruthless – reconstruction using the original plans. Surprisingly, this was carried out after the war by the Communists who, like many Czechs (including some Catholics), looked kindly on Hus as a Czech nationalist and social critic as much as a religious reformer.

The outward appearance of the nearby church of **sv Jiljí** (St Giles), on Husova, suggests another Gothic masterpiece, but the interior is decked out in the familiar white and gold excess of the eighteenth century. The frescoes, by Václav Vavřinec Reiner (who's buried in the church), are full of praise for the Dominican Order who commissioned the work, having taken over the church after the Protestant defeat in 1620. Other paintings depict the tale of Thomas Aquinas, the thirteenth-century Dominican theologian, and the unhappy story of Giles himself, a ninth-century hermit who is thought to have lived somewhere in Provence. Out one day with his pet deer, Giles was chased by the hounds of King Wanda of the Visigoths and struck by an arrow meant for the deer. The hounds were rooted to the spot by an invisible power, while the wounded Giles defended his pet – the hermit was later looked upon as the patron saint of cripples.

A short step away on Řetězová is the **House of the Lords of Kunštát and Poděbrady** (Tues–Sun 10am–noon & 1–6pm), who owned the building from 1406 onwards. It's not exactly gripping, but it does give you a clear impression of the antiquity of the houses in this area, and of the way in which the new Gothic town was built on top of the old Romanesque one. Thus the floor on which you enter was originally the first floor of a twelfth-century palace, whose ground floor has been excavated in the cellars.

Drifting towards the river from Betlémské náměstí, you pass the **Divadlo na zábradlí**, on Anenské náměstí, which Havel joined in the 1960s. Then it was the centre of Prague's absurdist theatre, with Havel working first as a stagehand and later as its resident playwright. Over by the weeping willow, which droops its tentacles over the embankment, is a statue of Smetana – the nineteenth-century Czech composer – sitting looking out over the Vltava. He gets more exposure in the adjacent **Smetana Museum** (daily 10am–5pm; closed Tues), for serious fans only but housed in a gaily decorated building that once did duty as the city's waterworks.

Josefov (The Jewish Quarter)

It is crowded with horses; traversed by narrow streets not remarkable for cleanliness, and has altogether an uninviting aspect. Your sanitary reformer would here find a strong case of overcrowding.

Walter White "A July Holiday in Saxony, Bohemia and Silesia" (1857)

And so they did. In less than half a century after Walter White's comments, all that was left of **JOSEFOV** was six synagogues, the town hall and the medieval cemetery. At the end of the nineteenth century, a period of great economic growth for the Empire, it was decided that Prague should be turned into a beautiful bourgeois city, modelled on Paris. The key to this transformation was the "sanitisation" of the ghetto which began in 1893, a process which reduced the notorious malodorous backstreets and alleyways of Josefov to ashes and replaced them with block after block of luxurious five-storey mansions. The Jews, gypsies and prostitutes were cleared out and the area became a desirable residential quarter, rich in Art Nouveau murals, doorways and decorative sculpture – the beginning of the end for a community which had existed for almost a millennium.

Geographically, Josefov lies to the northwest of Staroměstské náměstí, between the church of sv Mikuláš and the Vltava river. All the "sights" are part of the **State Jewish Museum** (April–Oct daily 9am–5pm; Nov–March daily except Sat 9am–4.30pm) and entry to them is covered by one ticket which you can buy from the box office in the Klaus Synagogue, next door to the Old Jewish Cemetery on U starého hřbitova.

Some history

Jews probably settled in Prague as early as the tenth century. To begin with, under Vratislav II, they were required to wear a yellow cloak as a distinguishing mark, but it wasn't until the thirteenth century that they were actually herded into a walled ghetto within the Staré Město, cut off from the rest of the town and subject to a curfew. As elsewhere, the Jews were used as scapegoats whenever there were social tensions – the pogrom of 1389 saw 3000 Jews massacred, some while sheltering in the Old-New Synagogue. But in comparison with other parts of Europe, the Renaissance in Prague was a time of cultural and economic prosperity for some Jews. Mordecai Maisl, who became Rudolf II's minister of finance, was the symbol of a successful generation, and his money bought Josefov a town hall, a cemetery and another synagogue. About this time, Rabbi Löw, who is buried in the old cemetery, wrote his famous stories about "the golem", a benign precursor of Shelley's Frankenstein. The ghetto was considerably enlarged during the seventeenth century, as the population grew to around 7000, but the Counter-Reformation meant difficult times for all non-Catholics and dress regulations were reintroduced. Although the Empress Maria Theresa abolished the law confining Jews to the ghetto, and Joseph II removed the gates (hence the ghetto's official name of Josefov, or Josefstadt) the racial restrictions on Jews weren't fully removed until 1848, after a particularly vicious pogrom. Even then, things did not really improve for the mixed ghetto population, who still inhabited what was the most densely populated area in Prague in the late nineteenth century.

As tensions between the German-speaking minority and the Czechs in Prague grew worse, the Jews found themselves caught in the firing line – "like powerless stowaways attempting to steer a course through the storms of embattled nationalities", as one Prague Jew put it. The increasingly chauvinistic German-speaking minority happily condemned Jews and Slavs in the same breath, whilst to the Czechs – since most of Prague's Jews spoke German or Yiddish – they were pigeon-holed as Germans. And when Hitler invaded, the Jews of the Czech Lands were transferred to Terezín (see p.175) to await their fate. The few relics left in the Jewish Quarter survived the war intact only because Hitler planned to turn the historic Prague ghetto into a museum to commemorate "the decadent culture of an extinct race". As Jews all over Europe were shipped off to the gas chambers, their religious artefacts were sent to Prague: put bluntly, the treasures survived but the people did not. As few as 40,000 Czech and Slovak Jews returned from the concentration camps, but many were scared off by the summary expulsion of German-speakers which took place after the war, and emigrated to Israel. Ironically, of those that did return, many joined the Communist Party, only to find themselves victims of Stalinist anti-semitic wrath during the 1950s. Nowadays there are fewer than 2000 Jews still living in Prague.

The sights

Josefov covered such a tiny area that under the new 1890s' street-plan, "three hundred wretched houses" became "eighty-one apartment palaces", and the number of streets was reduced to a mere handful. Through the heart of the old ghetto now runs the ultimate bourgeois avenue, **Pařížská**, a riot of turn-of-the-century sculpturing, spikes and turrets. It's Josefov's main street, a lively stretch of international airline offices and glitzy boutiques, though once you leave it, you are immediately in the former ghetto, now one of the most restful parts of the old town.

Halfway down Pařížská, on the left, is the steep brick gable of the **Old-New Synagogue** (Staronová synagoga), completed in the fourteenth century and now the oldest surviving synagogue in Europe. Originally, it was known simply as the New Synagogue, but by the time the ghetto had been gutted by fire several times, it had become the oldest of the "new" synagogue buildings in the quarter – hence its name. It's still the religious centre of Prague's Jewish community and you'll find it closed to visitors on the sabbath. Since Jews were prevented by law from becoming architects, the building was put together by a Cistercian workshop and its five-star ribbing is unique for Bohemia. Inside, you pass through one of the two low vestibules from which women were allowed to watch the proceedings, before reaching the grubby medieval hall, originally reserved for men only. There's little natural light here and only the low glow from the chandeliers lights up the central lectern on which the *torah* sits. In 1357, Charles IV allowed the Jews to fly their own municipal standard, a moth-eaten remnant of which is still on show. The other tattered banner which hangs in the hall was a gift to Prague's Jews from the Emperor Ferdinand II for helping fend off the Swedes in 1648. On

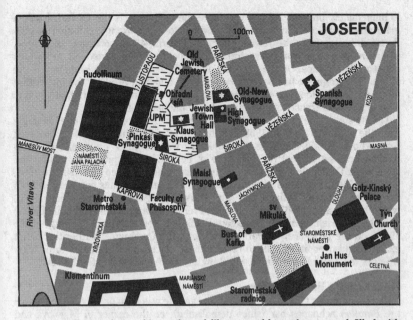

the west wall is a glass cabinet, shaped like two tablets of stone and filled with tiny personalised light bulbs, which light up on the anniversary of that person's death (there's even one for Kafka).

Opposite the synagogue is the **Jewish Town Hall** (Židovnická radnice), founded and funded by Maisl in the sixteenth century and afterwards turned into a creamy-pink Baroque house crowned by a wooden clock tower. In addition to the four main clocks, there's a Hebrew one stuck on the north gable which (like the Hebrew script) goes "backwards". Next door is the **High Synagogue**, once part of the town hall, whose rich interior stands in complete contrast to its dour, grey facade. The huge vaulted hall into which you descend is now used to display a mere fraction of the many hundreds of **Jewish textiles**, dating from the sixteenth to the early twentieth century, gathered here by the Nazis for their infamous museum.

The Old Jewish cemetery and the other synagogues

The main reason most people visit Josefov is to see the **Old Jewish Cemetery** (Starý židovský hřbitov), or *Beth Chaim* in Hebrew, meaning House of Life. Established in the fifteenth century, it was in use until 1787 when another site was established in the suburb of Žižkov, by which time there were some 100,000 graves here, one on top of the other, the majority buried far below the uneven crust. Get there before the crowds, and it can be a poignant reminder of the ghetto, its inhabitants subjected to inhuman overcrowding even in death. The rest of Prague recedes beyond the sombre lime trees and cramped perimeter walls, the haphazard headstones and Hebrew inscriptions casting a powerful spell. Small messages left on graves, held there by pebbles, wait for the wind to blow them away, only to be replaced by more.

Immediately on your left, as you leave the cemetery, is the **Obřadní síň**, a grim nineteenth-century house now devoted to a harrowing exhibition of children's drawings from the Jewish ghetto in Terezín, 40km northwest of Prague, where most Czech Jews were transported before being carted off to various concentration camps. On the opposite side of the entrance to the cemetery is the **Klaus Synagogue**, a late seventeenth-century building, used for the interesting temporary exhibitions put on by the State Jewish Museum. It's here that you buy your ticket for entrance to most of Josefov's buildings and sights.

On the south side of the cemetery, the **Pinkas Synagogue** juts out at an angle from the perimeter wall. In 1958 a chilling memorial to the 77,297 Czechoslovak Jews who were killed during the Holocaust was unveiled – a simple *menorah* (candelabra) set against the backdrop of never-ending names carved into the stonework. Disappointingly, though, the synagogue has been closed since 1968, allegedly due to problems with the masonry. The same fate has befallen Josefov's two other surviving synagogues: the **Maisl Synagogue** (closed since 1986), which houses an exhibition of gold and silverwork, *torah* scrolls and cult objects; and the Moorish **Spanish Synagogue** (closed "for electrical rewiring" since 1980), on the other side of Pařížská. Clearly, the Communist authorities didn't exactly bend over backwards to restore these places, and it remains to be seen whether the new administration will show any more enthusiasm for the task.

Franz Kafka: a life in Josefov

Kafka spent most of life in and around Josefov. He was born on July 3, 1883 above the *Batalion* schnapps bar (since demolished), on the corner of Maislova and Kaprova, now marked by a modern bust of the writer on the opposite side of the street. His father was an upwardly mobile small businessman who ran a fancy-goods shop on Staroměstské náměstí. In 1889, the family moved out of Josefov and lived for seven years in the beautiful Renaissance Dům U minuty, next door to the Staroměstská radnice, during which time Kafka attended the *Volksschule* on Masná (now a Czech primary school), followed by a spell at an exceptionally strict German *Gymnasium*, located on the third floor of the Golz-Kinský Palace. At eighteen, he began a law degree at the German University in Prague, where he met his lifelong friend and posthumous biographer and editor of his works, Max Brod. Shortly after graduating he became a clerk for the Workers Accident Insurance Company, whose offices were on Na poříčí, a job he held until he was forced to retire through ill-health in 1922. Illness plagued him throughout his life and he spent many months as a patient at one of the innumerable spas in German-speaking *Mitteleuropa*. He was engaged three times, twice to the same woman, each time without success, finally leaving home at the age of thirty-one for bachelor digs on the corner of Dlouhá and Masná, where he wrote the bulk of his most famous work *The Trial*. He died of tuberculosis in a Viennese sanatorium on June 3, 1924, at the age of forty, and is buried in the New Jewish Cemetery in Vinohrady.

As a German among Czechs, as a Jew among Germans, and as an agnostic among believers, Kafka had good reason to live in a constant state of fear, or *Angst*. Life was precarious for Prague's Jews and the destruction of the Jewish Quarter which continued throughout his childhood – the so-called "sanitisation" – had a profound effect on his psyche, as he himself admitted. It comes as a surprise to many Kafka readers that anyone immersed in such a beautiful city could write such claustrophobic and paranoid texts; and that someone who mixed in the café society of the time could write in a style so completely at odds with his verbose, artistic friends. It's also hard to accept that Kafka could find no publisher for *The Castle* or *The Trial* during his lifetime, though after his death this problem became even more acute. His works were banned in Nazi Germany, then across Europe, and even after the war, in his native Czechoslovakia, his works were deliberately overlooked, along with those of most German-Czech authors. It was the 1962 Writers' Union conference (which many see as the beginning of the Prague Spring) which finally rehabilitated him, though the Soviet invasion saw the removal of Kafka's bust from Josefov and another tacit ban on his works. It would be surprising, to say the least, if a Kafka Museum did not appear soon in Josefov to make amends for this past neglect.

Around Josefov

As Kaprova and Široká emerge from Josefov, they meet at the newly christened **náměstí Jana Palacha**, previously sporting a red star-shaped flower bed and going by the name of náměstí Krasnoarmejců (Red Army Square). It was this, as much as the fact that one of the buildings on the square is the Faculty of Philosophy at which Palach (see "Václavské náměstí", below) was a student, that prompted the new authorities to make the first change of street names here in 1989. By a strange coincidence, the street which intersects the square from the north is 17 listopadu (17 November), originally commemorating the students' anti-Nazi demonstration of 1939, but now equally good for more recent events.

The north side of the square is taken up by the **Rudolfinum**, a self-important nineteenth-century building, designed by Josef Zítek and Josef Schulz to house an art gallery, museum and concert hall for the Czech-speaking community. In 1918, however, it became the seat of the new Czechoslovak parliament, only returning to its original artistic purpose in 1946; these days, it's one of the capital's main concert halls. Across 17 listopadu from here, the **UPM**, or Uměleckoprůmyslové muzeum (Tues–Sun 10am–6pm), is installed in another of Schulz's creations. Literally speaking, this is a "Museum of Decorative Arts", though the translation hardly does justice to what is one of the most fascinating museums in the capital. From its foundation in 1885, through to the end of the First Republic, the UPM received the best that the Czech modern movement had to offer, from Art Nouveau to the avant-garde, and judging from previous catalogues and the various short-term exhibitions mounted in the past, its collection is unrivalled. Unfortunately, the permanent exhibition, a tasting sample from each of the main artistic periods from the Renaissance to the 1930s, only hints at the wealth of exhibits stored away in the museum's vaults. If you're interested in modern Czech art, there's a **public library** in the building (Mon noon–6pm, Tues–Fri 10am–6pm; closed July & Aug), which specialises in catalogues and material from previous exhibitions.

Nové Město

NOVÉ MĚSTO is the largest and most cosmopolitan of Prague's five towns, taking in most of the city's nightclubs, cafés, fast-food outlets and department stores. A relatively prosperous area of state-sponsored consumerism, it's now taking off under the free market with impromptu stalls, soap-box speakers,

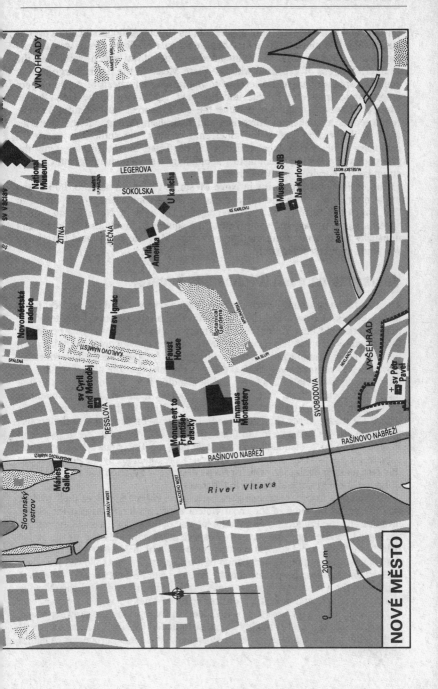

NOVÉ MĚSTO

hustlers and buskers ever more apparent in its streets. Although it comes over as a sprawling late nineteenth-century bourgeois quarter, Nové Město was actually founded in 1348 by Charles IV, intended as a new town which would link the southern fortress of Vyšehrad with the Staré Město to the north. Large market squares, wide streets, and a level of town-planning far ahead of its time, were employed to transform Prague into the new capital city of the Holy Roman Empire. However, it quickly became the city's poorest quarter after Josefov, renowned as a hot-bed of Hussitism and radicalism throughout the centuries until, in the second half of the nineteenth century, the authorities enacted a campaign of slum clearance similar to that inflicted on the Josefov. Only the churches and a few important historical buildings were left standing, but Charles' street lay-out survived pretty much intact.

The easiest **starting point** in Nové Město is Václavské náměstí, hub of the modern city and – with the surrounding streets – somewhere you're bound to find yourself returning to again and again. The rest of Nové Město, which spreads out northeast and southwest of the square, is much less explored, and unusually for Prague, using the trams and the Metro to get around here saves you some unnecessary legwork.

Václavské náměstí (Wenceslas Square)

The natural pivot around which modern Prague revolves, and the political focus of the events of November 1989, is **Václavské náměstí**, once the site of the horse market in Charles' new town, now more of a wide, gently sloping boulevard than a square. It's scarcely a conventional – or even convenient – space in which to hold mass demonstrations, yet every night for two weeks following the November 17 *masakr*, over 250,000 people crammed into the square, calling for the resignation of the KSČ leaders and demanding free elections. After the first night, the Socialist Party, previously just a puppet member of the Communist government, handed over the well-positioned balcony of the party's newspaper offices (*Svobodné slovo*, The Free Word), halfway up on the right, to the opposition speakers of Občanské fórum (Civic Forum). On November 27, the whole of Prague came to a standstill, many converging on the square to show their support for the two-hour nationwide general strike called for by the Forum. It was this last mass mobilisation which proved decisive – by noon the next day, the Communist old guard had thrown in the towel.

The square's history of protest goes back to the Prague Spring of 1968, when it was the scene of some of the most violent confrontations between the Soviet invaders and the Praguers. Towards the top end of the square, a small impromptu **shrine** of candles and messages of respect commemorates the death of Jan Palach, the 21-year old student who set himself alight in January 1969 in frustration against the continuing occupation of his country. He was followed four days later by another four people around the country, and on February 25 – the anniversary of the Communist coup – came a fifth death, that of Jan Zajíc. Nearby, stands the simple and majestic **Monument to sv Václav**, by the sculptor Josef Václav Myslbek, finally unveiled in 1912 after thirty years on the drawing board. Wenceslas sits astride his mighty steed, surrounded by smaller representations of the other patron saints of Bohemia – his mother Ludmilla, Procopius, Adalbert and Agnes.

Václavské náměstí is lined with self-important, six- or seven-storey buildings erected in the boom of the first half of this century (for more on which see below), and is awash with neon signs – as it was even under the Communists, then advertising things like the indissoluble friendship between Czechoslovakia and the Soviet Union, the Bulgarian State Import-Export Company and, of course, Coca-Cola. There's plenty to keep you occupied in the shops, bars and cinemas of the gloomy arcades, while outside, Václavské náměstí has always been the place to parade your new luxury motor. In the past, unfamiliarity with Western vehicles meant that even a Vespa was treated as if it were a recently landed inter-galactic spaceship, though these days, a little post-revolutionary cynicism accompanies the stares. Come back at night and it's the one place in Prague where life goes on after midnight – the hotels and nightclubs buzzing, and the police playing cat-and-mouse with the pimps and hustlers, turning a blind eye to most of the nation's new-found vices.

A stroll up the square: cafés and buildings

At the bottom, northwestern end, the post-modern adminstrative building for Prague's giant *ČKD* engineering works, built in steel and stone, is a favourite place to meet up before hitting town. It's an organic part of the new Můstek Metro station, with a record store and bookshop (open seven days a week) on the ground floor, and a roof-top café with an unbeatable view straight up Václavské náměstí. For a street-level look-out post, the place to be is the terrace of **Café Fórum**, part of the newly established headquarters of the revolution's prime political mover, Občanské fórum.

With so much going on, it's easy to overlook the wealth of **modern architecture** which the square has accrued over the course of this century. Most obvious is the giant wedge of sculptured concrete, the **Palác Koruna**, built in 1914 and best known for its cheap and seedy stand-up *bufet* on the ground floor. It's the masterpiece of Antonín Pfeiffer, one of Kotěra's pupils, whose rare mixture of constructivism and ornament has been frequently copied, but seldom matched.

The functionalist **Dům obuv** (House of Shoes) opposite, designed by Kysela in the late 1920s and touted at the time as the ultimate glass curtain-wall building, is the perfect expression of the optimistic mood of the newly established Czechoslovak Republic. Before the wholesale nationalisation of the late 1940s, it belonged to the Baťa family, respected patrons of avant-garde Czech architecture, whose functionalist factory-town in Moravia is one of the greatest monuments to the First Republic (see "Zlín", p.237).

Another outstanding example of Czech functionalism is the **Hotel Juliš**, a few doors further up at no. 22 (now called the *Tatran*), designed by Pavel Janák who made his name as one of the leading lights of the pre-First World War Czech Cubist movement.

Built a generation earlier, the *fin de siêcle* **Hotel Evropa**, halfway up on the left, represents everything the Czech modern movement stood against; chiefly, ornament for ornament's sake. Not that this lessens the indelible impression which the Art Nouveau decor has on its visitors, exuding a richness which only intensifies as you reach the flashy restaurant at the back. The terrace café has always had a reputation for low-key cruising, a great deal of posing and good coffee.

From the National Museum to the hlavní nádraží

At the southeastern end of the náměstí, the **National Museum** (daily 9am–5pm, Mon & Fri 9am–4pm; closed Tues) looms on the horizon like a giant eagle with its wings outstretched. Along with the National Theatre (see below), it's one of the great symbols of the nineteenth-century Czech national revival, with its monumental gilt-framed glass cupola, worthy clumps of sculptural decoration and narrative frescoes from Czech history. However, unless you're a geologist or a zoologist you're likely to be unmoved by most of the exhibits – room after room of stuffed animals and endless display cases full of rocks – but it's worth taking at least a quick look at the **Pantheon***, a celebration of (non-Communist) Czech science and culture. From the grand central staircase you enter a domed hall with forty-eight busts and statues of distinguished Czechs* (and a couple of Slovaks), including the universally adored T. G. Masaryk, the country's founding President, whose statue was removed by the Communists from every public place except the Pantheon itself. Also present are the museum's co-founders, Count Šternberk and Josef Dobrovský, and just two women – the writer Božena Němcová and the poet Eliška Krásnohorská. Since the revolution, the appeal of the museum's temporary exhibitions (on such themes as Masaryk himself) has increased dramatically, so it's always worth checking to see what's on.

Some of the worst town-planning this century was inflicted upon this part of the city, not least the building of the six-lane freeway which now separates the Nové Město from the residential suburb of Vinohrady to the east, and effectively cuts off the National Museum from Václavské náměstí. Previously known as Vítězného února (Victorious February), after the Communist coup, the road has now been renamed **Wilsonova**, in honour of the American President, a personal friend of the Masaryk family, who effectively gave the country its independence from Austria in the 1919 Treaty of Versailles. Even crueller was the fate of the Prague Stock Exchange building during the post-war reconstruction. Built in the 1930s, but rendered entirely redundant by the 1948 coup, the architect Karel Prager was given the task of designing a new "socialist" **Federal Assembly** building on the same site, without destroying the old bourse. He opted for a supremely unappealing bronze-tinted, plate-glass structure, supported by concrete stilts and hovering uncomfortably on top of its little predecessor. At least it's no longer the sham, rubber-stamp body it was on completion in 1973, as it now houses both chambers of the new parliament for which multi-party elections were held in June 1990.

Next to the Parliament building, the once grand **Smetanovo divadlo**, built by the Viennese duo Helmer and Fellner, now looks stunted and deeply affronted by the traffic which tears past its front entrance. It was opened in 1888 as the *Neues Deutsches Theater*, second fiddle to the Tyl and no match for the Czechs' new National Theatre; a sign of the fading fortunes of Prague's once all-powerful German minority. The velvet and gold interior is still as fresh as it was when the Bohemian-born composer Gustav Mahler brought the traffic to a standstill, conducting the premiere of his *Seventh Symphony*; nowadays the theatre serves as the city's second opera house.

The last building on this deafening flyover is the **Praha hlavní nádraží**, Prague's main railway station and the last great station of the dying Empire, officially opened in 1909 as the *Franz Josefs Bahnhof* (though the Emperor himself

---

* A brief background history of most of those present in the Pantheon can be found in "An A to Z of Czech and Slovak Street Names" in *Contexts*.

failed to attend). Trapped in the overpolished subterranean modern section, it's easy to miss out on the station's surviving Art Nouveau parts. The original entrance on Wilsonova still exudes imperial confidence, with its wrought-iron canopy and naked figurines clinging to the sides of the towers; on the other side of the road, the two great glass protrusions signal the new entrance in the Vrchlického sady.

Along Národní and Na příkopě

The borderline between the Staré and the Nové Město is made up by the partially pedestrianised boulevards of **Národní** and **Na příkopě**, a boomerang curve which follows the course of the old moat, filled in in 1760. The city's most flamboyant Art Nouveau buildings, as well as a variety of other stylish edifices, are ranged along much of its length. It's also Prague's busiest shopping street and promenade, lined with banks, boutiques and bookshops, and along with Václavské náměstí, it forms what's known as the *zlatý kříž* – the "golden cross" of the city's commercial centre, set to become the most expensive slice of real estate in the country once the market economy takes off.

The National Theatre and around

At the western end of Národní, looking out over the Vltava, is the gold-crested **National Theatre** (Národní divadlo), proud symbol of the Czech nation. Refused money by the Austrian state, Czechs of all classes dug deep into their pockets to raise funds for the venture themselves. The foundation stones, gathered from various historically significant sights in Bohemia and Moravia, were laid in 1868 by Palacký and Smetana, and the architect Josef Zítek spent the next fifteen years on the project. Then, in August 1881, just two months after the opening night, fire ripped through the building, destroying everything except the outer walls. But within two years the whole thing was rebuilt, this time under the supervision of Josef Schulz (who went on to design the National Museum), and it opened once more to the strains of Smetana's *Libuše*. The grand portal on the north side of the theatre is embellished with suitably triumphant allegorical figures, and inside, every square inch is taken up with paintings and sculptures by leading artists of the národní obrození. Tickets are relatively cheap, but most productions are in Czech, so unless there's an opera or ballet on, content yourself with a quick peek at the decor.

Opposite, the famous **Café Slavia** has been a favourite haunt of the city's writers and artists (and, inevitably, actors) since the first decade of the Republic. The instigators of the Czech avant-garde movement, *Devětsil*, used to hold their meetings here, recorded for posterity by the poet and Nobel Prize winner Jaroslav Seifert (see "Žižkov", p.95) in his *Slavia Poems*. It's been carelessly modernised since those arcadian days but it's as close as you'll get in Prague to a riverside café.

In direct contrast with these grand projects is the ultra-modern glass box of the **Nová scéna**, behind the National Theatre, designed by the leading architect of the Communist era, Karel Prager, and completed in 1981. It's one of those buildings most Praguers love to hate, decribed by one Czech friend as looking like "frozen piss" – not that that puts off the swarms of theatre-goers who choose to eat here before the show. Its concrete courtyard is a popular spot for skateboarding and is the preferred daytime meeting-place for Prague's small (and harmless) punk population.

Along Národní

A little way up Národní, on the left, are two of the city's most memorable **Art Nouveau buildings**, both designed by Osvald Polívka in 1907–08. The first one, at no. 7, was built for the Prague Insurance Company (*pojišťovna Praha*), hence the beautiful mosaic lettering above the windows advertising *život* (life) or *kapital* (insurance), as well as help with your *důchod* (pension) or *věno* (dowry). Next door, the former *Topič* publishing house provides the perfect accompaniment, slightly more ornate and now the headquarters of *Československý spisovatel*, the official state publishers – who, no doubt, have a great deal on their hands trying to work their way through the forty-year backlog of previously censored material.

Once you reach the tacky and transparent *Máj* department store, Národní breaks out into a modest consumerist flourish of shops and galleries. The streets ends at the chunky charcoal-coloured cubes of the **Adria Palace**, designed by two of the country's most innovative inter-war architects, Pavel Janák and Josef Zasche, for yet another insurance company, the *Reunione Adriatica di Sicurta*. Upstairs, there's a good café-terrace from which to observe life on the náměstí below, while the basement has been converted into a studio theatre, **Laterna magica** (Magic Lantern). This became the underground nerve-centre of the Velvet Revolution when Civic Forum found temporary shelter here shortly after their inaugural meeting on the Sunday following the November 17 demonstration. Against a stage backdrop of Dürenmatt's *Minotaurus*, the Forum thrashed out tactics in the dressing-rooms and gave daily press conferences in the auditorium during the crucial fortnight before the Communists reliquished power. Having now reverted to its former use, the theatre's multi-media shows are as popular as ever, and you'll find it almost impossible to buy tickets from the theatre box office, which lurks in the dark arcade.

Right by the Adria Palace, **Jungmannovo náměstí** gets its name from the pensive, seated figure of Josef Jungmann (1772–1847), a leading light of the národní obrození, and a prolific writer and translator. Just up from here by Prague's unique 1912 Cubist streetlamp, are the iron gates of the church of **Panna Marie Sněžna** (St Mary-of-the-Snows), once the great landmark of Václavské náměstí, when it towered over the old two-storey houses that lined the square, but now barely visible from the street. The gates are usually shut, forcing you to go through an unpromising courtyard behind Jungmann himself. Like most of Nové Město's churches, it was founded by Charles IV, who envisaged a vast coronation

THE *MASAKR*: NOVEMBER 17, 1989

On the night of Friday, November 17, 1989, a 50,000-strong, officially sanctioned student demo, organised by the students' union, *SSM* (League of Young Socialists), worked its way down Národní with the intention of reaching Václavské náměstí. Halfway down the street they were confronted by the *bílé přílby* (white helmets) and *červené barety* (red berets) of the hated riot-police. For what must have seemed like hours, there was a stalemate as the students sat down and refused to disperse, some of them handing flowers out to the police. Suddenly, without any warning, the police attacked and what became known as the **masakr** (massacre) began – no-one was actually killed, though it wasn't for want of trying by the police. Under the arches of Kaňka's house (Národní 16), there's a small symbolic bronze relief of eight hands reaching out for help, a permanent shrine in memory of the hundreds who were hospitalised in the violence.

church on a scale comparable with the St Vitus Cathedral, on which work had just begun. But the money ran out and the Hussite Wars began, with only the presbytery complete. The result is curious: a church whose hundred-foot high vaulting – added later by the Franciscans who inherited the half-built building in the seventeenth century – does little to stave off claustrophobia, further compounded by the oversized Baroque altar. However, you can get an idea of the intended scale of the finished structure from the small, green Franciscan Gardens, which lie to the south of the church.

Na příkopě to náměstí Republiky

Back on the course of the old moat, you can skip across the bottom end of Václavské náměstí and join the crush of bodies rambling down **Na příkopě** (literally "On the Moat"). The street was once lined on both sides with elegant buildings, like the former department store at no. 4, built in 1869–71 and now housing some swish boutiques. But some were replaced during the enthusiastic construction boom of the inter-war Republic, including the Art Nouveau *Café Corso*, and the earlier *Café Francais*, once the favourite haunts of Prague's literary set. Now only *Café Arco*, on nearby Hybernská, still stands – though in an unrecognisable and unremarkable form, frequented more by people with time to kill before their train than literary cronies.

There'll almost certainly be queues inside the country's first and foremost fast-food restaurant, *Arbat* at no.29, named after a notorious suburb in Moscow and serving paltry hamburgers all day long. Upstairs there's a much less popular Russian sit-down restaurant, *Moskva*, briefly renamed *Morava* (by judicial letter-removing) during the 1968 disturbances. The rest of the street degenerates into a collection of monumentally brutal banks from the 1930s, which fan out into **náměstí Republiky**, an unruly space, recently made more so by the construction of a new Metro station and the ugly *Kotva* department store. The square's name derives from the fact that the First Republic was declared here on October 28, 1918, a fortnight before the official surrender of the Austro-Hungarian army.

The Obecní dům and Hybernská

Right on the square, the **Obecní dům** was the last great Czech building of the expiring Empire, and along with the *Hotel Evropa* on Václavské náměstí, still manages to conjure up images of Prague's café society. Intended as a cultural centre for an ascendant Czech nation, the complex was begun in 1903, and executed in an extravagant Art Nouveau style – decorated inside and out with the help of almost every artist connected with the Czech Secession. It's changed little since its completion in 1911, and the simplest way of soaking up the hall-like interior, peppered with mosaics and pendulous brass chandeliers, is to have a beer and a bite to eat in the *restaurace*, or sit around the fountain at the far end of the equally cavernous *kavárna*. It's worth wandering upstairs too, for a peek at the central Smetanova síň, where the opening concert of the Prague Spring Festival – traditionally a rendition of Smetana's *Ma vlast* (My Country) – is held in the presence of the President of the Republic. Recently, there have been **guided tours** of the rest of the building, showing off its abundant treasures (including paintings by Alphonse Mucha, Max Švabinský and other leading Czech artists), but it's not certain whether these will become a regular feature; ask at the *PIS*. Otherwise, the restaurant and café are open regular hours (the café from 7am), and you may or may not be able to get into the other parts by just turning up and strolling in.

Large international art exhibitions – occasionally worth a look – are held in the early nineteenth-century church, **U hybernů**, opposite the Obecní dům, while a hundred metres or so further down Hybernská are the headquarters of the now miniscule Social Democratic Party. In 1912, the Sixteenth Congress of the Russian Social Democratic Labour Party (which Lenin himself attended) took place here – a fact which proved sufficient for the Communists to install a vast Lenin museum in the building, which, not surprisingly, is now defunct. At the end of the street, you run up against **Masarykovo nádraží**, Prague's first railway station, opened in 1845, though a modest, almost provincial affair compared to the later hlavní nádraží.

South of Národní

The streets which spread **south of Národní**, towards Vyšehrad, try hard to be grand Parisian avenues, though in fact they still run along the old medieval lines of Charles IV's grandiloquent fourteenth-century town plan. Of the many roads which fan out from Václavské náměstí, Vodičkova is probably the most impressive, running southwest for half a kilometre to **Karlovo náměstí**. This is Prague's biggest square, though the tree-planted park which now occupies it only manages to obscure its grand proportions. At the northern end of the square, the **Novoměstská radnice** (currently being renovated) was once a Gothic town hall to rival that of the Staré Město, but after 1784 it was converted into a prison and criminal court. It was here that Prague's **first defenestration** took place on July 30, 1419, when the radical preacher, Jan Želivský, and his penniless religious followers stormed the building, mobbed the available Catholic councillors and burghers and threw several of them out of the town hall windows onto the pikes of the Hussite mob below. Václav IV, on hearing the news, suffered a stroke and died just two weeks later. These were the first fatalities of the long and bloody Hussite Wars, which finally ended in the fratricidal Battle of Lipany in 1434.

Walk the square's length and the southern end is marked by the so-called **Faust House** (Faustův dům), a late Baroque building with a long and diabolical history of alchemy carried out within its walls. An occult priest from Opava owned the house in the fourteenth century, while the Irish alchemist and international con-man, Edward Kelly, was summoned here two centuries later by the eccentric Emperor Rudolf II to attempt to turn base metal into gold. Later, the Czech version of the Faust legend was played out here, with the arrival one rainy night of a penniless and homeless student, Jan Šťastný (meaning *Faustus* or lucky). He found money in the house, which he kept – only to discover that it was put there by the Devil, who then claimed his soul in return. Seemingly unperturbed by the historical fate of past chemists on this site, a modern pharmacy has set up shop on the ground floor.

West off Karlovo náměstí, halfway down Resslova (on the right), is the eighteenth-century church of **sv Cyril and Metoděj**, now the centre of the Orthodox church in the west of the country, but originally constructed for the Roman Catholic church by Bayer and Dientzenhofer. It's difficult now to imagine the scene here on June 18, 1942, when seven of the Czechoslovak secret agents involved in the most "successful" assassination of World War II (see below) were holed up in the church by over 300 members of the SS and Gestapo. For several hours the Nazis fought a pitched battle, using explosives, flooding and any other method they could think of to drive the men out of their stronghold in the crypt.

THE ASSASSINATION OF REINHARD HEYDRICH

The assassination of Reinhard Heydrich in 1942 was the only attempt the Allies ever made on the life of a leading Nazi. It's an incident which the Allies (at the time) and the Communists (ever since) billed as a great success, in the otherwise rather dismal seven-year history of the Czech resistance. But, as with all acts of brave resistance during the war, there was a price to be paid. Given that the reprisals meted out on the Czech population were entirely predictable, it remains a controversial, if not suicidal, decision to have made.

The target, **Reinhard Tristan Eugen Heydrich**, was a talented and upwardly mobile anti-semite (despite rumours that he was partly Jewish himself), a great organiser and a skilful concert violinist. He was a late recruit to the Nazi Party, signing up in 1931, after having been dismissed from the German Navy for dishonourable conduct towards a woman. However, he swiftly rose through the Party ranks to become, in the autumn of 1941, Protector of the puppet state of *Böhmen und Mähren* – effectively, the most powerful man in the Czech Lands. Although his rule began with brutality, it soon settled into the tried and tested policy which Heydrich liked to call *Peitsche und Zucker* (literally, "whip and sugar").

On the morning of May 27, 1942, as Heydrich was being driven by his personal bodyguard in his open-top Mercedes, from his manor house north of Prague to his office in the Hradčany, three Czechoslovak agents (parachuted in from England) were taking up positions in the northern suburb of Libeň. As the car pulled into Kirchmayer Boulevard (now V Holešovičkách), one of them, a Slovak called Gabčík, pulled out a gun and tried to shoot. The gun stuck but Heydrich's bodyguard, rather than driving out of the situation, slowed down and attempted to shoot back. At this point, another agent, Kubiš, threw a grenade at the Mercedes. The blast injured Heydrich and stopped the car, but failed to harm his bodyguard, who immediately jumped out of the car and began chasing Gabčík down the street, shooting. Gabčík pulled out a second gun, shot the bodyguard dead and hopped on board an approaching tram. Back at the Mercedes, Kubiš had been badly injured himself and, with blood pouring down his face, jumped on his bicycle and rode into town. Heydrich, seemingly only slightly wounded, flagged down a delivery van and hitched a lift to the nearest hospital. However, eight days later he died from shrapnel wounds and was given full Nazi honours at a funeral service in Berlin, in the presence of the Führer. Revenge was quick to follow. The day after Heydrich's funeral, the village of **Lidice** (see p.121) was burnt to the ground.

The plan to assassinate Heydrich had been formulated in the early months of 1942 by the Czechoslovak government-in-exile in London, despite fierce opposition from the resistance within Czechoslovakia. Since it was clear to them that the reprisals would be horrific, the only logical explanation for the plan is that this was precisely the aim of the government-in-exile's operation – to forge a solid wedge of resentment between the Germans and Czechs. In this respect, if in no other, the operation was ultimately successful.

The seven finally committed suicide rather than give themselves up, and at street level on the south wall there's a plaque commemorating those who died: in the crypt itself, there's a small exhibition with photos, detailing the incident.

East of Karlovo náměstí: Ke Karlovu

East of Karlovo náměstí, Ke Karlovu runs south to the southernmost edge of Nové Město, where it dips down into the Botič valley below Vyšehrad. A third of the way down this unassuming street, set back from the road in a modest garden, the russet country house behind wrought-iron gates is the **Vila Amerika** (Tues–Sun 10am–4pm), one of the most successful secular works of Kilian Ignaz Dientzenhofer. Finished in 1720, it now houses a museum devoted to **Antonín Dvořák**, easily the most famous of all Czech composers, who for many years had (literally) to play second fiddle to Smetana in the orchestra at the National Theatre, where Smetana was the conductor. In his forties, Dvořák received an honorary degree from Cambridge before leaving for the "New World", and his gown is one of the very few things of his to have found its way into the museum, along with the programme of a concert given at London's Guildhall in 1891. But what the display cabinets may lack is compensated for by the airy Rococo house and the music which wafts through it.

Tour groups who have ventured this far south tend to ignore the museum, parking instead around the corner in Na bojišti, and piling into the pub, U **kalicha**, immortalised in the opening passages of the consistently popular comic novel, *The Good Soldier Švejk*, by Jaroslav Hašek. In the story, on the eve of the Great War, Švejk (often written as *Schweik* in English) walks into *U kalicha*, where a plain-clothes officer of the Austrian constabulary is sitting drinking and, after a brief conversation, Švejk finds himself arrested in connection with the assassination of Archduke Ferdinand. Whatever the pub may have been like in Hašek's day (and even then, it wasn't his local), it's now unashamedly orientated towards the Deutschmark, and about the only authentic thing you'll find inside is the beer.

Having a beer and heading back towards the centre is the most obvious option from here, though if you've got a few hundred more metres left in your legs you could continue south down Ke Karlovu. At the end of the street stands what was, in its prime, one of the most fascinating museums of the old regime, the **Museum SNB**, or Museum of the Ministry of Interior (Tues–Sun 10am–5pm; closed July & Aug). Works by Trotsky, photos of Bob Dylan, plays by Havel, contraband goods and illegal drugs were all displayed in the grand room of dissidence, closed-circuit TV watched over your every move, and the first thing you saw on entry were 200 police pistols pointing at you from the wall. But the most famous exhibit was undoubtedly a stuffed alsatian called Brek, who saw twelve years' service on border patrols, intercepted sixty "law-breakers", was twice shot in action and eventually retired to an old dogs' home. With the barbed wire and border patrols all but disappeared, and the police at the nadir of their popularity, there are moves afoot to turn the whole thing into a museum of road and traffic police – which would be a bit of a shame.

From the neighbouring Na Karlově church, there's a great view over to Vyšehrad, across the Botič valley, to the twin delights of the skyscraper *Hotel Forum* and the low-lying **Palác kultury** (Palace of Culture), the country's biggest concert venue. But unless you're heading for Vyšehrad (see below), this is a bit far to come just for views. It's another 500 metres' walk west to the waterfront (or you can take tram #7 from the bottom of the valley, below the church).

North along the waterfront

The magnificent turn-of-the-century mansions which line the Vltava's right bank stretch north, almost without interruption, for some two kilometres, from the rocky outcrop of Vyšehrad to the Charles Bridge and beyond. At Palackého náměstí, the buildings recede for a moment to reveal the city's first great Art

Nouveau sculpture, the **Monument to František Palacký**, the great nineteenth-century Czech historian and ardent nationalist, by Stanislav Sucharda. Like the Hus Monument, which was unveiled three years later, this mammoth project – fifteen years in the making – had almost missed its moment when it was finally completed in 1912, but thanks to the sheer audacity of Sucharda's work it remains an impressive piece. Extravagant ethereal bodies of copper clamber over the monument, contrasting sharply with the plain stone mass of the plinth and the giant seated figure of Palacký himself.

Further along the embankment, the striking white functionalist mass of the **Mánes Gallery** (Tues–Sun 10am–1pm & 2–6pm) spans the narrow channel between the Šitek water-tower and the waterfront itself. Named after Josef Mánes, a fairly traditional nineteenth-century landscape painter and Czech nationalist, the gallery was a centre of activity during the Velvet Revolution. There's a friendly, youthful atmosphere in the riverside café here, while the gallery itself puts on some of the more unusual exhibitions in Prague

The adjacent island of **Slovanský ostrov** came about as a result of the natural silting of the river in the eighteenth century. By the late nineteenth century it had become one of the city's foremost pleasure gardens, where, as the composer Berlioz remarked, "bad musicians shamelessly make abominable music in the open air and immodest young males and females indulge in brazen dancing, while idlers and wasters . . . lounge about smoking foul tobacco and drinking beer". On a good day, things seem pretty much unchanged from those heady times. The occasional concert can still be heard, though hardly up to the standard Berlioz would have wished for, and there are rowing boats for hire, too, from May to October.

Closer to the opposite bank, and accessible via the Legií bridge, **Střelecký ostrov**, or Shooters' Island, is where – from the fifteenth century onwards – the army held their shooting practice. Later, it was a favourite spot for a Sunday promenade and remains a popular place in summer. The first May Day demonstrations took place here in 1890, and, one hundred years on, having been used and abused by the Communists for propaganda purposes, the demonstrations have returned. The first post-Communist gathering was held in 1990.

HAVEL ON THE WATERFRONT

Since the beginning of the Charter 77 movement, **Václav Havel**, his wife Olga and his brother Ivan have lived in the top-floor flat of Rašínovo nábřeží 78. So permanent was the surveillance on Havel (apart from his four-and-a-half years in prison) that the secret police set up a small prefab hut (since removed) on the other side of the road from which they could monitor his movements in relative comfort.

Following Havel's much publicised rejection of the draughty, pompous rooms of the hrad (the traditional place of residence for the President), his house has become something of a shrine. After forty years of Stalinist heroics, it's a fittingly modest object of pilgrimage – a typical four-storey mansion, no doubt beautiful when it was first designed (and owned) by his grandfather, a respected Art Nouveau architect, but now shabby and run-down. There's no armed guard, no name on the bell, no plaque, yet despite the lack of anything to see, there are usually one or two people talking *sotto voce* and pointing up to the top floor, not to mention the lines of goodwill graffiti scrawled on the wall.

Vyšehrad

Around 3km south of the city centre, the rocky red-brick fortress of **VYŠEHRAD** has more myths attached to it per square inch than any other place in Bohemia. According to Czech legend, this is the place where the Slav tribes first settled in Prague: the "wise and tireless chieftain" Krok built a castle here, and his youngest daughter Libuše went on to found *Praha* itself. Alas, the archaeological evidence doesn't bear this claim out, but it is clear that during the eleventh and twelfth centuries Vyšehrad surpassed even the hrad in importance. Vratislav II (1061–92), the first Bohemian prince to be crowned king, built a royal palace here, though within half a century the royals had moved to a new palace at the hrad, and from then on Vyšehrad began to lose its political significance. Charles IV linked Vyšehrad to the newly founded town of Nové Město by a system of walls, most of which were destroyed in a two-month siege and battle between Prague's Hussites and Emperor Sigismund's Catholic crusaders. Subsequently, the Habsburgs kicked out the population of Vyšehrad and rebuilt the palace as a fortified barracks, only to tear it down two centuries later and turn it into a public park.

With only the red-brick fortifications left as a reminder of its former strategic importance, the Czech národní obrození movement became interested in Vyšehrad, rediscovering its history and its legends, and gradually transforming it into a symbol of Czech identity.

However, for all its national historical significance, Vyšehrad is a pretty unremarkable set of buildings these days, more of an afternoon's escape from the human congestion of the city than a must on a tourist itinerary. To **get there**, without walking the length and breadth of Nové Město, hop on tram #17 at any point along the waterfront, and get off just before the road tunnels through the rock face.

The fortress

The best way of approaching the **fortress** is from the waterfront, from where a series of steep steps leads up through the trees to a small side entrance in the walls. You come out right in front of the blackened sandstone church of **sv Petr and Pavel**, rebuilt in the 1880s in neo-Gothic style on the site of an eleventh-century basilica. The twin openwork spires are the fortress' most familiar landmark, but since the archaeologists got their hands on the site some years ago in their search for remains of the eleventh-century royal palace, the church itself has been out of bounds.

One of the first moves of the národní obrození movement was to establish the **Slavín Cemetery** alongside the church. It's a measure of the part that artists and intellectuals played in the foundation of the nation, and the respect with which they are still treated, that the most prestigious graveyard in the city is given over to them: no soldiers, no politicians, and not even the Communists, managed to muscle their way in here. It's cosy and well-kept, and though to the uninitiated there are only a handful of well-known figures, for the Czechs the place is alive with great names. Dvořák's grave is one of the more expensive, behind the iron railings under the arches, his mosaic inscription glistening with gold stones. Smetana, who died twenty years earlier, is buried at the opposite end, in comparatively modest surroundings. The focus of the cemetery is the Slavín monument, by Antonín Wiehl, communal resting-place for a number of twentieth-century Czech artists, including the painter Alfons Mucha, the sculptors Josef Václav Myslbek and Ladislav Šaloun, and the architect Josef Gočár. Perhaps more significantly, the grave of the Romantic poet Karel Hynek Mácha was the assembly point for the November 17 demonstration which triggered the Velvet Revolution. The demonstration was organised to commemorate the fiftieth anniversary of the funeral of Jan Opletal, a student at the university, who was killed during the earlier student protests against the Nazi occupation. His funeral took place on November 17, 1939, amid more violent disturbances, to which the Nazis responded by executing various student leaders, packing thousands off to the camps and shutting down all higher education institutes. A 50,000-strong crowd gathered at the cemetery and attempted to march to Václavské náměstí, only to be stopped short in Národní, where the infamous *masakr* took place (see box, p.86).

The rest of the deserted fortress makes for a pleasant enough stroll, though the small museum of historical drawings in one of the bastions, and the exhibition in the new deanery, are both pretty dull. It's better to head for the patch of grass to the south of the church of sv Petr and Pavel, where you'll come across Myslbek's gargantaun statues of four mythological couples, which used to grace the city's Palackého most.

Cubist Vyšehrad

Even with only a passing interest in modern architecture, it's worth spending some time seeking out the **Cubist villas** of Vyšehrad. In 1911, the *Skupina výtvarných umělců* (Group of Fine Artists) was founded in Prague, and quickly became the organising force behind the Czech Cubist movement. Over the next six years, the influence of French Cubist painting was felt by Czech painters and sculptors, and – uniquely – architects. **Pavel Janák** was the *Skupina*'s chief theorist, **Josef Gočár** its most illustrious exponent, but **Josef Chochol** was the most successful practitioner of the style in Prague.* He completed a number of single houses, neatly clustered below Vyšehrad, using prismatic shapes and angular lines to produce the sharp geometric light and dark shadows characteristic of Cubism. Outside Czechoslovakia, only the preparatory drawings by the French architect Duchamp-Villon, for his *Maison Cubiste* (never undertaken), can be considered as remotely similar.

The most impressive example, if only for its perfect angular location, is the corner house (no. 30) on **Neklanova**, dating from 1913. Further along the same street, at no. 2, is another apartment block, and around the corner is the most ambitious project of the lot – Chochol's family house on the **Rašínovo nábřeží**, designed right down to its zig-zag garden railings, though presently concealed behind some over-enthusiastic trees and shrubbery.

---

* If you've got a taste for the style and want to pursue the matter outside Vyšehrad, make for Gočár's Dům U černé Matky boží, on Celetná in the Staré Město, or, outside Prague, Janák's house on the main square at Pelhřimov in South Bohemia. Incidentally, the two buildings that started the whole thing off are Gočár's spa building at Bohdaneč and his department store in Jaroměř, both in East Bohemia.

The suburbs

By the end of his reign in 1378, Charles IV had laid out his city on such a scale that it wasn't until the industrial revolution of the nineteenth century that the first **SUBURBS** began to sprout up around the boundaries of the old town. Only the wide expanse of Letná, east of the Hradčany ridge, and the twin suburbs of Vinohrady and Karlín were actually planned; the rest grew with less grace, trailing their grey tenements across the surrounding hills. While you're not going to spend too much time in any of the suburbs, there are a few places worth visiting, and most of them are quick and easy to reach by Metro.

East: Vinohrady, Žižkov and Karlín

Just on the other side of the Wilsonova freeway is the smart nineteenth-century suburb of **VINOHRADY**, home over the years to many of Czechoslovakia's most notable personages. Although it has a run-down air about it these days, it's still a desirable part of town to live in, boasting two spacious parks: the Riegrovy sady and the Havlíčkovy sady. If Vinohrady has a centre, it's **náměstí Míru**, accessible by Metro line A, a leafy square centred on the church of sv Ludmila. From here, block after block of decaying residential mansions, each covered in their own individual garment of sculptural decoration, form grand bourgeois avenues which spread eastwards to the city's great cemeteries (see below). Vinohrady's other fine square – and only other real sight, apart from the cemeteries – is **náměstí Jiřího z Poděbrad**, halfway between náměstí Míru and the cemeteries and also accessible on Metro line A. The modern church here, built by Jože Plečnik in 1928, the Slovene architect responsible for much of the remodelling of the hrad, is highly respected now, but for the most part was shunned by contemporary artists. It's a marvellously eclectic and individualistic work, employing a sophisticated *pot-pourri* of architectural styles, which include a temple-like pediment, a traditional Gothic rose window, and a preference for good old bricks and mortar.

The cemeteries

Approaching from the west, the first and the largest of Prague's vast cemeteries – each of which is bigger than the entire Jewish Quarter – is the **Olšany cemetery**, founded after the great plague epidemic of 1680. The perimeter walls are lined with glass reliquaries, stacked like shoe-boxes, while the graves themselves are a mixed bag of artistic achievements, reflecting the funereal fashions of the day as much as the character of the deceased. At each gate, there's a map, divided into districts and criss-crossed with cobbled streets, and an aged janitor ready to point you in the right direction at the mention of a famous name. Probably the most famous person who *was* buried here was Jan Palach, the philosophy student who set fire to himself in protest against the 1968 invasion. Over 500,000 people attended his funeral in January 1969, and in an attempt to put a stop to the annual vigils at his graveside, the secret police removed his body in 1973 and reinterred it in his home town, 60km outside Prague. To reach the cemetery, take Metro line A to Flóra station, from where the entrance is just over the way.

One stop down the line, on the other side of Jana Želivského, which runs along the eastern edge of the Olšany cemetery, the **New Jewish Cemetery** (Nový židovský hřbitov; April–Aug daily 8am–5pm; Sept–March daily 8am–4pm; closed

---

KOTĚRA IN VINOHRADY

For devotees of Czech modernism, **Jan Kotěra** (1871–1923) is the key figure behind much of the country's extraordinary architectural achievements during the first half of this century. Born in Brno, he studied under Otto Wagner in Vienna during the height of the Viennese Secession. His first buildings in Prague – like the Peterkův dům at Václavské náměstí 12 (1899–1900) – displayed all the characteristic traits of his new schooling. Yet even at this early stage, Kotěra showed a marked preference for rectilinear and minimalist decoration, rather than the effusions of mainstream Art Nouveau. In 1908, he built his own **family house** in Vinohrady, at Hradešinská 6, almost devoid of decorative forms and rendered entirely in brick, signalling the final break with the past. It may not be conventionally beautiful, but for its time, it's as remarkable as any of those of his better known Western European contemporaries. Kotěra is buried in Vinohrady's fourth great cemetery, the Vinohrady cemetery, 200m or so east down Vinohradská from the New Jewish Cemetery.

Fri & Sat) was founded in 1895. It's the repository of some of Prague's most beautiful funereal art, though most people come here to see the graves of Franz Kafka and family, as well as those of the poet Rainer Maria Rilke (1875–1926), and the writer Franz Werfel (1890–1945): ask for directions at the entrance.

Directly to the north of here (the entrance is 200m up Jana Želivského, on the right), the **War Cemetery** (Vojenský hřbitov) remembers a more popular Soviet invasion, that of 1945. It's a small, tufty meadow, dotted with simple white crosses, and nearby, the marked graves of the Czechs who died fighting for the Habsburgs in World War I on the Italian front are laid out in a semi-circle.

Žižkov and Karlín

From the cemeteries, it's about a fifteen-minute walk north up Jana Želivského (or a couple of stops on tram #16) to **Vítkov Hill**, a thin green wedge of land dividing the districts of **ŽIŽKOV** and **KARLÍN**. From its westernmost point, you get probably *the* definitive panoramic view over the city centre. On July 14, 1419, Vítkov was the scene of the Hussites' first and finest victory under the inspired leadership of the one-eyed general, Jan Žižka (hence the name of the district), whose equestrian statue crowns the hill. Ridiculously outnumbered, but fanatically motivated, Žižka and his Táborite troops routed the Emperor Sigismund and his papal forces. The giant granite **monument** was actually built between the wars as a memorial to the new nation, though its pompous brutality was perfectly suited to its post-war use as a Communist mausoleum: Presidents Gottwald, Zápotocký and Svoboda are all buried here, along with various other Party hacks. Vítkov was an ideal resting place for a number of reasons. Suitably prominent, it also lay in the heart of the old "red" districts of Žižkov* and Karlín, from which

---

* Czechoslovakia's Nobel Prize-winning poet, **Jaroslav Seifert** (1901–1986) was born and bred in the Žižkov district. He was one of the founding members of the Czechoslovak Communist Party, and in 1920, helped found *Devětsil*, the most daring and provocative avant-garde movement of the inter-war Republic. Always accused of harbouring bourgeoise sentiments, Seifert and eight other Communist writers were expelled from the Party when Gottwald and the Stalinists hijacked the Party at the Fifth Congress in 1929. After the 1948 coup, he became *persona non grata*, a position made worse by his later involvement in Charter 77. In 1984 he became the one and only Czech to win the Nobel Prize for Literature.

the Communists drew their large working-class support. However, both areas have been much altered since the war, and the monument itself – which has been shut for years – looks unlikely to re-open in the near future.

North: Holešovice and Bubeneč

The districts of **HOLEŠOVICE** and **BUBENEČ**, tucked into a huge U-bend in the Vltava, have little in the way of magnificent architecture, but they both make up for it with two huge splodges of green: to the south, Letná, where Prague's greatest gatherings occur; to the north, the Stromovka park, bordering the Výstaviště amusement park. Across the river, meanwhile, is Prague's only genuine chateau.

Letná

Reachable on tram #8 from Karlín, or #26 from náměstí Republiky, the flat green expanse of the **Letná plain**, laid out as a public park in the mid-nineteenth century, offers little in the way of distraction most of the time. Its main post-1948 function was as the site of the May Day parades, when thousands of citizens were dragooned into marching past the south side of the Sparta Stadium, where the old Communist cronies would take the salute from a giant red podium. On November 26, 1989, though, the park was the scene of a more genuine expression of popular protest, when over 750,000 people joined in the call for a general strike against the Communist regime. Unprecedented scenes followed in April 1990, when a million Catholics came to hear Pope John Paul II speak, on his first visit to an Eastern Bloc country other than his native Poland.

Letná's most famous monument is one which no longer exists. The **Stalin Monument**, the largest of its kind in the world, was once visible from almost every part of the city – a thirty-metre-high granite sculpture portraying a procession of people being led to Communism by the Pied Piper figure of Stalin. Designed by Otakar Švec, who committed suicide before it was unveiled, it took 600 workers 500 days to erect the 14,000-ton monster, revealed to the cheering masses on May 1, 1955. It was the first and last celebration to take place at the monument. Within a year, Krushchev had denounced his predecessor, and after pressure from Moscow the monument was blown to smithereens by a series of explosions spread over a fortnight in 1962. All that remains is the vast concrete platform on the southern edge of the Letná plain where it used to stand, now a favourite spot for skateboarders and the perfect position from which to view the central stretch of the Vltava, spanned by its several bridges and glistening in the afternoon sun. If you're feeling thirsty, head for the café outside the nearby Hanava Pavilion, which shares a similar view.

The Museum of Technology and the Museum of Modern Art

At present, Holešovice boasts only one museum, the **Museum of Technology** (Tues–Sun 10am–5pm), which lies just east of the plain on Kostelní, and contains a host of antique road vehicles, including the carriage in which Archduke Franz Ferdinand drove through Sarajevo on the fateful day of his assassination in 1914. The showpiece, though, is the hanger-like main hall, packed with machines from Czechoslovakia's motoring heyday between the wars, when the country's *Škoda* cars and *Tatra* limos were really something to boast about.

A brand new **Museum of Modern and Contemporary Czech Art** is planned in the district (optimistically scheduled to open in 1991), ten minutes' walk away at Dukelských hrdinů 7. This is the site of the newly restored 1928 Trade Fair building, a seven-storey glass curtain-wall design and in many ways the ultimate functionalist masterpiece. It certainly blew Le Corbusier's mind, as he himself admitted in 1930: "When I first saw the Trade Fair building in Prague I felt totally depressed, I realised that the large and convergent structures I had been dreaming of really existed somewhere, while at the time I had just built a few small villas".

Výstaviště and Stromovka park

Five minutes' walk north up Dukelských hrdinů (or tram #5 from náměstí Republiky, tram #12 from Malostranské náměstí, or tram #17 from Národní) takes you right to the front gates of the **Výstaviště**, a classic turn-of-the-century amusement park centred on the flamboyant glass and iron Průmyslový palác, where the Communist Party held its rubber-stamp congresses from 1948 until the late 1970s. At the weekend, hordes of Praguers push prams, drink beer and listen to traditional brass band music, while others wander around the planetarium and the lavish (and pricey) exhibitions, which take place in the park's motley assortment of buildings.

Behind the amusement park is the Královská obora (Royal Enclosure), more commonly known as **Stromovka park**, for centuries used as a game park for the noble occupants of the hrad. From here, you can wander northwards to Troja and the city's zoo, by way of a path under the railway which leads straight on to the Císařský ostrov, and from there to the right bank of Vltava.

Troja

A pleasant country retreat, though still very much part of Prague, Jean Baptiste Mathey's **Troja Chateau** (April–Sept Tues–Sun 9am–5pm; bus #112 from the end of Metro line C) was built for the Šternberk family towards the end of the seventeenth century. It's a rather plain design, and, despite its recent renovation and rusty red repaint, is no match for the excited, blackened figures of giants and titans who battle it out on the balustrades of the chateau's monumental staircase. Inside, gushing Baroque paintings depicting the victories of Emperor Leopold I over the Turks cover every inch of the walls and ceilings of the Great Hall, but if none of this appeals, it's enough to appreciate the chateau's perfect formal park (where Kafka worked briefly as a gardener). The park stretches down to the river, where you can hire rowing boats (May–Oct), and west to the city's **Zoo** (daily April 7am–5pm; May 7am–6pm; June–Sept 7am–7pm; Oct–March 7am–4pm).

West: Dejvice, Střešovice and beyond

Dotted across the hills to the west of the city centre are the leafy suburbs of Dejvice and Střešovice, which are littered with villas built between the wars for the upwardly mobile Prague bourgeoisie and generally command magnificent views across the north of the city. Further west is the battlefield of Bílá hora and the park and museum at Hvězda, though only the latter is worth making a special effort to see.

Dejvice and Střešovice

While wealthy Praguers moved out to Střešovice in the 1920s in search of the perfect living space, a group of leading architects affiliated to the Czech Workers' Alliance initiated a series of radical housing projects to provide inexpensive single-family villas in **DEJVICE**. The best-known and most remarkable of these experiments was the **Baba** development in the north of the district (bus #125 from Revoluční or #131 from Metro Hradčanská), a model neighbourhood of 33 functionalist houses, each individually commissioned and built under the guidance of Pavel Janák. Rather than using expensive materials, they achieved a new kind of luxury through judicial use of space and open-plan techniques. They have stood the test of time better than most utopian social visions, not least because of the fantastic positioning of the site, facing south and looking down on the city. Some of the houses remain exactly as they were when they were first built, others have been quite thoughtlessly altered, but, sadly, it's impossible to explore any of the houses yourself: you'll have to be content with surreptitious peeping from the street.

The architects of **STŘEŠOVICE** had no such social conscience, and the houses here were for the wealthy only. The most famous example is the **Müller Haus** (at Na hradním vodojemem 14), designed by the Brno-born architect, Adolf Loos, a typically uncompromising white box, wiped smooth with concrete rendering, though now grey with pollution. Completed in 1930, it was one of Loos' few commissions (it took eleven attempts to get planning permission). It's not exactly a wonder to behold, and since you can't get inside, you get no hint of the careful choice of rich materials and minimal furnishings which were Loos' hallmark. It's surrounded by hundreds of inferior, but identikit, box houses, all similarly inaccessible, and you might well wonder now what all the fuss was about.

Bílá hora and Hvězda

A couple of kilometres southwest of Střešovice, trams #8 and #22 (from outside the Strahov Monastery) terminate close to the once barren limestone summit of **Bílá hora** (White Mountain). There's nothing to see, bar a new housing estate, but here on November 8, 1620, the fate of the Czech nation was sealed for the following three hundred years. The Protestant forces under Count Thurn and the "Winter King" Frederick of Palatinate were trounced by the Catholic troops under the command of Maximilian of Bavaria (whose army, incidentally, included Descartes). The battle was over in little more than an hour, and the Czechs lost their aristocracy, their religion, their scholars and, most importantly, their sovereignty.

A last ditch counter-attack was launched by the Moravian Protestants near the hunting park of **Hvězda**, a short walk north of Bílá hora (or tram #2 from Metro Dejvická, trams #1 and #18 from Metro Hradčanská), now one of Prague's most beautiful and peaceful parks. Soft, green avenues of trees lead to a bizarre star-shaped building designed by Ferdinand of Tyrol for his wife. Fully restored in the 1950s, it now houses a **museum** (Tues–Sat 9am–4pm, Sun 10am–5pm), devoted to the writer Alois Jirásek (1851–1930), who popularised old Czech legends during the národní obrození, and artist Mikuláš Aleš (1852–1913), whose drawings were likewise inspired by Czech history. Nevertheless, it's the building which is the greatest attraction – decorated with grand stucco work and frescoes, and hosting the occasional chamber music concert.

South: Zbraslav

For a quick jaunt out of the centre, but still within the city boundaries, head for the former monastery at the village of **ZBRASLAV** (*ČSAD* bus from Praha-Smíchov train station), 10km south of the city. In the grounds, the National Gallery's open-air **Museum of Modern Czech Sculpture** (Tues–Sun 10am–6pm) is a perfect picnic destination, with sculptures imaginatively strewn about the chambers, courtyards and gardens of the Baroque buildings. Works by all the leading figures are here; Gutfreund, Šaloun, Sucharda, Bílek and Štursa – not to mention *The Motorcyclist* by Otakar Švec, the only extant work by the man responsible for the Stalin Monument (see "Letná" above).

FOOD, DRINK AND NIGHTLIFE

There's no comparison between Prague and other cities in Czechoslovakia: the capital has the widest choice of **restaurants** and cafés, the busiest concert season, and the only clubs and discos which stay open until the small hours. Other **entertainment** – specifically film and theatre – is less accessible due to the language barrier, though even there the options are increasing as Prague becomes more responsive to Western visitors. The city, incidentally, is also a business and operational centre, encompassing all the country's embassies and airline offices, and you'll find a full set of **listings** at the end of this section.

Eating and drinking

Cheap **self-service** stand-up *bufet* or *občerstveni*, selling canteen-style food are thick on the ground in Prague, but getting a table at a real **restaurant** is becoming almost as difficult as finding a room. Demand far outstrips supply, and although private outfits are beginning to open, there's still a long way to go before some sort of equilibrium is achieved. In the meantime, you are at the mercy of the *Panívrchní* or head waiter, who may remain unmoved by any financial incentives that you offer, and simply declare the place *výprodano* (literally, "sold-out"). There are, however, a number of ways around the problem: book a table one (or more) nights in advance; eat your main meal at lunchtime (as most Praguers do), when the rest of the city's tourists are busy sightseeing; or try somewhere a bit further from the centre. Failing that, you can console yourself with **drinking** Bohemia's world-class beers in any pub, where you'll always be able to ask for some bread, cheese and ham to soak it up.

Eating: restaurants and wine bars

There are two main types of establishment in Prague where you can get something to eat: a **restaurace** (restaurant), where eating is (ostensibly) the main preoccupation; and a **vinárna** (wine bar), which tends to think of itself as a notch up in the exclusivity stakes, and specialises in wine. Often, you'll also be able to eat in that most typical of Czech institutions, the *pivnice* (pub), though these are largely concerned with the serious business of drinking beer (and are covered in more detail in the next section). In practice, these strict definitions are blurred, with some places having *restaurace* and *pivnice* sections under the same roof, some *vinárna* offering food, some only wine and so on. The **lists** below feature *restaurace* and *vinárna* only, and are grouped according to district. One thing to remember is that the Czechs – if they eat out at all in the evening – do so early (rarely after 9pm), and in all but the poshest *vinárna* the chef packs up well before 10pm. You may well need to **reserve a table** at many establishments, and where it's necessary we've given a telephone number.

Prague's **cuisine** is confined to the simple things of life – ham and beer, and, of course, the standard Bohemian fare of pork, beef, dumplings and sauerkraut. It's difficult to avoid the ubiquitous indigenous cooking even at the so-called "ethnic" restaurants (which usually employ Czech chefs), making life hard for vegetarians or anyone who prefers something a bit less calorific. Quality is still fairly uneven, too – lukewarm meals and a lack of fresh vegetables are both fairly widespread. Food **prices** used to be strictly controlled and subsidised, with each establishment given a price category, but this system is gradually being broken down by the introduction of market forces. However, although food prices are rising, even the most expensive restaurants are still cheap by European standards.

Hradčany

U labutí, Hradčanské náměstí 11 (☎53 94 76). Top-notch restaurant offering Bohemian steaks and Moravian wine. There's a cheap snack bar, too, with outside tables in summer. Open Mon–Sat 7pm–1am.

U ševce matouse, Loretánské náměstí 4 (☎53 35 97). Small restaurant with a resident *švec* (cobbler) to fix your shoes while you wait. Open Tues–Sat noon–9pm.

Vikárka, Vikárská 6 (☎53 51 58). A restaurant built into the Romanesque walls of the hrad, and one of the President's favourite locals. Good wine cellar. Open daily 11am–10pm.

U zlaté uličky, U Daliborky. The food's not bad, nor is it the rip-off you might expect given its prime location in the hrad. However, a long wait for a table is likely. Open Tues 2–6pm, Wed–Sun 11am–6pm.

Malá Strana

Lobkovická vinárna, Vlašská 17 (☎53 01 85). Fresh asparagus and mushrooms washed down with Mělník wine. A popular and relatively expensive restaurant. Open daily 4pm–midnight.

Regent, Karmelitská 22. An unpromising restaurant from the outside, and consequently little known to out-of-towners, despite its Malá Strana location. Good for occasional vegetable dishes and Prague's own *Staropramen 12°* beer. Open Mon–Fri 10am–10pm.

U malířů, Maltézské náměstí 11 (☎53 18 83). A popular but very reasonable *vinárna* serving delicious food in a converted sixteenth-century house, which used to belong to a *malíř* (artist) called Jiří Šic (pronounced "Shits") whose frescoes adorn the walls. Open Mon–Sat 11am–3pm & 6–11pm.

U Mecenáše, Malostranské náměstí 10, (☎53 38 81). Well-known medieval *vinárna* where Václav IV used to drink. Occasionally has Bulgarian moussaka on the menu. Open daily except Sat.

U Schnellů, Tomášská 2. Tends to catch too much of the tourist crowd to be really good value, but it's a convenient restaurant with full meals and *Plzeňský Prazdroj* on offer.

U svatého Tomáše, Letenská 12. A restaurant in an old monastery, serving traditional grub and dark *Braník 12°*. There's a barbecue on the patio, Germans in the cellar, and the occasional tune on the Hammond organ. Open daily 11am–11pm.

U tří pštrosů, Dražického náměstí 12 (☎53 61 51). Exclusive, expensive and over-rated food at this traditional Czech restaurant. Reservations are a must, though you may have more luck at lunchtimes. Open daily 11am–3pm & 6–11pm.

Staré Město

Berjozka, Rytířská 31 (☎22 38 22). The best (and most expensive) Russian restaurant in town. Open Mon–Sat 11am–11pm.

Modré štiky, Karlova 20. Reasonably priced trout and *Plzeňský Prazdroj* on a regular basis, but not exclusively a fish restaurant. Open daily 11am–11pm.

Paříž, U Obecního domu 1 (☎232 20 51). A dearer (and tastier) restaurant than the one in the nearby Obecní dům, but no match for it in terms of decor. You must reserve in the evening.

U prince, Staroměstské náměstí 29. An unpretentious, medium-priced restaurant serving traditional Czech food. Inevitably, due to its location, it attracts a fair few tourists, particularly at lunchtime when you'll be lucky to get a table. Open daily 9am–11pm.

U Supa, Celetná 22. Lively fourteenth-century pub serving full meals and very strong, dark *Braník 14°*, either inside or on the cobbles of its cool, vaulted courtyard. Open Mon–Sat 11am–9pm.

Vegetárka, Celetná 3. Don't believe a word of it – this is no vegetarian restaurant. However, it is cheap and does have a few more veggie dishes than usual, served up in its grim self-service room. Open Mon–Fri 11.30am–2.30pm.

Vietnamská restaurace, Havelská 29. Cheap, vaguely Vietnamese food, and a better-than-average selection of meatless dishes. Open Mon–Fri 11am–6pm.

Josefov

Krušovická pivnice, Široká 20. Traditional food and vast quantities of *Krušovice 12°*, a beer from deep in the Žatec hop region, which many consider to be the best Bohemian brew.

Košer jídelna, Maislova 18. Indifferent self-service kosher restaurant in the Jewish town hall, frequented mostly by Prague's dwindling Jewish community. Open 11.30am–1pm.

U Golema, Maislova 8 (☎23 18 00). Small, swish and intimate restaurant serving some tasty Jewish specialities. Reasonably priced, too. Open Mon–Fri 10am–10pm.

U Rudolfa II, Maislova 5 (☎231 26 43). A good, reasonable *vinárna* in the Jewish Quarter which serves everything with rice. If there are no tables, ask to eat at the bar. Open daily 10am–10pm.

U staré synagogy, Pařížská. Outside on the terrace is for serious drinking, but inside it's a fairly ordinary and convenient Czech restaurant near the Old-New Synagogue.

Nové Město

Alfa, Václavské náměstí, 28. Unpretentious restaurant and café with a wide range of cocktails and aperitifs. On the first floor of the now delapidated 1920s' Alfa arcade.

Arbat, Na příkopě 29. Until *McDonalds* gets a foothold, this bland, but extremely popular, hamburger outlet is the only fast-food joint in town. Open daily 7.30am–11pm.

Hlavní nádraží, Wilsonova. Sleazy restaurant on the first floor of Josef Fanta's once exhuberant Art Nouveau station. Architectural curiosity-value only.

Indická restaurace, Štěpánská 61 (☎236 99 22). An "Indian" restaurant, two doors down from the *BA* offices, which despite the lack of imported spices, makes a change from standard Bohemian fare. Prices are moderate and reservations advisable. Open Mon–Sat noon–4pm & 6–11pm.

Nad Karlovem, Legerova 12 (☎20 24 95). Pleasant place with "Chinese" and Czech cuisine, and *Plzeňský Prazdroj* at moderate prices. Reservations advisable; closes around 9pm.

Obecní dům, náměstí Republiky. The service may be slow and the food nothing special, but the palatial Art Nouveau decor is infinitely more satisfying than any Czech meal. Open daily until 11pm.

Palace, Jindřišská. A new hotel/restaurant complex, ranging from jacket, tie and credit card at the upstairs restaurant to a less pretentious café downstairs (6–11am & noon–midnight), which has the best salad-bar in town.

U Fausta, Karlovo náměstí 4 (☎29 01 12). Quiet, intimate *vinárna*, well off the tourist track. Food served all day. Open Mon–Fri noon–2am.

U šupů, Spálená. A *vinárna* which specialises in mushroom dishes; there's even a take-away booth in the same building dispensing *krokety se žampiony*.

U zlatého tygra, Husova 17. Typical Czech restaurant/pub, serving traditional food, and frequented by Prague's literary crowd including the writer and colourful bohemian, Bohumil Hrabal.

Viola, Národní 7. Small Italian restaurant with the menu in Czech and Italian, but fairly indifferent pasta dishes. Poetry readings, too, and a clientele of ageing intellectuals.

The suburbs

Chang-Chou, Janáčkovo nábřeží 1, Smíchov (☎54 91 64). Genuine Chinese cuisine, hence the high prices, popularity and obligatory reservation. For around 1000kčs, you're allowed to drink and eat as much as you like all day. Open daily 11.30am–midnight.

International, náměstí Družby 1 (shortly to be renamed), Dejvice (Metro *Dejvická*, then tram #20 or #25). If you're hankering after a bit of lost Stalinism, this 1950s' marble and granite hotel may be just the thing. Restaurant downstairs or open sandwiches upstairs in the lobby.

Myslivna, Jagellonská 21, Vinohrady (☎27 62 09). Specialises in game dishes – wild boar, venison, and so on. Expensive but filling. Open 11am–3pm & 6–10pm.

Peking, I. P. Pavlova 64, Vinohrady (☎29 35 31). Good Chinese food, and triple-glazing to keep out the noise of the traffic.

Praha EXPO 58, Letenské sady, Bubeneč (☎37 45 46). Pricey restaurant and café on the seventh floor of this period piece, built, as the name suggests, for the 1958 World Expo in Montreal. A great view over the Vltava.

ÚKDŽ, náměstí Míru 9, Vinohrady. An old nineteenth-century *Národní dům* (now owned by the Railway Workers' Union) far from the tourist-infested centre of town, with a good restaurant, and ballroom dancing on the first floor. Convenient for the Vinohrady theatre.

U pastýřky, Bělehradská 15, Vinohrady (☎43 40 93). Open spit and *cimbalom* folk music, washed down with Slovak food and wine. Reasonably priced and popular, so reserve ahead. Open Mon–Sat 5pm–1am.

Drinking: cafés, pubs and bars

Prague had a thriving café society in the first half of this century, which was all but killed off under the Communists. Today, with plenty to talk about, the **cafés** are blossoming again, and the choice is pretty varied – from the Art Nouveau relics of earlier times to swish expresso bars (both of which are called *kavárna* and are licensed), alongside the simple sugar and caffeine joints you'll find all over the city (known as *cukrárna*). For evening drinking and no-nonsense alcoholic injection, you need to head for a **pivnice**, a Czech pub, which invariably serves excellent beer by the half-litre, but closes around 10 to 11pm. Drinking any later than this in Prague is difficult, though not impossible: you'll need to go to one of the posh wine bars or hotel bars, where you should be able to keep going until after midnight.

Hradčany and Malá Strana

Café de Colombia, Mostecká 3, Malá Strana. French radio, Colombian coffee, but very few tables under its Gothic vaults. Open daily noon–midnight.

Malostranská kavárna, Malostranské náměstí 28, Malá Strana. Originally the *Radetsky Café*, founded in 1874 in a late eighteenth-century palace. Despite the changes, still a good place to meet for coffee and cakes, and with a summer terrace.

U Bonaparta, Nerudova 29. Serves *Staropramen 12°* and some basic food. Conveniently situated halfway up the hill to the hrad.

U černého vola, Loretánské náměstí 1. Does a brisk business providing the popular light beer *Velkopopovický kozel 12°* in huge quantities to thirsty local workers. Starts and finishes early.

U kocoura, Nerudova 2. Newly converted Baroque ale-house on the corner of Malostranské náměstí, serving simple food and *Plzeňský Prazdroj* and in close competition with *U Bonaparta*, further up the hill.

U Lorety, Loretánské náměstí, Hradčany. The cafe's terrace facing the Černín Palace is a great place for watching the sunset and listening to the Dutch bells chime.

Staré Město

Bellevue, Smetanovo nábřeží. Café (and restaurant) with a summer balcony overlooking the the river, the bridge and the hrad.

Bílý jelínek, U radnice. Tiny designer cakes on tiny designer tables, just off the Staroměstské náměstí.

Blatnička, Michalská. Student hangout, which reputedly stocks the cheapest wine in town.

U dvou koček, Uhelný trh. Packed *Plzeňský Prazdroj* pub, mainly for drinking but with some cheap and basic food available. Open Mon–Sat 10am–11pm.

U medvídků, Na Perštyné 7. Serves traditional food and *Budvar*, the original light Budweiser beer from South Bohemia. Open daily 9am–11pm.

U rychtáře, Staroměstské náměstí, A no-nonsense workers' pub by the Golz-Kinský Palace. Serves *Staropramen 12°* and cheap food.

U vejvodů, in a passage off Na Perštýné. Cheap and cheerful *pivnice* that's happy to serve food for lunching workers. Closed at the weekend.

U zlatého hada, Karlova 18. Black leather seats, loud music and tables for two make this café a popular meeting-place for young Praguers.

U zlaté štiky, Dlouhá 9. A small wine and spirits bar near the Staroměstské náměstí. Open daily 5pm–2am.

Vyčer vino, Štupartská. A tiny but popular wine-drinking bar in a sidestreet off the Staroměstské náměstí, where the clientele spills out on to the street.

Nové Město

Arco, Hybernská 16. Don't expect authentic furnishings from the café which gave its name to the *Arconaut Circle* (Kafka, Kisch, Brod et al), though it's very handy for the Masarykovo nádraží.

Branický sklípek, Vodičkova 26. One of the few places where you can down the lethal *Braník 14°* brew.

ČKD dům, Na příkopě 1. Prague's denim crew fight for tables on the fifth floor of this post-modern building, whose rooftop terrace has a superb view up Václavské náměstí. Known as a low-key gay hangout, too. Open daily 10am–11.30pm.

Evropa, Václavské náměstí 25. *The* place to be seen on Wenceslas Square is on the *Evropa*'s summer terrace. But to appreciate the Art Nouveau decor, take breakfast inside. Open daily 10am–11.30pm.

Fórum, 28 října. Housed at the side of the former Czechoslovak-Soviet Friendship House, now the *Občánské fórum* (Civic Forum) headquarters. Tables and chairs outdoors in summer.

Obecní dům, náměstí Republiky. The *kavárna* is in the more restrained south hall of this huge Art Nouveau complex. Open daily 7am–11pm.

Paris-Praha, Jindřišská. Small, chic café selling *Gauloise* singles; next door to the French delicatessen of the same name. Open Mon–Fri 8.30am–7pm, Sat 8.30am–1pm.

Slavia, Národní 1. The *Slavia* has always attracted a mixed crowd – artists, theatregoers, old women, tourists and German trendies – since the days when *Devětsil* used to hang out here in the 1920s.

U Fleků, Křemencova 11. Famous, raucous *pivnice* where the waiters rarely bother to ask what you want, since most people are here to sample the dark *Flek 13°* beer, brewed and consumed exclusively on these premises since 1499. Despite seats for over a thousand drinkers, you may still have to fight for a bench. Open daily 9am–11pm.

U kalicha, Na bojišti 12. Once the unassuming local of Hašek's fictional hero, the *Good Soldier Švejk*, now overrun by tour groups for whom the place is set up as a typical Prague pub. Open daily 11am–3pm & 5–11pm.

U Nováků, Vodičkova 30. Popular café on the first floor, with cards, dominoes and *kulečník* (Czech billiards).

U Pinkasů, Jungmannovo náměstí 15. Typical Prague *pivnice*, despite its proximity to Václavské náměstí. Full of Czechs downing bread, cheese and some of the best *Plzeňský Prazdroj* in town.

Entertainment: music, theatre and film

For many Praguers, **entertainment** is confined to an evening's drinking in one of the city's beer-swilling *pivnice*. But if you're looking for something a bit different, there's plenty to keep you from the night-time frustration normally associated with the old Eastern Bloc capitals. As far as **live music** is concerned, the classical scene still has the edge over more contemporary styles – there's a great opportunity to hear some of the lesser-known works of the big Czech composers. Jazz, though less prevalent, also has a long and worthy tradition in Prague, aided by the international jazz festival held here in even-numbered years. The homegrown rock scene has yet to find its feet outside of its pre-1989 underground ghetto, but new clubs are opening (and closing) thick and fast. With the newfound freedom of the Nineties, **discos and nightclubs** are literally booming all around Václavské náměstí, but – with few notable exceptions – they serve more as an indoor red-light district than what most Westerners would understand by the term "nightclub". Predictably enough, with a playwright as President, **theatre** in Prague is thriving – for a start, there's a twenty-year backlog of censored material to be unleashed on the public. Without a knowledge of the language, however, your scope is more limited, though there's a tradition of innovative mime, puppetry and black theatre in the city.

For **what's on listings**, *The Month in Prague* details theatre and concert events, while a weekly broadsheet, *Kino*, lists the films showing around Prague – both available from *PIS* on Na příkopě. As yet, there's no guide to the more offbeat circuit, and you'll simply have to scour the flyposters in the centre of town to find out what's on. **Tickets** for most events are infinitely cheaper than in London or New York (at least while the state subsidies continue) and are available from the *Sluna* oulets in the Alfa arcade on Václavské náměstí and Černá růže arcade on Panksá. Don't despair if everything is officially sold out, as standby tickets are often available on the night at the venue's box office. Lastly, you should bear in mind that most theatres and concert halls are **closed in July and August**.

Live music

There's a wide choice of live music venues throughout the city and there should be something to suit all tastes. The city's **classical music** calendar is impressive, while less formally there's a burgeoning **jazz, rock and pop** scene which bears investigation.

Classical music, opera and ballet

Classical concerts take place throughout the year in Prague, though the biggest event is the *Pražské jaro* (Prague Spring) **international music festival**, which traditionally begins on May 12, the day of Smetana's death, with a performance of *Ma vlast*, and finishes on June 2 with a rendition of Beethoven's Ninth Symphony. As well as the main venues (see below), watch out for concerts in the city's churches and palaces, while throughout the summer, chamber music concerts take place in the gardens and courtyards of the Left Bank. All classical concerts tend to be booked out by a combination of groups and season-ticket holders, but it's generally fairly easy to get hold of standby tickets from the venue itself, an hour or so before the performance.

Smetanovo divadlo, Wilsonova, Nové Město (☎26 97 46). The former German opera house, and the city's second-choice venue for opera and ballet.

Smetanova síň, Obecní dům, náměstí Republiky, Nové Město (☎232 98 38). Beautiful Secessionist hall and home to the Czech Philharmonic Orchestra (ČF). Closed July & Aug.

Tylovo divadlo (Tyl Theatre), Železná 11, Staré Město (☎22 32 95). Prague's main, eighteenth-century opera house (due to re-open in 1991 after a lengthy renovation).

Jazz, rock and pop

Live **contemporary music** – mainly jazz, rock and pop – has undergone something of a renaissance since 1989, so much so that the listings below should not be taken as the last word on the emerging scene: you'll need to check out the flyposters around town. For the time being, gigs (and drink once inside) are still remarkably cheap.

Club 007, Kolej Strahov, Spartakiádní 7, Strahov (☎35 44 41). Student club with indie gigs Thurs & Fri. Open until 2am or later.

Lidový dům, Emanuela Klímy 8, Vysočany (☎82 34 34). Ever popular with the thrash and metal crowd. Open until 1am.

Malostranská Beseda, Malostranské náměstí 21, Malá Strana. An occasional jazz venue on the left bank, serving up the same kind of musical mix as *Reduta* (see below).

Metro, Národní 20, Nové Město (☎26 20 85). All kinds of jazz, Tues–Fri until 2am.

Na Chmelnici, Koněvova 219, Žižkov (☎82 85 98). The main venue for domestic indie bands. Doubles as an alternative theatre venue, too.

Palác kultury, 5 května 65, Nusle (☎417 27 41). Prague's main indoor venue for big-name acts. The action is on six floors with smaller concert halls, a cinema, nightclub, restaurant and café all thrown in.

Reduta, Národní 20, Nové Město (☎20 38 25). Prague's best jazz club, anything from trad to modern, but increasingly popular so get there early. Open Mon–Fri until 2am, though the music stops at midnight.

Rock Café, Národní 20, Nové Město. Acts as both venue, art space and general nerve centre of the old underground music scene. Open late.

Sněhobílá kočka, Českomoravská 15, Vysočany. Proved too much for the new Prague authorities at first, who closed it down, but now a regular and beery rock venue. Open until 4am.

Újezd, Újezd 18, Malá Strana. Post-punk thrash and underground groups are the main course at this increasingly popular all-nighter. Open until 6am.

Nightclubs and discos

Prague's **nightclubs and discos** are not for the serious club-goer – naff live bands and glass dance-floors are very much in, while the city is currently experiencing a (hopefully shortlived) explosion of *striptýz* acts in its dance venues. Many of the places in and around Václavské náměstí feature at least one of these dubious attractions. The following listings only scratch the surface of the phenomenon, and while none are exactly recommended, you may end up enjoying yourself, despite everything. Entrance fees everywhere are comparatively stiff, but many places now stay open all night.

Alhambra, Václavské náměstí 5, Nové Město. Probably the most famous of the striptease clubs on the square. Open until 3am.

Admirál, Botel Admirál, Hořejší nábřeží, Smíchov. Laser disco on a boat ,with the obligatory glass dance-floor lit from below.

Monica, Charvátova 11, Nové Město. All-nighter usually featuring Ivana Mládka's banjo band (!) and, of course, a striptease act.

Narcis, Melantrichova 5, Staré Město. Gained notoriety thanks to a sensational article in *The Independent*, which thought it was a den of thieves, though in fact it's no better, or worse, than most of Prague's late-nighters.

Varieté, Vodičkova 30, Nové Město. Here since before the revolution, its sub-*Folies Bergère* show has now been subverted by a rash of striptease acts.

Theatre

Theatre has always had a special place in Czech culture, one which the Velvet Revolution only strengthened. It was the actors who first went on strike, along with the students, and it was the capital's theatres which served as information centres during the revolution.

Most plays in Prague are performed in Czech, although visits from British, American and Irish companies are on the increase. There's also a strong tradition of black theatre and mime, as well as puppet theatre and the multi-media spectacles of the *Laterna magika*, all of which communicate their message without the need for any knowledge of Czech. The list below includes a broad cross-section of companies and theatres, from which you should find something interesting to watch.

Braník Theatre of Pantomime, Branická 63, Braník (☎46 05 07). An adventurous mixture of Czech mime and pantomime, attracting the country's top artists, including Boris Polívka and his troupe. The international festival of mime is based here every June.

Disk, Karlova 8, Staré Město (☎26 53 77). During term time, the theatre is the main venue for the city's drama students' productions, while in summer it's given over to black theatre.

Divadélko říše loutek, Žatecká 1, Nové Město (☎232 34 29). Puppet theatre for children.

Hudební divadlo, Křižíkova 10, Karlín (☎22 08 95). Puts on mostly Western musicals in Czech.

Laterna magika, Národní 40, Nové Město (☎26 00 33). Theatre showing the multi-media extravaganza which went down well at the Montreal EXPO 58. It's been going ever since and is a bit too obviously tourist-orientated for some.

Na Vinohradech, náměstí Míru 7, Vinohrady (☎25 70 41). A nineteenth-century theatre that's a traditional testing ground for up-and-coming Czech actors, putting on mostly classics.

Na zábradlí, Anenské náměstí 5, Staré Město (☎236 04 49). Havel's old haunt back in the 1960s, now run by Ladislav Fialka, the great-grandfather of Czech mime. Alternately shows straight theatre and dumb shows.

Národní divadlo, Národní 2, Nové Město (☎20 53 64). Prague's grandest nineteenth-century Czech theatre puts on a wide variety of plays, opera and ballet. Worth visiting for the decor alone.

Nová scéna, Národní 40, Nové Město (☎20 62 60). This is Prague's most modern and versatile stage. Mostly straight theatre, but also hosts the occasional opera, ballet and *Latern magika* show.

Semafor, Alfa arcade, Václavské náměstí, Nové Město (☎26 14 49). Another multi-media venture founded in the 1960s, now catering mostly for Prague's foreign visitors.

Spejbl a Hurvínek, Římská 45, Vinohrady (☎25 16 66). The indomitable puppet duo created by Josef Skupa earlier this century and still going strong at this, the one traditional puppets-only theatre in the country.

U věže, náměstí M. Gorkého 28, Nové Město (☎22 51 41). Children's puppet shows most days – adult shows on Wed evenings.

Film

As many as half the films shown in Prague cinemas at any one time are the latest British or American productions, dubbed into Czech (a small white square on the poster means the film is dubbed). Slightly more off-beat English-language films are left in the original, with Czech subtitles. For mainstream films, look around Václavské náměstí, which boasts seven cinemas, or check the shortlist below for other options. The *PIS* on Na příkopě has a comprehensive listings broadsheet of the week's films.

Alfa, Václavské náměstí 28, Nové Město. One of the few big 70mm screens in Prague, and the most popular place to see new releases.

British Cultural Section, Jungmannova 30, Nové Město. Shows English films on Thurs & Fri only; closed July & Aug.

Ponrepo, Veletržní 61 (☎37 92 78). The exception to the rule – regularly shows old black-and-white films from all over the world in their original language.

Listings

Airlines *Aeroflot*, Václavské náměstí 15, Nové Město (☎26 08 62); *British Airways*, Štěpánská 63, Nové Město (☎236 03 53); *ČSA*, Revoluční 1 (☎21 46); *Lufthansa*, Pařížská 5, Staré Město (☎232 74 40); *Pan Am*, Pařížská 11, Staré Město (☎26 67 47).

American Express There's an office inside *ČEDOK* on Na příkopě (for opening hours see below).

Banks and exchange Most banks open Mon–Fri 7.30am–3pm only. There's a 24-hour exchange service at the airport.

Boats You can hire rowing boats (15kčcs per hour) from two of the Vltava's islands; the Slovanský ostrov and the Císařský ostrov .

Books English-language books are in short supply, but try Na příkopě 27, Nové Město. For secondhand books, try the bookshops on Mostecká and on Újezd, in Malá Strana. *Waterstones* are planning to open a store in a converted church on Melantrichova,

Car hire From *Pragocar*, at the airport and at Štěpánská 42, Nové Město (☎235 28 09).

Car repairs *Austin Rover*, Jeseniova 56, Žižkov (☎27 23 20); *BMW, Ford, Mercedes & VW*, Severní XI, Spořilov (☎76 67 52); *Fiat*, Na stráži, Krč (☎42 66 14); *Renault*, Ďablická 2, Kobylisy (☎88 82 57).

ČEDOK Na příkopě 18, Nové Město (☎212 71 11); open June–Sept Mon–Fri 8.15am–4.15pm, Sat 8.15am–2pm; Oct–May Mon–Fri 8.15am–4.15pm. For guided tours and international train tickets.

Chemist There's 24-hr service at Na příkopě 7, Nové Město (☎22 00 81).

Dentist Emergency service at Vladislavova 22, Nové Město (☎26 13 74).

Embassies *Canada*, Mickiewiczova 6, Hradčany (☎32 69 41); *Denmark*, U Havlíčkových sadů, Vinohrady (☎25 47 15); *France*, Velkopřevorské náměstí 2, Malá Strana; *Germany*, Vlašská 19 (☎53 23 51); *Hungary* Mičurinova 1, Hradčany (☎36 50 41); *Italy*, Nerudova 20, Malá Strana (☎53 06 66); *Norway*, Na Ořechovce, Dejvice (☎35 66 51); *Poland*, Valdštejnská 8, Malá Strana (☎53 69 51); *Soviet Union*, Pod kaštany 1, Bubeneč (☎38 19 40); *Sweden*, Úvoz 13, Malá Strana (☎53 33 44); *UK*, Thunovská 14, Malá Strana (☎53 33 47); *USA*, Tržiště 15, Malá Strana (☎53 66 41). The nearest embassies for nationals of Eire, Australia and New Zealand are in Vienna.

Emergencies Police ☎158; ambulance ☎155; fire brigade ☎150.

Football Prague's best team is *Sparta Praha*, which supplied five of the country's 1990 World Cup squad, and play every Sunday at the Sparta Stadium ,opposite the Letná park (the season runs from Sept–Dec & March–June). Prague is also home to three other clubs: *Slavia Praha* and *Bohemians*, who both play in Vršovice, the former just south of Vršovické náměstí, the latter further out on Vladivostocká (tram #4 or #22 for both from Metro Náměstí Míru); the currently supporter-less army side, *Dukla Praha*, who play in Dejvice (bus #125 from the Švermův most).

Gay and lesbian life. For up-to-date information on the Prague gay scene, phone ☎52 73 88; 6–10pm only (English spoken). The official Czechoslovak organisation for gays and lesbians is *Lambda Praha*, c/o Jan Lány, Pod Kotlářkou 14, Smíchov (phone as above).

Ice-hockey As in football, the best team is *Sparta Praha* and the stadium is next door to the Sparta Stadium. Games are played on Tues and Fri and the season runs from Sept–May.

Late-night shops Self-service *bufet* food and various grocery supplies are available in the Můstek Metro station (Tues–Fri 6am–10pm, Sat & Sun 2–11pm); general provisions at *Večeerka* on Kaprova, Staré Město (same times as above).

Laundry Self-service laundromats (called *prádelna*) at Mostecká 2, Malá Strana (Mon–Fri 7am–6pm) and Václavské náměstí, Nové Město (7am–6pm).

Left-luggage There's a 24-hr service at Praha hlavní nádraží and Praha-Holešovice, as well as lockers at most bus and train stations.

Libraries At the *British Cultural Section*, Jungmannova 30, Nové Město (☎22 45 50; Mon–Fri 8am–noon & 1–4pm) you can browse through the books and old newspapers, but there's a waiting list to gain borrowing rights. The *American Library*, Vlašská 11, Malá Strana (Mon–Fri 10am–5pm ; closed Aug), has lectures and discussions on American history and culture throughout the week, plus a wide-ranging selection of newspapers, magazines and books.

Lost property Go to Bolzanova 5, Nové Město (☎24 84 30).

Maps There's a specialist *Olympia* map shop on Hybernská, Nové Město.

Markets People sell anything and everything at Prague's *tržnice* (markets). The biggest ones are at V kotcích, Staré Město (daily); Letná plain, Holešovice (every Sun 8am–2pm; Metro Hradčanská); Vltavská (Mon–Sat 9am–6pm; a 10-min walk from Metro Vltavská); and Pankrác (Mon–Sat 7am–6pm; Metro Pankrác).

Newspapers The bookshop above Metro Můstek regularly receives English-language newspapers (open seven days a week), as does the *Zahraniční noviny* outlet in the Rokoko arcade on Václavské náměstí.

Opticians The most central ones are at Mostecká 3, Malá Strana, and Národní 37, Nové Město.

Petrol stations All-night service at Olšanská, Žižkov; Argentinská, Holešovice; and Plzeňská, Smíchov. Lead-free petrol is available at the last two stations only.

Photos Passport photos from Bartolomějská 1, Staré Město; express film developing at Nad alejí 29, Břevnov.

Post Office The main post office is at Jindřišská 14, Nové Město (☎26 48 41). A 24-hr service for parcels, telegrams and telephones. Pick up Poste Restante here.

Posters and art There's a poster shop in the arcade between Celetná and Templová, while old prints and artwork can be found at Karlova 16, Staré Město.

Sauna At the *Slavia Praha* stadium, Vršovice (open daily 8am–10pm).

Second-hand shops Clothes at Žitná 41, Nové Město and Karlovo náměstí; watches at Národní 18, Nové Město and Pštrossova 24, Nové Město; *objets d'art* at Nerudova 46, Malá Strana.

Swimming pools Indoor and outdoor pools at Podolská 74, Podolí (Mon–Fri 6am–10pm, Sat & Sun 8am–8pm; tram #3, #17 or #21 from Palackého náměstí).

AROUND PRAGUE

Few people who visit Prague take the trouble to leave the city limits and head off into the surrounding countryside, which is a shame since few capitals can boast such unspoilt tracts of woodland so near at hand. Once you leave the cosmopolitan streets of the city behind, the traditional small-town feel of Bohemia immediately makes itself felt. Basically, there are four directions in which to head, ranged around the points of the compass. To the **north** is the wine-producing town of **Mělník**, and beyond, the wooded hills of **Kokořínsko**. **East**, you can head towards the modern spa of **Poděbrady**, taking in the open-air folk museum at **Přerov nad Labem** before continuing on to the medieval mining town of **Kutná Hora**. The route **south** lies along a trail of castles and chateaux, up the **Sázava valley**, or, further, to **Konopiště**. And to the **west** is **Karlštejn**, the most evocative medieval castle in Bohemia, the unspoilt countryside around **Křivoklát**, and the village of **Lidice**, a sad testimony to the Nazi occupation of the last war.

With your own transport, most of these places are less than an hour's drive from Prague, but by **public transport**, some are going to take take two hours or more to reach – which means several destinations would be better considered as overnight stops. The biggest attraction out of Prague, Kutná Hora, deserves more than a day anyway.

North to Mělník and Kokořínsko

One of the quickest and most rewarding trips out of the capital is to follow the Vltava as it twists northwards across the plain to meet the Labe at Mělník. This is the beginning of the so-called **záhrada Čech** (Garden of Bohemia), a fertile region whose cherry blossoms are always the first to herald the Bohemian spring, and whose roads in summer are lined with stalls overflowing with fruit and vegetables. But the real reason to venture into this flat landscape is to visit the chateaux which lie along the banks of the river, all easily reached from Prague by public transport.

Kralupy nad Vltavou

The Nobel Prize-winning poet, Jaroslav Seifert, didn't beat around the bush when he wrote that **KRALUPY NAD VLTAVOU** "is not a beautiful town and never was". It paid an unusually heavy price in the last war, bombarded from the air,

BOAT TRIPS FROM PRAGUE

If you want a change of pace in the summer months, it's worth considering taking a **boat trip on the Vltava river**. The traditional mode of water transport – the *vor*, or raft – is no longer an option, but there are a number of less romantic ferries which offer a variety of trips, setting off from the jetty on the right bank, just south of Jiráskův most in Nové Město. Buy all tickets at the jetty, or ask in advance at *ČEDOK*.

● The quick jaunt **in and around Prague** (May–Sept hourly 10am–4pm) is pleasant enough, although the route runs through the suburbs, all of which have their bleak spots. Since the construction of huge dams further upriver, the Vltava has come a long way from its riotous youth, when it swept away bridges in its path, and nowadays these boat trips are more likely to be cancelled due to lack of water than stormy weather.

● Boats also leave for **Císařský ostrov** (2 daily; 50min), the Vltava's biggest island, now exclusively given over to industry. However, it's worth the trip, since Stromovka park and Výstaviště lie to the south, while a few minutes' walk over to the right bank brings you to the chateau at Troja and the nearby zoo (see "The Suburbs" above for details).

● For the trip **north to Roztoky**, one boat a day leaves at 10am on the two-hour journey, which also doles out its fair share of industrial panoramas around Karlín and Holešovice. Things get better in the last hour as the boat leaves the city proper and approaches Roztoky, though unless it's a good day for a picnic, you might as well get the train straight back into town as Roztoky castle isn't up to much.

● Few travellers are prepared to take the time to travel **south to the Slapy dam** (2 daily; 4hr), which is a pity because the river is at its best here, snaking through the great swathe of wooded hills south of the city. For Praguers this is *the* place to have a *chata* (summer house), and the sides of the valley are littered with little brown huts. Although there are around 2000 boats moored on the river, there's virtually no traffic allowed (except water-skiing) – an attempt to preserve the precarious balance of nature which has suffered so much from pollution over the last forty years. From the dam itself, you can continue by boat through the placid waters further south, to the castles of Orlík and Zvíkov (see "South Bohemia", p.128 for details).

and post-war industrial development left it with "smokestacks . . . like phantom trees, without branches, without leaves, without blossoms, without bees". Now, Kralupy's oil refineries and chemical plants have spread across both sides of the river, but it's still worth making the 45-minute train journey from Prague, as just a few kilometres to the north, on either side of the Vltava, are two chateaux worth visiting: Nelahozeves on the left bank, and Veltrusy on the right.

Nelahozeves

Shortly after pulling out of Kralupy, the train passes through a short tunnel and comes to rest at NELAHOZEVES ZASTÁVKA station, below the plain, barrack-like chateau of **Nelahozeves** (mid-April to mid-Oct Tues–Sun 9am–5pm), recently given a new lease of life by a sgraffito face-lift. The chateau was built by a group of undistinguished Italian builders for one of the lackeys of the Habsburg Emperor, Ferdinand I, and now, stripped of its furniture, it serves as an art repository for European paintings from the collections of three great aristocratic families; the Pernštejns, the Rožmberks and the Lobkovics. The best stuff, sadly, is either housed in Prague galleries or on permanent loan elsewhere, leaving little to gloat over here, but there are some good portraits spanning the centuries, and you might chance upon a local wedding, usually held on Saturdays in one of the chateau's wings.

The country's most famous composer, Antonín Dvořák, was born and bred in the house (no. 12) next door to the post office, which sits under the shadow of the chateau. The local teacher suggested that Dvořák, who was originally apprenticed to a butcher, should be sent to the Prague Organ School instead – he never looked back, though he continued to draw inspiration from his homeland throughout his life. If there's someone around at the house (officially open Tues–Thurs, Sat & Sun 9am–noon & 2–5pm), you can have a quick look at the great man's rocking-chair, but it's an experience that's somewhat short of exciting.

Veltrusy

The industrial suburbs of Kralupy stop just short of the gardens of the chateau of **Veltrusy zámek** (March, April & Sept daily 9am–noon & 1–4pm; May–Aug daily 8am–noon & 1–5pm; closed Mon), over the bridge from the main station in Nelahozeves (one stop on from Nelahozeves zastávka). The classic Baroque symmetry of Veltrusy is an altogether more satisfying experience, its green shutters and henna-dyed wings pivoting round a bulbous, green-domed building, recalling earlier country houses in France or Italy. It was built in the early eighteenth century as a plaything for the upwardly mobile Counts of Chotek, its 290 acres of surrounding woodland perfect for a little light hunting.

If you fancy staying, there's a very good **campsite** (April to mid-Nov) just outside the chateau grounds – a great spot from which to watch the barges on the Vltava, but no place for a healthy dip given the pollutants that pour into the river further upstream. On the road to the campsite, there's an isolated row of houses offering cheap **private rooms,** too.

Mělník and around

Occupying a commanding site at the confluence of the Vltava and Labe rivers, **MĚLNÍK**, 33km north of Prague, lies in the heart of Bohemia's wine-growing region. Viticulture here goes back to the tenth century, but it became the town's mainstay only when Charles IV, aching for a little of the French wine of his youth, introduced grapes from Burgundy. There's no direct train service from Prague, so you're more likely to arrive by bus, which takes around an hour; to reach the older part of town from the bus station, simply head uphill in the direction of the big church tower.

The town is pleasant – and old – enough for some casual strolling, but you're likely to be drawn soon enough to Mělník's greatest monument, the Renaissance **zámek** (daily March, April & Sept 9am–4pm; May–Aug 8am–noon & 1–5pm; closed Mon), visible for miles around. Below it, vines cling to the south-facing terraces, as the land plunges into the river below. The present building, covered in the familiar sgraffito patterning, houses more of the apparently unending art collection of the last owners, the Lobkowitz family – displayed in magnificently proportioned rooms, which also provide great views out over the landscape. From beneath the great tower of Mělník's priory church, next door to the chateau, there's an even better view of the river confluence, and the subsidiary canal, once so congested with vessels that traffic lights had to be introduced to avoid accidents.

If you're hoping **to stay**, the *Zlatý beránek*, on the main square (at no. 10), one block east of the chateau, is your best bet for a cheap and vacant room. As for **food and drink**, the chateau restaurant is as good a place as any to sample some of the local wine: the red *Ludmila* is the most famous of Mělník's wines, but if you prefer white, try the fresh trout (thankfully not pulled out of the Vltava or Labe below) washed down with a bottle of *Tramín*. If the tour groups are monopolising the chateau restaurant, you're left with the basic food served at the *Zlatý beránek*, or the beer at the lively *Zámecká pivnice*, opposite the main chateau gateway.

Liběchov

Seven kilometres downriver (ten minutes' by train from Mělník), and just out of sight of the giant coal-fired power station which provides most of Prague's electricity, is the rhubarb-and-custard coloured **zámek** (Tues–Sun 9am–noon & 1–3.30pm) at **LIBĚCHOV**. Even without the sickly colour scheme, it's a bizarre chateau; formal and two-dimensional when viewed from the French gardens at the front, but bulging like an amphitheatre around the back where the entrance is. Inside is another surprise, a **Museum of Asian Cultures**, featuring endless Buddhas, Mongolian printing equipment, Balinese monster gear and Javanese puppets: they all make for a fascinating half-hour tour. The main dining hall, now full of Asian musical instruments, is curious, too, kitted out in its original barley-sugar decor with little sculpted jesters crouching mischievously in the corners of the ceiling.

For all the chateau's excesses, the village itself is little more than a *hostinec* and a bend in the road, but straggled up the valley are the remains of what was once an attractive spa resort for ailing Praguers. Many of the old *Gasthäuser* are still standing, including the *Pension Stüdl* where Kafka spent the winter of 1918. It was here that he met and got engaged to Julie Wohryzek, daughter of a Jewish shoemaker from Prague, a match vigorously opposed by his father and which prompted Kafka to write his vitriolic, but unsent, *Letter to His Father*. The only place to stay nowadays is the **campsite** (mid-April to Sept), one kilometre up the Liběchovka valley, which has some good hiking possibilities in to the Kokořín region (see below).

Roudnice nad Labem

A short bus ride west of Mělník (or accessible by train from Nelahozeves), **ROUDNICE NAD LABEM** lies in the Labe basin in flat surroundings, except for the occasional cypress tree and the odd volcanic molehill. It's only really worth stopping off if you're keen to climb the mythical mound of **Říp** (459m), the most prominent of these hills, south of the town. Here, the leader of a band of wandering Slavs, Čech, sat down, surveyed the land and decided to set up home, thus founding Čechy (Bohemia). His brother Lech, meanwhile, headed further north to found Poland. If you feel inspired by their example, follow the red-marked **path** from Roudnice, which takes you to the summit (marked by a twelfth-century church) in around an hour.

Kokořínsko

Northeast of Mělník, you leave the low plains of the Labe for a plateau region know as **Kokořínsko**, a hidden pocket of wooded hills which takes its name from the Gothic castle which rises through the tree-tops at its centre. The sandstone plateau has weathered over the millennia to form sunken valleys and rocky outcrops, and given the local well-preserved, half-timbered villages, it comes as a surprise that the whole area isn't buzzing all summer.

However, the only place everyone heads for is the village of **KOKOŘÍN**, whose spectacular fourteenth-century **hrad** (April & Oct Sat & Sun 9am–4pm; May–Aug Tues–Sun 8am–5pm; Sept Tues–Sun 9am–5pm) and dramatic setting greatly attracted the Czech nineteenth-century Romantics. The castle is a perfect eagle's lair, ideal for the robbers who used it as a base after it fell into disrepair in the sixteenth century. Not until the end of the nineteenth century did it get a new lease of life, from a jumped-up local landowner, Václav Špaček, who bought himself a title and refurbished the place as a family memorial. There's precious little inside and no incentive to endure the half-hour tour, as you can explore the ramparts and climb the tallest tower without the guide.

The village itself is fairly nondescript, but there's a lot of scope for some gentle hiking in the area, with a series of marked paths emanating from the picturesque **Pšovka valley** below the castle. With a couple of **hotels** and at least four **campsites**, Kokořín is also the easiest place to find somewhere to stay in the locality. In summer, there's one direct **bus** a week from Prague's Praha-Holešovice bus station (leaving at 7.45am); otherwise, take the regular buses to Mělník and change there. Alternatively, take the local train from Mělník to MŠENO, from where it's a 3-kilometre walk west on the green-marked path.

East to Poděbrady

The scenery immediately **east of Prague** is even less varied than that around Mělník, a rich blanket of fields spreading over the plain as far as the eye can see. If you're in a hurry, you'd be advised to take in only Kutná Hora (see p.114) and then move straight on to East Bohemia. With more time, though, there are a couple of nearer towns on the same route which merit a stop: one, Poděbrady, even makes a possible overnight destination if Prague is full.

Přerov nad Labem

One place that *is* worth a visit as you head east – whatever your destination – is the **skansen** (folk village) at **PŘEROV NAD LABEM**. The first of its kind when it was founded in 1895, skansens became quite a fad in post-war Czechoslovakia, as collectivisation and urbanisation wiped out traditional rural communities, along with their distinctive folk culture and wooden architecture. Přerov's skansen is busy during the summer with tour groups from Prague, wandering through various half-timbered and stone buildings, some brought here plank by plank from nearby villages, some from Přerov itself. Particularly evocative is the reconstructed eighteenth-century village school, with a portrait of the Austrian Emperor taking pride of place amid the Catholic icons and a delicate paper theatre for drama lessons.

To get to the village, take one of the slow buses from Prague to Poděbrady, get off at the crossroads just after the turn-off to MOCHOV, and it's a kilometre further north on foot.

Poděbrady

For a spa resort on the Labe, **PODĚBRADY** is, nevertheless, a pretty ugly town, and until the nearby motorway is completed it will remain badly scarred by the heavy traffic ploughing eastwards from Prague. All this is par for the course: the spa waters were only discovered earlier this century and Poděbrady owes its existence, for better or worse, to its strategic position on the east–west trade route.

The town's only real claim to fame is as the birthplace of **George of Poděbrady**, the one and only Hussite King of Bohemia (and the last real Czech), whose copper green equestrian statue stands in the main square, náměstí Jiřího. But apart from the statue, there's scarcely a trace of George anywhere – although he was born in the **zámek** (May–Oct Tues–Sun 9am–5pm), which fronts on to the main square (and backs on to the river), the present structure was built a hundred years after his death and houses only the minutest of historical exhibitions. The **spa** itself, laid out with a stunning lack of imagination earlier this century, is not much better, though its waters are popular enough judging by the queue of people at the concrete rotunda on Riegrovo náměstí, which is a couple of blocks northeast of the main square. Fifteen thousand patients a year pass through Poděbrady, and around tea-time most of them can be seen promenading through the town's park, inspecting the window displays of Bohemian crystal and admiring the fully functioning floral clock. For a glimpse of the town's halcyon days, in the last years of the Empire, check out the local **museum**, at Palackého 68 (Feb–April Mon–Fri 9am–noon & 1–4pm; May–Oct Tues–Sun 9am–5pm), two minutes' walk from the castle.

Despite its limitations, Poděbrady is a convenient halt on the road to Prague, less than an hour by train from the city. Its two **hotels**, both on Riegrovo náměstí, regularly have vacancies and there's a **campsite** (May to mid-Sept) a little further upstream from the castle. With visitors of one kind or another all summer, there's a fair selection of films and classical concerts on offer in town, not to mention some intriguing **eating** options – a Chinese restaurant, a Japanese garden café, and a pizzeria on the main square.

Kutná Hora

For two hundred and fifty years or so **KUTNÁ HORA** (Kuttenberg) was one of the most important towns in Bohemia, second only to Prague. By the late Middle Ages its population was equal to that of London, its shanty-town suburbs were straggled across what are now green fields and its ambitious building projects set out to rival those of the capital itself. The road to prosperity began with the discovery of silver deposits in the surrounding area. German miners were invited to settle and work the seams, and in 1308 Václav II founded the royal mint here and sent for Italian craftsmen to run it. The town's sudden wealth allowed it to underwrite the construction of one of the most magnificent churches in central Europe, and a number of other prestigious Gothic monuments.

The town suffered badly during the Hussite Wars, besieged and eventually taken by Žižka's fanatical Táborites in 1421, only to be recaptured by Sigismund and his papal forces a few years later. While the silver stocks remained high the town was able to recover its former prosperity, but when the mines dried up at the end of the sixteenth century, Kutná Hora's wealth and importance came to an abrupt end – when the Swedes marched on the town during the Thirty Years' War, they had to be bought off with beer and not silver. The town never fully recovered, shrivelling to less than a third of its former size, its fate emphatically sealed by a devastating fire in 1770.

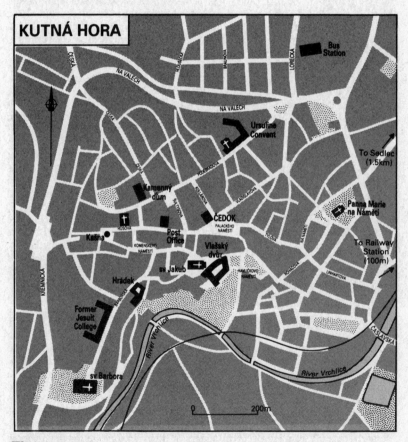

The town

The small, mean houses which line the town's medieval lanes give little idea of its former glories. The same goes for **Palackého náměstí**, nominally at least the main square, but now thoroughly provincial in character. A narrow alleyway on the south side of the square leads to the leafy Havlíčkovo náměstí, off which is the **Vlašský dvůr** (Italian Court), originally conceived as a palace by Václav II, and the town's bottomless purse for three centuries. Here, Florentine minters produced the Prague Groschen (*pražské groše*), a silver coin widely used throughout central Europe until the nineteenth century. The building itself has been mucked about with over the centuries, lastly – and most brutally – by nineteenth-century restorers, who left the chestnut trees and a fourteenth-century oriel window (capped by an unlikely looking wooden onion dome) as the Court's only redeeming features. The town council now occupies much of the complex, with civil weddings conducted in the Gothic main hall, and since the small exhibition on the process of minting (April–Sept 8am–5pm; Oct–March 8am–4pm; closed Mon) is none too absorbing, you'd do better to take a turn in the court gardens, which climb down in steps to the Vrchlice valley below. It's undoubtedly Kutná Hora's best profile, with a splendid view over to the church of sv Barbora (see below).

Behind the Vlašský dvůr is **sv Jakub** (St James), the town's oldest church, begun a generation or so after the discovery of the mines. Its grand scale is a clear indication of the town's quite considerable wealth by the fourteenth century, though its artistry pales in comparison with Kutná Hora's other ecclesiastical buildings. Its leaning tower is a reminder of the precarious position of the town, the church's foundations prone to subsidence from the disused mines below.

The Jesuits arrived a trifle too late to exploit the town's silver stocks, but with their own funds they built a palatial **Jesuit College** on the ridge to the southwest of town. With its gallery of saints and holy men, it was a crude and vainglorious attempt to dent the achievements of the neighbouring church of **sv Barbora** (Tues–Sun 8am–noon & 1–5pm), arguably the most beautiful church in central Europe. Not to be outdone by the great monastery at Sedlec (see below) or the St Vitus Cathedral in Prague, the miners of Kutná Hora began financing the construction of a great Gothic cathedral of their own, dedicated to Saint Barbara, the patron saint of miners and gunners. The foundations were probably laid by Parler himself in the 1380s, but work was interrupted by the Hussite wars, and the church remained unfinished, despite a flurry of building activity at the beginning of the sixteenth century.

From the outside (best viewed from the gardens of the Vlašský dvůr) it's an incredible sight; bristling with pinnacles, finials and flying buttresses supporting its most striking feature, a roof consisting of three tent-like towers, which culminates in unequal needle-sharp spires. Inside, cold light streams through the plain glass windows, lighting up a playful vaulted nave whose ribs form branches and petals stamped with coats of arms belonging to Václav II and the local miners' guilds. The wide spread of the five-aisled nave is remarkably uncluttered: a Gothic pulpit – half wood, half stone – creeps tastefully up a central pillar, and black and gold Renaissance confessionals hide discreetly in the north aisle. On the south wall is the Minters' Chapel, decorated with fifteenth-century wall frescoes showing the Florentines at work, while in the ambulatory chapels there are some fascinating paintings of local miners at their job, unique for their period.

West of the main square, the squat, many-sided **Kašna** (fountain) strikes an odd pose in the Rejskovo náměstí – anything less like a fountain would be hard to imagine. Another Gothic building to survive the 1770 fire was the **Kamenný dům**, built around 1480 and now converted into a fairly unexceptional local museum. From later times, Kilian Ignaz Dientzenhofer's **Ursuline convent**, on the northern edge of the old town, promised to be the best of Kutná Hora's

Baroque monuments, but it was never completed. Only three sides of the convent's pentagonal plan were finished, its church added in neo-Baroque style in the late nineteenth century while sv Barbora was being restored.

A few practical details

Fast trains from Prague's Masarykovo nádraží to Kutná Hora are fairly frequent, and take around an hour. The railway station is a few minutes' walk east of the town centre, where all the sights are within easy walking distance of each other. In addition, the town has a highly efficient system of aluminium orientation signs, and at almost every street corner a pictorial list of the chief places of interest keeps you on the right track. They even point the way to the **youth hostel** (*turistická ubytovna*; reception open 6–8pm) which lets out its rickety bunk beds for very little, but insists on an 8am start to the day. For a more leisurely night, try the *Mědínek* **hotel,** at Palackého náměstí (☎0327-2741/2743), which also serves seven different varieties of coffee in its foyer. The nearest **campsite** (mid-May to mid-Sept) is by a lake near Malešov, 5km southwest of Kutná Hora by local bus or train.

Around Kutná Hora: Sedlec and Kačina

There's a couple of easy side trips to be made from the town. Bus #1 or #4 runs the 3km northeast to **SEDLEC**, once a separate village but now a suburb of Kutná Hora. Adjoining Sedlec's defunct eighteenth-century Cistercian monastery (now the largest tobacco factory in Europe), is the surviving fourteenth-century **monastery church**, a work of great originality redesigned by Giovanni Santini, who specialised in melding Gothic with Baroque. Here, given a plain French Gothic church gutted during the Hussite wars, Santini set to work on the vaulting, adding his characteristic sweeping rib patterns, relieved only by the occasional Baroque splash of colour above the chancel steps. However, for all its attractions, the church seems to be permanently closed except for the occasional service.

Cross the road, following the signs, and you come to the monks' graveyard where an ancient Gothic chapel leans heavily over the entrance to a macabre subterranean **kostnice**, or ossuary, full to overflowing with human bones. When holy earth from Golgotha was scattered over the graveyard in the twelfth century, all of Bohemia's nobility rushed to be buried here, the bones mounting up until there were over 10,000 complete sets. In 1870, worried about the mounting supply, the authorities commissioned František Rint to do something creative with them. He rose to the challenge and moulded four giant bells, one in each corner of the crypt, out of the bones, designed wall-to-ceiling skeletal decorations and, as the centrepiece, put together a chandelier made out of every bone in the human body.

Nothing quite so ghastly confronts you at the early eighteenth-century chateau of **Kačina**, a 4-kilometre hike or hitch northeast of Sedlec. It's a colossal neoclassical affair, the facade stretching for over 200m across the lawn. For the owners, the up-and-coming Chotek family (who also owned Veltrusy), the chateau grounds came first, and planting began a full fifteen years before a stone was laid. Appropriately, perhaps, the chateau now houses a museum of agriculture (April–Sept Tues–Sun 8am–5pm), which used to extol the virtues of (forced) collectivisation, though this is now undergoing reform. It's the wide expanse of parkland, however, which draws car loads of Czechs here throughout the summer.

To the Sázava Valley

A short train ride **southeastwards** from Prague is enough to transport you from the urban sprawl of the capital into one of the prettiest regions of central Bohemia. Until the motorway to Brno and Bratislava tore its way through the area in the 1970s, the roads and railways linking the three big cities took the longer, flatter option, eastwards along the Labe valley. As a result, commerce passed the **Sázava Valley** by, and it remains undeveloped, unspoilt and out-of-the-way. A handful of castles and chateaux on the way to, and along, the Sázava Valley make convenient day trips and are the main reason for heading out this way.

Průhonice

Barely outside the city limits, and just off the country's one and only motorway, the chateau of **Průhonice** (May–Aug Tues–Sun 10am–6pm; Sept–April Sat & Sun 10am–6pm) throngs with Czech weekenders even outside the summer season. For the great majority, it's the 625-acre park they come to see and not the castle itself, which is a motley parade of neo-Renaissance buildings most of which are closed to the public anyway. The park is a botanical and horticultural research centre, so the array of flora – not to mention fauna – is unusually good here. Though few do, it's worth paying a passing visit to the chateau's **art gallery**, which features a permanent collection of twentieth-century Czech paintings and sculpture, including a hefty series of canvases by the Czech Cubists.

Průhonice is about 15km from Prague, and there's a regular *ČSAD* **bus** service from Praha-Chodov bus station (Metro Upatov).

Sázava and Český Šternberk

Rising majestically from the slow-moving waters of the river Sázava below, **Sázava monastery** (April & Sept Sat & Sun 9am–4pm; May–Aug Tues–Sun 8am–noon & 1–5pm) was founded by the eleventh-century Prince Oldřich, on the instigation of a passing hermit called Prokop (St Procopius), whom he met by chance in the forest. The Slavonic liturgy was used at the monastery and, for a while, Sázava became an important centre for the dissemination of Slavonic texts. Later, a large Gothic church was planned, and this now bares its red sandstone nave to the world, incomplete but intact. The chancel was converted into a Baroque church and later still the Tieg family bought the place and started to build themselves a modest chateau. Of this architectural hotchpotch, only the surviving Gothic frescoes – in the popular "Beautiful Style", but of a sophistication unmatched in the Bohemian art of the time – are truly memorable.

The village of **SÁZAVA** itself thrived on the glass trade, and the rest of the monastery's over-long guided tour concentrates on the local glassware. Without your own transport, it'll take a good hour and a half by bus or train to cover the 55km from Prague to Sázava. Of the two, the **train** ride (change at ČERČANY) is the more visually absorbing, at least by the time you join the branch line which meanders down the Sázava valley. There's a **campsite** (June to mid-Sept) and a reasonably priced **motel** by the river, should you need a place to stay.

Several bends in the Sázava river later, the great mass of the **hrad** (April & Oct Sat & Sun 9am–4pm; May–Aug Tues–Sun 8am–5pm; Sept Tues–Sun 9am–5pm) at ČESKÝ ŠTERNBERK is strung out along a knife's edge above the river; a breathtaking sight. Unfortunately, that's all it is, since apart from its fiercely defensive position, little remains of the original Gothic castle. Add to the dull guided tour, the full two-hour journey by train or bus from Prague (again, change trains at Čerčany), and you may decide to skip it altogether.

Konopiště

Other than for its proximity to Prague, the popularity of **Konopiště** (April, Sept & Oct Tues–Sun 9am–noon & 1–4pm; May–Aug Tues–Sun 8am–noon & 1–5pm) remains a complete mystery. From the opening of the season to the last day of October, coach parties from all over the world home in on this unexceptional Gothic castle, stuffed with dead animals and dull weaponry. The only interesting thing about the place is its historical associations: King Václav IV was imprisoned in the castle's distinctive round tower, and the Archduke Franz Ferdinand lived in the castle until his assassination in Sarajevo in 1914. It's he whose prime interest seems to have been killing any living creature foolish enough to venture into the castle grounds: between 1880 and 1906, he killed no fewer than 171,537 birds and animals, the details of which are recorded in his *Schuss Liste* displayed inside. There's a choice of two equally tedious **guided tours** – the shorter forty-minute tour of the Zámecké sbírky takes you past the stuffed bears, deer teeth, and assorted lethal weapons; the tour of the Zámecké salony is less gruesome but ten minutes longer. There are occasionally tours in English, French and German, too, so ask at the box office before you sign up. Or simply head off into the surrounding deer park for a pleasant stroll.

As Konopiště is only 45km from Prague you shouldn't have to stay the night, though there is a **campsite** (May–Sept) and **motel** not far from the castle car park. The castle is a fifteen-minute walk west from the railway station at BENEŠOV.

Jemniště

Castle enthusiasts are better advised to visit the simple Baroque **zámek** (same times as Konopiště above) hidden in the woods above the nearby village of JEMNIŠTĚ. To get there, you'll need to change trains at Benešov, heading for POSTUPICE, twenty-five minutes down the line, and then walk the fifteen minutes from there. It's worth the effort because the chateau is rarely visited (it should come as no surprise if you're the only taker for the brief guided tour), yet it contains an impressive collection of seventeenth-century pictorial maps and plans, and a small selection of Empire furniture.

West of Prague

The green belt area to the west of Prague has its fair share of rolling hills too, but spend more time here and you'll find it's easily the most varied of the regions around the city, and consequently one of the most popular destinations for urban Czechs. Although it takes in the huge steel and coal town of **Kladno**, for the most part there are few big settlements. As you drift further south, the landscape becomes harsher and more thickly forested and around **Křivoklát**, the Berounka river carves itself an enticingly craggy valley. Beyond Rakovník, the woods thin out and the hop fields begin to take over, but further downstream there's no such respite around the most popular destination of all, Charles IV's magnificent country castle at **Karlštejn**.

Around Karlštejn

KARLŠTEJN, 28km southwest of Prague, is a small T-shaped village strung out along one of the tributaries of the Berounka – pretty, but not enough to warrant a coach park the size of a football pitch. It's the **hrad** (March, April, Oct–Dec daily 9am–noon & 1–4pm; May–Sept daily 8am–noon & 1–6pm; closed Mon), occupying a defiantly unassailable position above the village, which draws in the mass of tourists. Built in the fourteenth century by the Emperor Charles IV as a giant safe-box for his crown jewels, it quickly became Charles' favourite retreat from the vast city he himself had masterminded. Women were strictly forbidden to enter the castle, and the story of his third wife Anna's successful break-in (in drag) became one of the most popular Czech comedies of the nineteenth century.

The hrad looks much better from a distance. Inside, only the top two chambers deserve attention, and of those, only the **Mariánská věž** is open to the public at the moment. Here Charles shut himself off from the rest of the world, with any urgent business passed to him through a hole in the wall. The castle's finest room, the **Chapel of sv Kříž**, at the highest point of the castle, remains closed: only the Emperor, the archbishop and the electoral princes could enter this guilded treasure-house, whose walls alone contain 2200 semi-precious stones and 128 painted panels, the work of Master Theoderich, Bohemia's greatest four-teenth-century painter. All it lacks are the crown jewels themselves, now stashed away in the cathedral in Prague.

Český kras

While nowhere near as extensive or impressive as the karst regions of Moravia and Slovakia, the **Český kras** (Bohemian Karst), about 5km west of Karlštejn, has all the same ingredients as its rich relations. Geologically, the region has fascinated scientists since the early nineteenth century, but the one set of caves open to the public, the **Koněpruské jeskyně** (daily April–Oct), lay undiscovered until 1950. Nowadays, they're not so easy to miss, thanks to the Hollywood-style giant white lettering on the hillside above. But much more fascinating than the dripstone decorations was the simultaneous discovery of an illegal mint in the upper level of the caves. A full set of weights, miners' lamps and even the remains of food were found here, dating back to the second half of the fifteenth century.

Practical details

Slow **trains** for Karlštejn leave Praha-Smíchov station roughly every hour, and take about forty minutes. To reach the caves, you'll need to catch one of the infrequent **buses** from the soap-producing town of BEROUN (50min by train from Praha hlavní nádraží), a couple of kilometres to the north of Karlštejn.

Hotels are hard to come by, but **campsites** like the one by the river at Karlštejn are much more common. ŘEVNICE (two stops before Karlštejn) is the unlikely village in which Martina Navrátilová spent her tennis-playing childhood, but perhaps more importantly it has a hotel by the station, a supermarket in town, and a campsite (open May–Sept) with bungalows, just across the river.

Křivoklátsko

The beautiful mixed woodland that makes up the UNESCO nature reserve of **Křivoklátsko**, 40km due west of Prague, is just out of reach of the day-trippers, making it an altogether sleepier place than the area around Karlštejn. The epileptic twists (*křivky*) of the Berounka cast up the highest crags of the region, which cluster round the castle of **Křivoklát** (April, Sept & Oct daily 9am–4pm; May–Aug daily 8am–noon & 1–5pm; closed Mon) – somehow elevated above everything around it. With such a perfect location in the heart of the best hunting ground in Bohemia, Křivoklát naturally enjoyed the royal patronage of the Přemyslids, whose hunting parties were legendary. From the outside it's a scruffy but impressive stronghold, dominated by the round tower in which the Irish alchemist, Edward Kelly, found himself incarcerated after falling out with Rudolf II. The one-hour guided tour takes in most of the castle's good points, including the Great Hall and the chapel, dating back to the thirteenth century, both of which have an austere beauty quite at odds with the castle's reputation as a venue for bacchanalian goings-on.

Practical details

Apart from a direct Saturday morning service, all journeys by **train** from Prague to Křivoklát require a change at Beroun. **Buses** from Praha-Dejvice station run frequently only at weekends, and take around an hour and a half. Křivoklát castle is the region's only real "sight", though you could happily spend days exploring the surrounding countryside on the network of well-marked footpaths. However, unless you're staying at one of the two **campsites** (June–Sept), a short walk up the river near ROZTOKY, you'll have to hole up in RAKOVNÍK (30min up the line from Křivoklát), a deeply provincial town with just one posh **hotel** and a good local beer to offer.

Lidice

The small mining village of **LIDICE**, 18km northwest of Prague, hit the world headlines on June 10, 1942, at the moment when it ceased to exist. On the flimsiest of evidence, it was chosen as scapegoat for the assassination of the Nazi leader Reinhard Heydrich (see "Nové Město", p.89). The men of the village were rounded up and shot, the women sent off to various camps and the children sent to "good" German homes, while the village itself was burnt to the ground.

Knowing all this as you approach Lidice makes the modern village seem almost perversely unexceptional. At the end of the straight tree-lined main street, 10 června 1942, there's a dour concrete memorial with a small but horrific **museum** (April–Sept daily 8am–4pm; Oct–March daily 8am–5pm), which regularly shows a short film about Lidice, including footage which the Nazis themselves shot as the village was burning. The spot where the old village used to lie is just south of the memorial, now merely smooth green pasture punctuated with a few simple symbolic reminders; the foundations of the old school, a wooden cross and a common grave.

After the massacre, the "Lidice shall live" campaign was launched and villages all over the world began to change their name to Lidice. The first was Stern Park Gardens, Illinois, soon joined by villages in Mexico and other Latin American countries. From Coventry to Montevideo, towns twinned themselves with Lidice, so that rather than "wiping a Czech village off the face of the earth" as Hitler had hoped, it became a symbol of anti-fascist resistance.

There's no place, nor reason, to stay and most people come here as a daytrip from Prague on one of the regular buses from Praha-Dejvice.

Around Kladno

KLADNO, 10km further west, is a pretty grim town, made even grimmer by the expansive grey 1950s' architecture which the town received in reward for its strong support for the 1948 coup. Nowadays, it typifies the contradictions and problems of the post-Communist state: what will happen to a town of over 70,000 people whose existence is rooted in heavy industries which are both economically and ecologically unsound? What remains of the staré město is a dusty, dirty run-down mess into which there seems little point in venturing. The town's definitive museum of the working-class (the Czechoslovak Communist Party was founded in Kladno) is closed for "technical reasons", and apart from the local **puppet theatre** near *ČEDOK* on the main square, there's nothing else to see.

Buses for Kladno leave Praha-Florenc bus station roughly every half-hour. The only reason to come here is to catch one of the buses which leave Kladno around midday for Lány (see below), though you can avoid it altogether by taking the slow train to CHOMUTOV from Prague's Masarykovo nádraží, getting out at STOCHOV, 3km northeast of Lány.

Lány

At the weekend, Škoda loads of Czech families, pensioners and assorted pilgrims make their way to **LÁNY**, 12km beyond Kladno, a plain, grey village on a hill by the edge of the Křivoklát forest. They congregate in the town's pristine cemetery to pay their respects to one of Czechoslovakia's most important historical figures, Tomáš Garrigue Masaryk, the country's founding father and President from 1918 to 1935.

Tomáš Garrigue Masaryk – known affectionately as TGM – was born in 1850, in Hodonín, a town in a part of Moravia where Slovaks and Czechs mixed happily with one another. His father was an illiterate Slovak peasant who worked for the local bigwig, his mother a German, while Tomáš himself trained as a blacksmith. From such humble beginnings, he rose to become professor of philosophy at the Charles University, a Social Democrat MP in the Viennese Reichskrat, and finally the country's first, and longest-serving, President. A liberal humanist through and through, Masaryk created what was, at the time, probably the most progressive democracy in central Europe, featuring universal suffrage, an enviable social security system and a strong social democratic thrust. At the time of his death in 1937, it was one of the few democracies left in Central Europe, "a lighthouse high on a cliff with the waves crashing on it on all sides", as Masaryk's successor, Edvard Beneš put it. The whole country went into mourning – a year later the Nazis marched into Sudetenland.

After the 1948 coup, the Communists began to dismantle the myth of Masaryk, whose name was synonymous with the "bourgeois" First Republic. All mention of him was removed from textbooks, street names were changed and his statue was taken down from almost every town and village in the country. However, during liberalisation in 1968, his bespectacled face and goaty beard popped up again in shop windows, and again in 1989, his image returned to haunt the beleagured Communists.

The Masaryk plot is separated from the rest of the cemetery (*hřbitov*) by a little wooden fence and flanked by two bushy trees. Tomáš is buried alongside his American wife, Charlotte Garrigue Masaryková, who died some fifteen years earlier, and his son Jan, who became Foreign Minister in the post-1945 government, only to die in mysterious circumstances shortly after the Communist coup (see "Hradčany", Prague). After laying their wreaths, the crowds generally wander over to the other side of the village, where there's a Presidential summer **zámek** with the obligatory blue-liveried guards. Its rooms are strictly out of bounds, but the large English gardens, orangerie and deer park are open to the public at weekends and public holidays.

travel details

Trains
From Prague (Praha hlavní nádraží) to Poděbrady/Hradec Králové (up to 6 daily; 1hr 10min/2hr 5min); Benešov (every 30min; 55min–1hr 10min); Tábor/České Budějovice (up to 7 daily; 2hr/3hr); Plzeň/Mariánské Lázně/Cheb (up to 12 daily; 1hr 45min/3hr 20min); Brno (up to 14 daily; 3hr 30min); Bratislava (7 daily; 5hr 30min); Poprad/Košice (7 daily; 9–10hr/10–11hr).

From Prague (Praha-Smíchov) to Karlštejn (every 30min; 40min); Plzeň (16 daily; 1hr 30min–2hr 30min).

From Prague (Masarykovo nádraží) to Nelahozeves (up to 15 daily; 1hr 10min); Kutná Hora (7 daily; 1hr); Karlovy Vary (6 daily; 4hr–5hr 30min); Turnov/Liberec (2 daily; 2hr 10min/3hr 10min).

From Prague (Praha-Holešovice) to Kutná Hora (up to 4 daily; 1hr); Pardubice (8 daily; 1hr 30min); Brno/Bratislava (up to 10 daily; 3hr 30min/5hr 30min).

Buses
From Prague (Praha-Florenc) to Mělník/Liběchov/Děčín (up to 4 daily; 45min/1hr/2hr 30min); Poděbrady/Hradec Králové (up to 10 daily; 55min/2hr); Kladno (30min; 40min); Karlovy Vary (up to 14 daily; 2hr 25min–3hr 20min); České Budějovice (up to 6 daily; 2hr 30min); Brno (up to 13 daily; 2hr 40min).

From Prague (Praha-Pankrác) to Český Šternberk (2 daily; 2hr).

From Prague (Praha-Holešovice) to Veltrusy (up to 6 daily; 45min); Mělník (up to 30 daily; 45min–1hr); Kokořín (1 daily at the weekend; 1hr 20min); Litoměřice (up to 6 daily; 1hr 20min–1hr 40min).

From Prague (Praha-Strašnice) to Kutná Hora (up to 7 daily; 1hr 30min).

From Prague (Praha-Dejvice) to Křivoklát (up to 3 daily; 1hr 30min); to Lidice (20 daily; 25min).

From Prague (Praha-Vysočany) to Poděbrady (7 daily; 1hr 15min); Turnov (6 daily; 2hr 40min).

CHAPTER TWO

BOHEMIA

The ring of mountains which forms the natural borders of **Bohemia** (Čechy) has proved ineffective over the years as an obstacle to the region's more powerful neighbours. In the Middle Ages the region profited from being at the centre of Europe's overland commerce, but the Bohemian golden age, bumped up by the region's medieval silver mines, didn't last long. By the seventeenth century, the Czech Lands had been torn apart by the almost continuous religious wars, of which the Thirty Years' War was the final and most destructive. Wandering round Bohemia at the turn of the eighteenth century, Henry Crabb Robinson declared it "a veritable back settlement of Germany . . . thoroughly Catholic . . . and under a very Egyptian darkness" – the latter a reference to the dark ages of the Counter-Reformation, one of the saddest periods in Bohemian history but one which paradoxically endowed the region with much of its architectural wealth. Most towns still follow a medieval pattern: their central marketplaces are lined with medieval arcades and rich facades; on every hill of any significance, there's a castle, in every woods, a chateau.

For the sake of its wealth and beauty, Bohemia has suffered more than most of Czechoslovakia: its rivers can no longer sustain life forms, its forests are among the worst affected by acid rain, and its citizens are choking to death from the sulphur emissions of the power stations which keep the rest of the country supplied with energy. As for the **people** themselves, rather than being "bohemian" or unconventional, they share a lot of characteristics with the Germans – in their cuisine, their habits and not least in the early-to-bed early-to-rise routine, which – while it doesn't preclude all nightlife – does start and finish things off a lot earlier than in other parts of the country. There are good reasons for these national similarities: German was the language of power, business and culture in Bohemia until well into the nineteenth century, and Czechoslovakia itself had an enormous German-speaking population, living mostly in the border regions (commonly referred to as the Sudetenland). It was the German annexation of this area that was one of the catalysts of World War II: afterwards, the entire ethnic German population was forcibly ejected for alleged "mass collaboration" with the Nazis.

Prague, dealt with in the previous chapter, is the natural centre and capital of the region; the rest divides easily into four geographical districts. **South Bohemia** is the least spoilt, bordered by the Šumava mountains – a largely undiscovered part of central Europe. Its chief attraction, aside from the thickly forested hills, is a series of well-preserved medieval towns, whose undisputed gem is **Český Krumlov**. Neighbouring **West Bohemia** has a similar mix of rolling woods and hills, despite the industrial nature of its capital **Plzeň**, home of Pilsen beer and Škoda cars. Beyond here, as you approach the German border,

Bohemia's famous **Spa Region** unfolds, with magnificent resorts such as **Mariánské Lázně**, **Karlovy Vary** and **Františkovy Lázně** enjoying sparkling reputations, based for the most part on their unrivalled social life at the turn of this century.

North Bohemia has real problems. Despite being similar to the lands to the south and west, it has been devastated by industrialisation, rendering many parts virtually uninhabitable – even traditionally "healthy" spa resorts like **Teplice-Šanov**. There are respites, though, and in the far north, the rocks and ravines of the **Český Švýcarsko** are far enough removed to be attractive. **East Bohemia** has suffered indirectly from the polluting industries of its neighbour, but remains relatively blight-free. Its lowlands are richer (and duller) and its mountains more impressive than the rest of Bohemia. Two areas of freak sandstone rock formations – the **Český ráj** and the area **around Broumov** – make great walking and climbing country, infinitely preferable to the crowds and dead trees of the more popular **Krkonoše** mountains. And there are two finely preserved towns worth visiting on the flat Labe basin – **Hradec Králové** and **Pardubice**, both boasting fascinating new and old towns.

Transport throughout Bohemia is fairly easy, thanks to a comprehensive network of railway lines and regional bus services, though connections can be less than smooth, and journeys slow. The only exceptions are parts of the Šumava and Krkonoše mountain ranges, which are a little thin on public transport – the idea being, of course, to walk.

SOUTH BOHEMIA

The rolling hills of **South Bohemia** (Jižní Čechy) have emerged virtually unscathed from a century of conspicuous industrialisation and the destruction of two world wars. The result is a plethora of walled medieval towns suffused with a bucolic calm. **České Budějovice** – the largest town by far – boasts a good-looking old town (and a beer of no less standing); smaller places, like **Český Krumlov**, are even better preserved.

The **Šumava** mountain range, which forms the natural border with Austria and Germany, proved no barrier to the German-speaking foresters and traders who settled on the northern slopes and left their mark on the Bohemian towns and villages in that area. They've now been replaced by a seasonal population of walkers, fishermen, canoeists and inland beachniks, drawn by the region's natural beauty – probably the least affected by acid rain.

The **Vltava**, Bohemia's chief river, provides the setting for the region's most popular **castles**, some almost monastic in their simplicity, like **Zvíkov**, and others almost choking on aristocratic decadence, such as **Orlík**, **Hluboká** and **Rožmberk**.

Regional transport in South Bohemia isn't as bad as might be expected, given the overwhelmingly hilly, rural nature of the terrain. Travelling by train allows you to experience more of the countryside, and even parts of the Šumava are served by a scenic one-track railway which winds its way from Český Krumlov, along the shores of Lake Lipno and then north to Prachatice. Buses go virtually everywhere, and they're almost invariably less frequent, more expensive but quicker.

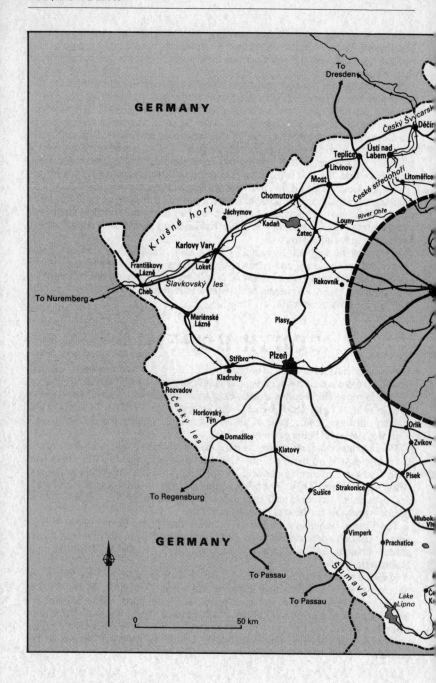

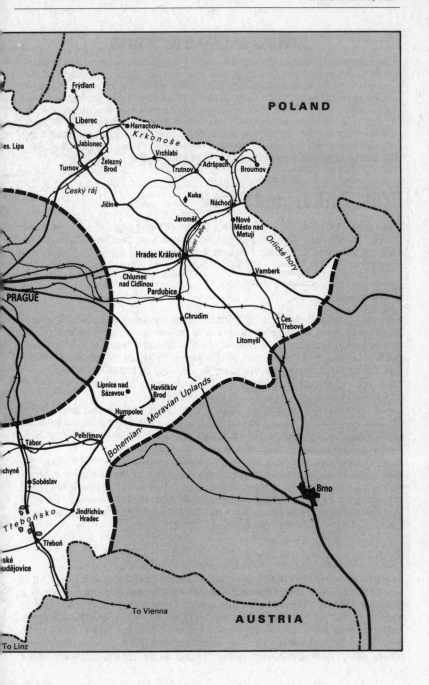

Orlík, Zvíkov and Písek

South from Prague and the Slapy Dam, there are two castles and a town worth visiting. The castles – Orlík and Zvíkov – both overlook the River Vltava and are most easily accessible by boat; Písek on the river Otava is approachable by more conventional means.

Orlík

If you arrive by boat, avoiding the scourge of the *souvenyry* stands which punctuate the walk from the bus terminal, you're unlikely to be disappointed by the creamy nineteenth-century castle of **Orlík** (literally "eagle's nest"), which reaches out into this wide stretch of the Vltava. No doubt the view was a great deal more spectacular before the valley was flooded in the 1960s; nowadays the water laps rather tamely at the foot of the castle and concrete has been injected into its foundations to prevent it from being swept away.

After disembarkation, the fun stops. At the height of the summer, it's not unusual to wait an hour and a half for the privilege of joining a guided tour of the castle (daily every 10min; April, Sept & Oct 9am–noon & 1–4pm; May–Aug 8am–noon & 1–5pm; closed Mon) which pays sycophantic homage to the region's greatest self-propagandists, the Schwarzenbergs, who turned this historic pile into a pseudo-Gothic money-waster. There's nothing among the faience, weaponry and Schwarzenberg military memorabilia to hint at its 700-year history, and even the gardens were only laid out last century. Unless you're drawn by the lakeside **campsite**, 2km downriver, the best plan is to catch the late-afternoon ferry upriver to Zvíkov as soon as you can.

Zvíkov

Fourteen kilometres upstream, the spartan rooms of **Zvíkov** (April & Sept Sat & Sun 9am–noon & 1–4pm; May–Aug Tues–Sun 8am–noon & 1–5pm) come as a welcome relief after the "romantic interiors" of Orlík, especially as you're free to wander around at will. The light stone buildings, left to rack and ruin by the Rožmberks as early as the 1500s, are hidden amid the woods of a rocky promontory at the confluence of the Vltava and the Otava. A small dusty track passes under three gatehouses before leading to the central courtyard which boasts a simple early Gothic two-storey arcade, reconstructed in the nineteenth century from the few remaining bays that still stood. Even the meagre offerings in the museum are more than compensated for by the absence of tour groups, the cool stone floors and the wonderful views over the water. If you required further incentive, the chapel has faded fifteenth-century frescoes "where nimbed souls in underpants float uncomfortably through a forest" as a critic aptly described it.

Písek

The only guaranteed methods of covering the 20km from Zvíkov to **PÍSEK** are waiting for the afternoon bus in ZVÍKOVSKÉ PODHRADÍ, a couple of kilometres up the road, or walking 6km south to the train station at VLASTEC. A one-horse rural market town, it gets its name from the gold-producing *písek* (sand) of the river Otava. Gold fever* has waxed and waned in the town over the centuries but if recent prospecting discoveries prove correct, the gold under the ground at nearby Mokrsko will be enough to repay the country's entire foreign debt (around $6 billion) – providing, that is, the government prevails over the region's strong environmental lobby.

The town experienced its first gold rush in the thirteenth century, but the Thirty Years' War demolished Písek's prosperity, and all that remains is a **stone bridge**, which predates even the Charles Bridge in Prague, and which likewise accrued a fine selection of beatific Baroque statuary during the Counter-Reformation. Looking south down the river, the ancient remnants of Písek's castle look like they're about to slip gracefully into the water; north, a monotony of concrete socialist constructions hopefully will. Walking up Šrámkova from the cramped main square, you come to the Putimská brána, the only remaining bastion, adjoined by a number of quiet backstreets. These lead to a small vegetable **market** which takes place under the aegis of the 74-metre onion-domed *hláska* (watchtower) of the Dominican church. The small **photographic gallery** opposite features the occasional engaging exhibition.

Practical details

Písek is low-key and quiet enough to make a night's stay an attractive possibility. The top hotel is the *Otava*, Chelčického 56/8 (☎0362-28 61), smothered in a pictorial history of the town by the nineteenth-century Romantic painter (and local student) Mikoláš Aleš. More modest are the *Bílá růže*, Fráni Šrámka 169 (☎0362-49 31), and the *U tří korun* (☎0362-44 41), on the main square; or even the ugly and inconvenient *Sport* (☎0362-45 93), north of the bridge on Žatavské nábřeží.

In the novel by Jaroslav Hašek, the *Good Soldier Švejk* made his fictional appearance at Písek, in a blizzard, handcuffed to a lance-corporal in the Austrian constabulary "for comfort", before moving on to Tábor on the next train. Should you wish to do the same, the **bus** and **train stations** are both south of town, at the end of Nádražní (bus #1 from the main square).

---

* Small deposits of gold can still be found along the silty banks of the Otava and gold-panning has recently emerged as quite a popular sport in this part of Bohemia. An annual gold-panning championship is now held every summer on the river at nearby Slaník.

TEMELÍN – CHERNOBYL OF THE FUTURE?

TEMELÍN, 20km or so southeast of Písek, is soon to be the site of one of the largest nuclear power stations in the world, built to a Soviet design similar to the one used at Chernobyl – reason enough to give the town a wide berth. Many of its constituent parts have never been built or tested before, yet despite a long campaign of protest by local and international groups (including the draping of a hundred-foot "STOP ČSFRNOBYL" banner from one of the cooling towers by Greenpeace), the project is to go ahead. So much money has been already spent, and so much of the country devastated by the effects of its coal-produced energy, that a scaled-down version of the reactor is due to come into operation in 1992. For more on this issue see "The Environment" in *Contexts*.

Tábor and around

Founded in 1420, **TÁBOR**, 88km south of Prague, was the spiritual and strategic centre of the Hussites' social and religious revolution, which swept through Bohemia in the first half of the fifteenth century. It gave its name to the radical wing of the Hussite movement, the Táborites, whose philosophy that all people should be equal on earth as in heaven found few friends among the feudal-minded nobility of the time, Hussite or Catholic. Under constant threat of physical attack, they developed into a formidable fighting force (Tábor means literally "fortified camp"), declaring war on the Catholic church and remaining undefeated until 1452, when the town was taken by a force led by the moderate Hussite King George of Poděbrady. Two centuries later, the town rose up again in support of the rebellion against the Catholic Habsburgs, and was one of the last to be captured in 1621 after the Protestant defeat at the Battle of Bílá hora.

Yet for all its grand history, Tábor is the quietest of places today, especially its old quarter, devoid of traffic and with precious few shops within its walls. Centuries of inactivity have turned its vast maze of narrow medieval streets, designed to confuse the enemy, into dusty dilapidated back-alleys, and aside from their very real attractions, the Hussite Museum is the only specific "sight" in town.

The Town

To reach the staré město, walk west from the train or bus **station** through the park by the town barracks. En route, you'll pass an unusual and passionate **statue of Hus** by local sculptor František Bílek. It was one of Kafka's favourite works of art, a view not shared by the rest of the citizens of Kolín (where the statue used to reside), who had it transferred here by popular request. For the old town, continue past the statue down třída 9 května until you reach the busy square which straddles the ridge between the new and old towns, then head up Palackého.

In the staré město, only the central square, **Žižkovo náměstí**, hints at Tábor's former glory, with its wide variety of gables and gargoyles, rebuilt after the fires of the fifteenth and sixteenth centuries. It was here in 1420 that the people of Tábor threw theological caution to the wind and set up a religious commune under the principle of *není nic mé a nic tvé, než všecko v obec rovně mají* ("nothing is mine, nothing is yours, everything is common to all"). Large urns were set up in the square and anyone – male or female – wishing to live in the commune had first to place all their possessions in the urns, after which they were given work on a daily rota. Men and women were given equal rights, there was a ban on alcohol, and from the stone table which still stands outside the radnice, communion was given to the people "in both kinds" – as opposed to the Catholic practice of reserving the wine (the blood of Christ) for the priesthood. The Táborites had this last symbolic act emblazoned on their flag – a red chalice on a black background – which, like the rousing religious war songs they sang before battle, struck fear into the crusaders from thirty nations who came against them.

The radnice's huge concert chamber is the venue for the town's **Museum of the Hussite Movement** (Tues–Sun 8.30am–5.15pm), which should open again sometime in the early 1990s. It gives access to a small section of the huge network of **underground passages** which formed part of the town's fortification system, as well as containing a medieval "tank" invented by the Táborites' blind but brilliant military leader Jan Žižka, whose statue (traditionally depicted with one eye still functioning) tops the square in front of the church. As for the rest of the town, its hotchpotch of backstreets, enlivened by the occasional decorative flourish, are perfect for aimless wandering. If you want more direction to your strolling, head off by bus or train to one of the local destinations detailed in "Around Tabor", below.

THE PIKARTS AND ADAMITES

When news of Tábor reached the rest of Europe, all manner of foreign heretics gravitated to this small Bohemian town, which became something of a haven for unorthodox religious sects. One of the most numerous were the so-called **Pikarts**, who, as their name suggests, came from Picardy in France. The Pikarts took the Táborite heaven-on-earth philosophy one step further, preaching "that the perfect soul does not need to practise acts of virtue". This liberal message was beyond the pale for the more puritanically inclined Táborites, and the Pikarts were expelled from Tábor and forced to set up in the nearby castle of Příběnice (now in ruins) on an island in the Lužnice. Their leader, Martin Húska, was eventually captured and taken to Roudnice castle where he was tortured and burnt to death.

The Pikarts may have raised a few eyebrows in Tábor but they were nothing compared to the **Adamites**, who came to the fore in Příběnice. To become an Adamite, it was necessary to undergo a period of harsh asceticism after which you were "born again". The new soul could then indulge in whatever he or she desired – theft, perjury, sex – with impunity. This gave way to ritual nudism and "love-feasts", as one shocked (and fascinated) contemporary chronicler recalls – "wandering through the forests and hills, some of them fell into such an insanity that men and women threw off their clothes and went naked . . . from the same madness they supposed that they were not sinning if they had intercourse with one another". When rumours of such activities reached the Táborites, Žižka sent an expedition against them, taking the prisoners to Klokoty (see below) and personally seeing to the burning of fifty of them, before handing over another twenty-five to his fellow townsfolk.

Practical details

Fast trains from Prague take under two hours to reach Tábor, so at a pinch, you could actually come here on a day trip. However, if you'd prefer to stay, Tábor has four **hotels**, of which the *Slovan*, on třída 9 května (☎0361-236 97), and the nearby *Jordán* (☎0361-234 02), are both cheap and usually full. The *Slávia* by the station (☎0361-235 74), is also often full, but the high-rise *Palcát* – also on třída 9 května (☎0361-229 01) – is relatively inexpensive and regularly has vacancies, as well as playing host to the occasional live band and the regular *P Club* nightclub. For the possibility of a cheap, **hostel bed**, follow the signs from the town's western gate, Bechyňská brána, to *TJ Vodní stavby*, Pinkova 2101. If it's **food** you want, bear in mind that the **pizza bar** (the only alternative to the uniform hotel restaurants) closes by 9pm.

All the **campsites** are well out of the centre. Very few buses run to the *Malý Jordán* (mid-June to mid-Sept), situated north of the town, in the woods between Lake Jordán (where the Táborites used to baptise their children) and its smaller sister lake, but it's a pleasant 3km walk by marked track along the lakeside. There's a bigger site, *Knížecí rybník* (open all year), also by a lake, a short walk from SMYSLOV train station, 6km (and one stop on the Pelhřimov line) east of Tábor.

Around Tábor: Chýnov Caves, Klokoty and Bechyně

With an afternoon to spare, several trips are possible around Tábor, all of which are within an easy walk or short train journey from the town.

The dry **Chýnov Caves** (Chýnovská jeskyně) are a 3km walk across the fields from CHÝNOV train station (three stops east of Tábor). Amid gentle meadows and orchards, the entrance to the caves consists of a fifty-metre plunge down narrow, precipitous steps into the earth, to the sounds of Bach's *Toccata in D minor*. The whole experience is a lot more like real potholing than the larger caves in Moravia and Slovakia and consequently is not recommended for claustrophobics. Tours last thirty minutes (Tues & Wed 10am–5pm, Thurs & Fri 10am–4pm, Sat & Sun 9am–5pm).

Just 4km west of Tábor, **KLOKOTY** boasts one of the most endearing and least pompous of Bohemia's Counter-Reformation monasteries, though sadly there's no admission. An ensemble of nine green onion domes rises above the pristine whitewashed walls, from which you get the best views in the region, across to Tábor.

Bechyně

Every hour and a half, a dinky red electric train – the Empire's first such service when it was built in 1902 – covers the 24km journey from Tábor to the small soporific spa and pottery-producing town of **BECHYNĚ**. As you enter the town, rail and road both cross a spectacular viaduct over the Lužnice gorge. Unfortunately, after this dramatic introduction things start to disintegrate: the Rožmberks' Renaissance chateau is closed to the public, the monastery is now a school, and the main square has long since lost its function as a marketplace. Content yourself instead with the **Museum of Pottery** (whose collections of turn-of-the-century vases are worth investigating) and the small **Folk Art Museum**, on the opposite side of the square (whose collections aren't).

Unless you decide – for some unaccountable reason – to stay at the *Lužnice* in the centre of town, make sure you don't miss the **last train back to Tábor** which leaves at around 8pm.

The East: Kámen, Pelhřimov and Lipnice nad Sázavou

The sporadic branch-line service between Tábor and Pelhřimov skirts the one-street village of **KÁMEN** ("Rock"), whose hrad was once a fortified staging-post between these two strongly pro-Hussite walled towns. It's worth a detour since in 1974, after centuries of neglect, the castle was reopened – incongruously – as the **Museum of the International Motorcycle Federation** (April & Oct Sat & Sun 9am–4pm; May–Aug daily 8am–5pm; Sept daily 9am–5pm; closed Mon). Some wonderful old Czech bikes are on display, from the very first Laurin & Klement Model TB from 1899 – not much more than a bicycle with a petrol tank tacked on – to the heyday of Czech biking between the wars. Other machines include ČZs and Jawas, which may have cut some ice back in the 1940s when they were designed, but now only exacerbate the country's environmental problems. To trace the sad demise of the Czech motorcycle industry, you have to join the short guided tour of the castle.

Pelhřimov

If you're heading east into Moravia and need a place to stay, the tiny medieval town of **PELHŘIMOV** is only 16km further along the road. Barely 200m across, the walled town still retains two sixteenth-century tower gates, some beautiful Renaissance houses, and, on the main square, a masterpiece of Cubist architecture by Pavel Janák, who in 1913 adapted the Baroque house at no. 13 to suit his new theories without forsaking the intentions of the original. Always the first to be renovated, the seat of the sgraffitoed *národní výbor* (town council) contains the occasional local exhibition (Mon–Fri 2–5pm, Sat 9–11.30am), while the local **museum**, next to the church of sv Bartoloměj, holds more permanent fare. The *Hotel Slávie*, overlooking the old square, is the best situated of the town's three equally cheap **hotels**.

Lipnice nad Sázavou

It's another 20km by bus to the dull textile town of HUMPOLEC, just beyond which is the village of **LIPNICE NAD SÁZAVOU**. Here, Bohemia's ultimate bohemian, the writer **Jaroslav Hašek**, died on January 3, 1923, his most famous work still unfinished. Stories about Hašek's life – many propagated by the author himself – have always been a mixture of fact and fiction, but at one time or another he was an anarchist, dog-breeder, lab assistant, bigamist, cabaret artist and People's Commissar in the Red Army. He alternately shocked and delighted both close friends and the public at large with his drunken antics and occasional acts of political extremism. When, towards the end of his life, he made his home in the *Česká koruna* pub in Lipnice, Hašek wrote happily, "Now I live bang in the middle of a *pivnice*. Nothing better could have happened to me". Few friends attended his funeral and none of his family, with the exception of his eleven-year-old son, who had met his father only two or three times. In a final act of contempt, the local priest would only allow his body to be buried alongside the cemetery wall, among the unbaptised and suicides. Before long, however, Hašek's *Good*

Soldier Švejk had become the most famous (fictional) Czech of all time, culminating in his canonisation by the Communist regime – his works even published by the military publishers, *Naše Vojsko* (Our Army).

The village has changed little over the intervening years; the aforementioned pub is being renovated, as are parts of the castle, ruined even in Hašek's day; a flattering bust of the author has been erected on the way up to the castle, and his gravestone is a little less ignominious these days. Beside the castle, in the house where he died, the **Memorial to Jaroslav Hašek** (daily April–Sept 8am–noon & 1–4.15pm; Oct–March 8am–noon & 1–3pm; closed Mon) is respectfully vague about the many contradictions in Hašek's life, not least the alcoholism which eventually cost him his life.

If you want to pay homage to Hašek at Lipnice, roughly five buses a day make the 10km trip from Humpolec, though once here you'll have to backtrack to Humpolec or Pelhřimov to find a bed for the night, unless you stay at the **campsite** just east of the village (mid-May to Sept).

Třeboňsko

The **Třeboňsko** region – with the town of Třeboň at its heart – is unlike the rest of Southern Bohemia; characterised not by rolling hills but by peat bogs, flatlands and fish ponds. This monotonous, unhealthy marshland, broken only by the occasional Gothic fortress, was moulded into an intricate system of canal-linked ponds as early as the fifteenth century, ushering in profitable times for the nobles who owned the land. The fish industry still dominates the region and around September the ponds are drained to allow the fish to be "harvested". Larger ponds, like the Rožmberk, are drained only every other year and for three days people from the surrounding district gather to feast, sing and participate in what is still a great local event, and one worth heading for if you're anywhere nearby. Wildlife also thrives on the soggy plains and in 1977 UNESCO declared a large area, from Soběslav south as far as the Austrian border, a nature reserve.

Jindřichův Hradec

JINDŘICHŮV HRADEC (Neuhaus) is a small sleepy town built amongst Třeboňsko's fish ponds. It's typical of the region: hemmed in by walls and water, and typical too in that no sense of this is given as you approach the staré město from the stations, ten minutes' walk north of the town. Here the walls have long since been replaced by a park, and you simply drift into the old quarter, ripped apart by a fire in 1801, which robbed the place of much of its rich medieval dressing. The main square displays a subdued array of wealthy merchants' houses but the rest of the town's crusty buildings, huddled around the castle walls, recall an earlier feudal era. Havlíčkova leads down from the square to a bridge which separates two fish ponds, creating a small harbour. The thirteenth-century **zámek**, mirrored in the water below (and presently closed to the public), gives little hint of the sixteenth-century renovations inside by Italian architects, who transformed the inner courtyards of this grim fort.

Few visitors stray from the environs of the chateau and therefore miss the flaking alleyways in the north of the old town. Most of the ecclesiastical buildings in the town are out of bounds but the local **museum** (Tues–Sun 8.30am–5pm) is set above the cloisters in the old Jesuit seminary. One room is devoted to Ferenc Rákóczi II, leading light of the Hungarian War of Independence (1703–11), who studied here, while another honours the composer Bedřich Smetana (see p.201), who seems to have moved from one brewery to another; born in one in Litomyšl, between 1831 and 1835 he lived in another here, below the castle.

Places **to stay**, if you're taken by the slow pace of life, boil down to the two hotels, the _Grand_ (☎32 46) and the _Vaygar_ (☎172), and possibly the _Zlatá husa_ (Golden Goose) restaurant, all reasonable and located on the main square.

Červená Lhota

In the middle of nowhere, halfway between Soběslav and Jindřichův Hradec, the pink sugar-lump castle of **Červená Lhota** is reflected perfectly in the still waters which surround it. It _is_ a remarkable sight – a Gothic water-fort converted into a Renaissance retreat for the rich – and one which appears on almost every tourist handout, but, without your own transport, its isolated location makes it a nightmare to reach on public transport. Given this, and the unremarkable nature of the chateau's interior, it's really only for dedicated fans of Karl Ditters von Dittersdorf (the composer died here in 1799).

Třeboň

Right in the middle of the fish ponds, the spa town of **TŘEBOŇ** is as medieval and minute as Pelhřimov, its staré město made up of just four streets, a four-teenth-century monastery and a chateau. The walls and three gateways (includ-ing the impressive double south gate, next to the local brewery) have survived from the sixteenth century, though the houses all suffered from the last great fire of 1781. Out of all proportion to the rest of the town is the huge Renaissance **zámek** (April & Oct Sat & Sun 9am–4pm; May–Aug daily 8am–4pm; Sept daily 9am–4pm; closed Mon), built by Petr Vok, a colourful character, notoriously fond of sex, drugs and alchemy, and the last heir of the Rožmberk family. The chateau, daubed in blinding white sgraffito and taking up almost a fifth of the town, is clumsy in the extreme, though there's an adjacent "English park", equal in size to the staré město, for the town's spa patients to stroll in. South of the town is the Svět pond where the _Státní rybářství_ (State Fishery) on Novohradská handles the region's huge fish harvest, but more specifically, its _kapr_ (carp) culling. Carp, not turkey, is the centrepiece of the Christmas Day meal in the Czech Lands, tradi-tionally sold alive and flapping from town squares across the country.

The Schwarzenberg mausoleum

Třeboň was the first Bohemian town to be bought up by the Bavarian-based Schwarzenberg family in 1660 who, having sided with the Habsburgs in the Counter-Reformation, became the unofficial heirs of ousted or defunct aristocrats like the Vítkovci and Rožmberks. In 1875, when the family owned more estates in Bohemia than anyone else, they "honoured" Třeboň by establishing the **Schwarzenberg mausoleum** (Schwarzenberská Hrobka) here (daily April & Oct 9am–3.30pm; May–Aug 8am–4.30pm; Sept 9am–4.30pm; closed Mon). It's a strangely subdued, out-of-the-way sight for a family so fond of ostentatious displays of wealth; hidden among the silver birch trees south of the Svět pond. After 1945 the family's possessions were expropriated and, along with all their fellow German-speakers, they were thrown out of the country. Today, the most famous descendant is probably Karl von Schwarzenberg, recently returned from exile and one of President Havel's closest advisors.

Practicalities

There are two **hotels**: the *Svět* (0333-30 46) is huge, ugly and out of town; the *Bílý koníček* (☎0333-22 48), sporting turreted Renaissance gables, is small, central and pretty, but also usually full. **Camping** and **swimming** take place at the *Domanín* campsite (mid-May to Sept), south of the fish pond, near the mausoleum.

While carp is often on menus around town, there is actually no fish **restaurant** in Třeboň at the moment. You'll have to try your luck at one of the hotels, or better still, if you're camping and cooking your own food, buy fresh fish from the *rybárna* (fishmonger) under the arcades in Březanova.

Třeboň is on the main train line from Prague to Vienna, so it's possible to **cross into Austria** by catching one of the two daily expresses – the train station is five minutes east of the old town. **Motorists** must cross the border further northeast at NOVÁ BYSTŘICE. Alternatively, frequent **buses** run west to České Budějovice or east to Jindřichův Hradec; the bus station is five minutes west of the old town.

České Budějovice and around

The flat urban sprawl of **ČESKÉ BUDĚJOVICE** (Budweis) comes as something of a surprise after the small-town mentality of the rest of South Bohemia. But first impressions are deceptive, for at its heart it's no more cosmopolitan than anywhere else: stuck in a Bohemian backwater, contact with the outside world is still restricted to Bavarians and provincial Austrians. Yet since its foundation in 1265, the town has been a self-assured place, convinced of its own importance. Its wealth, based on medieval silver mines and its position on the old salt route from Linz to Prague, was wiped out in the seventeenth century by the twin ravages of war and fire. But perhaps because it remained a loyal Catholic town in a hotbed of Hussitism, the Habsburgs lavishly reconstructed most of České Budějovice in the eighteenth century. The result may not be the "Bohemian Florence" of the *ČEDOK* brochures, but the staré město at least has been well preserved in the face of two centuries of rapid industrial growth. Besides, its real renown is due to its local brew *Budvar*, better known abroad under its original German name, *Budweiser*. Needless to say, although lighter than the average Bohemian lager, it bears little resemblance to the bland American *Bud*.

Arriving and finding somewhere to stay

České Budějovice has a compact old town that's only a five-minute walk from the **train** or **bus station**, both situated to the east of the city centre, along the pedestrianised maršála Malinovského.

Given České Budějovice's popularity with neighbouring Austrians and Germans, **hotel rooms** can be difficult to find even out of season. To find out what's on offer, go to the first floor of the excessively plush *ČEDOK* offices on the main square or try the hotels themselves, which are usually more inclined to suddenly discover vacancies. There are no really cheap options so you might as well start your search at the once grand, now moderately priced *Slunce* (☎038-367 55), just down from *ČEDOK*, and hope to get a view onto the square.

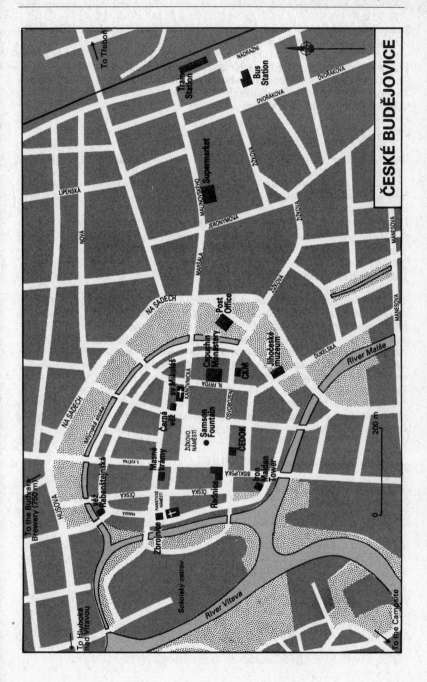

ČESKÉ BUDĚJOVICE

In July and August rooms are available in **student hostels**, and it's worth trying even if you haven't booked in advance. First go to *CKM*, Osovobzeni 14 (☎038-361 38), and find out the addresses for the current year's hostels and (if *CKM* say they're full) then go to the hotels themselves and beg. The only guaranteed cheap sleep is to bring your own tent and **camp**, or rent the **bungalows** either at the *Dlouhá louka* site (April–Oct), accessible by bus #6 or #16, or out at Hluboká nad Vltavou (see below).

The Town

At the end of maršála Malinovského you hit Na sadech, the busy ring road flanked by small parks which enclose the staré město in place of the old town walls. From here, the medieval grid plan leads inevitably to the town's showpiece, the magnificent central **Žižkovo náměstí**, one of Europe's largest squares. The buildings are elegant enough, testifying to the last three centuries of German burgher power (it wasn't until the 1890s that the first Czech was able to buy one of the valuable houses here), but it's the square's arcades and the octagonal **Samson's Fountain** – once the only tap in town – which make the greatest impression. It was German merchants, too, who paid in silver and salt for the 72-metre status symbol, the **Černá věž** (Black Tower), one of the few survivors of the 1641 fire, which leans gently to one side of the square; its roof gallery (Tues–Sun 9am–5pm) provides a superb view of the staré město. The streets immediately off the square – 5 května, Česká and N. Frýda – house the odd *cukrárna* (cake and coffee shop) and (relatively) chic clothes shops.

When the weather's fine people tend to promenade by the banks of the Malše, where parts of the original town walls have survived along with some of České Budějovice's oldest buildings. All that is left of the bishop's palace is his serene **garden** (daily May–Sept 8am–6pm), accessible through a small gateway in the walls. Round the corner, on Piaristické náměstí, you can pick up a live goose complete with take-out canvas carrier from the old women who run the lively **market** that spreads out in front of the rough-looking, thoroughly medieval **zbrojnice** (salt house), once the most important building in town.

Drinking, eating and nightlife

Drinking is obviously an important activity in České Budějovice, though serious *Budvar* drinkers will be disappointed to learn that the grim brewery gates on U Trojice (bus #2, #4, #6 or #12) are firmly closed to the public – though you can at least be sure of getting the real thing at the grimy modern restaurant next door. The liveliest place in town is *Masné krámy* (5 května 23), formerly a sixteenth-century covered meat market, which now serves huge quantities of *Budvar*, and a little food, all day until 10pm. If you're looking for an early jar, try the station's faded 1908 *restaurace* where the beer flows freely from 6am – if you don't believe it, look at the tab of the bloke next to you.

As for **eating**, České Budějovice abounds in *cukrárnas*, such as the swish *U klaštera* on Piaristická, while a bigger **breakfast** can be had at one of the many stand-up *bufets* – there's one on the ground floor of the *Hotel Zvon*. Picnic fodder can be assembled at the big **supermarket** on maršála Malinovského or at the fruit and veg market on Piaristické náměstí.

Sit-down meals are much of a muchness at the big hotels. So for something different, the **fish restaurant**, *U železné panny* on Biskupská (open till 10pm; closed Sun), serves carp and trout fresh from the ponds northwest of town.

Nightlife is thin on the ground: the locals seem to opt for hanging around the hotel lobbies or tipping each other into the fountain – neither exactly a fun night out.

Up the Českobudějovická pánev

Regular buses run from České Budějovice to **HLUBOKÁ NAD VLTAVOU** (Frauenburg), 8km northwest across a flat basin of soggy land. A Přemyslid stronghold was founded above the village as early as the thirteenth century, but it was sequestered from its Protestant Czech owners in 1622 for their part in the anti-Habsburg rebellion, and given to the arriviste Schwarzenberg family, who spent some of their considerable fortune turning it into the Disneyland-style **zámek** (daily May–Aug 8am–5pm; Sept 9am–5pm; April & Oct 9am-4pm; closed Mon) that pulls in the crowds today. The result – a deliberate copy of Windsor Castle – is both impressive and excessive. In 1945, when all the German estates were nationalised, the Schwarzenbergs decamped with most of the loot, but the odds and sods they left behind at their numerous other castles have been brought here, making the interior similarly over-the-top. The forty-minute guided tours, in Czech and (occasionally) German, run every ten minutes.

From the main square where the buses unload passengers, it's a stiff climb up to the chateau. If you're arriving by train, two out-of-the-way stations (nominally) serve the village: Hluboká nad Vltavou station, 3km southwest on the Plzeň line; and Hluboká nad Vltavou-Zámostí station, 2km east on the main line to Prague.

If the surrounding mock-Tudor fails to move you, it's possible to seek sanctuary in the former **Riding School**, which now exhibits Gothic religious art and the occasional interesting contemporary exhibition. Alternatively, head off into the chateau's very English grounds, where South Bohemia's wild boars are reputed to hang out. Should you wish **to stay** overnight here, rather than fight for rooms in České Budějovice, there are two hotels in the village, and a **campsite** (mid-May to Sept) in KŘIVONOSKA, 5km to the north.

Holašovice

If you've got your own transport, it's worth making a quick detour to the village of **HOLAŠOVICE**, 12km west of České Budějovice. There's no specific "sight" here – it's a working village – but the entire settlement stands as far and away the most perfect example of **Baroque Folk architecture**, unique to this part of Bohemia. All the farmhouses (including the one and only *hostinec*) date from the first six decades of the nineteenth century, and face on to the original village green. Every house on the square follows the same basic design though the decorative detail of the barn doors and gables are unique to each one. There are other nearby villages displaying similar architectural treats – like ZÁBOŘÍ and DOBČICE – but none compete with the consummate effect of Holašovice.

Kratochvíle

Further west, 2km outside NETOLICE, **Kratochvíle** (Kurzweil) is without doubt the most charming Renaissance chateau in Czechoslovakia. It stands unaltered since its rapid six-year construction by Italian architects between 1583 and 1589, commissioned by the last generation of Rožmberks to while away the time – the literal meaning of *kratochvíle*. The attention to detail is still clearly visible in the exquisite stucco work and painted vaults, but the rest of the place is now given over to the **Museum of Animated Film** (open Tues–Sun April & Sept 9am–noon & 1–4pm; May–Aug 8am–noon & 1–5pm; Oct 9am–noon & 1–5pm), which caters for a young, domestic audience with original puppet "actors" and drawings from kids' cartoons like *Boris*, illiciting yelps of recognition from the Czech kids and studied approbation from their parents. If, however, you're expecting enlightenment on international figures like Jan Švankmajer, you'll be disappointed.

There's nowhere to stay in Netolice – other than the **campsite** (May–Sept), southwest of the town centre – but it's only a forty-minute bus ride from České Budějovice. The last 2km to Kratochvíle are best covered on foot.

Český Krumlov (Krumau)

To Egon Schiele **ČESKÝ KRUMLOV** appeared as a dense autumnal collage, a farrago of rose-brown houses tumbling down to the blue-green river below. The Austrian painter (who set up a studio here in 1911) was inspired by this hilly southern Bohemian town, which has hardly changed in the last three hundred years and which ranks as one of the most beautiful in central Europe. UNESCO is trying to save it from its gradual disintegration and has turned much of the town into a medieval building site. Consequently, only the castle gets any serious attention from the crowds, leaving the town's warren of narrow streets – which are the real attraction – relatively undisturbed.

The town's **history** is dominated by the great seigneurs of the region, the Rožmberks and the Schwarzenbergs. Thanks to special privileges won after the Battle of Leipzig in 1813, the Schwarzenbergs were permitted to keep a private army of twelve soldiers dressed in Napoleonic uniform (who also doubled as the castle's private orchestra). Every morning at 9am, one of the liveried guards would sound the bugle from the thirteenth-century round tower. In 1945, Krumau awoke abruptly from this semi-feudal coma when the Schwarzenbergs and the majority of the town's inhabitants, who were also German-speaking, were booted out. Now a thoroughly Czech town, its economy still relies on the foul polluting paper mill a few kilometres upstream.

Practical points

The **railway station** is five minutes' walk north of the old town, down a precipitous set of steps, while the **bus station** is closer to the heart of town, on the right bank – either way, the best method of exploring Český Krumlov is on foot. As for **orientation**, the town is divided into two separate quarters by the twisting snake of the River Vltava: the circular staré město on the right bank and the Latrán quarter on the hillier left bank.

Before losing yourself in the town's maze of streets it's best to find some **accommodation**. The *Hotel Růže*, on Horní (☎0337-22 45), originally built by the Rožmberks to house their guests, and the *Krumlov* on the main square (☎0337-22 55) are both beautiful old hotels in the staré město, offering moderate doubles. At the same price, the *Vyšehrad* (☎0337-23 11), near the train station, is modern and

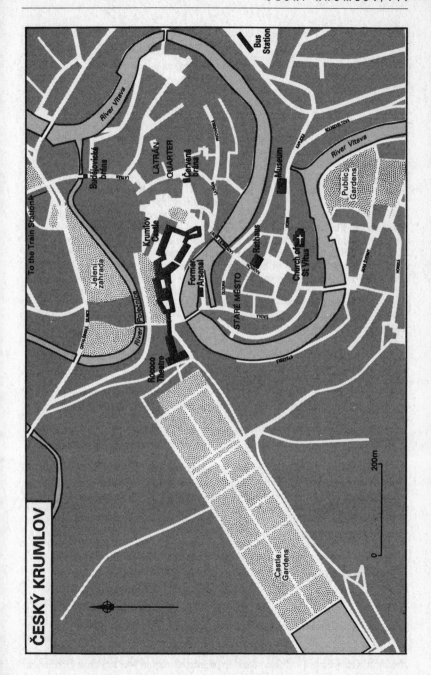

ČESKÝ KRUMLOV

Bus Station

River Vltava

Budějovická brána

LATRÁN QUARTER

Červená brána

Museum

River Vltava

Public Gardens

To the Train Station

Jelení zahrada

Krumlov Castle

Rathaus

Church of St Vítus

Former Arsenal

STARÉ MĚSTO

River Polečnice

Rococo Theatre

Castle Gardens

200m

0

ugly. If, as is likely, all three hotels are full, there is always the primitive **camp-site**, 2km south on the road to Větřní. As far as **eating** goes, there's nowhere to recommend outside the hotel restaurants.

The Town

For centuries, the focal point of the town has been the omnipresent **Krumlov Castle** (daily April & Oct 9am–noon & 1–4pm; May–Aug 8am–noon & 1–5pm; Sept 9am–noon & 1–5pm; closed Mon), in the Latrán quarter, as good a place as any to begin a tour of the town. The first courtyard belongs to the older, lower castle but it's the smaller sgraffitoed courtyards of the upper castle, added in the fifteenth century, which contain the castle's treasures – though much of the Schwarzenbergs' best stuff has been taken off to Hluboká. The fifty-minute tour doles out rich helpings of feudal opulence: the Rococo excesses of the blue and pink marble chapel, followed by the garishly decorated *Maškarní sál* (Ballroom). The covered Plášťový most – a minor Bridge of Sighs with a superb view over the town – leads to the castle's highlight, the eighteenth-century Rococo theatre, one of the few left in the world to have kept its original gold and blue galleries, its stage and twelve changes of backdrop. Another covered walkway puts you high above the town in the unexpectedly expansive and formal **terraced gardens** (open all year) whose tranquillity is disturbed only by the annual Drama Festival, performed in the garden's modern, revolving open-air theatre.

The shabby houses leaning in on Latrán lead to a wooden ramp-like bridge which connects with the staré město. Just before the bridge, on the left, an almost medieval scene unfolds in the cobbled courtyard of the *Krumlovská pivnice*. There's a compelling beauty at work in the old town, whose precarious existence is best viewed from the circling River Vltava. Turn right down Dlouhá, where the houses glow red at dusk, and continue on to the slip of land which houses the town's former arsenal. From here, if the river's not swollen, you can walk across the gangplanks of the footbridge to Rybářská, which then follows the left bank to the southernmost bridge, taking you back into the old town.

Alternatively, head straight up the soft incline of Radniční to the main square, looking backwards and upwards to the castle. On one side of the square a long, white Renaissance entablature combines two-and-a-half Gothic houses to create the old **Rathaus**, while on the other, the high lancet windows of the church of St Vitus rise vertically above the ramshackle rooftops. Continuing east off the square, down Horní, the beautiful sixteenth-century Jesuit college now provides space for a driving school, and the *Hotel Růže*. Opposite, the local **museum** (Tues–Sat 9am–4pm, Sun 9am–noon) includes a reconstructed seventeenth-century shop interior among its exhibits.

The Šumava

The original inhabitants of the dense pines and peat bogs of the Šumava region, southwest of Český Krumlov and stretching along the Austrian and German borders, were German foresters who scraped a living from the meagre soil – their Austrian lilt and agricultural poverty separating them from their "civilised" Sudetenland brothers in western and northern Bohemia. Up to the declaration of the First Republic in 1918 this sparsely populated region was kept in a permanent semi-feudal state by the all-powerful Schwarzenberg and Buquoy dynasties. The peasants had to have permission from their landlords to marry, and their customary greeting to the local squire was *Brotvater* (literally "Breadfather"). However, few links remain with the past since the expulsion of the German-speakers in 1945 and the Šumava remains underpopulated despite financial incentives for Czechs to move here.

Apart from the region's one truly medieval town, **Prachatice**, the majority of visitors come here for the scenery, which is among the most unspoilt in the country – thanks to the absence of industry (and, thus, acid rain fallout) on either side of the border. Most tourists crowd round the northern shore of the artificial **Lake Lipno**, creating their own peculiar brand of beach culture, while others head for the hills – less impressive than on the Austrian and German side but also less touristed. If you're considering **hiking**, three maps, available at most bookshops, cover the area from southeast to northwest: *Českobudějovicko*, *Šumava Prachaticko* and *Šumava Klatovsko*. The three most scenic ways of **getting around** the region are the Český Krumlov–Volary branch line, the boat service across Lake Lipno and, of course, walking; often more convenient are the local buses, though at weekends you may find it necessary to hitch.

Rožmberk nad Vltavou and Vyšší Brod

Buses from Český Krumlov follow the Vltava valley to the pretty village of **ROŽMBERK NAD VLTAVOU** (Rosenberg), its subtle charm completely upstaged by the fortress towering above it. As the name suggests, its *raison d'être* in the thirteenth century was as the headquarters of the powerful and single-minded Rožmberk family, regional supremos until their extinction in 1611. Nowadays, though, the castle speaks little of that family, but volumes instead of the later French owners, the Buquoys, who stuffed the dull, mannerless rooms with heavy neo-Gothic furnishings and instruments of torture. Czech tour groups fall over one another for a place on the 45-minute guided tours, which leave every fifteen minutes (April & Oct Sat & Sun 9am–noon & 1–4pm; May–Sept Tues–Sun 9am–noon & 1–5pm), but one look at the cooped-up gibbon in the forecourt will give you a suitable foretaste of what's to come.

Further south upriver and fifteen minutes by bus is **VYŠŠÍ BROD** (Hohenfurth), notable for its dazzling white Cistercian monastery, founded by Austrian monks during the thirteenth century. Its proximity to the border and its extreme wealth gave rise to a set of immodest fortifications, which withstood two sieges by the needy Hussites. The essentially Gothic monastery church was, despite its pews, for the exclusive use of the monks, except on religious holidays when the locals were allowed in at the back. In the blue side chapel rests Petr Vok, the last of the Rožmberks, who died of drink and drugs – but still given pride of place as the monastery's rich patron. The popular guided tours end with the monastery's main attraction, a 24-carat gold Rococo library accessible only via a secret door in one of the bookcases.

There's a hotel in Vyšší Brod and a campsite (May to mid-Oct) back in Rožmberk, but it's not very far by foot or infrequent local bus or train to Lipno nad Vltavou by Lake Lipno, where a host of other facilities are available (see below). If you are walking westwards be sure to take the red route to the viewpoint at **Čertova stěna** (Devil's Rocks), a giant scree of granite slabs which tumble into the river below.

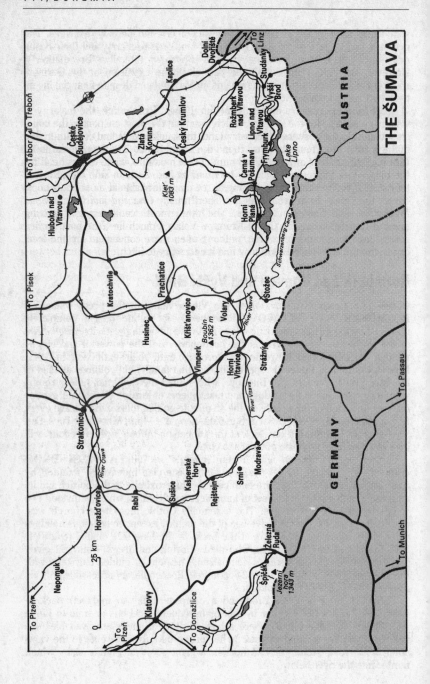

THE ŠUMAVA

If you're planning on crossing the border into Austria, it's only 7km from Vyšší Brod to the border crossing at STUDÁNKY, and another 7km east to HORNÍ DVOŘIŠTĚ, where you can cross the border on one of the international expresses which pause there, or continue to the E55 border crossing (open 24 hours) at DOLNÍ DVOŘIŠTĚ, another 8km northeast.

Lake Lipno

Just before Lipno nad Vltavou, a dam marks the southeastern end of **Lake Lipno**. On the face of it, there's not much to get excited about. The barrage turns the turbines of a huge underground hydroelectric power station, while the lake's scenic southern shore was for years occupied by the military – who are only gradually relinquishing their hold. However, the **northern shore** is punctuated by small beach resorts which have developed rapidly over the last twenty years, mostly created to give workers some well-needed fresh air. The area is popular, and the few hotels invariably full, but you're rarely far from a campsite, which often have cheap bungalows for rent too. **Buses** link most places, supplemented by trains from Černá v Pošumaví westwards, while *ČSAD* **ferries** run between Lipno nad Vltavou and Horní Planá, stopping at various points on the way. If you're planning to spend some time here it might be worth buying the very detailed *Lipenská přehrada* map.

Aside from LIPNO NAD VLTAVOU – which has just one hotel and a choice of **campsites**, complete with takeaway stalls playing loud West Coast music – the southernmost villages are the least developed and **FRYMBURK**, with its delicate white octagonal spire jutting out into the lake, is arguably the best place for which to head, with two low-key campsites south of the village. At nearby **DOLNÍ VLTAVICE**, on a secluded thumb of land, a small crowd enjoys the grassy "beach" with a view over to the short stretch on the opposite shore belonging to Austria. To get there, it's necessary to change buses at **ČERNÁ V POŠUMAVÍ**, little more than an averagely-priced hotel and a collection of campsites, but one of the few places which rents out *lodí* (boats). There's not much more to **HORNÍ PLANÁ** – one hotel, a supermarket, two pubs and a concrete caravan site – but it's the main resort hereabouts, and in summer the village becomes an extension of the beach as pink flesh and beachwear graces the little village square. The Czechs happily soak up the sun, cheek-by-jowl on the almost sandy beach, surrounded by a dubious combination of crazy golf, candyfloss and beer.

Forest walks beyond the dam

The main road from Horní Planá northwest to Volary was, until recently, punctuated at regular intervals by little red signs warning about the impending iron curtain; all villages west of the Vltava were closed to road vehicles, with trains the only legal means of transport. All this should soon be a thing of the past as the state-induced paranoia surrounding the border recedes, allowing access to a much greater area.

From Ovesná station at the top of Lake Lipno, the yellow-marked route heads northwest through gigantic boulders and thick forest to Perník (1049m), before dropping down to JELENÍ, where the **Schwarzenberg Canal** emerges from a tunnel. Built at the turn of the eighteenth century in order to transport the Šumava's valuable timber straight to the Danube (less than 40km due south), the canal was abandoned as a waterway in 1962. A little further on you reach the

Bären Stein, marking the spot where the last bear in the Šumava was shot in 1856. The only potential threat now are 25 lynx which were resettled hereabouts in 1985. Moving on, you should reach the station at ČERNÝ KŘÍŽ in around six hours from Ovesná. Here, the railway divides and you should head north to **VOLARY** (Wallern), where there's little reason to stop, unless you chance upon a vacancy at the *Bobík* hotel, or need to change trains for Prachatice or Vimperk.

Prachatice and Husinec

Where the slopes of Libín (1096m) merge into the Bohemian plain lies the amiable little market town of **PRACHATICE** (Prachatitz) – "Gateway to the Šumava". Most people come here en route to the Šumava, but it's also a useful base for visiting Husinec, birthplace of Jan Hus (see below). A short walk uphill from the bus and train stations brings you to the main square, outside the old town, which contains *ČEDOK*, a supermarket complex and a self-service *restaurace* packed with workers, policemen and cheap grub. Everything else of use or interest is contained within the walls of the tiny circular **staré město**, reached through the bulky fifteenth-century Pisecká brána, a gateway whose faded mural shows Vílem of Rožmberk on horseback and above it, in among the battlements, the red rose symbol of the family who acquired the town briefly in 1501.

The gate's double arches open out on the small Kostelní náměstí where old women sell spices and vegetables in the shade of the trees. The Gothic church of **sv Jakub** is the oldest building in town, its steep, rather peculiar red-ribbed roof the town's landmark. Prachatice is best known to the Czechs for the exquisitely decorative **Literátská škola** to the left, complete with miniature Renaissance battlements, which local boys Hus and Žižka are said to have attended, although the bizarre depictions of men clubbing each other to death seem more akin to its present use as a butchers.

At this point the cobbles open out into the old town square, which gives off a thoroughly Germanic air. Its most striking aspect is the riot of **sgraffito** on the facades of the buildings. If you haven't already come across the phenomenon, Prachatice is as good a place as any to get to grips with it. The technique – extremely popular in the sixteenth century and revived in the nineteenth – involves scraping away plaster to form geometric patterns or even whole pictorial friezes, producing a distinctive lacework effect. The most lavish example of this style is without doubt the sixteenth-century stará **radnice**, decorated with copies of Hans Holbein's disturbing, apocalyptic parables. The arcaded **Rumpalův dům** is similarly smothered, as is the former **solnice** or salt house, at the far end of the square, from which the town accrued its enormous wealth in the Middle Ages.

Accommodation in Prachatice is supplied by the cheap *Národní dům* or *Zlatá stezka* hotels on the old town square. To get to the primitive **campsite**, by the lake at KŘIŠŤANOVICE (July & Aug only), there's an infrequent bus service from Prachatice, followed by a 1500-metre walk from the bus stop on the Volary road.

Husinec and Jan Hus

> "*You may burn the goose* [hus],
> *but one day there will come a swan,*
> *and him you will not burn.*"
>
> Martin Luther

Six kilometres north of Prachatice is the unassuming ribbon village of **HUSINEC**, birthplace of **Jan Hus** (1369–1415). From a childhood of poverty here on the borders of the Czech and German-speaking districts, this mild-mannered Bohemian enjoyed a meteoric rise through the education system to become rector of the Charles University in Prague in 1403. Soon afterwards he became embroiled in a largely national dispute between the Germans and Czechs at the university, causing controversy with his radical sermons criticising the social conditions of the time. Even though many of the more famous tenets of Hussitism were evolved after his death – for example, he never actually advocated communion "in both kinds", nor did he ever denounce his Catholicism – his outspoken comments against the sale of indulgences to fund papal wars led to his unofficial trial by the Council of Constance in 1415. There, he was burned at the stake as a heretic, despite having been guaranteed safe conduct by the Emperor Sigismund. The Czechs were outraged and Hus became a national martyr overnight, inspiring the people to rebel against their masters and kings.

In the nineteenth century, when interest in Hus began to emerge after the dark years of the Counter-Reformation, the poet Jan Neruda visited Husinec, and was horrified to see Hus's former home shabby and neglected. No expense has been spared since, with the family house converted into a **museum** (Tues–Sun 8am–noon & 1–5pm), and many of Hus's old haunts in the surrounding region becoming points of pilgrimage over the last century. That said, you're likely to be alone exploring the museum's small exhibition and the one original room, a tiny garret on the top floor.

Getting here is easiest on one of the afternoon **buses** from Prachatice; coming by train, the station is 3km east of the village.

From Volary to Vimperk

The scenic train ride from Volary to Vimperk takes you deep into the Šumava forest, and it's worth breaking the journey at some point and delving further into the woods. One stop is at the primaeval **Forest of Boubín**, 3km from Zátoň station – there's camping from mid-May to mid-September, 1.5km from the station. It is forbidden to walk among the pines and firs, some of which are over four hundred years old, but green markers take you around the perimeter and on to a small **deer park**. To get back to the railway without retracing your steps, follow the blue-marked path from the deer park to the campsite and station at KUBOVA HUŤ (6km). From May to September trains skirting the south slope of Boubín also stop at the station high above the village of **HORNÍ VLTAVICE**. The two-kilometre scramble down through the forest is worth it for the justly popular **campsite** and *hostinec* below. From Horní Vltavice, a few local buses cover the 13km to STRÁŽNÝ and one or two may now continue over the border (open 24 hours), heading for Kleinphilippsreuth in Germany.

On to the West Bohemian Šumava

The rest of the Šumava strictly lies in West Bohemia, though is only accessible by bus from the east. Two buses a day from Vimperk make it to **KAŠPERSKÉ HORY**, an old mining village below the ruined castle of Kašperk, built in Charles IV's reign. There are a couple of **hotels** here, and a smart Renaissance radnice embellished with three perfect eighteenth-century gables, and the town

museum, which serves as a repository for some wonderful Bohemian glassware, once manufactured by Johann Loetz in the neighbouring town of KLÁŠTERSKÝ MLÝN (Klöstermühle). In the late nineteenth century Loetz won many prizes in Brussels and Paris for his Tiffany-style vases in iridescent glass and weird vegetal shapes, many of which inexplicably escaped the auctioneer's hammer and ended up here.

Down in the narrow Otava valley, the nearby village of REJŠTEJN retains an Austrian flavour, but a short bus ride south, along the newly surfaced road, the once isolated hamlet of **SRNÍ** tells a different story. Here, the traditional timber tiles and shingles of the old mountain cottages exist alongside the likes of the multistorey *Hotel Šumava*, with more of the same in the pipeline.

A cluster of wooden buildings 6km south at ANTIGL provide **camping** and a useful base for exploring the cool cascades of the **Vydra river gorge**. Most buses continue the 3km upstream as far as **MODRAVA**, where the pseudo-Alpine buildings have all but won the day. From here, there's access to some of the wildest, boggy, woody scenery in the Šumava – though you'll have to walk every step of the way.

The northwestern tip of the Šumava is best approached by train from Klatovy (see p.154). It centres around the ski resort of **ŽELEZNÁ RUDA** (Eisenstein), 2km from the German border, and just over an hour by train from Klatovy. At ŠPIČÁK, the chair lift to the top of **Pancír** (1214m) operates all year, and you can reach either of two local glacial lakes – Černé jezero or Čertovo jezero – by the yellow-marked path from the Špičák station. If you're considering walking, the *Šumava Klatovsko* map is a worthwhile investment. Neither the *Javor* nor the *Slávie* in Železná Ruda could be described as cheap or pleasant places to stay, and it's probably better to go for the **campsite** or bungalows, 4km back down the track at Hojsova Stráž-Brčálník. The railway, which used to run on to Germany, was closed during the Cold War, but there's a border crossing, a short walk from the station at Železná Ruda, from where it's even less distance to the local *Bahnhof* in Bayerisch Eisenstein.

WEST BOHEMIA

For centuries, the rolling hills of **West Bohemia** (Západní Čechy) have been a buffer zone between the Slav world and the great German-speaking lands. The border regions were heavily colonised by neighbouring Germans from the twelfth century onwards. At first they were welcomed by the Czech Přemyslid rulers, providing urgently needed skilled craftsmen and miners for the Bohemian economy, but when the newcomers began to enrich themselves while maintaining their separate ethnic identity, political complications inevitably followed. Every momentous event in Bohemian history found the population split along ethnic lines, until finally in 1938 the excesses of the Sudeten German Party provided the impetus for a violent break with the past. For North and West Bohemia the forced removal of the German-speaking population after World War II left vast areas of the countryside and a number of large towns, empty of people. In the years after the war, Czechs and Slovaks were encouraged to resettle the towns and villages, but even now the countryside in particular remains eerily underpopulated.

The economic mainstay of the region for the last century has been the big industrial city of **Plzeň**: home of the Škoda engineering works, centre of the beer industry, and the region's capital. Within easy reach of Plzeň, though, are the deserted monasteries of **Kladruby** and **Plasy**, monuments to the architectural genius of Giovanni Santini, the master of "Baroque-Gothic". Further south, the historic border town of **Domažlice** offers easy access to the colourful **Chod region**. The so-called spa region, to the northwest, although an integral part of West Bohemia, and source of much of its foreign currency revenue, is dealt with separately – see p.156.

As one of the most sparsely populated regions in the country, **public transport** is somewhat patchy. However, excellent rail links exist between the major towns, so unless you're heading for the back of beyond, getting around should present few real problems.

Plzeň

Even the constant drizzle can't wash the dirt off the buildings of **PLZEŇ**, the largest city in Bohemia after Prague with a population of 175,000. Parts of the city defy description, such is their dereliction, and the skyline is a symphony of smoke and steam, the results of which can be seen in the colour of the city's tap water. Yet despite its overwhelmingly industrial character, there are compensations – a large number of students, eclectic architecture and an unending supply of (probably) the best beer in the world, all of which make Plzeň a justifiably popular stopoff on the main railway line between Prague and the West.

Some history
Plzeň (or Pilsen as it is still called in the West) was built on beer and bombs. In 1850 it was a small town of 14,000, of whom 10,000 were German. Then in 1859 an ironworks was founded and quickly snapped up by the Czech capitalist **Emil Škoda**, under whose control it drew an ever-increasing Czech population from the countryside: within thirty years the overall population had trebled while the number of Germans had decreased. Although initially simply an engineering plant, the Austrian government transformed it into a huge armaments factory during World War I, second only to Krupps in Germany, which inevitably attracted the attention of Allied bombers during World War II. Nowadays, apart from producing the country's rolling stock, it also has the dubious privilege of manufacturing all the nuclear reactors for the Warsaw Pact countries. However, since cancelled orders are mounting up, and the wisdom of nuclear power is being openly questioned, the factory may soon have switch tack again.

Arrival, orientation and accommodation

Plzeň's two **railway stations** are works of art in themselves: of the two, your likeliest point of arrival is the hlavní nádraží (main station), east of the city centre, rather than the Jižní předměstí (south station), 750m southwest of the centre. The unsavoury **bus terminal**, for all national and international arrivals, is on the other side of town. From either the bus or train station, the city centre is only a short walk away, or a few stops on tram #1 or #2.

Finding a vacancy in one of Plzeň's **hotels** presents few problems. Besides the faded splendour and Hollywood stairways of the moderate *Slovan*, Smetanovy sady 1 (☎019-335 51), and the *Hotel Continental*, Zbrojnická 8 (☎019-330 60), or the ugly and expensive *Central*, náměstí Republiky 33 (☎019-326 85), there's always the cheap and charming high-rise *Hotel Plzeň*, Žižkova 66 (☎019-27 26 56; tram #1 or #4 from outside the Tyl Theatre). In July and August, **student hostels** offer cheap dorm accommodation – go to *CKM* on Dominikanská to find out the latest addresses. Bus #20 will drop you at the *Bílá hora* **campsite**, in the northern suburb of the same name, where Plzeňites go **swimming** on summer days.

The City

Stepping out of the main station onto Moskevská (shortly to be renamed, though no one's quite decided what yet), you're confronted with a variety of bad-taste Communist buildings, some still in the process of completion. A recently unveiled plaque at the end of the street commemorates the liberation of Plzeň by the Americans – something the Communists consistently refused to acknowledge. Close by, the River Radbuza, one of four rivers running through Plzeň, doesn't bear close inspection, but the historical core of the city beyond it almost certainly does. The main square, **náměstí Republiky**, presents a full range of architectural styles, starting with the exalted heights of the Gothic church of **sv Bartoloměj**, abandoned awkwardly in the middle of the square, its bile-green spire reaching up more than one hundred metres. Over the way, a splash of local colour is provided by the weekly round of civic weddings which take place, with characteristic Czech restraint, in and around the Italianate **Stará radnice**, self-importantly one storey higher than the rest of the square.

Here and there other old buildings survive, and the overall layout has remained unchanged since medieval times. But the vast majority of Plzeň's buildings hale from the city's heyday during the industrial expansion around the turn of the century. In the old town, this produced some wonderful variations on neo-historical themes and Art-Nouveau motifs, particularly to the north and west of the main square. The largest surviving **synagogue** in the whole country stands disused by the main north–south thoroughfare, its once red bricks caked in dirt. West of here, there are still more blocks of late nineteenth-century residential apartments, boasting vestiges of ornate mosaics and sculpturing, now barely visible under the pollutants which have eaten away at their fanciful facades.

Beer and the brewery

The real reason most people come to Plzeň is to sample its famous 12° beer *Plzeňský Prazdroj*, or **Pilsner Urquell** (its more familiar Germanised export name). Beer has been brewed in the town since it was founded in 1295, but it wasn't until 1842 that the famous *Bürgerliches Brauhaus* was built by the German banker Bleichröder, after a near-riot by the townsfolk over the declining quality of their beer. The new brew was a bottom-fermented beer which quickly became popular across Central Europe, spawning thousands of paler imitations under the generic name of *Pilsner* – hence the addition of the suffix *Prazdroj* (Urquell, meaning "original") by the brewers, to show just who thought of it first.

Trying to get on a guided tour of the **brewery** can be a frustrating business, since *ČEDOK* say that they will only arrange tours at fourteen days' notice, and even then only for groups. Others have occasionally succeeded in getting hold of

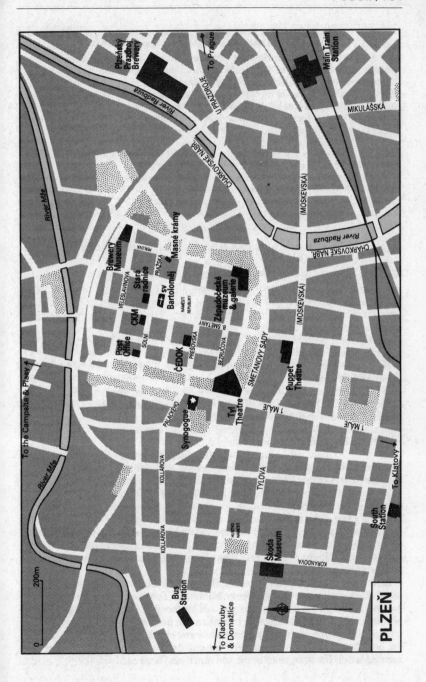

PLZEŇ

ŠKODA: THE CARS AND THE JOKES

For Czechs, the **Škoda industrial empire** is a great Czech achievement and a source of national pride. It's doubly ironic, then, that the word *škoda* means "shame" or "pity" in Czech – a marketing own-goal were it not the name of the founding father of the Czech car industry, **Emil Škoda**. The latest Škoda model, which is actually assembled at the company's Mladá Boleslav plant, has been very favourably received, even in the West (whence a large proportion of its components derive), and is in great demand from the new Czech bourgeoisie. In 1989, there was a three-year waiting list, despite a retail price of over 90,000 Czech crowns (over twice the average yearly salary). At the time of writing, Volvo and Renault had just been outbid by Volkswagen for a 49-percent stake in the firm.

Škoda cars have, however, long been the laughing stock of Western European car buffs. A few sample groaners:

Customer to garage mechanic: "Have you got a petrol cap for a Škoda?"; garage mechanic to customer: "It's a fair swop".

Q: What do you call a Škoda convertable? A: a skip.

Q: What's the difference between a Jehovah's Witness and a Škoda? A: You can close the door on a Jehovah's Witness.

Q: How do you double the value of your Škoda? A: Fill up the petrol tank.

Q: Why do Škodas have heated rear windows? A: To keep your hands warm as you're pushing it along. . .

someone at the brewery itself (☎019-21 64) who speaks English, and persuading them to give impromptu tours. Most people, though, give up and head for the Brewery Museum instead (see below), and/or go for a glass of the real thing at the *Restaurace Prazdroj* at U Prazdroje 1, next to the brewery's triumphal arch, which was built in 1892 to commemorate its fiftieth birthday – and which has appeared on every authentic bottle of *Plzeňský Prazdroj* ever since. Plzeň's annual **beer festival**, incidentally, is held in October.

Museums and galleries

Plzeň has a fair few museums, the biggest being the copper-topped **Západočeské muzeum** (soon to reopen after an extensive renovation). A neo-Baroque extravaganza, it was built in the nineteenth century to educate the peasants who were flocking to the city, and while few of its mammoth selection of exhibits deserve close attention, there are some notable exceptions. The **Západočeské galérie** boasts some of the best examples of twentieth-century Czech painting outside Prague. Around the corner, beneath the elongated vaults of the neo-Gothic **Masné krámy** (Butchers' Stalls), the gallery puts on its temporary art exhibitions (Tues–Fri 10am–6pm, Sat 10am–1pm, Sun 9am–5pm; concerts Sun mornings).

At the end of the beautiful, narrow, *fin-de-siècle* Veleslavínova is the most popular of Plzeň's museums, the **Brewery Museum** (Tues 1–4.30pm, Wed–Sun 9am–4.30pm), a more than sufficient consolation for those who fail to get into the brewery itself. The friendly anglophile custodian can furnish you with an *anglický text*, and get the old *Würlitzer* organ going while you check out the exhibits: the smallest beer barrel in the world (a mere one-centimetre cube), casement after casement of kitsch Baroque beer mugs, and much else besides.

Unfortunately, unless you're an automotive engineer or an early-riser you won't get much from the **Škoda Museum** by the factory on Korandova (Mon–Fri 6.30am–3pm), which displays the insides of train engines and suchlike.

Eating, drinking and entertainment

All the hotels in town have **restaurants** attached to them – the *Plzeň* even offers "Italian" cooking – but for really cheap meals try the *bufet* under the *Central*, or the takeaway stands on Moskevská, where large quantities of *brambory* are consumed by the folk queueing for buses. On the same street is a **late-night shop** (open Sun mornings), always a hive of activity when the big supermarket opposite is shut. **Drinking** is obviously a serious consideration in a city that produces not just one but two world-class beers. Apart from the aforementioned *Restaurace Prazdroj* (see above), you can get *Plzeňský Prazdroj* at the older and more famous *U Salzmanů* on Pražská. *Gambrinus*, Plzeň's other beer, is best drunk at *U Žumbery* on Bezručova. As for cafés, try the one by *CKM* on Dominikánská, near the university, or down a *fernet* and tonic at *U Bedřicha* on B. Smetany.

Plzeň's wonderful Beaux Arts **Tyl Theatre** (by the Smetanovy sady) is the city's main venue for opera and ballet. Other concerts and cultural events stick mainly with the *Dům kultury* on Moskevská, but in the summer the **Festival of Folk Songs** (July) is just one of the events held at the *Přírodní divadlo*, Plzeň's open-air theatre, set in the botanical gardens of Lochotínský park, near the medical faculty (tram #3 or #4 from outside the Tyl Theatre). Czechoslovakia's longest-running puppet duo, Spejbl and Hurvínek, originated at Plzeň's **puppet theatre**, *Divadlo dětí Alfa* at Moskevská 17 (entrance is on Jungmannova), which still puts on daily performances and also the occasional film.

Around Plzeň: Plasy and Kladruby

Within easy reach of Plzeň are two monasteries which bear the hallmark of Giovanni Santini, arguably the most original Baroque architect to work in the Czech Lands. Of the two sights, Plasy – 20km north of Plzeň – is the easiest to get to (accessible by train or bus), though Kladruby – over 30km west – is without doubt a more rewarding day trip.

Plasy

The **Cistercian monastery** of **PLASY** (Plass) is submerged in a green valley, 24km north of Plzeň. Originally founded in the twelfth century, the present muddle of flaking Baroque outbuildings is the work of two of Prague's leading architects, Jean Baptiste Mathey and Giovanni Blasius Santini-Aichl. Of the two, **Santini** (1667–1723), the Prague-born son of north Italian immigrants, is the more interesting: a popular architect whose personal, slightly ironic style produced some of the most original works in the country. The brilliant white cloisters harbour palatial pretensions, while the rest of the monastery (April & Oct 9am–noon & 1–4pm; May & Sept 9am–noon & 1–5pm; June–Aug 9am–noon & 1–6pm; closed Mon) is now an art gallery, the highlight of whose over-long guided tour is the side chapels, containing Santini's superb frescoes.

Shortly after its Baroque redevelopment, the monastery was dissolved, and in 1826 fell into the hands of **Prince Clarence von Metternich**, the arch-conservative Austrian Chancellor and political architect of the post-Napoleonic European order. Over the road, obscured by willow trees, is the cemetery church hijacked and transformed by the prince into the family mausoleum. In tune with his politics, its oppressively Neoclassical forms dwarf the commoners' graveyard behind it.

Kladruby

If Plasy failed to move you, the **Benedictine monastery** at **KLADRUBY** (Kladrau) should do the trick. It's an altogether less gloomy affair, once the richest monastery in Bohemia, gutted during the Thirty Years' War and then transformed under Santini's supervision once the Counter-Reformation had set in. The main attraction is the huge monastery church, where the original Romanesque and Gothic elements blend imperceptibly with Santini's idiosyncratic additions. The original lantern tower has been converted into an extravagant Baroque cupola, which filters a faded pink light into the transepts, themselves covered in stars and zigzags mirrored on the cold stone paving below. It's the perfect expression of Santini's so-called Baroque-Gothic style, and a work of consummate skill.

To get to Kladruby, take the train from Plzeň to **STŘÍBRO** (Mies), where you'll have to change on to one of the fairly frequent local buses. Dramatically poised over the Mže (Mies) river, Stříbro was previously the vague frontier post between the German- and Czech-speaking districts, its tidy square sporting arguably the most beautiful Renaissance radnice in Bohemia, paid for by the town's long-extinct silver mines. There's no other reason to pause here unless it's to stay the night at the moderate *Evropa* (☎24 60) hotel on the main square.

Klatovy and around

Just over an hour by train from Plzeň, **KLATOVY** (Klattau) is another possible day trip from Plzeň, or alternatively a potential base for exploring the northwest tip of the nearby Šumava region (see p.148). Either way, there's enough to keep you occupied for at least a couple of hours before moving on.

Tightly walled in and nervously perched on high ground, Klatovy warns of the approaching border with Germany. Its best feature is the cluster of tall buildings jostling for position on one side of the cramped town square. Tucked in beside the Renaissance radnice, the sixteenth-century **Černá věž** (blackened by past burnings) is evidence of past prosperity – and the need for a lookout post to protect the town. From its pinnacled parapet you can see the forests of the Bavarian border and, across the rooftops, the smaller and later **Bílá věž**. Next to it, the white Jesuit church exudes incense and cooled air from its curved interior, though it's more fascinating for its musty **catacombs** (daily April–Sept), where Jesuits and other wealthy locals are preserved in varying stages of decomposition. Next door at *U bílého jednorožce* (The White Unicorn) is a seventeenth-century **apothecary** (daily April–Sept 8am–4pm), which was functioning intact until 1964, but has since become a UNESCO registered monument. The bottles and pots are all labelled in Latin, with swirling wooden pillars flanking the shelves; the back room where the drugs were mixed comes complete with horror-movie flasks of dried goat's blood and pickled children's intestines.

For **practical matters**, visit *ČEDOK*, opposite the apothecary, which dispenses a free brochure and map of town, and can help find you a room in one of Klatovy's three cheap **hotels**. Alternatively, there's a rudimentary **campsite** (open mid-June to mid-Sept), by the River Úhlava, a couple of kilometres' bus ride west of the town.

Domažlice and the Chods

Fifteen kilometres from the German border, **DOMAŽLICE** has always been inextricably linked with the Chod people (see box) who had the task of containing the German *Volk's* inexorable drift eastwards from Bavaria. For centuries the town was the local customs house, but it lost much of its former importance when the border was fixed in 1707, and apart from the weekend **Chod Folk Festival** in August, Domažlice's gentle snoozing goes undisturbed.

The Town

Like many small Bohemian towns it starts and ends at its main square, which extends for 500 metres along a perfect east–west axis. Flanked by uninterrupted arcades under every possible style of gable, the cobbled square seems like a perfect setting for a Bohemian-Bavarian skirmish. Halfway down one side, the thirteenth-century church steeple used to double as a lookout post for the vulnerable town, and ascending its 196 steps provides you with a bird's-eye view of the whole area. The two streets running parallel, either side of the main square, are scruffier relatives and mark the boundaries of what was the medieval town.

The town's other remaining thirteenth-century round tower is part of the **Chodský hrad**, seat of the Chods' self-government until it fell into the hands of Wolf Maximilian Laminger. The castle museum worthily traces the town's colourful history, but you're more likely to want to spend time in the **Jindřich Jindřich Museum**, northeast of the old town (Tues–Sun 8am–2.30pm) – founded by a local composer, Jindřich Jindřich, who gathered together Chod folk costumes, ceramics and anything else linked to the region. If you can't catch the annual festival, this amazing collection, as well as the mock-up cottage interior, do much to compensate. Under the Communists, there was a pathetic attempt to link the Chods' history as border guards with the activities of the Cold War frontier patrols (they even set up their union headquarters here). One room in particular had displays of neo-Nazi propaganda from West Germany alongside a book by Václav Havel – a kind of guilt by juxtaposition.

Some practicalities

Arriving at the railway station or the bus terminal, you should avoid **sleeping** at the nearby *Chodský Hotel*, and walk the ten minutes into town to check on vacancies at the *Slávia* (☎45 63) or *Koruna* (☎22 79), both of which are cheaper and occupy prime sites on the main square. Apart from the hotel **restaurants**, there are at least two other places to eat, though at all of them the clientele – and staff – seem more intent on drinking. Given the absence of nightlife you won't be missing anything by staying instead at the riverside *Babylon* **campsite** (May–Sept), 6km south by bus, or at the *Hájovna* site (mid-May to mid-Sept), 1km or so north of KDYNĚ (which is 20min by train from Domažlice).

THE CHODS

"The spearhead of the Slavic march into Central Europe" as writer Josef Škvorecký described them, the **Chods** (*Chody*) are one of the few Czech tribes to have kept their identity. Very little is certain about their origin, but their name comes from *chodit* (to walk about), and undoubtedly refers to their traditional occupation as guardians of the frontier. Since the earliest times their proud independence was exploited by a succession of Bohemian kings who employed them as border guards, in return for granting them freedom from serfdom and various other feudal privileges.

However, after the Battle of Bílá hora, the Habsburgs were keen to curb the Chods' power, and the whole region was handed over lock, stock and barrel to one of the victorious generals, Wolf Maximilian Lamingen. At first the Chods tried to reaffirm their ancient privileges by legal means, but when this proved fruitless, with the encouragement of one Jan Sladký – better known as Kozina – they simply refused to acknowledge their new despot. Seventy of the rebels were thrown into the prison in Novoměstská radnice in Prague, and Kozina was singled out to be publicly hanged in Plzeň on November 28, 1695, as an example to the rest of the *Chody*.

Although the Empire prevailed, the Chods never allowed the loss of their freedoms to quash their natural ebullience or the peculiar local dialect which still survives in the villages. Stubbornly resistant to Germanisation, they carried the banner of Czech national defiance through the dark ages. Even now, of all the regions of Bohemia, Chodsko is closest to its cultural roots, known above all for its rich local costumes, still worn on Sundays and religious holidays, and for its *dudy* (bagpipes), now played only in folk ensembles and at festivals.

THE SPA REGION

Czechoslovaks make the most of their 176 spa resorts, and the big three West Bohemian spas – **Mariánské Lázně**, **Františkovy Lázně** and **Karlovy Vary** – are always packed with patients and tourists. This famous triangle of spas, conveniently scattered along the German border, was the Côte d'Azur of Habsburg Europe, attracting the great names of *Mitteleuropa*. But what was once the prerogative of the mega-wealthy has long since become the right of the toiling masses. Since the nationalisation of the entire spa industry, every factory and trade union has received an annual three weeks' holiday at a *lázně dům* (spa pension): perks aimed at proving the success of socialism. *Die Kur* is still very popular among all central Europeans, but spas are not to everyone's taste. Even at the most active of the lot – Karlovy Vary – the plethoric and elderly predominate. To avoid cure-seekers, head instead for **Cheb** or **Loket**, both beautifully preserved towns and largely crowd-free.

Mariánské Lázně (Marienbad)

At the beginning of the nineteenth century, the area around **MARIÁNSKÉ LÁZNĚ** was unadulterated woodland. Only in 1818 did the local abbot, Karel Reichenberger, and a German doctor, Josef Nehr, take the initiative and establish a spa here. Within a century **Marienbad** (as it is best known) had joined the clique of world-famous European spas, boasting a clientele from writers to royalty. That inveterate spa-man Goethe was among the earliest of the VIPs to popularise the place, and a few generations later it became the favourite holiday spot of King Edward VII, a passion he shared with his pal, the Emperor Franz Josef. During World War I, even the incorrigibly infirm Franz Kafka spent a brief, happy spell here with Felice Bauer, writing "things are different now and good, we are engaged to be married right after the war"*.

Today, though, Mariánské Lázně is the mere ghost of turn-of-the-century Marienbad. What was once fashionable, elegant and expensive is now plebeian, dilapidated and cheap; where there was intrigue and excitement, there is now banality and melancholy. That said, what was an exclusive fat-farm for the rich and famous only two generations ago, is now eminently accessible to all and sundry. The air of neglect and grand decay is also preferable to the thoughtless development that's been foisted on other, more popular resorts. In any case, it's an expansive place, with as many opportunities for retreating into the surrounding woods as strolling *en promenade* through the streets.

Around the spa

Mariánské Lázně was the last, but by no means the least, of Bohemia's famous spas. As far as the eye can see, sumptuous, regal spa buildings rise up from the pine-clad surrounds, most dating from the second half of the nineteenth century, ensuring an intriguing homogeneity in their *fin-de-siècle* opulence. On one side of the main drag, Hlavní třída, the four-storey luxury mansions are festooned with shapely balconies – built for kings and now used by the mob – overlooking the former *Anlagen* (spa gardens). This part of town, once patrolled by special spa police who imposed strict fines on those discovered smoking or committing other crimes against health, is now given over to pedestrians and silent, smokeless trolley buses. Frédéric Chopin stayed at the *Bílé labuť* (The White Swan), the modest two-storey *dům* at no. 47, on his way from Paris to Warsaw. Upstairs in the **Chopin Museum** (Mon–Fri 10am–noon & 2–5pm) you can sink into an armchair and listen to a crackly recording of the composer. A few doors away, there's a shop selling tins of *oplatky*, the sugar- or chocolate-filled wafers for which the spa is famous, and which make the waters you are about to taste infinitely more palatable.

Around the Kreuzbrunnen Colonnade

The focal point of the spa, overlooking the town, is the **Kreuzbrunnen Colonnade**, now named after Maxim Gorky, who once vacationed here. The most beautiful wrought-iron colonnade in Bohemia, it gently curves like a whale-ribbed railway station, the atmosphere relentlessly genteel and sober despite the tasteless acid-house frescoes. In summer, Bohemian brass bands give daily **concerts** (also at the Lesní pramen), and German tourists buy up the Bohemian crystal in the upstairs gallery. Access to the colonnade's life-giving faucets is restricted (daily 6am–noon & 4–6pm), though the spa's first and foremost spring, Křížový pramen, should shortly be reopened after a face-lift.

---

* The title of Alain Resnais' 1961 film *Last Year in Marienbad* is, like the film itself, misleading. The action is shot entirely in a French chateau, though the plot (what there is of it) is based on an incident that may (or may not) have occurred the year before in Marienbad. With a script by *nouveau roman* iconoclast Alain Robbe-Grillet, it's either absolute rubbish or totally seminal, depending on your view.

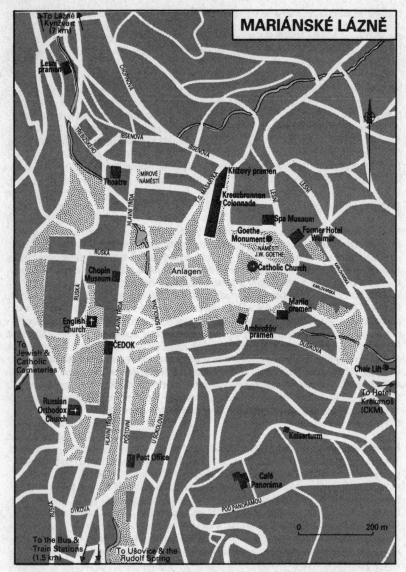

Rising up behind the Kreuzbrunnen Colonnade are yet more giant ochre spa buildings, including the **Hotel Weimar** (now the *Kavkaz*) in which King Edward VII preferred to stay and, two doors down, the **Spa Museum** (Mon–Fri 9–11am & 2–3pm; films shown on Tues & Thurs at 1pm), which now occupies the house in which Goethe stayed on his last visit in 1823. Marienbadalia – including a collection of beautiful tins in which the spa's famous wafer-thin *oplatky* (*Oblaten*)

used to be packaged – fills the ground floor; upstairs you can find some of the original furnishings. Since the 1989 revolution Goethe has had the additional posthumous privilege of having the square named after him, just recompense for the removal of his statue from its granite plinth (which now supports a commemorative plaque) by the retreating Nazis.

Walks around the town

Unless you're booked in for treatment, you'll have to content yourself with sipping the waters, wolfing down the wafers and taking the obligatory constitutional. Mariánské Lázně's altitude lends an almost subalpine freshness to the air, even at the height of summer, and **walking** is as important to "the cure" as the various specialised treatments. To this end, the expert nineteenth-century landscape gardener, Václav Skalník, was employed to transform the valley into an open park, providing an intricate network of paths leading to the many springs dotted around the surrounding countryside. At the end of the Kreuzbrunnen Colonnade, there's a map showing the various marked walks around the spa; armed with a *plán města* (available from most hotels, bookshops and newsagents) you can strike off on your own.

Goethe's favourite walk, up to the *Miramonte* for morning coffee, is retraced by most visitors, though since the café was converted into a *lázně dům* (spa home) for kids, you have to delve deeper into the woods to the *Červená karkulka* café for refreshments. From here, it's not far to the lower town of Ušovice whence you can return to town via the Neoclassical Rudolf Spring, where, according to ČEDOK, "hypotonic calcareous-magnesium-hydrogen carbonate-ferrugineous acidulous waters" are to be had. On the opposite side of the valley, behind the hotel *Atlantik*, are the decaying remnants of a small red-brick **English church**: its inwards gutted and windows boarded up, long since abandoned by its royal patrons – "as melancholy a sight as anything to be seen in Central Europe" lamented Richard Bassett. Further along Ruská, the neo-Byzantine **Russian Orthodox church** is in better shape, and, if you can get in, its altar is reputedly the largest piece of porcelain in the world. From here, tracks slope up to the town's Catholic cemetery, followed by the **Jewish cemetery** (still in use) where Professor Theodor Lessing, the first Czech to be murdered by the Nazis (in 1933), is buried. Less exertion is necessary to enjoy the **panoramic view** from the roof of the old **Kaiserturm** (*rozhledna*), on the hillside southwest of the spa.

Practicalities

On **arrival**, passengers are unloaded from their buses and trains at a suitably discreet distance from the spa. Trolley bus #5 then covers the 3km up the former *Kaiserstrasse* to the *Hotel Excelsior*, where the pedestrianised zone of the spa proper begins. Many of the central **hotels** retain a decadent ambience without being ridiculously expensive, but to save a lot of fruitless legwork – since everything's likely to be full during high season – your best bet is to visit ČEDOK in the *Atlantik*, on Hlavní třída, to enquire about the vacancies which appear at 10am and 5pm daily. If you're an *IYHF* member, or a student, then rooms in the *Hotel Krakonoš* at Zádub 53 (☎0165-2624; bus #12 or the chair lift, east of the spa on Dusíkova) cost next to nothing (though a lot more to non-members). Otherwise there's *Motel Start* (☎0165-2062) on Plzeňská, which has a small **campsite** next door offering cheap **bungalows** (May–Sept). The bigger *Luxor* campsite is awkwardly located, several kilometres west of the station (take bus #6 to Velká Hleďsebe, then walk 1km south down the Plzeň road).

Food and drink

Hlavní třída is punctuated with cafés, shops and restaurants, most hinting at bygone opulence. *Café Polonia*, Hlavní třída 50, offers stucco decoration as rich as its cakes; coffee is served on the terrace of *Maxims*, further up on the same side, and at the *Sadová kavárna*, Poštovní 195. The spa's top **restaurant** is in the *Hotel Golf*, 2km east of town (bus #12), and is almost exclusively patronised by German-speakers. For something different, try and get your mouth round some *vepřové po Ščchuansku* (Szechuan pork) at the *Cínský restaurace*, above the *Atlantik* at Hlavní třída 46. Constitutional food halts include the *Lunapark* (1km north of town) and the *Červená karkulka* (see "Walks around the spa").

The interior of the *B-Bar* (by the *Hotel Palace*), is wall-to-wall *Coca-Cola* posters, hence its popularity with the denim crew, but it purports to serve *Italské špagety* until midnight. Other **late-night spots** include the *Hodonínská vinárna* for nourishment, or the closest you'll get to a nightclub at the nearby *Lil-Club* and at the "American nightclub" in *Hotel Corso*. The more youthful locals, however, prefer the disco at the *Atlantik* or up at the *Lunapark*.

Lázně Kynžvart and Teplá

If you're looking for a longer excursion out of Mariánské Lázně, spend a leisurely afternoon walking over to **LÁZNĚ KYNŽVART** (Königswart), 8km northwest of town. Now a spa for children, it was for many years the private spa of the Metternich family who entertained Goethe, Beethoven and Dumas (among others) at their Empire chateau, 2km from the railway station (but closed for renovation until 1992). A longer day trip is to **Teplá Monastery**, 15km east, whose abbots used to own the springs at Mariánské Lázně. Despite the Baroque topping, the plain stone facade of the monastery church is a striking reminder of Teplá's twelfth-century origins. The rest of the monastery carries the universal stamp of the Baroque Counter-Reformation, but the real reason to come here is to see the Neoclassical *Nová knihovna* (New Library). Built in the 1900s, it boasts almost edible stucco decoration, triple-decker bookstacks and swirling black iron balconies framed by white pilasters.

Cheb (Eger)

For many Western visitors, **CHEB**, 10km from the German border, is their first taste of Czechoslovakia. Most people leave shortly after arriving in a state of some confusion and disillusion, concluding that although (or because) it's the westernmost border town, there has been no effort to make it a showpiece for the country. In fact money has been poured into the town, but Cheb's post-war haemorrhage has left it with less than a third of its pre-war population, and a collective identity crisis of mammoth proportions. Cheb is a beautiful historic town, yet despite incentives offered by the previous Communist government, Czechs have been reluctant to move here. The root of the malaise lies in the authorities' ambivalence to Cheb, simultaneously encouraging its future and denying its past. Nevertheless, it's worth an afternoon's stopoff – if only to escape the spa towns all around.

EGERLAND

Most Germans still refer to Cheb as **Eger**, the name given to the town by the German colonists who settled here from the eleventh century onwards. The town was at the centre of the (anti-semitic) **Pan-German Schönerer movement** of the late nineteenth century, which fought desperately against the advance of Czech nationalism, aided and abetted (as they saw it) by the weak and liberal Austrian state. The most famous protest against the 1897 Badeni Decrees, which granted the Czech language equal status with German throughout the Czech Lands, took place in Eger.

Thus, in the 1930s the pro-Nazi **Sudeten German Party** (SdP) found Egerland receptive to their anti-semitism as much as their irredentism. Although it's estimated that a quarter of the German-speaking voters stubbornly refused to vote for the SdP, the majority of Egerländer welcomed their incorporation into the Third Reich, completed in 1938. At the end of World War II, only those Germans who could prove themselves to have been actively anti-fascist (Czechs were luckily exempted from this acid test) were permitted to remain on Czechoslovak soil; the others were forced out, reducing the population of Cheb to 27 percent of its pre-war level. The mass expulsions were accompanied by numerous acts of vengeance, and the issue remains a delicate one. Havel's suggestion in his first presidential address that an apology to the Germans was in order outraged most Czechoslovaks, who prefer to forget this episode in their nation's history.

The City

Cheb's **railway station** is an unpromising place at which to arrive, and the ten-minute walk into town does little to dispel the unease. En route down the main avenue, you pass *ČEDOK*, where it's easy to arrange a **place to stay** in one of Cheb's three or four cheap and central hotels. If *ČEDOK* is closed, try the cheap *Hradní dvůr* (☎220 06) on Dlouhá, or the slightly sleeker *Hvězda* (☎225 49) on the main square.

Most visitors feel slightly self-conscious strolling through town, and this has made the locals equally conscious of foreigners. The backstreets of the old town are full of seventeenth-century German merchants' houses, though at first glance many appear more like slums. Given the option, most Czechs shun this part of town, in preference for the modern flats which have shot up on the outskirts. Instead it's the local Gypsy population who are forced to live here, and who, since the Velvet Revolution, have been subjected to a spate of attacks, particularly in the border regions of West and North Bohemia. However, as a foreigner, you're unlikely to experience anything other than innocuous curiosity and a little gentle hustling.

It's not unusual to heave a sigh of relief – aesthetic at any rate – once you reach the town square, **náměstí krále Jiřího z Poděbrad**. This is the old *Marktplatz*, established in the twelfth century as the commercial and political heart of Egerland. Street life has moved to the ugly superstore on the main shopping street, though, leaving the beautiful seventeenth-century square strangely empty but for the occasional group of German tourists. The batch of half-timbered buildings huddled together at the bottom of the square, called **Špalíček**, form a ruthlessly unCzech ensemble – originally a cluster of medieval shops, now housing just a small café.

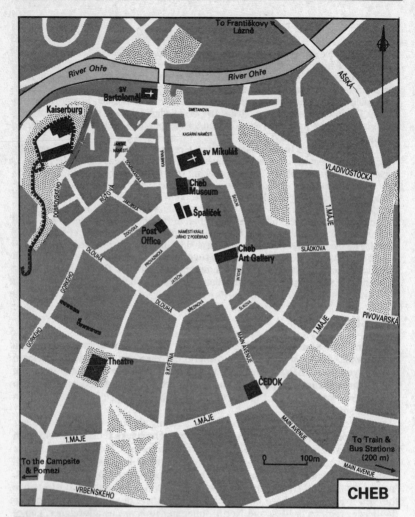

CHEB

The Cheb Museum and art gallery

Behind Špalíček lurks the **Cheb Museum** (Tues–Sun 8am–noon & 1–4pm), in
the former *Stadthaus* where **Albrecht von Wallenstein** (*Albrecht z Valdšejna*),
Duke of Friedland (Frýdlant) and generalissimo of the Thirty Years' War, was
murdered in 1634 by an Irishman on the secret orders of Emperor Ferdinand II.
A converted Catholic, Wallenstein took it upon himself to raise, fund, and lead the
Habsburg Imperial army to victory against the rebellious Protestant nobility,
procuring for himself no fewer than sixty estates in northeast Bohemia. Having
routed the Saxons, Bavarians and Swedes, he began negotiating with them on the
emperor's behalf, but the suspicion that he intended to set up his own kingdom

led Emperor Ferdinand to order his assassination. The museum studiously avoids Cheb's more recent history, but 1634 gets close attention and the heavy Gothic woodwork provides an evocative setting for Wallenstein's murder, graphically illustrated on the bedroom walls.

Great efforts have been made to establish a new cultural life in the vacuum left by the post-war expulsion of Germans. The **Cheb Art Gallery** (Tues–Sun 9am–noon & 1–4pm), at no. 16 on the square, ranks as one of the best in the country for inter-war twentieth-century Czech art, concentrating on both the 1890 generation led by Jan Preisler and the Czech fusion of Expressionism and Cubism exemplified by the works of Antonín Procházka, Emil Filla and Josef Čapek.

Down by the River Ohře (Eger), the small Gothic church of **sv Bartoloměj** has been converted (with large helpings of Bulgarian marble) into a spacious setting for a superb collection of fourteenth- and fifteenth-century Bohemian sculpture.

Sv Mikuláš and Kaiserburg

Cheb's two largest buildings, dating from the town's early history are out of keeping with the red-roofed uniformity of the seventeenth-century *Altstadt*. The church of **sv Mikuláš** has a bizarre multi-faceted roof like the scales of a dinosaur, though since the renowned Austrian architect Balthasar Neumann (who was born here) restored it in the eighteenth century, only the bulky towers remain from the original thirteenth-century building, conceived as a monumental Romanesque basilica. In the northwestern corner of the town walls, the **Kaiserburg** (Chebský hrad; May–Sept Tues–Sun 9am–noon & 1–5pm) is an unpromising sprawl of ruins, built on and with volcanic rock: a remnant of the twelfth-century castle bequeathed by that obsessive crusader, the Holy Roman Emperor Frederick Barbarossa. In among the Baroque fortifications, the Gothic Černá věž (Black Tower) presents an impressive front and offers peeks at Cheb's chimneys and roof-tiles through its tiny windows. Stroll down to the lower storey of the ruined chapel in the northeastern corner for a glimpse of the castle in Barbarossa's time.

Františkovy Lázně (Franzensbad)

"The present Františkovy Lázně has nothing of historic interest", wrote Nagel's Guide in the 1960s, casually writing off a town hailed by Goethe as "paradise on earth". But, although **FRANTIŠKOVY LÁZNĚ**, 6km north of Cheb and linked by regular trains, may not boast any individual architectural gems, it is *the* archetypal spa town. The early nineteenth century's obsession with symmetry ensured a regular grid plan, barely five streets across, surrounded on all sides by parks and woods. Every conceivable building has been daubed in *Kaisergelb*, a soft ochre colour, set against a backdrop of luscious greenery.

Originally known as *Egerbrunnen*, the spa was founded in 1793 and named Franzensbad after the then Habsburg Emperor. The Neoclassical architecture of the Empire period finds its way into every building – even the cinema has Doric pilasters. The virtual absence of vehicles and rowdy nightlife make it the most peaceful of the spas, though as patients stagger about and people in white coats scamper between buildings, it can sometimes resemble a large open lunatic asylum.

The Town

From the crumbling yellow station, the road opens out onto the former *Kurpark*, whose principal path leads diagonally to a white wooden bandstand. This stands at the head of **Národní**, the spa's main boulevard, dotted with potted palms and ornamental cherry trees. Beethoven stayed at no. 7 in 1812, as the German plaque at the front and the eponymous garden café round the back recall. The diminutive splendour of the *Slovan* hotel's salons is also perfect for a coffee or something more substantial. At the opposite end of Národní, the **Františkův pramen** (Franzensquelle) is enclosed under a plain Classical rotunda. While the faithful queue to have their receptacles filled from the dazzling brass pipes, real spa snobs retire to drink from their beakers under the nearby colonnade. Like most spa water it's pretty unpalatable, on this occasion due to its high salt content. A different kind of faith drives women to touch the feet (and other parts) of a repulsive bronze cherub, who sits holding a phallic fish not far from the spring: Františkovy Lázně specialises in the treatment of gynaecological problems and popular myth has it that such a gesture will ensure fertility.

The 1820 church of **sv Kříž** strikes an appropriately imperial pose at one end of Jiráskova: another riot of princely mansions with wrought-iron balconies. Františkovy Lázně's finest spa pension, *Villa Imperiale*, is set apart from the other spa buildings, and nowadays is full of nouveaux (Western) imperialists enjoying a spa holiday for the price of a bed and breakfast. Older imperialists are on view in the **Spa Museum** (dr. Pohoreckého 8; Mon–Fri 9am–noon & 2–5pm), being subjected to gruesome nineteenth-century cures; don't miss the man with a leech on each buttock, held in place by two jam-jars.

The spa's formal parks quickly give way to untamed woodland, where there's a two-kilometre walk through the silver birches to Lake Amerika (in dry weather a *mikrovláčka* (mini-train) runs every 30min), though swimming is not advisable. On the other side of town, a path marked by red hearts leads to the popular *Zámeček Café*, hidden away amidst the acacia.

Practical details

Františkovy Lázně may not be the busiest spot in Bohemia, but there are so few **beds** available that it's often difficult to find a place. Try *ČEDOK* on Národní for the latest information. Luckily, there's a good **campsite** with **bungalows** 1500m southwest of the town, by the lake (open May–Sept), and Cheb is only 4km away across country (follow the red markers south down Klostermannova). If you walk to Cheb, incidentally, you go via Komorní Hůrka, a spinney on a hill that's the only surviving volcano in Bohemia – though no longer active.

Karlovy Vary (Karlsbad)

KARLOVY VARY, king of the famous triangle of Bohemian spas, is also one of the most cosmopolitan Czech towns. Its international clientele annually doubles the local population, which is further supplemented in the summer by thousands of able-bodied tourists. The narrow valley resounds with German, as well as the multifarious languages of central Europe, and, of course, Russian. Traditionally given the red carpet treatment, those Soviets with sufficient roubles continue to frequent the resort. Such a high density of foreigners has always ensured that the shops of Karlovy Vary are positively teeming with treats, at least by Czech standards; and the clientele looks set to diversify further in the 1990s.

Karlovy Vary is still better known throughout the world as **Karlsbad** (Carlsbad in its anglicised form), the nineteenth-century watering place of European notables, but its origins go back much further. Tradition grants Charles IV (or rather one of his hunting dogs) with discovery of the springs (hence Karslbad): in fact, the village of Vary (which means "boiling" in Czech) had existed for centuries before Charles' trip, though the king did found a German town here in around 1350, and set a precedent for subsequent Bohemian rulers by granting Karlsbad various privileges. By the nineteenth century its position at the meeting of two great German-speaking empires, and the much heralded efficacy of its waters, ensured the most impressive visitors' book in Europe.

> The telephone code for Karlovy Vary is ☎017.

Arriving and finding a place to stay

The **bus station** and the **main train station** are on opposing sides of the Ohře (Eger), both in the modern northern part of town. The shops and hotels in this part of town are cheaper than elsewhere, providing the otherwise invisible local residents with daily necessities. Half a kilometre south, the spa quarter stretches along the winding Teplá valley and is closed to motor vehicles, so like all good spa patients, you'll have to walk.

Accommodation

Since Karlovy Vary is packed out all summer, it's best to start looking for **accommodation** early in the day. The *ČEDOK* office at Tržiště 23, in the *Hotel Atlantic* (☎243 78), will find you a cheap **private room**, but may insist you stay for a minimum of three nights.

Of the **hotels**, the *Grand Hotel Pupp*, on Mírové náměstí 6 (☎221 21), starts the ball rolling with doubles for an arm and a leg. Equally grand and central, but less than half the price, is the *Atlantic*, Tržiště 23 (☎241 15). Nearer the station but further from the spa, the *Národní dům*, Masarykova 24 (☎233 86), is a cheap and seedy nineteenth-century option, while the prices at the *Turist*, Dimitrovova 18 (☎268 37), are rock bottom.

One of the country's few **youth hostels**, with dormitory beds for next to nothing, is part of *Juniorhotel Alice*, in the woods south of the spa at Pětiletky 1 (☎243 79); take bus #7 from behind the *Národní dům*. Just before the hostel is Karlovy Vary's **campsite**, behind *Motel Březova* (open May–Sept), which also lets out reasonable rooms.

Exploring the spa

By the time you reach the Poštovní most, 500m or so south of the bus station, the late nineteenth-century grandeur of Karlovy Vary begins to unfold along the river banks. The post office itself is a riot, inside and out, and a fitting introduction to

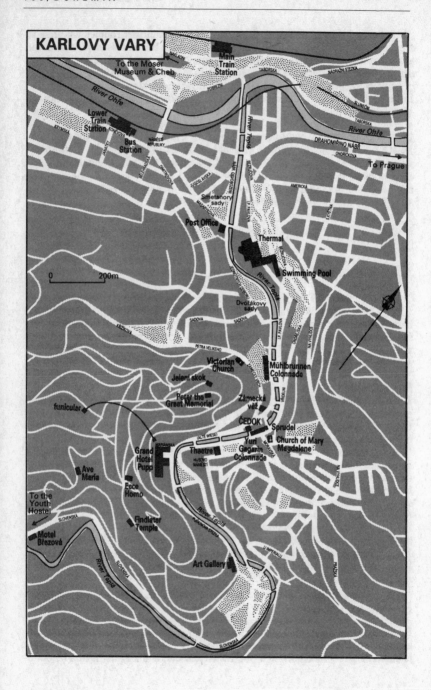

KARLOVY VARY

the row of stately spa pensions which line Jednotných odbarů. Difficult to miss is the **Thermal** sanatorium, an inexcusable concrete scab but a useful source of information for happenings in town (Mon–Fri 8am–5pm, Sat 9–11am) and a clear signpost for the open-air *bazén* (Mon–Sat 2–9.30pm, Sun 9am–9.30pm; closed third Mon in month), a spring-water **swimming pool** high up above the river. The poolside view over the town is wonderful, but don't be taken in by the clouds of steam – the water is only tepid. As the valley narrows, the river disappears under a wide terrace in front of the graceful **Mühlbrunnen Colonnade**, whose four separate springs are each more scalding than the last. If you've forgotten your cure cup, you can buy the tasteless *becher* vessels from one of the many souvenir shops, or cut costs and buy a plastic cup for half a crown. Popular wisdom has it that "when the disorder becomes a disease, doctors prescribe the hot waters of Carlsbad": in the eighteenth century, the poor were advised to drink up to five hundred cups of the salty waters to cure the disease of poverty. The German playwright Schiller (who came here in 1791) drank eighteen cups and lived to tell the tale, but generally no more than five to seven cups are recommended.

Sprudel and shopping

Most powerful of the twelve springs is the **Sprudel** (*Vřídlo* to the Czechs), which belches out over 2500 gallons of water every hour. The smooth marble floor of the new **Yuri Gagarin Colonnade** (he came here in the 1960s) allows patients to shuffle up and down contentedly, while inside the glass rotunda the geyser pops and splutters, shooting hot water forty feet upwards. Ensuing clouds of steam obscure what would otherwise be a perfect view of Dientzenhofer's Baroque masterpiece, the **Church of Mary Magdalene**, pitched nearby on a precipitous site. The light, pink interior is a refreshing interlude from the nineteenth-century, almost Victorian air of the rest of the town.

South of the Sprudel was Karlovy Vary's most famous shopping street, the former **Alte Wiese**, described by Le Corbusier as "a set of *Torten* (cakes) all the same style and the same elegance". Its shops, which once rivalled Vienna's Kärntnerstrasse, still exude the snobbery of former days, and though the new Moser glassware in the windows is in many ways inferior to stuff in the antique shop a few doors down*, the tea and cakes served on marble tables at the *Elefant Café* is a reminder of Karlovy Vary's halcyon days.

At the end of the Alte Wiese is the **Grand Hotel Pupp**, founded in 1701 as the greatest hotel in the world. At the turn of the century *Pupp*'s was *the* place to be seen, and became a meeting place for Europe's elite. Despite its lacklustre upkeep and careless modernisation, it can't fail to impress, and the cakes are still made to Mr Pupp's own recipe. On the opposite bank, the former *Kaiserbad* (Lázně no. 1) is another sumptuous edifice, styled like a theatre but actually the only socialist **casino** to survive the 1948 revolution. Even if you don't fancy a flutter (in hard currencies only; open from 4pm daily), it's worth checking out the luscious velvet and marble interior.

---

* A wider range of glassware can be seen at the **Moser museum** in the factory suburb of DVORY (take bus #1, #9 or #16). Everyone who's anyone has had a Moser glass made for them, from Stalin to the Shah, and can still buy the stuff direct from the factory (though you'll have to pay up to 100-percent duty on it at the border).

A certain Mr Charles Marx from London (as he signed himself in the visitors' book) visited the spa several times towards the end of his life, staying at the *Hotel Germania* (now predictably enough called the *Marx*), at Zámecký vrch 41, above the Mühlbrunnen Colonnade. He was under police surveillance each time, but neither his daughter Eleanor's letters (she was with him on both trips) nor the police reports have much to say about the old revolutionary, except that he took the waters at 6am (as was the custom) and went on long walks. The Communists couldn't resist setting up a Karl Marx Museum, just down from the Mühlbrunnen Colonnade: it used to pad out the flimsy connection, but now faces an uncertain future.

Walking in the hills

Of all the spas, Karlovy Vary's constitutional **walks** are the most physically taxing and visually rewarding. You can let the **funicular** (*lanovka*) take the strain by hopping aboard one of the trains (9.30am–4.30pm; every 15min) from behind *Hotel Pupp*, which drop you at a café and viewpoint. Alternatively, you can climb up through the beech and oak trees to the wooden crucifix above the Alte Wiese, and then on to the spectacular panorama where the **Peter the Great Memorial** commemorates the Russian Tsar and a dozen or so royal hangers-on. In season, you can enjoy the (not so savoury) view northwards from the **Jelení skok** restaurant, which serves food and drink (Tues–Sun 10am–6pm). The road below slopes down to Zámecký vrch, which the English aristocracy used to ascend in order to absolve their sins at the red-brick **Victorian Church**. Clearly visible, high on the opposite bank, is the **Imperial**, a huge fortress hotel, built in 1912 to rival *Pupp*'s and flying in the face of the popular Art-Nouveau architecture of the spa.

The most popular level walk is along the Puškinova stezka towards Karlovy Vary's main **art gallery** (Tues–Sun 9am–noon & 1–5pm), which contains some unremarkable twentieth-century Czech canvases and a disappointingly limited selection of glassware.

Eating, drinking and entertainment

What I indulged in, what I enjoyed
What I conceived there
What joy, what knowledge
But it would be too long a confession
I hope all will enjoy it that way
Those with experience and the uninitiated..

Needless to say, Goethe had a good time here. His coy innuendos are a reference to the enduring reputation of spas like Karlovy Vary for providing romantic distraction. Dancing, after all, was encouraged by the spa doctors as a means of losing weight. These days, however, there are few places, except *Pupp*'s, in which you can indulge yourself in a similar fashion.

The *Francouzská restaurace* at the *Grand Hotel Pupp* is without doubt the place **to eat**, not least because of the decor; but it's not cheap, and you must reserve a table. Otherwise, you'll have to make do with the less exclusive *Plzeňská restau-*

race, situated in the hotel's modern wing (and dubbed "the crematorium" by the locals). If you'd rather mix with Czechs, Slovaks and Gypsies, head for the *Národní dům*'s restaurant or the *Jizera* on Dimitrovova. Serious beer **drinking** goes on at the *Budvar*, I.P. Pavlova 8, and at the *Gambrinus* pub on Moskevská.

Coffee and cakes are in better supply. Apart from the *Elefant* and the cafés up in the woods, cheaper places include the *Continental* at Tržiště 27, or the *Italská cukrárna*, opposite the *Národní dům*. *Café Pupp*'s **breakfast** is legendary but expensive.

Karlovy Vary's **cultural life** is pretty varied; from classical concerts at the former *Kurhaus* (Lázně #3) and occasionally at *Pupp*'s, to the hysterically bad variety shows at the *Národní dům*. The town also plays host to Czechoslovakia's **International Film Festival**, held in August in even-numbered years. For details of what's going on, ask at the box office (open Mon–Fri 8am–5pm, Sat 9–11pm) in the *Thermal* complex.

Around Karlovy Vary: Loket and Jáchymov

Halfway between Karlovy Vary and Loket, to the southwest, as the beautiful blue-marked track crosses over to the left bank of the River Ohře, the giant pillar-like rocks of the **Svatošské skály** (Hans Heiling Felsen), which have inspired writers from Goethe to the Brothers Grimm, loom out of the wooded river bank. After 10km you reach **LOKET** (Elbogan), which gets its name – *loket* means elbow – from the sharp bend in the Ohře that provides a dramatic setting for this minute hilltop town. The thirteenth-century **hrad**, which slots into the precipitous fortifications is due to reopen as a **Museum of Porcelain**, displaying wares which have been manufactured in the town for centuries. Also on display should be the meteorite, weighing nearly a ton, which was found at the bottom of a well in 1775.

Loket's picturesque houses form a garland around the base of the castle, the narrow backstreets sheltering Saxon houses and secluded courtyards like Sklenařská, where the redundant German sign *Glaser Gasse* has been left unmolested. On the main square, the only **accommodation** available is at the *Weisses Ross* (now the *Bílý kůn*), a sky-blue neo-Gothic hotel where Goethe met his last love, Ulrike von Lewetzow: he in his seventies, she a mere seventeen.

The uranium mines at Jáchymov

JÁCHYMOV (Joachimsthal), 20km northeast of Karlovy Vary and only 5km from the German border, will probably never recover from its past. In the early 1950s literally thousands of citizens (many of them former Communist Party members) were rounded up during the country's Stalinist terror and sentenced to hard labour in the **uranium mines** to the north of the town. Underfed and subject to harsh treatment by their Soviet gaolers, untold numbers died of exhaustion, starvation and leukaemia.

Joachimsthal was founded in the sixteenth century, when silver deposits were discovered. The royal mint established here struck the famous *Joachimsthaler* (eventually giving rise to the *Dollar*, a corrupt form of the abbreviation *Thaler*). In 1896 the Frenchman Henri Bequerel discovered uranium, and it was from Joachimsthal uranium that Marie and Pierre Curie discovered radium earlier this century. The experiment proved as fatal to them as it did to the generations of German miners who worked the pits: even under the First Republic their average life expectancy was forty-two years. Although the mine was closed down in 1964, radiation levels far in excess of World Health Organisation (WHO) safety levels were recorded in the town in the 1980s, and calls for the immediate evacuation of the village were made by the youth journal *Mladá fronta* even before the Velvet Revolution. Despite this, the citizens of Jáchymov continue to work in the local tobacco factory and the Marie Curie spa pension, where patients are "cured" by the town's radioactive springs. Our advice is don't hang around.

NORTH BOHEMIA

North Bohemia (Severní Čechy) splits conveniently into two roughly equal halves, divided by the River Labe (Elbe). Historically part of Bohemia since the first Přemyslid princes, but ethnically Teutonic for most of the millennium, there are now no more than a few thousand Germans left. In the eastern half, where the frontier mountains are less pronounced, two rich German cities developed: **Liberec** (Reichenberg), built on its cloth industry, and **Jablonec** (Gablonz), which relied on jewellery, with smaller mixed settlements in the very north producing Bohemia's world-famous crystal and glass. The western part has its borders in the forests of the **Krušné hory** (Erzegebirge or Ore Mountains) which – as their name suggests – have long been a source of great mineral wealth, providing material for porcelain, and, more latterly, uranium. Thousands of Saxons drifted over the ill-defined border in the Middle Ages, some taking up their traditional wood-based crafts, others working in the mines which sprung up along the base of the mountains. By the end of the nineteenth century **factories** and **mines** had become as much a part of the landscape of North Bohemia as mountains and chateaux. Then, with the collapse of the Empire, the new-born Czechoslovak state inherited three-quarters of the Habsburg industry, and at a stroke became the world's tenth most industrialised country.

German and Czech miners remained loyal to the Left throughout the slump of the 1930s, but the majority of North Bohemia's *Volk* put their trust in the proto-Nazi Sudeten German Party or SdP, with disastrous consequences for the country – and for Europe. Allied bombings took their toll during the war and, in accordance with the Potsdam agreement, the German population was expelled in 1945. However, economic necessity ensured that the region was quickly rebuilt and resettled, and the ensuing Five Year Plans intensified industrial development.

Areas of outstanding natural beauty like **Český Švýcarsko**, and towns of architectural finesse, like **Litoměřice**, still exist, but the last forty years of unbridled industrialisation have irrevocably marred the land and lives of North Bohemia. While the rest of Europe was belatedly tempering sulphur emissions and increasing fuel efficiency, the Czechs were steadily sinking to fortieth place in the world league of industrial powers, and rising to first place for male mortality rates, cancer and still-births. It's easy to blame all these calamities on the factory fetishism of the Communists, but damage to the forests of the Ore Mountains was noted even before World War II, and smog levels have irritated the citizens of local towns for the best part of this century. Yet now that the voices of dissent have been unleashed, the outlook is not all bleak. It's worth remembering that the first demonstration of the 1989 revolution took place not in Prague but in **Teplice** – against environmental pollution. For more on this issue, see "The Environment" in *Contexts*.

West up the River Ohře

There are three walled towns on the **River Ohře** (Eger), foolishly neglected by most travellers eager to reach Karlovy Vary and the spas of West Bohemia. With your own transport, all three can be easily covered in a day; by public transport, it's best to take your pick and concentrate on just one or two towns.

Louny

LOUNY is the first of the medieval fortified towns on the Ohře, its perfect Gothic appearance all but entirely destroyed by fire in 1517 – all, that is, except the strikingly beautiful church of **sv Mikuláš**, whose triple pyramidal roof was rebuilt by the German mason Benedikt Ried who died here in 1534. There's a small art gallery named after him on the main square, next door to the town museum, and a good second-hand bookshop opposite, but otherwise little reason to stay the night at the *Union* hotel, just off the square.

Žatec

ŽATEC (Saaz), 24km up the Ohře from Louny, is the centre of the hop-growing region which supports Czechoslovakia's famous beer industry. From here south as far as Rakovník (Rakonitz) the roads are hemmed in by the endless tall, green groves of hop vines. No one quite knows why Czech hops are the best in the world for brewing beer, but everyone accepts the fact, and even German beer giants like *Stella Artois* import them in preference to their own. As long ago as the twelfth century, Bohemia's *Žatec Red* hops have been sent down the Elbe to the Hamburg hop market, and Žatec's biggest annual binge is still the September hop festival held in the town square.

The **old town** itself, on the hilltop opposite the train station, is a scruffy, vaguely medieval affair, with two of its fifteenth-century western gates still intact. In those days the town was predominantly Czech but the next three centuries brought wave upon wave of German immigrants, until it became a distinctly German town. The central square, headed by the plain pink Renaissance radnice, is not exactly impressive despite its age – "spoiled by Classicist adaptations" according to the unusually critical *ČEDOK* brochure. Behind it, the town's Jesuit church is guarded by a wonderful gallery of beatific sculptures, while the town **brewery** (no admission) occupies pride of place in the old thirteenth-century hrad.

If you're given a choice between the town's two **hotels**, *Družba* (on the main square; ☎32 26) and *Zlatý lev* (on Oblouková; ☎28 20), make for the faded net curtains and musty chandeliers of the latter, which preserve the hotel's 1920s origins. For something cheaper, *ČEDOK* (on the main square) may be able to arrange a bed for the night in one of the town's two cheap **hostels**.

Kadaň

Very much in the same mould as the other two towns, **KADAŇ** (Kadaan), 22km west, is nevertheless the most substantial halt on the Ohře before Karlovy Vary. From the train station, enter the old town walls through the round whitewashed barbican of the Žatec gate. The church on the main square is down to its bricks and mortar in places, and the rest of the town maintains a dusty air of neglect about its eighteenth-century buildings. On the opposite side of the square is **Katovská** ("Hangman's street" – his house is below the gate at the end) which must be Bohemia's narrowest street, barely more than a passage, the light straining to make its way past the maze of buttresses. At the southern tip of town, Kadaň's recently renovated **hrad**, a modest domestic seat, sits over the Ohře, one wing now a hotel, *vinárna* and exhibition gallery. From a gate by the side of the hrad you can gain access to the best preserved part of the town **walls**.

If you need to stay over, there's a choice of three **hotels**: the *Zelený strom* (Green Tree) on Jiráskova, which couldn't be more inappropriately named, *Svoboda* on the main square, and the flash set-up in the castle.

The North Bohemian coal basin

The **North Bohemian brown coal basin** contrives to be even less enticing than it sounds. It forms an almost continuous sixty-kilometre rash of mines, factories and prefabricated towns, from Kadaň to Ústí nad Labem. Not only are the notorious Hamr uranium mines located in this region, but 75 percent of all Czechoslovakia's brown coal is mined here, the majority of it from just ten metres below the surface. Huge tracts of land at the foot of the **Krušné hory** have been transformed by giant insect-like diggers which crawl across fields of brown sludge like the last surviving cockroaches in a post-nuclear desert. Around one hundred villages have been bulldozed, the rail and road link east of Chomutov shifted south, and the entire town of Most flattened to make way for the ever-expanding mines. Not only is the stuff extracted here, much of it is burnt locally too, and brown coal is particularly nasty stuff – far and away the filthiest and most harmful of all fossil fuels. You can't fail to see the lethal white clouds billowing out of the country's power stations at Tušimice and Prunéřove, both less than 5km north and east of Kadaň.

Most to Duchcov

The only building in **MOST** (Brüx) to survive the town's recent migration was the early sixteenth-century church, which was moved brick by brick to the new location, 841 metres away. Otherwise, there's only the familiar prefab desolation here. At **LITVÍNOV** (Oberleutensdorf), 6km north of Most, the unwelcome bonus of a huge chemical plant just south of the town, coupled with the constant sulphur emissions, creates a bank of cloud which regularly blots out the sun and reduces all light to a grey haze. At the side of the road there are special lights which switch on above the simple command "RED LIGHT STOP! SWITCH OFF YOUR ENGINE!" when the authorities deem the chemical levels too dangerous. Somewhat incredibly, Litvínov still has the leftovers of its nineteenth-century *Ringstrasse*, now boarded up and long since overtaken by the town's new constructions. At first **DUCHCOV** (Dux), 8km further east, appears no different, encircled as it is by coal mines. But in this unlikely location a grandly conceived, though unexceptional, Baroque **zámek** contains a small exhibition dedicated to the world's most famous bounder, **Casanova**, who whiled away his final years as librarian in these staid surroundings, writing his steamy memoirs.

Teplice-Šanov

In the midst of this polluted region lies the traumatised town of **TEPLICE-ŠANOV** (Teplitz-Schönau), the forgotten fourth spa of the once celebrated quartet of Bohemian resorts that included Karlsbad, Marienbad and Franzensbad. In the nineteenth century it became "the drawing room of Europe", prompting the likes of Chopin, Liszt and Beethoven to appear on its *Kurliste*. But already in the 1880s, the all-too adjacent mining industry had inflicted its first blow to Teplice's idyllic way of life: the nearby Döllinger mine breached an underwater lake, flooding the natural springs which have had to be artificially pumped to the surface ever since. The lingering smell of lignite was just one of the town's more memorable characteristics, now enhanced by the addition of other noxious chemical vapours. But the accumulative cost of this assault on the environment is more serious. Teplice is no place to winter, as the smog wraps itself round the town for weeks and the sulphur dioxide levels sometimes reach 25 times the WHO safety maximum.

The Town

Arriving at the old *Aussiger Bahnhof* (now Teplice v Čechách nádraží) injects a sense of hope in innocent minds, with its rich neo-Renaissance frescoes adorning the vaulted ceiling, though this is soon dispelled by block after block of silent and peeling nineteenth-century houses which stand between the station and the centre. Even the old **Kur Garten** has a somewhat deseased air about it, despite the lively sounds of birdlife. The white concrete box of the **Dům kultury** is the dominant feature of the park now, fronted by the **New Colonnade**, a glorified greenhouse made up from some of Bohemia's great glass surplus. Only when you cross the valley to the monumental **Schloss** is it just about possible to make the imaginative leap into Teplice's arcadian past. The Schloss was the seat of the Clary-Aldringen family until 1945 when they, and most other Teplitzers, took flight from the approaching Red Army. The countless rooms of the castle museum (Tues–Sun 9am–noon & 1–5pm) contain memorials to Goethe, Beethoven and Pushkin, wall-to-wall Biedermeyer and much else besides.

Outside the main gates, the Zámecké náměstí, a narrow lane past the Catholic church, leads to a series of brightly coloured houses in austere Empire style, including the *Zlaté slunce* (Golden Sun) where Beethoven once stayed. South of here, a splendid staircase takes you past the twin turrets of the *U Petra* restaurant to the **Schlossgarten**, which spreads itself around two lakes.

The rest of the spa lies in the eastern part of town, once the separate village of Šanov (Schönau), linked by Lipová (Lindenstrasse), which still clings on to its lime trees, despite the acid onslaught.

Staying, drinking and eating

In order of preference, Teplice's two **hotels** are the *Hotel de Saxe* (☎66 48) on the corner of Masarykova and Husitská, near the main station, and the *Thermia* (☎21 51), both moderately priced. Teplice's top **restaurant** is, without doubt, *U Petra* by the Schloss, but you'll get just as good stuff for half the price at the *restaurace* on Zámecké náměstí. Assembling a **picnic** or grabbing a quick snack are both best done in the dark, old-fashioned interior of the shop opposite the *Thermia*.

Litoměřice and around

Once you've reached **LITOMĚŘICE** (Leitmeritz), at the confluence of the Ohře and the Labe, you've left the worst of North Bohemia behind. And despite the sight of the Lovosice chemical works on the horizon, the town feels safely out of danger, its feet firmly in the food basket of Bohemia which lies to the south. Litoměřice was the third or fourth city of Bohemia in the Middle Ages, but the dislocation of the Thirty Years' War is still visible in the town. Nowadays, it has a dusty neglected air, much like the other towns on the Ohře, and the main reason people come here is to pay their respects at Terezín, the country's most infamous concentration camp, just south of the town.

Even if you're here for the same reason, you'd be wrong to dismiss the town itself, for Litoměřice is a virtual museum for **Octavio Broggio**. Broggio was born here in 1668 and, along with his father Giulio, redesigned the town's many churches, following the arrival of the Jesuits and the establishment of a Catholic bishopric in the mid-seventeenth century. The reason for this zealous re-Catholicisation was Litoměřice's rather too eager conversion to the heretical beliefs of the Hussites and its disastrous allegiance to the Protestants in the Thirty Years' War.

The Town

Stepping out of the train station, you'll notice the town's last remaining bastion across the road; behind it lies the historical quarter, which is entered via the wide boulevard of Dlouhá. There's no better place to understand the town's rich religious heritage than at the hybrid church of **All Saints** at the top of the street. It started life as a Romanesque church and now boasts the only Gothic spire left on the skyline, a beautiful wedge-shaped affair reminiscent of Prague's right bank. But its grand Broggio frontage is misplaced, raising expectations which are quickly disappointed by the oppressively low ceiling and the dusty furnishings.

The town's vast cobbled marketplace is best known for the **Mrázovský dům** (at no. 15), whose owner, a devout Hussite, had a huge *kalich* (chalice) – the symbol of all Hussites – plonked on the roof in 1537. West of the square, the **Severočeská galerie** (Tues–Sun 9am–noon & 2–5pm) is set in a wonderfully rambling sixteenth-century building on Michalská, its inner courtyard draped in ivy and echoing to the trickle of a modern fountain. Exhibitions doing the Bohemian circuit stop off here, supplementing the already handsome permanent collection of Czech works and the sculpture terrace round the back.

Cathedral hill

On a promontory 500m southwest of the town centre, the **Cathedral hill**, where the bishop and his entourage once held residence, was originally an entirely separate entity, with its own fortifications. On its northern slope, the small, pasty chapel of **sv Václav** is in many ways the younger Broggio's finest work, grand despite its cramped proportions and location. But the reason to come this far is to wonder at the former cathedral of **sv Štěpán**, on the grassy Dómské náměstí, which Giulio Broggio (among others) redesigned in the second half of the seventeenth century. This work marked the start of the extensive rebuilding of Litoměřice and the cathedral's interior is full of light touches missing from the later churches, set against the dark wood and gloomy altar paintings from the school of the German master Lucas Cranach. Outside, the freestanding *campanile* adds a peculiarly Tuscan touch.

A path along the north side of sv Štěpán leads down to the *vinárna* at no. 177, where the Czech poet **Karel Hynek Mácha** died in 1836. The house next door – built after Mácha's untimely death – contains a small exhibition (Tues–Sun 10am–5pm) on the life of the old Romantic, whose most famous poem *Máj* (May) was hijacked by the Communists as their May Day anthem. He was once buried in the local cemetery, but when the Nazis drew up the Sudetenland borders Litoměřice lay inside Germany, so the Czechs dug him up and reinterred him in Prague. Once you've reached the bottom of the cathedral hill, the stairway of the Máchovy schody will take you back up into town.

Practicalities

The **train station** and **bus terminal** are southeast of the old town. Cross the road and walk a short way up Dlouhá, and you'll come to *ČEDOK* who can help you find **hotel** vacancies. The cheapest option – which *ČEDOK* may not mention – is the *Hotel Rak* (☎24 36) on the main square, which lets out its dirty doubles for next to nothing. Otherwise, it's the high-rise *Sechezy* (☎24 51), Vrchlického 10, in the housing estate northeast of town. There's a **campsite** with **bungalows** (and an open-air cinema) open June to September in the woods between the railway line and the river.

Don't go looking for **nightlife** – you won't find any – though you could try the *Vinárna Vikarka* (closed Thurs), where Mácha met his death, and where you can sample some of the local wine, *Müller-Thurgau*. Alternatively, you can get basic **food** and go for some local beer at *Pivnice Kalich* (closed Sat & Sun), north off the main square.

Terezín (Theresienstadt)

The main road from Prague to Berlin passes right through the fortress town of **TEREZÍN**, just 3km south of Litoměřice. Purpose-built in the 1780s by the Habsburgs, and capable of accommodating 14,500 soldiers and hundreds of prisoners, it defended the northern border against Prussia. Although the **Main Fortress** itself was never put to the test in battle, Terezín remained – as it does today – a garrison town. As you enter, the red-brick fortifications are still an awesome sight, though the huge moat has been put out of action by the local gardening enthusiasts. As a town it's an eerie, soulless place, built to a dour eighteenth-century grid plan, its bare streets still ringing with the sounds of soldiers and military police.

The Lesser Fortress

On the other side of the River Ohře, east down Pražská, lies the **Lesser Fortress**, built at the same time as a military prison*, and now a memorial and museum to the 35,000 or more who died here during the darkest period of Terezín's history – the Nazi occupation of the fortress during World War II.

---

* The prison was used by the Habsburgs to encarcerate enemies of the Empire, such as the young Bosnian **Gavrilo Princip**, who succeded in shooting the archduke Ferdinand in 1914, thereby precipitating World War I.

Between 1941 and 1942, the whole town was turned into a transit camp and **ghetto** for Jews and other Nazi prisoners en route to their deaths at Buchenwald and other nearby camps. Although the main fortress was theoretically not an extermination camp, the SS prison, established in the lesser fortress in 1940, had all the trappings of a concentration camp.

Yet one of the sickest ironies of Terezín is that it was billed by the Nazis as a model camp: when the International Red Cross asked to inspect one of the Nazi camps, they were brought here and treated to a week of Jewish cultural events, including the staging of an opera, a jazz band concert and a host of other activities, the like of which – needless to say – were never seen before or after their visit.

There is no guided tour to the lesser fortress, so it's worth buying the brief broadsheet guide to the prison in English. The infamous Nazi refrain – *Arbeit Macht Frei* (Work brings freedom) – is daubed across the entrance on the left, which leads to the exemplary washrooms, built for the Red Cross tour of inspection and still standing. The rest of the camp has been left empty but intact, and graphically evokes the appalling, cramped conditions under which the prisoners were kept half-starved and badly clothed, subject to indiscriminate cruelty and execution. The main **exhibition** is housed in the smart eighteenth-century mansion set in the prison gardens, home to the Camp Kommandant, his family and fellow SS officers. There's a short documentary, intelligible in any language, regularly shown in the cinema which was set up in 1942 to entertain the prison officers.

The lesser fortress and exhibition are open daily (9am–5pm). The town itself is accessible by bus or a short walk from Litoměřice. It's difficult to imagine a less appealing place to stay, but stay you may, at the *Parkhotel*, Máchova 1, or the nearby **campsite** (May to mid-Sept).

Ploskovice and Úštěk

On a lighter note, just 6km northeast of Litoměřice is the crisp, light summer **zámek** (30-min guided tour; April–Oct Tues–Sun 8am–4pm) in the village of **PLOSKOVICE**. The rusting scaffolding which accompanies all Czech renovation jobs is still in place, but hopefully the fountains will soon issue forth and the whole place – sometimes frivolous, sometimes tasteless, always fun – and its beautiful walled grounds will flourish once more.

Bypassed by the main road – and, it seems, by life itself – for the last three centuries, **ÚŠTĚK** (50min by train from Litoměřice) originally grew up around the now-ruined medieval fortress. It's not sufficiently picturesque to go out of your way for, but if you're **camping** (May–Sept) out by the pleasant sandy-beached Chlemař lake, behind the railway station, you should definitely wander into town. On one side of the main street there's a line of fourteenth-century burgher houses, which – uniquely for Bohemia – still retain their original triangular gables made of wood or slate. Down by the Úštěcký stream to the southwest of the town, in among the geese and hens, there are some fascinating wooden shacks, known as the **ptačí domky** (birds' houses). Perched on top of each other on the highest ledge of the steeply terraced banks, they provided ad hoc accommodation for the Italian workers who built the town's railway link in the late nineteenth century.

Český Švýcarsko

The sandstone rocks of **Český Švýcarsko** (Bohemian Switzerland), at a sharp crack in the geographical defences of Bohemia, have delighted visitors on both sides of the border for centuries. Like the other "rock-cities", in the Český ráj (see p.183) and the Broumov region (see p.193), the whole area was formed when volcanic rock thrust its way to the surface, causing fissures and cracks in the land which later widened. The result is probably the most impressive geological amusement park in the country; a dense network of mini-canyons and bluffs all covered in a blanket of woodland. At the centre of the region lies Děčín, a busy inland port straddling the Elbe, whose tourist attractions are limited but which serves as a convenient base for exploring the surrounding hills.

Děčín

Despite being in German hands for most of the last thousand years, **DĚČÍN** has long been the gateway to Bohemia. Its castle, which rises up to the east as you enter the country from Dresden, was once the stronghold of the Slav tribe Děčané. Modern Děčín is really two towns – **Děčín** (Tetschen) itself and **Podmolky** (Bodenbach) – divided by the River Labe, which has always been the driving force behind the town's economy.

The main point of **arrival** is the grubby hlavní nádraží in Podmolky, which looks out on to the *Grand Hotel*'s mass of grey concrete, and an unsightly state supermarket. It's not a great start, but then Podmolky was a late developer, only coming into existence in 1850 through the amalgamation of three villages on the left bank. Sixty years of furious building followed, funded by the town's flourishing shipping industry, the results of which are still visible in the four or five blocks west of the station, where the local Gypsies and neighbouring Saxons while away the hours window-shopping and wolfing down ice cream. To cross the river to Děčín, take any of the buses outside the station.

Despite its superior antiquity, Děčín itself is hampered by the fact that its showpiece, the **Schloss Tetschen-Bodenbach** – a simple but beautiful eighteenth-century pile, elevated above the town on an isolated lump of rock – is now a barracks and therefore closed to the public. Visitors have to content themselves with a stroll through the rosebeds of the castle's Baroque gardens, up the steps on the north face of the rock.

With time to kill, and an interest in seamanship and navigation, you can spend a happy hour in the **Museum of Elbe Transport**, situated in a former hunting lodge behind the *Hotel Sever* in Podmolky. Alternatively, head for the meringue-coloured mansion (ultra-violet at night), atop the **Pastýřská stěna** (Shepherd's Rock), accessible by a lift (*výtah*) cut into the rock on the left bank of the river: the return trip costs four local bus tickets. There's a small café here, with an incredible view over Děčín, and, nearby, a small zoo.

Practical details

Hotels divide into those in Podmolky – the moderate *Grand* (☎0412-270 41) and even more reasonable *Sever* (☎0412-223 61), both by the main station – and the cheap *Pošta* (☎0412-228 31), on the main square in Děčín (bus #8 or #9 from Podmolky). There's a small **campsite** on the south side of the castle rock, but there are much nicer sites in the Český Švýcarsko itself, for more on which see below. *ČEDOK*, at Prokopa Holého 8 in Podmokly, can give you the times of the daily **ferries** to HŘENSKO and DRESDEN which depart from just past the Tyršův most on the Děčín side.

Walking in the Český Švýcarsko

The Český Švýcarsko splits neatly in half with Děčín as the meeting point. Whichever part you're heading for, it's a good idea to get hold of the 1:50,000 *Český Švýcarsko* **map** which marks all campsites and footpaths in the area. The popular **Jetřichovické stěny**, to the northeast of Děčín, are topographically more interesting and cover a much greater area than their western counterparts. At their base runs the Kamenice river, accessible in parts only by the popular boat trips. The smaller range to the west, the **Děčínské stěny**, are less spectacular, but don't suffer from the same human traffic jams and, what's more, can be easily reached from Děčín itself as a hiking day trip.

Jetřichovické stěny

The only way to get to the Jetřichovické stěny and the Kamenice gorge is by bus, since the railway line from Děčín follows the left bank, which falls into German territory. Three or four weekday **buses** make the roundabout journey to Jetřichovice, via Hřensko, Tří prameny, Mezní Louka and Mezná, or you can take one of the two morning **boats** (May–Aug), which run from D ěčín to Hřensko.

Despite its mountainous setting, **HŘENSKO** (Herrnskretchen), at 116m above sea level, is the lowest point in Bohemia. It's a pretty village on the right bank of the Labe, lined with half-timbered houses and redolent of Saxony, which faces it on the opposite bank. Todays Hřensko makes its living out of the German day-trippers flocking to the nearby rocks, and its one hotel, the *Labe*, which is usually full.

By far the most popular destination is the **Pravčická brána**, at 30m long and 21m high the largest natural stone bridge in Europe. It's a two-kilometre hike up from Tří prameny, a clearing 3km up the road from Hřensko. It's a truly breath-taking sight, though not one you're likely to enjoy alone unless you get there very early or out of season. The German border is less than 1km away, but the red-marked path which appears to head towards it actually rejoins the road 4.5km further east at **MEZNÍ LOUKA**, whose hotel of the same name is invariably full in season, but whose **campsite** has cheap bungalows (May–Sept) for rent.

From Mezní Louka, the path continues another 14km to Jetřichovice, meandering through the southern part of the complex of mini-canyons, taking in the **Malá Pravčická brána**, a smaller version of the bridge, and a couple of very ruined border castles. **JETŘICHOVICE** itself is an old Saxon hamlet made up of huge wooden farmsteads typical of the region, their present-day Czech owners keeping up Germanic standards of cleanliness and domesticity. Just south of the village, across a ford, there's a **campsite** and swimming pool (open in high season only).

The Kamenice gorge

Another option from Mezní Louka is to walk the 2km southwest to **MEZNÁ**, an unassuming little village which basks in a sunny meadow above the Kamenice. From the village green, a green-marked path plunges a hundred feet down to the cool, dank shade of the river, traversed by means of the wooden Mezní můstek

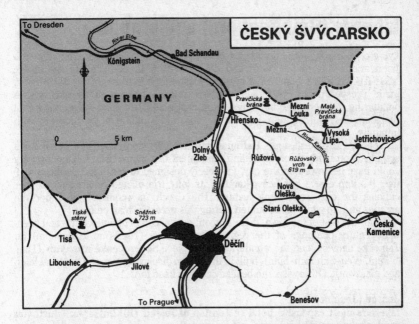

ČESKÝ ŠVÝCARSKO

bridge. Here, you have a choice of heading up or down the **Kamenice gorge** to the landing stages, from where boatmen will take you on a short but dramatic boat trip down (or up) the river. The trips (May to mid-Sept) are justifiably popular so be prepared to wait a couple of hours at least in high season. The downstream trip drops you a few kilometres from Hřensko, while the upstream one unloads its passengers close to Dolský Mlýn. If you're keen to do some more walking, take the latter trip and continue along the yellow-marked path up a shallower gorge to Jetřichovice.

Děčínské stěny

If your sole aim is to see the rocks, it's simplest to catch a bus from Děčín to Tisá; or take the train to LIBOUCHEC station and walk the 2.5km north to Tisá. If, however, you're intent on a day's walking, follow the red-marked path from the bridge by the castle in Děčín 10km to **Sněžník** (728m), a giant rock plateau which has thrust itself up above the decaying tree line. From here, there's a great view over the flat, forested landscape into Germany, and back over to the Jetřichovické stěny. The path then swings north to OSTROV, the last village before the border, before returning to the main road at Tisá. Alternatively, you could shortcut by walking straight to Tisá along the tarmacked road.

From the village of **TISÁ** itself, the **Tiské stěny** are hidden from view, but climb the hill and the whole "sandstone city" opens up before you. Sandy trails crisscross this secret gully and it's fairly simple to get to the top of one or two of the gigantic boulders without any specialist equipment. You could spend hours here, exploring, picnicking and taking in the panoramic views. It's a full day's walk from Děčín, so if you want to hole up here for the night, there's a **motel** and **campsite** just off the road west to Nový Dvůr (open all year).

Liberec (Reichenberg) and around

Lying comfortably in the broad east–west sweep of the Nisa valley, framed by the Jizera mountains to the north and the isolated peak of Ještěd to the south, **LIBEREC** couldn't hope for a grander location. Sadly though, the town itself, made prosperous by its famous textiles, doesn't live up to its environs. A smattering of interesting buildings and a couple of fairly good museums are all that's on offer, and, if you're in a hurry, you could continue on your journey with impunity.

Liberec's cathedralesque **Rathaus** which totally dominates the small main square, is probably the most telling monument the chauvinistic Reichenbergers could have bestowed on the city. Purposely designed to recall its Viennese relative, it's impressive but heavy-handed, its lofty trio of neo-Renaissance copper cupolas the only redeeming feature. The Czech "newcomers" sit under the arcades and sip white wine, contemplating this great German edifice.

As for the rest of the town, there's an offbeat collection of nineteenth- and twentieth-century paintings at the regional **art gallery** (Tues–Sun 10am–6pm) on Zámecké náměstí, and the wonderful period piece **Severočeské muzeum** (Tues 1–5pm, Wed–Sun 9am–5pm), built in the 1890s, displaying some of the local linen and glasswork. Otherwise, the best advice is to head for . . .

Ještěd (Jeschken)

Liberec's most expensive hotel sits on top of **Ještěd** (1012m), from which you can look over into Poland and Germany on a clear day. Even if you don't decide to

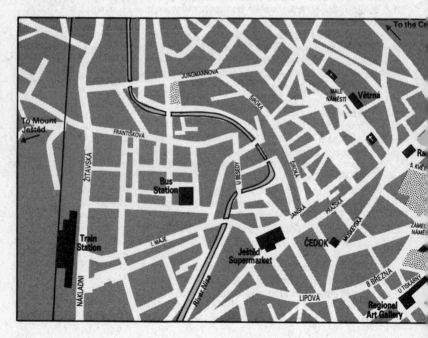

KONRAD HENLEIN IN REICHENBERG

Had Liberec been a little further northwest, it could have lived on in the post-war world as **Reichenberg**. Sited just the wrong side of the historical borders of Germany, the Reichenbergers made up for this geographical oversight with their ardent Pan-Germanism. It was the home town of Czechoslovakia's ultimate fifth columnist, **Konrad Henlein**, born in the nearby village of Reichenau (Rychnov) in 1898 and destined to become the leader of the pro-Nazi Sudeten German Party (SdP). Henlein played an unheroic role in World War I, and after a spell as a bank clerk in Reichenau he became a gym teacher in the pure German town of Asch (Aš) in West Bohemia. The combined effects of the slump and the events in the neighbouring German Reich excited the Sudeten Germans, who proclaimed Henlein their *Führer* at a huge rally outside Saaz (Žatec) in 1933. When the newly formed SdP won roughly two-thirds of the German votes in the 1935 elections (thus becoming the largest single party in the country), Reichenberg became a centre of pro-Nazi sentiment. However, few of the Germans survived the post-war expulsions and Liberec (unlike Cheb) was swiftly repopulated and successfully Czechified after the war.

stay the night (not a cheap option by any means), be sure to check out the bar-cum-diner and the restaurant with its crazy mirrors, either of which wouldn't look out of place in an episode of *Thunderbirds*. From the centre of town, take tram #3 to the end of the line and then follow the signs to the **cable car** (*lanovka dráha*), which runs to the summit and hotel from 6am to 10pm all year.

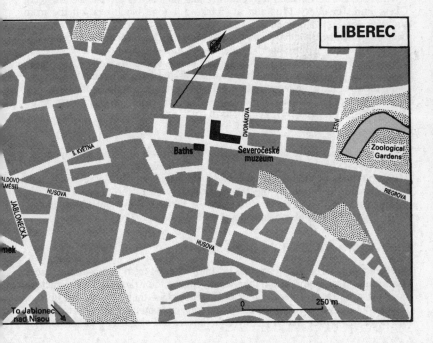

Practical matters

From the **train station**, you can reach the centre on foot in ten minutes, or take any of the trams or buses waiting outside. The **bus terminal** is fractionally closer to town, on Na rybničku. Next door to the bus terminal, the *Česká Beseda* (☎231 61) is the first of Liberec's rock-bottom **hotels**. Others include the *Terminus* (☎243 68), between the two stations, and *U potůčku* (bus #15 from the main theatre to the end, then walk up Na výběžku) – though it's probably best to check on vacancies first through *ČEDOK*, at Revoluční 66.

Jablonec nad Nisou (Gablonz)

JABLONEC NAD NISOU starts almost before the southwestern suburbs of Liberec end. It began life as a small Czech village but was cut short in its prime by the Hussite Wars, when the whole area was laid waste by the neighbouring Catholic Lusatians. Apocryphally, the only survivor was the large apple tree (*jabloň*) which stood on the village green, and gave the subsequent town its name. From the sixteenth century, it was better known as Gablonz, by the Saxon glass-makers who began to settle in the area, but it wasn't until the late nineteenth century that the town's **jewellery trade** really took off. By the turn of the century Gablonz was exporting its produce to all corners of the globe, and its burghers grew very rich indeed, building themselves mansions fit for millionaires and endowing the town with lavish public buildings – all in the contemporary Secession style that was beautifying Prague and Vienna.

The one and only reason for venturing into Jablonec is to visit the engaging **Glass and Jewellery Museum** at Jiráskova 4 (one block east off the main square; Tues–Sun 9am–noon & 1–4pm), which traces the history of the two intertwined industries. Chandeliers and garnets are the two Bohemian specialities to look out for, as is the superb collection of turn-of-the-century and Art-Deco pieces. Outside, despite the obvious former wealth of the town, the Art-Nouveau houses and Gablonz' famous *Americanische Wolkenkratzer* (quasi-skyscrapers) along the river have not been well looked after. A prime example is the Helmer & Fellner theatre, a couple of blocks west of the main square, a wonderful Secessionist structure slowly peeling itself out of existence.

Practical details
You can reach Jablonec on tram #11 from Liberec, which winds its way up the Nisa valley. If you'd prefer to stay here rather than Liberec, there's a wide choice of cheap **hotels**, so head for *ČEDOK* on Mírové náměstí, or if they're closed, start your search at *Na baště* by the big red-brick church to the north of the town centre. On warm summer days, the folk of Jablonec head out to the nearby Mšeno lake for a spot of sunbathing and swimming (bus #1 or #7 from town).

The Jizera Mountains and Frýdlant

Northeast of Liberec, and reachable by tram #3 or #4 from the town, the **Jizera Mountains** (Isergebirge) form the western edge of the Krkonoše range which, in turn, make up the northern border of Bohemia. Like their eastern neighbours, they have been very badly affected by acid rain, compounded by the proximity of the Bogatynia power station just over the border in Poland. The mountains rise suddenly from Liberec's northern suburbs to over 1000m high – and that's part of the problem, since at such a height they soak up every cloud of filth that floats by. The upper reaches, once covered in thick pine and even the odd patch of virgin forest, are now desolate and depressing. The Czechs, seemingly unperturbed, flock there still, but it's best to steer clear of the mountains themselves altogether.

Frýdlant (Friedland)

> *It was neither an old stronghold nor a new mansion, but a rambling pile consisting of innumerable small buildings closely packed together and of one or two storeys; if K had not known that it was a castle he might have taken it for a little town.*
>
> Franz Kafka, *The Castle*

The hybrid sprawling *Schloss* at **FRÝDLANT** (40min by train from Liberec), a town on the north side of the frontier mountains, was one of the models for Kafka's novel *The Castle*. Like his fictional character *K*, Kafka came here on business, not as a land surveyor but as an accident insurance clerk, a job which he did for most of his brief life. In Kafka's time the castle was still owned by the Clam-Gallas clan, but its most famous duke was Albrecht von Wallenstein, whose statue still stands in the town's main square. The **castle** (daily April, Sept & Oct 9am–noon & 1–3pm; May–Aug 8am–noon & 1–4pm) is ensconced on a rock over the river, a short walk from the town centre along a pretty tree-lined avenue. The two-hour guided tour is a bit too much for most people, except perhaps those with a passion for Baroque bric-a-brac.

There's a large, friendly **campsite** by a bend in the river below the approach to the castle, the only accommodation available at the time of writing. In HEJNICE, 10km southeast (30min by train; change at RASPENAVA), the *Perun* usually has rooms. There's a Polish border crossing 13km north of Frýdlant, on the road to Zgorzelec (Görlitz).

EAST BOHEMIA

East Bohemia (Východní Čechy) is more varied than the other regions of Bohemia, dividing into three distinct areas. Along the northern border with Poland, the hills of **Krkonoše** and the **Orlické hory** form an almost continuous mountain range. However, the havoc wreaked by acid rain is depressing and unavoidable, and only in the foothills of the **Český ráj**, to the south, and the area **around Broumov** to the east, are its effects less noticeable. Further south still, the terrain on either side of the River Labe is flat, fertile and, for the most part, fairly dull. But the towns of the river basin (the *Polabí*) do much to make up for it – places like **Hradec Králové**, the regional capital, its historic rival **Pardubice**, and **Litomyšl**, Smetana's birthplace, down by the Moravian border.

Český ráj

Less than 100km from Prague, the sandstone rocks and densely wooded hills of the **Český ráj** (Bohemian Paradise) have been a popular spot for weekending Praguers for over a century. Although the Český ráj is officially limited to a small nature reserve south of Turnov, the term is loosely applied to the entire swathe of

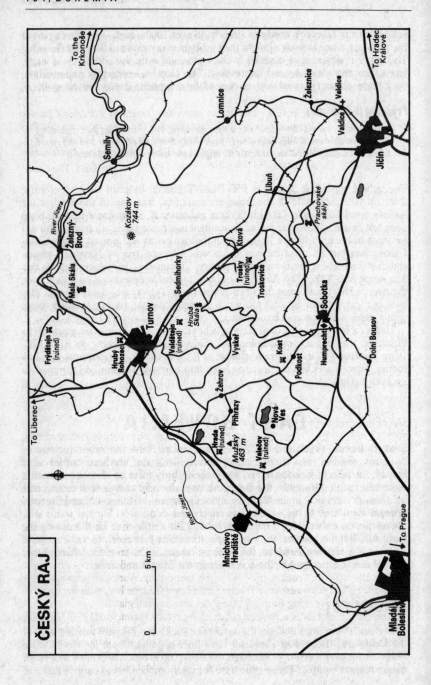

ČESKÝ RAJ

To the Krkonoše
To Hradec Králové
Lomnice
Železnice
Valdice
Semily
River Jizera
Kozákov 744 m
Železný-Brod
Libuň
Prachovské skály
Jičín
Malá Skála
Sedmihorky
Ktová
Trosky (ruined)
Troskovice
Sobotka
Frýdštejn (ruined)
Turnov
Valdštejn (ruined)
Hrubá Skála
Hrubý Rohozec
Žehrov
Vyskeř
Kost
Podkost
Humprecht
Dolní Bousov
To Liberec
Přihrazy
Nová Ves
Hrada (ruined)
Mužský 463 m
Valečov (ruined)
To Prague
River Jizera
Mnichovo Hradiště
Mladá Boleslav
0   5 km

hills from Mnichovo Hradiště to Jičín. **Turnov** is the most convenient base for exploring the region, but there's little incentive to stay there. Infinitely more appealing is **Jičín**, which has preserved its seventeenth-century old town intact. But more interesting than either of the towns is the surrounding **countryside**: ruined fortresses, bizarre rock formations and traditional folk architecture, all smothered in a blanket of pine forests.

From Turnov, local **trains** run roughly every two hours to Jičín; local **buses** from both towns infrequently wind their way through the otherwise inaccessible villages nearby. Generally, though, the distances are so small – Turnov to Jičín, for example, is just 24km – that you might as well buy the *Český ráj Poděbradsko* map and **walk** along the marked footpaths.

Turnov and around

TURNOV (Turnau) is somewhat short on excitement. Aside from the **Český ráj museum**, containing an interminable collection of semiprecious stones dug out of a nearby hillside, and temporary exhibitions of nature photography, there's nothing to see here except grimy streets. If you're spending your days walking, though, you may find it convenient **to stay** overnight here; *Hotel Sport* (☎636; near the football stadium) or the cheaper *Slavie* (just off the main square) occasionally have vacancies. Alternatively, *ČEDOK* (on the main square) may be able to rustle up a hostel bed or a hotel room in a nearby town. One place worth heading for is the chateau of **Hrubý Rohozec** (daily April, Sept & Oct 9am–noon & 1–4pm; May–Aug 8am–noon & 1–5pm; closed Mon), high up on the left bank of the Jizera river, on the outskirts of Turnov. A welcome contrast from the rest of the town, the hour-long guided tour dishes out some great views, but its Renaissance chambers contain no great surprises. On the road up to the chateau, there are some **private rooms** to rent – probably the best accommodation in Turnov, if there's space.

Valdštejn and Hrubá skála

Just a two-kilometre walk through the woods from the Turnov-město railway station (one stop down towards Jičín from Turnov) is the former Gothic stronghold of **Valdštejn** (May–Sept 15 Tues–Sun 9am–4.30pm), the ancestral castle of the Wallenstein family for many years. Already in ruins by the late sixteenth century, it was occupied by vagrants, and later attempts to restore it never came to fruition, though its position remains impressive – as does the eighteenth-century stone bridge, flanked by Baroque statues.

Another 2km southeast, **Hrubá skála** (Big Rock), the first (and arguably the best) of Český ráj's sandstone cities, unfolds amidst the trees. It's easy to spend hours clambering up and down the bluffs and dodging the crevices, whose names – *Myší díra* (Mouse Hole), *Dračí věž* (Dragon's Tower) and *Sahara* – give some idea of the variety of rock formations to be found here. Various viewpoints, like *Zamecká vyhl* or *Marianské vyhl*, range high above the tree line, with the protruding stone slabs emerging from the pine trees like ossified giants.

The nearby **zámek** is a colossal nineteenth-century reconstruction of the original Gothic castle: very popular with Czech film crews, but closed to the public. From here, a green-marked path descends through the *Myší díra* and the *Dračí skály*, zigzagging down to a small lakeside **campsite** (April–Oct) near the Karlovice-Sedmihorky station on the Turnov–Jičín branch line.

Trosky

The spectacular ruined hrad of **Trosky** (5km southeast of Hrubá skála) is the Český ráj's number-one landmark. Its twin Gothic towers, *Bába* (Grandmother) and *Panna* (Virgin), were built on volcanic basalt rocks which burst through the sandstone strata millions of years ago. You can climb Bába for a far-reaching view of the Jizera basin, but Panna, the higher of the two, is suitably out of bounds. Although the brooding rubble is officially only open at the weekend (April–Sept), it's easy to gain access at other times by climbing over the wooden fence. There's a flash new **hotel** and restaurant complex by the castle car park, with cheap doubles, and a **campsite** 2km back along the path to Turnov. Getting here, three or four daily **buses** run from Turnov, but it may be quicker to take the train to Ktová station on the Jičín line, and walk 2km uphill.

Sobotka and around

Compared to Turnov or Jičín, **SOBOTKA** is off the beaten track: 13km from either place, hotel-less, and only easily accessible by train from Jičín (50min; change at LIBUŇ).

Unless you're camping (see below), it's no good as a base for exploring the region, though it does harbour some good examples of the local brightly painted half-timbered architecture and – just northwest of the town, on a strange conical hill – a striking seventeenth-century **Humprecht hunting lodge** (April–Sept Tues–Sun 8am–noon & 1–5pm). It's a bizarre building, worth a peek inside if only for the central *trompe l'oeil* dining room, a windowless sixteen-metre-high oval cylinder with the acoustics of a cathedral. On the other side of the hill from Sobotka is a rudimentary **campsite** (mid-June to Sept) and swimming pool.

Podkost

One bus daily (at around 1pm) covers the 3km northwest from Sobotka to **PODKOST**, a small settlement by a pond at the edge of the Žehrov forest. The village is dominated in every way by **Kost** (guided tour, lasting 50min April, Sept & Oct Tues–Sun 9am–noon & 1–4pm; May–Aug 8am–noon & 1–5pm) it's castle, sitting atop its gigantic sandstone pedestal, with a characteristic rectangular keep. Thanks to a fire in 1635, after which it was used as a granary, Kost retains the full flavour of its fourteenth-century origins, and the late Gothic art exhibition is well worth seeing, too – but to do so, you have to endure the guided tour, and since Kost is now the best preserved castle in the Český ráj, the tour groups begin to congregate early. Down in the village, *Hotel Podkost* (☎931 27), although cheap, is usually fully booked up.

You're more likely to find room another 4km northwest along the scenic red-marked path through the Žehrov forest, at **NOVÁ VES** by the Komárovský lake, which has three **campsites** and a **hotel** on its banks. North of the lake lies a matrix of paths which crisscrosses the complex rock systems, leaving the forest after 3km at the hotel and campsite in **PŘÍHRAZY**. Paths spread out west from here, back into the woods, emerging only to ascend Mužský (463m), but other-wise continuing for 2km to the **prehistoric burial ground** of Hrada and the rocky viewpoint at Drábské světničky. The ruined fort of **Valečov** lies another 2km to the south at the southwestern edge of the woodland. On a day's hike, you could easily do a round trip from Nová Ves or Příhrazy, by heading east from

Valečov, or else continue for another 3km west to the station at MNICHOVO HRADIŠTĚ, on the main railway line to Prague.

Jičín and around

At the southeastern tip of the Český ráj, where the fertile plain of the River Labe touches the foothills of the Krkonoše, **JIČÍN** (Gitschin), an hour by train from Turnov, is easily the most rewarding stop in the region. Its location, close to some of the Český ráj's most dramatic scenery, makes it a convenient base for some easy hiking, while its Renaissance chateau and arcaded main square are attractive surroundings for a night or two's stay.

The town is closely associated with the infamous **Albrecht von Wallenstein** (*Albrecht z Valdštejna*), Duke of Friedland, who during his meteoric rise to eminence (see p.162) owned almost every chateau in the region. Wallenstein confiscated Jičín early on in the Thirty Years' War, and chose this rather unlikely town as the capital of his new personal empire. He rebuilt the main square in stone in the 1620s, in a style which drifts in and out of the late Renaissance and early Baroque. One side is still dominated by Wallenstein's **zámek**, which now contains the town museum and art gallery and the great conference hall in which the leaders of the three great East European powers, Russia, Austria and Prussia, signed the Holy Alliance against Napoleon in 1813. A covered passage connects the chateau's eastern wing with the Jesuit church next door, allowing the nobility to avoid their unsavoury subjects while en route to mass. But this steeple-less Baroque church is eclipsed by the mighty sixteenth-century **Valdická brána** close by, whose tower gallery offers a panorama over the town.

One of Wallenstein's more endearing additions to the town is the avenue of lime trees which leads to the princely garden of **Libosad**, now an overgrown spinney, but still worth a wander. The melancholy of the Renaissance loggia, last repaired at the end of the First Republic, is overshadowed by the horror of one of the country's most brutal Communist prisons, in nearby **VALDICE**. Originally a seventeenth-century Carthusian monastery it was converted into a prison by the Habsburgs, and used after 1948 to keep the regime's political prisoners in a suitably medieval state of deprivation.

At present **accommodation** in Jičín is limited to the *Astra* (☎324 31), east off the main square, and *Start* (☎332 31), a more expensive, modern hotel, out on the road to Valdice. A kilometre out on the Mladá Boleslav road is the *Rumcajs* **campsite** with wooden **chalets** (May–Sept). The only surprise on the **eating** front is the new ice cream and mulled wine bar (11am–8pm), opposite the former Jesuit college, west off the square down Chelčického.

Prachovské skály

The real reason to come to Jičín is to see the **Prachovské skály**, a series of sandstone and basalt rocks hidden in woods 3km northwest. There's an occasional local bus, but it's a relaxed walk, via the *Rumcajs* campsite, to the rocks. They lack the subtlety of the Hrubá skála formations, but make up for it in sheer size and area; their name derives from the *prach* (dust) which covers the forest floor, forming a carpet of sand. In high season, swarms of climbers cling to the silent, grey rocks like a plague of locusts, but out of season it's possible to find a tranquil spot.

Železný Brod and Malá Skála

Heading northeast from Turnov, the railway follows the course of the Jizera river to ŽELEZNÝ BROD (Eisenbrod), one of the main centres of Bohemia's world-famous glass-making industry. It's a town of contradictions, its factories and high-rises spread along the banks of the river, while half-timbered cottages in the traditional Český ráj colours cover the hillside. The tiny main square is a typical mix of styles: one side is taken up by two wholly uninspiring 1950s buildings – the glass and crystal factory, and the *Hotel Cristal*, while the other side shelters the nineteenth-century town hall and the timber-framed local **museum**, which displays local arts and crafts. Up the hillside by the town church, which sports a nifty little wooden belfry, are outstanding examples of **folk architecture**, usually confined to more inaccessible villages.

Six kilometres back down the valley towards Turnov (and also accessible by train) is the village of **MALÁ SKÁLA**. A steep red-marked path leads from the village to the **Suché skály** ("Silent Rocks") and a number of rock caves, used during the Counter-Reformation as safe houses for persecuted Protestants. The view across the valley to the ruined castle of Frýdštejn is the reward you get for your pains, and there are a **hotel** and **campsite** back down in Malá Skála should you wish to stay the night.

The Krkonoše

The **Krkonoše** (Giant Mountains) are the highest in Bohemia, and formed part of the historical northeastern border of the ancient kingdom of Bohemia. They remained uninhabited until the sixteenth and seventeenth centuries, when glass-making and ore-mining brought the first German and Italian settlers to the Riesengebirge, as they were then known. The mountains' undoubted beauty ensured an early tourist following, and for resorts like Špindlerův Mlýn it's now the sole industry. Since the war – despite being one of the few protected national parks in the country – thousands upon thousands of trees have become fatally weakened by **acid rain** (the annual rainfall here is among the highest in the country). Once the trees are badly affected, insects do the rest, transforming the trees into grey husks, devoid of foliage. Extensive felling is the government's hopelessly inadequate response, aimed at stopping the spread of the destructive insects – rather like a smoker removing a set of lungs to prevent cancer.

For many people, the fate of Bohemia's ancient forests is the most damning indictment of the Communists' forty years of mismanagement. And as if to rub the matter in, despite the irretrievable damage, the focus over the last ten years has been on new hotels and chair lifts rather than environmental measures. Since the Velvet Revolution, though, all political parties have given environmental issues a high priority, but it remains to be seen whether – in the rush to transform the country into a market economy – such principles will be preserved. For the tourist in the Krkonoše, the situation is worse the further west and the higher up you go, though in winter the snow obscures much of the damage. In summer, walking is the main mode of transport, making it well-nigh impossible to ignore the rain's effects – though in the relative safety of the largely unspoiled valley bottom the problem can seem a long way away.

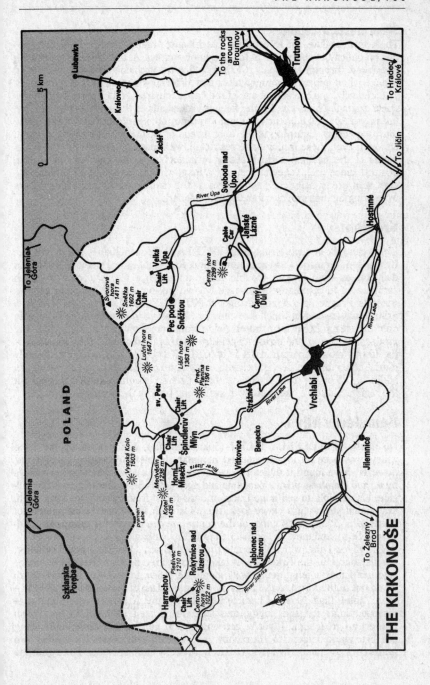

THE KRKONOŠE

Some practical details

These grim realities fail to deter the coachloads, which makes cheap **accommodation** difficult to get hold of at the height of summer. At the moment, everything is booked through the main *ČEDOK* office in Vrchlabí, though this should change when private accommodation, now officially sanctioned, starts to spread. Theoretically, you can stay at one of the *bouda* (chalets), dotted across the mountains, originally hide-outs for the fleeing Protestants of the seventeenth century, but in practice you'll be lucky to find a vacancy at any except *Labská bouda*, the most expensive. **Camping** is the only means of ensuring a place for the night, although even these facilities are restricted, with just two sites within the boundaries of the national park. Walking is undoubtedly the best way of **getting around**, since each valley is basically a long, winding dead-end for motor vehicles, with pretty hefty car parking fees at the end aimed at dissuading drivers from bringing their vehicles into the national park.

Vrchlabí

If you can talk in such terms, then **VRCHLABÍ** (Hohenelbe) is the hub of the Krkonoše for transport and accommodation. Reservations are essential for the six daily **buses** from Prague (double that number on a Friday), some of which continue on to Špindlerův Mlýn (see below), but not for the *Krakanoš* express (departs Prague at 5.20pm; change at KUNČICE, 4km south). Vrchlabí is a grimy, one-street town which stretches for 3km along the banks of the Labe, with only the sleazy *Labuť* for a **hotel**. Aside from some low-key "attractions" – the gardens and zoo of the sixteenth-century chateau, and a small **folk museum** – the town's most important asset is its *ČEDOK* (☎0438-3180), which is the only tourist office that can deal direct with every hotel and *bouda* in the Krkonoše. In addition, *CIS* on the main square can book **private accommodation** throughout the region. There's a **campsite** with swimming pool on the Semily road.

Špindlerův Mlýn

No doubt **ŠPINDLERŮV MLÝN** (Spindlermühle), 15km north up the Labe valley, was once an idyllic, isolated mountain hamlet. Successive generations, however, have found it difficult to resist exploiting a town where seven valleys meet, and countless private pensions and ugly hotels lie scattered across the hillside. It's possible to see huge tracts of dead forest from Špindlerův Mlýn itself, but should you want a closer look, there's a chair lift to just below summit of **Medvědín** (1235m); it's north of the centre, on the way to the **campsite** (mid-May to Sept), and must be approached from the left bank.

The **River Labe**, which flows into the North Sea (as the Elbe) near Hamburg, has its source in the Krkonoše. It takes about three hours to reach the source (pramen Labe): a long, gentle walk along the valley, followed by a short, sharp climb out of the forest to the modern, expensive *Labská bouda* (☎0438-932 21) – more **hotel** than *bouda*. Characteristically for the Krkonoše, the summit is disappointingly flat and boggy, and the source itself (500m from the Polish border) no great sight. If you're carrying a pack, continue for three hours along the blue-marked track to Harrachov (see below). Otherwise, it's around two hours back to Špindlerův Mlýn, via Horní Misečky and Medvědín. For a **glimpse** of **Poland**, you should catch a bus from Špindlerův Mlýn to *Špindlerova bouda*, where dead trees, Polish border guards and the odd grazing sheep provide the entertainment.

The west: Harrachov

Five buses and one train (change at nearby TANVALD) make the daily journey from Prague to the westernmost resort in the Krkonoše, **HARRACHOV**, whose cottages are scattered about the Mumlava valley. A glassworks was established here in 1712, and the local **glass museum** has a small sample of its wares throughout the ages. Harrachov's **hotels** are usually full, with the possible exception of *CKM*'s moderate *Juniorhotel*, which has a – largely theoretical – special cheap rate for *IYHF* members. Alternatively, there's a **campsite** near the border crossing on the road from Prague to Szczecin. For cheap thrills, Harrachov's brand new **chair lift** sends you over the dry tobogganing course to the top of Čertova hora (1022m), high enough to view the pollution damage all around.

The east: Pec pod Sněžkou and Janské Lázně

PEC POD SNĚŽKOU (Petzer) is the main hiking base for climbing **Sněžka** (Schneekoppe or "Snow Peak"), at 1602m the highest mountain in Bohemia, and the most impressive in the entire range. Its bleak, grey summit rises above the tree line, relieving walkers of the painful sight of gently expiring pines, and making for a fine panorama. If you don't fancy the six-kilometre ascent, take the **chair lift** from the village. The border, signified by discreet white and red stone markers, divides the rounded summit; on the Czech side there's a restaurant. But unless Czech–Polish relations take a dramatic turn for the worse, the Polish border guards are unlikely to use the Kalashnikovs which swing nonchalantly at their sides. To the east of the summit, a path follows the narrow mountain ridge (which also marks the border) 2.5km to another peak, Svorová hora (Czarna Kopa to the Poles). To the west, there's a steep drop, again along the ridge, to *Slezská bouda* (on the Polish side). To reach Špindlerův Mlýn from here (a three-and-a-half-hour walk), follow the blue markers (via *Luční bouda*), and not the red and blue ones, which veer into Polish territory.

There are regular **buses from Prague** to Pec pod Sněžkou, plus the occasional one to Janské Lázně (see below), and the *Úpa* express from Prague ends at Svoboda nad Úpou, 3km east of Janské Lázně. As for **accommodation**, Pec has no campsite and little likelihood of vacancies in any of the hotels, so you may have to rely on locals touting private rooms, or on finding a secluded spot to pitch your tent.

JANSKÉ LÁZNĚ (Johannisbad), hidden away in a sheltered, fertile valley on the southern edge of the national park, has a different atmosphere from the other resorts. Visitors come here to imbibe its mineral waters, not climb its surrounding peaks (although even the lazy can reach the top of Černá hora by the hourly cable car). On a hot summer's day all the classic images of spa life converge on the central stretch of lawn; a brass band plays its Germanic tunes in slightly lackadaisical fashion, while the elderly and infirm spill from the tearoom on to the benches outside. The *Lesní dům, Praha* and *Zátiší* are Janské Lázně's **hotels**, in ascending order of price – all fairly cheap and usually full, but worth a try.

Trutnov and the rocks around Broumov

The modern factories and housing complexes which ring Bohemia's easternmost textile town, **TRUTNOV** (Trautenau), signal the end of the national park, though the town is a useful fall-back for the Krkonoše in the height of summer, and makes a good base for exploring the Adršpach rocks and the Stěnava valley to the east. The busy arcaded main square, downstream and uphill from the railway station, has been beautifully restored and is closed to vehicles. Even the fountain is working, depicting Krakonoš (Rübezahl), the sylvan spirit who guards the Giant Mountains and gave them their Czech name. All this can be best appreciated from the café terrace just behind the radnice. If you've got some time to kill, there's the odd exhibition at the **museum** in the former *stará škola*, around the corner from the café. Trutnov's greatest claim to fame is that for some time in the early 1970s, **Václav Havel** used to work in the local brewery, where they produce a very good 14° light beer called *Krakonoš*. His experiences later provided material for *Audience*, one of three plays centred around the character *Vaněk* (a lightly disguised version of Havel himself).

Trutnov's **accommodation** is out of town: the pricey *Horník* hotel is 1km east, towards Poříčí, the not much cheaper *Motel Horal* is 2km out on the Vrchlabí road, and the nearest **campsite** (mid-June to mid-Sept) is by a small lake, 2km southwest of town.

The rocks around Broumov

Between Trutnov and Broumov (see below) lie two seemingly innocuous hilly strips smothered in trees, which closer inspection reveals to be riddled with sandstone protrusions and weird rock formations on the same lines as those in Český ráj. Distances here are small and the gradients gentle, making it ideal for a bit of none too strenuous – but no less spectacular – **hiking**. If you're thinking of exploring the rocks, get hold of the detailed *Teplicko-Adršpašské skály/Broumovské stěny* map before you get there, which shows all the colour-coded footpaths and the campsites. And since the region is served by train from Trutnov to Broumov (via Teplice), it seems a shame not to take advantage of this slow but scenic service, rather than suffer on the local buses.

The Adršpach rocks

The **Adršpach rocks**, 15km east of Trutnov, rise up out of the pine forest like petrified phalluses. Some even take trees with them as they launch themselves hundreds of feet into the air. This region has been popular with German tourists since the nineteenth century, though nowadays they are outnumbered by Czech rock-climbers and ramblers. Once you enter the "sandstone city", the outside world recedes and you're surrounded by new sensations – sand underfoot, the scent of pine, boulders and shady trees. Most of the rocks are dangerous to climb without the correct equipment and experience, so you'll probably have to content yourself with strolling and gawping at the rocks, best described by their nicknames: *Babiččina lenoška* (Grandmother's Armchair), *Španělská stěna* (Spanish Wall) and the ironic *Trpaslík* (Dwarf).

ADRŠPACH railway station lies at the northern extremity of the rock system. On arrival you can't really miss it, since some of the rocks have crept right up to the station itself. But after an initial burst of bold and dramatic formations, everything settles down for a kilometre or so as you work southwards. Then to the right, the Anenské údolí heralds another theatrical burst of geological abnormalities. Just 1km west of the woods' edge, **TEPLICE NAD METUJÍ** provides a functional base for the rocks, with a hotel, supermarket and cinema. There's no official campsite, but people are bound to be camping nearby: try attaching yourself to one of the more legitimate-looking clusters of tents.

If you're a keen rock-climber, the annual **festival of mountaineering** held here in early September is of interest. It's basically an excuse for a lot of boozing and showing off, but specialist climbing films are also shown. It attracts people from all over Europe, who come and share their experiences, many demonstrating their skills on the local formations.

Broumov and the Broumov Wall

BROUMOV (Braunau), 30km due east of Trutnov, is itself no great attraction: a thoroughly German town before the war (a feeling it still retains), it's stuck in the middle of nowhere, and there's no real reason why you should end up here unless you're hiking along the Broumov wall. It's more impressive from a distance, with the colossal Baroque monastery perched on a sandstone pedestal above the river; but apart from an interesting wooden Silesian church on the Křivinice road out of town, there's not much else to keep you here: unless that is you need to make use of either of the town's two **hotels**.

The **Broumov wall** is a thin sandstone ridge that almost cuts Broumov off from the rest of the country. From the west, there's no indication of the approaching precipice, from which a wonderful vista sweeps out over to Broumov and beyond into Poland, but from the east your target is more clearly spread out before you. The best place to appreciate the view is from Dientzenhofer's chapel of **Panna Marie Sněžna**, situated in among the boulders at the high point of the ridge (4km east of Police nad Metují railway station). The best rock formations are 6km south of here, close by the the highest point of the wall, **Božanovský Špičák** (733m), only a few hundred metres from the Polish border. There's a little **campsite** in MACHOV, 2km to the west, and another one in the bigger town of POLICE NAD METUJÍ, whose station is 3km further along the road from Machov.

Náchod and Nové Město nad Metují

South of the sandstone rock formations, **NÁCHOD** (which means "entrance") was one of the few border towns not annexed by the Nazis when they marched into the Sudetenland in 1938, since at the time there were only four German-speaking families in the whole town. It's a scruffy place, cowering at the base of its large sgraffitoed chateau, built to guard the road from Silesia into Bohemia. These days the town has been undergoing a slow and painful restoration, and most people just stop off in order to break the journey (and spend their last remaining crowns) en route to Poland – the border is a couple of kilometres east of the town centre. The only reason to stay any longer is to visit the chateau at Nové Město nad Metují (see below). To that end, when restoration is completed, the Art-Nouveau *Hotel U Beránků* promises a theatre, restaurant and *kavárna*. Meanwhile, the only vaguely functioning **accommodation** is the *Hron* (☎0441-207 52), out on the Dobrošov road, or the **campsite** (mid-May to mid-Sept) 2km east at BĚLOVES.

THE COWARDS IN NÁCHOD

The exiled writer **Josef Škvorecký** was born and bred in Náchod – a "narrow cleavage between the mountains", as he characteristically dubbed it. During his wartime childhood he was joined by film-director-to-be Miloš Forman, then only a young boy, who came to stay with his uncle when his parents were sent to a concentration camp from which they never returned. Later, in the cultural thaw of the 1960s, before they were both forced to emigrate, the two men planned (unsuccessfully) to make a film based on *The Cowards*, Škvorecký's most famous novel. Set in "a small Bohemian town" (ie Náchod) in the last few days of the war, the book caused a sensation when it was published (briefly) in 1958 because of its bawdy treatment of Czech resistance to the Nazis.

Nové Město nad Metují

NOVÉ MĚSTO NAD METUJÍ, 9km south of Náchod, sits on a high spur hemmed in by a tributary of the River Labe. The old town is nothing more than the restored sixteenth-century houses which line each side of the rectangular arcaded main square. No doubt once a busy marketplace, it now stands aloof from the bustle of the modern new town to the north, maintaining a museum-like silence only occasionally disturbed by the arrival of coach parties. Their reason for being here is the seventeenth-century **zámek** (April & Oct Sat & Sun 9am–noon & 1–4pm; May–Aug Tues–Sun 8am–noon & 1–5pm; Sept 9am–noon & 1–5pm), which looks out across the Labe basin (known as the *Polabí*) from the northeast corner of the square. After piecemeal alterations over the centuries, it was redesigned at the beginning of this century by the quirky Slovak architect **Dušan Jurkovič**, who was responsible for the wall-to-wall leather vaulting of the Žebrový sál (Ribbed Hall). The other rooms are lavishly furnished in every period from the original Renaissance to highly unusual works by Czech Cubists like Pavel Janák. Your most likely point of **arrival** is the **main railway station**, 2km northwest of the chateau, in Nové Město's modern new town. Local (and *ČSAD*) buses link the old town square with the station, while it's also possible to catch a direct *ČSAD* bus to Náchod or Hradec Králové from the old town square. If you want to stay the night, the only **hotel** in town is the cheap *Metuj*, off Kominského, the main drag running north–south through the new town.

Hradec Králové

Capital of East Bohemia, and the largest city on the fertile plain of the Upper Labe, **HRADEC KRÁLOVÉ** is a typically attractive Bohemian town, with a handsome historical quarter paid for by the rich trade which used to pass through the town en route to Silesia. But there's another side to the town, too. To the west of the medieval centre is one of the great urban projects of the inter-war Republic, built by some of Czechoslovakia's best modern architects. The two towns don't blend – in fact they barely communicate – and these days, the staré město is little more than a museum piece. Even if you don't particularly take to the new town, it's a fascinating testimony to the newly emerging modern Czechoslovak state, and gives the whole of Hradec Králové a unique, expansive and prosperous atmosphere.

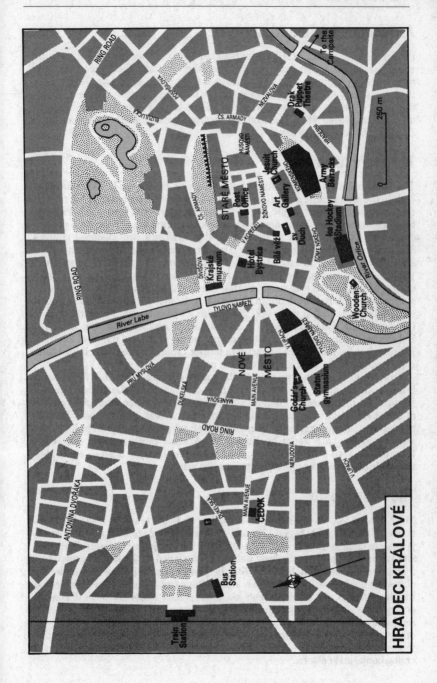

Arriving and orientation

Hradec Králové spreads itself out on both banks of the Labe: on the left bank, the **staré město** sits on an oval rock between the Labe and the Orlice rivers; the **nové město** begins as soon as you leave the old town, straddling the river and then composing itself in fairly logical fashion between the river and the station to the west. By **train** and **bus**, you arrive in the nové město; to reach the staré město, take a #5, #6, #8, #11, #15 or #20 bus from the station down the main street (formerly Leninova) into town.

The staré město

The **staré město** was once entirely surrounded by zig-zag red-brick fortifications built in the eighteenth century, though they've now been replaced by the modern ring road which keeps traffic out of the old quarter. With most daily business being conducted over in the new town, a small supermarket and a couple of bookshops are all that remain to disturb Hradec Králové's two medieval squares, **Žižkovo náměstí** and the smaller **Husovo náměstí**. At the western end of Žižkovo náměstí rise five towers, two of which belong to the church of **sv Duch** (Holy Ghost), one of the country's few great brick churches, a style more commonly associated with neighbouring Silesia. Given its grand Gothic scale, its whitewashed interior is a letdown, despite Petr Brandl's *St Anthony* and a superb stone tabernacle dating from 1497. The church's twin towers are outreached by the once-white **Bílá věž**, built in the sixteenth century from the profits of Bohemian–Polish trade. Also in this corner of the square is the town brewery, invisible but for the terrace of Baroque former canons' houses which lead to its gate, bristling in their garish new coats of paint.

To the east, where the two sides of the square converge, the older Renaissance houses on the north side have kept their arcades, while the Bishop and the Jesuits built their Baroque "barracks" opposite. Next door, an impressive **gallery** of twentieth-century art and sculpture includes a real gem in Josef Váchal's mysterious *Satanic Invocation* (*Vzývači ďabla*), which spills over onto its carved wooden frame, plus works by Kupka and Mucha. Further down, the **Jesuit Church** has been beautifully maintained, its mighty Baroque altarpiece providing a suitable repository for more of Petr Brandl's work.

The nové město

Most of what you now see outside the old town is the result of an architectural master plan outlined between 1909 and 1911 and carried out over the next twenty years. Building began on a grand scale with the **Krajské muzeum** (Tues–Sun 9am–noon & 1–5pm), on the leafy waterfront, designed by the father of the Czech modern movement, **Jan Kotěra**. With the rest of central Europe still under the obsessive hold of the Viennese Secession, Kotěra's museum, crowned with one of his characteristic domes, represents his greatest shot across the bows of contemporary taste, finished in an unconventional mixture of red brick and concrete rendering. The entrance is guarded by two colossal sphynx-like janitors, but otherwise the ornamentation is low-key – as is the exhibition inside, a straightforward though attractive display of nineteenth- and twentieth-century arts and crafts, books and posters.

It's difficult to see beyond the pollutant-caked rendering of the **Hotel Bystrica**, built immediately after the museum, again by Kotěra. The rehashed *kavárna* exudes the dour feel of the 1930s, but the Art-Nouveau restaurant is the fruit of an earlier work by Kotěra, adorned with murals by Jan Preisler and František Kysela's graceful stained-glass cranes. Kotěra's contribution to the new town stopped with his death in 1923, and his place was taken by **Josef Gočár** who, in the same year, won a competition for a school building south of the old town. His biggest, most brutal building was the **Statní gymnasium**, on the right bank, a four-storey red-brick structure which sets the tone for the rest of the town: chunky, monumental and not altogether appealing. The right bank is dominated by block after block of similar buildings, painted in mute pastel colours and decorated with neon lettering, a hangover from the city's last brief period of càpitalism between the wars.

Practicalities and entertainment

Accommodation can be hard to find, particularly when there's a big match on at the ice hockey stadium, so it's worth enquiring about vacancies at *ČEDOK* at no. 63 (☎049-325 86) on the main street (formerly Leninova) in the new town. The town's **hotels**, in ascending order of price, are: *Paříž* off Mánesova (☎049-326 31); *Bystrica* on the inner ring road (☎049-242 01); the *Zimní stadión*, Komenského 1214 (☎049-239 11); the high-rise *Alessandria*, SNP 733 (☎049-415 21), impossible to miss on bus route #6, #12, #21, #22 or #25 from the station; and the *Černigov* opposite the station (☎049-340 11), which will cost you an arm and a leg. Alternatively, take bus #17 to the *Stříbrný rybník* **campsite** (mid-May to mid-Sept), where you can swim in the lake and even hire **bicycles**.

The best place in town for **eating** is Kotěra's *Bystrica* hotel restaurant (daily 11.30am–2.30pm & 6–9.30pm), especially for lunch, when the waiters pull out all the stops with Viennese aplomb. Plainer service and faster, cheaper **beers** can be had at *Pod věží* on Žižkovo náměstí, or *Na hradě* on Špitálská.

Entertainment

Hradec Králové is home to *Drak*, Czechoslovakia's internationally renowned **puppet theatre** company, who specialise in adult as well as kids' shows. Using actors, singers, dancers and puppets, they've gone a long way towards breaking down the boundaries between conventional theatre and puppet theatre. *Drak*'s theatre is south of the old town on Hradební.

As for **sport**, the ice hockey stadium by the Jiráskovy sady hosts the odd international match as well as the local team's fixtures – and the town swimming baths reputedly have artificial waves.

Around Hradec Králové

The flat expanse around Hradec Králové, known as the *Polabí*, is a fertile region whose hedgeless cornfields stretch for miles on end. It's pretty dreary stuff to look at, baking hot in summer and covered in a misty drizzle most of the winter, though a few places within easy striking distance from Hradec Králové merit a stop: the area **around Jaroměř** and Santini's summer chateau at **Chlumec nad Cidlinou**, in particular.

Jaroměř

JAROMĚŘ, 36km northeast of Hradec Králové and accessible by train, is a grey and uninviting town for the most part, blighted by the proximity of the Josefov barracks (until recently full of Soviet soldiers). The one sight worth writing home about is Josef Gočár's **Wenke department store** (Mon–Fri 9am–4pm, Sat & Sun 9am–noon), situated on the busy main road from Hradec Králové to the Polish border. In this exceedingly unpromising street (now called Husova), Gočár undertook one of the first self-conscious experiments in Cubist architecture in 1911. It's an imaginative, eclectic work, quite unlike the Cubist villas of Prague's Vyšehrad or the nearby spa of Bohdaneč, the plate-glass facade topped by a Neoclassical top-floor, the monochrome, geometric interior still intact (though no longer packed with goods). Instead, it now serves as the venue for displays of local school exam work and the like, but upstairs there's an art gallery with exhibits by all three of Jaroměř's home-grown artists: Otakar Španiel, Josef Wagner and Josef Šima. The first two were sculptors, while Šima was an artist whose wilfully optimistic painting of Jaroměř forms the centrepiece of the gallery.

You can **stay the night** at the moderate *Černý kůn* hotel on the main square, rather than visit on a day trip, should you so wish.

Josefov (Josefstadt)

On the left bank of the river, where the Labe and the Metují rivers converge, is the fortress town of **JOSEFOV**. In the 1780s the Habsburgs created three fortified towns along the northern border with their new enemy, Prussia: Hradec Králové (Königgrätz), which has since lost its walls, Terezín and Josefov – the last two purpose-built from scratch and still in existence. Terezín was put to use by the Nazis during World War II, but Josefov remains the great white elephant of the Empire, never having witnessed a single battle. Their mutual designs are unerringly similar, two fortresses (one large, one small), identikit eighteenth-century streets and a grid plan whose monotony is only broken by the imposing **Empire Church** on the main square. Again, like Terezín, Josefov is still a garrison town, packed with soldiers and posses of military police cruising around in jeeps. All in all, it's not a great day out, but the thick zigzag trail of red-brick fortifications, now topped by beautiful tree-lined paths, is eminently strollable, with far-reaching views across the wheat fields of East Bohemia.

Kuks

The great complex of Baroque spa buildings at **KUKS**, just 5km north of Jaroměř, on the banks of the Labe, was the creation of the enlightened Bohemian dilettante Count Špork. Work began, largely according to Špork's own designs, in 1695, and by 1730 he had created his own private **spa resort** kitted out with a garden maze, a hospital, a concert hall (complete with its own orchestra) and a racecourse (surrounded by statues of dwarves). On December 22, 1740, disaster struck when the river broke its banks, destroying all the buildings on the left bank, and worse still, the springs themselves. All that remains is an overgrown monumental stairway leading nowhere, and, on the right bank, the hospital building fronted by Matthias Bernhard Braun's famous terrace, now the chief reason for visiting Kuks. Špork invited Braun to Prague in 1710, and became the

Tyrolean sculptor's chief patron in Bohemia, commissioning him to execute a series of **allegorical statues** to elevate the minds of his spa guests: to the west, the twelve *Vices* culminate in the grim *Angel of Grievous Death*; to the east, the twelve *Virtues* end with the *Angel of Blessed Death*. Over the years the elements have not been too kind to Braun's work, whose originals have had to retreat inside the hospital building and now provide the highlight of the 45-minute guided tour (May–Sept Tues–Sun 9am–noon & 1.30–5pm; Oct Sat & Sun only). Also on show is the beautifully restored eighteenth-century pharmacy and Špork's gloomy subterranean mausoleum.

Kuk's **train station** lies to the south of town. One stop further west or a pleasant two-kilometre walk along the banks of the river, is **Betlém**, Braun's open-air sculpture park, again sponsored by Špork. This time the theme is more explicitly religious and sculptured groups like *The Coming of the Magi* are seemingly half-created, still an organic part of the boulders strewn about the woods.

Chlumec nad Cidlinou

CHLUMEC NAD CIDLINOU, 29km west of Hradec Králové, makes an easy day trip. In the middle of the featureless dusty *Polabí*, its chateau, **Karlova Koruna** (April & Oct Sat & Sun 9am–4pm; May–Aug Tues–Sun 8am–5pm; Sept Tues–Sun 9am–5pm), stands on a rare patch of raised ground, built in 1721–23 to a design by Giovanni Santini. The well-kept grounds, only a few blocks south of the station, are perfect for a picnic, followed by a quick wander round this modest Baroque pleasure house, filled with copies of Braun's statuary. Santini's ground plan is a simple but intriguing triple-winged affair, dominated by a central circular hall whose pink and grey marble dome fills two storeys, with a grand staircase leading to the upper balcony. If you've forgotten your picnic, there's a cheap **restaurant** in one of the outbuildings (closed Mon & Tues).

Pardubice

There's always been a certain amount of rivalry between the two big towns of the *Polabí*. **PARDUBICE**'s historical core is more immediately appealing than Hradec Králové's, but its new town lacks the logic and cohesion of its neighbour – which means that, on balance, there's slightly less to see here. You could easily come on a day trip from Hradec Králové (only 30min away by train); not a bad idea when you consider the fact that Pardubice is also the capital of the country's chemical industry and not the healthiest of places to spend the night.

The Town

The **train** and **bus** stations lie at the end of Palackého in the new town, a busy thoroughfare and the beginning of Pardubice's seemingly endless parade of shops. It's a good ten-minute walk from here (or a short ride on trolley bus #3, or bus #6, #9, #12 or #13) to **náměstí Osvobození**, which marks the transition from the new town to the old. At one end, the seriously striking Art-Nouveau **theatre** is a deliberately Czech structure, designed by Antonín Balšánek, whose magnificent facade is flanked by multicoloured mosaics: of Libuše founding Prague on one side and a blind Žižka leading the Hussites into battle on the other. The other truly arresting building on the square is the church of **sv Bartoloměj**, originally Gothic but more memorable for the Renaissance additions to its exterior, which makes up for a lack of tower with a syringe-like central spike. Gočár worked in Pardubice too: the squat grey *Statní banka* and the *Hotel Grand* opposite, the hub of all Pardubice's nightlife, are both his.

Beyond the soaring Gothic gateway, the centre of old Pardubice, **Pernštýnovo náměstí**, is almost claustrophobically cramped, an effect made all the more pronounced by the tall three-storey buildings on each side, handsome gabled sixteenth- and eighteenth-century houses for the most part. The most striking is **U Jonáše**, whose plasterwork includes an exuberant depiction of Jonah at the moment of digestion by the whale. Its Gothic diamond vaulting can be appreciated as you step into the modern art gallery housed inside.

What little else there is of the staré město spreads north from here, either down the buttressed beauty of Bartolomějská or the crumbling facades of Pernštýnská. Both lead eventually to the still more intimate Wernerovo nábřeží, its drooping willow trees providing a perfect spot for the town's budding artists, music wafting across the courtyard from the almost chic *bistro* at no. 100. At this point, all that's left of the old town is the **zámek** (Tues–Sun 10am–5pm). An impressive series of walls, gates and barbicans lead to a rather colourless courtyard, entrance to the all too familar Czech art gallery, housed in one of the wings.

SEMTEX

Pardubice is the home of Czechoslovakia's most famous export, **Semtex**. This plastic explosive became a firm favourite with the world's terrorists during the 1980s because of its ability to avoid detection by electronic means in customs halls. Approximately 1000 tons of the explosive is reckoned to have gone to Libya alone (and from there – it seems – into the hands of the IRA), and researchers are now looking into ways of tagging it to prevent misuse in the future. It's still produced at (though no longer exported from) the huge chemical complex in the village of Semtín (from which it gets its name), a few kilometres northwest of Pardubice – until recently the village was etched out of all maps. Selling arms and explosives is not at all new to Czechoslovakia, but it sits ill with the country's new squeaky clean image, and President Havel, in particular, is committed to stopping what used to be one of the country's most successful – and deadly – export industries.

Practicalities – and horse-racing

Pardubice's **hotels** are much of a muchness, but given a free choice, the *Hotel Grand* (☎040-203 21) is the most central, followed by the *Zlatá štika*, Jägermannova 127 (☎040-207 21), and the *Nádraží*, predictably enough located near the station (☎040-207 59). The *Hotel Labe* (☎040-367 11) is in a league and price range of its own; strictly a last resort.

Pardubice has the best **steeplechase course** in the country and races take place every other weekend. The traditional big race (which celebrated its centenary in 1990) is the *Velká Pardubická* in early October, at which time it is impossible to get anywhere to stay in town. The racecourse (*závodiště*) is 2km out of town; take bus #4 or #14.

Chrudim

Twelve kilometres south of Pardubice, the otherwise provincial town of **CHRUDIM** springs into life every June and July when it hosts its annual **Puppet Festival**. At other times of the year, it's still worth the short train ride to visit its marvellous **Puppet Museum** (Muzeum Loutkářských kultur) in the sixteenth-century Mydlářovsky dům, just off the main square. Czechoslovakia has a long tradition of puppetry, going back to the country's peasant roots, and the museum acts as a repository for marionettes and puppets donated from all over the world.

Down the hill from the square, there's a cheap beery restaurant in the huge nineteenth-century town museum; while of Chrudim's two **hotels** the *Centrál*, Husova 246, is the cheaper.

Litomyšl

LITOMYŠL (Leitomischl) sits on the border between Bohemia and Moravia in a kind of no-man's-land between the two provinces. The **train station** is five minutes' walk northwest of the old town, a pleasant stroll along (and across) the river Loučná. Everything there is to see is close at hand. The picturesque main square, strung out like a juicy fat Czech sausage, is lined with almost uninterrupted arcades, a pastel parade of Baroque and Neoclassical facades. The sixteenth-century **U rytířů** at no. 110 (and now an art gallery) is the finest – decorated with medieval knights and merchants holding bags of money, clinging rather mischievously to their carved columns.

To the east, a knot of ramshackle backstreets, punctuated by churches in need of, or under, repair, leads up to the Pernštejn's **zámek** (daily April, Sept & Oct 9am–noon & 1–4pm; May–Aug 8am–noon & 1–5pm; closed Mon), a smart, sgraffitoed affair which bursts into frivolous gables and finials on its roof, and boasts Bohemia's finest triple-decker loggia inside. It now houses a fascinating exhibition of old musical instruments, mostly classical, which you wander around at your leisure to appropriate musical accompaniment from a temperamental Czech tape recorder. The inspiration for the museum comes from the brewery next door, where the most Czech of all Czech composers, **Bedřich Smetana**, was born in 1824, one of eighteen children born to an upwardly mobile brewery manager. The family's stay at Litomyšl was uneventful, and when Bedřich was only seven his father got a job in Jindřichův Hradec. Catalysed by the events of 1848, Smetana became a leading figure in the Czech national revival, helping to found the National Theatre in Prague, and throughout his life promoted the nationalist cause through works like *Ma vlast* ("My Country"), a symphonic poem inspired by Czech legends and – in its most famous passage – by the meandering River Vltava, which forms the backbone of Bohemia. Like others before him, Smetana became deaf towards the end of his life (during which time he composed some of his most famous works), and ended his days in a mental asylum, driven insane by syphilis. Every year in his honour, the town puts on a **festival** of Smetana's music at the end of June.

The ugly but moderate *Zlatá hvězda* (☎23 38) on the main square should be able to provide **food** and **accommodation**, but if not, the no less ugly *Dalibor* near the station will oblige. There's a **campsite** (May–Sept) 2km east of the town centre.

travel details

Trains

From Tábor to Písek (8 daily; 1hr 30min); Chýnov/Pelhřimov (up to 8 daily; 15min/1hr 30min); České Budějovice (up to 11 daily; 1hr–1hr 30min).

From České Budějovice to Jindřichův Hradec (3 daily; 1hr 5min); Plzeň (8 daily; 2hr–3hr 30min); Český Krumlov/Horní Planá/Volary (up to 7 daily; 1hr/2hr 15min/3hr 10min).

From Plzeň to Domažlice (up to 15 daily; 1hr–1hr 40min); Klatovy/Železná Ruda (up to 14 daily; 1hr–1hr 20min/2hr 30min); Stříbro/Mariánské Lázně/Cheb (10 or more daily; 30–50min/1hr 15min–1hr 30min/1hr 40min–2hr 20min); Žatec (8 daily; 2hr–2hr 45min).

From Domažlice to Klatovy (7 daily; 1hr 10min).

From Mariánské Lázně to Teplá/Karlovy Vary (11 daily; 40min/1hr 50min).

From Cheb to Františkovy Lázně (15 daily; 8min); Karlovy Vary (15 daily; 50min–1hr 10min).

From Karlovy Vary to Kadaň (17 daily; 50min–1hr 10min).

From Litoměřice to Děčín (5 daily; 1hr 10min); Mělník (9 daily; 30–45min); Ploskovice/Úštěk (11 daily; 12min/35min); Liberec (7 daily; 3hr 15min).

From Liberec to Frýdlant (up to 11 daily; 40min); Jablonec nad Nisou/Železný Brod (8 daily; 30min/2hr); Turnov (16 daily; 50min).

From Turnov to Jičín (11 daily; 50min–1hr 10min); Železný Brod (16 daily; 20min); Hradec Králové (up to 16 daily; 2–3hr).

From Hradec Králové to Jaroměř (20 daily; 20–30min); Kuks (10 daily; 40min); Chlumec nad Cidlinou (15 daily; 20–40min); Pardubice (26 daily; 30min).

From Pardubice to Chrudim (15 daily; 30min).

Buses

From Tábor to Kámen (up to 6 daily; 30min).

From Pelhřimov to Kámen (up to 7 daily; 30min); Humpolec (up to 10 daily; 30min); Jihlava (up to 8 daily; 45min).

From Jindřichův Hradec to Slavonice (up to 8 daily; 1hr 30min); České Budějovice (12 or more daily; 1hr 10min).

From České Budějovice to Hluboká nad Vltavou (20 or more daily; 20min); Holašovice (up to 8 daily; 40min); Prachatice (up to 10 daily; 1hr 15min).

From Český Krumlov to Rožmberk/Vyšší Brod/Lipno nad Vltavou (up to 10 daily; 40min/55min/1hr 15min).

From Plzeň to Karlovy Vary (up to hourly; 1hr 30min).

From Karlovy Vary to Loket (up to 14 daily; 25min); Jáchymov (up to 18 daily; 50min); Děčín (up to 4 daily; 3hr 45min).

From Teplice to Litoměřice (7 daily; 1hr 10min); Děčín (up to 6 daily; 1hr 20min).

From Děčín to Liberec (up to 3 daily; 2hr 10min).

From Liberec to Vrchlabí (up to 6 daily; 2–3hr); Hradec Králové (up to 5 daily; 1hr 50min).

From Hradec Králové to Jaroměř/Trutnov (up to 14 daily; 25min/1hr 10min); Pec pod Sněžkou (up to 8 daily; 2hr); Náchod (up to 6 daily; 1hr); Nové Město nad Metují (up to 5 daily; 1hr 20min); Litomyšl (5 or more daily; 1hr 10min).

CHAPTER THREE

MORAVIA

Wedged between Bohemia and Slovakia, **Moravia** (Morava) is the smallest of the three provinces which make up Czechoslovakia, and as such, shares characteristics with both its big brothers. Like Bohemia, much of Moravia is heavily industrialised (and even more densely populated), while the region's folk roots, traditions and even its religion are as strongly felt here as in parts of Slovakia.

Geographically, Moravia stretches from the Bohemian-Moravian Uplands or *Vysočina*, which form the ill-defined western border, to the Slovak Carpathians beyond the River Morava in the east. But the administrative divisions are the ones which persist: South Moravia centred around the regional capital, Brno, and North Moravia, written off by some as an industrial wasteland, actually containing Moravia's most diverse countryside.

Lying on the railway line between Prague and Bratislava, **Brno** is the one place in Moravia InterRailers might easily think of going to. Few do, yet it's no bad place to hang out, a once-grand nineteenth-century city, and within easy striking distance of a whole host of sights, most notably Moravia's **karst region**. South of Brno a whole string of Germanic medieval villages, towns and castles perch on a ledge above the Vienna plain.

By contrast, the uplands of the *Vysočina*, which separate Bohemia and Moravia, are poor and sparsely populated, viewed by most travellers from the window of their coach or train to Brno. If you do stop – and parts of it are definitely worth visiting – make sure you dig deeper than **Jihlava**, the area's most convenient starting point. It's worth taking the trouble to visit either **Telč** or **Slavonice**, arguably the country's most perfect architectural set pieces. And even if you're not a devotee of Santini's Baroque confections, the pilgrimage church at **Žďár nad Sázavou** is something special. To the east of Brno, the landscape around the **River Morava** is – visually, at least – undeniably flat and boring, and for most travellers the wine is the only (very good) reason to stop. That said, some towns on and around the River Morava stand out on their own merit: the provincial treasure house and graceful gardens of **Kroměříž**, and at the other end of the scale, the modernist aesthetics of **Zlín**.

In the northern half of the province, the Baroque riches of the Moravian prince-bishopric have left their mark on the old capital, **Olomouc**, now a thriving university town and the region's main attraction. The rest of the North Moravian corridor which forms the gateway into Poland is a virtual rerun of North Bohemia, a black hole into which few venture voluntarily flanked by the **Jeseníky** and **Beskydy** mountains. Of the two, the latter win hands down in terms of variety, with sights ranging from the antique cars in **Kopřivnice** to the country's largest folk skansen in **Rožnov pod Radhoštěm**.

If the number of Moravians who want independence is small, there are many more who feel justifiably grieved at Moravia's plight. Having had a certain degree

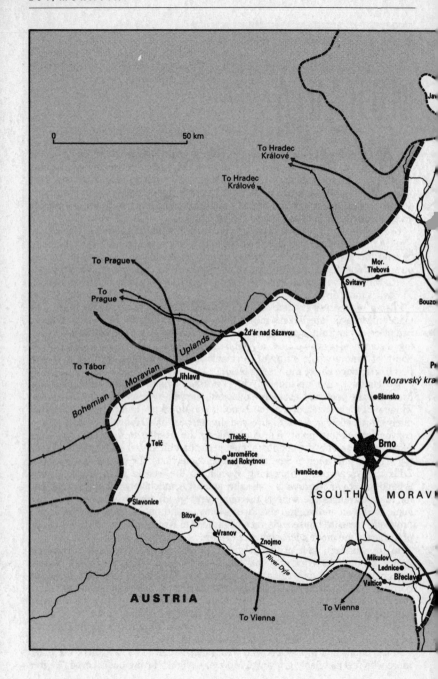

of autonomy between the wars, Moravia has been subordinated to Prague since the Communists took control in 1948; federalisation in 1969 favoured only the Slovaks, while Moravia remained part of the Czech Republic. Until Moravia has its own self-governing body, it is argued, it will continue to subsidise the Czech (ie Bohemian) half of the country which in turn subsidises the Slovaks. General discontent has boosted the prospects of the Moravian Nationalist party, the HSD-SMS, who performed surprisingly well in the country's first free elections, gaining even more votes than the Slovak nationalists.

Transport is fairly good throughout Moravia, though the **train system** is not quite as comprehensive as that of Bohemia, petering out in the *Vysočina*, and degenerating into a series of overcomplex branch lines along the more industrialised River Morava and in the north of the region. In such instances, **buses** are invariably quicker and more direct. **Accommodation** suffers from the usual shortcomings, but the situation in the big towns like Brno and Olomouc is a vast improvement on the difficulties of Prague.

SOUTH MORAVIA

The landscape of **South Moravia** (Jižní Morava) appears little different from that of much of Bohemia – gentle hills, forests and cultivation – but as you approach the Austrian border the land becomes richer, the orchards and vineyards getting thicker with the move south.

Brno, the most obvious starting point, presents the other side of the region – a town based on heavy industry, but also suffused with a refreshing cosmopolitanism. You'll inevitably find yourself here at some point and, although its attractions are often underrated, it's a good idea to allow for some time out of the city, since it forms a good base for much of South Moravia. To the south and west, smaller, more manageable towns like **Mikulov**, **Telč** and **Slavonice** retain a great deal of their medieval origins. Further east, the landscape **around the River Morava** becomes monotonous, although there are a couple of specific sights worth stopping off for: **Kroměříž** for its Baroque chateau and gardens, and **Zlín** for its vision of industrial utopia.

Brno

BRNO "welcomes the visitor with new constructions", as one *ČEDOK* brochure euphemistically puts it. In fact, the ugly grey suburbs which sprawl across the surrounding hills play a major part in discouraging travellers from stopping in the city. But as one of the country's few really grand cities with a couple of really good museums and galleries, a handful of other sights and a fair bit of nightlife, it's worth two or three nights at the least. As yet, though, the city receives few visitors outside the annual Trade Fairs. This has its advantages of course: tourists here are welcomed rather than alternately shunned or ripped off as in Prague, and life still maintains some of the endearing (and infuriating) affectations of a provincial Vienna, itself only an hour away by car.

Brno was a late developer, being no bigger than Olomouc until the late eighteenth century. The town's first cloth factory was founded in 1766, and within fifteen years was followed by another twenty, earning Brno the nickname of *rakouský Manchestr* (Austrian Manchester). With the building of an engineering plant early in the next century the city began to attract Czech workers, along with Austrian, German, English and Jewish entrepreneurs, making it easily the second largest city in the Czech Lands at the end of the nineteenth century. Between the wars Brno enjoyed a cultural boom, heralded by the 1928 Exhibition of Contemporary Culture which provided an impetus for much of the city's **avant-garde architecture**. After the war, German-speakers (some 25 percent of the population) were given their marching orders and sent packing to Vienna. Brno's capital fled along with its capitalists and centralised state funds were diverted to Prague and Bratislava, pushing Brno into third place – where it has remained. However, with the recent switch to decentralisation, the city's fortunes seem to be looking up at last.

Arriving and getting around

For a whole generation, Brno's main **railway station** was covered in a web of scaffolding. A quick glance out of the carriage was enough to convince most travellers to move on. Then in a flurry of activity in the first half of 1989, the scaffolding was stripped off, paint was splashed on and brass fittings slapped in to mark the 150th anniversary of the Brno–Vienna railway. Now, as you leave the fresh and creamy late nineteenth-century splendour of the station, it only serves to point up the rot and decay which has been the lot of the rest of the city's buildings. Arriving at Brno's main **bus station**, situated five minutes' walk south of the train station, is a lot less impressive, but easy to escape from: simply follow the overhead walkway which descends into the train station. Both stations have lockers and there's a 24-hour left luggage office at the train station.

Most of Brno's sights are within easy walking distance of the train station, although **trams** will take you almost anywhere in the city within minutes. Tickets (which are half the usual width) must be bought beforehand from *PNS* newsagents, hotel lobbies or yellow ticket machines, and validated in the punching devices on board. Some trams run all night (signified by a red number on the tram stop), gathering together in front of the station on the hour, every hour. For one day in early summer, all the old rolling stock – right back to the first horse-drawn street cars – is brought out from retirement. The same tickets are valid for the city's **buses** and **trolley buses**, but you're unlikely to need to use them, since they tend to plough the more obscure suburban routes. **Taxis** can be hailed or picked up at one of the ranks outside the train station or the city's international hotels.

Trying to obtain even the most simple tourist **information** in Brno presents serious problems. *ČEDOK* at Divadelní 3 (☎254 66) might provide you with a few glossy brochures (though rarely in English), otherwise your best bet is to try the hotel receptionists at the *Grand* or *International* who are used to dealing with foreigners. If you want a more detailed map than the one we've printed, ask for a *plán města* from the bookshop near the station on Masarykova.

The Brno area telephone code is ☎05.

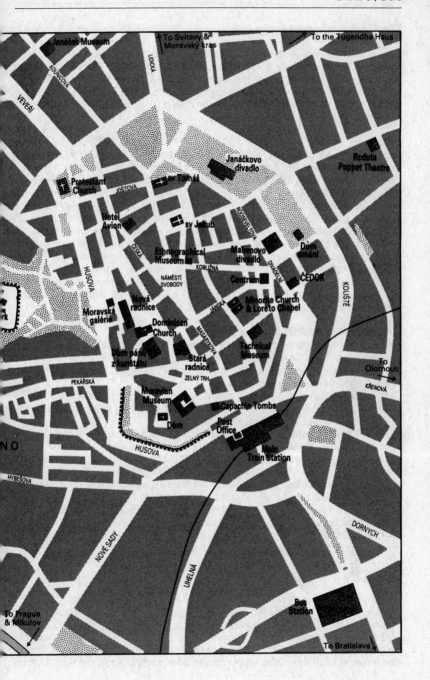

To Svitavy &
Moravsky kras

To the Tügendha Haus

Janáček Museum

KOUNICOVA

LIDICKÁ

VEVEŘÍ

Janáčkovo
divadlo

Reduta
Puppet Theatre

Protestant
Church

JOŠTOVA

sv Tomáš

ROOSEVELTOVA

Hotel
Avion

ČESKÁ

sv Jakub

DIVADELNÍ

Ethnographical
Museum

Mahenovo
divadlo

Dům
umění

HUSOVA

KOBLIŽNÁ

NÁMĚSTÍ
SVOBODY

Centrum

ČEDOK

KOLIŠTĚ

Nová
radnice

JÁNSKÁ

Minorite Church
& Loreto Chapel

Moravská
galérie

Dominican
Church

MASARYKOVA

Dům pánů
z kunštátu

Stará
radnice

Technical
Museum

To
Olomouc

PEKÁŘSKÁ

ZELNÝ TRH

KŘENOVA

Moravian
Museum

Capuchin Tombs

NO

Dům

Post
Office

HUSOVA

Main
Train Station

HYBEŠOVA

DORNYCH

NOVÉ SADY

UHELNÁ

To Prague
& Mikulov

Bus
Station

To Bratislava

Finding a place to stay

Accommodation is in the same uncertain state as in the rest of the country. However, you're unlikely to have trouble getting a room, except during the International Consumer Goods Fair in April. ČEDOK can arrange rooms, but will try and steer you towards the more expensive hotels. Since nearly all hotels are within easy walking distance of the train station, you might prefer to hunt for something cheaper yourself.

Hotels

Brno's **hotels** are all fairly central: the **cheapest** are the *Morava*, Novobranská 3 (☎275 26), and the *Evropa* at the corner of of Jánská and Masarykova (☎266 11). The *Družba* (if it's still called that), Kounicova 90 (☎435 45), is north of the city on tram routes #13, #16 and #22, but only opens between July and September. Up one notch, but still reasonable, Brno's **moderate** hotels are *U Jakuba*, Jakubské náměstí 6 (☎229 91), the *Avion*, Česká 20 (☎276 06), and the *Slovan*, Lidická 23 (☎74 55 05). More **expensive** but equally central are the *Grand Hotel* (☎264 21), practically opposite the station, and the *Slavia*, Solničnií 15/17 (☎237 11). For a secluded (and inconvenient) location in the woods to the west of town, try the *Myslivna* (☎33 95 96), bus #68 from Mendlovo náměstí to the end of the line. Modern, unwelcoming and overpriced, the *International* on Husova (☎213 41 11) and the *Continental* on Kounicova (☎75 05 01) are both worth avoiding, as are the two high-rise hotels, *Veroněž I* and *Veroněž II*, south of the city.

Private rooms, hostels and campsites

ČEDOK (Mon–Fri 9am–5pm, Sat 9am–noon) on Divadelní arrange cheap **private rooms**, but at the time of writing were sticking to their old ways and demanding a minimum stay of four nights. This may change if and when they start to be seriously undercut by private operators.

In July and August, it's possible to stay in one of the city's **student dorms**. As addresses change from year to year, the best thing to do is go straight to the CKM office at Česká 11 (☎236 41) and ask there.

Brno's three **campsites** are a train or bus ride out of the city centre. Best of the bunch is the *Obora* site (April–Oct), 10km northeast of the city on the shores of the brněnská přehrada (Brno Dam). A ČSAD bus runs hourly, and in summer you can get there by tram #3, #10, #14, #18, #20 or #21, followed by a boat across the dam. Somewhat less picturesque is the *Bobrava* site, 10km south at Modřice (March–Oct). Take the local *osobní* train three stops to Popovice (last one around 11pm). In the summer, with your own transport, it's possible to camp (rather uncomfortably) at the Grand Prix circuit, Masarykův Okruh; take the motorway in the direction of Prague to the Kývalka exit, then follow the signs. Buses between Brno and the circuit are laid on during the Grand Prix.

The City

Despite its 400,000-plus population, the centre of Brno is compact. The city's main action goes on within the small egg-shaped old town, pedestrianised for the most part and encircled by a swathe of parks and the inner ring road. Around **Zelný trh** and **náměstí Svobody** you'll find most of the city's shops and markets. In the southwestern corner of the old town are the quieter streets around Petrov, the lesser of Brno's two hills, topped by the **dóm**. Further west, the squat fortress of **Špilberk** looks down on the old town to the east and Staré Brno to the south, site of the original medieval settlement. Worth a visit, but still further from the centre, are Brno's modern architectural sights, the exhibition grounds of **Výstaviště** and – on the opposite side of town – Mies van der Rohe's **Tugendhat Haus**.

Zelný trh and the stará radnice

Every tram in Brno congregates in front of the station, and there's an infectious buzz about the place in the early afternoon, after work. A steady stream of people plough up and down **Masarykova**, a somewhat hazardous cocktail of cobbles, steaming manholes and tram lines. Don't let that stop you from looking up at the five-storey mansions, laden with a fantastic mantle of decoration, grotesquely disfigured by pollutants.

To the left as you head up Masarykova is **Zelný trh** (cabbage market), the low-key vegetable market on a sloping cobbled square not yet back to the brisk trade of its pre-war days, and somewhat ill-served by the mishmash of buildings which line its edges. At its centre is the petrified diarrhoea of the huge *Parnassus* fountain by Fischer von Erlach: in the good old days when it worked properly, live carp was sold from its waters at Christmas. At the top of the square, the plain mass of the Dietrichstein Palace, sporting a severe extra top pediment, leads to an intimate arcaded courtyard which forms the entrance to the **Moravian Museum** (Tues–Sun 9am–6pm), a worthy though not entirely convincing collection of ancient and medieval artefacts, with emphasis on the Great Moravian Empire.

Much more interesting, if only for their macabre value, are the **Capuchin tombs** (Tues–Sat 9–11.45am & 2–4.30pm, Sun 11–11.45am & 2–4.30pm) to the far south of the square, a gruesome collection of dead monks and top nobs, mummified by chance in the crypt of the Capuchin church. Until the eighteenth century, Brno's moneyed classes forked out large sums to be buried here in the monks' simple common grave, in the hopes of finding a short cut to heaven – righteousness by association, perhaps. The bodies lie fully clothed, some with the hollow expressions of skeletons, others still frozen in the last painful grimace of death. Just to drive the point home, signs in Czech chime in with "What we are, they once were, what they are, we will be". Not an experience for the faint-hearted.

Clearly visible from Zelný trh is the **stará radnice**. Anton Pilgram's Gothic doorway is its best feature, the thistly pinnacle above the statue of Blind Justice symbolically twisted as if it's about to fall onto your head – Pilgram's testament on the corrupt town aldermen who shortchanged him for his work. Inside, the radnice's courtyards and passageways are a confusing mixture of styles, jam-packed with whatever tour groups are passing through town, here to see the *Brněnský drak* (Brno dragon) – actually a stuffed crocodile – a gift from the Turks to Archduke Matthias, which is suspended from the ceiling rather like a cheap inflatable space shuttle*. If you're still a bit hazy on the geography of the old town, the tower of the radnice is worth a climb for the panorama across the city's red-tiled rooftops.

---

* The other town mascot displayed here is the *Brněnské kolo* (Brno wheel), made in 1636 by a cartwright from Lednice, who bet a friend that he could fell a tree, make a wheel and roll it to Brno (some 50km away) all before sunset. He won the bet and the wheel has been given pride of place in the stará radnice ever since, though the story goes that following his great feat people began to suspect that he was in league with the Devil. His business fell off and the cartwright died in poverty.

From the nová radnice to the dóm

Round the back of the stará radnice, the cobbled square below the Dominican Church serves as a car park for the grey functionaries of the present city council who hold office at the **nová radnice**. It's a passable attempt by Mořic Grimm, the city's chief Baroque architect, "a provincial talent but a sound craftsman" as one critic described him. There's nothing to see here, unless someone's getting married, despite the pretty sundials in the echoing first courtyard. The handful of hilly streets which lead south from here to the Petrov hill are the nearest Brno gets to a secluded, intimate spot. As you walk up Dominikanská from the cobbled square, take a quick look inside the **Dům pánů z Kunštátu**, one of Brno's few Renaissance buildings, now serving up some pretty good art exhibitions around its galleried courtyard.

The Petrov hill, on which the **dóm** stands, is one of the best places in which to make a quick escape from the choked streets below. The needle-sharp Gothic spires of Brno's dóm dominate the skyline for miles around, but close up, the crude nineteenth-century rebuilding has made it a lukewarm affair. Still, it holds a special place in Brno's history for having been instrumental in saving the town from the Swedes in 1645. After months besieging the town, the Swedish general Tortennson decided to make one last attempt at taking the place, declaring that he would give up at midday if the town hadn't surrendered. In a fit of inspiration, the bell-ringer, seeing that the town was on the brink of defeat, decided to ring the midday bells an hour early. The Swedes gave up their attack, the city was saved, and as a reward the Habsburg emperor switched the Moravian capital from Olomouc to Brno (well, so the story goes).

Inside the lofty nave, the most interesting art treasures are the aluminium *Stations of the Cross*. Constructed in the 1950s, these get progressively more outrageous and abstract as the story unfolds, until the final relief is no more than flailing limbs and anguished metal. Other than this, it's not really worth venturing into the dóm, despite its recent facelift, unless you're in need of sanctuary from the heat of the day.

The dóm is not the only reason to climb Petrov: there's a far-reaching view over the great plain which extends south to Vienna and, from the leafy Petrov park tucked into the city ramparts, an interesting angle on the dóm itself. In among the trees of the park, a slender white obelisk commemorates the Napoleonic Wars (the Battle of Austerlitz took place just outside Brno – see p.223), lining up perfectly with the avenue of Husova which leads to the red-brick Protestant Church and, beyond it, the bright white former Party headquarters, known affectionately as the Bílý dům (White House). When it was at the planning stages in the 1950s, the more committed cadres wanted to remove the offending Protestant Church which blocked the view up Husova. Fortunately, aestheticism triumphed over atheism and the plan was somehow foiled.

Náměstí Svobody

Back down on Masarykova, follow the flow north and you'll end up at **náměstí Svobody**, nominally the city's main square and focus of the November 1989 revolution for Brno's 400,000 population. Far short of magnificent, it's nonetheless the place where most of Brno come to do their shopping. In summer, you can sit and drink coffee *al fresco* under the shadow of the square's golden plague column (see box) – and admire the square's three finest buildings which span almost four centuries. The earliest is the **Dům pánů z Lipé**, with an ornate Renaissance facade in need of a cleaning. Opposite, and totally lacking in subtlety, is **Dům u čtyř mamlasů**, belonging to one of Brno's richest nineteenth-century industrialists, whose four muscle-bound employees struggle to hold up both his building and their loincloths. And in the northwest corner of the square, Bohuslav Fuchs' functionalist **Moravská banka** (now significantly just the *státníbanka*) has turned a rather nasty green since its inception in the 1930s. On the northeast corner of the square is the **Ethnographical Museum** (Tues–Sun 9am–6pm), which contains a large permanent collection of Moravian folk costumes, ceramics, painted easter eggs and an album of old photos, as well as occasionally hosting exhibitions on ethnographic themes from other countries.

PLAGUE COLUMNS

Plague columns are a frequent feature of Catholic towns and cities, an expression of civic gratitude for having been delivered from the Black Death. Later regarded by Protestants and Czech nationalists as symbols of the Austro-Hungarian hegemony, many were demolished during the celebrations following the foundation of the Czechoslovak Republic in 1918. Brno's column, erected in 1648 after the unsuccessful Swedish (Protestant) siege of the city, was one of the lucky survivors.

North and east of náměstí Svobody

Mořic Grimm's finest architectural work in Brno is the **Minorite church and Loreto chapel** on the corner of Minoritská and Jánská, whose vivacious frontage makes the most of its cramped site. Inside, it's much the best Baroque in town, high to the point of giddiness. The right-hand portal leads to the main church, a gilded, frescoed hall packed with religious kitsch and linked to the church next door, an even more over-the-top affair with a Hollywood-style altar staircase whose red-carpeted steps must be ascended on bended knee. The Loreto chapel, plonked in the middle of the church and taking up most of the nave, is everything it should be: an identical replica of the one in Prague (and, of course, Loreto in Italy).

Further along Minoritská into Josefská, the **Technical Museum** (Tues–Sun 9am–6pm, Sun 9am–2pm) has a wonderful stock of old trams, bicycles and cars from which to stage their temporary exhibitions. One permanent exhibit worth seeking out is the **Panorama** (for which you need a separate ticket), a large wooden stereoscope built in 1890 and designed to allow several viewers to see its rotating slides simultaneously. Usually it's loaded with old photos of Czechoslovakia (but the slides are changed every fortnight or so). Backtrack for one block and walk down to the bottom of Jánská, where the department store **Centrum**, built in 1928 by the shoe magnate Tomáš Baťa still cuts a bold figure sixty years on.

Brno's finest nineteenth-century building is the **Mahenovo divadlo**, a forthright building exuding the municipal confidence of its original German patrons in its Corinthian columns and pediment. Its insides are suitably smothered in gold sculpturing and glittering chandeliers, and it has the distinction of being the first theatre in the Austro-Hungarian Empire to be fitted with electric light bulbs. It would be difficult to think up a more ugly accompaniment to the Mahenovo than the squat **Dům umění**. This does, however, contain the city's most innovative art gallery and theatre venue, specialising in modern, controversial exhibitions and even the occasional gig.

A little further up Rooseveltova, the grey and unappealing **Janáčkovo divadlo** was built in the 1960s as the city's – indeed the country's – largest opera house. Although he was born in the very north of Moravia, **Leoš Janáček** moved to Brno at the age of eleven and spent most of his life here, first as a chorister and then teacher and choirmaster at the local Augustinian monastery. Battling against the prejudices of the German town administration, he managed to drag Czech music out of the pubs and into the concert hall, eventually founding the Brno Conservatoire and Organ School in 1882, but as a composer he remained virtually unknown outside Moravia until well into his sixties, when he began the last and most prolific creative period of his life (see "Beskydy", p.255). Across the park and a short way up Kounicova, there's a modest **museum** celebrating Janáček's life and work, where you can sit back and relax to his music.

Heading north from náměstí Svobody up **Česká**, a steady stream of people flows past the concentration of book and record shops, pubs and cafés, wolfing down takeaways and *zmrzlina*, and, at the top, waiting for the trams and buses which congregate on Joštova, which marks the end of the old town. At its western end Joštova forms a grand approach to the church of **sv Tomáš**, whose adjoining monastery houses a museum of the working-class movement, at present closed while undergoing a post-1989 rethink.

West of the old town

Moving west from the centre, on the other side of Husova, the old town gives way to the woods of the Špilberk hill. On Husova itself is the country's best collection of modern art, the **Moravská galérie** (Tues–Sun 10am–6pm). The only permanent collection is the top floor's exhibition of "applied arts" – anything from avant-garde photomontages to swirling Art-Nouveau vases. The rest of the building is given over to consistently good temporary exhibitions – check the fly posters about town to see what's on offer.

Skulking on a thickly wooded hill to the west of Husova and barely visible through the trees, the ugly squat fortress of **Špilberk** (Spielberg) acquired a reputation for being one of the most god-awful prisons in the Habsburg Empire. As you walk up through the castle grounds, a monument of Romulus and Remus commemorates the many Italians who died here, having been incarcerated fighting for their country's freedom in the northern borders of what is now Italy. The testimony of one Italian inmate, the poet Count Silvio Pellico, so shocked the Austrian middle classes that the prison was closed down in 1857. Less than a hundred years later, it was put back into use by the SS who confined, tortured and killed some 80,000 prisoners during the war. Knowing all this, the tour round the dimly-lit dungeons is depressingly evocative stuff, but until 1994 the place is undergoing a lengthy overhaul. As a consolation, stroll around the brooding battlements or visit the castle's swish *vinárna*.

The area south of the Špilberk hill, where the first settlements sprang up in the early Middle Ages, is known as Staré Brno. Few traces of these survive and nowadays there's nothing particularly old or interesting about this part of town, with the exception of the fourteenth-century **Augustinian monastery** on Mendlovo náměstí. Despite its unpromising locale – the square is little more than a glorified bus terminal – it's one of Brno's finest Gothic buildings, its pillars and walls smothered in delicate geometric patterning. The monastery is best known for one of its monks, **Gregor Mendel** (1822–1884), whose experiments in the abbey gardens with peas and bees eventually led to the discovery of the theory of heredity and subsequently genetics. Despite publishing several seminal papers outlining his discoveries, his work was ignored by the scientific establishment and in 1868 he gave up his research to become the monastery's abbot. Only after his death was he acknowledged as one of the greats of modern biology, and there's a room dedicated to him in the small anthropological museum housed in part of the monastery.

Výstaviště and the Tugendhat Haus

To the west of the city centre, where the River Svratka opens up to the plain (tram #1 or #18 from the station), is the **Výstaviště Exhibition Ground**. The main buildings were laid out in 1928 for the city's Exhibition of Contemporary Culture, and most of the leading Czech architects of the day were involved in the scheme, which prompted a flurry of functionalist building projects across the city's burgeoning suburbs. Even if you've no interest in modern architecture, the various fairs and exhibitions staged here are big social events, particularly the annual Consumer Goods Trade Fair which takes place at the end of April. Such fairs, once the showpieces of socialism, are now more an opportunity for foreign companies to try and flog their goods. The most arresting (and largest) building on the site, the circular crystal and concrete **Z pavilion**, is actually one of the post-war additions, but one which kept to the spirit of the original concept. The only building which predates the complex is the **Zámeček**, which features an interior by Brno-born arch-minimalist Adolf Loos.

The part of the 1928 exhibition which really caused a sensation was the **Nový dům** (New House; no admission), worth a look if you're keen on Bauhaus-style architecture. Inspired by the Weissenhofsiedlung built one year earlier in Stuttgart, Bohuslav Fuchs and various others designed a series of boxy white concrete villas by the woods of the Jiráskův les, 1km north of Výstaviště. The brief for each architect was to create modest two-storey houses for middle-income families, using standard fittings and ordinary materials to keep the unit costs down. Now grey, peeling and overrun by vegetation, it takes a leap of imagination to appreciate the shock of the new which these buildings must have aroused at the time. To get there, take tram #18, getting off halfway down Kamenomlýnská.

On the opposite side of town, in the northeastern suburb of Černá Pole, Modernist guru Mies van der Rohe built the **Tugendhat Haus** (Černopolní 45; tram #5, #9, #17 or #21) in the same functionalist style, but to a very different brief: the Tugendhats, an exceptionally rich Jewish family who ran a number of the city's textile factories, wanted a state-of-the-art house kitted out in the most expensive gear money could buy. Completed in 1930, the family had barely eight years to enjoy the luxury of the place before fleeing to South America (with most of the period furniture) in the wake of the Nazi invasion. For the last fifty years it has been put to many uses – both the Nazis and Communists were particularly partial to it for exclusive social functions – and until the November 1989 revolution it was virtually impossible to gain access to the place. Gradually it's being opened up to the public (daytime weekends seem to be the best bet). Entering through the top floor, the main living space is actually downstairs, open-plan for the most part, and originally decked out in minimalist monochrome furnishings offset by colourful Persian carpets. The Communists' "modernisation" after the war was depressingly thorough and the huge unbroken front window, which looked out over the garden and the whole cityscape beyond it, has been replaced by a series of much smaller panes, the largest the Communists' glassworks could muster.

FUCHS, FUNCTIONALISM AND SWIMMING POOLS

While Brno produced two great modern architects in Adolf Loos and Jan Kotěra, they spent most of their time in Vienna or Prague; it was left to another Moravian, **Bohuslav Fuchs**, who began working here in 1923, to shape the face of modern Brno. Fuchs and his functionalist cohorts turned their hand to everything from the town's brutal crematorium (Jihlavská; tram #7, #8 or #15) to the Protestant church on Botanická, its interior decoration as "low-church" and prosaic as you can get. His own hand is everywhere in the city, in the now gloomy arcade off Jánská, in the slimline *Hotel Avion* and in Výstaviště itself. His most famous works are the open-plan boarding school and Vesna girls' school (on the hilly Žlutý kopec just north of Výstaviště), two simple four-storey functionalist buildings, way ahead of their time *at* the time, but already gone to seed in the intervening years. But perhaps the best way to appreciate Fuchs' work is to head out to the outdoor swimming pool he built in the suburb of Zábrdovice (tram #2, #8, #16, #19 or #21), where you can laze by the pool and take in the culture at the same time.

Eating, drinking and nightlife

There's no shortage of places **to eat and drink** in Brno. The restaurants retain an old-fashioned air of good service, while the pubs are lively if nothing else – though most close around 10pm, leaving only the posh hotels and exclusive *vinárna* open after midnight. As for **nightlife**, classical music and opera are well catered for and, with a large contingent of students, there's usually something a bit less staid going on.

Stand-up buffets and street food

Česká is a good place to look for takeaway foods like *bramborák* or *hranolky* and, of course, ice cream, or you could try the vast *Sputnik* complex at the bottom of the street. If you need provisions, there's a daily vegetable market in Zelný trh, and the bakery on the north side of náměstí Svobody is worth heading for. One of the best stand-up eateries is the new *Bufet Tranzit*, opposite the station. For fish specialities, try *Rybena* on Běhounská. It's also worth remembering that the *bufet* at the station is open late into the night, though it's not recommended.

Restaurants and wine-cellars

Sit-down restaurants start out pretty cheap; try the *Academická* on Gorkého for lunch or *U Luzerna* on Slovákova, both of which are inexpensive and close to the university. Nearer the centre of town, *Opera*, diagonally opposite the Mahenovo divadlo, is popular with foreign students and reasonably priced. Fresh from chef school, the young apprentices at *U Jakuba* try a bit harder than most Moravian cooks, and surprisingly enough, the renovated Habsburg-style *restaurace* at the station is actually not a bad choice.

As yet, the *Galérie* on Smetanova, which also gives space to local artists, is the only pizza place in town, though the *San Marco*, west off Masarykova, also serves up quasi-Italian grub. As time goes on, the choice and variety of restaurants should increase as private outfits start up. Until they do, the swisher places are state-run eateries like the small and intimate *Černý medvěd* on Jakubské náměstí (advance reservation advisable). The best of the rest are all *vinárna* which stay open late, and generally require advance booking; try *Baroko*, Orlí 17, or *U královny Elišky*, Mendlovo náměstí 1 (☎33 8903).

Cafés and pubs

One of the best **cafés** in town is *U Kolbabi*, at the beginning of Kounicova. It's usually filled with students taking a quick break from the library next door, and is one of the few places in Brno that serves a good espresso. During the summer, outside drinking takes place at various cafés around náměstí Svobody and Zelný trh.

Brno is hotter on **pubs** than cafés, though of course you can get a coffee in either. The local brew is *Starobrno* but the best places are actually the ones which don't serve it. *Špalíček* at the top of Zelný trh is a good bet, with tables outside in summer and lashings of *Gambrinus* from Plzeň. *Stopka* on Česká, once the best *pivnice* and restaurant in town, has hiked up its prices after a revamp, though downstairs is still good for a jar of dark beer or *Plzeňský Prazdroj*. Dark beer is also served at *Černohorská* by the Capuchin church. If you're still keen to taste the local stuff, try *U tří knížat*, Minoritská 2, which opens at 8am, or better still rough it at *Pivovarská*, right by the brewery itself on Mendlovo náměstí. Like the street itself, *U formana* at Česká 29 is full of Moravian youth in all its various forms, and serves Prague's *Staropramen*.

Nightlife

Ballet, opera and orchestral concerts are the most accessible of the **classical** arts for those without any Czech, and the Mahenovo and Janáčkovo divadlo, both off Rooseveltova, share the load. It's true that the best Moravian singers are eventually lost to Prague, but they make their reputations here as much as anywhere, and productions are usually competent if a little conservative. There's a lively fringe theatre scene, but unless you chance upon a particularly physical, visual show, the language is going to be an insurmountable barrier. Tickets for all shows can be bought in advance from the **box office** at Dvořákova 11 (☎263 11), or (much cheaper) from the venue itself, half an hour before the performance starts.

It's not that there aren't any **clubs** in Brno – it's just that there aren't many. Best of the lot is the *Vysokoškolský klub*, Gorkého 43, which is the main venue for indigenous folk, jazz and anything in between – check out the monthly posters dotted round town. There's a more youthful club on Křenová, with the emphasis on imported Western rock videos and records, and featuring the occasional gig. The student club *Topas* functions during term time at the Kounicové koleje, a hall of residence down Mučednická (tram #3, #10, #14, #20 or #21 from the top of Česká), and on the other side of town live gigs occasionally take place at an on/off club on Musilova (tram #3 or #12). A wide selection of international films are shown at the cinemas around town, including the occasional subtitled US blockbuster. *Ponrepo* at Hybešova 51 specialises in black and white films from the 1940s to the 1960s.

Clubs in the **big hotels** stay open latest, and serve up the usual Western pap. The *Hotel International* on Husova and the *Evropa* on Masarykova usually have a bash every night except Sundays and Mondays. The *Rozmarýn* "variety-club" on Žerotinovo náměstí is one of Brno's dingiest sleaze-pits.

Listings

Books and prints A bizarre collection of books in English grace the shelves of *Zahraniční literatura*, náměstí Svobody 18. Second-hand books in all languages and a good range of old prints, maps and artwork can be had from the bookshop at Česká 28.

Car hire *Brnocar* (☎254 75) at Solniční 6.

ČEDOK Main office for foreign tourists is at Divadelní 3 (☎254 66).

Chemists All-night service at Kobližna 7 (☎222 75).

Crystal and glass The best two outfits at the moment are *Krystal*, Masarykova 33, and *Universal*, Minoritská.

Currency exchange *ČEDOK* will only accept credit cards and foreign cash. All other matters are dealt with by the *státní banka* at náměstí Svobody 21 or Rooseveltova 18/20.

Hospital Bratislavská 2; emergency medical attention ☎155.

Motorcycle Grand Prix Brno hosts the grand prix at the end of August at the Masarykův okruh. Special buses are laid on during the competition, otherwise take bus #65 and walk for five minutes west.

Police The main police station is at Kounicova 46.

Post office The central post office is next to the train station. It runs a 24-hour telephone exchange.

Supermarket Brno's biggest supermarket lies between the bus and train stations. Late-night shopping Thursdays.

Taxis The main taxi ranks are outside the station and on Solni ční, or dial ☎245 04 or ☎256 06.

Around Brno

Brno has plenty to keep you occupied, but if you're staying any amount of time, follow the advice of the health authorities and get out of the city at the weekend. One of the few good things about living in the grey concrete suburbs is that you can walk straight out into the woods and bump into a deer. If that doesn't take your fancy, the most popular day trip is to the limestone caves of the **Moravský kras**, closely followed by the castle of Pernštejn and the battlefield at **Slavkov** (Austerlitz). Potentially more interesting than any of those is the Renaissance chateau at **Moravský Krumlov**, which houses a museum of the work of the Art-Nouveau painter Alfons Mucha.

The Moravský kras

Number-one destination for all tour groups passing through Moravia is the limestone **karst region** of the **Moravský kras**, just over 25km northeast of Brno. It's definitely worth a visit, but unless you're part of a coach tour (book yourself on one at *ČEDOK* in Brno), it can be pretty tricky to reach the caves. The best thing to do is to get the morning train from Brno out to BLANSKO (get off at Blansko-Macocha station), and then follow the crowd to the nearby bus terminal. From Blansko bus station it's possible to buy an all-inclusive ticket which will get you into all three caves and pay for your journey there and back (tours set off at 8am & 11am). Although this is good value, by the third cave, the novelty of the karst experience begins to wear off. The alternative is to pay up, leave the tour halfway and then hitch, pray for a bus or walk the 5km back through the woods along the green-marked path.

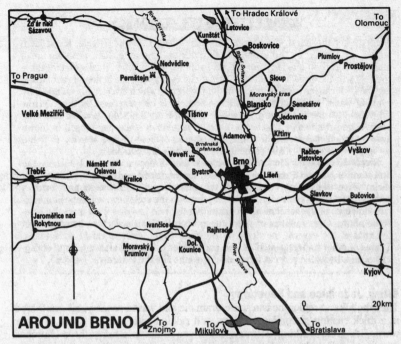

AROUND BRNO

The most popular tour target is the **Punkevní jeskyně**, the largest cave system and the deepest part of the gorge – get there early if you want to avoid the queues. Daily tours run every fifteen minutes (April–Sept 7am–4.30pm; Oct–March 7.30am–2.30pm) and take around fifty minutes. It's pointless cataloguing the fantastic array of stalactites and stalagmites; suffice to say it really is worth the hassle of getting there. After a series of five chambers, you come to the bottom of the Macocha Abyss, a gigantic 138-metre mossy chasm created when the roof of one of the caves collapsed. The first man to descend into the abyss and return alive was Father "Lazerus" Erker in 1728, almost two hundred years before the caves themselves were properly explored. From the abyss, you're punted half a kilometre along the slimy Punkva river which gives the cave its name.

The two other caves open to the public are only slightly less spectacular, but with the added advantage that the queues are correspondingly smaller. The **Kateřinská jeskyně** (30min tour; April–Sept 7.30am–3.30pm; Oct–March 8.30am–3.30pm), one and a half kilometres before the Punkevní jeskyně at the point where the Punkva river re-emerges, is basically one huge "cathedral" of rock formations, a hundred metres long and twenty metres high. The smallest of the lot is the **Balcarka jeskyně** (April–Sept 7.30am–3.30pm; Oct–March 8.30am–3.30pm), which lies 2km east of the Macocha Abyss. A fourth cave system called Sloupsko-Šošůvské jeskyně sits on the southern edge of the village of SLOUP, but is really only worth visiting for the occasional concerts which take place there.

KARST TOPOGRAPHY

Named after the Karst, the barren limestone plateau around Trieste, **karst** land-scapes are formed by the action of rainwater on limestone. Rain picks up small amounts of carbon dioxide from the atmosphere, which, when it falls on limestone rock, slowly dissolves it. Gradually, over millions of years, the action of rain attacking the rock causes hairline cracks in the limestone, which are steadily enlarged by running water. In its early stages, karst scenery is characterised by thin, narrow ridges and fissures; as these grow and deepen, the dry limestone is raked into wild, sharp-edged fragments, practically bare of vegetation since any topsoil is blown away – and bleached bright white, like shards of bone. Karst scenery is found throughout Czechoslovakia, particularly in **Moravia** and **Slovakia**.

Rivers do odd things in karst landscapes: they disappear down holes where the limestone is weakest, and flow for miles underground, suddenly bursting from rocks when the geology changes. If an underground river widens and forms a cavern, the drips of rainwater percolating through the soil above will deposit minuscule amounts of the calcium bicarbonate that the rain has dissolved from the limestone above. Over millions of years these deposits form stalactites hanging from the roof of the cavern; the drips on the floor form columns called stalagmites. Traces of other minerals such as iron and copper colour the stalactites and stalagmites, and the whole process forms cave systems like the **Punkevní jeskyně**.

Křtiny, Jedovnice and Senetářov

The whole karst region boasts some dramatic and varied scenery, all smothered in a thick coating of coniferous forest and riddled with marked paths. In other words, it's great **walking country**, and if you're not in a hurry three churches deserve a visit and provide a more relaxed alternative to the crush along the Punkva river. If you're serious about heading off into the hills, try and get hold of the elusive *Okolí Brna východ* map.

You can avoid all the crowds by getting off the Blansko train at ADAMOV station and walking east up the Josefovské údolí, a steep craggy valley with remnants of the original primaeval forest cover and open-air stalagmites. After 3km, at the top of the valley, there's a special nature trail round a mini-karst region of around five caves, none of which are actually accessible. Another 3km further east and out of the woods leaps the enormous dome and tower of the unfinished pilgrimage church of **KŘTINY**, started by the Baroque builder, Giovanni Santini. One of the doors is usually open to let you inside, where the nave has been handed over to a series of frescoed domes which fuse into one, giving the church a Byzantine feel. Only one set of curvaceous cloisters to the south was completed, now filled with the gifts and remembrances of a thousand pilgrims.

Taking the yellow-marked path, skirt the edge of the woods to the north, which rise gently past the understated peak of Proklest (574m). Six kilometres on from Křtiny, you emerge from the trees at the small lake which accompanies the village of **JEDOVNICE**, no beauty itself thanks to a fire in 1822 which also torched the late eighteenth-century village church. From the outside the latter looks hurriedly restored, but a group of Moravian artists redesigned the interior in the 1960s, filling it with symbolic art, stained glass and, as the centrepiece, the striking **altar** painting by Mikuláš Medek, *persona non grata* in Czechoslovakia in the 1950s for his penchant for surrealism and social comment. His choice of colours is didactic: a blue cross for hope, red for the chaos of the world. Unless it's a Sunday, you'll have to get the key from the *kaplan* who lives opposite the church, and who can also furnish you with an *anglický text*.

There's no escaping the modernity of the concrete church at **SENETÁŘOV**, 4km down the road to Vyškov; it's built in the shape of a ship, its "mast" visible as you approach from the plateau – though as a concept, its symbolism is reminiscent of the work of Santini. It's an uncompromising building, with huge plateglass panels at the west end through which you can clearly see Medek's vivid blue altarpiece. But it's his *Stations of the Cross*, lost in a corner of the north wall and difficult to see without getting inside, that are the church's masterpiece. Starting with a deep red crown of thorns, the pictures progress in bold simple colours and symbols, fusing into one long canvas and signalling a new and original working of an otherwise hackneyed theme.

On a completely different score, there's a minute **folk museum** (April–Oct Sat & Sun 8am–6pm) in a thatched cottage opposite the church, with a mock-up display of a typical Moravian home around the end of the last century.

Practical details

A regular bus service runs between Brno and Jedovnice, passing through Křtiny and occasionally continuing to Senetářov, making all the above places easy to visit on a day trip from Brno. If you want to stay the night, try the *Dukla* (☎0506-50 01) or *Macocha* (☎0506-10 10) in Blansko, but get *ČEDOK* in Brno to ring through to check vacancies for you. Alternatively, there's a campsite (May–Oct 15) by the lake at Jedovnice. There's a good private restaurant called *U lišky bystroušky* (☎654 39) in BÍLOVICE, halfway between Brno and Blansko on the main railway line.

The Northwest

Just as Brno's housing estates peter out to the northwest, you come to the long, snake-like **Brněnská přehrada** (Brno Dam), a favourite place for the folk of Brno to go on a sunny weekend (tram #3, #10, #14, #18, #20 or #22). The further you get from the lake's bulbous southern end, the thinner the crowds and the thicker the woods along the shoreline. In the summer, boats zigzag their way to VEVERSKÁ BÍTÝŠKA, passing the thirteenth-century clifftop fortress of **Veveří**, currently undergoing a lengthy restoration. There's a pretty path through the spruce on the left bank, should you miss the boat back.

Pernštejn

The Gothic stronghold of **Pernštejn** is a lot of people's idea of what a medieval castle should look like, and consequently one of the most popular targets around Brno. The train up the Svratka valley takes over an hour from Brno, but it's a pleasant journey (you may have to change at Tišnov), making it one of the easiest and most rewarding day trips. Stepping off the platform at NEDVĚDICE, the castle is immediately visible on the cusp of a low spur to the west. And as you approach by the yellow-marked track, it becomes increasingly intimidating. After a series of outer defences, the **hrad** (April & Oct Sat & Sun 9am–4pm; May–Aug Tues–Sun 8am–5pm) proper is a dramatic sight, kestrels circling the dizzying sheer walls. Originally built in the thirteenth century, various reconstructions have left it a jumble of unpredictable angles and extras, including a death-defying covered wooden bridge which spans the castle's main keeps. The hour-long guided tour is short on specific treasures, but makes up for it in atmosphere and spectacular views across the mixed woodland of the nearby hills. Should you wish to stay, the *U sokolovny* near the station in Nedvědice should have rooms.

The Southwest: Moravský Krumlov

South of Brno, the landscape lacks the variety and beauty of the karst to the north. Here the hills roll gently and smoothly towards Vienna, pleasant to travel through, plump and fertile. To the west the hills have more purpose, and before you know it, the Bohemian-Moravian Uplands begin.

Moravský Krumlov

One place southwest of Brno worth making the effort to see is **MORAVSKÝ KRUMLOV**, squeezed into a tight bend of the Rokytná river, which can be reached (well, almost) by train from Brno. The station is actually 2km east of the town, which, like a lot of small Moravian towns, has the feel of a mud-spattered working farmyard – there's just one **hotel**, the moderate *Jednota*, located on the main square. The local **zámek** to the west of town is similarly earthy, despite its lofty Italianate pretensions. Its delicate arcaded loggia from 1557 now resounds with the noise of the fifteen-year old railway workers who learn their trade here, and you'll have to sneak past the foreman to get a look. If you haven't got the bottle, content yourself with the **Mucha gallery** (April–Oct Tues–Sun 9am–noon & 1–4pm), housed in one of the outbuildings, which contains the paintings and drawings of one of Czechoslovakia's better-known artists, **Alfons Mucha** (1860–1939).

Mucha was actually born in the even grubbier mining town of Ivančice, a few kilometres to the north, a odd starting point for an artist who is best known for his delicate Art-Nouveau posters. In the West he is known solely for the stuff he did while working in Paris, where he shared a studio with Gauguin (there's a photo of the latter playing the piano with his trousers down just to prove it). In fact, Mucha came to despise this "commercial" period of his work, and when the First Republic was declared in 1918, he threw himself into the national cause like no other artist, designing its stamps, bank notes and numerous posters.

It was left to an American millionaire to commission him to do what he saw as his life's work: a cycle of twenty monumental canvases called the *Slovanská epopej* (*The Slav Epic*), which constitute the bulk of the work on display here. In Czech terms they're well-worn themes – Komenský fleeing the fatherland, the Battle of Vítkov – but they were obviously heartfelt by Mucha, and in these damp and badly-lit rooms, his gloomy, melodramatic paintings take on a fascination all of their own. In the end he paid for his nationalism with his life: dragged in for questioning by the Gestapo after the 1939 Nazi invasion, he died shortly after being released.

Slavkov (Austerlitz) and Bučovice

Twenty kilometres by train across the flat plain east of Brno, **SLAVKOV** is just another dour one-street village, swamped by the great mass of its late Baroque **zámek** (April, Sept & Oct Tues–Sun 9am–noon & 1–4pm; May–Aug Tues–Sun 8am–noon & 1–5pm) and accompanying Neoclassical church. Like so many chateaux close to the Austrian border, the contents were quickly and judiciously removed by the owners before the arrival of the Red Army in 1945, but the 45-minute guided tour is still worth it for the incredible acoustics of the central concave hall. Every whisper of sound in the giant dome echoes for a full ten seconds, while outside not one word can be heard.

On December 2, 1805, in the fields between Slavkov and Brno, now peppered with simple crosses, the Austrians and Russians received a decisive drubbing at the hands of the numerically inferior Napoleonic troops in the **Battle of Austerlitz**. The Austrians and Russians committed themselves early, charging into the morning fog and attacking the French on both flanks. Napoleon, confident of victory, held back until the enemy had established its position and then attacked at their weakest point, the central commanding heights of the Pratzen Hill, splitting their forces and throwing them into disarray. It was all over by lunchtime, with over 24,000 troops dead. After the battle, the Treaty of Pressburg was signed by the big three, marking an end to Napoleon's eastern campaign until the fateful march on Moscow in 1812. There's a graphic description of the battle in Tolstoy's epic novel *War and Peace*.

Over a hundred years later, on the strategic Pratzen Hill to the southwest of Slavkov (now known as the Pracký kopec), the **Mohyla míru** (Monument of Peace) was erected on the instigation of a local pacifist priest, and paid for by the governments of France, Austria and Russia, who within three years would once more be at war with one another. The battlefield round about is now just another ploughed field, dotted with the odd little Calvary, but the tent-like stone monument designed by the Art-Nouveau architect Josef Fanta contains a small **museum**, including the obligatory toy soldier mock-up of the battle. Military enthusiasts without wheels will have to walk the 2km from PONĚTOVICE station (25min) to the battlefield.

Bučovice

Ten kilometres further east, the **zámek** (April & Oct Sat & Sun 9am–noon & 1–4pm; May–Aug Tues–Sun 8am–noon & 1–5pm; Sept Tues–Sun 9am–noon & 1–4pm) at **BUČOVICE** (50min by train from Brno) gets a fraction of the visitors who turn up at Slavkov. Part of the explanation must lie with its unpromising exterior: a dull grey fortress with four ugly squat towers. None of it prepares you for the subtle, slender Italianate arcading of the courtyard's loggia, with each set of supporting columns topped by a different carved motif. At the centre of the courtyard a stone fountain was added a few generations later, "a little too robust" as the guide puts it, and out of keeping with the rest of the masonry. The towers, the gardens and countless rooms once matched the charm and elegance of the courtyard, but the Liechtensteins, who obtained the house through marriage in 1597, soon turned the place into little more than a storage house for the family records, scattering its original furnishings between their many other Moravian residences.

The only things they couldn't remove were the original sixteenth-century **ceiling decorations**, a fantastical mantle of sculpture and paint which coats just five or so rooms, none more than twenty feet across. The first few are just a warm-up for the thick stucco of the **císařský sál**, with the bejewelled relief figures of Mars, Diana, a half-naked Europa and, most magnificent of all, the Emperor Charles V trampling a turbanned Turk into the paintwork. But the decoration of the **zaječí sál** (The Hall of Hares) is the real star turn, an anthropomorphic work reckoned to be one of the few of that period still in existence. It's an hysterical scene, with the hares exacting their revenge on the world of man and his closest ally – the dog. The aftermath of the hares' revolution sees them sitting in judgement (wigs and all) over their defeated enemies, as well as indulging in more high-brow activities – hare as Rembrandt, hare as scholar and so on.

Along the Austrian border

Historically, the land on either side of the River Dyje (Thaya), which runs parallel with the border between Moravia and Austria, has for centuries been German-speaking, its buildings designed by Austrian architects and its eyes set firmly on Vienna, just 60km to the south. But, as in the rest of the country, the ethnic German population was forcibly removed from South Moravia after 1945 and their private vineyards handed out to the demobilised Czech heroes of the liberation. The region's viticulture is one of the few industries that kept going on private plots even after nationalisation in 1948, but in every other way the last forty years have driven a great wedge between two previously identical regions on either side of the river. The neat, prim and expensive Austrian Weinviertel to the south now seems worlds apart from the shabby, unkempt and dirt-cheap Moravian side of the Dyje, but there are one or two real high spots which make this a region worth exploring. The recent reopening of the border may yet bring a greater parity, as Austrian Schillings begin to filter through, and the region begins to wake from its enforced slumber.

Mikulov and around

Clinging on to the southern tip of the Pavlovské vrchy, the last hills before the Austrian plain, **MIKULOV** (Nikolsburg) is one of South Moravia's minor gems. Slap bang in the middle of the wine-producing region, it's been a border post for centuries – hence the narrow streets and siege mentality of much of the architecture. The town still functions as a busy crossing point between the two countries; if you're driving from Vienna, it's a great introduction to the country and, given its strategic locale, surprisingly untouristed.

Raised above the jumble of red roof tops is the **Schloss** (April–Sept Tues–Sun 8am–4pm), an imposing complex which sprawls over a rocky hill on the west side of town. It's a bland, rather characterless building: blown to smithereens by the Gestapo in the last days of the war in a final nihilistic gesture, it was rebuilt in the 1950s to house the town museum. While that's being hastily "redesigned", you can still give the exhibits on viticulture a quick once-over and check out the amazing view into Austria.

In 1575 castle and town fell into the hands of the fervently Catholic Dietrichsteins, who established various religious edifices and institutions here. They're also responsible for the hint of Renaissance in the town – the occasional arcade or pictorial sgraffito – and the main square itself, appealingly misshapen and huddling below the castle. Later, behind the oversized plague column, they built the church of **sv Anna**, originally intended to be the family mausoleum, a strange, monstrous and half-finished building which looks a bit like the Karlskirche in Vienna, with its combination of smooth classical columns and stumpy Baroque towers. On the exposed limestone hill on the east side of town, the family also set up a series of chapels. It's a bleak windblown outcrop, but well worth the sweat of the climb for the view across the vineyards to Vienna.

Mikulov boasted a thriving Jewish community until the advent of the Nazis, and on the other side of the castle lies what used to be the Jewish ghetto. The town's seventeenth-century **synagogue** on Husova is slowly being renovated in order to turn it into a museum of Jewish culture, and round the corner in

Brněnská, a rugged path leads to the town's overgrown medieval **Jewish cemetery** (židovský hřbitov) with finely carved marble graves dating back to 1618. To get into it, you'll need to pick up the key from Brněnská 28, but failing that there's a hole in the wall towards the top of the cemetery.

The town is rarely busy, the majority of visitors pausing for a couple of hours at the most before moving on, since at the time of writing there was no **accommodation**. Being in the wine region, the best time to come here is after the grape harvest, when the first bouquet of the year is being tried and tested in vast quantities at the local *sklepy* (wine caves) on the edge of town.

Pavlovské vrchy

Mikulov is the starting point for hiking and exploring the **Pavlovské vrchy**, a thin low ridge of limestone hills, rugged and treeless in a thoroughly un-Czech way. Since the damming of the Dyje and the creation of the artificial Nový mlýn lake, the rare plant life on the Pavlovské vrchy has suffered badly. In a rather belated and empty gesture, the authorities declared the region a protected landscape region. With or without its original vegetation, it's good gentle **hiking country**, with wide-angle views on both sides and a couple of picturesque ruined castles along the ten-kilometre red-marked path to DOLNÍ VĚSTONICE. Archaeological research has been going on here since 1924, when an early Stone Age settlement was discovered. Wolves'-teeth jewellery and a number of clay figurines were found here, and the best stuff is now displayed in the Moravian Museum in Brno, including the voluptuous *Venus of Věstonice*, a tiny female fertility figure with swollen belly and breasts. At Dolní Věstonice you can either walk another 4km to the station at POPICE, or catch one of the hourly buses back to Mikulov.

Valtice and Lednice

To the southeast of Mikulov, nose to nose with the Austrian border, are the twin residences of the **Liechtenstein family**, one of the most powerful landowners in the country until 1945. At their peak they owned no fewer than 99 estates – one more and they would have had to maintain a standing army in the service of the empire. The one who benefited most from all this wealth was Prince-Bishop Karl Eusebius von Liechtenstein-Kastelcorn, who came into the family fortune in 1627 and whose motto – "Money exists only that one may leave beautiful monuments to eternal and undying remembrance" – can be seen in practice all over Moravia.

Both chateaux are laid out in one magnificent stately park, the Boří les, and in many ways that's the best feature of the whole area. At **VALTICE** (Feldsberg), the family's foremost residence (20min by train from Mikulov), was cleaned out just before the end of the war, and its endless rooms are relentlessly bare. The whole place is currently undergoing renovation, and its east wing has been converted into a posh hotel and restaurant which does a brisk trade with holidaying Austrians. From the end of the garden, you can still see the watchtowers (now unmanned) and the chateau's vineyards, which produce a good Moravian red, pure and unadulterated, unlike most of the country's wines, and one of the few to be exported. A red-marked path from the train station leads you on a scenic wander through the woods of the **Boří les**, which the family's nineteenth-century heirs took pleasure in embellishing with the odd quasi-historical monument – here a triumphal arch, there a temple to Apollo. The path skirts one of the two fifteenth-century fish ponds, eventually winding up in Lednice itself (3hr).

Although just 7km from Valtice (hitching or walking is probably quicker than waiting for the infrequent local bus), the family's summer residence at **LEDNICE** (Eisgrub) couldn't be further away in style. Part of the family estate since 1243, it was one of the last to be subjected to a lavish rebuild job in the 1840s, which turned it into a neo-Gothic extravaganza. In contrast to Valtice, there's plenty to look at, romantic interiors crowd every one of its wooden-panelled rooms. Bear in mind that Lednice is one of Czechoslovakia's most visited chateaux (April & Oct Sat & Sun 9am–noon & 1–4pm; May–Aug Tues–Sun 8am–noon & 1–5pm; Sept Tues–Sun 9am–noon & 1–4pm), so if you want to avoid the tour groups, try the Orangerie – or better still head off into the chateau's watery grounds, home to numerous herons and laughing gulls. Piqued by local objections to their plan for a colossal church, the Liechtensteins decided to further alienate the village by building the largest minaret outside the Islamic world: it dominates the view of the park from the chateau, but apart from a few resident swallows, there's nothing to see inside.

As for **accommodation**, Valtice and Lednice have just one hotel apiece, both of which tend to be swiftly booked out each summer, particularly in August when there's a Baroque Music Festival at Valtice. Other than camping at the *Apollo* **campsite** (May–Sept) by the Lednice fish pond, the only alternative is to stay in the rather drab town of BŘECLAV, 8km east of the two chateaux (and accessible by the occasional train from Lednice), which has three moderately priced hotels.

Znojmo and around

Further up the Dyje valley, about 45km west of Mikulov, **ZNOJMO** (Znaim) is not as immediately appealing as Mikulov. It's a much bigger town – and a fair hike to the old town from the station – with the last hundred years' industry and suburbs falling in unsightly fashion all around. Initial impressions do nothing to dispel the gloom. The sloping market square has a weary air about it: damaged in the last war, its cobbles have literally gone to seed and the Capuchin buildings at the bottom of the square are as uninspiring as the concrete supermarket which squats at the opposite end.

Hope rears up in the shape of the **radniční věž**, a soaring romantic affair which twists its uppermost gallery at an angle to the main body. The view through its wooden hatches is little short of spectacular and it's a good way to get your bearings and a feel for this decidedly seedy old town. To climb up the tower, enter through an alleyway on the opposite side of the street, which also serves as the starting point for touring the warren of *podzemí* or **underground tunnels** which run for miles under the old town. A minimum of ten people are needed for a tour, but the armless guide is open to persuasion, since he seems to relish his task of getting visitors lost and confused in this medieval labyrinth, originally built for defensive purposes, later used for storing wine.

At this point you can head off in a number of directions, but the most interesting is the narrow lane of Velká Mikulášská, left off the square, which leads to the oldest part of Znojmo – a tight web of alleyways woven round the church of **sv Mikuláš**, a plain Gothic hall church, sporting an unusual panelled gable. Set at a right-angle to it is the much smaller **chapel of sv Václav**, now handed over to the Orthodox community and invariably locked. Nevertheless it's a curious building, on a north–south axis and tucked into the town walls, from which you get a commanding view down the Dyje valley as it blends into the Austrian plain.

"Better a living brewery than a dead castle" goes one of Czechoslovakia's more obscure sayings, and as far as Znojmo's **hrad** goes it's not difficult to agree, but it's more of a tragedy that the most valuable twelfth-century paintings in the country, including contemporary portraits of the Přemyslid princes which adorn the walls of the rotunda of sv Kateřina, should fester in a factory-cum-castle forecourt – the hrad has been turned into brewery. As the paramilitary mentality surrounding industrial installations subsides, it may become easier to get past the factory gates, but until then the nearest you'll get is Přemyslovců at the end of Velká Františkánská, where the former **Minorite monastery** puts on the occasional contemporary art exhibition and classical concert in the cloisters.

The location of Znojmo's old town, perched high above the deep gorge of the Dyje to the south, means that leaving the safety of the town walls at the end of Přemyslovců plunges you straight into thickly wooded countryside. It's a gentle wander round the foot of the hrad to the chapel of sv Václav, but for a longer walk, take the path down to the dam and, keeping on the same side of the river, climb up to the village of Hradiště for an unbeatable vista of Znojmo and the Dyje.

Architecture freaks may want to take a look at the huge yellow colossus of the Premonstratensian convent at Louka (Klosterbruck), begun but never finished by the Baroque architect Johann Lukas von Hildebrandt, and now swallowed up in Znojmo's suburbs. From a distance it still manages to make an impression, but closer to, the smashed windows and the watchtowers of the Czechoslovak Army, who use the place as a barracks, are a miserable end for such a place.

Practical details

Trains run fairly frequently from Mikulov to Znojmo, taking around an hour, while trains from Brno often take over two. If you're heading into Austria, the 24-hour border crossing is at HATĚ on the E84 (the occasional bus goes there). The cheapest and most central **hotel** in town is the *Černý medvěd* (☎0624-4271) on the main square. If it's full, go to the *ČEDOK* office, also on the main square, to reserve a place at one of Znojmo's slightly more expensive hotels. The **campsite** is 3km from the train station at SUCHOHRDLY (bus #1). As for **food**, the old town's northernmost square is a good place to head for *zmrzlina* or *langoše*, but for more substantial fare, try the hot and beery *Znojemská Libuše* behind the main supermarket. Incidentally, pickled gherkins are Znojmo's speciality, though you needn't feel any compulsion to join in.

Vranov and Bítov

Twenty kilometres west of Znojmo, the River Dyje has been dammed just above the village of Vranov (see below), and whatever the implications for the equilibrium of the ecosystem, it provides a summer playground for large numbers of holidaying Czechs, with a couple of interesting chateaux and some great opportunities for swimming and generally lazing around. Without your own transport, getting around can be a time-consuming business, so it's best to plan to stay at least one or two nights.

VRANOV (Frain) itself is a regular South Moravian village, entirely dominated by its cliff-top **zámek** (April & Oct Sat & Sun 9am–noon & 1–4pm; May–Aug Tues–Sun 8am–noon & 1–5pm; Sept Tues–Sun 9am–noon & 1–4pm), originally a medieval stronghold, but after a fire in 1665 converted into a Baroque chateau by the Viennese architect Fischer von Erlach and made all the more magnificent by its position on a knife's edge above the Dyje. There's no alternative to the one-kilometre hike up the steep road which leads round to the back of the castle. Nothing in the rest of the sprawling complex can quite compare to Fischer's trump card at the far end and the real reason for trekking out here. The overall effect of the cavernous domed **Ancestors' Hall** is as much due to Rottmayr's wild frescoes as to Fischer's great oval skylights: its frenzied, over-the-top paintings depict the (fictitious) achievements of the Althan family who commissioned the work.

At the weekend buses run regularly from Znojmo to Vranov, less frequently during the week. Alternatively, you could take the more frequent train to ŠUMNÁ station and walk the 4km to Vranov. From Vranov, where there are three cheap hotels, it's only a fifteen-minute walk to the *přehrada* (dam) and the sandy beach known as Vranovská pláž; to get there, take the boat shuttle across the lake. From May to September there's a fair bit of life here: camping, chalets, boat hire, a couple of shops and a daily boat service up the lake to Bítov and beyond. The sun-worshippers are shoulder to shoulder on the beach in the high season, but it's easy to lose the crowd by picking a rocky spot further upstream.

The village of **BÍTOV**, 8km west up the lake, is more geared to vacationing Czechs than Vranov and of its two campsites, the *Kopaninky* site to the southeast is the more secluded. The only way to get from Vranov to Bítov – bar hitching – is to take the boat. Even buses from Znojmo to Bítov are infrequent, but connections with Jihlava (see below) are much better. The ruined castle which can be seen from the village is a fourteenth-century defence fort; Bítov's wholesome **hrad** is 1.5km further upstream. Like Vranov it boasts a classic defensive location on a spit of grey rock high above the river, which the flooding of the valley has diminished only slightly. For this reason alone, it's worth clambering up to enjoy the view, but inside it's not a patch on Fischer's genius touch at Vranov; contrived neo-Gothic decor and soulless, unlived-in rooms fail to come alive in the tedious guided tour.

Jaroměřice nad Rokytnou

One hour northwest by train from Znojmo, and a convenient place to break the journey to Jihlava, the village of **JAROMĚŘICE NAD ROKYTNOU** is completely overwhelmed by its russet and cream Baroque **zámek** (April & Oct Sat & Sun 9am–noon & 1–4pm; May–Sept Tues–Sun 8am–noon & 1–5pm), built over the course of 37 years by the wealthy and extravagant Johann Adam von Questenberg. No one seems very sure where to lay the architectural blame for this oversized chateau, but the two darlings of Vienna, Jakob Prandtauer and Johann Lukas von Hildebrandt, appear to be prime suspects. Although the project was never completed, there's far too much here already, turning the hour-long tour into something of an endurance test. The two exceptions are the elegant Rococo halls, the *hlavní sál* and the *taneční sál*, where Questenberg used to put on lavish classical concerts. Alternatively, you could skip the tour and spend the morning exploring the great domed chapel or pottering around the formal gardens. Should you wish to stay the night, the moderate concrete hotel *Opera* will no doubt oblige.

Jihlava (Iglau)

When silver deposits were discovered in the nearby hills in the 1240s, **JIHLAVA** was transformed overnight from a tiny Moravian village into one of the biggest mining towns in central Europe. Scores of German miners came and settled here, and by the end of the century Jihlava could boast two hospitals, two monasteries and, most importantly, the royal mint. The veins of silver ran out in the fourteenth century, but the town continued to flourish off the cloth trade, reaching its zenith around the latter half of the sixteenth century when over 700 master spinners worked in the town.

For all its history there's not that much to see in Jihlava. This is partly due to a fire in 1523 and the ravages of the Thirty Years' War, but most of all to the expulsion of ethnic Germans from this "language-island" in 1945. This move signalled the end of an era, or as Czech guidebooks prefer to put it "the beginning of a new stage in the development of Jihlava". In reality the town has been in decline ever since, plagued by an ignorant Communist council who in their comparatively brief forty-year rule have left the most indelible mark on the town – the mud brown multistorey car park/supermarket complex plonked in the middle of Jihlava's huge main square in place of a block of medieval houses.

If you can look beyond Jihlava's most glaring addition, the main square, **náměstí Míru**, is actually a wonderfully expansive space, lined with restrained Baroque and Rococo houses, sporting two fountains, a couple of outdoor cafés and plenty of street life to soak in. At the top of the square, next door to *ČEDOK*, is the **town museum** (Tues–Fri & Sun 9am–5pm, Sat 9am–1pm), worth a visit for the interior alone, being one of the few Renaissance houses to survive the 1523 fire. Its covered inner courtyard with an arcaded gallery and diamond vaulting is perfectly preserved and peculiar to Jihlava. You can see the same kind of interior design in the small **art gallery** round the corner in Komenského.

The Jesuit church of sv Ignác protrudes into náměstí Míru for no particularly good reason: far more appealing are the town's thirteenth-century churches set back from the square. The most attractive of these is the church of **sv Jakub** (St James), east of the square, best admired from afar where its two plain stone towers and steeply pitched roof rise majestically above the burgher houses around. There's little to get excited about inside, but for a closer look you'll have to ask round for the key, or hope a tour group arrives. The town walls run round the back of the church and in the valley below are the woods of the Březinovy sady, which contain a rather sad zoo. On a hot day, they're a cool and pleasant place for a stroll.

For a town originally built on silver, Jihlava lacks the vestiges of prosperity which grace, say, Kutná Hora. Just one fine gateway guarding the road from the west is all that's left of the town's five gates, along with a few finely carved portals, the remnants of fifteenth-century frescoes, and, in between, a lot of rubble.

Practicalities

It hardly seems worth staying the night in Jihlava, but if you're interested in seeing Telč and Slavonice it may well be the easiest place to grab a bed. The **train station** is 1km north of the old town (trolley bus A), but until the moderately priced *Grandhotel* (Husova 1) gets back on its feet, you're likely to have to take trolley bus C to the expensive *Jihlava* (Semilucká 7; ☎066-267 01). Similarly priced but more convenient is the recently renovated *Zlatá Hvězda* (☎066-294 21), in the sgraffitoed corner house at the bottom of the main square, which offers the town's only nightlife, with drinking and dancing in its cellars until 3am. If you're camping, the lakeside *Pávov* **campsite** (open all year) is 4km north of Jihlava, not far from the motorway. *ČEDOK*, on the main square, will let you know the times the local bus goes there, and provide the latest fixtures of the town's army ice hockey team *Dukla Jihlava*, one of the best in the country.

MAHLER IN IGLAU

"I am thrice homeless, as a native of Bohemia in Austria, as an Austrian among Germans and as a Jew throughout the world. Everywhere an intruder, never welcomed." **Gustav Mahler's** predicament was typical of the Jews of *Mitteleuropa*, and it only exacerbated his already highly-strung personality. Prone to Wagnerian excesses and bouts of extreme pessimism, he would frequently work himself into a state of nervous collapse when composing or conducting. It was this Teutonic temperament, more than his German-speaking background, that separated him from his more laid-back Czech musical contemporaries.

Born in 1860 in the nearby village of Kalischt (Kaliště), on the Bohemian side of the border, Mahler's parents took advantage of the 1860 law allowing the free movement of Jews within the Empire, and moved to Pirnitzergasse (Malinovského) in Iglau (Jihlava), where there had been a strong Jewish community since the mid-fourteenth century. Mahler's father Bernhard, "a man of humble origins", ran a distillery and a couple of pubs, drunken dives by all accounts and certainly too much for a sensitive vegetarian like Mahler. These business ventures nevertheless failed to drag the family out of their interminable poverty, which caused the untimely deaths of eight out of his thirteen brothers and sisters. He went to Iglau's German Gymnasium (some fifty years after Smetana), and at the age of ten made his first public appearance as a pianist at the town's municipal theatre, then in a converted church on Komenského. A local farmer persuaded Bernhard to send his boy to Vienna, where he was accepted as a student at the conservatoire. After a fairly stormy career as a conductor that included stints at Olomouc and Prague, Mahler finally settled in Vienna, the place with which he is most closely associated.

For over fifty years now there's been little mention of the town's greatest son, and the only place with any kind of memorial is HUMPOLEC, 25km northwest of Jihlava, a Bohemian town with precious little connection with the composer. Here, a local teacher has single-handedly amassed the largest collection of Mahleriana in the world, now on display on the ground floor of the town museum. Bear in mind, before you get too excited, that it is the remarkable achievement rather than the exhibition itself which is worthy of praise.

Žďár nad Sázavou

The highest point in the Bohemian-Moravian Uplands or *Vysočina* is around 40km northeast of Jihlava, though you'd hardly realise since the whole range is deceptively flat. This is and has always been a poor region, but one really good reason for venturing into the hinterland is to visit **ŽĎÁR NAD SÁZAVOU**, originally a small settlement pitched not far from its Cistercian monastery, established in the thirteenth century.

Since the war the population has increased tenfold, making it one of the largest (and bleakest) towns in the region. The monastery, which is the only thing worth seeing, is a two-kilometre walk north through the grey new town of Žďár – instructive if nothing else. As the woods and fish ponds approach, there's a small bridge decorated with the familiar figures of eighteenth-century saints. More of a working farmyard than a House of God, the great rectangle of ragged outbuildings spreads over a muddy paddock to your right. You'll need to get the keys from the priest (who speaks some German) to get into everything except the official museum. If it's a weekend, there's quite likely to be a few people looking round the place, so this may not be necessary.

The whole complex is the work of **Giovanni Santini** (who also had a hand in the monasteries of Plasy and Kladruby near Plzeň), perhaps the most gifted architect the Czech Counter-Reformation threw up. His two great talents were marrying Gothic and Baroque forms in a new and creative way, and producing buildings with a humour and irony often lacking in eighteenth-century architecture. The monastery church isn't a particularly good example, but the **Zelená hora** (Green Hill) cemetery church, hidden in the trees, undoubtedly is. It's a unique and intriguing structure, showy in every way except its size. The zigzag cemetery walls form a decagon of cloisters around the central star-shaped church, a giant mushroom sprouting a half-formed, almost Byzantine dome, dedicated to sv Jan Nepomucký (St John of Nepomuk). Details of his martyrdom (see Prague's St Vitus Cathedral) and symbolic references to the saint fill the church. On the pulpit, a gilded relief depicts his being thrown off the Charles Bridge in Prague by the king's men, while everywhere in macabre repetition is the saint's severed tongue and the stars which appeared above his head: above the pulpit, on the ceiling, in the five side chapels.

Back in the main part of the monastery, there's a book museum and a small exhibition dedicated to Santini (April & Oct Sat & Sun 9am–4pm; May–Sept Tues–Sun 8am–4pm). It's easy to get a room in Žďár, whose hotels include the *Bílý lev* (☎0327-3982) and the *Tálský mlýn* (☎0327-76534). A decent **restaurant** can be found by the monastery, and fifteen minutes' walk north up the road there's a lakeside **campsite** (June 15–Sept 15). Žďár is only an hour's fast train ride from Brno.

MORE SANTINI

For further exposure to Santini's work, a number of his more light-hearted minor buildings are dotted about the Žďár region. The first, a couple of hundred yards further north of the Cistercian monastery in Žďár, is the graveless and eerie **dolní hřbitov** (lower cemetery), whose three simple chapels symbolise the Trinity. The cemetery walls form gentle ripples that enclose the bare space, inhabited by a lonesome angel calling the tune for Judgement Day.

Down the road at **OSTROV NAD OSLAVOU** (7min by train), using a similar design to the one he employed in the chateau at Chlumec nad Cidlinou, Santini built a *hostinec* (pub) in the shape of a "W" in memory of his fellow mason Václav Vejmluv (in German his initials read as W.W.). It's seen a lot of use and abuse over the years, and is not in great shape today, but it's still the local village boozer: buy a pint and appreciate the architecture at leisure.

Just 2km northeast of Ostrov and within easy walking distance, the local church at **OBYČTOV** is another Santini design, built in the shape of turtle, one of the Virgin Mary's more obscure symbols. Four chapels mark each leg, a presbytery the neck, and the west onion-domed tower, the distorted head. Ask around for the key to the whitewashed interior, which features more mutant turtle symbolism.

Telč and Slavonice

Telč and Slavonice are two of the most beautiful Renaissance towns anywhere in Europe. Yet while Telč is a popular stopoff on whirlwind tours of the country, Slavonice – every bit as perfect – is invariably deserted. Both are feasible day trips from Jihlava, even on the superhumanly slow *osobní* **trains** which take up to an hour and a half to reach Telč and slightly over two hours to get to Slavonice (change at Kostelec for both). On the other hand, **buses** to Telč take just 45 minutes, but there's no direct service to Slavonice from Jihlava.

Telč

It's hardly an exaggeration to say that the last momentous event in **TELČ** was the great fire of 1530, which wiped out all its wooden Gothic houses and forced the town to start afresh. It was this fortuitous disaster which has made Telč what it is: a perfect museum-piece sixteenth-century provincial town, little more than two medieval gatetowers, one huge wedge-shaped square and a chateau. Renaissance arcades extend the length of the square, lined with gentle pastel-coloured houses (including, oddly enough, a Renaissance fire station) that display a breathtaking variety of gables and pediments, none less than two hundred and fifty years old.

At the narrow western end of the square, the **zámek** (April, Sept & Oct daily 9am–noon & 1–4pm; May–Aug daily 8am–noon & 1–5pm; closed Mon) in no way disturbs the sixteenth-century atmosphere of the town – it too was badly damaged in the fire, and had to be rebuilt in similar fashion. Like the chateau at neighbouring Jindřichův Hradec, it was the inspiration of Zacharias of Hradec whose passion for all things Italian is again strongly in evidence. It's not lined with treasure troves, but the period ceilings are exceptional and the whole place is refreshingly intimate and low-key after the intimidating pomposity of the ubiquitous Baroque. At the end of the tour you'll be let loose on the cloistered garden and the art gallery squeezed into the chateau's east wing.

Most people come here for a couple of hours and then leave, so theoretically it should be fairly easy to get a bed in the moderate *Černý orel* at no. 7 on the main square (☎96 22 21). But it only takes one pre-booked tour group to scupper your plans, so ring in advance if possible.

Slavonice (Zlabings)

SLAVONICE, 25km south of Telč and less than a mile from the Austrian border, is in many ways even more remarkable. It's a crumbling monument to a prosperity which lasted for just one hundred years, shattered by the Thirty Years' War which halved the population, and eventually disappearing off the map when the post road from Prague to Vienna was re-routed via Jihlava in the 1730s. To make matters worse, the forced removal of the German-speaking inhabitants in 1945 emptied Slavonice, and when the Iron Curtain wrapped itself around the village, road and rail links with the West were severed, border guards stalked the streets and the arrival of any visitor was treated with deep suspicion.

Even now, the old town – basically just one misshapen square and a church – has a strange and haunting beauty. The impression is further enhanced by the bizarre biblical and apocalyptic sixteenth-century "strip cartoons" played out on many of the houses in monochrome sgraffito, and in bad need of a Telč-style renovation. Slowly, though, life is coming back to Slavonice: the border crossing has yet to be fully reopened, but the Cold War paranoia has gone – there's even a trendy art gallery/café on the main square, and Austrians (some of whom no doubt once lived here) are gradually rediscovering the town.

Despite Slavonice's undoubted draws, it's difficult to kill more than an hour or so here. For a start, pick up an ice cream at the local *cukrárna*, if only for a closer look at the obligatory diamond vaulting in the entrance hall. Alternatively, go for a quick walk along the former Iron Curtain – a favourite local pastime – a few hundred metres south of the station. There's a hotel on the main square should you get stranded or wish to hang out here. If you don't fancy the slow train journey northwards, Slavonice is well connected by bus to Jindřichův Hradec and points west.

Up the River Morava

What the Labe basin is to the Bohemians, the **River Morava**, 50km east of Brno, is to the Moravians, who settled in this fertile land around the late eighth century, taking their name from the river and eventually founding the short-lived Great Moravian Empire, the first coherent political unit to be ruled by Slavs, and the subject of intense archaeological research (and controversy) over the last forty years. For the visitor, it's a dour, mostly undistinguished landscape – flat low farming country, with just the occasional factory or ribbon village to break the monotony – and most people pass through en route to more established sights. In summer this can be a great mistake, for almost every village in the area has its own folk festival, and in early autumn the local wine caves are bursting with life and ready to demonstrate the region's legendary and lavish hospitality.

Geographically the Morava (along with the River Oder) forms a natural corridor between east and west, difficult to defend against intruders, and consequently trashed by numerous armies marching their way across Europe, from the Turks to the Tartars. Nowadays, at various different points, it forms the border between Slovakia and Austria, then, moving north, Moravia and Slovakia. As a region, it's known as *Slovácko* – a kind of grey area between Moravia and Slovakia, the local dialect and customs virtually indistinguishable from West Slovakia.

Hodonín

As the Morava cuts across country from the Slovak–Austrian border to the southwest, the first place of any size is **HODONÍN**, an industrial town whose only claim to fame is **Tomáš Garrigue Masaryk**, the country's founding father and first president, who was born here in 1850. His mixed parentage – his mother was German-speaking, his father a Slovak peasant – was typical of the region in the nineteenth century. His statue, which had graced the main square since the foundation of the Republic in 1918, was removed by the Communists, and naturally enough it's back with a vengeance, unveiled by Havel himself shortly after the beginning of his own presidency.

Strážnice

For most of the year **STRÁŽNICE**, 17km upriver, sees perhaps a handful of visitors, but for one weekend at the end of June, thousands converge on this unexceptional town for the annual **International Folk Festival**, held in the three purpose-built stadiums in the castle grounds. During the festival, all hotels are booked solid for miles around and the only thing to do is to bring your own tent and try and squeeze onto the castle campsite (open all year round), or just crash out somewhere in your sleeping bag. If you're here at any other time of the year there's only enough to keep you occupied for an hour or two: the zámek, though no work of art itself, contains an exceptionally good **folk museum** (May–Oct Tues–Sat 8am–5pm, Sun 9am–6pm) which belongs to the Institute of Folk Art housed in the same building, and in a field to the south there's a newly established **skansen** (same times as above) with thatched cottages and peasant gear from the outlying villages.

Outside of the festival, it should be easy enough to stay at the *Černý orel* on Malinovského, or get a table at the *Zámecká vinárna* (in the castle) which serves up the local wine and features live music at the weekend.

Strážnice also makes a good base for visiting one or more of the private *sklepy* or **wine caves** which survived collectivisation, and now provide the focus of village life in the summer months before and after the grape harvest. Perhaps the easiest *sklepy* to visit for those without their own transport are the Plže caves at **PETROV**, a thin settlement strung out along the main road from Hodonín, one stop down the railway line from Strážnice. Hidden from sight, on the other side of the railway track, are around twenty or so whitewashed stone caves, over two hundred years old, some beautifully decorated with intricate floral designs, others with just a simple deep blue stripe. Most days around late September, there are one or two locals carefully overseeing their new harvest, who'll happily show you around and no doubt invite you to sample (and of course buy) some of their wine. During the rest of the summer, merrymaking goes on in the evenings at weekends. Those with their own transport and a taste for the stuff could check out POLEŠOVICE, 12km north, or MUTĚNICE, 15km west, or better still the thatched *sklepy* at PRUŠÁNKY. There are countless other festivals in the area, as in VLČNOV and HLUK at Whitsuntide, and pilgrimages to places like BLATNICE; check the listings in the local press for coming events.

Uherské Hradiště and around

UHERSKÉ HRADIŠTĚ, like many towns on the Morava, has sold its soul to industry, and the only time travellers stray into its shapeless centre is in their search for the **Pamatník Velké Moravy** (April–Oct Tues–Sun 8am–noon & 1–4pm), suspected site of the capital of the Great Moravian Empire. It's actually across the Morava in Staré Město, north of the centre (10min by foot or bus #1, #4 to the second stop after the bridge), in what looks like a concrete bunker from the last war. The foundations of a ninth-century church, discovered in 1949, are on display along with a lot of bones and broken crockery. A more accessible load of old rocks can be viewed, along with a good selection of folk costumes and suchlike, at the **Slovácké muzeum** (times as above) in the Smetanovy sady to the east of town.

The obligatory Jesuit church aside, the town's only other sight as such is the late Baroque apothecary *U zlaté koruny* on the main náměstí. It's still functioning as a *lékárna* (chemist), but the service area has been brusquely modernised and you can only peep through into the frescoed back room. On the same square is the town's oldest and cheapest **hotel**, the *Slunce* (☎015-34 40), best approached before the *Morava* (☎015-26 73) at Šafaříkova 855, or *Grand* (☎015-30 55) on Palackého náměstí, unless you're camping at the *Kunovice* site (bus #2).

Velehrad

The Cistercian monastery at **VELEHRAD**, just 9km across the fields from Uherské Hradiště, is one of the most important pilgrimage sites in

---

VELKÁ MORAVA – THE GREAT MORAVIAN EMPIRE

At its peak under the Slav prince Svätopluk (870–894), the territories of **Velká Morava** (the Great Moravian Empire) extended well into Slovakia, Bohemia, and parts of western Hungary and southern Poland. Arguments over the whereabouts of its legendary capital *Veligrad* have puzzled scholars for many years. At first the most obvious choice seemed to be Velehrad, but excavations there have proved fruitless. Opinion now seems divided between Nitra in West Slovakia, Mikulčice, right on the Slovak border southeast of Hodonín, and Staré Město, now part of Uherské Hradiště. The Slovaks in particular see themselves as the true descendants of the Great Moravian Empire while Staré Město is the site pushed for by most Czech archaeologists. Whatever the truth, the whole lot had been laid waste by the Magyar hordes by 906, not long after the death of Svatopluk, and Slovakia remained under Hungarian rule for the next millennium.

Czechoslovakia. It's an impressive sight, too, the twin ochre towers of its **church** (daily 9am–5pm) set against the backdrop of the **Chřiby hills**, a low beech-covered ridge which separates Brno from the Morava basin. There's no accommodation here – other than a campsite, 1.5km up the road to SALAŠ – but the village is served by regular buses from Uherské Hradiště.

The monastery's importance as an object of pilgrimage derives from the belief (now proved to be false) that it was the seat of Saint Methodius' archbishopric, the first in the Slav lands, and the place where he died in 885. The 1100th anniversary of this last fact attracted over 150,000 pilgrims from across the country in 1985, the largest single unofficial gathering the country had seen since the first anniversary of the Soviet invasion in August 1969. More recently, when Velehrad entertained Pope John Paul II on his lightning tour of the country in April 1990, half a million people turned up.

There's certainly something about the place that sets it apart: its historical associations, the sheer magnificence of its Baroque detailing, or its strange limitless emptiness, outside of the annual pilgrimage. The gigantic scale of the church is borrowed from the original Romanesque church on the same site, which after being sacked by marauding Protestants several times, burned down in 1681. Inside, the finer points of the artistry may be lacking in finesse, but the faded glory of the frescoed nave, suffused with a pink-grey light, and empty but for the bent old women who come here for their daily prayer, is bewilderingly powerful.

Buchlovice and Buchlov

Four kilometres west of Velehrad, still just out of reach of the Chřiby hills, is the village of **BUCHLOVICE**, easily accessible by bus from Uherské Hradiště. There's nothing to see here except the eighteenth-century **zámek** (40-min guided tour every half-hour; April & Oct Tues–Sun 9am–4pm; May–Sept Tues–Sun 8am–5pm), a warm and hospitable country house with a lovely arboretum bursting with rhododendrons, azaleas and peacocks. The house, made up of two symmetrically opposed half-circles, has been recently renovated, and the smallish suite of rooms still holds most of its original Rococo furniture, left behind in haste by the Berchtold family in 1945.

THE APOSTLES OF THE SLAVS

The significance of the Saints **Cyril** (827–69) and **Methodius** (815–85) goes far beyond their mere canonisation. Brothers from a wealthy family in Constantinople, they were sent as missionaries to the Great Moravian Empire in 863 at the invitation of its ruler, Rastislav, less for reasons of piety than to assert his independence from his German neighbours. Thrust headlong into a ready-made political minefield, they were given a hard time by the local German clergy, and had to retreat to Rome, where Cyril became a monk and died. Methodius meanwhile insisted on returning to Moravia, only to be imprisoned for two years at the instigation of the German bishops. The pope eventually got him released, but dragged him back to Rome to answer charges of heterodoxy. He was cleared of all charges and consecrated Bishop of Pannonia and Moravia, and continued to teach in the vernacular until his death in 885.

More important than their actual achievements in converting the local populace was the fact that they preached in the tongue of the common people. Cyril in particular is regarded as the founder of Slavonic literature, having been accredited with single-handedly inventing the Glagolithic script, still used in the Eastern Church and the basis of the modern Cyrillic alphabet that takes his name, while Methodius is venerated by both Western and Eastern Christians as a pioneer of the vernacular liturgy and a man dedicated to ecumenism. After Methodius' death, his followers were duly chased out and forced to take refuge in Bulgaria. The Czech Lands came under Rome's sway once and for all, and had to wait until the end of the fourteenth century before they once more heard their own language used to preach the gospel.

A stiff three-and-a-half-kilometre climb up into the forest of the Chřiby hills, the Gothic hrad of **Buchlov** (times as above) couldn't be more dissimilar. In bad weather, as the mist whips round the bastions, it's hard to imagine a more forbidding place, but in summer the view over the tree tops is terrific and the whole place has a cool, breezy feel to it. Founded as a royal seat by the Přemyslids in the thirteenth century, it has suffered none of the painful neo-Gothicising of other medieval castles – in fact the Berchtolds had turned it into a museum as early as the late nineteenth century. Heavy, rusty keys open up a series of sparsely furnished rooms lit only by thin slit windows, and dungeons in which the Habsburgs used to confine the odd rebellious Hungarian. If you're on for a bit of hiking, the stillness and extraordinary beauty of the surrounding beech forests are difficult to match, but make sure you stock up with provisions, as there are few shops in the area. The only place to stay is the *Smraďavka* campsite (open all year), 2km southeast of Buchlovice.

Luhačovice

Twenty-seven kilometres east of Uherské Hradiště, **LUHAČOVICE** is decidedly lush after the rather demure aspect of the Morava valley, but as a rather genteel spa town it can't hope nor does it try to compete with the pomp and majesty of the West Bohemian spas. Although the springs are mentioned as far back as the twelfth century, nothing much was done about developing the place until it was bought up in 1902 and the first of Dušan Jurkovič's quirky half-timbered villas, which have become the spa's hallmark, were built. The largest of these buildings, the **Jurkovičův dům**, dominates the central spa gardens which spread northeast from the train station. The beams are purely decorative, occasionally breaking out into a swirling flourish, and the roof is a playful pagoda-type affair – all in all a uniquely Slovak version of Art Nouveau. The blot on Luhačovice's copybook is the new colonnade, a graceless concrete curve, but nevertheless a good place to sit and watch the infirm pass by, sipping the waters from their grotesquely decorated mugs. The rest of the spa forms a snake-like promenade boxed in by shrubs and trees, with overly quaint bridges spanning the gentle trickling river. Soon enough you hit another cluster of Jurkovič buildings, one of which is the natural spring open-air **swimming pool**, good for a cheap unchlorinated dip. The villas continue into a spa-like surburbia, but unless you fancy a hike into the surrounding woods or are staying at the lakeside **campsite** a kilometre up the main road, there's no reason to continue walking.

To get to Luhačovice from Uherské Hradiště by train, you must change at Uherský Brod; buses run direct, though less frequently. The **bus** and **train stations** are at the southwestern end of the spa and the two **hotels** non-patients can stay at are within a few hundred metres of each other: the more expensive *Alexandria* (☎33 11), which runs a "traditional" variety show in its nightclub, and the down-to-earth *Litoval* (☎93 30 40). Check at *ČEDOK* near the train station for any other possibilities. Although buses from all over the country run regular services to Luhačovice, it's still a bit out on a limb, stuck halfway up the Šťávnice valley leading nowhere. If you're continuing into Slovakia though, the scenic train journey from Uherský Brod through the White Carpathians to Trenčianská Teplá is as good a way as any to get there.

Zlín and around

Hidden in a gentle green valley east of the Morava, **ZLÍN** is one of Czechoslovakia's most fascinating towns. Despite appearances, it's not just another factory town, it is *the* factory town – a museum of functionalist architecture and the inspiration of one man, **Tomáš Baťa** (pronounced "Batya"), son of a local cobbler who worked his way up from nothing to become the First Republic's most famous millionaire. He grew rich supplying the Austro-Hungarian army with its boots during World War I, and between the wars quickly became the largest manufacturer of shoes in the world, producing over 50 million pairs annually.

When Baťa set up his first factory at the turn of the century, Zlín's population was just 3000. Now, with suburbs trailing for miles along the River Dřevnice, it exceeds 85,000. Its heyday was during the First Republic when Baťa planned and started to build the ultimate production-line city, a place where workers would be provided with good housing, schooling, leisure facilities and a fair wage. All along the approach roads to the town centre you can see the red-brick shoe-box houses which Baťa constructed for his workers as "temporary accommodation" – houses which have lasted better than anything built after 1948. He died in a plane crash in 1932 at the peak of his power, and although his work was continued by his son (also called Tomáš), the combined effects of Allied bombing, nationalisation and economic stagnation have left only a hint of the model garden city Baťa had in mind. But while Zlín can't hope to be a top priority on anyone's itinerary, it does present an entirely different side of the country from the usual provincial medieval staré město.

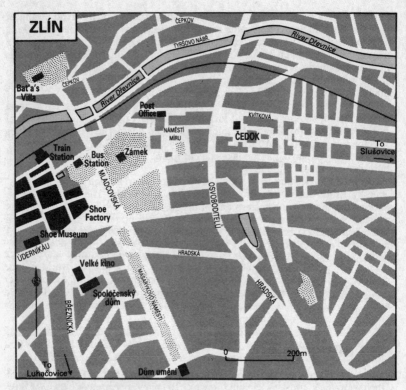

Arriving and accommodation

Arriving at Zlín's **train** or **bus station**, you're just a few minutes' walk from the centre and everything there is to see. *The* **hotel** to stay at is the expensive *Spoločenský dům* (☎067-2312), renamed the *Moskva* in the 1950s, though it may yet revert to its original name. Those of lesser means could try the *Družba* (☎067-277 85), 2km out on the road to Slušovice (bus #52), or *Ondráš* on Kvitkova. For **food**, your best bet are the hotel restaurants, or alternatively the vegetable market around náměstí Míru. The nearest **campsite** is 12km away in NAPAJEDLA (open all year), on the Morava.

The Town

Baťa was a longstanding patron of modern art, art which would reflect the thrust and modernity of his own business. In 1911 he had his own villa built on the north side of the river, by the leading Czech architect of the time, Jan Kotěra. In the late 1920s Le Corbusier was called in to design the town, but after an abortive sketch of the place, the job fell to local architect František Gahura, who had studied under Kotěra and who was given the chance of a lifetime – to design and build an entire city.

Unlike every other town in the country, Zlín does not revolve around the local zámek or marketplace but around the **shoe factory** itself, its sixteen-storey offices designed by one of Gahura's assistants, Vladimír Karfík. The style – concrete frame, red-brick infill and plate-glass windows – is typical of all the town's original 1930s buildings, slavishly copied and barbarised by undistinguished post-war architects. Bata's own office was a huge air-conditioned lift capable of visiting every floor. As well as serving as the corporation's administration, it now houses Zlín's main "sight", the **Shoe Museum** (Obuvnické muzeum) which works the same shift as the rest of the factory: Monday to Friday 7am to 2pm. Even if you're not a foot fetishist, it's a wonderful 1930s-style museum, with shoes from all over the world from medieval *boty* to the latest sad attempts of the Zlín factory (renamed *Svit* after nationalisation in 1948), plus a recently "revised" final section on Bata himself.

From out of the factory grounds rises the obligatory red and white striped chimney, industriously spewing black smoke over the town – in its own way a reassuring guarantee of further employment. When the siren goes at 2pm for the end of the day-shift, the workers pour out of the factory gates and onto the trolley buses, as if part of some strange Orwellian dumb-show. Directly opposite the main entrance across Úderníků is Karfík's plate-glass department store which naturally includes a shoe shop (Czechoslovakia still leads the world in one respect – shoe consumption, which stands at an annual rate of 4.2 pairs per capita). Beyond here, further up the slope, lies the faded white 1930s **Velké kino** which holds 2000 movie-goers and the eleven-storey **Spoločenský dům**, built by Karfík and Lorenz in 1933 and now a hotel.

Only the sloping green of the Masarykovo náměstí, flanked by more boxy buildings, gives some idea of the trajectory of Gahura's master plan. The first block on the left is Gahura's Masarykovy školy, where Bata pursued his revolutionary teaching methods still admired today. At the top of this leafy space is the **Dům umění**, designed by Gahura in 1932 as a memorial to Bata, where his statue, some memorabilia, and the wreckage of the biplane in which he crashed used to stand. Now it serves as the concert hall for the town's orchestra and for exhibitions of contemporary art – appropriate enough given Bata's tireless patronage of the **avant-garde**, which he not only utilised in his photographic advertising, but also produced in the film studios that were built here between the wars, and still churn out the many animation films for which the country is renowned.

ZLÍN – GOTTWALDOV

On old maps of the country and on the odd signpost on the roads leading to Zlín, you might see mention of **Gottwaldov**, the name given to the town by zealous local Party hacks in 1949, after the country's notorious first Communist president, Klement Gottwald, known as the "Stalinist butcher". It was no doubt seen as a just revenge on Bata, who rid his shop floor of Communists by decree in the 1920s. Not long into the Velvet Revolution, the idea of reverting to the original name became a local obsession. Banners were draped out of windows saying "at žije Zlín" ("Long live Zlín"), and shortly before the name-change, Tomáš Jnr paid his first visit to the town since going into exile in Canada shortly after the Communist coup. The whole town turned out, but perhaps more importantly, Bata promised to help the company through the difficult times ahead.

Gahura's master plan was never fully realised and the rest of the town is accidental and ill-conceived. The only other place of interest is the modest country **zámek**, set in the park opposite the factory, which contains a museum, art gallery and café and which now pays lavish tribute to, rather than denegrates – as in the past – Baťa's achievements.

Lastly, and a propos of nothing in particular, Zlín is the unlikely birthplace of that not so avant-garde playwright **Tom Stoppard**. His father was a Czech doctor by the name of Eugene Straussler, but barely two years after his birth, the family fled from the Nazis to Singapore, where his father died. His mother later married a major in the British army and settled in England. These two snippets explain two otherwise puzzling points: why Stoppard has a slight foreign accent and why the Tom Stoppard Prize is given to Czech or Slovak authors in translation.

SLUŠOVICE

It is no mere coincidence that the region that produced Baťa and Zlín should be home to **JZD Agrokombinát Slušovice**, less than 10km east of Zlín and probably the most thrusting and successful company of the Communist era. Reports of the scope and range of its activities have always been a mixture of fact and myth, but having started out as just another farming co-operative in the 1950s, it now produces everything from computers to cucumbers, running its own national chain of supermarkets, restaurants and hotels (including one in Vietnam), an international airport and even its own football team. If you've got your own transport, a quick spin up the newly resurfaced roads which surround Slušovice is a salutary experience. The white and yellow of JZD AK turns up everywhere: on garden fences, on the special bus stops, across the roofs of factories. Slušovice has also become something of a centre for the surrounding districts, hosting shambolic flea markets as well as horse-racing, cycling and football events. At the weekend the place is absolutely packed – though to be honest, there's no real reason why any traveller should want to go there.

The co-op has always enjoyed the enthusiastic patronage of the Party, but the real driving force behind Slušovice's meteoric success is František Čuba, the co-op's founder. Čuba's style of management has been nothing if not controversial, combining a Thatcherite disregard for labour laws and pay differentials with a head-hunting recruitment policy which perhaps uniquely for Eastern Europe was not based wholly on Party membership. The events of 1989 witnessed fairly vitriolic attacks against his autocratic practices, but Čuba seems to have ridden out the storm despite blunt statements like "democracy ends at the gates of the enterprise", landing himself the largest piece of the shareholding cake in the company's foreign trade section. However, the future looks bleak even for Czechoslovakia's most modern company, which basically knew all the loopholes of the old system but knows much less about the harsh realities of market-led economics.

Kroměříž

KROMĚŘÍŽ (Kremsier), to the west of the main Uherské Hradiště road, and seat of the bishops of Olomouc from the Middle Ages to the nineteenth century, is one of Moravia's most graceful towns. Its once-powerful German-speaking population has long since gone, and nowadays the town feels pleasantly provincial, famous only for its Moravian male-voice choir and folk music tradition. Quiet though it is, Kroměříž is definitely worth an afternoon's visit, if only for the chateau's rich collections and the town's extensive gardens.

Savagely set upon by the Swedish army in the Thirty Years' War, Kroměříž was rebuilt by order of **Prince-Bishop Karl Eusebius von Liechtenstein-Kastelcorn**, a pathological builder (see Valtice), and a member of the richest dynasty in Moravia at the time. Vast sums of money were spent not only hiring Italian architects, but also enriching the chateau's art collection and establishing a musical life to rival Vienna. Liechtenstein founded a college for choristers, maintained a 30-piece court orchestra and employed a series of prestigious *Kapellmeisters*, though aside from the chateau's extensive archives there's little evidence of courtly life extant today.

The old town

Standing on the southwest side of the River Morava, the centre of the **old town** is the former marketplace of Velké náměstí. A broad, generous space, it's gracious enough, but the houses themselves have suffered over the years. Jánská hides the town's finest ensemble: a flourish of terraced canons' houses with bright candy-coloured Empire frontages. On one side of the square the houses lean back, inviting you to approach the **Bishop's Palace** (1hr guided tour; April & Oct Sat & Sun 9am–5pm; May–Sept Tues–Sun 9am–5pm), a severe Baroque fortress relieved only by the fifteenth-century lanterned tower, sole survivor of the Swedes' rampage in the Thirty Years' War. Inside, the chateau is actually a more gentle Rococo than its uncompromising exterior might at first suggest. The dark wood and marble decor of the small **manský sál** where the bishops held court is overwhelmed by Maulbertsch's celebratory frescoes, which bear down on guests from the unusually low ceiling. The showpiece of the palace is the fiddly white and gold excess of the **sněmovní sál**, as high and mighty as anything in Prague, and a perfect setting for the concerts which still take place here. In the first three months of 1849, delegates from all parts of the Empire met to thrash out a new constitution, in the face of the revolutionary events of the previous year. The **Kremsier Constitution** which came out of these brainstorming sessions acknowledged "equality of national rights", only to be unceremoniously ditched by the Habsburgs who launched into their final bout of absolutism a few years later.

If you want, you can skip the tour entirely and just visit the **art gallery** (Zámecká obrazárna) which contains what's left of the Liechtenstein's vast collection, still the best selection of sixteenth- and seventeenth-century European paintings in Moravia. There's plenty of bucolic frolicking supplied by the Flemish masters, including an earthy Breughel, and a more sober portrait of Charles I and his wife Henrietta by Van Dyck. Others worth noting are Veronese's awestruck *Apostles*, Cranach's *Beheading of St John* (with a mangy dog lapping up the spillage), and Titian's equally gruesome *Apollo punishing Marsyas*.

Gardens and galleries

Like Olomouc, Kroměříž is a place as rich in gardens as in buildings. The watery **Zámecká zahrada** (daily 7am–6.30pm), established by one of the green-fingered Chotek family who held the archbishopric in the 1830s, stretch right down to the Morava, covering an area twice the size of the old town. Having long since dropped its formality, it's now a pleasantly unruly park, reeking of wild garlic and hiding an aviary, a deer park and a few stalking peacocks. Ten minutes' walk west of the zámek are the **Květná zahrada** (daily 7am–7pm), more formal but also more beautiful and generally in a better state of repair. They were laid out by the Liechtensteins in the 1670s, "ten years and no expense spared" as the Latin inscription reminds you. Its finest vista and one much snapped by photographers is the Neoclassical colonnade along the gardens' north side, with its parade of columns, 46 in all, each topped by a Roman bust.

Other than the bishop's palace and its two gardens, there's not much else on offer in Kroměříž. The **Galérie Švabinský** (Tues–Sun 8am–noon & 1–5pm) on the main square is mostly dedicated to the work of Max Švabinský, a turn-of-the-century artist and graphicist who was born here in 1872. There's no denying his skill nor his prolific output, but he's a mite too gushy and romantic for today's tastes, and the drawings of nudes and tigers displayed here are unlikely to convert the sceptical. Of the town's churches, the Gothic sv Mořic is the oldest, but its innards were ripped out by fire in 1836 and rebuilt without much feeling. A better bet is the Baroque church of **sv Jan Křtitel** at the top of Jánská, whose sensuous lines and oval dome represent one of the showpieces of Moravian Baroque. Lastly, it's worth wandering round to Moravcova in the easternmost corner of the old town, formerly the Jewish ghetto. Jewish communities in places like Kroměříž, Uherské Hradiště and Prostějov were among the largest in the Czech Lands before World War II, and since they provided many essential services the local bigwigs left them alone. The **Jewish Town Hall** (the only one outside Prague) in Moravcova is remarkable not for it's architectural beauty but for its mere existence, the result of a magnanimous gesture by the prince-bishop for services rendered in the Thirty Years' War.

Practicalities

The train station is on the north side of the Morava, and as you walk into town across the river, you should pay a quick visit to *ČEDOK* on Komenského náměstí, who somewhat unbelievably hand out free sketch-maps of the town. For **accommodation**, the *Straka* (☎0634-217 15) on Komenského náměstí is cheaper though not so well-situated as the moderate *Haná* (☎0634-204 68) on the main square.

NORTH MORAVIA

North Moravia (Severní Morava) is not the never-ending industrial conglomerate that its critics would have you believe, though it certainly has more than its fair share of ecological disaster zones, like the black coal basin in the far northeast. Yet at the same time it manages to boast some of Moravia's wildest and most varied countryside, from the region's highest peaks in the **Jeseníky** to the traditional communities in the nether reaches of the **Beskydy** hills. The two biggest towns typify North Moravia's contradictions: **Ostrava**, the country's largest mining and steel town, is somewhere no Moravian would ever recommend you to go (with some justification); **Olomouc** on the other hand is probably Moravia's most attractive and vibrant city, and a definite target for the region.

Olomouc

For the last twenty years, the chief sight in **OLOMOUC** (pronounced "Olla-moats" and known to the Germans as *Olmütz*) was the Soviet soldiers from the nearby garrison, who could be spotted a mile off by their flying-saucer hats and tightly fitting riding boots. Happily, this episode in the city's life is coming to a close, and its reputation as Moravia's most immediately appealing city is surfacing once again. There's a healthy quota of students thanks to the university, a great swathe of gardens which burst into life for the annual flower festival in May, and generally a lot more going on than in the average North Moravian town.

Occupying the crucial Morava crossing point on the road to Kraków, Olomouc was actually the capital of Moravia from the Middle Ages to the mid-seventeenth century and the seat of the bishopric for even longer. All this attracted the destructive attention of Swedish troops in the Thirty Years' War, and their six-year-long occupation left the town for dead. Only the wealth of the church and its strategic trading position kept Olomouc alive, while the military threat from Prussia confined the town to within its eighteenth-century red-brick fortifications, firmly in place until 1888.

The staré město

Despite being a quarter the size of Brno, Olomouc has the same exciting buzz of life, its main arteries chock-a-block with shoppers in the afternoon rush. The **staré město** is a strange contorted shape, squeezed in the middle by an arm of the Morava. Train and bus terminals are 1.5km east of the old town – and too far to walk – so on arrival, take any tram heading west up Osvobození and get off after three or four stops. Uniquely for Czechoslovakia, you must enter at the front and pay the driver.

Náměstí Míru

In the western half of the staré město, all roads lead to the city's two central cobbled main squares, which are hinged to one another at right angles. The lower of the two is more or less triangular, but the upper, **náměstí Míru** is thoroughly irregular, at its centre an amalgamation of buildings and styles that collectively make up the **radnice**. From its creamy rendering the occasional late Gothic or Renaissance gesture emerges, a free standing flight of steps, the handsome lanterned tower soaring up to its conclusion of baubles and pinnacles and a lonely oriel tucked round the back. Most people, though, stare at the north side with its crude arcade of shops (including the Civic Forum information centre) and astronomical clock, which, like its more famous successor in Prague, was destroyed in the war. The rather soulless workerist remake chimes allright, but the figures disappointingly don't budge.

Far more action-packed is the monumental **Holy Trinity Column**, to the west of the radnice, big enough to be a chapel and easily the largest plague column in the country. It's a favourite place for meeting up, eating takeaways from the Divadelní arcade, or just sitting and soaking it all in. Set into the west facade of the square is the **Divadlo Oldřicha Stibora**, previously the *Olmützer Stadttheater* where Mahler arrived as the newly appointed *Kapellmeister* in 1883. The local press took an instant dislike to him, in his own words, "from the

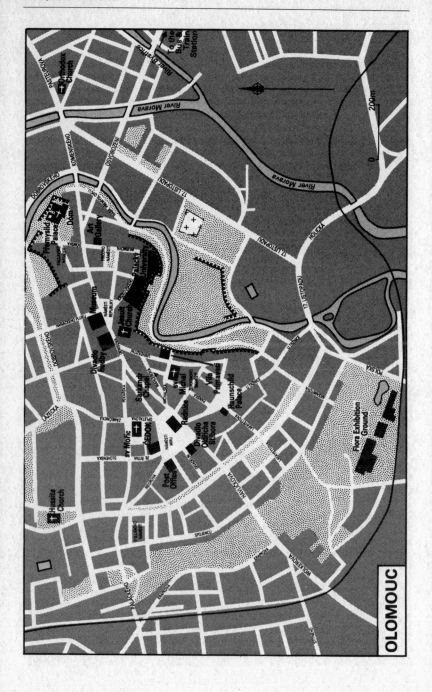

moment I crossed the threshold . . . I felt like a man who is awaiting the judgement of God". No doubt there was a strong element of knee-jerk anti-Semitism in his hostile reception, but this was not helped by Mahler's own autocratic style which caused a number of the local prima donnas to live up to their name. He lasted just three months.

Olomouc makes a big fuss of its sculpture, like that adorning the Edelmann Palace (no. 28 – now a bookshop), and even more of its **fountains** – though most don't actually work – which grace each one of Olomouc's six ancient market squares. Náměstí Míru boasts two of them: Hercules, looking unusually athletic for his years, and, to the east of the radnice, a vigorous depiction of Julius Caesar – the fabled founder of the city – bucking on a steed which coughs up water from its mouth. Jupiter and Neptune can be found in the lower square, which has a dustier feel to it, sloping down to the characteristically low-key church of the Capuchins, with only the single Renaissance oriel of the **Haunschild Palace** on the corner with Lafayettova, and its *pivnice* below, to lift the spirits.

Around Náměstí Míru

North off the upper square, the church of **sv Mořic** is, from the west at least, an oddly mutant building, defensive like a Norman fort, but inside overcome by a thick coat of pink paint making the original Gothic interior difficult to stomach. It does however boast the largest organ in the country, an ugly dark wooden affair with dirty grey pipes – you can only hope it sounds better than it looks. Back out through the west door, you're confronted with another typical socialist supermarket, which has muscled its way into the historic part of town with the connivance of the philistine Communist council.

Two of the city's best-looking backstreets, Školní and Michalská, lead southeast from náměstí Míru, up to the church of **sv Michal**, plain enough on the outside but inside cool, spacious and clad in the masterly excess of Baroquification. Three octagonal domes rise up in Byzantine-like fashion, raised up by Roman pilasters with capitals so large they're bearing fruit. It's like some neo-Romanesque basilica and, in the middle of Moravia, frankly quite disorientating. Gypsy families have been moved into the dilapidated streets round about, and as the bedclothes get aired and the sun beats down, there's a Mediterranean feel to the quarter. Alongside sv Michal, the exuberance of the turn-of-the-century **Vila Primavesi** is well hidden behind the nearby blossoming trees and a coat of blackened pebble dash. It's now a health clinic, but it's worth climbing the stairs – a blaze of gold and blue mosaic – to check out the Art-Nouveau decor of the waiting room. More obviously accessible is the mini-dome of the neo-Baroque **Sarkandr Chapel**, which replaced the old prison on the corner of Na hradě and G. Mahlera at the beginning of this century. It's hardly big enough to kneel in, though this is perhaps its main charm.

From the university east to the dóm

Firmly wedged between the two sections of the staré město is the obligatory **Jesuit Church**, deemed to be particularly necessary in a city where Protestantism had spread like wildfire in the sixteenth century. Jutting out into the road, it signals the gateway to the less hectic, quieter part of town. The great mass of the former Jesuit College, now the **Palacký University**, dominates the first square, náměstí Republiky. Opposite is the town **museum** (Tues–Sun 9am–5pm), housed in the convent and cloisters of sv Klara, with a pretty tame permanent display but the odd worthwhile exhibition of contemporary art on the ground floor. Trams and cars make this one of Olomouc's least accommodating squares, and apart from the sub-Bernini Triton fountain, you'd be as well to duck down Halasova to the leafy **Fričovo náměstí**, closed in on all four sides by fine Baroque buildings laid out after the Swedes had laid the place to waste, including the Archbishop's Palace financed by the multi-millionaire archbishop Liechtenstein in the 1660s. It's one of the most peaceful spots in town, popular with students easing their brains from a session in the library, and right by the local art gallery, just up Wurmova.

On the other side of the tramlines, the **dóm**, dedicated to sv Václav, is a nineteenth-century rehash job in the same vein as the dóm in Brno, but the secluded cathedral close on which it stands – Václavské náměstí – is a cut above its counterpart. The nave is bright and airy, its walls and pillars prettily painted in imitation of the great Romanesque churches of the West, and the **crypt** has a wonderful display of gory reliquaries and priestly sartorial wealth. Next door, the scanty remains of the original twelfth-century **Přemyslid Palace** are on display in the chapterhouse. The Gothic frescoes and Romanesque stonework are mildly impressive and the guide enthusiastic, but it's all a bit too earnest and specialised for most people. Right by the entrance is the Baroque chapel of sv Anna, and set back from it the deanery where the teenage King Václav III, the last of the Přemyslids, was murdered in mysterious circumstances in 1306, throwing the country into a blood-letting war of succession.

To the parks and the Flower Festival

The Habsburg defences to the west of the staré město were completely torn down in the late nineteenth century to make way for what is now a long, busy thoroughfare formerly known as Leninova. Starting in the north with the cinema, a late Secession building decorated with caryatids worshipping Edison light bulbs, it continues with the familiar trail of Habsburg bureaucracy. Halfway down on the right, a leftover water tower is the only survivor on a square that contained a synagogue until 1939, and where a statue of Stalin and Lenin subsequently stood. The former (and only the former) was defaced badly towards the end of the 1980s, apparently by an outraged Gorby-supporting Soviet soldier. Neither survived the iconoclasm of November 1989.

If you're tired of Olomouc's uneven cobbles, the best places to head are the parks which practically encircle the town. A couple of blocks of *fin-de-siècle* houses stand between the avenue and the long patchwork strip of crisscross paths, flowerbeds and manicured lawns. It's just a small sample of the annual **Flower Festival**, a mammoth international gathering of florists, held further south in the special Flora Exhibition Grounds at the beginning of May (there's a smaller affair sometime in August or September). Another pleasant walk is out of the southern end of the old town's lower square and left into the tiny Malé náměstí, which has a flight of steps which lead down to the Bezručovy sady, once the city moat, where the more youthful locals hang out.

Practical details

ČEDOK, on náměstí Míru, will book **rooms** for you; someone there usually speaks German and occasionally English. If it's closed, try the cheap *Hotelový dům* on Volgogradská (☎068-296 71) or the slightly more expensive *Morava* at

Riegrova 16 (☎068-296 71), followed by the nineteenth-century, moderate *Národní dům*, 8 května 21 (☎068-251 79), and the similarly priced *Palác* (☎068-232 84) on the corner of Komenského, before forking out an arm and a leg for the *Sigma* (☎068-271 53) by the station or the *Hotel Flora* (☎068-232 41), Krapkova 34. Rooms can be hard to come by in May when the Spring Music Festival follows the Flower Festival. For campsites, see "North to Šternberk", below.

For **restaurants**, try the *Národní dům* or any of the other larger hotels. More interestingly, the *Hanacká restaurace* on the lower square and the *Lidová jídelna*, 8 května 3, are traditional Moravian establishments, and the posh-ish *Asia* right at the end of Divadelní purports to sell "Asian" food (Tues–Sat; evenings only). For lighter snacks, typically Czech pizzas can be found in the Divadelní arcade, and a good range of cakes in the *cukrárna* next to *ČEDOK*.

In the **evenings**, there's still a bit of life in the two big squares, but inevitably most people head for a *pivnice* or *kavárna* like the *Opera*, by the main theatre, or the *Café Corso* on the other side of the square (open till 10pm and 11pm respectively). The *Divadlo Oldřicha Stibora* puts on a good selection of opera and the city's philharmonic orchestra regularly perform here. In late May, Olomouc has its own *Hudební jaro* (Spring Music Festival), when concerts are spread evenly around the town's venues and churches. The youthful *Divadlo hudby* (Denisova 47) puts on a more adventurous programme of gigs, films and video – anything from Jan Švankmajer to U2. The subsidiary *S-Klub* advertise their gigs and events here, which take place at the student college on 17 listopadu 43.

Around Olomouc

Olomouc sits happily in the wide plain of the **Haná region**, famous for its multifarious folk costumes and songs reflecting the fertility of the land. Naturally enough in a strongly agricultural area, the harvest festivals (*Hanácké dožínky* or *dožínkový slavnost*) are the highlight of the year. If you're in the region in the last half of September, you'll see posters up everywhere advertising them. All the places listed below are situated in the Morava plain, and are easily reached by bus or train on day trips from Olomouc, with the exception of the area round Bouzov which is really only for those who have their own transport.

North to Šternberk

If you're camping, the nearest site to Olomouc is *Dolní Žleb*, 14km north in Šternberk. En route, to the east, the ridge of the Jeseníky foothills drifts imperceptibly towards you, broken only by the twin towers of the Baroque pilgrimage church at **KOPEČEK**. Perched 200m above the plain and flanked by its whiter-than-white convent wings, the site and scale are truly spectacular. But it's only feasible to visit with your own transport, and, close up, it doesn't live up to expectations – it's only really worth making your way up here if you want to see the adjoining **zoo**.

You can enjoy just as good a view from the heights above **ŠTERNBERK** (Sternberg), where the annual *Ecce Homo* motor race is held in mid-September over the lethal switchbacks on the road to Opava. The town itself is not much more than its giant Baroque church and **zámek** (April & Oct Sat & Sun 9–4pm;

May–Sept Tues–Sun 8am–5pm), worth a visit not for its rooms, which are part of an overlong guided tour, but for its museum which houses a fabulous collection of clocks and watches from an ancient Chinese alarm clock to the substandard fare churned out by the state watch manufacturers *Prim*, who are based in the town.

Přerov and Prostějov

Twenty-three kilometres southeast of Olomouc, twenty minutes by train, **PŘEROV** (Prerau) is an ungainly town dedicated to the chemical and engineering industries. Aside from a brief annual Jazz Festival in late September, its single redeeming feature is the endearing old town square, a tight semicircle of colourful houses centred around a typically melodramatic statue by František Bílek of the sixteenth-century religious reformer Jan Blahoslav, holding up his translation of the New Testament. The straight side of the náměstí is taken up by the sixteenth-century zámek, which among other things commemorates Blahoslav's more famous successor in the Protestant Unity of Brethren, **Jan Ámos Komenský** aka John Amos Comenius. Komenský was actually born some fifty or sixty kilometres further south in Uherský Brod, but his Latin schooling took place at the Brethren's school in Přerov. As nominal leader of the Brethren, Komenský was forced to flee the Czech Lands after the Battle of Bílá hora, settling for a while in the Polish city of Leszno. He narrowly escaped being shipwrecked on his one and only voyage to Protestant England in 1641, where he tried unsuccessfully to set up a college of social reform. Of his many writings, his graded and pictorial Latin textbooks have proved more influential than his religious treatises. Throughout the eastern part of Moravia, the Brethren rode out the Counter-Reformation to emerge in significant numbers once Austrian liberalism began to take effect in the late eighteenth century.

Twenty kilometres and half an hour by train, the big textile town of **PROSTĚJOV** (Prossnitz) has a more spacious and grand old centre, but the highlight is Jan Kotěra's 1908 **Národní dům**: close to the last remaining bastion of the Gothic town walls, this now houses a theatre and restaurant.

As with his museum at Hradec Králové, Kotěra was moving rapidly away from the "swirl and blob" of the Secession, but here and there the old elements persist: in the sweep of the brass door handles, in the pattern on the poster frames. Apart from its furniture, the restaurant has been left unmolested, and the bold Klimt-like relief of the *Three Graces* above the mantlepiece is still as striking as ever.

Five kilometres west of Prostějov, two good lakeside **campsites** (May–Oct) provide plenty of opportunities for swimming, and on a high mound above the westernmost reservoir stands the imposing slab of the zámek at **PLUMLOV** (Plumenau), another of the Liechtenstein's fancies. Designed by Prince-Bishop Karl Eusebius von Liechtenstein-Kastelcorn himself, only one wing out of the four planned got off the drawing board, and it's been under reconstruction for a long time now, but it makes a good piece of scenery under which to swim.

Around Bouzov

The northernmost tip of the Drahanská vrchovina around Bouzov – an extension of the hills of the Moravský kras – has enough to keep you occupied on a lazy weekend. **BOUZOV** itself is nothing but its **hrad** (1-hr guided tour; April & Oct

9am–4pm; May–Sept 8am–5pm; closed Mon) – a stunning thirteenth-century Gothic fortress right on the high point of the vrchovina, and perfectly suited as a base for its former owners, the Teutonic Knights. It also took the fancy of the Nazi SS who based their Czech headquarters here during the last war. Whether because of this last fact, or just because of the usual revulsion at the pompous neo-Gothicising, the guided tour might be considered worth skipping for a walk in the surrounding hills instead.

Four kilometres south at **JAVOŘÍČKO**, the local SS burnt the village to the ground and shot 38 of the inhabitants in the last days of the war. This futile and tragic act aside, the reason for coming here is to visit the **Javoříčské jeskyně**, limestone karst caves on a par with the ones near Brno, but without the crowds and queues. Five kilometres east of Bouzov, **BÍLÁ LHOTA** has a eighteenth-century zámek distinguished only by its beautiful arboretum. The **Mladečské jeskyně**, a more extensive and popular limestone cave system another couple of kilometres on, are just off the main Olomouc–Prague road and at the end of the most twig-like of branch lines from LITOVEL (which has rooms at the cheap *Záložna* hotel (☎22 90) on the main square). Given that there are no official camp-sites in the area, the only other place you might be able to stay the night is at the cheap *Bouzov* (☎932 06), below the hrad.

The Jeseníky mountains

The **Jeseníky mountains** are the highest mountains in what is now Moravia. It's a region that's worlds apart from the densely populated industrial centres of the north and east of the province or even the vine-clad hills of the south, having more in common with the Bohemian Krkonoše (of which it is a natural eastern extension). The highest reaches rise up to the northwest between Šumperk and Jeseník, but these have been extensively damaged by acid rain and are worth avoiding. To the south, the hills drift into a gentle high plateau. Perhaps the best area to head for is the foothills on either side of the big peaks, which harbour some low-key spa resorts like Lázně Jeseník and the historical remains of Czech Silesia.

Around Šumperk

ŠUMPERK (Schönberg) is the gateway to the upper Jeseníky, though it actually gets surprisingly few visitors. It has the feel of a mountain town, despite the fact that the shift from the plain to the hills is much less dramatic here than at Šternberk. For the last two centuries it was a thriving German textile town, at the vanguard of the language frontier. The Germans may have fled but the town still relies on its cloth-making tradition.

Unlike most provincial towns, there's no obvious centre to Šumperk; its neo-Renaissance radnice stands on the quiet and insignificant náměstí Míru, while the action – so to speak – goes on along the town's long shopping mall (previously known as Red Army Avenue), and the unruly park which lies to the north of the train station. Unreconstructed street names were a feature of most towns pre-November 1989, but Šumperk topped the lot with a Stalin Square, a Stalingrad Street and a statue of the man himself in a nearby car park by the old town walls. This last attraction having gone, there's not much to see here, but if you end up staying over, there's a modicum of nightlife. The South Tyneside Pipe Band were playing when I was last there, but for details of the latest entertainment ask *ČEDOK*, 100m east from the *Grand Hotel*.

Grabbing a **room** for the night should present few problems. In descending order of price the choices are the *Grand Hotel* (☎0649-21 41) by the park, the *Moravan* (☎0649-35 91), Odborářů 3, and the *Praha* (☎0649-35 85) at the top end of the shopping mall. If you don't fancy stopping off at Velké Losiny, Jeseník is a scenic two-hour train ride from Šumperk.

Velké Losiny

One good reason for staying in Šumperk is to visit the Renaissance chateau in the tiny Moravian spa of **VELKÉ LOSINY** (Gross-Ullersdorf), twenty minutes away by train, and one of the last oases of civilisation before you hit the deserted heights of the Jeseníky. The **zámek** (45-min guided tour; April & Oct Sat & Sun 9am–noon & 1–4pm; May–Sept Tues–Sun 8am–noon & 1–5pm) is set in particularly lush grounds beside a tributary of the River Desná. It's a three-winged, three-storeyed structure which opens out into a beautifully restored sixteenth-century arcaded loggia, and for once the guided tour is really worthwhile. It was the northernmost property of the extremely wealthy Žerotín family, but inhabited for less than a hundred years. As strong supporters of the Unity of Brethren, the Žerotíns were stripped of their wealth after the Battle of Bílá hora and the chateau left unused – except as a venue for the region's notorious witch trials of the Counter-Reformation.

The train station is in the spa itself, and it's a pleasant one-kilometre walk along the blue-marked path through the verdant gardens peppered with the familiar faded ochre spa buildings. The *Praděd*, on the crossroads by the station, serves food and may even have a bed for the night.

Over the pass to Jeseník

The railway and the Desná river peter out before the real mountains begin. A bus from Šumperk runs roughly every two hours via the last station, KOUTY NAD DESNOU, continuing over the saddle of Černohorské sedlo (1013m). The ascent from Kouty is a dramatic series of hairpins, but the top of the pass is a disappointment. The tourist board may prefer to talk of "mountain meadows and pastures" but the reality is low-lying scrub and moorland: any spruce or pine trees which dare to rise above this are beaten down by acid rain. Some fairly bad-news development is nevertheless ploughing on, but for the moment there's just an impromptu **campsite**, 500m from the saddle. If you want to enjoy a better view, it's a 45-minute walk to **Červená hora** (1333m) and another hour and a half to **Šerák** (1351m), which looks down onto the Ramzovské sedlo, a much lower pass to the west which the railway from Šumperk to Jeseník opts for. There's a chair lift to take you down to the campsite at RAMZOVÁ should you so wish. Two hours in the opposite direction bring you to **Praděd** (1491m), the highest and most barren peak in the range. From there you can easily drop down to **KARLOVA STUDÁNKA** on the Bílá Opava, the nearest the Jeseníky get to an old Silesian mountain resort, with the cheap *Džbán* (☎932 38) and cheaper *Opava* (☎932 30) hotels theoretically able to accommodate you. Rough camping in these parts is fairly acceptable, especially if you manage to befriend a passing hiking group.

Jeseník and around

On the other side of the pass, the road plunges down with equal ferocity to **JESENÍK** (Gräfenberg), a town that's pleasant without being at all picturesque. There are several reasonably priced hotels which make finding a room a mere formality, after which you should head up to **Lázně Jeseník** (Bad Gräfenberg), 2km above the town, where local farmer Vincent Priessnitz established one of the many famous Silesian spas in the nineteenth century. There's a wonderful Art-Nouveau monument to the spa's founder in the Kurpark, presiding god-like over the skinny sick on his right and the "cured" (or at least plump) on his left. Gogol took the cure here, but such days are only really recalled in the grandish Priessnitz Sanatorium. The natural springs are actually scattered about the surrounding countryside, providing hot and sulphuric refreshments *en promenade*. If you'd prefer to get clean away from people and particularly spa patients, the viewpoint from the summit of Zlatý chlum, 2km east of Jeseník, fulfils the requirements. There's a **campsite** with swimming pool less than 2km along the valley towards another spa resort, LIPOVÁ LÁZNĚ.

If you're serious about a bit more **hiking**, two long but gentle hikes are possible around here. Follow the blue-marked path from Lázně Jeseník over the hills to Velké Špičák (12km) where weird rocky outcrops and a mini-karst cave system can be explored (take the local train back to Jeseník); or take the red-marked path from Lázně Jeseník over to ŽULOVÁ (13km) where the local fortress was turned into a church. At Žulová, the countryside flattens out as it slips into Poland, but you might consider hopping on the train (30min) to **JAVORNÍK** (Jauernig) where the local zámek features a collection of historical pipes and ornate smoking devices.

Around Opava (Troppau)

Hard by the Polish border and on the road from Jeseník to Ostrava, **OPAVA** is one of the oldest towns in the country, an important trading centre on the Amber Road from the Adriatic to the Baltic Sea, but perhaps better known as **Troppau**, capital of Austrian (and later Czech) Silesia (see box). Badly damaged in the last few weeks of the war, when ninety percent of the town was reduced to rubble, it's a big, busy, if fairly nondescript, town. Much has been rebuilt since 1945, and while the town may not merit a detour, it's a place to break a journey or do a bit of chateau-seeing.

Nothing too spectacular remains of the town's Silesian days: the huge four-teenth-century red-brick church has survived more or less intact on the old fish market – now a car park for the spanking new red-brick monstrosity of the *Kamyšin* nightclub-cum-hotel complex. The **Silesian Diet*** used to meet in the old Jesuit seminary at the top end of Masarykovo třída – Opava's best-looking street, boasting a couple of Baroque palaces – and later moved to the Minorite monastery further down on the left. Lastly, the grand nineteenth-century **Silesian Museum**, set in the town's pretty semicircle of parks, has been painstakingly restored since the war and houses a worthy though dull exhibition that avoids most of the controversies of Silesian history.

---

* It was at here at the Troppau Conference that the "Holy Alliance" of Austria, Russia and Prussia met late in 1820, to thrash out a common policy towards the revolutionary stirrings of post-Napoleonic Europe.

1990 saw the founding of a (Czech) Silesian University in Opava, something which is sure to bring some excitement to an otherwise dead nightlife. The two cheapest **hotels** are the *Zimní Stadion* (Zámecký okruh 8) round by the museum and the more central *Orient* on Ostrožná.

Three chateaux

There are three Silesian chateaux of varying interest, all within easy reach of Opava. **Hradec nad Moravicí** (currently no admission), 8km away at the end of its own little branch line, was visited by Beethoven, Liszt and Paganini, and every June there's a Beethoven music competition held here. Since 1982 the chateau and park have been undergoing a slow restoration programme and the exhibits have been transferred to the chateau at **Raduň**, 6km southeast of Opava (15min by bus). In contrast to the snail's pace renovation of Hradec, the handsome Baroque chateau at **Kravaře**, 8km east of Opava, was rapidly and lavishly rebuilt to house an exhibition (opened in 1970 shortly after the second Soviet "liberation") devoted entirely to the Soviet army's costly Ostrava Operation of May 1945.

Krnov and Bruntál

The nearest border crossing into Poland from Opava is 25km away at **KRNOV** (Jägerndorf), famous for the organs manufactured here since 1873. It, too, was flattened in the last war, but should you wish to stop over before heading into Poland, there's an offbeat and pricey hotel in the former Augustinian monastery, called the *Moravan*.

On the main road from Olomouc to Krnov, **BRUNTÁL** (Freudenthal) is only worth a mention for its Baroque chateau, another hang-out of the Teutonic Knights, which, if you're passing through, doles out all the usual attractions – an arcaded courtyard with loggia, "valuable furnishings" – without actually pulling off any surprises.

SILESIA

From 1335 onwards **Silesia** (*Slezsko* in Czech) was an integral part of the Historic Lands of the Bohemian Crown. In the 1740s, the majority of it was carelessly lost to the Prussians by the young Empress Maria Theresa. The three remaining Duchies – Troppau (Opava), Jägerndorf (Krnov) and Teschen (Těšín) – became known as Austrian Silesia with Troppau as their capital, separated from each other by the Moravian salient around Ostrava. The population, though predominantly German, contained large numbers of Czechs and Poles – a mishmash typical of the region, and one which caused interminable territory disputes. In 1920 – after a few bloody skirmishes – the new state of Czechoslovakia lost part of Těšín to Poland and gained part of Hlučín from Germany, and in 1928, Silesia was amalgamated with Moravia. This last act, in particular, annoyed the violently irredentist pre-war German population. But, like the majority of the country's German-speaking minority, they were booted out in 1945, making the whole issue of a separate Silesia fairly redundant. Nevertheless, the post-1989 Moravian nationalists (HSD-SMS) still carefully distinguish between Moravia and Silesia in their propaganda, in an empty gesture which is unlikely to stir the Polish minority, nor the Czechs and Slovaks, who have colonised the region since the war.

Ostrava

If you told a Czech you were going to **OSTRAVA**, they'd probably think you were mad. The city is regularly shrouded in a pall of grey smog, and although efforts have been made in the last ten years to clean up the centre, they can't cover up the fact that it's coal and steel that have made the town what it is – rich and dirty. It is, however, Czechoslovakia's fourth largest city (pop. 330,000 – many of whom are Polish migratory workers) and the main gateway into Poland (though the Polish side is little better). And, should you wish to stay in the North Moravian coal basin, Ostrava is as good a place as any, with a goodish cultural and sporting life.

The Town

Ostrava divides into three distinct districts: **Slezská Ostrava** to the east, where the first black coal deposits were discovered back in 1763, **Vítkovice** to the south where the first foundry was set up in 1828, and **Moravská Ostrava** where most of the town's "sights" are located. If you've any sense you'll spend your time exclusively in the latter, largely pedestrianised part of town where Ostrava's shops and department stores bunch up around the old marketplace and main square. Though hardly an architectural masterpiece, it's still able to vaunt a handful of swanky turn-of-the-century facades put up by the rich German and Austrian capitalists who owned the mines here until nationalisation in 1945. Until recently it was known as náměstí Lidových milicí (People's Militia Square) – a once-proud reference to the city's strong working-class traditions and post-war support for the Communist Party. This largely unspoken alliance ensured Ostrava's stores were (relatively) well stocked, and for the last twenty years the commercial district was always crowded with Poles and Soviet soldiers gaping in awe at what to them was an unbelievably wide range of products.

Ostrava's most lavish museum was the one dedicated to the working class, on Dimitrovova: now it lies abandoned, awaiting some new, post-revolutionary exhibits. The **town museum** on the main square contains few thrills, but the city **art gallery** (Tues–Fri 10am–6pm, Sat & Sun 10am–3pm), a block west of ČEDOK, is good on turn-of-the-century painting. One of the most distinctive features of Ostrava is the proximity of much of its industry to the centre. The Karolina **coking plant**, only a step away from the city's commercial district, was closed down a few years ago, having spewed out lethal carcinogenic filth over the city's main shopping district for over a century. Even now, antiquated pitheads are very much a part of the cityscape: an awesome sight, lit up at night like proverbial satanic mills, their immediate future – like that of the city itself – looks very bleak indeed.

Some practical points

Ostrava's main **train station**, the hlavní nádraží, is to the north of the city centre (tram #2, #8 or #12), while the local station, Ostrava střed, and the bus terminal are just a few minutes' walk west of the centre. **Hotels** tend to be booked up with Polish migrant workers, so if you're here during office hours go straight to ČEDOK, Dimitrovova 9. Cheapest hotels are the *Moravia* (☎069-22 60 46), Dimitrovova 172, and the *Odra* (☎069-23 22 80) and the *Beseda* (☎069-35 33 22) out in Vítkovice (trams #12, #13, #14 and #15), but you'll be lucky to be that choosy.

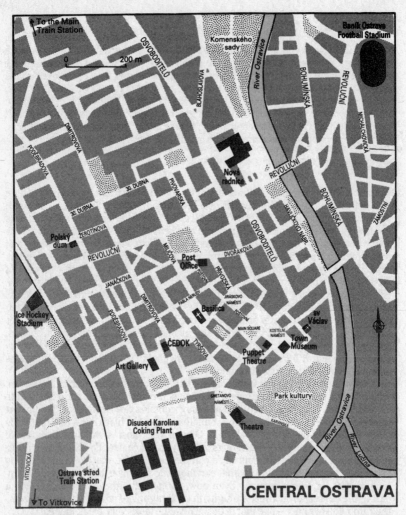

CENTRAL OSTRAVA

Things to do

With big state funds behind it, Ostrava boasts a good **philharmonic orchestra** and the usual range of opera, ballet and theatre, while Janáček, who died in Ostrava, is the subject of the city's **May Music Festival**. At the other end of the cultural spectrum, the country's youngest annual event, **Miss Czechoslovakia** (banned by the Communists when it was first mooted in 1968), takes place here – top prize last year was the latest Škoda.

The city that produced Ivan Lendl is the country's most important sports centre after Prague. Predictably enough, as a working-class city *par excellence*, Ostrava's strongest tradition is in football, with both *Baník Ostrava* and *Vítkovice* enjoying long stretches in the country's *první liga* (First Division). A large number of the country's big sporting events are held here, so check the listings in *ČEDOK* and on fly-posters around town for the latest fixtures.

The Beskydy region

Despite the short distance between them, the hilly **Beskydy region** couldn't be further from the apocalyptic filth of the Ostrava coal basin. In the foothills there's a whole cluster of interesting sights not far from (and including) **Nový Jičín**. Further south and east, into hiking country proper, the old Wallachian traditions of the region have been preserved both *in situ* in the more inaccessible villages, and at the skansen at **Rožnov pod Radhoštěm**.

Nový Jičín

NOVÝ JIČÍN is a typical one-square town on the main road from Olomouc to Ostrava. As squares go, it's a particularly fine one, with wide whitewashed arcades tunnelling their way under a host of restrained late Baroque facades. Only one building stands out (literally), the **stará pošta**, with a pretty two-storey loggia dating from the town's boom-time in the sixteenth century when it bought its independence from the Žerotín family. The chief attraction of the town is now its **Hat Museum** (*Kloboučnické muzeum*; Tues–Fri 8am–noon & 1–4pm, Sat & Sun 9am–noon), laid out in the Žerotíns' old chateau, through the covered passageway of Lidická, which unrealistically claims to be the only such museum in the world. Thankfully, the present exploits of the state hat enterprise *Tonak* (based in the town) are only lightly touched on, leaving most of the museum to a wonderful variety of hats produced in Nový Jičín since 1799. The bit that gets the Czechs going is the array of hats worn by famous national personages – a bit esoteric for non-Czechs, though some might be stirred by the sight of Masaryk's topper.

Nový Jičín has two train termini, both at the end of obscure and inconvenient branch lines, making **bus** by far the easiest way to come and go. *ČEDOK* are on the main square and it should be no hassle getting a **room** in one of the town's many hotels.

One place you can reach by train is the village of **HODSLAVICE**, 8km south of Nový Jičín and birthplace of **František Palacký** (his house is now a museum), one of the chief political figures of nineteenth-century Czechoslovakia. More exciting than this last fact for most people is the village's sixteenth-century **wooden church** of sv Ondřej, a first hint of the local Wallachian culture.

■ WALLACHIAN CULTURE ■

As far as anybody can make out, the **Wallachs** or **Vlachs** were semi-nomadic sheep farmers who settled the mountainous areas of eastern Moravia and western Slovakia in the fifteenth century. Although their name clearly derives from the Romanian Vlachs, it is thought that they arrived from eastern Poland and the Ukraine, and the name Vlach is simply a generic term for sheep farmer. Whatever their true origins, they were certainly considered a race apart by the surrounding Slav peasants. Successive Habsburg military campaigns against the Vlachs in the seventeenth century destroyed their separate identity, and nowadays Wallachian culture lives on only in the folk customs and distinctive wooden architecture of the region.

Štramberk

Eight kilometres east of Nový Jičín by irregular bus, or an easy two-hour walk away, the smokestack settlement of **ŠTRAMBERK** is actually one of the best places to take your first dip into Wallachian culture. Clumped under the conic Bílá hora (not to be confused with *the* Bílá hora in Prague) like an ancient funeral pyre, Štramberk feels very old indeed, yet many of its wooden cottages were built as late as the first half of the nineteenth century. Its virtue is in seeing a working Wallachian community, its cottages simply constructed out of whole tree trunks, unpainted and untouristed rather than cooped and mummified in a sanitised skansen. Despite being no more than a village, Štramberk does have a nominal main square with three stone buildings in "folk Baroque" at one end and the Jesuit church at the other, beside which there's a small **museum** displaying archaeological findings from the nearby Šipka cave, where remains of Neanderthal Man were discovered. You can see the galleried wooden tower of the original church, halfway up the walls to the castle, laid to waste by the Tartars and never rebuilt. Its one remaining roundtower, **Trúba**, is now a lookout post, with a restaurant nearby.

Kopřivnice

On the other side of Bílá hora from Štramberk (and an easy half-hour walk), **KOPŘIVNICE** is an ugly sprawling factory town, but nevertheless worth a quick visit for its **Tatra Museum** (April–Nov daily 8am–4pm; Dec–March Mon–Fri only), situated in the hangar-like building next door to the train station. Even if spark plugs don't fire your imagination, there are some wonderful vintage cars here. Unlike the popular and ubiquitous Škoda, the luxury Tatra cars have always aimed to be exclusive: the first model which came out in 1897 was called the *President* and from 1948 onwards that's exactly who drove them. The silent and powerful black Tatra, looking like something out of a gangster B-movie, became the ultimate symbol of Party privilege. Ordinary mortals could buy any colour they liked – as long as it *wasn't* black – a colour reserved for Party functionaries. When you've seen the Tatra 87 and the 603, it's a slightly hysterical and somewhat frightening thought to imagine the country's top Stalinists cruising around in these cars, succeeded in the 1970s by the Soviet-looking Tatra 613. Characteristically, Havel and his entourage parade around in BMWs to avoid the stigma of the Tatra, and with the Party no longer in a position to pay for its usual bulk order, the firm may well ditch the luxury motors in favour of the Tonka-tough lorries it also excels in.

Kopřivnice's other museum contains a small tribute to the famous Olympic medallist and long-distance runner of the 1950s, **Emil Zátopek**, who was born in the town in 1922. One thing the museum doesn't tell you is that his wife, Dana Zátopková, was also an Olympic record holder in the javelin. The museum also features a tame section on the controversial subject of Lachian culture (see "Frýdek-Místek", p.258).

Příbor (Freiberg)

Five kilometres and one train station north of Kopřivnice, **PŘÍBOR** appears at first to be a scruffier rerun of Nový Jičín – which it is – except that it has a much greater claim to fame as the birthplace of **Sigmund Freud**. Although the family's financial problems forced them to leave for Vienna when Sigmund was only four, it's difficult to resist the chance to visit the place where Freud went through his oral and anal phases. The town **museum**, situated in the town's former monastery on Lidická, has only one room out of four devoted to the man (Tues & Thurs 8am–noon & 2–4pm, Sun 9am–noon). Sadly there are no pictures of baby Sigmund, only dull official photos of learned and bearded men (including Jung) at conferences on psychoanalysis. In the rest of the town, few associations present themselves, apart from Freud's bust which sticks out of the ground by the local supermarket.

FREUD IN FREIBERG

Born in 1856 to a hard-up Jewish wool merchant and his third wife, Freud himself had no hesitation in ascribing significance to events which took place during the family's brief sojourn in the ten-metre-square rented room above Zajík the blacksmith at Zámecnická 117 (now a locksmith's). "Of one thing I am certain," Freud wrote later in life, "deep within me, although overlaid, there continues to live the happy child from Freiberg [Příbor], the first-born child of a young mother who received from this air, from this soil, the first indelible impressions." Things were not always so idyllic, and Freud later used a number of events in his early childhood to prove his own psychoanalytical theories. The family maidservant, "my instructress in sexual matters" in Freud's own words, was a local Czech woman who used to drag him off to the nearby Catholic church and in Freud's eyes was responsible for his "Rome neurosis". She was eventually sacked for alleged theft (and for encouraging baby Sigmund to thieve, too) and sent to prison. Things weren't too bad on the Oedipal front either, with Freud suspecting his adult half-brother of being the father of his younger sister, Anna

---

Hukvaldy

Moravians hold Janáček much dearer to their hearts than Freud, and the village of **HUKVALDY**, 6km east of Příbor, has become a modest shrine to the composer. Born just two years before Freud, **Leoš Janáček** was the ninth of fourteen children, too many for his impecunious father who taught at the local school. Thus at the age of eleven Janáček was sent to Brno to be a chorister and from then on he made his home in the city, battling against the prejudices of the powerful German elite who ruled over the Moravian classical music scene. When at last he achieved recognition outside Moravia, through the success of the opera *Jenůfa*, he was already in his sixties. Having bought a cottage in Hukvaldy, he spent his last, most fruitful years based in Brno and Hukvaldy, composing such works as the *Glagolithic Mass*, *The Cunning Little Vixen* and *The House of the Dead*. He was fired by his obsessive love for a woman called Kamila Strösslová, wife of a Jewish antique dealer in Písek, who had sent him food parcels throughout World War I. Although he never left his wife, Janáček kept an almost daily correspondence with Kamila for over ten years. In August 1928, he caught a chill searching for her son in the nearby woods and died in a hospital in Ostrava.

Even if you've no interest whatsoever in Janáček, Hukvaldy is a homely little village, sheltering happily under the woods of a thoroughly ruined castle that comes complete with a deer park. The composer's **museum**, housed in his cottage, is pleasantly low-key (May–Sept Tues–Sun 9am–noon & 1–4pm; April & Oct Sat & Sun only), containing just a little modest furniture and his lectern: he always composed standing up. Really though, it's the gentle pastoral setting, a constant textural element which underlies all Janáček's music, which remains the most instructive impression of the place.

Frýdek-Místek

Ten kilometres or so northeast and accessible by bus from Hukvaldy, **FRÝDEK-MÍSTEK** is a rather rude re-entry into the Ostrava coal basin. Its charms are few and its soulless industrial quarter has assumed a much greater importance than either of its twin old towns that straddle the River Ostravice: **Místek**, on the left bank, and **Frýdek** opposite. The main square of the latter is a dusty neglected corner, with a statue of Saint Florian superintending a waterless fountain – a sad comedown for the patron saint of firemen. For an indication of the whole town's popularity, there's just one hotel by the train station, the fairly cheap *Beskyd* (☎27 51).

The town's landmark is its **zámek**, containing a small folk museum and a tribute not only to Janáček, but also to the Silesian poet Petr Bezruč who stayed in Místek for a while, championing the grievances of the poverty-stricken local miners. There is as yet no mention of the Frýdek-born poet **Óndra Łysohorsky** who died shortly after the upheavals of 1989. The simple reason for this is that Bezruč wrote in Czech while Łysohorsky chose to write in Lachian, a dialect (or language, depending on your point of view) somewhere between Czech and Polish which, at its peak between the wars, was spoken by around a million people (mostly miners) in the Beskydy region. The ninth child of a Lachian miner, Łysohorsky (whose real name was Erwin Goy*) was brought up speaking German and Lachian, and after writing his first verses in his German mother-tongue, decided to change to Lachian. Łysohorsky's obstinacy on this point eventually brought him into conflict with the post-war Communist authorities, who accused him of supporting the region's Polish irredentists. Apart from a brief reprise in 1958, his verse remained unpublished in Czechoslovakia, despite his being one of the country's better-known poets abroad (see "Poetry and Fiction" in *Contexts* for a sample of his work). The winds of change since 1989 have meant that the poet's vast archives can now be safely deposited in Frýdek castle and in the future there may yet be a memorial alongside Bezruč's.

Into the hills of the Beskydy

Between the sparsely wooded pastureland which stretches from Nový Jičín to Frýdek-Místek and the Rožnovská Bečva valley are the **hills of the Beskydy**. Starting off in North Moravia and entering Poland, they actually extend right over into the Ukraine, shadowing the ridge of the higher Carpathian range to the south. Spruce has gradually given way to pine, as yet not too badly affected by pollutants, and in the westernmost reaches patches of beech forest still exist. If you're planning on any serious **hiking**, get hold of the 1:100,000 *Beskydy* map which marks all the hiking paths in the area.

---

*Óndra Łysohorsky took his pen-name from the local Robin Hood rebel Ondráš who was imprisoned in, and escaped from, Frýdek castle back in the seventeenth century, at the time owned by the wicked Duke Pragma. His surname comes from the highest peak in the Beskydy, Lysa hora.

FRENŠTÁT POD RADHOŠTĚM is the main resort in the hills, previously a fairly grim town dominated by the local Russian barracks, one of the first to shut up shop in the 1990 troop withdrawals. Since it's not exactly in the thick of the Beskydy, it's only really worth staying here if **hotels** are your only option for accommodation, with the *Radhošť* and *Sport* in town and the more expensive *Hotel Vlčina*, 1.5km up the hill from town on the green-marked path.

Radhošť (1129m), the mountain which Rožnov and Frenštát both dub themselves as under (*pod*), is the most famous – thanks to its legends – but not the tallest, though the view from the top is still pretty good. Close to the summit there's a primitivistic wooden totem featuring Radegast, the mountain's legendary pagan god, and a fanciful wooden Uniate chapel, done out in neo-Byzantine style. With the help of a chair lift (*lanovka*), the less athletic can make do with **Pustevny**, just east of Radhošť, a high saddle rather than a peak (and also accessible by road), where the fantastical *Tanečnica* hotel and a number of other nineteenth-century timber-slat buildings survive, including a nifty, carefully balanced *zvonička* (belfry). Though they rarely have space, it's worth trying *Skalíkova louka* on the green-marked path which drops down to the campsite in POST ŘEDNÍ BEČVA.

Rožnov pod Radhoštěm and around

Halfway up the Rožnovská Bečva valley, **ROŽNOV POD RADHOŠTĚM** is home to the biggest and most popular skansen of folk architecture in the country. To the west the town displays its post-war industrial development, while on the other side of the river from the station, where the town's spa gardens once were, is the main entrance to the **skansen** (May, June & Oct daily 8am–6pm; July & Aug 8am–7pm; Oct 8am–5pm). The museum is divided into three parts, of which only two are presently complete. The moving force behind the first part, the **Dřevené městečko** (Wooden Town), was local artist Bohumír Jaromek, who was inspired by the outdoor folk museum in Stockholm (from which the word *skansen* derives). In 1925, Rožnov's eighteenth-century wooden radnice was moved from the main square to the site of the present museum, followed by a number of other timber buildings from the town and from neighbouring villages like Větřkovice u Přibora, which supplied the imposing seventeenth-century wooden church. There are Wallachian beehives decorated with grimacing faces, a smithy and even a couple of *hospoda* selling food and warm *slivovice*. The second part of the museum, the **Valašká dědina** (Wallachian Village), built in the 1970s on a hillside, takes a more erudite approach, attempting to recreate a typical highland sheep farming settlement – the traditional Wallachian community complete with live sheep and organic crops. The third section, **Mlynska dolina** – yet to be completed – will concentrate on an old water mill.

Coach parties are frequent visitors to Rožnov, and in July and August folksy festivities are put on for the tourists, making the chances of finding a vacancy in one of the two **hotels** slim. **Campsites**, however, are thick on the ground, with one on either side of the road to Postřední Bečva and one 3km up the road in DOLNÍ BEČVA.

If you want to see Wallachian folk architecture in its natural habitat, head further south to the villages of the Vsetínksá Bečva valley which runs parallel to the Rožnovská Bečva. From Postřední Bečva, you can walk over the hills via the predominantly wooden hamlets of Bzové, Jezerné and Raťkov before descending into Velké Karlovice, a mixture of of vernacular architecture and the new industry foisted on the region after the war.

travel details

Trains

From Brno to Prague (hourly; 3hr 15min–4hr 30min); Žďár nad Sázavou (hourly; 1hr–1hr 40min); Jihlava (up to 11 daily; 2hr–2hr 40min); Blansko (up to 16 daily; 25–40min); Slavkov/Bučovice (up to 12 daily; 25–40min/40–50min); Znojmo (6 daily; 1hr 40min–2hr 20min); Olomouc (up to 20 daily; 1hr 30min–2hr 40min); Bratislava (up to 20 daily; 1hr 45min–3hr 30min); České Budějovice (2 daily; 4hr 30min); Liberec (2 daily; 6hr 40min); Poprad/Košice (2 daily; 11hr 15min).

From Znojmo to Mikulov/Valtice (11 daily; 1hr 10min/1hr 30 min); Jaroměřice nad Rokytnou (12 daily; 45min–1hr 15min); Jihlava (3 daily; 1hr 45min).

From Olomouc to Prague (over 25 daily; 3hr 20min–5hr 50min); Prostějov (up to 16 daily; 15–30min); Přerov (up to 20 daily; 20min); Šumperk/Jeseník (up to 10 daily; 1hr–1hr 30min/2hr 10min–4hr); Bruntál/Krnov/Opava (up to 8 daily; 1hr 30min/2hr/3hr); Ostrava (up to 10 daily; 1hr 30min–2hr 30min); Poprad (5 daily; 6hr 30min); Banská Bystrica (1 daily; 5hr 15min); Košice (4 daily; 7hr); České Budějovice (1 daily; 6hr 20min).

Buses

From Brno to Prague (hourly; 2hr 35min); Křtiny/Jedovnice (up to 10 daily; 45min/1hr); Znojmo (up to 11 daily; 1hr 10min); Mikulov (up to 14 daily; 1hr 20min); Hodonín (up to 8 daily; 1hr 20min); Buchlovice/Uherské Hradiště (up to 10 daily; 1hr 10min/1hr 20min); Zlín (up to 16 daily; 2hr–2hr 40min); Kroměříž (up to 14 daily; 1hr 30min); Luhačovice (up to 4 daily; 2hr 10min).

From Uherské Hradiště to Velehrad (up to 14 daily; 25min); Buchlovice (up to 15 daily; 20min); Strážnice/Hodonín (up to 4 daily; 45min/1hr); Luhačovice (up to 5 daily; 40min); Zlín (up to 16 daily; 40min–1hr); Kroměříž (up to 6 daily; 1hr); Trenčín (up to 6 daily; 1hr 15min).

From Olomouc to Opava (up to 4 daily; 2hr); Nový Jičín (up to 10 daily; 1hr 15min); Příbor/Frýdek-Místek (up to 8 daily; 1hr 30min/1hr 50min); Rožnov pod Radhoštěm (2 daily; 1hr 15min).

From Nový Jičín to Štramberk (up to 19 daily; 15–40 min); Kopřivnice (up to hourly; 35min); Příbor (up to 20 daily; 25min); Frýdek-Místek (up to 8 daily; 45min); Frenštát pod Radhoštěm (up to hourly; 40min).

CHAPTER FOUR

SLOVAKIA

The federal republic of **Slovakia** (Slovensko) consists of the long, narrow strip of land that makes up the 500-km-long fish-tail of Czechoslovakia. Outside of the Alps, it's perhaps Europe's most exhilarating landscape, ranging from the parched plains of the Danube basin to the dense forests of the central mountainous ridges, where June, July and August are often the wettest months of the year. The mountains are without doubt the republic's biggest pull, but only the High Tatras have borne the brunt of the recent upsurge in tourism. Acres of unspoilt countryside are still the general rule, mostly out of reach of the average coach tour, but far from impossible for the independent traveller to reach.

Slovak **history** is one of relentless cultural repression by the neighbouring Magyars whose feudal seats, now mostly in ruins, are visible on almost every hillock in the country (for a brief history of Slovak nationalism, see p.272). Despite this, the Slovaks emerged from a millennium of serfdom inside the kingdom of Hungary with their language and national identity pretty much intact. For the first-time visitor, perhaps the most striking cultural difference on entering Slovakia is in the attitude to religion. Catholicism is almost as strong here as in parts of Poland, the churches are full to overflowing on Sundays, and even during the week there's a steady flow of after-work worshippers. In the remoter hill regions, despite the onslaught of collectivisation, centuries-old peasant communities still live much as they have done for years. In other respects, though, change has come all too rapidly to parts of Slovakia, and often the new industrial and urban landscape can be depressingly similar to post-war developments all over Eastern Europe and the Soviet Union.

Slovakia divides conveniently into three distinct regions: Bratislava and West Slovakia, the Central Mountains and East Slovakia. As an introduction to the republic, **West Slovakia** is uncharacteristically flat, and the federal capital, **Bratislava**, potentially disappointing, especially for those expecting a Slovak Prague, though taken on its own terms, it's a rewarding place. On the other side of the Danube basin, the **Central Mountains** are the real heart of Slovakia, though many of the more interesting towns like **Banská Bystrica** and **Banská Štiavnica** are in fact old German settlements. Not surprisingly, the most alluring of the mountains, the **High Tatras**, are also the tallest of the lot, pulling in tourists from all over Europe. If you want to avoid the international crowd, head for the **Low Tatras** or better still the **Malá** and **Veľká Fatra** ranges, where the Slovaks themselves prefer to go.

Poprad, the transport hub for the High Tatras is also the starting point for exploring **East Slovakia**, the least touristed region in the entire country. Some of the most outstanding areas of natural beauty are located here, in the ravines of the **Slovenský raj**, close to the Tatras, and in the limestone karst region of the **Slovenský kras** further south. Architecturally, the **Spiš region**, settled by Saxons back in the Middle Ages, is the east's most fascinating, less than an hour's drive from Poprad. Further afield still, **Carpatho-Ruthenia** is a land apart,

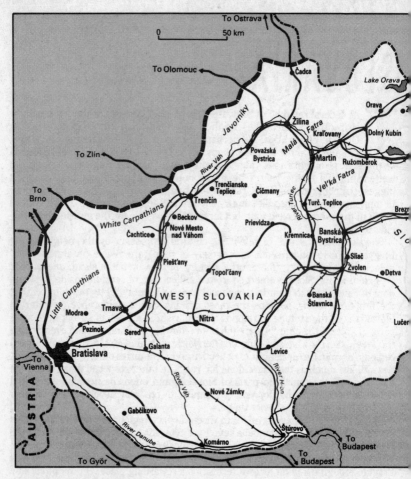

still partially inhabited by Rusyns, whose wooden Uniate churches are among the most remarkable sights in the country. Finally, Slovakia's second largest city, **Košice**, is tucked away in the far east of the republic, a good starting point for exploring the deserted beech forests of the **Vihorlat** and the sandy beaches of the **Slovak Sea**.

As far as **transport** goes, not only are distances that much greater in Slovakia, but you'll inevitably find yourself taking that bit longer to reach places. The railway system is much less extensive, although it does make for exceptionally scenic travelling, trundling up every conceivable valley there is. Buses make up for the shortfall in trains, but there are still mountain villages and parts of the far east that are quite simply a pain to get to. If you are planning to venture into such regions, it's as well to buy the relevant **hiking maps** before you get there, and be prepared to do a considerable amount of legwork. Hiking is an enormously popular pastime in Slovakia, and the best hiking **routes** are highlighted in the text.

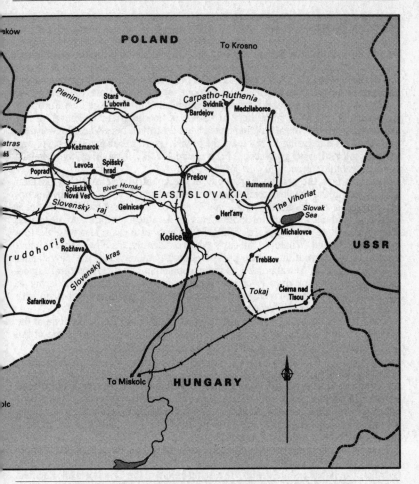

BRATISLAVA AND WEST SLOVAKIA

In many ways, the western third of Slovakia is the least typically Slovak. For a start, the capital **Bratislava**, although today thoroughly Slovak, was for centuries basically an Austro-Hungarian city in which the Slovaks, like the Gypsies and Jews, were in a distinct minority. The great flat plain of the Danube to the east has always been (and still is) inhabited by Hungarian-speakers – well over half a million at the last count. Its two major cities – **Trnava** and **Nitra** – contain some of the most important religious institutions of the Hungarian Kingdom. The region's one range of limestone hills, the **Small Carpathians** to the north, are within easy reach of the capital, but too tame to compare with the more typical central mountains further east.

Bratislava

Caught between the westernmost tip of the Carpathians and the flat plain of the Danube, with both Austria and Hungary tantalisingly close, **BRATISLAVA** has two distinct sides to it. On the one hand, the old quarter is quite simply a manageable and attractive slice of Habsburg Baroque; at the same time, the rest of the city has the brash, crass and butchered feel typical of the average East European metropolis. Those who come here in search of unadulterated medieval streets will be disappointed: more buildings have been destroyed here since the war than were bombed out during it. Not least the Jewish quarter, bulldozed to make way for the colossal new suspension bridge, most SNP, symbol of the capital's upwardly mobile thrust.

Although now the second largest city in the country, most of the population actually live in the mushrooming high-rise estates, which means that the historical centre is much smaller than you'd expect. The penchant for national museums and Slovak cultural monuments is a rather obvious and desperate attempt to imitate Prague; yet in reality, Bratislava's virtues are less tangible, less easily pigeonholed. Whatever the city's previous identity, it's Slovak through and through now, its youthful centre packed out with students and the new denim-clad generation of Slovakia's burgeoning population. The multicultural atmosphere of the pre-war days is only vaguely echoed in the city's smattering of Magyars, Gypsies, and day-tripping Austrians – but it's a cosmopolitanism with which neither Prague nor Brno can compete.

You'll need a couple of days at least to soak the place in, and with none of the accommodation hassles of Prague, the relaxed feel of the city and some of the best weather in the country, you'll probably want to stay longer.

A brief history

For centuries Bratislava was *Pressburg* to the German world, who supplied around half the inhabitants until the 1945 expulsions, and *Pozsony* to the Hungarians, who used the place as their capital for several centuries – crowning their kings and queens in the cathedral and holding their Diet here until the Turks were finally beaten back from the Hungarian plain.

At the turn of the century the city had barely 60,000 inhabitants, most of whom were German, Hungarian and/or Jewish, with a smattering of Gypsies and Slovaks. The balance shifted with the establishment of the Czechoslovak Republic in 1918, which gave a leg-up to the Slovaks who took over the cultural and political institutions and renamed the place Bratislava after Bratislav, the last Slav leader of the Great Moravian Empire. Since then, the population has increased sevenfold and overtaken Brno as the country's second largest metropolis.

The Bratislava area telephone code is ☎07.

Arrival and orientation

"East of Vienna, the Orient begins." Metternich's much-quoted aphorism rings true in the multi-ethnic chaos of Bratislava's **hlavná stanica**, the city's none too splendid main train station where most international or long-distance **trains** pull in. Once you've fought your way past the melée of scaffolding and stand-up *bufet*s, go down to the big tram terminus below the station and, having bought your ticket from one of the machines on the platform, hop on a #1 or #13 into town. Some trains, particularly those heading for destinations within West Slovakia, pass through Bratislava's **Nové Mesto** station, linked most easily to the town centre by tram #6 or #14.

Buses tend to arrive at the autobusová stanica on Bajkalská, also in Nové Mesto, northwest of the town centre. The best thing to do is turn right, walk 100m to the junction with Vajnorská and jump on any tram going down into town.

Bratislava does have an **airport** of sorts, but at present there are no direct flights to or from the West. There are, however, several domestic flights a day to Prague, as well as two to Košice and one to Poprad. Bus #24 goes from the airport to the main train station or else you could catch the ČSA bus, which regularly runs a shuttle service to and from the ČSA office on Mostová.

Getting around and information

The best way to see Bratislava is to walk – in fact that's the only way to see the pedestrianised staré mesto and the hrad to the west, where most of the city's sights are concentrated. However, if you're staying outside the city centre or visiting the suburbs, you'll need to make use of the city's cheap and comprehensive **transport system**. Buy your ticket beforehand (from newsagents, kiosks, hotel lobbies or ticket machines), validate it as soon as you get on, and use a fresh ticket each time you change. **Night buses** congregate at námestie SNP, every quarter to the hour.

Like Prague, Bratislava boasts a proper **tourist information office**, *Bratislavská informačná a propagačná služba* or *BIPS* for short (Leningradská 1; Mon–Fri 8am–6pm, Sat 8am–1pm), good for general queries (some English spoken) and getting hold of the monthly listings magazine, *Kam v Bratislave* (mostly in Slovak but with two pages of English info); they don't, however, offer an accommodation service (see below). You can buy a detailed *Orientačná mapa* from the *Deutsche Bücher* shop two doors further up from *BIPS* on Rybárska.

Finding a place to stay

Bratislava has none of the logistical problems of overcrowding that plague Prague, but nor does it have anything like the range of hotels. If you're staying for three nights or more, the best option is to take a private room. Otherwise you'll have to take what's thrown at you by ČEDOK, and probably pay through the nose for it.

Private rooms and hostels

The cheapest alternative, **private rooms**, can be arranged through ČEDOK's office on Štúrovo (☎520 81), where the staff speak a little English. With the market opening up, there may be private operators hanging about outside, but this isn't something you can rely on.

CKM run one of their plush hostel-cum-hotels, *Juniorhotel Sputnik*, on Drieňová (☎22 78 83) in Nové Mesto (bus #34 or #54). Theoretically YHA members can get a very good deal here (everyone else pays hotel-type prices), but the place is invariably full. A better option are the **student hostels** which *CKM* runs in July and August, offering cheap dorm beds. The drawback is that it's a pretty chaotic system with venues changing from year to year, so check at the *CKM* office, Hviezdoslavovo námestie 16 (☎33 16 07; Mon–Fri 1–4pm), about this year's arrangements before setting out.

BRATISLAVA

Dom Odborov

To the
Campsite
& Bus Station

To Bratislava
Nové Mesto
& Airport

MALINOVSKÉHO

Tržnica
(Covered Market)

ŠTEFANOVIČOVA

MÝTNA

ŠTEINEROVA

ZÁHRADNICKÁ

NÁMESTIE
SLOBODY

RADLINSKÉHO

AMERICKÉ
NÁMESTIE

ovich

OBCHODNÁ

ČESKOSLOVENSKEJ ARMÁDY

Ondrej
Cemetery

DUNAJSKÁ

Office

Hummel
Museum

KYJEVSKÉ
NÁMESTIE

VINGRADSKA

Modrý
kostolík

ica

Slovak
National
Theatre

ŠTÚROVA

ČEDOK

BEZRUČOVA

DOSTOJEVSKÉ HO RAD

Reduta

Palacký
University

ŠAFÁRIKOVO
NÁMESTIE

0   250 m

Slovak
National
Museum

Hydrofoil

River Danube

To Petržalka

Hotels and camping

For the moment, ČEDOK (details above) has a monopoly on all hotels in Bratislava, none of which are particularly good value. Steer clear of the *Fórum*, the business person's hotel, and the next most expensive options, the *Devín* and *Kyjev*. Given a free choice, the more moderate *Carlton* (☎582 09) on Hviezdoslavovo námestie does at least have atmosphere and a very central location.

If you're **camping**, two fairly grim sites are 8km northeast of the city centre, out near the swimming lake at Zlaté Piesky (tram #4 from the station; tram #2 from town). Bungalows are on offer all year round; tent camping May to September only. In addition, there's a cheap hotel here called the *Flora,* which can be booked through ČEDOK.

The staré mesto

Trams from the main train station offload their shoppers and sightseers behind the *Hotel Fórum* in Obchodní – literally Shop Street – which descends into Harbanovo námestie, a busy whizzing junction on the northern edge of the staré mesto. Here you'll find a couple of large bookshops, the city's biggest shoe store and, unmoved by the vulgar clamour of it all, the hefty mass of Galli da Bibiena's **Trinity Church**. Despite a tired and faded air inside its single-domed nave, it's one of the city's finest churches, its exuberant *trompe l'oeil* frescoes creating a magnificent false cupola on the ceiling, typical of the Bibiena family who excelled in theatrical design. If this is your first Slovak church though, probably the most striking feature is the constant flow of worshippers, young and old, who shuffle in and out genuflecting all the while: a far cry from the wizened penitents who occasionally turn up at Czech churches.

Opposite the Trinity Church, a footbridge passes under the first tower of the city's last remaining double gateway. Below, in what used to be the city moat, is an open-air *čitáreň* (reading room), a tiny garden which hosts the odd literary event in amongst the modern sculpture and the shrubbery. It belongs to the **Baroque Apothecary** called *U červeného raka* ("At the Red Lobster"), immediately on your left between the towers, which now houses a **Pharmaceutical Museum** (Tues–Sun 10am–5pm), displaying everything from seventeenth-century drug grinders to Slovak herbal tea bags. Upstairs, period pharmacies have been reconstructed but if you'd rather see a fully functioning *lekáreň*, try the neo-Renaissance *U Salvatora*, Nálepkova 35.

The second and taller of the two gateways is the **Michalská brána** (daily 10am–8pm), an evocative and impressive entrance to the staré mesto whose outer limits are elsewhere hard to distinguish. You can climb it, giving a quick glance en route to the vertical **museum of arms and armaments**, for a great rooftop view of the old town. Michalská and Jirásková – which make up the same street – are lined with some of Bratislava's finest Baroque palaces, but the talk and chatter which issues from the cafés and bars is that of students, shoppers and young politicos. The former, taking breaks from the university library, exit from the building that once held the Hungarian Diet, and congregate around the Baroque palace of the **Mozartov dom**. Here Verejnosť proti nasiliu (People Against Violence), the Slovak sister of Civic Forum, seconded the old Institute for Political Education into their headquarters during the student strike of 1989. There's a relaxed atmosphere and it's a good place to meet up with people, either at the **information centre** downstairs or in the swanky **café** upstairs. The building itself is strikingly beautiful and, in keeping with the cultural traditions of the place (Mozart once performed here), there are exhibitions, talks and film shows in the rooms off the leafy balconied courtyard.

Opposite the *VPN* headquarters is the **Academia Istropolitana**, the first Hungarian (or, if you prefer, Slovak) university. Founded in 1465 by Matthew Corvinus, it continually lost out to the more established nearby universities of Vienna, Prague and Kraków, and was eventually forced to close down in 1490. The buildings and the inner courtyard were modernised in the 1960s for the faculty of performing arts, who put on some interesting shows and exhibitions of their work in the chapel and crypt.

The palaces of the Austro-Hungarian aristocracy continue right into Nálepkova, starting with the **Pálffy Palace** (only one of three in Bratislava), today a trendy **art gallery** (Tues–Fri 10am–8pm, Sat & Sun 10am–5pm) with the occasional live "happening" in the basement, where contemporary exhibitions also take place. The rest of the building has a mediocre collection of European paintings from the fourteenth to the twentieth centuries, only worth bothering with for Janko Alexy's two smooth pastel canvases and the occasional one-off expo on the top floor. Further down, next to the Esterházy Palace, is the **kaplnka Božieho tela** (Corpus Christi Chapel), a richly decorated intimate space packed with illuminated manuscripts, jewellery and ecclesiastical wealth.

Námestie 4 apríla, Dibrovovo námestie and around

A little east of here are the twin main squares of the staré mesto: **námestie 4 apríla** (the day the city was liberated by the Red Army in 1945), a patch of green focused on a fountain sporting the usual cherubs seemingly peeing out of fishes' mouths, and the shady extension of **Dibrovovo námestie**. No longer at the centre of things, they now provide a leafy respite from the city's busy shopping malls. Opposite the fountain is the **stará radnica**, a modest two-storey building and a lively hotchpotch of styles. Gothic in its core, Renaissance in its innards and nineteenth-century in its reconstruction, it surpasses itself in the serene half-moon gables and fragile arcading of the inner courtyard. Next door to the town hall, the **Viticultural Museum** (Tues–Sun 10am–5pm) is the scholarly tribute to the fact that Bratislava is at the centre of the country's wine industry, but it's the building and not the exhibition which wins first prize.

The Counter-Reformation, which gripped the parts of Hungary not under Turkish occupation, issues forth from the **Jesuit Church**, filled to the brim with the usual post-Baroque kitsch. Not far from here, opposite the gaudy yellow Franciscan Church, is the **Mirbach Palace** (Tues–Fri 10am–6pm, Sat & Sun 10am–5pm; concerts Sun 10.30am), arguably the finest of Bratislava's Rococo buildings, and preserving much of its original stucco decor. That said, the Baroque art inside isn't up to much, save for the wall-to-wall miniatures set into the wooden panelling and a series of seventeenth-century Dutch tapestries, discovered by chance while renovating the Primate's Palace (see below).

Round the back of the stará radnica, with the stillness of a provincial Italian piazza during siesta, is the **Primaciálne námestie**, dominated by the Neoclassical **Primate's Palace**, whose pediment frieze is topped by a 300-pound cast-iron cardinal's hat. The palace's main claim to fame is as the place where Napoleon and the Austrian Emperor signed the Treaty of Pressburg in 1805. When it's been fully renovated, it too will house another of the city's unremarkable art collections.

All over the staré mesto, commemorative plaques make much of Bratislava's musical connections, but apart from the reflected glory of its proximity to Vienna and Budapest and the pre-war presence of a large German population who ensured a regular supply of Europe's best, the city has produced only one (mildly) famous composer, **Johann Nepomuk Hummel** (1778–1837), who was in any case very much an Austrian at heart. Still, it's as good an excuse as any for a **Hummel Museum** (Tues–Sun 10am–5pm; concerts late afternoon Thurs), housed in the composer's birthplace, a cute apricot-coloured cottage swamped by its neighbours and hidden away behind two fashionable shops on Klobučnícka. Like Mozart, his tutor and friend for a while in Vienna, Hummel was a *Wunderkind* who began performing at the tender age of ten. Although he wrote many pretty Classical works, his real talents lay in his virtuoso piano-playing, which, lacking the permanence of composition, has confined his fame to the musical cognoscenti.

The dóm, the Jewish Quarter and the hrad

On the side of the staré mesto nearest the hrad, the most insensitive of Bratislava's post-war developments took place. As if the annihilation of the city's large and visible Jewish population by the Nazis wasn't enough, the Communist authorities tore down virtually the whole of the **Jewish Quarter** in order to build the brutal showpiece bridge, the most SNP (see below). Quite apart from the devastation of the ghetto, the traffic which tears along the busy thoroughfare of Staromestská has seriously undermined the foundations of the Gothic **dóm**, coronation church of the kings and queens of Hungary for over 250 years, whose ill-proportioned steeple is topped by a tiny gilded Hungarian crown. In all probability it was never very attractive from the outside, but with the new road missing the west door by a matter of metres, coupled with the noise and fumes, the best policy is to take refuge inside where, against all odds, it's pleasantly cool and light, if unspectacular.

Passing under the approach road for the new bridge, two old, thin houses stand opposite one another, both now converted into museums. The first, a yellow Rococo fancy called *U dobrého pastiera* (At the Good Shepherd), is a **clock museum** (daily 10am–5pm; closed Tues) with a display of – depending on your tastes – nauseously vulgar or brilliantly kitsch Baroque and Empire clocks; the second is (nominally) a **folk museum** (times as above) which consists of a few period dining rooms and a lot of fairly ordinary arts and crafts gear.

Up to the hrad

From these twin museums, Beblavého begins the steep climb up to the castle. For many years this was one of the city's more infamous red-light districts, serving both town and barracks from its strategic point between the two, and described evocatively by Patrick Leigh Fermor who passed through Bratislava en route to Constantinople in 1934: "During the day, except for the polyglot murmur of invitation, it was a rather silent place. But it grew noisier after dark when shadows brought confidence and the plum-brandy began to bite home. It was only lit by cigarette ends and by an indoor glow that silhouetted the girls on their thresholds. Pink lights revealed the detail of each small interior: a hastily tidied bed, a tin basin and a jug, some lustral gear and a shelf displaying a bottle of solution, pox-foiling and gentian-hued; a couple of dresses hung on a nail." Like the Jewish cafés Leigh Fermor also hung out in (along with, though not necessarily at the same table as, the young Ludvík Hoch – aka Robert Maxwell), all this has long since gone, but there's still a hint of the bohemian about the ramshackle houses now slowly being turned into swish galleries or chic boutiques.

The **hrad** itself, frequently referred to as the "inverted bedstead", is an unwelcoming giant box built in the fifteenth century by the Emperor Sigismund in expectation of a Hussite attack, and burnt down by its own drunken soldiers in 1811. Only recently restored, it now houses half of the pretty uneven collections of the **Slovak National Museum** (Tues–Sun 10am–noon & 2–4pm). Numismatologists will have fun among the coins on the top floor, but the rest of us could happily skip the whole museum and concentrate on the view from outside the castle gates south across the Danube plain, which is nothing short of spectacular. Sadly, most of the immediate foreground is taken up with the infamous Petržalka estate, detracting somewhat from the romantic thought that, as you gaze out over the meeting point of three countries, you are looking at the heart of *Mitteleuropa*.

PETRŽALKA AND PETROCHEMICALS

The **Petržalka housing estate** is a symbol of the new Slovak nation, dragged forcibly into the twentieth century – but at a cost. Over a third of the city's population – an incredible 150,000 people – live on Petržalka, whose estates still retain cruelly ironic names like Háje (Woods) and Lúky (Meadows) in what is now a virtually treeless expanse of mud and high-rise, with the added attraction of being surrounded (until recently) by the barbed wire and watchtowers of the Iron Curtain. In many respects it can't compete with certain housing estates in the West, but with the highest suicide rate in the country it's not a place anyone would choose to live in.

The Petržalka problem is just one of the many social and ecological issues which were brought to light by *Bratislava nahlas* (Bratislava Aloud), a "green" booklet published in October 1987 by an officially recognised environmental organisation, but quickly suppressed by the Communists (though not before it had been passed round almost every household in Bratislava). The two biggest polluters lambasted in the report were the *Slovnaft* oil refinery, a vast petrochemical complex just 2km east of Petržalka, and the chemical works to the northeast of the city centre, which pumps some 9000 litres of sulphuric acid into the Danube every year.For more on ecological issues, see "The Environment" in *Contexts*.

Hviezdoslavovo námestie, the waterfront and around

Between the staré mesto and the waterfront lies the graceful, tree-lined boulevard of **Hviezdoslavovo námestie**, with a swish Hungarian restaurant and a couple of cafés along one side, and the seedy splendour of the *Hotel Carlton* on the other. Pride of place in the square and prime spot for casual loitering is the larger-than-life statue of Pavol Országh Hviezdoslav, "father of Slovak poetry", whose life as minor government official in the Orava region was pretty uneventful, but whose poetry is still a source of great national pride. All this brings you to the square's eastern end, where the Hungarians and Germans (who were in the majority at the time) erected two magnificent late nineteenth-century edifices: the first, fronted by an elaborate fountain depicting the mythological figure of Ganymede, is now the **Slovak National Theatre**, a top-quality Viennese-style opera house; the second, diagonally opposite, is the later, more Secessionist **Reduta Theatre**, home to the Slovak philharmonic orchestra.

The River Danube and the most SNP

Down past Štúrovo námestie is the **waterfront**, separated from the water itself by the fast dual carriageway of Rázusovo nábrežie. Once you've navigated this, you can stroll along the banks of the (far from blue) **River Danube** – *Dunaj* in Slovak. At this point the Danube is fast, terrifyingly (and unnaturally) so – witness the speed to which the massive double-barges are reduced by the current and, by contrast, the velocity of those hurtling downstream. There's a regular (and hazardous) ferry service across the river, an alternative to crossing by either of the two bridges. The larger of these is the infamous **most SNP** (Bridge of the Slovak National Uprising), for which the old Jewish Quarter was ripped up. However brutal its construction, it's difficult not to be impressed by the sheer size and audacity of this single open suspension bridge. Its one support column leans at an alarming angle, topped by a saucer-like penthouse café reminiscent of the Starship Enterprise. The view from the café is superlative (except after dark when you can't see a thing due to the reflection of the café's lights), but the cost of the lift and a drink will set you back more than usual: for a cheap alternative there's just as good a view from the loo. The best place from which to view the bridge is the rather forlorn funfair in the **Janko Kráľ Park** on the opposite bank – all that's left of what Baedeker described in 1904 as "a favourite evening-promenade . . . with café and pleasant grounds".

A BRIEF HISTORY OF SLOVAK NATIONALISM

It's not just today's nationalists who see Slovakia as separate from the rest of Czechoslovakia. For most of the last thousand years, it *was* a different country – Hungary. If the Slovaks ever had sovereignty over their own land (and even this is debatable), it went under with the defeat of the Great Moravian Empire (much of which was in present-day Slovakia) by the Magyars in 906. From that time on, virtually without interruption, the majority of Slovaks remained tied by serfdom to their Magyar or Magyarised feudal lords.

All things considered, it's hardly surprising that there was little in the way of a Slovak national revival, or národné obrodenie, until **the nineteenth century**. But while many of the new leaders were pan-Slavists who viewed all Slavs, be they Slovak, Czech, Polish or Russian, as brothers, few singled out the Czechs for special attention. When they did, briefly in 1848 and later in 1918 with the formation of the Czechoslovak Republic, it was on the grounds of expediency, to scupper any of the compromise plans put forward by the Hungarians. When the Czechs began behaving uncannily like their previous Hungarian masters – taking all the top jobs, imposing their own language – many Slovaks became disillusioned with the Republic and viewed its demise in 1938 as a blessing in disguise.

The pros and cons of Slovakia's brief period of **independence** from 1939 to 1944 under the leadership of Jozef Tiso – in practice just another Nazi puppet state – are the subject of much public and private discussion at the moment. Whereas some Slovaks saw it as a genuine expression of Slovak statehood, just as many took to the hills and fought against it in the 1944 anti-Fascist uprising. Right now, the most crucial thing is to open up the debate – which in the black-and-white world of Communism was impossible.

Whatever their differences over World War II, few Slovaks were happy with the **post-1945 situation**. Once more, Czech promises of Slovak autonomy set out in 1945 were reneged upon. The Communists, by far the largest party in the Czech

The Slovak National Gallery

When the Slovaks took control of Bratislava in 1918, a town in which they had previously made little impression, they set about establishing their own cultural monuments to rival those of the Austrians and Hungarians. Three such buildings were put up in the waterfront district, of which the **Slovak National Gallery** (Tues & Sat 11am–6pm, Wed–Fri & Sun 10am–5pm), housed in a converted naval barracks, is probably the most worthwhile. The problem with modern Slovak art is that, until the foundation of the Republic, there was no living tradition outside the skilful and infinite folk art of the countryside. Between the wars, Slovak artists began to establish themselves in much greater numbers, but the work is mostly derivative Expressionist stuff, whose major achievement was in the depiction of peasant life as a subject worthy of "high art" and, later on, in recording the privation which was commonplace in the rural areas of Slovakia in the 1930s. Three artists stand out: **Janko Alexy**, the only Slovak artist to have made any impression internationally; **Miloš Bazovský**, whose naive, robust portrayal of peasant life is redolent of the Mexican artist Diego Rivera; and **Ľudovít Fulla**, whose urgent, colourful canvases are the very opposite of Bazovský's calm, smooth technique. The post-1948 selection is a uniformly predictable celebration of the Slovak National Uprising and the brave new socialist world. For those not heading further east, the section on East Slovak **icon**

Lands trailed behind the newly formed Democrats in the Slovak polls. True to form, though, the Slovak Communists were put into positions of power by their comrades in Prague. After 1948, centralisation was one of the cornerstones of Stalinist economics, putting paid to any hopes Slovak Communists might have had of running their own affairs. And in the 1950s, the victims of the show-trials and purges were more often than not Slovak and/or Jewish.

In January 1968, Alexander Dubček was elected First Secretary of the Communist Party, the first Slovak to hold such a high position. Nevertheless, **the events of 1968** were primarily Prague-inspired, and while the Czechs got nothing out of the Warsaw Pact invasion, the Slovaks did at least get federalisation, a bilingual national media, and a large injection of state money to help to adjust the economic imbalance between the two republics. It was a sop to the Slovak Communists – classic divide and rule tactics – and one which worked, at least for a while.

From the dissident movement of Charter 77 to the Velvet Revolution of November 1989, events over the last twenty years have been focused on Prague, but it wasn't long before old differences began to emerge, most famously in the summer of 1990, when it came to deciding on a new name for the country in what became known as the **great hyphen debate**. The Slovaks' insistent demand that a hyphen be inserted in "Czechoslovakia" was greeted with ridicule by most Czechs. The messy compromise formula of "Czech and Slovak Federative Republic" (for use only in the Slovak half of the country) pleased no one and it remains a volatile issue. Then, in the **1990 elections**, the differences between the two republics became clearer than at any time since the 1930s. While Civic Forum romped home in the Czech Lands, the VPN, Civic Forum's Slovak partners, were defeated by the more conservative Catholic Christian Democrats under the wily leadership of Ján Čarnogurský. Despite the electoral failure of the extreme Slovak Nationalist Party, the threat of UDI remains real, but is most useful as a political lever for gaining yet more concessions from the Czechs.

paintings is definitely worth catching. Some, like the *Posledný súd* (Last Supper), are an untutored personal nightmare of the apocalypse, with the Devil employing a whale-like monster to gobble up the damned as they fall from grace.

Further along the quayside, past the hydrofoil launch, is the unremarkable natural history section of the **Slovak National Museum** (Tues–Sun 9am–5pm), housed in a dark and dingy 1930s building. Further east along Vajanského nábrežie stands the **Palacký University**, an equally dour building, founded along with the Republic in 1918 and, like the nearby bars and cafés, brimming with young students. Otherwise, waiting around for buses is the main object of the folk milling around Šafárikovo námestie. The only specific sight around here is Ödön Lechner's Art-Nouveau **Modrý kostolík** (Little Blue Church), on Bezručova, decorated, inside and out, with the richness of a central European cream cake and dedicated to Saint Elizabeth, who was born in Bratislava in 1207.

Námestie SNP and around

At the top end of Štúrova is **Kyjevské námestie**, where the whole city seems to wind up after work, to grab a beer or takeaway from one of the many stand-up stalls, to jabber away the early evening and above all to catch the bus or tram home. It's not difficult to think of a more picturesque setting than under the shadow of the high-rise *Hotel Kyjev* and the city's biggest department store, but this is where the action is. Further up the road, **námestie SNP** is a bit more accommodating, with at least a few trees and a host of outdoor cafés: it's where the Slovaks gathered in their thousands for their part in the Velvet Revolution. At its centre is the inevitable Monument to the Slovak National Uprising, the anti-Fascist coup against the Nazis in the summer of 1944 which cost the country so dear. A macho bronze partisan guards the eternal flame, while two Slovak women (heads suitably covered) maintain a respectful distance. To most Slovaks, it's just another of those ugly but invisible celebrations of militarism with which the city and indeed the whole republic has been "blessed" over the last forty years.

Behind námestie SNP is the brown marble and onyx abomination of the *Hotel Fórum*, the city's flashiest hotel. It looks out onto **Mierové námestie**, one of the city's busiest intersections and little more than a cacophony of cars and lorries now, though no doubt once a princely foil for the **Grassalkovich Palace**, which cowers in the top corner. Until recently this was the Klement Gottwald House of Young Pioneers – the Communist youth organisation – now disbanded, though only the gardens, which excel in ugly modern fountains, are open to the public for the moment. There's not much reason to be in this part of town unless you want to pay your respects to the **Slovak Federal Assembly**, two blocks north up Banskobystrická, which occupies the former summer residence of the archbishop of Esztergom.

The other side of Mierové námestie is a better place to wander, where block after block of dowdy yet colourful late nineteenth-century buildings squat under the Slavín hill. The only sight as such is the pale blue and exceedingly plain **Lutheran Lycée** on Konventa (closed to the public), outside which a tall granite column commemorates the many leading Slovak men of letters who were educated here in the nineteenth century. Surprisingly enough for a fervently Catholic peasant country, the Protestants produced Slovak leaders far in excess of their actual numerical strength, including the entire 1848 triumvirate of Štúr, Hodža and Hurban.

The Slavín Monument

The Slavín hill is crowned by the gargantuan **Slavín Monument**, ceremoniously completed in 1960 to mark the fifteenth anniversary of the city's liberation, and which must now rank as the largest Soviet monument still standing in the entire country. Visible from virtually every street corner in Bratislava, it's the kind of thing every tour group in the capital is taken to see at some point or other. It's all horrifically militaristic, not to say phallic, its giant ribbed obelisk thrusting into the sky topped by an anguished Soviet soldier holding the victory banner outstretched. Not only is it in exceedingly poor taste, but it was overshadowed eight years later by the second Soviet "liberation".

The villa quarter just below the monument has always been a well-to-do suburb, settled by the wealthy German middle classes in the inter-war period and until recently the exclusive territory of the Party bosses. At no. 46 Mišikova (Mouse Street), the mild-mannered **Alexander Dubček** still lives. In 1968, he became probably the only Slovak ever to achieve world fame, a feat he achieved by becoming the somewhat unlikely leader of a deeply divided Communist Party as it attempted to bring about *perestroika* twenty years ahead of its time. Crushed by the Soviet invasion, he spent his twenty years of internal exile here too, under constant surveillance, working for the Slovak equivalent of the local forestry commission.

Eating, drinking and nightlife

Food is taken more seriously in Bratislava than in Prague, and it's worth splashing out now and then for a really good spread at one of the city's more exclusive spots. In addition to the usual Slovak fare, **Magyar cuisine** finds its way onto most menus in various shapes and forms, though authentically only in the city's handful of truly Hungarian restaurants. The preference for wine over beer also lends a more cosmopolitan touch to the city's many cafés and bars – indeed getting hold of a draught beer can be difficult in the centre of town.

Breakfast, snacks and cafés

Like the Czechs, the Slovaks tend to skip **breakfast**, settling for the usual grainy black coffee instead. This leaves you at the mercy of the self-service joints around town, whose standard *párok* (or any other type of sausage), roll and mustard is too much for most people first thing in the morning. Most also serve *polievka*, a range of salads, which you buy by the 100g dollop, and the most famous Slovak speciality of all, *bryndzové halušky*, a kind of pasta dish in a heavy Slovak cheese sauce. You can get the latter at the *Mliečne špeciality* outlets on Gorkého and námestie SNP – simply ask for *bryndzaký* (vegetarians should note that it usually contains small flecks of bacon or salami). One of the best self-service restaurants is actually next door to the snobby *Fórum* hotel on Mierové námestie.

Street **snacks** are best grabbed on Kyjevské námestie where the usual *langoše*, *gofry*, chips and so on are on offer. Pizza places are opening up thick and fast all over Slovakia at the moment. Bratislava's is just opposite the *Kyjev* hotel, one block northeast of Kjevské námestie and, as usual, the choice is fairly limited and the product a very liberal interpretation of the Italian dish. If none of the above sounds appealing, you could amass something resembling a picnic from the covered *tržnica* (market) opposite the Dom Odborov (formerly Dom ROH).

Bratislava abounds in **cafés**, some – like the *Lýra* on Jiráskova, *Zelený dom* on námestie 4 apríla, and the student hang-out *U dežmara* by the university library – just right for a quick caffeine hit; many more have outdoor tables perfect for soaking up the street life. Of these, perhaps the best are the *Muráň* and *Tisovec* grouped round the námestie SNP. Another prime spot is Hviezdoslavovo námestie, with the *Hungaria*, a Magyar establishment as you'd expect, the indoor *kaviareň* in the seedy *Hotel Carlton*, or, for a good range of cream cakes, the *Park*. Further afield, there's the roomy turn-of-the-century *Štefánka* overlooking Mierové námestie, and of course the *Bystrica*, stuck on top of the most SNP.

Restaurants, wine bars and pubs

For cheap and unpretentious Slovak food you could do worse than the *Slovenská reštaurácia*, above the *Luxor* café on Štúrovo, or the *Diétna reštaurácia* on Michalská. Fish specialities (thankfully not pulled out of the Danube) are on offer at the slightly more expensive *U zlatého kapra*, on Prepošská, and *Rybásky cech*, situated in a former fisherman's house down by the waterfront below the hrad on Žižkova.

Bratislava's ethnic options are pretty limited at the moment, but the *Maďarská reštaurácia* on Hviezdoslavovo námestie is without doubt the best, serving superb (though none too cheap) Hungarian meals occasionally to the accompaniment of a *cimbalom*. Alternatively, you could try the *Perugia* on Zelená, which serves Italian food of sorts.

The *Stará sladovňa*, at the end of Cintorínska, is probably Bratislava's most famous eating and drinking establishment. It served as the city's malthouse until 1976, when it was converted into what claims to be the second largest restaurant in Europe (it seats 1600 at a pinch). Certainly there's rarely any problem getting a seat, and the food isn't at all bad, though they stop serving around 8 or 9pm. It's also one of the few places in the centre of town where you can drink draught Bohemian beer – *Velkopopovický kozel* and *Budvar* – not to mention listen to big band music and the usual rowdy singing. Two other places with beer and similarly lively clientele are *Smíchovský dvor* on Heydukova, which serves Prague beer, and *Pivovarská reštaurácia* out on Steinerova which serves the local brew.

Wine bars, which generally also serve food, tend to be open a bit later than ordinary restaurants. Try the Hungarian *Tokaj vináreň* on Leningradská; the *Moravská vináreň*, a student dive dubbed the *ponorka* (submarine); and the reputedly trendier *Veľkí františkáni* on Dibrovovo námestie, which features Slovak Gypsy music.

Nightlife

Aside from the pubs, cafés and wine bars, Bratislava's most established **nightlife** is heavily biased towards high culture, with opera and ballet at the **Slovak National Theatre**, and orchestral concerts at the **Reduta**, as well as the varied programme put on at the modern **Dom Odborov** complex (tram #2 or #14 from the station; tram #4, #6 or #10 from town). Tickets for the first two venues are available in advance from the box office (noon–8pm) behind the National Theatre, and for the Dom Odborov from a box office inside the building from 3pm onwards. If (as is likely) it's sold out, you can usually get stand-by tickets, available thirty minutes to an hour before the performance.

Bratislava hosts a couple of large-scale festivals, starting with its own **Spring Music Festival** in April – without the big names of Prague's, but a lot easier to get tickets for. The **Bratislava Jazz Days** take place in October and often head-line with the same folk who've just trundled through Prague and Kraków. In September there's an international arts festival with groups from all over Europe taking part, mostly, but not exclusively, highbrow.

Otherwise, if you're looking for something a bit more alternative, forget it. There are no regularly alternative venues: such gigs and events that do take place are often forced to use the formal setting of the Dom Odborov. During term-time things are a bit more lively, since most action revolves around the university – scour the noticeboards and fly-posters for the up-and-coming events. Another good place to head for is the **Mozartov dom** on Jiráskova – run by *VPN*, the Slovak equivalent of Civic Forum – which has an interesting cultural programme, and is a good place to go for insider tips. If you're still at a loss as to what to do, pick up this month's *Kam v Bratislave* for cinema listings, exhibitions and (sporadically) gigs.

Listings

Airline *ČSA* & *Slov-Air*, Mostová 3 (☎33 85 71–4).

BIPS Leningradská 1 (☎33 43 70). Open Mon–Fri 8am–6pm, Sat 8am–1pm.

Boats up the Danube: *Česko-Slovenská plavba dunajská*, Fajnorovo nábrežie (☎59 527).

Books Good selection of second-hand guides and English-language books at *Antikvariát*, Kyjovské námestie 5.

Car hire *Pragocar*, Hviezdoslavovo námestie 14 (☎33 32 01).

Embassies and consulates At present there's just one embassy – *Finland*, Gorkého 15 (☎55 870) – and one Western consulate – *Austria*, Červeňova 19 (☎33 51 77) – but with a separate Slovak ministry of international relations recently set up, other consulates should be open in the near future.

Football Bratislava's premier team is *Slovan Bratislava*, the only Czechoslovak club to have won a European competition within living memory. *Slovan*'s ground is the *Tehelné Pole* stadium, built during the last war and also used for the country's international games. For details of how to get there, see "Sport facilities" below.

Left luggage Lockers and 24-hour deposit at both train and bus stations.

Maps *Slovenská kartografia* kiosk on Kyjevské námestie sells a good selection of town and hiking maps of Slovakia.

Markets The best fruit and veg market in town takes place daily (except Sun) in the Tržnica covered market hall opposite the Dom Odborov. Early Saturday morning is the busiest and best time to go.

Newspapers Main outlet for foreign newspapers is on Leningradská. Failing that, try the more upmarket hotels.

Pharmacies 24-hour pharmacies at Mýtna 5, Trnavská 1 and Bebravská 24.

Post office Main post office is at námestie SNP 35. 24-hour service (telephone, telex, tele-gram) at Kolárska 12.

Sport facilities There are two main sports complexes, *Tehelné pole* and *Pasienky*, both next to one another in Nové Mesto (tram #2 or #14 from the station; tram #4, #6 or #10 from town). An ice hockey stadium, a cycle track and the big *Slovan* football stadium are just some of the facilities on offer.

Taxis Can be hailed or found in long lines outside the top hotels like the *Fórum*, *Kyjev*, *Carlton* and so on. Alternatively, telephone ☎508 51/508 52.

Telephones International calls can be made at the main post office or (for a hefty surcharge) at any of the big hotels.

Out from the city

Most people find enough in the centre of town to occupy them for the average two- or three-day stay. But if you're staying around for longer, or would prefer to be among the vine-clad hills which encroach on the city's northern suburbs, there are several places where you could happily spend a lazy afternoon, all within easy reach of the city centre.

Zlaté Piesky and other swimming possibilities

Out on the motorway to Piešťany, just past the city's huge chemical works, the **Zlaté Piesky** (tram #2 from the train station; tram #4 from town) is a popular destination for weekending Bratislavans. Despite its name, which means "Golden Sands", it's a far cry from the Côte d'Azur, though on a baking hot day in August, that, or even the stench from the local chemical factory, fails to deter large numbers of sweltering Slovaks from stripping off and throwing themselves into the lake's lukewarm waters. If you'd prefer a genuinely clean swimming environment, try the outdoor pool in the sports complex on Odbojárov (tram #2 or #14 from the station; tram #4, #6 or #10 from town).

Kamzík

North of the station, the city immediately gives way to the vineyards and beech-wood slopes of the suburb of Vinohrady (a world apart from its vine-less namesake in Prague), perfect for making a quick escape from the city and indulging in a bit of aimless wandering through the undergrowth. If you need a target, follow the yellow markers from the station, which take you 2.5km up to, and through, the woods to the summit of **Kamzík** (440m), topped by a TV tower with a viewpoint café that serves food of sorts. If you don't fancy the walk, take bus #33 to the chair lift on the north side of the hill, or simply take the strain out of the trip by catching trolley bus #213 to the last stop and walking along the red-marked path for 1km.

Devín

Bus #29 or #59 will get you to the village of **DEVÍN**, 9km northwest of Bratislava, whose ruined castle perches impressively on a rocky promontory over the Danube. With the West just a stone's throw away across the river, border precautions were particularly excessive on the road to Devín – a continuous twenty-foot barbed-wire fence, punctuated at regular intervals by fifty-foot watchtowers and hidden cameras that monitored all vehicles which passed along the road. Today, such Cold War images seem about as far removed from reality as the traditional Slovak legends which surround Devín. In 864 and again in 871, the Slavs of the Great Moravian Empire gave the Germans two serious drubbings at Devín, the last of which is said to have left the Germans with so few prisoners with which to barter that they could only succeed in retrieving one half-dead hero named Ratbod. In the nineteenth century, Ľudovít Štúr and his fellow Slovak nationalists made Devín into a potent symbol of their lost nationhood, organising a series of publicity stunts in and around the castle in the run-up to 1848.

Apart from the view over into Austria, there's not a great deal to see at Devín, but *BIPS* have details of possible performances at the open-air amphitheatre in amongst the ruins. Alternatively, if you fancy doing some walking, it's a nice two-hour walk through the woods along the red-marked path from just above the last stop on tram #4 and #9.

Rusovce

In 1918, when drawing up the Versailles frontiers, the new Czechoslovak Republic was handed a small stretch of forested marshland on the right bank of the Danube to shore up its exposed western flank. Much of this land is now taken up with the unmissable Petržalka housing estate, but there are at least a couple more villages before the Hungarian border, one of which, **RUSOVCE**, makes a possible half-day trip – bus #116 from most SNP. Originally the Roman camp of Gerulata, there's now a small museum (May–Oct Tues–Sun 10am–5pm) containing the results of extensive archaeological excavations which have uncovered two large Roman burial sites. Nearby, a mock-Tudor **zámok** provides a neat country retreat for the Slovak Folk Ensemble, a pleasant park for picnicking and a lake for naturist swimming.

DANUBE TRANSPORT

From mid-April to mid-September there's a daily shuttle service by **hydrofoil** between Bratislava and Vienna (1hr), but it tends to be heavily booked up in advance. Less frequently, there's a service to Esztergom and Budapest (3hr 30min). All boats leave from the jetty on Fajnorovo nábrežie, near the Slovak National Museum. For this year's timetable go to the *Slovakoturist* office in the passage between Hviezdoslavovo námestie and Nálepkova, or the ticket office at the jetty. To find out about summer sightseeing cruises on the Danube in and around Bratislava, go to *BIPS*.

The Small Carpathians

From the Bratislavan suburbs to the gateway into the Váh valley, the **Small Carpathians** form a thin abrasive strip of limestone hills altogether different from the softer, pine-clad hills of the Czech Lands. These are the modest beginnings of the great Carpathian range which sweeps round through the back door into Romania. A thoroughly Balkan heat bounces off the sun-stroked plains of the Danube and permeates even these first foothills, whose south-facing slopes are excellent for vine-growing. There's also a smattering of castles and a whole host of hiking opportunities, all making for a welcome release from the Bratislavan smog.

The Small Carpathians really do force their way into the city boundaries, and you could use Bratislava as a starting point for **hiking** into the hills – just get hold of the *Malé karpaty* double map. Kamzík (440m) is the first peak (see previous page), and the view from its television tower on a clear day is difficult to beat, but if you want to do some serious trekking in unmolested countryside, continue along the red-marked path (previously known as the *cesta Hrdinov SNP*) which wiggles its way along the ridge of the hills all the way to Brezová, 75km away at the end of the range. There are campsites and hotels peppered along the route and it's easy enough to drop down off the hills and grab a bed for the night before moving on.

Modra

If you're going in search of *víno*, **MODRA**, just under 30km from Bratislava and entirely surrounded by the stuff, is the most convenient place to head. It's a typical ribbon-village with one elongated square lined with barn-door cottages growing fancier the nearer you get to the centre. The town's pottery factory sells its folk ware at *Slovenská ľudová majolika* (no. 62), while the local wines are best imbibed at the co-op headquarters further down on the other side of the street. Gracing the square at its widest point is a light stone statue of Ľudovít Štúr who is buried in the local cemetery (see box). The nearby Štúr Museum (Tues–Fri 8am–4pm, Sat & Sun 10am–4pm) is predictable enough and of course a classic Slovak school trip, though the kids are generally more interested in the ice cream outlet, judiciously placed next door. Close by, *langoše* and sandwiches are sold to the local workers and anyone else who wants them.

There are two reasonable hotels in Modra itself and a fancier one up in the hills at the *chata* and camping colony of PIESOK, 6km north of Modra. Quite the most rewarding peak in terms of views is Vysoká (754m), a five-kilometre walk from Piesok, but for a more gentle stroll, you could do worse than head 5km east from Piesok for the hulking zámok of Červený Kameň (Red Rock). Its defensive position and big fat bastions (designed, apparently, by Albrecht Dürer) were made to put fear into any enemies approaching from the plain, but the powerful Pálffy dynasty later transformed it into yet another luxurious family pad, adding gardens and various other creature comforts. It should eventually serve as a museum of period furniture with a medieval torture chamber and a seventeenth-century apothecary, but make sure the reconstructions are over before setting out.

ĽUDOVÍT ŠTÚR

Son of a Protestant pastor, Ľudovít Štúr (1815–1856) rose to become the only Slovak deputy in the Hungarian Diet prior to 1848. In the turmoil of 1848 itself, he ended up siding with the reactionary Habsburgs and leading a band of motley Slovak recruits *against* the equally chauvinistic Magyar revolutionaries. Even though the Slovaks shared the modest victory with the Habsburgs, they failed to extract any concessions from them. Disappointed and disillusioned, Štúr retreated to Modra, where he lived until his premature death in 1856, the result of a gun accident. In his later years, he became convinced that Slovakia's only hope lay with Tsarist Russia – now a distinctly unpopular viewpoint. Perhaps his most lasting achievement was in the formation of what is now the official Slovak written language, based on the Central Slovak dialect, although even this was only achieved in the face of vehement opposition from the more Czechophile scholars who advocated either Czech or its nearest equivalent, West Slovak.

Trnava

The fact that **TRNAVA**, 45km northeast of Bratislava, is one of the few towns on the plain to have survived with its walled-in medieval character intact is reason enough to visit the place. Calling it the Slovak Rome, though, as *ČEDOK* tend to, won't fool anyone. It is, however, a useful pointer to the town's rich ecclesiastical history, which began with the establishment of the Hungarian archbishopric here in 1541 and reached its zenith during the Counter-Reformation, with the founding of a Jesuit university.

Though no longer Slovakia's religious capital, it is one of the oldest towns in the republic, celebrating the 750th anniversary of its royal charter in 1988, an event which provided the much-needed impetus for restoration work on the town's various monuments. Today, however, none of this can hide the fact that

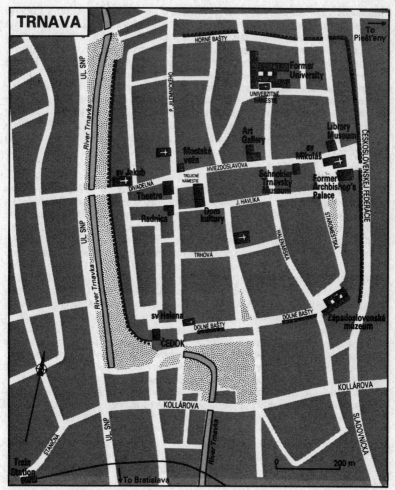

Trnava's golden days are over, and aside from a pleasant old town, a couple of fine churches and a fairly good museum, there's nothing to make you linger longer than a day. And with fast trains from Bratislava taking just 35 minutes, it's even feasible as a day trip.

The old town

From the bus and railway stations, walk up Staničná to the main ring road, ulica SNP, and walk north along the River Trnavka which runs parallel with the most impressive section of the old **town walls**, reinforced in the sixteenth century (and up to 6m thick in places) in anticipation of the marauding Turks. The red-brick Bernolákova brána is the only surviving gateway, popularly known as the

Franciscan gate, after their nearby church of **sv Jakub**. It leads swiftly to **Trojičné námestie**, the spacious main square where Trnava's institutions old and new congregate: the sixteenth-century **mestská veža**, the Neoclassical **radnica**, a Biedermeier **theatre** and, last but in no way least, the **Dom kultúry**, just one of a number of spanking-new buildings in Trnava which provide a bizarre contrast with the rubble piled up all over the old quarter.

The focus of life – and the anniversary showpiece – is the newly paved avenue which leads south from here, a pleasant window-shopping stroll which ends at the church of **sv Helena**, the town's oldest and, in its own small way, most impressive church, in a bare and miniature Gothic happily free from the suffocating hand of the Counter-Reformation. Next door is the town's former hospital from the same period.

Around sv Mikuláš

East off Trojičné námestie, Trnava's one-time cathedral, **sv Mikuláš**, beckons with two rather clumsy, eye-catching Baroque steeples. It was promoted from a mere parish church following the Battle of Mohács in 1526, which caused the Hungarians to retreat behind the Danube: the royalty moved to Pozsony (Bratislava), while the archbishop transferred his see to Nagyszombat (Trnava), setting up shop next door to sv Mikuláš. A century later Trnava's position as a haven for Magyar cultural institutions seeking refuge from the Turks was further bolstered by the establishment of a university. In common with all Habsburg institutions of the time, it was under the iron grip of the Jesuits, and Trnava soon became the bastion of the Counter-Reformation east of Vienna. The importance of religious over purely scholarly matters is most clearly illustrated by the sheer size of the **University church**, down Hollého, one of the largest in Slovakia and possessing quite the most intimidating altarpiece anywhere. The glory days were short-lived: with the expulsion of the Jesuit order from the Habsburg Empire and the defeat of the Turks, Trnava lost its university to Budapest, its archbishop's see to Esztergom and consequently its political and religious clout.

Staromestská, the broad leafy street which sets off south from the archbishop's palace, is probably the prettiest street in town, with a cathedral-close feel about it. At the end the plain off-cream mass of the seventeenth-century convent of sv Klara, now the **West Slovak Museum** (Tues–Sun 9am–5pm), offers a variety of exhibitions including (temporarily) the contents of the Schneider-Trnavský museum (see below). If you've been wondering what Slovak folk ceramics look like, eight rooms of gear by local potter Štefan Cyril Parrák should put you in the picture, but best of all are the few bits and bobs salvaged from the now-defunct **Jewish community**. Trnava's Jews were actually expelled from the city in the sixteenth century, when, on the usual trumped-up charge of ritual murder, the Emperor Ferdinand sent them packing through the Sereď gate, walling it up with ripped-up Jewish gravestones to bar their return. For three hundred years, Trnava was *Jüdenfrei*, then in 1862 the gate was removed and the Jews began to filter back to the unofficial ghetto, located about where the car park of the main supermarket now stands. The only remaining landmarks are two disused and weed-ridden **synagogues** on ulica J. Havlíka, on the brink of either restoration or collapse.

Trnava's two other museums have been undergoing restoration for the last few years. In the decaying street of the same name, the **Schneider-Trnavský Museum** celebrates the Slovak composer who was choirmaster at sv Mikuláš from 1909 until his death in 1958. But apart from confirming that he had very good taste in 1920s furniture, you won't learn much else here. The **Library Museum**, on the corner by sv Mikuláš, is no doubt designed to stress the contribution Slovak scholars like Bernolák and others made at what the Hungarians like to claim was an exclusively Magyar university.

Practical points

If you want to **stay the night**, finding a room should present few problems at the *Park* on ulica SNP (☎019-233 27), *Koliba* on Kamenný mlyn (☎019-249 07) or the slightly more expensive *Karpaty* (☎019-246 71) at the south end of town. If you're very hard up, try the *Kriváň* hostel on Bernolákova. If you have any problems, ČEDOK, across the road from the church of sv Helena, may be able to help.

Nitra

While Trnava is stuck in the past, **NITRA**, 40km east across the plain, has effectively shed its old skin and rushed headlong into the twentieth century. The result is a clearly divided town: on the one hand, the battered and forgotten old quarter clings on for dear life at the foot of the castle rock; on the other, the ungainly sprawl of modern Nitra, agricultural capital of the nation and proverbial bustling market town, gets on with the business of the day. Sadly, there's not much to choose between the two, but the sights, such as they are, are all situated in the old town, which has a certain kudos attached to it as the centre of Slovak Catholicism, ancient and modern.

Eating and sleeping

ČEDOK have their office located near the main market, but will undoubtedly attempt to book you into the expensive high-rise *Hotel Nitra* (☎087-333 96), Slančíkovej 1. Insist instead on staying at the *Zobor* (☎087-250 60) on the main avenue, which is less expensive, or the *Slovan* (☎087-287 82), Saratovská 16, which is cheaper still. The only time when finding a room might not be so straightforward is during the agricultural fair and the music festival, both of which take place every September.

Nitra is not too bad for **eating**, with pizzas at a small joint on Malinovského, and traditional fare at the no-smoking *Diétna reštaurácia* (closed Sat & Sun) on the corner of Gorazdova. There's nowhere particularly special to sample the local white wine, *Nitria* – just head for any of the *vináreň* in town.

The city centre

The central axis of the nové mesto, where you're most likely to arrive, is the busy crossroads by the city's main **market** (*tržnica*), where the region's produce is sold daily. The staré mesto and all the main sights are north of here, except for the **Kalvária**, a kitsch mock-up of the Crucifixion which crowns the summit of a small limestone hill southeast of the train station. The brutality of Nitra's modern development serves as the apocalyptic backdrop for three ugly concrete crosses, the two robbers grey and unpainted on either side of a technicolour Jesus.

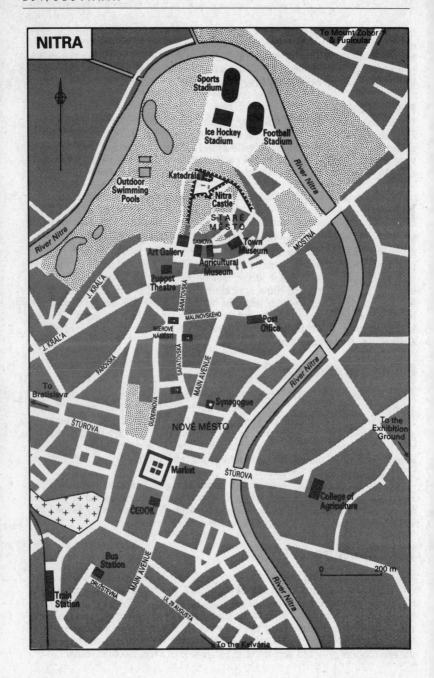

To the east of the market, as you cross over Štúrovo, is the country's main **College of Agriculture**, a flying-saucer-shaped building whose research department recently invented a strain of tree that could withstand acid rain – progress indeed. On Gorazdova, just off the main avenue (formerly Leninova), the sheer size of Nitra's Moorish **synagogue** is an indication of the strength of the town's pre-war Jewish community but, predictably enough, it lies abandoned and disused. Saratovská, which wins the prize for the nové mesto's most pleasant street, leads you away from the chaos of the new town to the sights around the castle.

The staré mesto

Nitra's **staré mesto** is actually very small, consisting of just a handful of streets huddled under the hrad. The entrance is formed by the former župný dom, which now houses the town's **art gallery** (closed for restoration), through whose arches you pass in order to reach the steeply sloping main square – a very modest affair but quite pretty and totally peaceful after the frenetic activity of the lower town. At its centre stands a recent (and typically clichéd) statue of **Prince Pribina**, the ninth-century ruler of Nitra, who erected the first church in what is now Czechoslovakia here in 833. Though no great believer himself, he shrewdly realised such a gesture would help him keep on good terms with his German neighbours. There's also a good wodge of evidence to suggest that Saint Methodius, the first bishop of (Great) Moravia, was stationed at Nitra and not at Velehrad in the Morava valley, as is often claimed.

Nitra's two museums are on the lower side of the square. The **Agricultural Museum** (Poľnohospodárske múzeum) housed in the former Franciscan monastery is the better of the two, but still a tad disappointing. Far from being an illuminating journey through the violent fortunes of Slovak agriculture, it differs very little from your average town museum, save for the odd stuffed seven-legged mutant calf. The **Town Museum**, a few doors along, shares its quarters with the *Divadlo pod hradom*, a fringe theatre venue who were putting on a feminist version of *Salomé* last time I was here.

The **hrad** itself is a scruffy little hybrid, saved only by its lofty position above the river. A fortress since the time of the Great Moravian Empire (of which it may have been the capital), it provided refuge for various Hungarian kings over the centuries until convincingly destroyed by the Turks in the seventeenth century. The walk up to the hrad is littered with crusty saints, a very fine plague column, and two massive gateways before you reach what's left of the castle, most of which has been turned over to the Archaeological Institute and is closed to the public. The one sight left in the hrad complex is the **katedrála** (only sporadically open), an old Gothic structure, now cluttered with uninspiring eighteenth-century adornments, which adjoins the Bishop of Nitra's cosy Baroque pad. It does, however, contain the remains of two tenth-century Slovak saints, Ondrej Svorad and Benedict Junior, both religious hermits who lived in the hills near Trenčín and spent most of their lives tending their gardens and vineyards. The locals, who had little time for able-bodied young men who wanted to devote their lives to spiritual contemplation, gave both of them a hard time. Ondrej Svorad escaped the villagers' wrath by diplomatically giving away a portion of his harvest, but Benedict Junior failed to appease his enemies, who threw him off a nearby cliff and then drowned him in the River Váh.

The Danube basin

To the east of Bratislava lies the rich agricultural region of the **Danube basin** (the *Felvidék* to the Hungarians), a flat, well-watered expanse of land which benefits from the warmest temperatures in the country and which, since being handed over to the Slovaks in 1918, now forms the border between Czechoslovakia and Hungary. It's one of the few places in Slovakia where you can go for miles without seeing a tree, and is the traditional haunt of most of Slovakia's Hungarian minority – 600,000 and rising at the last count. Sadly, it was also one of the regions which suffered badly during the last war, making one place very much like another. The only reason to come here at all is to drink, eat and lie by the region's many artificial lakes in true hedonistic fashion. The one exception is **Komárno**, which, while not worth a detour in itself, has enough to make you pause en route to Hungary.

THE GABČIKOVO-NAGYMAROS DAM

A question mark still hangs over the **Gabčikovo-Nagymaros hydroelectric barrage**, a megalomaniac joint project dreamed up in 1978 by the old guard, with the cynical collusion and capital of the Austrians who were on the lookout for cheap electricity at someone else's environmental expense. The Hungarians and Austrians have since both pulled out, following intense protest by environmentalists from all three countries. Meanwhile, on the Czechoslovak side, work has continued, even after the November 1989 revolution. The latest news is that there will now be a two-year pause while the new government assesses the ecological pros and cons of completing a toned-down version of the dam, which would produce a quarter of the electricity originally planned. The real difficulty on the Czechoslovak side is that the country has already committed vast amounts of money and resources to the project, and is desperately searching for alternative (and cheap) sources of energy to brown coal – the pollution from which is killing off the country's forests. Sadly, the damage caused by the dam appears to be just as devastating, and has already taken its toll. Once-perfect cropland is beginning to dry up around the construction sites, and many scientists believe that Bratislava's precious underground water table has already been adversely – if not irrevocably – affected.

Senec: sandy beaches and swimming pools

The towns of the Danube basin are probably the nearest Czechoslovakia comes to seaside resorts, and in the summer the "beaches" are packed with windsurfers, canoeists and idle sun-seekers slobbing out along reservoirs, lakes, swimming pools and any stretch of water they can find. If you're staying in Bratislava, **SENEC**, 26km east and just over thirty minutes by train, is the easiest place to get to and fairly indicative of the region. The Turks left one of their few monuments here, the **Turecký dom**, and a few other odds and sods which relieve the town's monotonous concrete. The place where the crowds head is the **Slnečné jazerá** (Sunny Lakes), a couple of reasonably sandy-beached artificial lakes within sight of the train station. There are two campsites (by the lake) and two hotels – *Amur* by the lake and *Lúč* in town – but the whole place is full to bursting in the hot months, especially during August.

Komárno (Komárom)

No question about it, **KOMÁRNO** is a Hungarian town through and through. Even the Slovak regional authorities have been forced to admit this fact and erect bilingual street and shop signs. In the shops you'll be greeted with the unfamiliar *tessék* ("what do you want?") rather than the ubiquitous *prosím*. But these ethnic niceties aside, Komárno is not going to win over many people's hearts; it's only worth stopping off should you pass through on the way to Budapest.

The Town

When the Czechoslovak border was dreamed up in 1918, the Hungarians of Komárom found their town split in two, with by far the most significant part – and what few sights there are – on the Slovak side of the border. The **train** and **bus stations** are northwest of the town's main drag, Zahradnícka Slovanská, which continues over the river into Hungary.

The town is best known for its huge fortress at the confluence of the Váh and the Danube, which has served as a strategic base for everyone from the Romans to the Russians. But Komárno's main "sight" is the **town museum** (Tues–Sun 10am–noon & 2–4pm) on ulica Gábora Steiner, right before the bridge, which pays tribute to the town's two most illustrious sons: the composer **Franz Lehár**, whose father was military bandmaster with the local garrison, and the nineteenth-century Hungarian writer **Mór Jókai**. Lehár enjoyed the dubious privilege of having written one of Hitler's favourite works, the operetta *Die Lustige Witwe*, and, despite the fact that his mother tongue was Hungarian and his own wife Jewish, found himself much in demand during the Third Reich. Jókai, on the other hand, was an extremely nationalistic Hungarian who wrote a glowing account of the Hungarian aristocracy and would have had nothing good to say about Komárno's modern-day split nationality. You won't get much from either of the exhibitions unless you know either Slovak or Hungarian. More fascinating is the disorientating sight of a small **Orthodox church** in the museum grounds, testifying to the Serbian colonists who settled around Komárno in the early eighteenth century in a desperate attempt to escape the revengeful Turks. Small pockets of Orthodox believers still exist in the region, and the seventeenth- and eighteenth-century Greek and Serbian icons on display here constitute one of the best collections outside Serbia.

Practicalities

ČEDOK on the main street can organise **accommodation** for you in one of the town's three moderately priced hotels; there's a **campsite** (May 15–Sept 15) by the Danube, 6km east in NOVÁ STRÁŽ (8min by train). Basic **food** can be had in the cellars of the *Reštaurácia pri radnici* (predictably enough opposite the town hall), though don't expect anything more Magyar than *guláš*. The *Café Lehár*, a big nineteenth-century building in the middle of Zahradnícka Slovanská not far from the Danube bridge, is the place to hang out in your best Budapest denim and sip a Coca-Cola. For those with the language, there's a Hungarian theatre down by the docks to the east of the big bridge.

Moving on, a daily **hydrofoil** runs to Budapest from the launch on the island by the bridge; enquire at *ČEDOK* for the exact times of sailings. **Trains** bound for Hungary leave Komárno station very early in the morning – more frequently at the station on the Hungarian side, a short walk from the border checkpoint.

Štúrovo

"The Danube threads towns together like a string of pearls" wrote Claudio Magris, but it's doubtful he had ŠTÚROVO* in mind at the time. Its only saving grace is the unbeatable view of Esztergom's great domed basilica on the Hungarian side of the river. Still, it is the last town on the Slovak Danube and the main **border crossing** for international trains – which is just about the only good reason for being here. Having said that, it's no bad place to break your journey, since, with the easing of border restrictions, it should become straightforward to cross over and admire the treasures of Esztergom (for which see *Hungary: the Rough Guide*).

The **train and bus stations** are actually an inconvenient 2.5km west of the town, with bus #1 covering the distance only infrequently. In the summer the focus of life alternates between the two outdoor swimming pools: *Kúpalisko Vadaš*, by the local **campsite** (May–Sept 15) just north of the town, and the other right by the river near the **car-ferry** launch, whence boats leave hourly for Esztergom. If you need to stay the night, there are two cheap hotels, the *Dunaj* (☎23 92) and *Šport* (☎20 80).

Piešťany and the Váh valley

Finding its source in the Tatras and carving its southwesterly course right the way to the Danube at Komárno, the **Váh** is one of the great rivers of Slovakia. It's common currency in tourist office circles to talk of the "Slovak Rhine", but despite the consistent appearance of ruined cliff-top castles at every turn of the river, there's nothing here to suggest the magic of the Rhine valley. Heading north up the Váh from Piešťany to Trenčín, the dramatics are played down, the mountains on either side keep their distance and the whole area still has the feel of the Danube basin. Beyond Trenčín, industry, the damming of the river, and a lorry-congested highway all dampen the effects of brigand hideouts like Vršatec and Považský hrad. The best way to weigh up the relative merits of the region is on one of the fast and frequent **trains** which leave Bratislava and twist their way up the Váh valley en route to the Tatras.

Leopoldov and Jaslovské Bohunice

As you approach from Bratislava, two landmarks provide an ominous entrance to the valley proper. The first is **LEOPOLDOV**, 18km south of Piešťany, once a vital fortress in the defence against the Turks, then converted into a prison in 1854 by the Habsburgs and later used by the Communists to encarcerate Slovak dissidents. The second is clearly visible on the western horizon. Out of the flat fields to the southwest of Piešťany rise the eight cooling towers of the country's first

---

*Like many towns in the Hungarian-speaking parts of Slovakia, Štúrovo was actually known by its Hungarian name Párkány until 1948 when the Communists dedicated it to the Slovak nationalist Ľudovít Štúr. Depending on how much political clout the Hungarian population can muster, it would come as no surprise if it reverted to its original title some time in the near future.

nuclear power station at **JASLOVSKÉ BOHUNICE**, built in the 1960s and recently the cause of heated exchanges between the Austrians (who want the plant closed down immediately on safety grounds) and Havel's government, who are trying to hold out until the new Mochovce nuclear reactor, some 50km further east, is fully operational.

Piešťany

The most convincing claim the local tourist board make about **PIEŠŤANY**, just over an hour by train from Bratislava, is that it's the largest spa town in Slovakia. In every other respect it's a disappointingly dour place, overrun with the unhealthy wealthy from different parts of the German-speaking world, for the sake of whose hard currency millions of crowns have been poured into the spa facilities, with precious little left over for the town itself. Still, green spaces, clean swimming pools and a host of other resources to which the public does have access, make it a more pleasant place to laze in the sun than most of the "beachy" resorts further south.

The town divides conveniently into two parts: the spa island cut off from the mainland by a thin arm of the River Váh, and the rest of the town on the right bank between the main arm of the river and the **bus and train stations** to the west. It's a fifteen-minute walk into town down the main avenue (bus #3, #9 or #12) to Pavlovova, the main drag through the centre of town, lined with cafés and trinkety shops. The obligatory bandstand and spanking new **Dom umenia** (which puts on plenty of Bach and Mozart for the foreign guests) are laid out in the nearby park, but the rest of the spa is on the opposite bank, connected by the partly covered **Kolonádový most**, rebuilt "for the benefit of the working-class" in the words of the 1950s commemorative plaque.

One place that definitely wasn't built with the latter in mind is the *Thermia Palace* hotel, which retains a hint of its turn-of-the-century opulence and – if the BMWs and Audis parked outside are anything to go by – now serves the new European aristocracy. The woods and park on the spa island are decidedly verdant, with the odd sculpture peeping out of the shrubbery and a host of old annexes still used for the spa's "mud wrapping and electrotreatment" for rheumatic illnesses. If you fancy a dip, the old-fashioned *Eva* swimming pool, 100m further north, is open to the public (closed Mon). From here the sleek, ultra-modern *Balnea* sanatorium spreads its luxurious wings the full length of the island, finishing up at the spa information centre and, behind it, the mini golf course.

If you haven't come here for treatment, you'll have to stay in one of the hotels on the right bank, of which the *Lipa* (Pavlovova 16) is currently the least expensive. If you're looking for cheap sustenance, try the *Vináreň v uličku*, hidden on Park pasáž, a side street off Pavlovova. **Camping** (May–Sept) is possible at either side of the mouth of the action-packed Sĺňava lake (bus #6, #13 or #12). If you'd rather lose the water-sport crowds, however, cross over to the left bank of the river where the Považský Inovec hills immediately begin, or walk 4km along the green-marked path to **MORAVANY NAD VÁHOM**. Here the sixteenth-century zámok has become a country retreat for the Slovak Artists' Union, surrounded by an open-air sculpture park – the former closed, the latter open to the public.

The ruined castles at Čachtice and Beckov

Halfway between Piešťany and Trenčín, to the north, is the industrial town of NOVÉ MESTO NAD VÁHOM, not a place to hang about in if you can help it, but a necessary halt if you're changing trains or buses to get to the ruined castles of Čachtice and Beckov.

Čachtice

Of these two lofty piles of rubble perched on opposing sides of the Váh, ČACHTICE's, 8km southwest of Nové Mesto, has the edge on views and legends, for it was here that the "Blood Countess" **Elizabeth Báthori** was walled in for almost four years before her death in 1614 to pay for her crimes and misdemeanours – which included the murder of over six hundred women (see below). Čachtice was her favourite castle; "she loved it for its wildness", wrote one of her posthumous biographers, "for the thick walls which muffled every sound, for its low halls, and for the fact of its gloomy aspect on the bare hillside". There's virtually nothing left of the castle today, and only an impassive portrait of Elizabeth herself in the village museum, 2km out of sight to the east. The quickest way to get up to the hrad is actually the stiff climb from VIŠŇOVÉ train station (15min

---

THE BLOOD COUNTESS OF ČACHTICE

Born in 1560, **Countess Elizabeth Báthori** was the offspring of two branches of the noble Báthori family, whose constant intermarriage may have accounted for her periodic fainting spells and fits of uncontrollable rage: other Báthoris, such as Prince "Crazy" Gábor, were similarly afflicted. As a child she was intelligent and well educated, being fluent in Latin, Hungarian and German at a time when many nobles, including the ruling prince of Transylvania, were barely literate. Brought up in the family castle at Nagyecsed, a humble town near the Hungarian-Romanian border, she absorbed from her relatives the notion that peasants were little more than cattle – to be harshly punished for any act of insubordination.

As was customary in the sixteenth century, her marriage was arranged for dynastic reasons, and an illegitimate pregnancy hushed up. Betrothed in 1571 – the same year that her cousin István became Prince of Transylvania – she was married at fifteen to twenty-one-year-old Ferenc Nádasdy. Over the next decade Ferenc was usually away fighting Turks, earning his reputation as the "Black Knight", and Elizabeth grew bored at their home in Sárvár Castle. There she began to torture serving women, an "entertainment" that gradually became an obsession. With the assistance of her maids Dorothea Szentes and Anna Darvulia (with whom she had a lesbian relationship), Elizabeth cudgelled and stuck pins into servants to "discipline" them; even worse, she forced them to lie naked in the snowy courtyard and then doused them with cold water until they froze to death. On his return Ferenc baulked at this (although he too enjoyed brutalising servants) and it wasn't until after his demise in 1604 that Elizabeth started torturing and murdering without restraint. Her victims were invariably women or girls, and – most importantly – always peasants.

Killing peasants could be done with impunity. Poor women could always be enticed into service at Beckov and Čachtice – Elizabeth's residence after she quit Sárvár, both then located within the borders of Transylvania (in modern-day Romania) – and, should word of their deaths leak out, the authorities would hardly

from Nové Mesto), rather than the slower, longer haul from Čachtice village itself.

Beckov

There's substantially more of a hrad above the village of **BECKOV** (presently closed for reconstruction), 5km northeast of Nové Mesto and accessible only by bus. This was another of Báthori's torture chambers, ruined by a fire which ripped through its apartments in 1729. There's a *reštaurácia* just under the rock, where you can relax and watch the rock-climbers risk life and limb on the cliff below the castle, and a small **folk museum** (Tues–Sun 10am–5pm) in which to while away half an hour.

Trenčín and around

Despite the usual high-rise accompaniments, **TRENČÍN**, 42km north of Piešťany, is the most naturally appealing of the towns on the Váh. Its central historical core sits below the most impressive **hrad** in the valley: part ruins, part reconstruction, it's a fiercely defensive sprawl of vaguely connected walls and ramparts on a

believe the accusations of the victims' parents against the Countess Báthori. With the assistance of Szentes, Darvulia, her son's former wet-nurse Helena Jo, and one man, the diminutive Fizcko, Elizabeth allowed her sadistic fantasies full rein. On occasion she bit chunks of flesh from servants' breasts and necks – probably the origin of the legend that she bathed in the blood of virgins to keep her own skin white and translucent.

In this fashion Elizabeth murdered over six hundred women, and could probably have continued doing so undetected, had not Darvulia died. Grief-stricken, the Countess formed an attachment to a local widow, Erzsi Majorová, who encouraged her to seek aristocratic girls for her victims. Enquiries by *their* parents could not be so easily ignored by the authorities who, in any case, by now had their own motives for investigating "Die Blutgräfin". Ferenc Nádasdy had loaned the Habsburg crown 17,000 gulden, which Elizabeth had persistently – and vainly – demanded back. Should she be found guilty of serious crimes this debt would be forfeited. Others also had the knives out – notably Paul, Elizabeth's son, who had grown up apart from her at Sárvár, and one Count Thurzo, both of whom were anxious to prevent the confiscation of the Báthori estates and gathered evidence against her throughout 1610.

On December 29 Thurzo's men raided Čachtice castle, and on entry almost tripped over the corpse of a servant whom Elizabeth had just bludgeoned for stealing a pear. Thurzo secretly imprisoned the "damned woman" in her own castle immediately, so that (in his words) "the families which have won such high honours on the battlefield shall not be disgraced. . . by the murky shadow of this bestial female". Due to his cover-up the scandal was mainly confined to court circles, although when Elizabeth died in 1614 the locals protested at her burial in Čachtice cemetery. She was later reburied at Nagyesced in the precincts of the family vault. Due to her sex (then considered to be incapable of such deeds) and rank, records of her trial were hidden, and mention of her very name subsequently prohibited by royal command.

steeply pitched and craggy site, spectacularly lit at night. Once it's fully restored it'll be a great place to explore, but as yet the only complete part is the galleried **Hodinová veža**, which gives the best view out across the valley. Slovakia's one and only **Roman inscription** of any worth is carved into the rockface below the castle, commemorating Marcus Aurelius' victory over the German hordes in 179 AD . Much later, the castle became the centre of Matúš Čák's short-lived independent kingdom. Čák was little more than a rebellious feudal despot who set up a mock-royal court, crowning himself "King of the Váh and the Tatras". He supported the young Přemyslid Václav III in his unsuccessful quest for the Hungarian crown, and had John of Luxembourg and the Hungarian King Charles Robert on the run for a number of years. Defeated only once, near Košice, he remained in control of his fiefdom until his death in 1321, and is now happily lauded one of the first great Slovak heroes.

Back down the castle's cobbled lane, in the elbow of the first sharp bend, is a radiant white and yellow **church** set in its own paved plateau – packed of a Sunday, closed of a weekday. A covered walkway leads down Hradná to the main square. Straight ahead is the **Piarist church**, ablaze with the fury of the Counter-Reformation and definitely worth checking out if it's open. Next door in the old monastery is the **Bazovský Art Gallery** (Tues–Sun 9am–5pm), named after the Slovak sculptor who died here in 1968 and whose statues stand in the courtyard. The building's heavy helpings of stucco are more memorable than a lot of the modern Slovak art displayed here, but the exhibitions do change regularly.

Pass under Trenčín's only remaining gateway, take a sharp right and you'll discover the town's former **synagogue**, a Moorish hulk of a building, completely ransacked during the war, but one of the few to have been fully restored: it now serves as an exhibition hall.

Practical matters

The **bus and train stations** are located next to each other to the east of the old town centre, which can be reached by crossing the park adjacent to the station. **Hotels** should be no problem: the *Tatra*, across the park from the station (☎0831-343 31), and the *Trenčan* (☎0831-214 06), Malinovského 7, are both cheaper than the *Laugaricio* on Vajanského (☎0831-378 41), though all are quite reasonable. The **camping site** (June to mid-Sept) is past the football stadium on an island in the Váh. Away from the big hotels, things go to bed very early in Trenčín, and the advice is to do the same yourself.

Trenčianske Teplice

While Trenčín bakes down in the valley, **TRENČIANSKE TEPLICE**, 12km northeast, marinates in the green glades of the Teplička valley. The nicest way to get to Trenčianske Teplice is on the narrow-gauge train-cum-tram which trundles up the valley from TRENČIANSKA TEPLÁ, itself less than ten minutes by train from Trenčín. Alternatively, you could hike the 9km across the hills from Trenčín following the red-marked path and ending your walk with a dip in Bohuslav Fuchs' pool (see below).

The spa itself is little more than a collection of sanatoria, ranging from the typical nineteenth-century ochre mansion of the *Sina* to the concrete *Krym*. The town's most unusual building is the stripy *Hammam* bathhouse whose Moorish interior is open only to spa guests, but you might be able to peep inside. Architectural buffs should check out the *Mahnáč* sanatorium, a top-notch Bauhaus-style building by Jaromír Krejcar; from the same period, Bohuslav Fuchs'* swimming pool complex, **Zelená žaba** (Green Frog), has a much wider appeal. Concealed in some woods to the north of the town and cut into the curve of the hillside, it looks as good as new sixty years on (daily noon–5pm), and swimming in the pool's spring water gives the weird sensation of swimming in warm lemonade. Like all spas, the strenuous stroll is an all-important part of the cure, so for the best views and a bit of mineral refreshment halfway, continue up the valley from the Zelená žaba, and, having reached the *Baračka* restaurant, head up to **Heinrich's spring**, and then on to Kráľovec (557m) for the definitive view over the Teplička valley. The whole trip should take around two hours. Should you wish to stay around, there are two **hotels** for non-guests.

THE CENTRAL MOUNTAINS

The great virtue of Slovakia is its mountains, particularly the **High Tatras** – which, in their short span, reach alpine heights and a bleak, stunning beauty. By far the republic's most popular destination, they are, in fact, the least typical of Slovakia's mountains, which tend on the whole to be densely forested and round-topped limestone ranges like the **Low Tatras** and **Malá Fatra** – less monumental but also somewhat less developed.

Geographically speaking, the region splits into two huge corridors, with the Váh valley to the north and the Hron valley to the south. The regional capital is **Banská Bystrica**, one of the many towns in the region originally settled by German miners, and still redolent of those times. Two other medieval mining towns worth visiting are **Banská Štiavnica** and **Kremnica**, set in the nearby hills. For the Slovaks, by far the most important towns historically are **Martin** and **Liptovský Mikuláš**, centres of the nineteenth-century národné obrodenie, both situated in the Váh valley. Generally, though, the towns in the valley bottoms have been fairly solidly industrialised, and are only good as bases for exploring the surrounding countryside, which can be easily done by a combination of hiking and busing. **Railways**, where they do exist, make for some of the most scenic train journeys in the country. As for the region's innumerable **villages**, from which many urbanised Slovaks are but one generation removed, they're mostly one-street affairs, it's true, but no less fascinating for that, and seemingly unchanged since the last century.

Banská Bystrica

Lying at the very heart of Slovakia's mountain region, **BANSKÁ BYSTRICA** (Altsohl) is a useful introduction to the area. Connected to the outlying disticts by some of the country's most precipitous railways, it's also a handsome historic town in its own right – although, as you arrive through the tangled suburbs of the burgeoning cement and logging industry, that may seem difficult to believe.

---

* For more on Fuchs' work, see p.216.

Banská Bystrica was a prosperous royal free town in the Middle Ages, the capital of the seven "Hungarian" mining towns colonised by German miners who, in this case, extracted silver and copper from the nearby hills until the seams ran dry in the eighteenth century. Since then, the town has shaken off its Teutonic past, and is perhaps best remembered today as the centre of the 1944 Slovak National Uprising, whose history, lavishly embellished and glorified by the Communists, is now undergoing a more critical reassessment.

> The Banská Bystrica area telephone code is ☎088.

Arriving and finding somewhere to stay

Banská Bystrica's main **bus and train stations** are in the modern part of town, ten minutes' walk east of the centre; if you happen to alight at Banská Bystrica mesto train station, cross the river and walk five minutes north to the main square. The local *ČEDOK* office is nearby on trieda SNP: it can book hotel

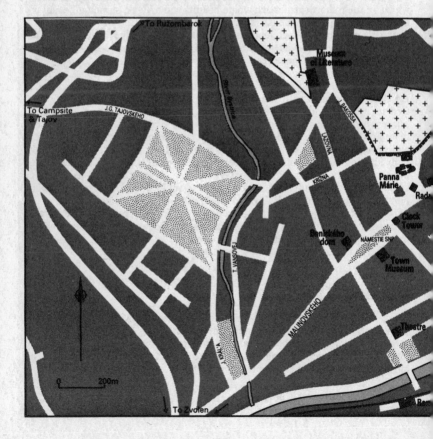

accommodation and change money, but precious little else. **Accommodation** can be thin on the ground in the high season so it's not a bad idea to check the vacancies at *ČEDOK* before traipsing round yourself. Incidentally – and importantly – it's here that you'll need to book rooms if you wish to stay in hotels in the southern approaches to the Low Tatras (see p.314). The cheapest place to stay in Banská Bystrica is the *Juniorhotel* opposite the main theatre (☎233 67), nominally run by the youth organisation *CKM*, and almost invariably full. If so, go round the corner to the *Urpín* (☎245 56) and *Národný dom* (☎237 37) before spending considerably more for the high-rise *Lux*, at the end of trieda SNP (☎241 418). Slightly out of town on the road to TAJOV is the *Turist* (☎330 12), usually booked out with groups but with a **campsite** situated next door. If you'd prefer a more rural setting, make for the campsite and bungalows (open all year) in the wooded vale just beyond Tajov, 5km west of Banská Bystrica by bus.

The town centre

On arrival, you'll find yourself stuck in the monumental part of town, built up after the war and obviously planned as a socialist showpiece. It's a thoroughly

alienating space with few redeeming features, designed to culminate in a statue of Lenin (now removed) and, behind him, the high-rise *Hotel Lux* (symbol of the town's inexorable progress and sophistication) and the **Múzeum SNP** (Tues–Sun 8am–6pm), looking something like a giant concrete mushroom chopped in half. For the sake of the Slovak National Uprising or SNP (see opposite) no expense was spared, with a lavish display of little actual substance. Groups were also treated to a film show projected onto a double TV screen, flanked by four separate slide shows which flashed up subliminal images of Lenin, Gottwald and other key figures to create an incredible imagistic film that charted the triumphant march from the SNP to socialism, rather than exploring the uprising itself. The whole thing will now have to be rewritten, if and when the Slovaks decide (and agree on) what the uprising actually means to them. Whatever the outcome eventually is, the facilities are there to create a very powerful exhibition. Outside on the grass you'll notice a few makeshift tanks and guns from the uprising sitting dejectedly beside the town's last two surviving medieval bastions.

From the giddy monumental heights of the múzeum SNP, it's just a short step up Š. Moyzesa to the humble and humane main square, **námestie SNP**. This modest space, from the charcoal black obelisk of the Soviet war memorial to the ensemble of buildings around the old castle, is basically where everything in Banská Bystrica happens. Sitting on the benches around the square's revolving fountain (which resembles nothing so much as a pile of black molten lava) is the usual cross section of Slovak society – drunks, denim-clad youths, Gypsies and shoppers.

One or two of the Renaissance burgher houses bear closer inspection, such as **Benického dom** at no. 16, the sgraffitoed building opposite (which contains an art gallery) and, a few doors up, the most imposing building on the square, the Thurzo Palace, decorated like a piece of embroidery and sporting some cute circular portholes on its top floor. The **town museum** (Mon–Fri 8am–4pm, Sun 9am–4pm) which now lives there can't quite match up to its setting, but there's a fair selection of folk and "high" art inside.

The rest of Banská Bystrica's historical sights are just beyond the northern end of the námestie. There's not much left of the old hrad except a few barbicans, a scabby royal palace and a rather undistinguished Baroque tower. The most important building is the church of **Panna Márie**, which dates back to the thirteenth century and contains the town's greatest art treasure, a carved late Gothic **altarpiece** by Master Pavol of Levoča, hidden away in one of the side chapels. At its centre stands the figure of Saint Barbara, the patron saint of miners, but more interesting are the side-panel reliefs, which include among others Saint Ursula and her posse of virgins. The place has been undergoing restoration, but if the work is complete be prepared also for Schmidt and Kracker's fiery German frescoes, the result of a heavy Baroquification in the eighteenth century.

Below the main church is the former **radnica**, a boxy little Renaissance building that now hosts an art gallery which shows temporary exhibitions of contemporary Slovak artists from the engaging to the laughable. Alongside the outer barbican a row of battered market stalls draws in the old folk from the surrounding villages to sell the meagre produce of their private plots. Shops and commerce continue further up Horná, but as far as specific sights go, the town has exhausted its potential.

THE SLOVAK NATIONAL UPRISING

The **Slovak National Uprising** was probably the most costly (and ultimately unsuccessful) operation undertaken by the Czechoslovak resistance during World War II. Like the Prague Uprising of May 1945, it was portrayed in unambiguous terms by the last regime as yet another glorious (Communist-inspired) episode in the struggle to defeat Fascism. But no event in the minefield of Slovak history is ever so clear cut, and the SNP is as controversial, in its own way, as the tragedy of the Warsaw Uprising.

As Hitler set about dismantling the western half of Czechoslovakia in 1938–39, the Slovaks under Jozef Tiso's Catholic People's Party established the first ever independent Slovak state. While this was an aspiration with which many Slovaks identified, it soon became clear that Tiso's hands were tied by his governmental allies, the proto-Fascist Hlinka Guards, and that Slovakia was really little more than a Nazi puppet state. Realising this, Slovaks began to desert the army and join the partisans in the mountains, so that by 1944, partisan activity and acts of sabotage had become widespread. It was at this point that the London-based government-in-exile authorised **Lieutenant-Colonel Ján Golian** to prepare a **national coup**, to be co-ordinated with the arrival of Soviet troops.

By the summer of 1944, the Soviet Army was massed on the Polish-Ukrainian side of the Carpathians, busy parachuting in Soviet partisans and seemingly poised to liberate Slovakia. Golian, meanwhile, had established a secret military centre at Banská Bystrica and began forming partisan units from escaped prisoners and army deserters. But while the mountains were perfect for concealing their activities, they were not so good for communication. In the end, the uprising stumbled into action prematurely, set off by default rather than according to any plan.

On August 24, 1944, the German military attaché for Bucharest, General Otto, along with his personal entourage was captured by Soviet partisans in Martin and shot. It was the most daring and provocative strike yet, immediately prompting Hitler to send five SS and two Wehrmacht divisions plus sundry other German troops into Slovakia. Realising they could delay events no longer, the uprising was officially declared by partisan radio from Banská Bystrica on August 29, and a Slovak National Council was set up, comprised of Communists and Democrats in roughly equal proportions.

Despite Soviet assurances of military assistance, only a few token gestures were made. As at Warsaw, the coup failed to prompt the expected Red Army offensive. The Soviets quite rightly suspected the political motives which lay behind the uprising, which smacked of Slovak nationalism and had been organised primarily from London. To be fair, though, Soviet supply lines were already stretched and breaching the Carpathians was no easy task – in the end it took the 4th Ukrainian Army over two months and some 80,000 lives to capture the Dukla Pass and reach Svidník, the first major town to be liberated. More disheartening was the Soviet refusal to allow the West to use Soviet air bases to drop essential equipment into Slovakia.

Even without Allied assistance, the Slovaks kept going for almost two months before the Nazis succeeded in entering Banská Bystrica on October 28. But apart from tying down a number of German divisions, it was a costly sacrifice to make. The reprisals went on for months and whole villages were given the "Lidice treatment" and worse – women and children were no longer considered sacrosanct. All in all, well over 30,000 Slovaks lost their lives as a result of the uprising, even though by October of the same year the Soviets had already begun to liberate the country.

Eating, drinking and nightlife

For **food and drink**, the *Bystrica*, an old nineteenth-century haunt on the corner of Horná, is a great place to hang out either in the café or the *reštaurácia*. The *Čerchova* next door to the town museum on námestie SNP has more youthful pretensions and its outdoor café round the back is a wonderful suntrap. The *vináreň* is more upmarket (if that's the word) with the occasional video-disco of an evening. There's also a pizza place on námestie SNP. Otherwise, the hotels, such as the *Urpín*, are always a good bet for basic sit-down meals. As in the rest of provincial Slovakia, **nightlife** is thin on the ground. The main opera house, *Divadlo J. G. Tajakovského* , is the town's bastion of high culture, while the local **puppet theatre** on J. Kollára regularly offers adult and kids' shows, and plays host to the occasional foreign touring company.

Zvolen and around

Once the effective capital of a Hungarian *župa* or regional district stretching as far as the Orava and Liptov regions, **ZVOLEN** (Neusohl), 20km and a forty-minute train ride south of Banská Bystrica, has come a long way down the scale of importance since those halcyon days. The main reason for coming here is to see the town's four-cornered **zámok** (Tues–Sun 10am–5pm), which squats scruffily on a big mound of earth at one end of Zvolen's excessively wide main thoroughfare. Built in the fourteenth century, the chateau fell to the exiled Czech Hussite leader Jiskra of Brandýs, who for nearly twenty years ruled over much of what is now Slovakia. Later, as the Turks got too close for comfort, it was transformed into the stern fighting fortress it now resembles.

Nowadays, few rooms contain any of their original decor beyond some fine Renaissance portals, but one room boasts a splendid wooden coffered ceiling decorated with no fewer than 78 portraits of successive Holy Roman Emperors. The rest of the apartments have been turned into an **art gallery** displaying a decent range of sixteenth- to nineteenth-century European masters, mostly lesser-known folk save for the odd Hogarth. Another section concentrates on Master Pavol of Levoča, easily the most original sculptor of the fifteenth century – a good opportunity to catch his work if you're going no further east.

The crude, makeshift armoured train below the castle was built for the Slovak National Uprising in Zvolen's railway workshops. Today, Zvolen lives off its logging business and its key position in the country's road and rail system. Polish, Hungarian and Yugoslav trucks litter the main street most days, as well as sundry car loads en route to somewhere more interesting. Although small, the **museum** at no. 43 is actually better than the one at Banská Bystrica, with a good selection of folk art that includes decorated crosses from Detva (see below).

Some practicalities

Zvolen is an easy day trip from Banská Bystrica, but you should find a hotel bed fairly easily at either the cheap *Grand* (☎22 11) or the moderate *Poľana* (☎243 60) on the main square. Failing that, there's the *Rates* (☎215 96) south of the river by the winter stadium (bus #6 to the end) or the nearby *Neresnica* **campsite** (May–Sept). Further out of town, on the other side of the village of KOVÁČOVÁ (bus #11) there's a better campsite (May–Oct) with a swimming pool.

Sliač and Hronsek

Between Zvolen and Banská Bystrica, a wide plain opens up and provides a perfect site for one of the largest Soviet air-force bases in the country, which by the time you read this should have been handed back to the Slovaks. The nearby airstrip has made little impression on the sleepy hillside spa of **SLIAČ**, 5km north of Zvolen by train. The springs were initially discovered back in the thirteenth century but were for years considered harmful rather than healing, since locals frequently came across the carcasses of birds and animals near the mouth of the source. Only in the eighteenth century was it discovered that fumes from carbonated waters, although therapeutic for humans, could, in sufficient concentration, asphyxiate small animals. A shot of the waters aside, there's nothing to do or see here as such, beyond a pleasant park, various mapped-out promenades and some far-reaching views across the valley basin. The **train station** lies between the village and Sliač-kúpele (the spa), up the hill by the edge of the woods.

Two stops further up the track is one of Slovakia's more unusual wooden churches, situated in the small village of **HRONSEK** by the banks of the river Hron. It's built using Silesian-style timber-framed techniques, but filled in with wood not plaster. If you can get hold of the key by asking round for the local priest, the interior features banked seating rather like a theatre in the round, capable of squeezing in over 1000 worshippers.

Detva and Lučenec

Heading south or east from Zvolen by train takes you through the wilds of southern Slovakia to the Hungarian border, though there's no particular reason to stop. Of the two, the southbound route is the most direct (and least interesting) if you're heading for Budapest. The eastbound railway via Lučenec does, however, at least have a few morsels on offer. Ten kilometres down the tracks, **DETVA** is only really worth visiting in mid-July when the folk festival is on, reputedly one of the best in Slovakia. The traditional skills of the community lie in woodcarving, particularly the *fujara*, a cross between a flute and a bassoon and an instrument common in folk music right across central Europe. Detva is also renowned for the **peasant headstones** in the local graveyard, carved in wood and looking more like totem poles than conventional Christian crosses.

Lučenec

Fifty-five kilometres southeast of Zvolen, **LUČENEC** (Losonc) is, for the most part, a scruffy, ramshackle place, typical of the Slovak-Hungarian border regions, with a population of Slovaks, Magyars and Gypsies in roughly equal proportions. It gets few visitors, but if you're passing through it's at least worth checking out the deconsecrated **Calvinist church** (Tues–Fri 9am–5pm, Sat & Sun 10am–1pm) on what's left of the old town square. A gaudy pink neo-Gothic affair from the outside, it's been sensitively restored inside and contains a stunning selection of Art-Nouveau ceramics. Before you move on, the temporary art exhibitions at the **Novohradská galéria** (times as church) occasionally merit a closer look, but don't expect miracles.

It's a good fifteen-minute walk to the church and gallery from the bus and train stations, but once you've hit the main drag through town (previously known as Marxova), there are a few places to break your journey into town. First off is the *ČEDOK* office, where you should be able to fix up a **room** without too much hassle in one of the town's four moderately priced hotels. For **food and drink**, try the pizza place a few doors down or the *cukráreň* at the end of the street, where you can enjoy a coffee and cake hit while sinking into your very own Parker-Knoll.

Banská Štiavnica

High above the Štiavnica river on the terraced slopes of the Štiavnické vrchy, **BANSKÁ ŠTIAVNICA** (Schemnitz), 25km southwest of Zvolen, couldn't wish for a more picturesque setting. The old town has suffered from centuries of sheer neglect, but a concerted effort in recent years by the Polish restorers *PKZ* is slowly taking effect. Nevertheless, there's no getting away from the fact that the town is little more than an ancient monument, as lifeless and isolated as it is beautiful – a place which sees few visitors and is only kept going by the new (yet already obsolete) industry in the blighted new lower town 800 feet below.

Practical matters

Built by "voluntary brigades" of Communist youth workers back in the 1950s, the **railway** is easily the most rewarding way of getting to Banská Štiavnica (1hr from Zvolen – you may have to change at Hronská Dúbrava). The station is south of the new town, from which the old town is a steep hike (there is the occasional local bus). *ČEDOK* have their office on Academická in the old town but with few visitors to compete with there should be no problem getting a room for the night. Campers have a wide choice of **campsites**, southeast of the town, on and off the road to Levice.

The old town

Banská Štiavnica earned its medieval wealth from the gold and silver deposits discovered here in the thirteenth century. As at Banská Bystrica, skilled German miners were brought in to work the seams, the town was granted special privileges by the Hungarian crown and the good times rolled – as testified by the handsome burgher houses erected on the main square, **Trojičné námestie**. Recently restored, they're back to their former glory, their names recalling their German heritage: Baumgartner, Rubigall and Hellenbach. The latter now houses part of the town's **Mining Museum**, a bit too heavy with geology for most, while the Jozef Kollár **art gallery** (Tues–Sun 10am–4pm) next door puts on more palatable exhibitions.

It's worth asking around for the key to the Gothic church of **sv Katerína** which graces the bottom of the square, alongside the old Rathaus which still serves the town council. Lutheranism caught on fast in Slovakia during the Reformation, especially among the German communities, and one of the most impressive Lutheran churches in the country is the ochre and green bulk of the **Protestant Church** opposite the Rathaus, built shortly after the 1781 Edict of (Religious) Tolerance.

Up the steps from the Rathaus, the fifteenth-century walled **starý zámok**, the town's most important building, is likely to be closed for restoration for the fore-seeable future. It was built on the same lines as Kremnica's castle (see below), as the town's strong box as well as a fortified residence for the local bigwigs; its central church-turned-fortress testifies to the panic which beset the Hungarian Kingdom during the peak of Ottoman expansion in the sixteenth century.

Below the castle, Sládkovičova leads up to the seventeenth-century **klopačka** (May–Sept Tues–Sun 8am–3pm). Topped by a miner's weather vane, whose bells used to raise the miners early from their beds, this now houses a more palatable section of the mining museum. From here the road continues uphill to the red-brick Frauenberg Church and the portly Baroque **Piargska brána**, one of the town's former gateways that's now stranded out on the road to Levice, giving an indication of Banská Štiavnica's original size when it was the third largest town in the Hungarian kingdom. On a nearby hillock, the white **nový zámok** (May–Sept Tues–Sun 8am–4pm) – a turreted cross between a sugar lump and a lookout tower – was yet another attempt by the town to guard against a Turkish attack.

For the best view of Banská Štiavnica, head northeast, past the Academy of Mining and Forestry, to the copper-coloured hilltop church of **Štiavnica kalvária** (via the green-marked path). A succession of Baroque chapels marks the zigzag trail up the hill to the lower church, and on the summit the climactic uppermost chapel contains a gruesome, fantastical tableau of the crucifixion.

North to Kremnica

The aluminium works which stains and pollutes the whole basin around ŽIAR NAD HRONOM, 18km west of Zvolen, is the largest in the world, and goes some of the way to explain the country's lethal supply of all things aluminium – from knives and forks to sculptures and buildings. It's not a place to hang around in (unless you want to get premature senile dementia from the dust particles) – and it's a good idea to opt for the hour-long train journey from Zvolen to Kremnica, which skirts Žiar, rather than the bus which takes you into the town. The other bonus of the train ride is the view as the track switches back and forth through the hills, climbing over 1500 feet in just 14km, and depositing you above the town, about a kilometre southeast of the centre.

Kremnica

KREMNICA (Kremnitz) isn't really what you'd expect from a rich gold-mining town. Sitting in a half-hearted plateau, midway up the Rudnica valley, it's a modest town, little more than its duo of castle and square, and certainly no match for the wealth and beauty of Banská Štiavnica – though it attracts a lot more visitors thanks to the extra pull of its gold mint.

Founded by the Hungarian King Charles Robert in 1320, Kremnica's gold seams were once the richest in medieval Europe, keeping the Hungarian economy buoyant and booming throughout the Middle Ages. The thick walls and bastions which still surround the town and castle were built to protect what was effectively the Bank of Hungary – the royal mint. Yet the steeply pitched main square on which the mint stands is nothing more than a scruffy provincial village green, dotted with ornamental beech trees, park benches and a particularly ornate

plague column which, topped with a flash of gold, is the only obvious reference to the town's wealth. The tatty fortifications of the **castle complex** above the square are now overwhelmed by fruit orchards, and the hrad itself is almost wholly taken up by the late Gothic church of sv Katerína, once the castle's main tower. At present it's closed to the public, undergoing badly needed restoration.

Back on the square there's a **Museum of Coins and Medals** (Tues–Sat 7.30am–3.30pm) which has been attracting visitors from all around the world since 1890. From Stalin to Churchill, they've all had anniversary *Kremnitzerducats* minted for them in their time. As well as some exceptionally beautiful Renaissance coins, there's a whole room of paper money, which, during the First Republic, was an art in itself, with designs by top artists like Alfons Mucha and Max Švabinský. The mines still produce a small amount of gold, and the odd commemorative coin is sporadically struck at the **Štátná mincovňa** (State Mint; no admission) on the northwest corner of the square.

An unlikely accompaniment to the coin museum, the **Ski Museum** (Tues–Sat 7.30am–3.45pm) at the bottom of the square has a collection of antique skis, tins of dubbin and a whole range of ski memorabilia. You can **drink** alfresco at the café by the steps up to the castle, but unless you're camping south of the town, there's nowhere to stay the night in Kremnica.

Up the Turiec valley to Martin

From Kremnica, the railway climbs another 18km or so before hitting the mill-pond flatness of the Turiec valley. Having climbed this far, you might expect something more spectacular: but for the cool mountain air and the Veľká and Malá Fatra in the distance, you could be back down in the Danube basin.

Turčianske Teplice

TURČIANSKE TEPLICE is the first stop on the railway as it romps its way across the valley floor to Martin. A modern and uninspiring spa town despite its fourteenth-century origins, it boasts very hot natural springs and a striking Bedouin-blue bathhouse, the Modrý kúpeľ. Theoretically, you could use the spa as a base for exploring the Veľká Fatra (the yellow-marked path from the station heads off into the hills), but you'll have to fight for the cheap rooms at the *Vyšehrad*, the only hotel in town. Two kilometres north by train, at DIVIAKY, there's a campsite (June 15–Sept 15) across the river from the pink seventeenth-century country house (closed to the public).

Martin

A town of considerable historic importance for the Slovaks, **MARTIN** and its industrial baggage occupy the last seven kilometres of the banks of the River Turiec before it joins forces with the mighty Váh. Perhaps unfairly, it's best known nowadays for its *ZTS* engineering works, which has had a monopoly on Warsaw Pact tank-production since 1948, but which is now, on President Havel's insistence, trying desperately to transform itself into a non-military enterprise. Yet there's more to Martin than a five-minute drive through the town might suggest – the country's most encyclopaedic folk museum, a better than average

Slovak art gallery and an open-air folk village on the outskirts of the town. There's also the possibility of a day's hiking in the less frequented southern range of the Malá Fatra, the Lúčanksá Fatra.

Some history

Established back in the fourteenth century, Martin remained the extremely average town of Turčianský Svätý Martin until well into the nineteenth century. Then, in 1861, a group of Slovak intellectuals and clergy gathered here to draw up the **Martin Memorandum**, which declared boldly that the Slovaks "were as much a nation as the Magyars" and rather more humbly asked the Austrian Parliament to establish a North Hungarian Slovak District (which would remain an integral part of Hungary) with Slovak as the official language. Their demands caused outrage among the Magyars and were studiously ignored by the Austrians.

Nevertheless, a number of important Slovak institutions were founded in the town, of which by far the most important was the **Matica slovenská**, set up to promote the embryonic national culture through education, literature and the arts. It was short-lived. The infamous *Ausgleich* of 1867, which effectively gave the Hungarians a free hand in their half of the empire, ensured that all Slovak institutions of higher education were closed by the mid-1870s.

During the next forty long years of fanatical Magyarisation, Martin remained the spiritual centre of the Slovak nation, and on May 24, 1918, Slovak nationalists of all hues gathered for the last time at Martin to sign the **Martin Declaration**, throwing in their lot with the Czechs, and scuppering the Hungarians' various proposals for a "Greater Hungary". At this point Martin was still seriously under consideration as the potential Slovak capital: it was centrally located, less exposed to attack and infinitely more Slav than the Austro-Hungarian town of Pressburg (Bratislava), the other main contender. Having lost that final bid for fame, the town never really recaptured the limelight, though the Matica slovenská remains active.

HIKING IN THE VEĽKÁ FATRA

To the east of the Turiec valley lie the **Veľká Fatra**, a line of craggy mountain tops surrounded by a sea of uninhabited, undulating forest. The ridge of brittle limestone peaks from Krížná (1574m) to Ploská (1532m), via the highest of the lot, Ostredok (1592m), is the most obvious area to aim for, but the thin craggy valleys which lead up to the mountains are actually much more enthralling to walk along: the two most accessible and geologically exciting are the Gaderská dolina and the Blatnická dolina. The return trip along either, including ascending at least one of the big peaks, is a full day's hike (6–7hr), for which it's a good idea to get hold of a *Veľká Fatra* hiking map. Both valleys begin at **BLATNICA**, one of the most idyllic villages in the Turiec valley. Half-timbered cottages spread along both sides of the village stream, while at their centre, the local manor house is now a **museum** (Tues–Sun 8am–4pm) dedicated to the great grandfather of Czechoslovak photography, **Karol Plicka**, whose images of the Slovak countryside are reproduced in countless coffee-table books. The only accommodation is a **campsite** (June 15–Sept 15) 1km south of Blatnica, and even that can be packed out in the summer season.

Around the town

There's not much to choose aesthetically between what might nominally be called the old town in the south and the industrial estates to the north, but the sights – such as they are – are all located in the south. From the train station, Martin's modern chessboard street-plan becomes quickly apparent as you hit the first major crossroads, on which stands the **post office** and the restaurant, *Hotel Slovan*, along with the **Turčianske múzeum** (Tues–Fri 7.30am–4pm, Sat & Sun 1–6pm), paradise for your average botanist but of limited appeal to anyone else. Of more general interest are the **Martin Benka museum** (Tues–Sun 9am–4pm), round the corner in Kuzmányho, and the **Turčianska galéria** (Tues–Fri 9am–5pm, Sat 9am–noon), which together house a whole series of paintings by the purportedly seminal (though thoroughly second-rate) Benka, as well as interesting offerings from the likes of his (more talented) disciples Janko Alexy, Miloš Alexander Bazovský and Ľudovít Fulla.

Straight ahead, two or three blocks down Muzeálna, is the barracks-like mass of the **Slovak National Museum** (Tues–Sun 8am–5pm), which houses the country's Institute of Ethnography and one of the best and most extensive folk collections in the country. Richly decorated costumes from every region of Slovakia are displayed here, along with every folk artefact you might expect to find in an average Slovak village – exhaustive stuff. On the other side of the open-air amphitheatre is the **Národný cintorín**, which, in imitation of the Slavín cemetery in Prague, contains the graves of most of the leading Slovaks of the národné obrodenie. It's nothing like as impressive as the Slavín, not least because of the subdued artistry of the headstones which Lutheranism – the religion of most of those buried here – demanded. If you search hard enough, you'll find the graves of Andrej Kmeť, Janko Kráľ, Janko Jesensky, Martin Benka, Andrej Švehla, Karol Kuzmány and Svet Hurban-Vajanovsky, all leading nineteenth-century Slovak nationalists.

Neither the old nor the new buildings of the **Matica slovenská**, founded in 1863, are anything to get excited about, although the latter, which looks like a giant domestic radiator, is easily spotted to the north of the Slovak National Museum. Perhaps the most rewarding place to visit in Martin is the **folk skansen**, 2km south of town (bus #15, #41 or #56, then walk), which gives some idea of the kind of place Martin was during the nineteenth century. It's also one of the biggest open-air museums in the country (after Rožnov in North Moravia) and contains buildings from all over Slovakia.

Of the town's two **hotels**, only the cheap *Turiec* (☎0842-386 03) near the Catholic church is actually still a hotel. Alternatively, try the even cheaper *Podstráne* (☎0842-389 18) in the village of the same name (see below). The nearest **campsite** (May 15–Sept 15) is in the woods west of VRÚTKY, an old working-class (now high-rise) suburb of Martin with its own train station conveniently situated on the main line from Bratislava to the Tatras.

WALKING IN THE LÚČANSKÁ FATRA

The southern ridge of the Malá Fatra (see below), the **Lúčanská Fatra**, rises swiftly and dramatically from Martin's westernmost suburbs, making the town a possible base for ascending the five big bare peaks of the southern Malá Fatra. If you're staying in town, a chair lift (*lanovka*) from PODSTRÁNE, 3km west of town (bus #40), deposits you just over 1km below the highest peak, **Veľká lúka** (1476m). If you choose to walk, it'll take nearly four hours to reach the top, though perhaps only half that to walk the 10km north along the ridge to the ruins at Strečno (see below). If you're camping at VRÚTKY, Martin's northernmost suburb, the nearest peak is the northernmost summit of **Minčol** (1364m).

The Malá Fatra

The **Malá Fatra** are the first real mountains on the road from Bratislava, and one of the most popular and accessible of the Slovak ranges. Severed in two by the sweeping sabre-like meanderings of the Váh, the northern ridge is by far the most popular, having the highest peaks and the most spectacular valley, Vrátna dolina. The southern ridge, including the Lúčanská Fatra (see above), is less geographically pronounced and drifts rather vaguely southwestwards, but contains a couple of non-hiking attractions. Most people use **Žilina** as a base simply because it's on the main line from Bratislava, though in fact it's just too far from the mountains to be really convenient. Basically, if you're serious about hiking, you'll solve a lot of logistical problems by bringing a tent.

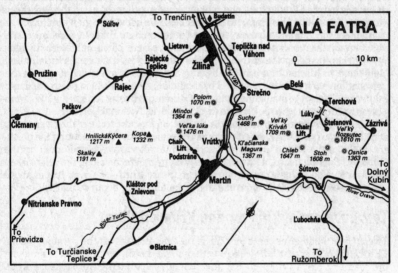

Žilina and around

The bile-green entrails of the train station at **ŽILINA** are no great introduction to the Slovak mountains, and now that the Museum of Friendship with the USSR has been closed down, the town itself has very little to offer. Not that this deters the crowds of coach parties, school kids and indigenous backpackers who throng the streets between the station and the old town to the west. Between the two is námestie SNP, unintentionally presided over by the back end of the Trinity church, with a low-key market and a gaggle of takeaway food outlets below, including some of the best *gofry* east of Prague. The old town's main square is actually quite pretty, arcaded for the most part, and dominated by the big yellow frontage of the Jesuit church. Next door, the old monastery has been converted into a relaxing exhibition space, **Považská galéria** (Tues–Fri 10am–5pm, Sat & Sun 11am–5pm) – unfortunately it's mostly given over to the sculpture of Rudolf Pribiš, whose sycophantic devotion to all things post-1948 ensured him a gallery of his own.

Accommodation

No one comes to Žilina to sightsee, but a lot of people end up staying here – so many in fact that it's not easy to get a cheap bed for the night in summer. The makeshift **hostel**, west of the old town, on Veľká Okružná, is in every way bottom of the pile, while ČEDOK, on the main square south of the old town, will help you with hotel vacancies, though they may fail to mention the cheapest of the lot, the *Dukla* on Dimitrovova (☎089-202 34). The *Metropol*, opposite the station (☎089-239 00) and the *Grand* on Sládkovičova 1 (☎089-210 56), both moderately priced, are also worth trying before resorting to expensive "international" hotels like the *Slovakia* (☎089-456 71).

Budatín and Strečno

On the right bank of the Váh (bus #22 or #30), the zámok of **Budatín** is a characteristically hybrid Slovak affair, now whitewashed over and housing the **Považské múzeum** (Tues–Sat 9am–5pm), which specialises in carved wooden furniture.

Infinitely more impressive are the fourteenth-century ruins of **Strečno** castle which crown the summit of a 200-foot cliff, 11km east of Žilina and fifteen minutes by train, commanding the entrance to the Váh valley as it squeezes through the Malá Fatra to Martin. You can climb up to the castle in a few minutes from the train station, but it remains obscured by scaffolding while it's being converted into a museum. Nearby is a monument to the **French partisans**, escaped POWs from a camp in Hungary, who took part in the 1944 Slovak National Uprising.

There's a **campsite** (July & Aug) in VARÍN, on the other side of the river: if you don't have your own transport, it's a more convenient base for ascending the northern peaks of the Malá Fatra than Vrátna dolina. Alternatively, you could try the *Chata pod Suchým* hostel, a two-kilometre walk from Strečno along the red-marked path via the Váh gorge's other ruined castle, **Starý hrad** – it's over 1000m above sea level, so expect a chilly night and don't count on there being vacancies.

Terchová and hiking around Vrátna dolina

Twenty-five kilometres east of Žilina, at the mouth of the Vrátna dolina, **TERCHOVÁ** is a neat little village with a cheap **hotel**, ten minutes' walk along the road to Zázrivá (☎089-951 85), and a handy supermarket for stocking up on provisions. It's also the birthplace of the Slovak folk hero **Juraj Jánošík** (see opposite), and a small **museum** (Tues–Sun 8am–4pm) draws links between Jánošík and the partisans who took part in the 1944 uprising. All the texts are in Slovak, but there's enough local folk art to keep you going throughout, not to mention Jánošík's celebrated brass-studded belt (thought to bring good luck) and jaunty hat. On the low hill overlooking the town stands a giant futuristic aluminium statue of the man himself, one of the many mass-produced in the region.

The **Vrátna dolina** actually owes its winsome reputation to the gritty cliffs of **Tiesňavy**, the sharp-edged defile which acts as the gateway to the valley. The occasional bus goes this way from Terchová, or it's a gentle twenty-minute walk. After such a dramatic overture the valley itself is surprisingly sheltered and calm. A short distance away is LÚKY, a major ski resort in winter and a justifiably popular **campsite** in summer, set against a scenic backdrop of thickly forested hilltops. The valley forks in two just before Lúky with most people heading south for the **chair lift** 3km away (get there early to avoid the worst of the queues), which takes you to Snilovské sedlo, a high saddle between **Veľký Kriváň** (1709m), the highest peak, and **Chleb** (1647m). The views are fantastic from either of the summits, but the coachloads of day-trippers who make it up here can be a bit overwhelming. Basically, the further you get from the chair lift, the more you'll lose the crowds. If you're out for the day from Žilina, you could descend Chleb's southern face, tracking the blue-marked path which runs via the Šútovský vodopád (waterfall) to ŠÚTOVO, fifty minutes by train from Žilina. Otherwise it's over six hours across the peaks to Strečno (see above).

In many ways a preferable alternative to the congestion of the chair lift and the peaks around Chleb is to turn left at the Vrátna dolina fork to ŠTEFANOVÁ (2km) which lies under the shadow of **Veľký Rozsutec** (1610m), whose sharply pointed rocky summit is arguably the most satisfying to climb. Follow the yellow-marked path to Podžiar, where you should change to the blue path up **Horné Diery**, an idyllic wet ravine which has to be traversed using ladders and steps. The ravine ends up at sedlo Medzirozsutce, the saddle between Malý and Veľký Rozsutec. Ascent takes around four hours, the descent via sedlo Medziholie about half that. For **accommodation**, try the cheap *Chata Vrátna* by the chair lift; but you stand a better chance of a room at the less reasonable but more luxurious *Hotel Boboty* (☎089-952 27), halfway down the road to Štefonová.

JÁNOŠÍK

Juraj Jánošík (1688–1713) is the most famous of the many Robin Hood figures who form an integral part of the songs and folklore of the Slovak mountain regions. Most originate from the turn of the seventeenth century when the central authority of the Habsburgs was at a weak point, worn down by the threat of Turkish invasion. Like many of the rural youth of his generation, Jánošík joined up with the anti-Habsburg army of the Hungarian rebel Ferenc Rákóczi II in 1703. When they were finally defeated by the Austrian Imperial forces at Trenčín in 1711, large numbers fled into the hills to continue the fight from there. Jánošík, however, opted for the priesthood and left for Kežmarok to complete his religious training. While he was away, his mother fell ill and died, and his father – who had absconded from work in order to build a coffin for her burial – was given a hundred lashes, which proved fatal for the old man.

Both parents dead, Jánošík finally took to the hills and gathered round him the obligatory band of merry men, indulging in the usual deeds of wealth redistribution. Sadly – though this too is typical of Slovak folklore – the crucial difference between Robin Hood and characters like Jánošík is that the latter nearly always come to a sticky end. In March 1713 Jánošík was captured by the lords of Liptov and sentenced to death in the central square of Liptovský Svätý Mikuláš, where he was hung by the ribcage.

It's impossible to overestimate the importance of Jánošík to both the oral and written Slovak literary tradition. More poems, novels and plays have been inspired by his exploits than by any other episode in Slovak history – except perhaps the Slovak National Uprising.

South of Žilina

Just south of Žilina, the cement works of LIETAVSKÁ LÚČKA coat the valley with a grey-white dust, before a bend in the River Rajčanka brings you into the verdant wooded spa town of **RAJECKÉ TEPLICE**, thirty minutes by train from

Žilina. Two hotels, two beautifully placed campsites – one in town and another 3km back along the valley – and a couple of thermal swimming pools make this a convenient base for a series of day **hikes** in the surrounding hills.

The most obvious is across the valley via the early twentieth-century zámok of **Kunerad** (closed to the public) and up Veľká lúka (1476m), which overlooks Martin and the Turiec valley. The blue-marked path is an alternative route back to the spa, and the whole trip is a full day's walking. A more leisurely afternoon's hike north along the green-marked path from the station takes you to the ruined castle of **Lietava**, a shade less spectacular than Strečno but still an impressive pile, some 300 feet above the village of the same name. The most popular destination, though, is across the hills to the **Súľovské skaly** (3hr on the yellow-marked path via ZBYŇOV), a "rock city" made up of contorted slabs of limestone, with the ruined castle of Súľov at its centre.

Čičmany

ČIČMANY is probably one of the most hyped villages in the whole of Slovakia, and with good reason. Lying in a wide, gently undulating valley, it's a Slovak village *par excellence*: a cluster of typical wooden cottages-cum-farms haphazardly strewn about the banks of the River Rajčanka, which at this point is little more than a mountain stream. What makes Čičmany special is the unique local tradition of **house-painting**. Each cottage is smothered in a simple, largely abstract decorative mantle of white snowflakes, flowers and crisscrosses, a feature entirely confined to the isolated Čičmany region. Electricity, telephone cables and the odd tractor are the only signs of modernity – as yet there aren't even any souvenir shops. Occasional tour groups break the spell, but even they don't stay for long, especially since the folk museum has been undergoing a major rebuild. The disadvantage with Čičmany's isolated position is its inaccessibility, with only infrequent **buses** covering the 38km from Žilina. You could try hitching, although the traffic is pretty light, especially on the last 7km from the main road. Somewhat remarkably there's a **hotel** in the village, the cheap *Kaštieľ*, should you make it out here.

The Orava region

Despite its wonderful mountainous backdrop and winding river valley, the **Orava region** that lies northeast of the Malá Fatra and flush with the Polish border is generally fairly bleak. For centuries it remained an impoverished rural backwater on the main road to Poland, so poor that when the Lithuanian army marched through in 1683 en route to Vienna, they burned most of the villages to the ground (including the former capital of Veličná) in disgust at the lack of provisions. Emigration to America was widespread throughout the late nineteenth and early twentieth century, and only after World War II was industry hastily foisted onto the region in an attempt to save it from extinction. As a consequence, the towns are short on excitement and long on eyesores, but the artificial **lake** to the north is recommended if you want to get some relatively clean swimming, and the **Western Tatras** provide a uniquely unspoilt alpine experience.

Accommodation can be a problem, so it's worth booking ahead from Dolný Kubín, the largest town in the region. Transport relies heavily on the branch line which stretches the length of the Orava valley from Kraľovany on the Váh to Trstená by the Polish border; elsewhere you're dependent on buses or hitching.

Istebné, Dolný Kubín and Orava castle

As an introduction to the Orava valley, the giant alloy plant and its attendant quarry at **ISTEBNÉ** (20min by train from Kraľovany) leave a lot to be desired. Until a few years ago, the level of dust in the atmosphere was intolerable, regularly blackening the skies over the valley at midday. Only in the mid-1980s, when the local population threatened to move out en masse, were dust separators finally fitted onto the factory chimneys. Miraculously, the pre-industrial settlement still exists, tucked into the hills to the north, fifteen minutes' walk from the bus and train station. Among its few remaining wooden buildings, it boasts a **wooden Lutheran church** with a richly patterned interior, one of only four in the country, built in 1686 on slightly raised ground above the village.

DOLNÝ KUBÍN, the regional capital, is not much better. True, its hilly locale is faultless and manages to lend a kind of surreal beauty to the gleaming white high-rise blocks which house most of the town's residents, but apart from the dull museum dedicated to the mild-mannered "father of Slovak poetry", Pavol Országh Hviezdoslav (1849–1921) who was born in nearby Vyšný Kubín, the only reason to stop here is to book some accommodation for further up the valley at the local ČEDOK office.

Eleven kilometres upstream from Dolný Kubín by train, **Orava Castle** (May, Sept & Oct 8am–4.30pm; June–Aug 8am–6pm; closed Mon) is one of Slovakia's truly spectacular cliff-top sights. Perched like an eyrie more than 100m above the village of ORAVSKÝ PODZÁMOK (literally "Below Orava Castle"), it's an impressive testament to the region's feudal past. Whoever occupied Orava castle held sway over the entire region and made a fortune taxing the peasants and milking the trade into Poland. Before you get suckered into signing up for a tour, though, be warned that it takes over an hour and a half and that there have to be at least 25 people outside the gates to coax the guides into action. If you do get inside, you'll be treated to hearty dollops of medieval kitchenware, instruments of feudal justice and wood-panelled dining halls. If you're unsuccessful, content yourself with the **mini-museum** of local artefacts down in the village and – with no accommodation available – head on up the valley.

Into the Western Tatras

At **PODBIEL**, thirty minutes by train from Oravský Podzámok, a collection of traditional wooden cottages has been converted into tourist accommodation. You could turn up at the *recepcia* at no. 101 during office hours just on the off chance, but it's better to try and book in advance from ČEDOK in Dolný Kubín. Quite frankly, you'll be lucky to get in there before the tour groups. In any case, the only reason to stop at Podbiel is to hitch, walk or catch one of the very few local buses going east up Studená dolina, the valley which leads to the Western Tatras, impressively arrayed on the horizon.

Thirteen kilometres east up the Studená dolina, just after ZUBEREC, lies the **Orava village museum** (Jan–April Mon–Fri 8am–3pm; May–Oct Tues–Sun 8am–4pm), a skansen of about twenty traditional wooden buildings from the surrounding areas, including a fifteenth-century **wooden church** from Zábrež, one of the few to escape the pillaging of the local Protestants. Its barn-like exterior gives no indication of the exuberant folk panel paintings inside, dating from the building's construction. Officially you're supposed to go round only with a guide, for which there must be at least fifteen visitors ready and waiting, but you could try pleading that you've come a long way – most countries seem exotically far away from Orava.

The Western Tatras

With the High Tatras increasingly reaching saturation point during most of the climbing season, the **Western Tatras** (Západné Tatry) present themselves as a refreshingly undeveloped alternative. They boast the same dog-tooth peaks and hand-mirror lakes, but with half the number of climbers. Unless you've managed to pre-book from Dolný Kubín, you'll find most of the *chata* or chalet-cum-hostels – the only accommodation in the Roháčska dolina – full up. The only alternative is to pick a discreet spot to pitch your tent in the neighbouring forests or make your base at **ORAVICE**, the only official **campsite** (July & Aug) on this side of the mountains. The main problem is getting to Oravice, which either means catching one of the few buses from TRSTENÁ (the last station on the Orava railway line) or walking 7km from the Orava village museum. Whatever you do, don't let the logistics get you down – you'll encounter the same problems in the other parts of the Tatras. More importantly, get hold of the *Orava* or better still the *Západné Tatry – Roháče* hiking map, plus the requisite camping gear and you'll have a smooth trip. Don't, however, undertake any mountain climbing if you've no experience, and always get a weather check before you start on a long walk which goes above 1500m. For more **information** on hiking and climbing, and important **safety hints**, see p.320.

HIKING ROUTES IN THE WESTERN TATRAS

From **Oravice**, two main trails cover the 6km to the Polish border of which the blue-marked one is the gentler. After a couple of very flat kilometres, a yellow path leads off to the right to **Osobitá** (1687m), a two- to three-hour climb from Oravice which gives a sweeping vista of the Western Tatras, weather permitting. Previously, walkers from the West had to avoid the path along the border, but these restrictions are likely to have been dropped by the time you read this. That being the case, once you reach the border, follow the blue-marked path up onto the ridge between the two countries which climbs up to **Volovec** (2063m) and **Ostrý Roháč** (2084m), 1km from the border. It could easily take four hours to reach the more spectacular scenery around Volovec, which makes a return trip a full day's hike. If you're carrying a pack, it's possible to drop down on the blue-marked path to the twin tarns of Jamnicke plesá and then continue for 8km to the Račková dolina **campsite** (May–Oct) or a little further to the *Esperanto* **hotel** in PRIBYLINA, probably the quickest way there is of approaching the High Tatras from the Orava region.

From **Roháčska dolina**, everything happens much more quickly. As you head down the valley the brooding grey peaks begin to gather round and by the end of the road (8km from the skansen; 3km from the final car park) it's only a steep kilometre-long walk on the green path to the still, glacial waters of **Roháčske plesá**, hemmed in by the Tatras' steep scree-ridden slopes. A punishing 2.5km (reckon on about 2hr) along the blue path leads to the Smutne sedlo ("Sad saddle"– sad because it's the mountain's cold north face) which lies on the main Roháč ridge. Ostrý Roháč is less than an hour to the east, while **Baníkov** (2178m) is the same distance west, but the king of the lot, **Baranec** (2184m), lies a good two hours' walk to the south.

Around Lake Orava

Back at Podbiel, the rail line continues to the village of **TVRDOŠÍN**, which boasts a fifteenth-century wooden church containing some fantastic primitive altar paintings that are contemporary with the building of the church itself. The last stop on the line is **TRSTENÁ**, 6km from the Polish border, which has two cheap hotels; if you're moving on to Poland, there's enough traffic to make hitching feasible.

What was once the Orava plain became **Lake Orava** in 1954 when five villages were submerged by the damming of the river. The wooded western shore has a fair smattering of *chata* settlements and two **campsites** (June 15–Sept 15). One of the lost villages, **SLANICA**, was the birthplace of one of the early pioneers of the Slovak language, the Catholic priest Anton Bernolák (1762–1813). Only the village church, hidden in the trees, still peeps its head above water, and has been converted into a museum of folk art and ceramics as well as a memorial to Bernolák. To reach it, take the boat from either campsite, or from NÁMESTOVO, the big new town to the far west of the lake (and thankfully out of sight from the main recreational area).

The Liptov region

The **Liptov region**, which lies to the south of the Orava region and the Western Tatras, offers a similar cocktail of traditional Slovak villages, obsolete heavy industry and a backdrop of spectacular mountains. **Ružomberok**, the first town you come to, at another T-junction on the River Váh, offers very little except accommodation, access to the beautiful Revúcka dolina and another stab at the Veľká Fatra. East of Ružomberok, the Váh valley widens into a vast plain, now partially flooded, whose main town, **Liptovský Mikuláš**, is similarly uninspiring but is best placed for exploring the Low Tatras.

As in the Orava, the traditional way of life in these parts has disappeared over the last two generations. But while few mourn the demise of subsistence farming as a way of life, more lament the fact that it was destroyed by forced collectivisation and industrialisation. Some things survive – the patchwork fields and terraces, the long timbered cottages, and of course the mountains – but give it a few more decades and the songs, dances and costumes will be of historical and folkloristic interest only.

Ružomberok and around

RUŽOMBEROK, like so many big towns on the Váh, has zero potential. The smell of synthetic fabrics wafts across its ungainly streets, splayed in an ungainly fashion around a central half-hill. Aside from the **Ľudovít Fulla Gallery** on Májekova (Tues–Sun 9am–5pm), devoted to Ružomberok's talented painter of the same name, the parish church is the place to head, pleasantly aloof from the rest of town. Before the war, the local priest was **Andrej Hlinka** (see below), spiritual leader of Slovak separatism, about whom the new officialdom is still ambivalent – as yet there's still no mention of him here.

ANDREJ HLINKA

Born in the neighbouring village of Černová in 1864, **Andrej Hlinka** served most of his life as a Catholic pastor of Ružomberok. He became a national martyr in 1906 when he was arrested by the Hungarian authorities and sentenced to two years' imprisonment for "incitement against the Magyar nationality", topped up by another eighteen months for "further incitement" in his inflammatory farewell address to the local parishioners.

Although at the time still in prison, he was also viewed by the authorities as the prime mover behind the peaceful demonstration of October 27, 1907, popularly known as the **Černová Massacre**, the "Bloody Sunday" of Hungarian rule in Slovakia. When the local Slovaks protested against the consecration of their church by a strongly pro-Magyar priest, the Hungarian police opened fire on the crowd, killing fifteen people and wounding countless others.

Not long after the foundation of Czechoslovakia in 1918, he began campaigning for Slovak independence and, having travelled to Paris on a false Polish passport to press the point at the Versaille Peace Conference, wound up in a Czechoslovak prison for his pains. He was only released after having been elected leader of the newly founded **Ľudová strana** (People's Party), strongly Catholic, vehemently nationalistic and the largest single party in Slovakia between the wars. While by no means openly fascistic, its slogan "Slovakia for the Slovaks" by implication excluded the Jews, Gypsies, Hungarians and Rusyns who made up much of Slovakia's population. His death in August 1938 was the only thing that saved him from the ignominy of participating in the Nazi puppet government, although his name lived on posthumously in the **Hlinka Guards**, Slovak equivalent of the SS. Jozef Tiso, Hlinka's successor, went on to become the Slovak Quisling, and was eventually executed as a war criminal in 1947.

Since November 1989, Slovak nationalists have launched a campaign to rehabilitate Hlinka, Tiso and company. An alarming number of Slovaks are very much in sympathy with such moves, and a plaque commemorating Hlinka was successfully unveiled in Černová. Similarly in August 1990, thousands of people turned up for a whole weekend of Hlinka celebrations held in Ružomberok.

Practicalities

The **train station** is northwest of the town centre, on the other side of the River Váh (bus #1 or #8). **Cheap rooms** are available at the *Liptov* (☎0848-225 09) and the only other downtown hotel, the *Kultúrny dom* (☎0848-224 19) – both situated on the main drag through town (as is *ČEDOK*). If you want to stay in either of the two out-of-town (and up in the hills) hotels it's best to book through *ČEDOK* to save a wasted journey. Take bus #3 or #4 from the town centre, both of which run regularly to the moderately expensive *Hotel Hrabovo* (☎0848-267 27), Ružomberok's poshest hotel, which has a grassy banked lake in which to swim. Behind it, on the hour, a four-seater cable car will take you to *Hotel Malina* (☎0848-250 70), a cheaper option with an even better view (and a swimming pool).

Short hikes around Ružomberok

One of the few redeeming features of Ružomberok is its proximity to the surrounding hills and villages. It's only a three-kilometre walk to the conic peak of **Sidorovo** (1099m) or 5km to **Malinné** (1209m), both of which are accessible via the cable car behind *Hotel Hrabovo*, and guarantee extensive panoramas over the Váh and Revúca valleys. Dropping down off the fell on the south side, head for the ribbon village of **VLKOLÍNEC**, set in a peaceful shallow valley south of Ružomberok (also reachable by bus #2 or #7 from Ružomberok to Biely Potok, then a 2-km walk). This is one of the best environments in which to see Liptov wooden folk architecture, though as ever there's a note of melancholy about the place. It was badly damaged by the Nazis in September 1944 in retaliation for the Slovak National Uprising, but those cottages that remain now form a natural skansen of timber structures.

With your own transport, you could explore the villages east of Ružomberok, starting with **ĽUDROVÁ**, 5km southeast, a beautiful village in its own right, but one whose white stone church has now been converted into a museum of Gothic art (you'll have to ask around for the key). The whitewashed manor house at nearby **LIPTOVSKÁ STIAVNIČKA**, though closed to the public, is also worth a look for its shingled turrets and onion domes. Five kilometres east, the **SLIAČE** villages – Nižný, Stredný and Vyšný – are also well known for their excellent folk architecture.

Liptovský Mikuláš and around

As in Orava, the broad sweep of the main Liptov plain east of Ružomberok has been turned, for the most part, into a vast lake, whose shoreline is too flat to scrape the label picturesque. Quite why it deserves the title Liptovská Mara (Liptov Sea) while the one in Orava is simply a lake remains a linguistic mystery, but a similar number of villages bit the dust in the name of "progess". On its easternmost edge sits **LIPTOVSKÝ MIKULÁŠ**, which, like Martin and Ružomberok, once played a part in the Slovak national revival or národné obrodenie, but has since fallen on more mundane times. Nowadays, it's really only worth coming here if you're intending to explore the Low Tatras.

The first rumblings of the Slovak národné obrodenie in Liptovský Mikuláš occurred in the late 1820s when a Slovak reading room was founded, followed much later by the *Tatrín* literary society established by the Lutheran pastor Michal Miloslav Hodža, one of the leading lights of 1848. Hodža's house at Tranovského 8 is now a not terribly enthralling **museum** (Tues–Fri 9am–noon & 1–4pm), which also touches on the events of May 10, 1848, in Mikuláš, when in response to the Hungarian uprising against the Habsburgs various leading Slovaks published the "Demands of the Slovak Nation" and quickly fled the country to avoid arrest.

A slightly better taste of the literary milieu of nineteenth-century Mikuláš can be had at the **Janko Kráľ Museum** (Tues–Fri 8.30am–3.30pm, Sat & Sun 9am–noon), housed in a Baroque building on the main square (the same one in which Jánošík was sentenced to death in 1713). Local boy Kráľ was the foremost Slovak poet of the Romantic movement, "a lawyer who preferred the company of shepherds", or the Slovak Lord Byron as some would have it. Needless to say he was a fervent nationalist, and only just escaped being executed for his beliefs in 1848.

At **PALÚDZKA**, a kilometre west of the town centre (bus #2 or #7 from Štúrova), is the largest wooden church in the whole of Slovakia, a big barn-like Lutheran structure, comfortably seating over two thousand worshippers, and as such worth the effort of tracking down the key. While you're in the area, you might as well cross the road to the **Jánošíkovo väzenie** (Jánošík's dungeon; Tues–Fri 9am–noon & 1–4pm) in the nearby *kaštieľ* (manor house) where the rebel hero was held before his public execution on Mikuláš's main square.

Accommodation

The **bus** and **train stations** are next door to each other, a ten-minute walk from the town centre (or any bus except #5 or #7). *ČEDOK*, on the main square, will only readily book you into the multistorey *Jánošík* (☎0849-227 26) by the river on Jánošíkovo nábrežie, the *Bystrina* (☎0849-221 83), 5km south at the mouth of the Demänová dolina (bus #5 then walk or take the *ČSAD* bus), or the slightly cheaper *Európa*, Štúrova 15 (☎0849-227 13). If you can't get in at any of those, you'll be lucky to get a look in further down the price scale – but try the *Kriváň*, Štúrova 5 (☎0849-224 15), or the *Lodenica*, nábrežie Janka Kráľa 8 (☎0849-223 49). The nearest **campsite** is the lakeside site at LIPTOVSKÝ TRNOVEC (20min by bus; June 15–Sept 15) on the northern shores of the Liptovská Mara, but if you're aiming to hike in the Low Tatras, you'd be better off at PODTUREŇ, 8km east (10min by train), or the Demänová site (mid-May to Sept) by the *Bystrina* (see above).

Východná and Važec

The annual **Slovak folk festival** held at the end of July in VÝCHODNÁ, 15km east of Liptovský Mikuláš and thirty minutes by train, is in every way equal to Strážnice's international affair (see p.233), attracting groups from every region of Slovakia. There's no accommodation in the village (a pleasant two-kilometre hike north from the station), but during the festival most people just crash out in the haylofts and barns of the local farmers (ask first). At any other time of the year, it's a modest little village whose succession of zigzag wooden gables is its only distinctive feature. VAŽEC, one stop further on, once renowned for being one of the most beautiful villages in Slovakia and built almost entirely from wood, without a brick or nail in sight, was destroyed by a catastrophic fire in 1931. Luckily, it was also a photographers' dream and you can get an impression of how things used to be from the small exhibition in the village **folk museum**. The purpose of most people's visit, though, is the **Važecká jaskyňa** (daily April–May 15 & Sept 15–Oct tours at 9am, 11am and 2pm; May 15–Sept 15 hourly 9am–4pm; closed Mon), a limestone cave system discovered back in the 1920s but only recently opened to the public. To get to the cave from the train station, walk to the other side of the village; to get to the *Hotel Važec*, continue for another 500m.

The Low Tatras

The impact of the **Low Tatras'** rounded peaks is nothing like as immediate as the sharp craggy outline of the High Tatras visible on the northern horizon. But they do constitute a more extensive range, in parts much wilder and less explored. The crudest development has gone on either side of the two tallest central mountains, **Chopok** and **Ďumbier**, but, particularly to the east, the crowds thin and – with the aid of a *Nízke Tatry* map – the countryside is yours for the taking. If you're not planning on doing anything so strenuous as hiking, you could happily spend a day or two visiting some of the caves in Demänovská dolina, swimming at the foot of the mountains at Tále or simply riding the chair lift to the top of Chopok and effortlessly soaking up the view.

On the practical front, **accommodation** really is a major problem, and it's worth planning ahead, either by booking in advance where possible, or at the

very least bringing your own tent. **Transport** is less problematic, with two railway lines serving the Váh and Hron valleys and buses taking you the rest of the
way into the mountains: of course, to get the most out of the region, you'll need to
walk – preferably armed with the map mentioned above and a stout pair of walking boots.

Demänovská dolina and the caves

Extremely overloaded buses wend their way fairly regularly up **Demänovská
dolina**, by far the most popular valley on the north side of the mountains. As
soon as you enter the narrow, forested part of the valley, signs point off to the left
to the **Demänovská ľadová jaskyňa** (May 16–Sept 15 Tues–Sun 9am–4pm), one
of Slovakia's two "ice caves". After a sweaty fifteen-minute walk up through the
woods to the entrance, it's an extremely chilly thirty-minute guided tour through
the cave. The first part leads through a vast hall-like chamber of mini-stalactites
and stalagmites, its walls covered in eighteenth-century graffiti testifying to the
early discovery of the caves. The second part descends into the claustrophobic
ice chamber, where the temperature even in summer is well below zero. Best
time to visit, though, is in the spring, when the ice formations are at their best,
creating huge stalactites of frozen water which drip down onto a massive frozen
lake. Two kilometres further on, signs indicate the **Demänovská jaskyňa
Slobody** (daily May 16–Sept 15 8am–4pm; Sept 16–May 15 tours at 9am, 11am &
2pm; closed Mon), used for storage by frostbitten partisans during World War II
– hence its name, "Cave of Freedom". It's an iceless cave (though no less freezing), much larger and more impressive than Demänovská ľadová jaskyňa when it
comes to the variety of rock formations.

A little further on, the road swings violently to the right and begins to climb
steeply for about 1.5km until it reaches **JASNÁ**, a major ski resort for this part of
the world, with sundry chair and ski lifts, as well as a smattering of (invariably
full) hotels, from the very reasonable *CKM Juniorhotel* (☎0849-915 71) to the
expensive *Družba*, and *Liptov* (☎0849 915 05); try enquiring about vacancies at
ČEDOK in Liptovský Mikuláš. It's also worth knowing that non-guests can use
the *Liptov*'s sauna. As for food, the *Tri domčeky*, by the main car park, offering
trout, and garlic soup, is probably the least pretentious option.

HIKING AROUND CHOPOK

Most people start walking from **Chopok** (2024m), the second highest peak in the
range, reached by two consecutive (and extremely popular) chair lifts from Jasná
(closed May, Oct & Nov). It's about two hours across the bare fell to the top of
Ďumbier (2043m), king of the Low Tatras and the easternmost limit of this central
ridge. From Ďumbier, it's five hours for each of the following routes: via Krupova
hoľa, back down the yellow-marked path to the campsite at the bottom of
Demänovská dolina; down Jánska dolina on the blue-marked path to the campsite
in Podtureň or further east to the campsite at MALUŽINÁ (turn right either at
sedlo Javorie or Pred Bystrou). Westwards, it's about five hours along the ridge to
the isolated hamlet of MAGURKA which has a *chata* but no official campsite; otherwise it's a good ten-hours' walk to the campsite and hotel at DONOVALY, at the top
of the pass from Banská Bystrica over to Ružomberok.

Approaching from the south

If you're coming from Banská Bystrica and the Hron valley, you'll end up approaching the Low Tatras from the south. The Hron valley up to BREZNO has been marred by industry, and the latter only has its three cheap hotels to recommend it. The main approach to Chopok from this side is via **Bystrá dolina**, the flip-side valley of Demänovská dolina. At its base, by the neat village of BYSTRÁ (5-km walk or bus from Podbrezová station), are the **Bystrianska jaskyňa** (daily May 16–Sept 15 9am–4pm; April–May 15 & Sept 16–Oct tours at 9am, 11am & 2pm; closed Mon), the only underground cave system on offer on this side. Two and a half kilometres up the valley is the main area of development known as **TÁLE**. There's a fully equipped campsite with a swimming pool (mid-May to Sept), a motel (☎0867-951 91) and a pricey hotel called the *Partizán* (☎0867-951 31). Buses will drop you (and a whole load of others) outside the moderate *Hotel Srdiečko* (☎0867-951 21) and the more expensive *Trangoška* (☎0867-951 30) at the end of the valley. From here, a chair lift rises in two stages to the top of Chopok, stopping just outside the moderately expensive *Hotel Kosodrevina* (☎0867-951 05). Whether you can afford any of the above hotels is academic unless you've **booked in advance** from *ČEDOK* in Banská Bystrica. If you're walking from Tále to the main ridge, it'll take you three to four hours along the yellow-marked path to the top of **Dereše** (2003m).

The eastern peaks

East of the central Chopok ridge, the real wilderness begins. The peaks are even less pronounced and rarely raise their heads above the turbulent sea of forest where Slovakia's last remaining wild bears, lynx and chamois hide out. Meanwhile, the villages in the Hron valley – which forms the southern watershed of the Low Tatras – are still stuck in the torpor of another era, and offer an insight into Slovak folk culture, though, naturally enough, virtually nothing in the way of conventional tourist facilities. If this has already whetted your appetite, the best thing to do is book rooms through *ČEDOK* at Banská Bystrica – or pack a tent and provisions and start walking.

The railway which climbs the Hron valley is one of the most scenic in the whole country, and if you pick the right train you can travel from Banská Bystrica through the Slovenský raj, finally coming to a halt at Košice, in three to four hours. The slower trains take significantly longer, stopping at even the most obscure villages, such as **HEĽPA** (1hr by slow train from Brezno), whose attractions include a cheap hotel and pristinely preserved folk architecture. To get the magnificent view from the top of **Veľká Vápenica** (1691m), follow either the yellow- or the blue-marked tracks from the station (2–3hr). One stop further on, **POHORELÁ** is similarly well endowed (though minus the hotel) and lies on the footpath to the next peak along, **Andrejcová** (1519m). The one and only campsite in the region is close by the next station on the line, Pohorelská Maša, but camping rough in the hills (though officially discouraged) is unlikely to cause any problems.

A lot of the slower trains pause for breath at ČERVENÁ SKALA, not a bad place from which to start one of the **best hikes** of the eastern range. Take the road to the village of ŠUMIAC, which looks like it's been plucked straight out of another century; then follow the blue-marked path up to **Kráľova hoľa** (1948m), the biggest bare-topped mountain east of Ďumbier. It's another three hours to **LIPTOVSKÁ TEPLIČKA**, one of the most fascinating and isolated communities in the Slovak mountains. You might be able to stay at the *turistická ubytovna* (☎092-925 30) but, failing that buses run to ŠTRBA, SVIT and POPRAD. If you want to remain in the Hron valley, there's the moderate *Telgárt* hotel in ŠVERMOVO (4km from Kráľova hoľa) where the railway doubles back on itself before climbing to its highest point (999m) shortly before Vernár station, on the edge of the Slovenský raj (see p.331).

The High Tatras

Rising like a giant granite reef above the patchwork Poprad plain, the **High Tatras** are for many people the main reason for venturing this far into Slovakia. Yet even after all the tourist board hype, they are still an incredible, inspirational sight – sublime, spectacular, saw-toothed and brooding. A wilderness, however, they are not. All summer, visitors are shoulder to shoulder in the necklace of resorts which sit at the foot of the mountains, and things don't get that much better if you take to the hills. The crux of the problem lies in the scale of the range, a mere 25km from east to west, some of which is shared with the equally eager Poles, the rest of which is out of reach to all but the most experienced climber. Part of the problem, though, is the saturation tactics of the tour operators, a logical extension of the region's overdevelopment. Yet when all's said and done, once you're above the tree line, surrounded by bare primaeval scree slopes and icy blue tarns, nothing can take away the exhilarating feeling of being on top of the world.

Arriving and practicalities

Most fast trains to the Tatras arrive at the **main train station** in Poprad (Poprad-Tatry), which is adjacent to the **bus station**. Unless you're staying in Poprad (for which see overleaf), take one of the little red electric trains (which connect all the main resorts), whose platforms are hidden round the corner, to STARÝ SMOKOVEC, the central resort whose *ČEDOK* office deals with all accommodation and information. From Poprad's tiny **airport**, west of the town (bus #12 or *ČSA* bus), there's just one flight a day to and from Prague via Bratislava – obviously a great deal more expensive than the train and heavily booked up during the summer (make your reservation at the *ČSA* office next door to the *Gerlach* hotel).

Accommodation in the High Tatras

Sorting out **accommodation** immediately is a priority at whatever time of the year you arrive, since finding anywhere to stay can be extremely difficult. The cheapest and most reliable option (providing the weather is warm enough) is **camping**, though having said that, the big swanky international sites are among the most expensive in the country. The best of the dear ones is the *Tatracamp pod lesom* (mid-May to Sept) in DOLNÝ SMOKOVEC (get off at Pod lesom station), with bungalows, hot showers and kitchen facilities. The two camps – *Eurocamp FICC* (open all year) and *Športcamp* (June 15–Sept 15) – just south of

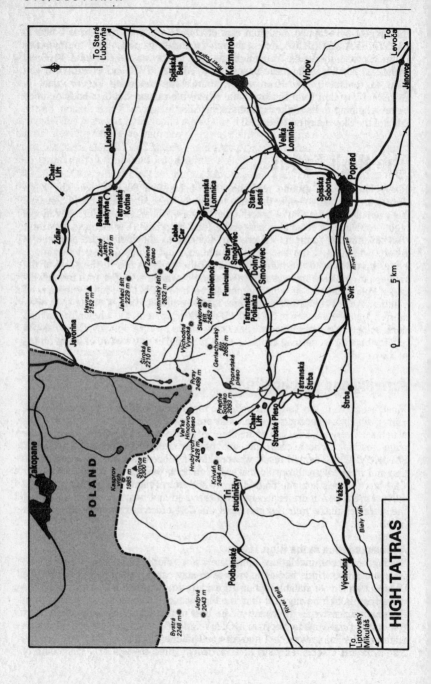

HIGH TATRAS

TATRANSKÁ LOMNICA (get off at Tatranská Lomnica-Eurocamp FICC station), are similarly priced but don't offer kitchen facilities, just takeaway roast trout instead. The TATRANSKÁ ŠTRBA site is the grottiest of the lot (May–Sept), while the cheapest and most basic is 1km south of STARÁ LESNÁ (June 15–Sept 15). If you have your own transport the *Šarpanec* site (May 15–Oct 15) is relatively secluded and, to the east, the VRBOV site (June–Sept) has many unforeseen advantages (see "The Spiš region", p.325).

As far as **hotels** are concerned, if you haven't booked in advance, you'll have to simply take what's on offer (within reason) – you may even find yourself farmed out to towns like Kežmarok (no bad thing – see p.325). *ČEDOK* near the main train station in Starý Smokovec deals with **all hotel bookings** in the Tatras, and if they're not yet offering to book private rooms for visitors, there are a growing number of *Zimmer Frei* (Rooms to Rent) signs in the area. If you're booking from abroad and want something cheap, try the *Bystrina* (☎0969-26 18) or, for something a bit more special (and a lot more expensive), the *Grandhotel*, both in Starý Smokovec (☎0969-21 54). The easiest thing to do, of course, is to stay a little further away from the mountains in Poprad (see below) where demand is much lower.

The situation with **hostels** is pretty much the same. *Juniorhotel CKM* (☎0969-26 61) in Horný Smokovec is (nominally) the region's *YHA* hostel, and theoretically very cheap for members. In reality, you won't get in unless you book a long time in advance. It's worth asking about this and the other hostels in the area at *ČEDOK* in Starý Smokovec, on the off chance.

The **mountain chata** which appear at various intervals across the mountains are primarily for climbers and as such are heavily in demand. To find out the latest on their availability, go to *Slovakoturist* (Mon–Fri 8am–4pm), a couple of minutes' walk east of the main station in Starý Smokovec. To take advantage of anything they offer, you'll have to be pretty flexible (most *chata* are only accessible by foot) and plan your hiking around your accommodation.

Poprad and around

It would be difficult to dream up a more unprepossessing town than **POPRAD** to accompany the Tatras' effortless natural beauty. A great swathe of off-white housing encircles a small, scruffy old town centre to the accompanying backdrop of spectacular snowcapped peaks. That said, it's refreshingly free of tour groups and the rather desperate pretentiousness of the higher resorts. In fact, if you can get in at the moderate *Hotel Európa* (☎092-327 44), it's no bad place to stay: slap bang next to the railway station, with a friendly, sleazy *kaviareň* and a slightly more upmarket restaurant. The *Gerlach* on Hviezdoslavovo námestie (☎092-337 59) is about the same price, minus the atmosphere.

Poprad was originally one of the twenty or so Spiš towns (see p.325), though the only hint of this is on the long village-like main square, five minutes' walk south of the train station, and useful for picking up provisions if you're planning any hiking. There's a good bakery and a small vegetable market on the north side of the square, while the south side is taken up with a host of indifferent new shops, including a bookshop where you might be able to pick up relevant **maps** – look out for the invaluable *Tatranské strediská* map which contains street plans of all the major resorts (excluding Poprad, which has its own map).

Spišská Sobota

If you do end up staying in Poprad, the village of **SPIŠSKÁ SOBOTA**, just 2km northeast (bus #2, #3 or #4), makes for an enjoyable cloudy afternoon's outing. Only a handful of the thousands of visitors who pass through Poprad make it here, yet it couldn't be more different from its ugly, oversized neighbour. Except during Mass on Sundays there are few signs of life in its leafy square, and the only clue that this was once a thriving Spiš town is the two-storey burgher houses, distinguished by their stone facades and the wooden gables whose eaves hang six feet or so over the square. At the eastern end of the square, an entire row has been recently renovated and smartly whitewashed, while in the centre huddle the old radnica, the obligatory Renaissance belfry and the church of **sv Juraj** (St George), whose origins go back even further than its present late Gothic appearance. Its vaulting is incredibly sophisticated for this part of the world, as are the font and a couple of the smaller chapels, but the real treat is the main **altar** carved by Pavol of Levoča in 1516, which includes a reworking of the famous *Last Supper* predella from the main church in Levoča. The **museum** (Mon–Sat 9am–4pm) at no. 33, opposite the south door of the church, is not really worth the effort except for the opportunity of seeing the inside of one of the typical town houses.

HIKING, SKIING AND CLIMBING IN THE HIGH TATRAS: SOME BASICS

It is as well to remember that the High Tatras are an alpine range and as such demand a little more respect and preparation than Czechoslovakia's other mountains. The whole area is part of the **Tatra National Park (TANAP)**, whose often quite strict rules and regulations are designed to protect what is a valuable, fragile environment. Most importantly you must stick to the marked paths, easy to spot since they are so well worn. Nevertheless, it's a good idea to get hold of a *Vysoké Tatry* map, which shows all the marked paths in TANAP, before you arrive in Poprad, where demand for such things frequently outstrips supply.

In the summer months, the most popular trails and summits are literally chock-a-block with Czech, German and Slovak walkers and, almost certainly, the best thing for the mountains would be if everyone gave them a rest for a few seasons. One of the reasons for the summer stampede is that many of the most exhilarating treks are only open from July 1 to October 30. This is primarily due to the **weather**, probably the single most important consideration when planning your trek. Rainfall is actually heaviest in June, July and August; thunderstorms and even the occasional summer snowstorm are also features of the unpredictable alpine climate. It may be scorching hot down in the valley, yet below freezing on top of Rysy.

Hiking: the golden rules

• Watch the **weather forecast** (easy enough to read even in Slovak – look for *počasie* in the paper).
• Set out **early** (the weather is always better in the morning).
• Don't leave the **tree line** (about 2000m) unless visibility is good, and when the clouds close in, start descending immediately.
• Bring with you: a pair of **sturdy boots** to combat the relentless boulders in the higher reaches; a **whistle** (for blowing six times every minute if you need help); and a **flask of water**.

The Tatra National Park (TANAP)

Cute red tram-like trains trundle across the fields, linking Poprad with the string of resorts and spas which nestle at the foot of the Tatras and lie within the **Tatra National Park** or **TANAP**. To be honest, they're all much of a muchness, a mixture of tasteless new hotels and half-timbered lodges from the last century set in eminently civilised spa gardens and pine woods – it's the mountains to which they give access that make them worth visiting.

Štrbské Pleso and around

ŠTRBSKÉ PLESO's life as a mountain resort began in earnest with the building of the rack railway which climbs 430m in just 5km from Štrba on the main line below. At 1351m, it's the highest Tatran resort. It's also the brashest, with reams of takeaway *gofry* stands and eyesore hotel hoardings, though this has more to do with its having hosted the 1970 World Ski Championships than anything else. The ski resort part of town is north of the *pleso*, the second largest of the glacial lakes from which the spa gets its name.

In summer, the only working lift is the chair lift to Solisko, from where the climb to the top of **Predné Solisko** (2093m) takes well under an hour. As with all

Skiing

The High Tatras are as popular for **skiing** in winter as they are for hiking in summer. The first snows arrive as early as November but the season doesn't really get going for another month. By the end of March, you can only really ski on the higher slopes reached by chair (as opposed to ski) lifts. The main ski resort is ŠTRBSKÉ PLESO which hosts the occasional international as well as national events; Hrebienok (near Starý Smokovec) and Sklanaté pleso (near Tatranská Lomnica) are the other two main ski areas. Queues for the lifts can be pretty horrendous – if so, head out to the quieter pistes around ŽDIAR or even JEZERSKO in the **Spišská Magura** hills. Wherever you go, you'd be best advised to bring your own equipment, although gear can be hired from *Hotel Patria* in Strbské Pleso. If you've got the cash to spare and want to have it all planned out before you go, international branches of *ČEDOK* organise skiing holidays to the High and Low Tatras – see "Information" in *Basics*.

Climbing

To go **rock-climbing** in the High Tatras you need to be a member of a recognised climbing club and be able to produce a membership card. Otherwise, you are required by law to hire a guide from the *Horská služba* (see below) which costs a fair whack, though up to five people can share the cost of one guide. It's possible to climb throughout the year, but as with skiing you should beware of avalanches. Note that *Cesta uzavretá – nebezpečenstvo lavín* means "Path Closed – Risk of Avalanches". The most popular climbs are in the vicinity of Lomnický štít, but since **Gerlachovský štít**, the highest peak in the Tatras, can only be ascended by legitimate climbers, it too is high on the hit-list.

For **advice** on where to and where not to climb, tips on the weather and emergency help, contact *Horská služba*, the mountain rescue service next door to *ČEDOK* in Starý Smokovec (☎0969-28 20/28 55). Again, it's best to bring your own climbing gear with you.

such lifts in the Tatras, book your ride well in advance to avoid the giant snake-like ticket queues which have usually formed by mid-morning. If you want to explore a whole ring of mystical glacial lakes which folk legends used to call "the eyes and windows of another sea", the trek over **Bystré sedlo** (2314m), which skirts the jagged Solisko range, is a round trip of around eight hours – you can cut an hour or so of this time by taking the chair lift to Solisko and then following the blue-marked path.

A gentle one-hour walk through the forest along the red-marked path to **Popradské pleso** is all many people manage on a lightning Tatra tour. It's a beautiful spot to have a picnic, although, given its popularity, by no means tranquil. Those with sufficient stamina can try the punishing climb to the **sedlo pod Ostrvou** (1959m), which gives a fantastic bird's-eye view of the lake. This red-marked path, known as the *Magistrála*, skirts the tree line all the way to **Zelené pleso**, 20km away in the far east of the range. If you don't have such boundless enthusiasm for walking, stroll along the yellow-marked track to the **symbolický cintorín** of wooden crosses set up to commemorate the considerable number of people who've lost their lives in the mountains.

One of the most popular climbs in the Tatras is **Rysy** (2499m) on the Slovak-Polish border, which Lenin himself once climbed. If you're planning on doing Rysy, you won't have time to picnic by the lake, since it's a good six hours' return trip from Popradské pleso via *Chata pod Rysmi*, at 2250m the highest (and coldest) of the mountain chalets, just below the first peak of Váha (2343m). If you can find a place to sit down on the crowded summit, it has to be one of the best views in Europe. Another possible climb from Popradské pleso is the eight-hour sweep over **Vyšoké Kôprovské sedlo** (2180m) via the largest lake of the lot, **Veľké Hincovo pleso**.

Kriváň (2494m), the westernmost Tatran peak (which is easy enough for anybody to climb) is a short, sharp seven-hour return journey from Štrbské Pleso via Jamské pleso. Like Rysy, it's a popular climb, and in summer, the top of the mountain is a great mass of boulders and walkers. If that sounds like your idea of hell, try some of the trails around PODBANSKÉ or even further afield in the Západné Tatry (see "The Orava region").

Tatranská Lomnica

TATRANSKÁ LOMNICA, 5km northeast of Starý Smokovec, is just a smaller version of that town – people come here on bad weather days, or to go up **Lomnický štít** (2632m), the second highest mountain in the Tatras, accessible by a hair-raising cable-car ride which sets off from beside the *Hotel Praha*. It's difficult to fault the view from Lomnický štít, but purists may disapprove of the concrete steps and handrails built to prevent the crowds from pushing each other off the rocky summit. If you prefer chair lifts to being cooped up in a cable car, there's one to Lomnický sedlo, the craggy saddle 500m below Lomnický štít.

Hiking options are not so good from Tatranská Lomnica, and most treks are best started from other resorts. Otherwise, cloudy days can be filled with horse-racing (Sundays only), outdoor chess and the **TANAP museum** (Mon–Fri 8am–noon & 1–5pm, Sat & Sun 8am–noon), whose smart displays of stuffed Tatran animals and plants accompany a brief history of the region. It was only explored for the first time in the late eighteenth century when a Scotsman, Robert Townson (see p.337), who was botanising his way round Hungary, ascended Kežmarský štít and a number of other peaks, against the advice of the local guides.

Hikes around Starý Smokovec

The old Saxon settlement of **STARÝ SMOKOVEC**, the most established and most central of the spas, scatters its constituent buildings for about 3km between Nový, Horný and Dolný Smokovec. The spa's old nucleus is the stretch of lawn between the half-timbered supermarket and the pricey *Grandhotel* (☎0969-25 01), built in 1905 in a vaguely kitch alpine neo-Baroque but still the finest guesthouse around. The remarkably unpretentious *Tatra* restaurant, a short step from the railway station and next door to *ČEDOK*, is a good place to have a large lunch or an early supper – note that it closes at 8pm.

If the weather's good, the most straightforward and rewarding climb is to follow the blue-marked path from behind the *Grandhotel* to the summit of **Slavkovský štít** (2452m), a return journey of nine hours. Again from behind the *Grandhotel*, a narrow-gauge funicular climbs 250m to HREBIENOK (45min by foot), one of the lesser ski resorts on the edge of the pine forest proper. The smart wooden *Bilíkova chata* (☎0969-24 39) is a five-minute walk from the top of the funicular. Just past the *chata*, the path continues through the wood, joining up with two others, from Tatranská Lesná and Tatranská Lomnica respectively, before passing the gushing waterfalls of the **Studenovodské vodopády**.

At the fork, just past the waterfall, a whole variety of trekking possibilities opens up. The right-hand fork takes you up the **Malá Studená dolina** and then zigzags above the tree line to the *Téryho chata*, set in a lunar landscape by the shores of the **Päť Spišských pleso**. Following the spectacular trail over the Priečne sedlo to *Zbojnicka chata*, you can return via the Veľká studená dolina – an eight-hour round trip from Hrebienok. Alternatively, continue from the *Téryho chata* to JAVORINA, nine hours one-way with the return trip by bus.

Another possibility is to take the left-hand fork to the *Zbojnicka chata*, and continue to Zamruznuté pleso, which sits in the shadow of **Východná Vysoká** (2428m); only a thirty-minute hike from the lake, this dishes out the best view of Gerlachovský štít there is for the non-climber. To get back down to the valley, either descend the Poľský hrebeň and return to Starý Smokovec via the *Sliezsky dom* (9hr round trip without the Východná Vysoká ascent), or continue north and track the Polish border to LYSÁ POĽANA, the Slovak border post (10hr one way), returning by bus to Starý Smokovec.

Tatranská Kotlina, Ždiar and around

The overkill in the central part of the TANAP makes trekking from the relative obscurity of **TATRANSKÁ KOTLINA** seem a positive delight. Most people, however, come here not to walk but to visit the **Belianska jaskyňa** (Tues–Sun mid-May to mid-Sept 9.30am–3.30pm; mid-Sept to mid-May tours at 9.30am, 11am & 2.30pm; closed Mon), fifteen minutes from the main road, whose pleasures include rock formations whimsically named the *Leaning Tower of Pisa* and *White Pagoda*, and an underground lake. Another bad-weather time-filler.

The **Zelené pleso** makes a good hiking target, surrounded by a vast rocky amphitheatre of granite walled peaks including the mean-looking north face of Lomnický štít. To get there, take the blue-marked path from the southwest end of Tatranská Kotlina, and turn right onto the green trail which ends at the ruined *chata* by Biele pleso (2–3hr). From here it's half an hour to the fully functioning *Brnčalova chata* which sits by the green tarn itself. If you've still got time and energy on your hands, traverse the ridge to the north and mount the summit of Jahňaci štít (2–3hr round trip).

The mountains of the **Belianske Tatry**, which form the final alpine ridge in the north of the TANAP, are out of bounds to everyone except the native chamois, but you can skirt round their southern slopes via the Kopské sedlo (30min on the blue trail from Biele pleso) and then on to Javorina (2–3hr).

On the other side of the Belianske Tatry, slightly off the main road to Javorina (and to Zakopane in Poland) is **ŽDIAR**, a traditional rural community founded in the seventeenth century which still lives off the land, but is now struggling to survive under the ever-increasing pressures of the neighbouring tourist industry. In all, there are around thirty or so wooden cottages in varying stages of modernisation, a half-timbered cinema and an unremarkable brick church. One of the houses has been converted into a modest **folk museum** (Mon–Fri 9am–4pm, Sat & Sun 9am–noon), while another will provide you with a meal and possibly a bed – if you've booked ahead from Starý Smokovec. So far, the place still resembles a muddy working village more than a tourist skansen – and it's all the better for it.

EAST SLOVAKIA

Stretching from the High Tatras east to the Soviet border, the countryside of **East Slovakia** (Východné Slovensko) is decidedly different from the rest of the country. The obligatory forests of pine and spruce give way gradually to acres of beech forests in the east, at their best in September and October when the hills turn into a fanfare of burnt reds and browns.

Ethnically, East Slovakia is probably the most diverse region in the country: even within a single valley different groups coexist. A third of the country's **Gypsies** live here, mostly on the edge of Slovak villages, in ghettoes of almost medieval squalor. In the ribbon-villages of the north and east, the **Rusyn** minority – hill-dwelling peasants whose homeland became part of the Soviet Ukraine after 1945 – struggle to preserve their culture and religion, while large numbers of **Hungarians** live along the southern border. Even the **East Slovaks** themselves are thought of as some kind of separate race by other Slovaks. Indeed, before 1918 there was a movement to create a separate state for East Slovaks. For more on the country's ethnic groups, see "Czechoslovakia's Ethnic Minorities" in *Contexts*.

A short train ride east of the High Tatras, the intriguing medieval towns of the **Spiš region** constitute East Slovakia's architectural high point, while to the south, the **Slovenský raj** offers some highly unorthodox hiking possibilities. Further south still, along the Hungarian border, the karst region of the **Slovenský kras** boasts one of the longest cave systems in the world. Along the northern border with Poland, **Carpatho-Ruthenia** – where the country's remaining Rusyn population lives – is a fascinating, isolated landscape, riddled with wooden Uniate churches, among the few monuments in the region to have survived the destruction of the last war. After spending time in the rural backwaters, **Košice**, the East Slovak capital, can be a welcome, though somewhat startling re-entry into city life, containing enough of interest for a stopover at least before heading east towards the Soviet border and the deserted beech forests of **the Vihorlat**.

Tourism comes to an abrupt halt east of Poprad, which means extra difficulties as regards both transport and accommodation outside the two main areas: the Spiš region and Košice, the regional capital. It's not that the hotels are full or the railways slow – it's just that they barely exist. The best advice is to take a tent as a fallback, and hope for the best.

The Spiš region

The land that stretches northeast up the Poprad valley to the Polish border and east along the River Hornád towards Prešov is known as the **Spiš region**, for centuries a semi-autonomous province within the Hungarian kingdom. After the dislocation and devastation of the mid-thirteenth-century Tartar invasions, the Hungarian crown was keen to repopulate the area as a stopgap against any further incursions by the eastern hordes. With the whiff of valuable ore deposits in the air, Saxon families were encouraged to colonise the area (to whom it was known as *Zips*), eventually establishing over twenty Zips towns which were were quickly granted special trading privileges and began to thrive like no other region around.

Today, minus its ethnic Germans, the whole of the Spiš region, along with its large Gypsy minority, shares the low living standards which are the rule throughout East Slovakia. The only glimmer of hope is in the growth of tourism, since architecturally the Spiš region has a substantial head start. The Saxon settlers had the wealth to build some wonderful Gothic churches, and later enriched almost every town and village with the distinctive touch of the Renaissance, imbuing the towns with a coherent and immediately likeable aspect.

Kežmarok and around

Just 14km up the road from Poprad, **KEŽMAROK** (Käsmark – derived from "Cheese Market") is one of the easiest Spiš towns to visit from the High Tatras. It's an odd place, combining the distinctive traits of a Teutonic town with the dozy feel of an oversized Slovak village. If you've visited nearby Spišská Sobota, the wooden gables, shingled overhanging eaves and big barn doors will all be familiar signs of a Spiš (as opposed to Slovak) town. But Kežmarok, which once rivalled the chief Zips town, Levoča, has the added attractions of a Renaissance castle and a fascinating clutch of buildings on its southern fringe.

The Town

From whichever direction you come, Kežmarok is dominated by the giant, gaudy **Protestant Church** (daily 8am–noon & 1–5pm), built by Theophil von Hansen, the architect responsible for much of late nineteenth-century Vienna, and funded by the town's wealthy merchants. It's a seemingly random fusion of styles – Renaissance campanile, Moorish dome, Classical dimensions, all dressed up in grey-green and rouge rendering – but a concoction of which Hansen, and presumably his patrons, were particularly fond. If you're accustomed to the intense atmosphere of Czechoslovakia's ubiquitous Catholic churches, the hall looks like it's been ransacked. On the right-hand side, swathed in the wreaths and sashes of the Hungarian tricolour, sits the tomb and mausoleum of **Count Imre Thököly**, the Protestant rebel who had the Imperial army on the run for eight years or so during the anti-Habsburg Kuruc revolt of 1677.

Next door is an even more remarkable, though significantly less imposing **wooden Protestant church**, again built by a German – this time Georg Muttermann from Poprad. Culturally speaking it couldn't be further from the Viennese cosmopolitanism of its neighbour and, by all accounts, it's a work of great carpentry and artistry inside, capable of seating almost 1500 people. Having said all that, it's firmly closed, apparently "for ten years".

One more building in this corner of town deserves mention – the **Lutheran Lycée**, architecturally fairly nondescript but soon to be restored and transformed into yet another museum of Slovak literature. Lutheranism, which was rife in the nether regions of the Hungarian empire, especially those parts colonised by Germans, was also the religion from whose ranks most of Slovakia's leading nationalists came. Men like the Czechophile Pavol Šafárik, the poet Martin Rázus, and the writer Martin Kukučín all studied here before the Hungarians closed the place down in the 1860s.

The old town itself is little more than two long leafy streets which set off from the important-looking though easily missable central radnica to form a V-shaped fork. The town's Catholic church, **sv Kríž** (Mon–Fri 9am–noon & 2–5pm), is tucked away in the dusty back alleys between the two prongs, once surrounded by its own line of fortifications, now protected by an appealing Renaissance belfry whose uppermost battlements burst into sgraffitto life in the best Spiš tradition.

The **castle** (Tues–Sun 9am–4pm), at the end of the right-hand fork, is the main reason the odd stray Tatran tour group makes it here. It was the property of the Thököly family for many years, until the Habsburgs confiscated it as punishment for the family's support of the aforementioned Kuruc revolt. To be honest, though, the museum of historical artefacts which now occupies its bare rooms doesn't really justify the compulsory hour-long guided tour.

Finally, if you've time to spare, you could do worse than take a quick turn under the sycamore trees of the local **cemetery**, just off the old Ringstrasse (at this point called Toporcerova, and the main road from Poprad). It's a fascinating testament to the diverse nationalities which have inhabited the region over the last century. The remaining Slovak peasantry continue to honour their dead with simple wooden crosses, while the vestigal German community stubbornly stick to their own language; *Ruhe Sanft!* (Rest in Peace) is something you'll see written on the more recent headstones, not just on the ornate (and uncared-for) turn-of-the-century graves which belong to the old German and Hungarian elite.

Practicalities

Arriving in Kežmarok by train is by far the most pleasant introduction to the town, thanks to the yellowing nineteenth-century Bahnhof. Kežmarok is near enough to the High Tatras to figure as a possible base for exploring the mountains, providing you have your own transport. That few people bother to do this is to your advantage, since **accommodation** is as a result fairly easy to find, although now and then the overspill does succeed in filling all three hotels. The *Lipa* on Toporecova (☎0968-20 37) is the most expensive, followed closely by the *Štart* (☎0968-29 15), which lies in the woods to the north of the castle; the *Tatra* (☎0968-27 95) in the old town is by far the cheapest of the three. The place where all the coach parties come to eat is the *reštaurácia* in the castle cellars, but if that's booked you'll do little worse at any of the hotel restaurants.

Vrbov

If you're a camper but also a hedonist, the hot sulphur springs at **VRBOV**, 5km south of Kežmarok, are the place to head. Without your own set of wheels, you'll have to rely on hitching or the infrequent bus service from Kežmarok and Poprad. The village itself is no more than a couple of grubby streets and the obligatory Gypsy ghetto but, continuing on the road south, there's a hotel and restaurant which go by the unlikely name of *Hotel Flipper* (no prizes for guessing it's a fish restaurant). All fairly innocuous, except for the rather dubious smell of bad eggs which emanates from the nearby sulphurised swimming pool and **campsite** behind, both of which are cheap and open from mid-June to mid-September. In the evening, the natural spring pool (daily 8am–10pm) becomes something of a floodlit social centre whatever the weather, as the locals immerse themselves in the fizzy, steaming, therapeutic water.

Stará Ľubovňa and the Pieniny

From Kežmarok, the railway draws a wide semicircle as it follows the Poprad river round to **STARÁ ĽUBOVŇA**, a scruffy, somewhat forlorn town, but marginally better placed for approaching the **Pieniny** than Kežmarok. As early as the 1930s, the Polish and Czechoslovak governments declared this small eruption of fissured limestone rocks which straddles the Dunajec river the **Pieniny national park** (PIENAP). Today, despite the continuing isolation of the nearby Zamagurie region (Zamagurie means literally "Behind the Spišská Magura hills"), tourism in the Pieniny on both sides of the border is flourishing, particularly the ever-popular **raft trips** down the Dunajec.

RAFT TRIPS AND HIKING IN THE PIENINY

Raft trips (daily June–Sept) are becoming big business for the folk on both sides of the Dunajec, which means that organisationally the whole thing couldn't be simpler. As soon as you arrive at ČERVENÝ KLÁŠTOR, the touts begin their hard sell, relieving you of your money and giving you a departure time and ticket. The *plti* (rafts) themselves are not much more than a series of mini-kayaks tied together, punted downstream by locals dressed up in the traditional rafters' costume. The rapids the rafts float down are positively benevolent compared to the brittle white cliffs which rise up on either side. River meanderings make the whole trip about an hour in length, but if you'd prefer to do your own thing, the trip can be made on foot by following the red-marked path 10km along the tree-lined river bank. At the end of the gorge, either try hitching a ride with one of the buses shipping people back, or else walk 3km along the road to LESNICA, then 5km across the hills back to Červený Kláštor, where there's a **campsite**, should you wish to stay over. In addition to the regular raft trips there's a canoe slalom competition on the river here every September. If you've time to spare at any other time of the year, pop into the fourteenth-century monastery near the campsite, now a museum of the region.

Stará Ľubovňa

If you've an hour or so to spare in Stará Ľubovňa waiting for the next bus, head in the direction of the mostly ruined castle which occupies a high spur overlooking the town. From the fifteenth to the eighteenth century, it was the main residence of the local Polish despot, who lorded it over the thirteen Zips towns pawned to the Polish crown by the Hungarians in the fifteenth century. Certain sections have remained intact and now serve as a **museum** (Tues–Fri 8am–4pm, Sat & Sun 9am–5pm) commemorating those who were tortured in the castle by the Nazis.

Far more interesting than the above, however, is the **folk skansen** (Tues–Sun 10–11.30am & 12.30–4pm), set up in the grassy meadow below the castle in the late 1970s to preserve the precious wooden architecture of the Zamagurie region to the west of Stará Ľubovňa. In the late nineteenth century, here as in other rural parts of East Slovakia, malnutrition was the norm and starvation by no means exceptional. People emigrated in droves to other parts of Europe and in particular to the United States. Many of the cottages brought here from the surrounding villages were simply abandoned, and some of them now contain mementoes and personal details of the last owners (in Slovak only). It's a well thought out museum, and includes an early nineteenth-century wooden church whose rich Orthodox interior can be viewed on request of the key (*kľúč*).

In the unlikely event of your needing a place to stay, try the *Vrchovina* across the river and up the hill from the train and bus stations, and for grub, the *vináreň* on the main square. If you're heading north into Poland, two slow trains a day crawl across the border to Muszyna (change at Plaveč on the Slovak side).

Levoča and around

Twenty-five kilometres east from Poprad across the broad sweep of the Spiš countryside, the walled town of **LEVOČA** (Leutschau), positioned on a slight incline, makes a wonderfully medieval impression. Capital of one of the richest regions of Slovakia for more than four centuries, its present-day population of around 11,000 is, if anything, less than it was during its halcyon days. The town's showpiece main square is hit by the occasional tour group from the Tatras, but otherwise its dusty backstreets are yours.

The first attempts at founding a town here were completely trashed by the Tartars. Then, in the wave of Saxon immigration which followed, Levoča became the capital of the Zips towns, a position it maintained until its slow but steady decline in the early nineteenth century. This led to a kind of architectural mummification, and it's the fifteenth and sixteenth centuries – the golden age of Levoča – which still dominate the town today.

The old town

The Euclidian efficiency with which the old town is laid out, chessboard-style, means that wherever you breach the walls, you'll inevitably end up at the main square, **Mierové námestie**, itself a long, regular rectangle. Most of Levoča's treasures are located here, not least the threesome of the Protestant church, town hall and Catholic church, which dominate the central space. To the north is possibly the least distinguished but most important building on the square, the former **Waaghaus** or municipal weigh-house, which was the financial might behind the town during its trading heyday. In 1321 King Charles Robert granted the town the Law of Storage, an unusual medieval edict which obliged every merchant passing through the region to hold up at Levoča for at least fourteen days, pay various taxes and allow the locals first refusal on all their goods. In addition, Levoča merchants were later exempted from such laws when passing through other towns. Small wonder then that the town burghers were exceptionally wealthy.

Of the three freestanding buildings on the main square paid for with these riches, it's the Catholic church of **sv Jakub** (May–Sept Tues–Sat 8am–4pm, Sun 1–4pm; Oct–April Tues–Sat 8am–4pm) that contains the most valuable booty. Every nook and cranny of the building is crammed with medieval religious art, star attraction being the early sixteenth-century wooden altarpiece by **Master**

Pavol of Levoča, topped by a forest of finials and pinnacles, which, at 18.6m in height, make it reputedly the tallest of its kind in the world. At the time, the clarity and characterisation of the figures in the predella's *Last Supper* must have seemed incredible: they were modelled on the local merchants who commissioned the work (Pavol and his apprentices can also be seen behind the figure of Saint James in the central panel). The disciples are depicted in various animated poses – eating, caught in conversation or, in the case of Saint John, fast asleep across Christ's lap. Only Judas, thirty pieces of silver over his shoulder, has a look of anguish, while Christ presides with serene poise. The work took over ten years to complete, and is only one of the many Gothic altars in the church which deserve attention, a clear indication of the town's wealth.

Before you can enter the church, it's necessary to buy a ticket from the former **Rathaus** (times as above) to the south, built in a sturdy Renaissance style. Downstairs, the local administration still holds sway, along with a few tables and chairs for ice-cream eaters; upstairs (where you get your ticket) there's a museum on the Spiš region and some fairly dubious contemporary Slovak art on the top floor. The third building in the centre of the square is the oddly squat **Protestant church**, built in the early nineteenth century in an uncompromisingly Neoclassical style, its bare pudding-basin interior not worth the search round for the key.

The rest of the square is lined with some fine sixteenth-century burgher houses, at their most eye-catching in the **Thurzov dom** – at first glance a flamboyant Renaissance structure, though in fact its most striking feature, the sgraffito decoration around the windows, dates from the restoration work of 1824. Further down on the east side of the square is a simple two-storey building which historians reckon to be the **House of Master Pavol of Levoča** (times as sv Jakub). All that's known about Pavol is what little can be gleaned from the town hall records: he was born around 1460, sat briefly on the town council, died in 1537, and his son was murdered by a man from Kraków. Even this much is missing from the house's exhibition, which concentrates more on the Kotrba brothers who made good the woodworm of the centuries in the 1950s. Unless you're a real fan of his stuff it hardly seems worth the effort, since it contains only later copies of the same work displayed in the church.

The rest of the town's grid plan is made up of one-storey hovels, once the exclusive abodes of Saxon craftsmen, now crumbling homes to the town's Slovaks and Gypsies. You could spend an enjoyable hour wandering the streets and doing the circuit of the run-down walls but, other than the curiosity value of the nineteenth-century German Gymnasium in the southwest of the town, there's nothing specific to see.

Practical details

Since Levoča lies at the end of a poorly served branch line that begins at Spišská Nová Ves, most people arrive at the **bus station**, close to the Košická brána in the northeast corner of town. Outside the annual pilgrimage (see below), **accommodation** shouldn't be hard to find, though the choice is limited to the *Družba* (☎0966-25 59) on the main road (whose name may well change) and the less expensive *Bielá pani* on the main square (☎0966-25 59). There's a **campsite** (June–Sept), a two-kilometre walk north of Levoča, in the woods by LEVOČSKÁ DOLINA.

THE MARIAN PILGRIMAGE

Once a year, Levoča goes wild. As the first weekend of July approaches, up to 250,000 Catholics descend on the town to attend the biggest of Slovakia's **Marian pilgrimages** which takes place in (and inevitably around) the church on Marianska hora, the sacred hill 2km north of the town. Families travel – in some cases walking – for miles to arrive in time for High Mass, which takes place around 6pm on the Saturday evening. From then on, the party goes on throughout the night, with hourly Masses being given in the church and singing and dancing (and drinking) going on outside in the fields until the grand finale at 10am Sunday morning, generally presided over by someone fairly high up in the church hierarchy. If you've never witnessed a Marian festival, this is the place to do it, though it only marks the beginning of a whole host of festivals which take place over the next two months in villages all over Slovakia. The main Greek-Catholic (Uniate) pilgrimage takes place some 40km northeast of Levoča, near the village of Ľutina on the third weekend in August.

Spišský Štvrtok

Easy to spot on the road between Poprad and Levoča, but not necessarily reason enough to get off the bus, is **SPIŠSKÝ ŠTVRTOK**, whose splendid thirteenth-century church sits atop the village hill, its masonry tower topped by an impressive wooden spire with four corner pinnacles. The perfect French Gothic side chapel from 1473 which emerges from the south wall was commissioned by the Zápoľskýs to be the family mausoleum, and is, without doubt, one of the most unlikely sights in East Slovakia.

Spišská Nová Ves

Thirteen kilometres south of Levoča, **SPIŠSKÁ NOVÁ VES** is the modern-day capital of the Spiš region, a relatively industrious town of around 35,000 whose origins are as old as Levoča's, but which has borne the brunt of the changes wrought on the region over the last century. Pawned to the Poles at the height of the Hussite Wars, along with twelve other Spiš towns, it fell to the Habsburgs in 1772, who immediately made it the Spiš capital, a fact which played a significant part in the demise of its old rival, Levoča. As a mining town, it was virtually guaranteed to get itself on the main Košice–Bohumín railway line when it was built in the nineteenth century. What that means today is that it's a good place from which to visit both the Slovenský raj and Levoča by train, but otherwise has only a few residual pleasures.

The main square is an excessively broad leafy avenue, in the style of Prešov and Košice, dotted with important-looking buildings, not least the municipal theatre in grand turn-of-the-century mood – definitely *the* place to hang out once it's refurbishment is complete. The yellow Gothic church contains a couple of minor works by Master Pavol of Levoča and there's a small museum – through an arch in the best-looking building on the north side of the square – which laboriously documents the mining history of the town. Other than this, you'll probably be most interested in the two hotels, *Metropol* (☎09665-21 41) and *Šport* (☎0965-222 17), of which the latter – by the ice hockey stadium – is by far the cheaper.

East to Spišský hrad

The road east from Levoča takes you to the edge of the Spiš territory, clearly defined by the Branisko ridge which blocks the way to Prešov. Even if you're not planning on going any further east, you should at least take the bus as far as Spišské Podhradie, for arguably the most spectacular sight in the whole country.

En route, you might spot the palatial neo-Baroque chateau at SPIŠSKÝ HRHOV peeping through its half-tamed grounds (only the latter are open to the public). There's no point in stopping off, at least until the village of NEMEŠANY, just past the artificial geyser Sivá Brada which shoots mineral water twenty feet up in the air. From here, walk along the road for a kilometre or so to the crest of the hill, where you should get your first glimpse (and the best one there is) of the **Spišský hrad**, its pile of chalk-white ruins strung out on a bleak green hill in the distance – an irresistably photogenic shot, and one which finds its way into almost every *ČEDOK* handout in the country. Predictably enough, the ruins themselves don't live up to expectations close to (May–Oct Tues–Sun 9am–5pm), though it's difficult to resist the impulse to get nearer, and the view from the top is undeniably good. If you do wish to wander round the castle, stay on the bus until SPIŠSKÉ PODHRADIE (literally "below the castle") and then start walking.

Around Spišský hrad

More rewarding is a closer inspection of the walled, one-street city of **SPIŠSKÁ KAPITULA**, the ecclesiastical capital of the Spiš region, whose plain monastic towers are often featured in the foreground of the aforementioned photographs. From the front, the **Cathedral of Sv Martin** is clearly a Romanesque church, built as a defiant outpost of Christianity shortly after the Tartar invasions. Later in the fifteenth century, the local patrons, the Zápoľskýs, tacked on a rather larger version of their family chapel up the road at Spišský Štvrtok. Inside, the combined effect produces an austere yet beautiful sense of space and light, enlivened by the soft colours of the fourteenth-century frescoes celebrating the coronation of King Charles Robert. Outside, a couple of graceful cypress trees stand at the top of the town's single street, lined with decrepit canons' houses, some inhabited by people, others only by bats and rats. With the recent re-establishment of a Catholic seminary here, however, the whole place is beginning to wake up from its forty-year religious slumber.

If you've time to spare, and energy to expend, take the path from Spišský hrad towards Dreveník, the limestone hill southeast of the ruins, and finish up at the village of ŽEHRA. The lure here is the perky thirteenth-century church sporting a natty shingled onion dome and matching white perimeter walls, which contains faded frescoes contemporary with the church, and an interior decor of Byzantine richness. If you're in need of accommodation, the cheap *Hotel Spiš* in Spišské Podhradie is the only place around.

The Slovenský raj

After the up-front post-glacial splendour of the High Tatras, the low-key pine forests of the **Slovenský raj** (pronounced "rye" – meaning "paradise"), 20km or so to the southeast of Poprad, might seem more than a little anti-climactic at first

SLOVENSKÝ RAJ

glance. No hard slog hiking or top-of-the-world views here, but, if your inclination is towards more frivolous outdoor pursuits, such as scrambling up rocky gorges and clinging on to chains and ladders beside shooting waterfalls, then the Slovenský raj may not be far from nirvana after all.

Covered in a thick coat of pine forest, the terrain – covering just twenty square kilometres – is typically karstic: gentle limestone hills which have been whittled away in places to form deep hairline ravines, providing a dank, almost tropical escape from the dry summer heat of the Poprad plain. To the north, the Hornád river has made the deepest incision into the rock, forming a fast-flowing, snaking canyon flanked by towering jagged bluffs which attract some of the country's dedicated rock-climbers. The most dramatic ravines climb up to the grassy plateau of the Veľká poľana at the centre of the region. To the south, the geography of the hills around Dedinky becomes more conventional and in winter the whole area turns into a popular ski resort.

Practicalities

It's perfectly possible to do the area from Poprad, by taking the **local train** to VYDRNÍK, LETANOVCE or SPIŠSKÉ TOMÁŠOVCE. Poprad being no great place to be, though, it might be more pleasant to hole up at the moderate *Flóra* hotel in ČINGOV (☎0965-911 30), which also lets out luxury bungalows, or even to use Spišská Nová Ves as a base (see "The Spiš region"). If you've got a tent, the PODLESOK **campsite** (mid-May to Sept) is the most convenient, but the one at Čingov (June 15–Sept 15) less crowded. From June 15 to September 15, you can camp at the makeshift Klaštorisko site in the middle of the forest.

Transport to the south of the region is likewise okay, with buses from Poprad and the picturesque Hron valley railway from Banská Bystrica. Dedinky is, however, only useful as a base for visiting the Dobšiná ice cave and less than useless for exploring the ravines. From north to south, there's nothing to take you bar your own feet – it's not much more than 10km cross-country from Podlesok to Dedinky, but take adequate provisions with you. **Walking** is also the only way of seeing the canyons and it's not a bad idea to try and get hold of the detailed *Slovenský raj* map which marks all the one-way tracks, *before* you arrive in the area. The most exhilarating tracks are those designated one-way – a strange concept to get your head round until you've been up one – and it's important to stick to the direction indicated. However much you're walking, it's best to bring a pair of sturdy boots, preferably with a good grip and at the very least splash-proof – it's extremely wet and slippery underfoot all year round. Bear in mind, too, that if you're at all scared of heights, you might encounter a few problems with some of the deeper canyons.

HIKING IN THE SLOVENSKY RAJ

With the 1:50,000 *Slovenský raj* hiking map, you can plan your own routes. If you're staying at Podlesok and follow the green markers, you immediately enter the **Suchá Belá**, one of the most exciting river beds to explore, but also one of the most accessible and therefore extremely popular at the height of the season, causing the occasional queue at crucial ladders. With so many obstacles en route, it takes nearly everyone a full two hours to stumble up this one-way ravine to the top. Similarly breathtaking stuff can be experienced up the gladed ravine of **Piecky**, which starts from 3km along the green-marked track to the Dobšinská ľadová jaskyňa.

Should you need a rest after the morning's exertions, head down to **Kláštorisko**, whose sunny sloping meadow is perfect for picnicking and sunbathing. If you've forgotten your packed lunch, the small *reštaurácia* at the top of the field might oblige. At the bottom of the clearing is an ongoing archaeological dig where the local panic-stricken Slavs built a monastery to give thanks for their safe deliverance from the Tartar invasions of the mid-thirteenth century.

If you continue for another half an hour past the bottom of Piecky, you come to the deepest one-way gorge of the lot, **Veľký Sokol**, another succession of wooden ladders slung over rock pools and rapids, up the side of waterfalls and riverine gulleys. From the top, you can either walk north across the Veľká poľana plateau to Kláštorisko (1hr 30min) or head west to the top of the Malý Sokol which swings round to join the last two-way quarter of the Veľký Sokol gorge.

The third main area to head for is the **Prielom Hornádu**, a sheer-sided breach (*prielom*) in the limestone rock forced by the Hornád river. Until recently it was impossible to enter the gorge except on ice-skates in winter or by kayak in summer. Now, in keeping with the vaguely vandalistic tendencies of the nation's trekkers, steel steps have been jammed into the rocks and rope bridges slung across the river, and the whole trip takes just three and a half hours from Podlesok to Čingov. If you're doing a round trip, take the yellow-marked path on the way back, which follows the limestone ridge high above the Hornád. The views are amazing, especially from the **Tomášovský výhlad**, a stick of exposed rock some 150m above the Prielom Hornádu.

Dedinky and the Dobšiná ice cave

Since the creation of the nearby lake, Palcmanská Maša, **DEDINKY** has become a thriving little tourist spot all year round. And with good reason. Nestling below Gačovská skala (1106m), whose spruce trees spill down to the grassy banks of the lake, it's the ideal recreational centre, with plenty of opportunities for swimming, wind-surfing, hiking and of course visiting the great Dobšiná ice cave itself. So popular is it, that unless you camp by the lake (June 15–Sept 15), you'll be pushed to find anywhere to spend the night. If you get no joy from the moderate *Priehrada* (☎0942-981 62), try the much cheaper *Geravy* (☎0942-932 27), 1km up the red-marked track behind the *Priehrada*, or the *Slalom* (☎0942-932 07), below the dam.

The most obvious day trip from Dedinky is the **Dobšiná ice cave** (Dobšinská ľadová jaskyňa; May 16–Sept 15 Tues–Sun 1-hr guided tours at 9am, 11am, 1pm & 3pm), by far the most impressive of Slovakia's two ice caves (the other is in the Low Tatras). It's basically one vast underground lake frozen to a depth of over 20m and divided into two halls, the biggest of which, the Veľká sieň, is over 100m across. Although the ice formations are a long way from the subtleties of your average limestone cave, it rarely fails to impress by the brute force of its size and weight. From Podlesok, it's a three-and-a-half-hour hike, mostly through the forest, or a short but very chancy hitch along the road. From Dedinky, simply take the train two stops in the direction of Brezno, after which it's a twenty-minute walk into the hills. It's worth bearing in mind that the caves are very popular (so get there early) and very cold (so take something warm to put on).

Moving on

Dedinky lies on the wonderful Banská Bystrica–Margecany branch line, built in the 1930s and one of the prettiest **train journeys** in Slovakia. It's a slow run if you're going all the way to Košice (3hr 30min), but the fast midday *rýchlik* takes an hour off the usual running time. If you're heading south to the Slovenský kras, you'll have to walk or bus the 4km to the old German mining town of DOBŠINÁ – either way it's a spectacular thousand-foot drop from the Palcmanská Maša. Most buses continue from Dobšiná to Rožňava, but if you prefer there are seven trains a day which also cover the route.

The Slovenský kras

Along with the Moravian karst region north of Brno, the **Slovenský kras** boasts some of Czechoslovakia's finest limestone caves, the highlight of which are the Domica caves which stretch right under the border into Hungary (where they're known as the Aggtelek caves). Even now, the surrounding hills are still plundered for their ores – copper, iron and once upon a time gold – and the largest town in the area, Rožňava, continues to make its living from the local mines, even if the original intrepid German miners have long since gone. The towns and villages are for the most part dusty, characterless places; people are by far the dominant feature of the landscape, large communities of Hungarians and Gypsies living side by side with the Slovak majority.

Rožňava and around

Once the seat of a bishopric and a flourishing German mining town, **ROŽŇAVA** (Rozsnyó) is now quite frankly a bit of a dump, though an undeniably useful one when it comes to making excursions into the karst region and the nearby aristocratic haunts of Krásna Hôrka and Betliar. All **transport** in the region has to pass through Rožňava at some point, although three railway stations still seems a mite excessive; the main one, called simply Rožňava, is a two-and-a-half-kilometre walk from town (infrequent bus #1 or #6 from the station, #2 from the nearby petrol station on the main road). The town's three **hotels**, all near or on the town square, are, in ascending order of price, the cheap *Gemer* (☎0942-28 29) – whose *reštaurácia* serves up lashings of goulash – the moderate *Kras* (☎0942-22 93) and the *Šport* (☎0942-21 79).

The town does have a couple of other redeeming features: it once boasted a mint, a cathedral and an episcopal palace. Of the three, only the Gothic cathedral (now just a parish church) is worth bothering about, largely on account of its sixteenth-century altarpiece depicting the life of the local miners. Secondly, there's the **Mining Museum** (Banícke múzeum; Tues–Sat 9am–4pm, Sun 9am–1pm), set in a long *fin-de-siècle* block (no. 43) on the road to Šafárikovo, and run by a lively retired Hungarian miner who does his best to make up for the lack of information in English. Ask to see the reconstructed (and somewhat over-clean) mine shaft tucked round the back of the building (along with an iron statue of the Hungarians' hero, Kossuth), bearing the traditional, though rather ominous inscription *ZDAR BOH* (Good Luck).

Krásna Hôrka

Plentiful buses run the 5km to **KRÁSNOHORSKÉ PODHRADIE** (literally "Below Krásna Hôrka"), the village sitting under the gaunt and seemingly unapproachable fortress of **Krásna Hôrka** (daily April–Sept 8am–noon & 1–4.30pm, Oct–March 9am–2.30pm; closed Mon), which tops the nearby limestone col. Such was the wealth of the regional bigwigs, the Andrássy family, that they were able to turn the whole place into a family museum in the late nineteenth century, having a number of other places in which to actually live. And that's basically what it is now, give or take the odd three-piece suite. In other words, fun for period furniture enthusiasts but, with compulsory guided tours lasting an hour and twenty minutes, not universally appealing. A better bet down in the village is the original Rožňava **mining museum** (May 15–Oct 15 Tues–Sun 9am–6pm), housed in a fabulous Secession building from 1906, and now given over to a display of folk gear from the surrounding region.

Within sight of both castle and village, and without doubt the most beautiful Art-Nouveau building in Slovakia, is the **Andrássy Mausoleum** (April–Sept 8am–noon & 1–6pm; Oct–March 9am–noon & 1–4pm). It was built in 1903–04 by Italian craftsmen at the great expense of Count Dionysus Andrássy, in memory of his wife, the Viennese opera singer Francesca Hablatz, who died in 1902. Dionysus himself was disowned by the family for marrying below his station, an action which no doubt stiffened his resolve to build an even more extravagant resting place for his lover. Set in its own carefully manicured gardens with sombre wrought-iron gates and characteristic sphynx-like janitors, the mausoleum itself, a simple dome structure, has an austere classicism. Inside, though, it bursts into an almost celebratory orgy of ornamentation: Venetian gold for the cupola, coloured marble from every corner of the globe and, as the centrepiece, two white Carrara marble sarcophagi in which Francesca and Dionysus (who died not long after the building was completed) are buried.

Betliar

The frivolous hunting zámok at **BETLIAR**, 5km northwest of Rožňava by train, couldn't be further from the brooding intensity of Krásna Hôrka, though it was owned by the same aristocratic posse. It was adapted as late as the 1880s in an "indefinite style" as the *ČEDOK* brochure puts it, to accommodate the Andrássys' popular hunting parties. A fairly standard array of period furniture, historical portraits and (naturally enough) reams of hunting trophies and stuffed animals greets those who sign up for the guided tour, but the large, well-groomed park steals the show, dotted with playful, folksy rotundas and mock-historic edifices. The only **accommodation** in the village is in the bungalows at the nearby campsite (June to mid-Sept).

Zádielska dolina and the caves at Jasov

One of the more bizarre karstic features of the Slovenský kras is the forested sheets of **planina** or tableland which rise above the plains like the coastal cliffs of a lost sea. In fact, the opposite is the case, the rivers having whittled their way down through what would otherwise be a featureless limestone plateau. Mostly, these erosions form broad sweeping valleys, but in a few cases, cracks appear in the more familiar form of riverine crevices. The most dramatic of these is the **Zádielska dolina**, a brief but breathtaking three or four kilometres of sky-scraping canyon. To get there, take the train or bus to DVORNÍKY, 25km east of Rožňava and 1km south of the Hungarian-speaking village, ZÁDIEL (Szádelö), which guards the entrance to the dolina. There's none of the Slovenský raj assault course on this hike, just a gentle yet magnificent stroll between the two bluffs. If you want something slightly more death-defying, return along the blue-marked track which ascends the right-hand ridge and shadows the canyon back to Zádiel, dropping down 2.5km east of Dvorníky near the cement works of TURNIANSKE PODHRADIE. For a longer hike of around 15km, you could either follow the blue-marked path over the hills to Jasov, or take the green-marked, then red-marked track to Pipitka (1225m), 10km away, and then return to Rožňava by bus from the Úhornianske sedlo down below.

Jasov

The Premonstratensian monastery at **JASOV** (Jászó) is visible across the fields long before you reach the town. It's actually much older than its thoroughly Baroque appearance would suggest, but is undergoing restoration work by the Polish restorers *PKZ*. Whether, once the work is done, the public will be able to view Kracker's fiery frescoes and suchlike is anybody's guess. The main motivation for visiting Jasov in the meantime is the **Jasovská jaskyňa** (daily April–May 15 & Sept 16–Oct tours at 9am, 11am & 2pm; May 16–Sept 15 9am–4pm; closed Mon), the least hyped caves in the karst region, though no less enjoyable for that, specialising in forests of "virgin stalactites" and containing some amazing graffiti scrawled on the walls by fugitive Czech Hussites in 1452. The only accommodation is the lively campsite and bungalows near the monastery, but if you're coming from Košice, Jasov can be done easily enough as a day trip.

There is a hotel 5km further up the railway track in MEDZEV, a town which hit the headlines in the summer of 1990 when the local Gypsy community began a rent strike – the first such action by the hardest-hit of all the country's minorities – to protest at the discriminatory housing policy of the local Slovak town council. The outcome, however, is somewhat less heartening – the Gypsy ghetto is to be bulldozed and the families rehoused in poorly constructed prefabs on the outskirts of the town.

The Gombasek, Domica and Ochtina Caves

The most impressive of the cave systems, the **Gombasecská jaskyňa** (times as at Jasov), is also one of the most accessible. To reach the caves, take the train one stop south of Rožňava to SLAVEC JASKYŇA station, whence it's 2km further south. There's a **campsite** near the caves, and every June the nearby village of GOMBASEK is the venue for the annual Hungarian folk bash.

Ten kilometres due south, hard by the Hungarian border, are the **Domica Caves** (daily May 16–Sept 15 tours at 9am, 11.30am, noon, 2pm & 3.30pm; Sept 16–May 15 9am, 11pm & 2pm): at 22km in length, one of the longest in the world. The short passage from Robert Townson (see below), one of the caves' earliest explorers, should give you an idea of the gushing prose which they often excite. The tours last for less than an hour and include a quick boat trip on the underground river. It should soon be possible to continue on a longer tour over the border into Hungary, where most of the cave system lies, something that's already possible from the Hungarian side.

Given Domica's inaccessibility, perhaps the easiest and most rewarding way of getting there is to follow the yellow-marked track from Gombasek up onto the *planina* and through the oak trees via the **Silická ľadnica** cave (1hr). The cave itself is closed to the public but its ominous entrance is impressively ice-encrusted throughout the summer, melting to a dribble by late autumn only to be replenished when the first cold spell of November arrives. Keep following the yellow markers east for 500m or so, then hang a right when you hit the red-marked path, whence it's a two-hour trek across the pockmarked tableland to Domica.

A JOURNEY THROUGH THE DOMICA CAVES

The following is an extract from Robert Townson's "Travels in Hungary", published in 1793. Townson, a Scottish scientist, botanised his way around the old kingdom of Hungary, staying with a lot of good-humoured Calvinists on the way, and in the passage quoted below recounts a visit to the Domica caves, long before the days of safety barriers and electric lighting.

I descended rapidly for a short distance and then I found myself in an immense cave . . . where large stalactites, as thick as my body, hung pendant from the roof, and I was shown others where the sides were ornamented in the manner of the most curious Gothic workmanship. In some the stalactites were so thick and close together that we were in danger of losing one another if we separated but a few yards. Here aged stalactites, overloaded with their own weight had fallen down, and lay prostrate; and there an embryo stalactite was just shooting into existence.

After I had wandered about for three or four hours in this awful gloom and had reached the end of the caverns in one direction, I thought it time to come out, and I desired my guide to return. After we returned, as we thought, some way, we found no passage further; yet the guide was sure he was right. I thought I recognised the same rocks we had just left, and which had prevented our proceeding further, but the guide was positive he was in a right direction. Luckily for us I had written my name on the soft clay of the bottom of the cave, which had been the extent of our journey; on seeing this the guide was thunderstruck, and ran this way and that way and knew not where he was, nor what to do. I desired him not to be frightened, but to go calmly to work to extricate us from this labyrinth.

As the wood which we burnt instead of lamps was nearly exhausted, and as I never adverted either to one of the guides whom we had left above, who by being charged with wood could not to get down the funnel-like hole, being so near; nor to the people of the village being acquainted with our being in the cavern, who no doubt would have taken every possible means of coming to our assistance had we stayed much longer than usual, I was a good deal alarmed for our safety and there was good reason; had our torches gone out, we should never have been able to find our way out; nor, had any accident have happened to our guide, could we by ourselves, though we had lights, have had any hopes of extricating ourselves. After wandering about till all our wood was nearly exhausted, we found a great stalactite from which, on account of its remarkable whiteness, I had been induced to knock off a specimen as I came by: I recollected how I stood when I struck it: this at once set us right, and after walking a little further we made ourselves heard to the other guide, from whom we got fresh torches, and we continued our route homewards without further difficulty.

So complete a labyrinth as these caverns are in some places, is not I am sure to be found in similar caverns: large open passages proved cul de sacs, whilst our road was over and under, through and amongst grotto work of the most intricate nature. I finally believe that though a man should have lights and food enough to last him a month – he would not be able to find his way out.

Ochtinská jaskyňa

Of all the cave systems, the **Ochtinská jaskyňa** (times as at Jasov) is without doubt the thinking person's cave. Set apart from the other cave systems, geographically and geologically, its unique feature is the spiky aragonite "flowers" which form like limpets on the cave sides – breathtakingly beautiful but by no means as spectacular in scale as the other limestone caves. From Plešivec, there's an infrequent train service to OCHTINÁ (35min), after which the cave is a three-kilometre walk uphill along the blue-marked path; from Rožňava, there's an equally infrequent bus service (40min).

Carpatho-Ruthenia

Carpatho-Ruthenia* is one of those places where people come from rather than go to. The media mogul Robert Maxwell and his cousin set off on foot, Andy Warhol's parents preferred to go by boat, and over a million others left this far northeastern corner of Slovakia by various means to seek fame and fortune elsewhere, mostly in North America, in the late nineteenth and early twentieth centuries.

They left, to escape not so much the unerring provinciality of the region, but the grinding poverty and unemployment whose stranglehold on the area has only quite recently abated. Even in the 1950s, an estimated 41 percent of Rusyn villages were still without electricity and, in 1968, enjoyed living standards of less than half the national average. Even today, the villages are visibly poorer and more isolated than their western counterparts. It's hardly an exaggeration to say that some villages have seen few visitors since the Russians passed through in 1945 (and again in 1968). Some things have changed, though, not always for the best: the whole area took a hammering in the last war, wooden buildings once the norm are gradually being replaced by concrete and brick, traditional costumes are now worn almost exclusively by the over-fifties, and industry has been somewhat crudely implanted here to try and stem the continuing emigration.

From a visitor's point of view, Prešov and Bardejov are both easy to reach and immediately appealing. Further afield, transport becomes a real problem (as it is to the local inhabitants), since the north–south axis of the valleys only hinders the generally eastbound traveller.

Prešov

Capital of the Slovak Šariš region, cultural centre for the Rusyn minority, **PREŠOV's** present-day split personality is indicative of its long and chequered ethnic history. Over the last few years it has been treated to a wonderful face-lift, and although there's not much of interest beyond its main square, it's a refreshingly youthful and vibrant town – partly due to its university – beyond all expectations this far east.

---

*Strictly speaking Carpatho-Ruthenia (*Podkarpatská Rus* in Slovak), a separate province during the First Republic, was taken as war booty by the Soviet Union in 1945. The term is here used loosely to refer to the East Slovak districts of Prešov, Bardejov, Svidník and Humenné, which border Poland, where the Rusyn minority still predominate.

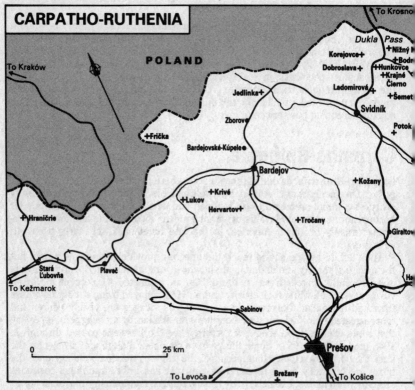

CARPATHO-RUTHENIA

POLAND

To Krosno
Dukla Pass
+Nižný
To Kraków
Korejovce+
+Bodr
Dobroslava+
+Hunkovce
Ladomirová+
+Krajné
Čierno
Jedlinka+
+Šemet
Svidník
Zborov
Potok
+Frička
Bardejovské-Kúpele●
Bardejov
+Kožany
+Krivé
+Lukov
Hervartov+
+Hraničrie
+Tročany
Giraltov
Stará
Ľubovňa
Plaveč
To Kežmarok
Ha
0   25 km
Sabinov
Prešov
To Levoča
Brežany
To Košice

The lozenge-shaped **main square** is flanked by creamy, pastel-coloured, almost edible eighteenth-century facades, topped by some exceptionally winsome gables and pediments, all beautifully preserved. Next door to *ČEDOK* (no. 1), at its southern tip, is the **Uniate Cathedral** (Grecko-katolická katedrála), in many ways a perfectly ordinary Rococo/late-Baroque church, except for the paraphenalia of orthodoxy, including a fabulously huge iconostasis. For the first time since the imprisonment of Pavol Gojdic (see p.342), the cathedral and the bishop's palace next door actually have an extant Uniate bishop and are enjoying a cultural renaissance.

On the opposite side of the square, the antique shop at no. 42 sells handy packs of art postcards by some genuinely gifted Slovak artists, whose original work is on display across the square at the town **art gallery** (Tues–Fri 10am–6pm, Sat & Sun 9am–1pm). Nearby is Prešov's **radnica**, from whose unsuitably small balcony Béla Kun's Hungarian Red Army declared the short-lived Slovak Socialist Republic. Searching desperately for a socialist tradition that simply never existed in this deeply religious country, the Slovak Communists made much of this brief episode in Prešov's history. In fact, it used to be the main subject of the town museum, situated in the dog-tooth gabled **Rákociho dom** at no. 86. Another tradition is no doubt hastily being sought while the museum is

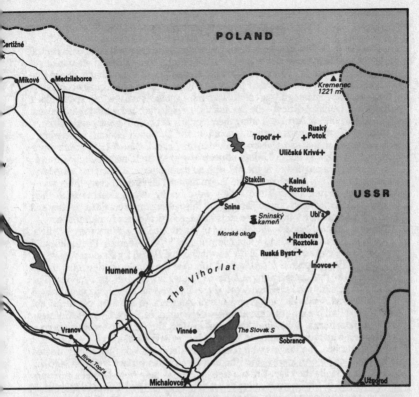

"under reconstruction", perhaps based on the Czechoslovak Legion's military victories which helped bring down the Kun's Bolshevik government.

Prešov's Catholic and Protestant churches vie with each other at the widest point of the square. Naturally enough, the fourteenth-century Catholic church of **sv Mikuláš** has the edge, not least for its modern Moravian stained-glass windows and its sumptuous Baroque altarpiece. Behind sv Mikuláš, the much plainer **Protestant Church**, built in the mid-seventeenth century, bears witness to the strength of religious reformism in the outer reaches of Hungary at a time when the rest of the Habsburgs' lands were suffering the full force of the Counter-Reformation. In the 1670s the tide turned, and a wave of religious persecution followed, culminating in the "1684 Blood Tribunal" in which 24 leading Lutherans were publicly hanged in Prešov's main square. The prime mover behind the trial was **Count Caraffa**, the Papal nuncio in Vienna, whose moustached statue stands above the grim memorial on the corner of the Protestant Lycée, next door to the church.

To the north of the main square, as to the south, lies "monumental Prešov", built in the optimistic days of the 1950s and presided over by the severe colossus of the Prešov district administration, which looks like something straight out of the Soviet Ukraine.

THE RUSYNS

The **Rusyns** or Ruthenians are without doubt one of the great lost peoples of central Europe. Even their name is a subject of some debate, since *Rusyn* is often taken to mean Little Russian or Ukrainian, but in the Hungarian kingdom simply referred to any non-Catholic Slavs. As to their political history, the picture is equally confusing. If they ever were an integral part of the Ukraine – whose language they speak, albeit a western or Lemkian dialect – the mountains in which they had settled soon became a permanent political barrier, dividing their territory between Hungary and Poland.

Meanwhile, their great cultural institution, the Orthodox church, underwent a series of crises and schisms which resulted in the Act of Union of 1596, which established the Greek-Catholic or **Uniate church** as part of the Roman Catholic Church. This unique religion, tied to Rome but with all the trappings of eastern Orthodoxy, became (and still is) the carrier of the Rusyn national identity. In every other way – dress codes, mores and folklore – they were hardly distinguishable from their Magyar and Slovak neighbours. Throughout this period, they remained, as they still do to a great extent, hill-dwelling peasants with no political or economic influence.

The first national leaders who emerged in the nineteenth century were predictably enough Uniate priests, and – like many of the Slovaks – fiercely Russophile and pro-Tsar. They played little part in the downfall of the Habsburg Empire, and when, in 1918, Ruthenia became a province of the new Czechoslovak Republic, it was largely due to the campaigning efforts of Ruthenian emigrés in America. The Slovaks laid claim to all the land west of the Už river, an area containing around 100,000 Rusyns, while the actual province of Ruthenia, to the east, contained not only 370,000 Ruthenians but large numbers of Hungarians, Jews, Gypsies, Germans and even Romanians. Following "liberation" in 1945, the Už river became a permanent border, with the annexation of Ruthenia by the Soviet Union.

On the surface, the Rusyns who remained in Czechoslovakia have been treated better than any other minority since the war. Scratch this surface, however, and the opposite is actually the case. Given a free choice (as they were between the wars and before 1948), the Rusyns tended to opt either for the local dialect or Russian as their language of instruction in schools. After the 1948 coup, however, the regime intervened and ruled that the term *Rusyn* was "an anti-progressive label" – all Rusyns became officially known as Ukrainians, and the language of instruction in Rusyn schools was changed to literary Ukrainian. The reaction of the Rusyns to the pedagogical chaos which ensued was to opt for Slovak schools rather than Ukrainian. Secondly, collectivisation, which disrupted all traditional peasant communities of Eastern Europe, encouraged urbanisation (and therefore Slovak assimilation). Lastly, and perhaps most cruelly of all, following the example of the Stalinist Ukraine, the Uniate church was forcibly amalgamated into the Orthodox church. Its priests and dissenting laity were, for the most part, rounded up and thrown in prison, including the church's one and only bishop, **Pavol Gojdic**, who received a life sentence and died in Leopoldov prison in 1960.

Hardly surprising then that in the last three censuses, fewer than 40,000 declared themselves as Rusyn. No one knows the real numbers, but it's estimated that between 130,000 and 150,000 Rusyns still live in East Slovakia. Since the Velvet Revolution things have begun to look up. As in 1968, when the ban on the church was finally lifted, the Uniates (who include large numbers of Slovaks) are busy arguing with the Orthodox community (reckoned to be as few as 30,000) over church property, all of which was handed over to the Orthodox church in the 1950s. Meanwhile, **Ján Hirka**, since 1968 the unofficial head of all Uniates, was ordained as a Uniate bishop in February 1990, and the martyr Pavol Gojdic canonised.

Practical details

The **bus** and **train station** are situated opposite one another about 1km south of the main square; any of the buses and trolley buses which stop outside will take you into town. **Accommodation** should be trouble-free, providing the number of Soviet tourists doesn't increase. The *Hotel Savoy*, right on the main square (☎091-310 62), is both cheap and convenient, as is the *Vrchovina* at Svätoplukova 1 (☎091-249 22). Prešov's two other hotels are both quite expensive: *Dukla* on the main square (☎091-227 41) and *Šariš* on Leningradská (☎091-463 53).

If you want to avoid **eating** at one of the big hotels, try the pizzeria on Svätoplukova (11am–7pm). Drinking or eating under the glistening chandeliers of the *Hotel Savoy* or beside the smoky mirrors of the *Vrchovina* is also a favourite local pastime. Prešov prides itself on its cultural traditions, with two large-scale **theatres** in town: the Divadlo Jonáša Záborského on the main square, and more famously, the Ukrainian National Theatre, based in a theatre on Jarková, west off the square. Plays at the latter are generally performed in Ukrainian or Slovak.

Bardejov and around

Over 40km north of Prešov and near the Polish border, **BARDEJOV** (Bartfeld) is an almost perfectly preserved medieval town comfortably positioned on its own rock with the obligatory sprawl of post-war development below. Bilingual shop signs and a parade of traditional costumes for the Saturday morning market are the most obvious signs of the local Rusyn minority. A possible day trip by train from Prešov, Bardejov's two moderate hotels make it equally good for an overnight stop, especially given the attractions of the nearby spa, Bardejovské kúpele (see below).

Built by Saxon colonists in the fourteenth century, the **old town** (five minutes' walk southwest of the train station) remains remarkably unchanged since those days, retaining most of its Gothic fortifications, including four of the original bastions along the eastern wall (and much of the original plaster judging by their state of disrepair). The rectangular main square, **námestie Osloboditelov**, is straight out of the German Middle Ages, both in its characteristic triangular gables (many of which are still faced with wooden slats) and in the central **Rathaus** (currently undergoing restoration), now part of the **Šariš museum**. It's worth a look inside, since it contains one of the richest collections of sixteenth- and seventeenth-century icons in Slovakia, taken from some of the many Uniate churches in the surrounding area. Along the north side of the square is the very serious-looking Gothic church of **sv Egídius**, the patron saint of goldsmiths, suitably vast given the burghers' wealth at the time. Inside, it's stuffed full of fifteenth-century carved wooden altars – eleven in all – including the *Altar of St Barbara* by Pavol of Levoča.

Bardejovské kúpele

A four-kilometre bus ride north of Bardejov, the spa town of **BARDEJOVSKÉ KÚPELE** was once a favourite playground of the Austro-Hungarian and Russian nobility. Nowadays, aside from a few remaining nineteenth-century mansions, there's nothing much to hint at its former glory. Instead, the major pull for non-patients is the spa's **skansen** (Tues–Sun 8.15am–noon & 12.30–4.15pm), which contains a whole series of timber-framed buildings, thatched cottages and an early eighteenth-century wooden church transferred from the surrounding Šariš region.

THE WOODEN CHURCHES OF CARPATHO-RUTHENIA

In the Rusyn villages around Bardejov, Svidník and Humenné, a remarkable number of **wooden Uniate churches** have survived to the present day. Most date from around the eighteenth century, when the influence of Baroque was beginning to make itself felt even among the carpenter architects of the Carpathians. A three-some of shingled onion domes, as at Dobroslavova, is the telltale sign, though the humbler churches opt for simple barn-like roofs.

Without your own transport, the possibility of reaching many of the churches *in situ* is limited, although there's a whole cluster within easy walking distance of the main road from Svidník to the Polish border. The easiest way of having a close look is to visit one of the skansens at Bardejovské kúpele, Svidník or Humenné, each of which contains a wooden Uniate church. If, however, you do make it out to some of the villages, you'll need to ask around for the local priest (*kňaz*) who'll have a key (*kľúč*).

The dark and intimate interior of a Uniate church is divided into three sections: (from west to east) the narthex or entrance porch, the main nave and the naos or sanctuary. Even the smallest Uniate church boasts a rich iconostasis all but cutting off the sanctuary, with the familiar icons of (from left to right) St Nicholas, the Virgin and Child, Christ Pantocrator and, lastly, the saint to whom the church is dedicated. Above the central door of the iconostasis (through which only the priest may pass) is the Last Supper, while to the left are busy scenes from the great festivals of the church calendar – the Annunciation, the Assumption and so on. The top tier of icons features the Apostles (with St Paul taking the place of Judas). Typically, the Last Judgement covers the wall of the narthex, usually the most gruesome of all the depictions, with the damned being burned, boiled and decapitated with macabre abandon.

The following is a varied selection of the most interesting churches, still *in situ*:

DOBROSLAVA, 7km north of Svidník. A delightful pagoda-style church, with a wide cruciform ground plan, distinctive triplet of shingled onion domes and an amazing Bosch-style *Last Judgement*.

LADOMIROVÁ, 4km northeast of Svidník. An eccentric mishmash of pagodas, baubles and cupolas on the main road to the Dukla Pass.

LUKOV, 14km west of Bardejov. Look out for the fantastic sixteenth-century diagrammatical depiction of the *Last Judgement* on the iconostasis.

MIROĽA, 12km east of Svidník. One of the most perfect examples of the triple Baroque cupolas descending in height from west to east.

NIŽNÝ KOMÁRNIK, 12km northeast of Svidník. An unusual modern wooden church not in the usual Lemkian style, with the central cupola higher than the other two.

TROČANY, 12km south of Bardejov. Simple cupolas like candle extinguisher caps. Renowned for its lurid, rustic icon of the *Last Judgement*.

ULIČSKÉ KRIVÉ, 2km from the Soviet border. Exceptionally rich in sixteenth-century icon paintings, including one relating the archangel Michael casually pulverising Sodom and Gomorrah.

Svidník and the Dukla Pass

Twenty kilometres or so due east of Bardejov and almost completely obliterated in the heavy fighting of October 1944, **SVIDNÍK** today is, not surprisingly, a characterless concrete sprawl. However, it does contain a clutch of intriguing museums and an open-air skansen of Rusyn folk architecture, and hosts a "Ukrainian" folk festival each year at the end of June. It's also by far the most convenient base from which to explore the wooden churches in the Rusyn villages, chiefly those near the Dukla Pass. For help with accommodation, the local ČEDOK office is 50m east off the town's main street.

Next door to ČEDOK is the **Museum of Ukrainian Culture** (Múzeum ukrajinskej kultúry), containing a fine array of Rusyn folk gear as well as numerous icons from East Slovakia and Russia. A ten-minute walk from the museum up the hill past the bus station, and clearly signposted round town, is the **Galéria Dezidera Millyho** (Tues–Fri 8.30am–4pm, Sat & Sun 9am–2pm), mostly given over to contemporary Rusyn artists, but with a couple of retrospective rooms devoted to Milly, one of the first Rusyn artists to win acclaim for his expressionist paintings of local peasant life. The gallery also houses some weird and wonderful sixteenth- to nineteenth-century icon paintings.

Looking something like the Slovak equivalent of New York's Guggenheim Museum, the spanking white **Dukla Museum** at the beginning of the Bardejov road is under reconstruction, but when complete it should house a gruesome exhibition on the battle for the "Valley of Death" (see "Dukla Pass" below). Instead, head about 1km northwest towards Bardejov, where a gigantic **Soviet war memorial** commemorates the many thousands who fell in the fighting. It's an exceptionally peaceful spot, interrupted only by the occasional coachload of Soviet war veterans, who stagger up the monumental staircase to lay wreaths to the sound of Beethoven's Funeral March blasting out from speakers strategically hidden in the ornamental shrubbery.

On the opposite side of the road, near the local football stadium, is Svidník's brand new, open-air folk **skansen** (times as Galéria Dezidera Millyho). If you're not planning on visiting any of the less accessible villages, this is a great opportunity to get a close look at some thatched Rusyn cottages, as well as a typical wooden Uniate church, brought here from the nearby village of Nová Polianka.

The Dukla Pass

The **Dukla Pass** (Dukliansky priesmyk), 15km north of Svidník by bus, was for centuries the main mountain crossing-point on the trade route from the Baltic to Hungary. This location has ensured a bloody history, the worst episode occurring in the last war, when over 80,000 Soviet soldiers and 6500 Czechoslovaks died trying to capture the valley from the Nazis. There's a giant granite memorial at the top of the pass, 1km from the Polish border, as well as an open-air museum – a trail of underground bunkers, tussling tanks and sundry armoured vehicles – strung out along the road from VIŠNÝ KOMÁRNIK, the first village to be liberated in Czechoslovakia (on October 6, 1944), to KRAJNÁ POĽANA.

Humenné and around

HUMENNÉ, like Prešov, is another basically Slovak town which serves as a centre for the neighbouring Rusyn villages. A modern and spacious place, with more charm than you'd expect from a town based on the chemical industry, the few visitors who do make it this far (mostly American emigrés) aim straight down the leafy main boulevard from the train station for Humenné's one and only sight, the stately seventeenth-century **zámok**. The museum inside the chateau is worth skipping for the enticing **skansen** (Tues–Fri 8am–4pm, Sat & Sun 9am–1pm) round the back of the chateau gardens. Set in a pretty little meadow-cum-orchard, there's a whole series of vivid blue-painted cottages and a characteristic eighteenth-century wooden church from Nová Sedlica; ask for the information sheet in English (*anglický text*).

Medzilaborce

Although actually closer to Svidník, **MEDZILABORCE** is best approached by train from Humenné, 42km to the south. The only conceivable reason to make the long journey out here is if the proposed **Andy Warhol Museum** becomes a reality. Although Andy Warhol himself was born in Chicago, USA (as Andrej Varchola), both his parents hailed from the Rusyn village of Miková, 8km northwest of Medzilaborce. His coal-mining father emigrated to the States shortly before World War I, the rest of the family joining him in 1918. Andy and his two brothers were brought up speaking Rusyn and English, but when fame and fortune hit in the 1960s, Warhol rarely made reference to his Slav origins, either in his work or conversation. Following his death in 1987, his home town began looking into the idea of establishing a museum. The fact that – as yet – no original works have been donated by the Andy Warhol Foundation in New York seems not to have perturbed the museum's enthusiasts: if the museum does take off, it could well be one of the most surreal experiences this side of the Carpathians.

Košice

Slovak towns never amount to much more than their one long main square, and **KOŠICE** – despite a population of over 200,000 – is no exception. Nevertheless, the buzz of city life can be quite reassuring, especially after a week or so in the Slovak back-of-beyond. Just 21km north of the Hungarian border, Košice also acts as a magnet for the Hungarian community – to whom the city is known as *Kassa* – and the terminally underemployed Gypsies of the surrounding region, lending it a diversity and vibrancy absent from small-town Slovakia.

Arriving and finding a place to stay

The **train** and **bus stations** are opposite each other, five minutes' walk east of the old town – an egg-shaped affair, no more than five or six blocks across from east to west. Head for the fanciful **Jakabov palác** across the park from the stations, which lies on gen. Petrova, one of several streets that take you to the main square.

Booking a **room** through ČEDOK (situated in the *Slovan* hotel at the southern end of the main square; ☎095-531 21) should be easy enough: ask about one of the city's cheap and central **hotel** options, like the *Tatra* and the late Baroque *Hotel Evropa*. The *Club* on Nerudova (☎095-202 14) is also fairly cheap, while the *Hutník* at Tyršovo nábrežie 6 (☎095-377 80) and *Imperiál* at gen. Petrova 16 (☎095-221 46) are both only moderately expensive. The *Slovan* (☎095-273 78) itself is Košice's most expensive hotel.

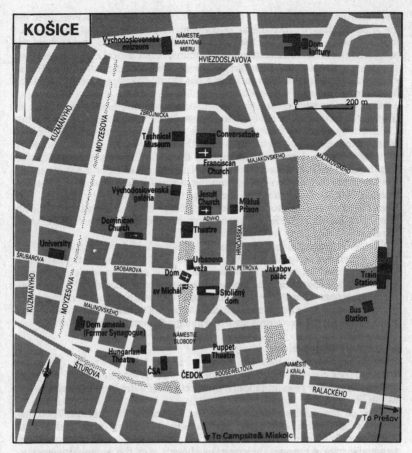

For information on the city's **student hostels**, open during July and August, enquire at the *CKM* office at no. 82 on the main square (☎095-278 58). The nearest **campsite** (mid-April to Sept) is 5km south of the city centre and also rents out bungalows; take tram #1 or #4, or bus #22 or #52 from the *Slovan* to the flyover, then get off and walk the remaining 500m west along Alejová, the road to Rožňava.

The old town

Almost everything of interest is situated on Košice's long main square, lined with handsome Baroque and Neoclassical palaces, but dominated by the city's striking charchoal-coloured **dóm**. Begun around 1390, it was paid for by the riches of the salt trade, which reached its peak in the following century. From the outside, it's an unusual building with striped roof tiles, like those of Saint Stephan's in Vienna, and two contorted towers. Inside, Gothic furnishings add an impressive touch to an otherwise quite plain nave – the main gilded altar depicting scenes from the life of Saint Elizabeth, patron saint of the dom, despite the fact that the city had a long and bitter row with her father, Charles of Anjou, over its monopoly of the salt trade. One of the best features of the church is the intricate relief work above the north and west doors, their tympana respectively depicting the frantic scenes of the Last Judgement, and Christ and his sleepy disciples squeezed onto the Mount of Olives.

South of the dóm is the similar, but much smaller, Gothic church of **sv Michal**, converted into a military storehouse during the sixteenth century when the threat of a Turkish invasion turned the town into little more than a military barracks and caused a mass exodus from the region. Visible from sv Michal, on the east side of the square, is the **Stoličný dom** where the post-war government was declared by President Edvard Beneš on April 4, 1945. For many observers, the fate of the country was sealed from the moment Beneš handed over four key ministries to the Communists, including the Ministry of the Interior. The Communists also saw this as a turning point – the house was subsequently chosen as the venue for Košice's (temporarily suspended) museum of the working class.

On the busy north side of the dom, Košice's handful of tourists dutifully climb the fourteenth-century **Urbanova veža** (Tues–Sat 9am–5pm, Sun 9am–1pm), which stands on its own set of mini-arcades, lined with gravestones discovered under the building during its nineteenth-century renovation. Lastly, the public park which runs down the centre of the main square is a favourite spot for loitering and makes an appropriately graceful approach to the city's grand Austro-Hungarian-built **theatre** (currently undergoing a thorough renovation).

Museums and galleries

Košice's most unusual museum, however, is the **Mikluš Prison** (Miklušova väznica; Tues–Sat 9am–5pm, Sun 9am–1pm), whose original dim-lit dungeons and claustrophobic cells graphically transport you into the house's murky history as the city prison.

Back on the main square, opposite the Franciscan Church, the **Technical Museum** (Tues–Sat 8am–5pm, Sun 8am–1pm) holds a large and eclectic selection of "technical" exhibits, from a giant pair of seventeenth-century bellows to a braille map of Europe. The emphasis, though, is on the wrought-ironwork for which the region is famous – everything from gates to lamp-posts and church bells. One block south at no. 72 is the better than average **Východoslovenská galéria** (Tues–Sat 10am–6pm, Sun 10am–2pm), which houses a variety of twentieth-century paintings and sculptures by Slovak, Hungarian and Austrian artists.

At the northern tip of the main square is námestie Maratónu mieru, a space dominated by the bulky nineteenth-century **Východoslovenské múzeum** (Tues–Sat 9am–5pm, Sun 9am–1pm), worth a look inside for its basement collection of extremely valuable fifteenth- to seventeenth-century **gold coins** – 2920 in all – minted at Kremnica, but stashed away by city burghers loyal to the Habsburgs when Imre Thököly's rebel force took Košice briefly in the 1670s. They were discovered by accident in 1935 by builders renovating no. 74 on the main square, appropriately enough the city's Finance Directorate. Hidden round the back of the museum is a wooden Uniate Church, originally from Carpatho-Ruthenia.

Eating, nightlife and the Herľany Geyser

Apart from hotel **restaurants** such as the *Imperiál*, it's worth trying the *Miskolc* (closed Sun) opposite the Technical Museum, which features Hungarian cuisine, or the more run-of-the-mill *Jalta*, further up on the same side, for sit-down meals. If you're into gathering your own provisions, there's a market by the Dominican Church, one block west of the main square. One place that's worth digging out is the crazy pink-and-blue ice cream parlour on the corner of Dostojevského and Adyho (open daily till 8pm).

Košice's **nightlife** revolves around the *vináreň* on the main square and the few streets on either side. But for something a bit more highbrow, Košice's Philharmonic Orchestra play regular **concerts** at the Dom umenia on Ždanovova and inside the dóm itself. The occasional opera is still performed at the main theatre, or at the Dom kultúry while the former is closed. Those with some knowledge of Hungarian might consider an evening at the *Thalia* Hungarian theatre on Mojmirova.

One of the most unusual sights in East Slovakia is the spectacular **Herľany geyser**, 22km northeast of Košice in the foothills of the Slanské vrchy, which shoots a jet of tepid water over thirty metres into the air for about twenty minutes or so every 32 to 34 hours. *ČEDOK* have the time of the next eruption, so you can time your arrival right on the irregular buses from Košice.

Michalovce and the Slovak Sea

East of Košice lies the **Dargov Pass**, which cuts through the low-lying north–south ridge of the Slanské vrchy, gentle enough to the eye, but a natural barrier that cost the Soviet army over 22,000 men to capture in World War II. A vast granite **monument** at the top of the pass records the fact. Coming down from the hills, the hazy **Zemplín plain** is visible below, stretching south into Hungary's Tokaj wine region and east into Soviet Carpatho-Ruthenia, territory which was an integral part of Czechoslovakia from 1918 to 1945.

Sixty kilometres east of Košice, and only 34km west of the Soviet border, **MICHALOVCE** is the main point of arrival for people heading for the Slovak Sea. Frequent buses run from Košice to Michalovce, but only one direct train, the *Zemplín* express, which leaves Košice at around 8.30am. Other than to change buses, there's no reason to hang around in Michalovce: if you do find yourself with an hour to spare between departures, head for the **town museum** (Tues–Fri 8am–4pm, Sat & Sun 8–11am), housed in the chateau opposite the bus station – marginally more exciting than sitting at the bus station.

The Slovak Sea

A large artificial lake created in the 1960s for industrial purposes, the **Slovak Sea** (Zemplínska šírava) to the east of Michalovce has become an extremely popular summer destination for Slovaks in the last few years. With such a late start in life, brash cheek-by-jowl *chata* colonies are the norm in the resorts which merge into one another along the lake's northern shores. Not everyone's cup of tea, to be sure, but there are compensations – it's hotter here than anywhere else in the country, and the sun continues to shine well into October. If you tire of the beaches, there are plenty of opportunities for **hiking** in the hills of the Vihorlat to the north of the lake (see below).

VINNÉ, the first settlement you come to from Michalovce, isn't actually on the lake shore, but has its own swimming possibilities in the mini-lake a short walk northeast of town, and there's even a ruined **hrad** above the village (1hr 30min by foot). Otherwise, the resorts are much of a concrete muchness, though the further east, the less crowded they get.

In high season, **accommodation** can be a problem without a tent, although many campsites have cheap **bungalows** to rent. There's a moderate motel in KAMENEC, and the more expensive *Merkur* hotel in HÔRKA, but failing that you'll have to fall back on Michalovce's three cheap hotels and bus it to the beach. Of the many **campsites** along the shores, head for the site just past KLOKOČOV (mid-May to Mid-Sept).

HIKING IN THE VIHORLAT

The volcanic hills of the Vihorlat offer some of the most rewarding **hiking** outside the main Tatra ranges: in particular, the trek up to the glacial lake of **Morské oko**. The best time to come is in late September, when the beech trees which cover the Vihorlat turn the hills a brilliant golden brown. The most difficult part is catching a bus further than the village of REMETSKÉ HÁMRE, which you'll need to do if you want to avoid walking the 9km up to the lake. In July and August, a daily bus runs from Michalovce to the car park just below Morské oko, but it passes along the southern shore of the Slovak Sea. The bus service which stops along the northern shore runs weekday mornings only.

From Remetské Hámre, it's a gentle two-hour hike along the pockmarked road to the lake; from the car park, it's just ten minutes. Unfortunately, it's not possible to swim in the lake since the whole area has been declared a nature reserve, but you can picnic wherever you please. Alternatively, it's an hour or so from the shores of the lake to **Sninský kameň** (1005m), a slab of sheer rock which rises up above the tree line, accessible only by ladder. The view from the top is outstanding – the blue-green splodge of Morské oko, the Slovak Sea and Zemplín plain beyond are all clearly visible, and on a good day you can see over into the Soviet Union, just 15km to the east. If you'd prefer not to backtrack, it's less than an hour's walk north to the village of ZEMPLÍNSKE HÁMRE, from where it's a further 5km to BELÁ NAD CIROCHOU (a short train ride from Michalovce).

If you're planning on hiking anywhere else in the Vihorlat, get hold of the hiking map *Bukovské vrchy/Laborecká vrchovina*, and ask at ČEDOK in Michalovce for the latest information on the area.

---

travel details

Trains
From Bratislava hlavná stanica to Trnava (14 daily; 35min); Štúrovo (up to 7 daily; 1hr 40min); Trenčín (14 daily; 1hr 50min); Žilina (15 daily; 3hr 15min); Poprad (12 daily; 6hr); Košice (7 daily; 7hr 30min); Prešov (1 daily; 7hr 15min); Brno (up to 20 daily; 1hr 45min–3hr 30min); Prague (7 daily; 5hr 30min).

From Bratislava Nové Mesto to Trnava (up to 15 daily; 35–50min); Komárno (7 daily; 2hr–2hr 30min); Zvolen/Rožňava/Košice (2 daily; 5hr/8hr/9hr); Banská Bystrica (1 daily; 5hr).

From Banská Bystrica to Zvolen (15 daily; 25–40min); Brezno (10 daily; 1hr 20min); Martin (6 daily; 1hr 50min).

From Zvolen to Detva (9 daily; 40min); Lučenec (15 daily; 1hr–1hr 30min); Kremnica (9 daily; 1hr).

From Žilina to Strečno/Šútovo (up to 12 daily; 15min/45min); Vrútky/Kraľovany (up to 20 daily; 30min/40min).

From Kraľovany to Istebné/Dolný Kubín/Oravský Podzámok/Podbiel/Trstená (13 daily; 16min/35min/55min/1hr 30min/2hr).

From Poprad (Poprad-Tatry) to Starý Smokovec/Štrbské Pleso (up to hourly; 45min/1hr 40min); Tatranská Lomnica (up to 15 daily; 25min); Kežmarok/Stará Ľubovňa (13 daily; 35min/1hr 35min); Košice (12 or more daily; 1hr 30min).

From Prešov to Bardejov (up to 12 daily; 1hr 30min); Humenné (11 daily; 1hr 15min–2hr); Košice (up to 14 daily; 50min).

From Košice to Rožňava (up to 10 daily; 1hr 15min–2hr); Lučenec (4 daily; 3hr 10min).

Buses

From Bratislava to Modra (up to 12 daily; 35min–1hr); Nitra (up to 18 daily; 1hr 30min).

From Poprad to Ždiar (2 daily; 1hr 10min); Levoča (up to 12 daily; 30–50min).

From Svidník to Prešov (up to 3 daily; 1hr 40min); Dukla Pass (up to 4 daily; 35min); Bardejov (up to 8 daily; 1hr 5min).

PART THREE

THE
CONTEXTS

THE HISTORICAL FRAMEWORK

Czechoslovakia has only been in existence since 1918. Before then, its constituent parts – Bohemia, Moravia and Slovakia – enjoyed quite separate histories: the first two under the sway of their German and Austrian neighbours; Slovakia under the Hungarian crown. In the early days of Slav history, all three loosely formed the Great Moravian Empire; later, Bohemia consistently played a pivotal role in European history, prompting the famous pronouncement (attributed to Bismarck) that "he who holds Bohemia holds mid-Europe". Since 1918, Czechoslovakia's tragedies have been exposed to the world at regular intervals – 1938, 1948, 1968 and most recently (and most happily), 1989.

BEGINNINGS

According to Roman records, the area now covered by Czechoslovakia was inhabited as early as 500 BC by **Celtic tribes**: the Boii, who settled in Bohemia (which bears their name), and the Cotini, who inhabited Moravia and parts of Slovakia. Very little is known about either tribe except that around 100 BC they were driven from these territories by two **Germanic tribes**, the Marcomanni who occupied Bohemia, and the Quadi who took over from the Cotini. These later semi-nomadic tribes proved awkward opponents for the Roman Empire, which wisely chose to use the River Danube as their natural eastern border.

The disintegration of the Roman Empire in the fifth century AD corresponded with a series of raids into central Europe by eastern tribes, firstly the **Huns** who displaced the Marcomanni and Quadi, and later the **Avars** who replaced the Huns around the sixth century, settling a vast area including the Hungarian plains and parts of Czechoslovakia. About the same time, the **Slav tribes** entered Europe from east of the Carpathian mountains. To begin with at least, they appear to have been subjugated by the Avars. The first successful Slav rebellion against the Avars seems to have taken place in the seventh century, under the Frankish leadership of **Samo**, though the kingdom he created died with him around 658 AD.

THE GREAT MORAVIAN EMPIRE

The next written record of the Slavs in Czechoslovakia isn't until the eighth century, when East Frankish (Germanic) chroniclers report a people known as the **Moravians** as having established themselves around the River Morava, a tributary of the Danube. It was an alliance of Moravians and Franks (under Charlemagne) which finally expelled the Avars from central Europe in 796 AD.

This cleared the way for the establishment of the **Great Moravian Empire**, which at its peak included Slovakia, Bohemia and parts of Hungary and Poland. At the political and religious crossroads of Europe, its first attested ruler, **Mojmír**, found himself under pressure from two sides: from the West, where the Franks and Bavarians (both Germanic tribes) were jostling for position with the papacy; and from the East, where the Patriarch of Byzantium was keen to extend his influence across Eastern Europe. Mojmír's successor, **Rastislav** (850–870), plumped for Byzantium, and invited the missionaries Cyril and Methodius to introduce Christianity using the Slav liturgy and Eastern rites. Rastislav, however, was given the elbow by his nephew, **Svätopluk** (871–894), who captured and blinded his uncle, allying himself with the Germans instead. With the death of Methodius in 885, the Great Moravian Empire fell decisively under the influence of the Catholic Church.

Svätopluk died shortly before the **Magyar invasion** of 896, an event which heralded the end of the Great Moravian Empire and a significant break in Czecho-Slovak history. The Slavs to the west of the River Morava (ie the Czechs) swore allegiance to the Frankish Emperor, Arnulf; while those to the east (ie the Slovaks) found themselves under the yoke of the Magyars. This separation, which remained for the next millennium, is one of the major factors behind the distinct social, cultural and political differences between Czechs and Slovaks.

THE PŘEMYSLID DYNASTY

During the tenth century, Bohemia began to emerge as a coherent political unit. Although under the shadow of the neighbouring Holy Roman Empire, it was ruled over by a native dynasty of Czech princes known as the **Přemyslids**. Nothing very certain is known about the early Přemyslid rulers, though many legends survive, most famously that of the proselytising **Prince Václav** (Saint Wenceslas) who was martyred by his pagan brother Boleslav the Cruel in 929. By the time the latter's son, Boleslav II (967–999), assumed the crown, Bohemia had officially become part of the Holy Roman Empire, its prince one of the seven electors of the emperor. During the eleventh century the Czech Lands (Bohemia and Moravia) were permanently united, though Moravia remained a separate province, usually ruled by a younger son of whoever was on the Bohemian throne.

The thirteenth century was the high point of Přemyslid rule over Bohemia. With the Emperor Frederick II preoccupied with Mediterranean affairs and dynastic problems, and the Hungarians and Poles busy trying to repulse the Mongol invasions from 1220 onwards, the Přemyslids were able to assert their independence. In 1212, **Otakar I** (1198–1230) managed to extract a "Golden Bull" (formal edict) from the emperor, confirming the royal title for Otakar and his descendents (who thereafter became *kings* of Bohemia). The discovery of silver and gold mines throughout the Czech Lands and Slovakia heralded a period of prosperity and large-scale **German colonisation**. Encouraged by the Přemyslids (and in Slovakia, the Hungarian Árpád dynasty), German miners and craftsmen founded whole towns in the interior of the country, such as Kutná Hora,

Jihlava, Banská Bystrica and Levoča. At the same time, the territories of the Bohemian crown were increased to include not only Bohemia and Moravia but also Silesia and Lusatia to the north (now divided between Germany and Poland).

A series of dynastic disputes at the beginning of the fourteenth century, culminating in the murder of the heirless teenage Václav III in 1306, led to the **end of the Přemyslid dynasty**. After more bloodletting, the Czech nobles offered the throne to John of Luxembourg, who was married to Václav III's niece and was the son of the Holy Roman Emperor.

THE GOLDEN AGE, HUS AND THE HUSSITES

King John spent most of his reign participating in foreign wars, with Bohemia footing the bill, and John himself paying for it first with his sight, and finally with his life, on the field at Crécy in 1346. It was his son, **Charles IV**, who ushered in the Czech nation's golden age. Although born and bred in France, Charles was a Bohemian at heart (his mother was Czech and his real name was Václav), as well as being an unusually intelligent monarch, speaking five languages fluently and even writing an autobiography. In 1346, he became not only king of Bohemia, but also, by election, Holy Roman Emperor. Two years later he founded a university in Prague and began promoting the city as the cultural capital of central Europe, erecting rich Gothic monuments – many of which still survive – and numerous ecclesiastical institutions. As emperor, Charles issued many Golden Bull edicts that strengthened Bohemia's position, promoted Czech as the official language alongside Latin and German, and presided over a period of peace in central Europe.

Following Charles' death in 1378, Václav IV assumed the throne. A legendary drinker, more interested in hunting than ruling, his reign was overshadowed by religious divisions within the Czech Lands and Europe as a whole, beginning with the **Great Schism** (1378–1417) in which rival popes held court in Rome and Avignon. This was a severe blow to Rome's centralising power, which might otherwise have successfully combated the assault on the Church which was under way in the Czech Lands towards the end of the fourteenth century.

JAN HUS

The attack was led by the peasant-born preacher **Jan Hus**, who was appointed to the influential position of Rector at Prague University in 1403. A follower of the English reformer John Wycliffe, Hus began to preach in the language of the masses (ie Czech) against the wealth, corruption and hierarchical tendencies within the Church at the time. A devout, mild-mannered man himself, as Rector he became embroiled in a dispute between the conservative German theologians and the Wycliffian Czechs at the university. For political reasons Václav backed Hus, and the Germans left the university in protest.

Hus's victory was short-lived. Widening his attacks on the Church, he began to preach against the sale of religious indulgences to fund the inter-papal wars, thus incurring the enmity of Václav (who received a percentage of the sales). In 1412 Hus and his followers were expelled from the university and spent the next two years as itinerant preachers spreading their reformist gospel throughout Bohemia. In 1414 Hus was summoned to the **Council of Constance** to answer charges of heresy. Despite a guarantee of safe conduct from the Emperor Sigismund, Hus was condemned to death and, having refused to renounce his beliefs, was burned at the stake on July 6, 1415.

Hus's martyrdom sparked off a **widespread rebellion** in Bohemia, uniting virtually all Czechs – clergy and laity, peasant and noble (including many of Hus's former opponents) – against the decision of the council, and by inference against the Catholic church. The Hussites immediately set about reforming church practices, most famously by administering communion *sub utraque specie* ("in both kinds", ie bread and wine) for the laity, as opposed to the Roman Catholic practice of reserving the wine for the clergy.

THE HUSSITE WARS

In 1419, Václav inadvertently provoked large-scale rioting by endorsing the re-admission of anti-Hussite priests to their parishes. In the ensuing violence, several Catholic councillors were thrown to their death from the windows of Prague's Novoměstská radnice. This defenestration is now taken as the official beginning of the **Hussite Wars** (1419–1434). Václav himself was so enraged (not to say terrified) by the mob that he suffered a heart attack and died. The pope, meanwhile, declared an international crusade against the heretics, under the leadership of the Emperor Sigismund, Václav's brother and heir to the Bohemian throne.

Already, though, cracks were appearing in the Hussite camp. The more radical Hussites, known as the **Táborites**, broadened their attacks on the Church hierarchy to include all figures of authority and privilege. Their message found a ready audience among the oppressed classes in Prague and the Bohemian countryside, who went round eagerly destroying church property and massacring Catholics. Such actions were deeply disturbing to the Czech nobility and their supporters who backed the more moderate Hussites – known as the **Utraquists** (from the Latin *sub utraque specie*) – who confined their criticisms to religious matters.

The common Catholic enemy prevented any serious divisions from developing amongst the Hussites for at least a decade or so, and under the inspirational military leadership of the Táborite **Jan Žižka**, the Hussites' (mostly peasant) army enjoyed some miraculous early victories over the numerically superior "crusaders". The Bohemian Diet quickly drew up the **Four Articles of Prague**, a compromise between the two Hussite camps, outlining the basic tenets about which all Hussites could agree, including communion "in both kinds". The Táborites, meanwhile, continued to burn, loot and pillage ecclesiastical institutions from Prague to the far reaches of Slovakia. At the **Council of Basel** in 1433 the Utraquists finally persuaded Rome to accept the Four Articles, in return for ceasing hostilities. The peasant-based Táborites (rightly) saw the deal as a victory for the Bohemian nobility and the status quo, and vowed to continue the fight. However, the Utraquists, now in cahoots with the Catholic forces, easily defeated the remaining Táborites at the Battle of Lipany in 1434.

By the end of the Hussite Wars, the situation for the majority of the population – landless serfs, and as such virtual slaves to the local feudal lords – had actually changed very little. The most significant development in the **social structure** was the growth of towns at strategic points on the continent's trade routes. In the new merchant class, Germans predominated, organising themselves into guilds, and preparing the ground for popular Czech resentment in later years.

COMPROMISE AND COUNTER-REFORMATION

Despite the agreement of the Council of Basel, the pope still refused to acknowledge the Utraquist church in Bohemia. The Utraquists nevertheless consolidated their position, electing the gifted **George of Poděbrady** as first Regent and then King of Bohemia (1458–71). The first and last Hussite king, George (Jiří to the Czechs) is remembered primarily for his commitment to promoting religious tolerance and for his far-sighted efforts in trying to establish some sort of "Peace Confederation" in Europe.

On George's death, the Bohemian Estates handed the crown over to the **Polish Jagiellonian dynasty** who ruled in absentia, effectively relinquishing the reins of power to the Czech nobility. In 1526, however, the victory of the Turks over the Hungarians at the Battle of Mohács led to the election of the Habsburg Ferdinand I as king of the Czech Lands and Hungary in order to fill the power vacuum, the **beginning of Habsburg rule** in what is now Czechoslovakia. Ferdinand adroitly secured automatic hereditary succession over the Bohemian throne for the Habsburgs, in return for which he accepted the agreement at the Council of Basel in 1537.

In 1546, the Utraquist Bohemian nobility provocatively joined the powerful Protestant Schmalkaldic League in their (ultimately successful) war against the Holy Roman Emperor, Charles V. When armed conflict broke out in Bohemia, however, victory fell to Ferdinand, who took the opportunity to extend the influence of Catholicism in the Czech Lands, executing several leading Protestant nobles, persecuting the Unity of Czech Brethren who figured prominently in the rebellion, and inviting Jesuit missionaries to establish churches and seminaries in the Czech Lands.

THE THIRTY YEARS' WAR

Despite the tolerance practised by Ferdinand's slightly loopy but liberal successor, Rudolf II (1576–1611), conflict erupted again during the reign of the ardently Catholic Matthias (1612–1617). The prospect of another Habsburg Catholic – Ferdinand II – acceding to the throne finally prompted the Bohemian Protestants to rebel. On May 23, 1618, two Catholic nobles were thrown out of the windows of Prague Castle – the country's second celebrated defenestration – an event which is now taken as the official beginning of the complex religious and dynastic conflicts collectively known as the **Thirty Years' War** (1618–1648).

Following the defenestration, the Bohemian Diet expelled the Jesuits and elected the youthful Protestant "Winter King", Frederick of the Palatinate, to the throne. In the first decisive set-to of the war, on November 8, 1620, the Czech Protestants were utterly defeated at the **Battle of Bílá hora** (Battle of the White Mountain). Twenty-seven Protestant nobles were executed on the Staroměstské náměstí in Prague and an estimated five-sixths of the Czech nobility went into exile, their properties handed over to loyal Catholic families from Austria, Spain and Italy.

THE DARK AGES

As a result of Bílá hora, the Czechs effectively lost their aristocracy, their religion and (for a while) their culture. The Thirty Years' War ended with the Peace of Westphalia in 1648, which, for the Czechs, was as disastrous as the war itself. The country was devastated, towns and cities laid waste, and the total population reduced by almost two-thirds. On top of all that, the Czech Lands were now decisively under the Catholic sphere of influence, and the full force of the **Counter-Reformation** was brought to bear on its people. All forms of Protestantism were outlawed, the education system was handed over to the Jesuits and, in 1651 alone, over two hundred "witches" were burned at the stake in Bohemia.

The next two centuries of Habsburg rule are known to the Czechs as the **dark ages**. Austria's absolutist grip over the Czech Lands catapulted the remaining nobility into intensive Germanisation, while fresh waves of German immigrants reduced Czech to a despised dialect spoken by peasants, artisans and servants. The situation was so bad that Prague and most other urban centres became practically all-German cities. By the end of the eighteenth century, the Czech language was on the verge of dying out, with government, scholarship and literature carried out exclusively in German. For the newly ensconced Germanised aristocracy, of course, the good times rolled and the country was endowed with numerous Baroque palaces and monuments.

The **rule of enlightenment** (1740–1790) during the reigns of Maria Theresa and her son Joseph II brought a degree of light to the dark ages. Having ruthlessly done their job, the Jesuits were unceremoniously expelled from the Empire, and the 1781 Edict of Tolerance allowed some freedom of worship for the first time in over 150 years. Such religious concessions were tempered by the inexorable centralisation and bureaucratisation which accompanied them, placing power in the hands of the Austrian civil service, and thus accelerating Germanisation. In addition, Maria Theresa involved the Czech Lands in a number of very costly wars, which resulted in the loss of most of the rich province of Silesia to Prussia.

THE NATIONAL REVIVALS

The Habsburgs' enlightened rule inadvertently provided the basis for the economic prosperity and social changes of the **Industrial Revolution**, which in turn fuelled the Czech national revival of the nineteenth century. The textile, glass, coal and iron industries began to grow, drawing ever more Czechs in from the countryside and swamping the hitherto mostly Germanised towns and cities. An embryonic Czech bourgeoisie emerged, and, thanks to Maria Theresa's educational reforms, new educational and economic opportunities were given to the Czech lower classes.

For the first half of the century, the Czech national revival or **národní obrození** was confined to the new Czech intelligentsia, led by philologists like Josef Dobrovský and Josef Jungmann at the Prague University. Language disputes (in schools, universities and public offices) remained at the forefront of Czech nationalism throughout the nineteenth century, only later developing into demands for political autonomy from Vienna. The leading figure of the time was the historian **František Palacký**, a Protestant from Moravia, who wrote the first history of the Czech nation, rehabilitating Hus and the Czech reformists in the process. He was in many ways typical of the early Czech nationalists – pan-Slavist and virulently anti-German, but not yet entirely anti-Habsburg.

SLOVAKIA

What the Czechs suffered in the three centuries following the Battle of Bílá hora, the Slovaks had to endure for almost a millennium, under **Hungarian rule**. For the entire duration, the territory of modern-day Slovakia was an integral part of the Hungarian Kingdom, known simply as Upper Hungary, and apart from a few German-speaking mining towns, it remained overwhelmingly rural and resolutely feudal. Those Slovaks who did rise to positions of power were swiftly "Magyarised".

The Battle of Mohács in 1526 signalled a temporary eclipse for the Hungarians as the Habsburgs assumed control of their kingdom. The eighteenth-century Enlightenment, on the other hand, boosted the Magyar national revival, and in 1792 Hungarian finally replaced Latin as the official state language throughout the Hungarian Kingdom. But Magyar nationalism was essentially chauvinistic, furthering the interests of the Magyarised nobility and no one else. The idea that non-Magyars might want to assert their own identity was regarded as highly subversive. Nevertheless, assert it they did.

With a thoroughly Magyarised aristocracy, and virtually no middle class, the Slovak national revival or **národné obrodenie** was left to the tiny Slovak intelligentsia that was made up mostly of Lutheran clergymen – passionately pro-Czech and anti-Magyar, but alienated from the majority of the devoutly Catholic Slovak peasantry on account of their religious beliefs. The leading Slovak figure throughout this period was **Ľudovít Štúr**, son of a Lutheran pastor, pan-Slavist but an ardent advocate of a separate Slovak language based on his own Central Slovak dialect.

1848 AND AFTER

The fall of the French monarchy in February 1848 prompted a crisis in the Habsburg Empire. The new bourgeoisie began to make political demands – freedom of the press, of assembly, of religious creeds – and in the nature of the Empire, its constituent nationalities also called out for more rights. In the Czech Lands, liberal opinion became polarised between the Czech- and German-speakers. Palacký and his followers were against the dissolution of the Empire and argued instead for a kind of multinational federation. Since the Empire contained a majority of Slavs, the ethnic Germans were utterly opposed to Palacký's scheme, campaigning for unification with Germany to secure their interests. Meanwhile, the radicals and students (on both sides) took to the streets in protest, giving the forces of reaction an excuse to declare martial law in June 1848.

In the Hungarian Kingdom, the **1848 revolution** successfully toppled the Habsburgs, and a liberal constitutional government was temporarily set up in Budapest. However, Hungarian liberals like Lajos Kossuth (himself from a Magyarised Slovak family) showed themselves to be more reactionary than the Habsburgs when it came to opposing the aspirations of non-Magyars. The "Demands of the Slovak Nation", drafted by Štúr, were refused point-blank by the Hungarian Diet in May 1848. Incensed by this, Štúr and his small Slovak army went over to the Habsburgs and into battle (unsuccessfully) against Kossuth's revolutionaries. Only in August 1849 was Habsburg rule reinstated, thanks to the intervention of Tsarist Russian troops on the streets of Budapest.

In both cases, the upheavals of 1848 left the absolutist Habsburg Empire shaken but fundamentally unchanged. The one great positive achievement in 1848 was the **emancipation of the peasants**. Otherwise, events only served to highlight the sharp differences between German and Czech aspirations in the Czech Lands, and between Hungarian and Slovak aspirations in the Hungarian Kingdom.

The Habsburg recovery was, however, short-lived. In 1859 and again in 1866, the new Emperor, Franz Joseph II, suffered humiliating defeats at the hands of the Italians and Prussians respectively. In order to buy some more time, the compromise or Ausgleich of 1867 was drawn up, establishing the so-called **Dual Monarchy** of Austria-Hungary – two independent states united by one ruler.

THE CZECH LANDS

For the Czechs, the Ausgleich came as a bitter disappointment. The Magyars became the Austrians' equals, while the Czechs remained second-class citizens. The Czechs' failure in bending the Emperor's ear was no doubt partly due to the absence of a Czech aristocracy which could bring its social weight to bear at the Viennese court. Nevertheless, the Ausgleich did mark an end to the absolutism of before, and the relatively liberal Austrians granted a wide range of civil liberties culminating in universal male suffrage in 1907.

Under such circumstances the Czech national movement flourished – and splintered. The liberals and conservatives known as the **Old Czechs**, backed by the new Czech industrialists, achieved a number of minor legislative successes, which outraged the German minority in the Czech Lands. By 1890, though, the more radical **Young Czechs** gained the upper hand and instigated a policy of non-cooperation with Vienna. The most famous political figure to emerge from the ranks of the Young Czechs was the Prague university professor **Tomáš Garrigue Masaryk**, who founded his own Realist Party in 1900 and began advocating the (then rather quirky) concept of closer cooperation between the Czechs and Slovaks.

SLOVAKIA

For the Slovaks, the Ausgleich was nothing less than a catastrophe. In the 1850s and 1860s, direct rule from Vienna had kept Magyar chauvinism at bay, allowing the Slovaks to establish various cultural and educational institutions. After 1867, the Hungarian authorities embarked on a maniacal policy of **Magyarisation** which made Hungarian (and only Hungarian) compulsory in both primary and secondary schools. Large landowners were the only ones to be given the vote (a mere six percent of the total population), while the majority of non-Magyars remained peasants. Poverty and malnutrition were commonplace throughout Upper Hungary and, by 1914, twenty percent of the Slovak population had emigrated, mostly to the USA.

Given the suffocating policies of the Magyars, it's a miracle that the Slovak národné obrodenie (and even the language itself) was able to survive. The leading Slovak political force, the Slovak National Party, was driven underground, remaining small, conservative and for the most part Lutheran throughout the latter part of the nineteenth century. The one notable exception was the Catholic priest, **Andrej Hlinka**, whose unflinching opposition to Magyar rule earned him an increasingly large audience among the Slovak people.

WORLD WAR I

At the outbreak of **World War I**, the Czechs and Slovaks showed little enthusiasm for fighting alongside their old enemies, the Austrians and Hungarians, against their Slav brothers, the Russians and Serbs. As the war progressed, large numbers defected to form the **Czechoslovak Legion**, which fought on the Eastern Front. Masaryk travelled to the USA to curry favour for a new Czechoslovak state while his two deputies, the Czech Edvard Beneš and the Slovak Milan Štefánik did the same in Britain and France.

In the summer of 1918, the Allies recognised Masaryk's provisional government and on October 28, 1918, as the Habsburg Empire began to collapse, the new **Czechoslovak Republic** was declared in Prague. In response, the German-speaking border regions (later to become the Sudetenland) declared their own *Deutsch-Böhmen* (German-Bohemian) government, loyal to the Austrians. Nothing came of the latter, and by the end of the year Czechoslovak troops had gained control of the Sudetenland with relatively little resistance.

In Hungary, a small group of leading Slovaks threw in their lot with the Czechs, while the rest of the country passively accepted its fate. The Hungarians, however, had other plans. Béla Kun's Red Army proceeded to occupy much of Slovakia, and it took an invasion by the Czechoslovak Legion to boot them out late on in 1919. In June 1920, the **Treaty of Trianon** confirmed the new Slovak–Hungarian border along the Danube.

Last to opt in favour of the new republic was **Ruthenia** (officially known as Sub-Carpatho Ruthenia), a rural backwater of the old Hungarian Kingdom which became officially part of Czechoslovakia in the Treaty of St Germain in September 1919. Its incorporation was largely due to the campaigning efforts of Ruthenian emigrés in the USA. For the new republic the province was a strategic bonus, but otherwise a huge drain on resources.

THE FIRST REPUBLIC

The new nation, Czechoslovakia, began postwar life in an enviable economic position – **tenth in the world industrial league table** – having inherited seventy to eighty percent of Austria-Hungary's industry intact. Less enviable was the diverse make-up of its population – a melange of minorities which would in the end prove its downfall. Along with the 6 million Czechs and 2 million Slovaks who initially backed the republic, there were over 3 million

Germans and 600,000 Hungarians, not to mention sundry other Ruthenians (Rusyns), Jews and Poles.

That Czechoslovakia's democracy survived as long as it did is down to the powerful political presence and skill of **Masaryk**, the country's president from 1918 to 1935, who shared executive power with the cabinet. It was his vision of social democracy which was stamped on the nation's new constitution, one of the most liberal of the time (if a little too bureaucratic and centralised), aimed at ameliorating any ethnic and class tensions within the republic by means of universal suffrage, land reform and, more specifically, the Language Law, which ensured bilinguality to any area where the minority exceeded twenty percent.

The elections of 1920 reflected the mood of the time, ushering in the left-liberal alliance of the **Pětka** ("The Five"), a coalition of five parties led by the Agrarian, Antonín Švehla, whose slogan "We have agreed that we will agree" became the keystone of the republic's consensus politics between the wars. Gradually all the other parties (except the Fascist and Communist parties) – among them Hlinka's Slovak People's Party and most of the Sudeten German parties – began to participate in (or at least not disrupt) parliamentary proceedings. On the eve of the Wall Street Crash, the republic was enjoying an economic boom, a cultural renaissance and a temporary *modus vivendi* between its minorities.

THE THIRTIES

The 1929 Wall Street Crash plunged the whole country into crisis. Economic hardship was quickly followed by **political instability**. In Slovakia, Hlinka's People's Party fed off the anti-Czech resentment that was fuelled by Prague's manic centralisation, consistently polling around thirty percent, despite its increasingly nationalist/separatist position. In Ruthenia, the elections of 1935 gave only 37 percent of the vote to parties supporting the republic, the rest going to the Communists, pro-Magyars and other autonomist groups.

But without doubt the most intractable of the minority problems was that of the Sudeten Germans who occupied the heavily industrialised border regions of Bohemia and Moravia. Nationalist sentiment had always run high in the Sudetenland, whose German-speakers resented having been included in the new republic, but it was only after the Crash that the extremist parties began to make significant electoral gains. Encouraged by the rise of Nazism in Germany, and aided by rocketing Sudeten German unemployment, the proto-Nazi **Sudeten German Party** (SdP), led by a gym teacher by the name of Konrad Henlein, was able to win over sixty percent of the German-speaking votes in the 1935 elections.

Although constantly denying any wish to secede from the republic, Henlein and the SdP were increasingly funded and directed from Nazi Germany after 1935. To make matters worse, the Czechs suffered a severe blow to their morale with the death of Masaryk late in 1937, leaving the country in the less capable hands of his Socialist deputy, Edvard Beneš. With the Nazi annexation of Austria (the Anschluss) on March 11, 1938, Hitler was free to focus his attention on the Sudetenland, calling Henlein to Berlin on March 28 and instructing him to call for outright autonomy.

THE MUNICH CRISIS

On April 24, 1938, the SdP launched its final propaganda offensive in the **Karlsbad Decrees**, demanding (without defining) "complete autonomy". As this would have meant surrendering the entire Czechoslovak border defences, not to mention causing economic havoc, Beneš refused to bow to the SdP's demands. Armed conflict was only narrowly avoided and, by the beginning of September, Beneš was forced reluctantly to acquiesce to some sort of autonomy. On Hitler's orders, Henlein refused Beneš' offer and called openly for the secession of the Sudetenland to the German Reich.

On September 15, as Henlein fled to Germany, the British prime minister, Neville Chamberlain, flew to Berchtesgarden on his own ill-conceived initiative, to "appease" the Führer. A week later, Chamberlain flew again to Germany, this time to Bad Godesburg, vowing to the British public that the country would not go to war (in his famous words) "because of a quarrel in a far-away country between people of whom we know nothing". Nevertheless, the French issued draft papers, the British Navy was mobilised, and the whole of Europe fully expected war. Then in the early hours of September 30, in one of the most treacherous

and self-interested acts of modern European diplomacy, prime ministers Chamberlain (for Britain) and Deladier (for France) signed the **Munich Diktat** with Mussolini and Hitler – without consulting the Czechoslovak government – agreeing to all of Hitler's demands. The British and French public were genuinely relieved, and Chamberlain flew back to cheering home crowds, waving his famous piece of paper that guaranteed "peace in our time".

Betrayed by his only Western allies and fearing bloodshed, Beneš capitulated, against the wishes of most Czechs. Had Beneš not given in, however, it's doubtful anything would have come of Czech armed resistance, surrounded as they were by vastly superior hostile powers. Beneš resigned on October 5 and left the country. On October 15, **German troops occupied Sudetenland** to the dismay of the forty percent of Sudeten Germans who hadn't voted for Henlein (not to mention the half a million Czechs who lived there). The Poles took the opportunity to seize a sizeable chunk of North Moravia, while in the "rump" Second Republic (officially known as Czecho-Slovakia), the one-eyed war veteran Emil Hácha became president, Slovakia and Ruthenia electing their own autonomous governments.

The Second Republic was not long in existence before it too collapsed. On March 15, 1939, Hitler informed Hácha of the imminent Nazi occupation of what was left of the Czech Lands, and persuaded him to demobilise the army, again against the wishes of many Czechs. The Germans encountered no resistance (nor any response from the Second Republic's supposed guarantors, Britain and France) and swiftly set up the Nazi **Protectorate of Bohemia and Moravia**. The Hungarians effortlessly crushed Ruthenia's brief independence, while the Slovak People's Party, backed by the Nazis, declared **Slovak independence**, under the leadership of the Catholic priest Jozef Tiso.

WORLD WAR II

In the first few months of the occupation, Nazi rule in the Protectorate was not yet as harsh as it would become: left-wing activists were arrested, Jews dismissed from their jobs, while the economy even enjoyed a mini-boom. Then in late October and November 1939, Czech students began a series of demonstrations against the Nazis, who responded by closing down all institutions of higher education. Calm was restored until 1941 when a leading SS officer, **Reinhard Heydrich**, was put in charge of the Protectorate. Arrests and deportations followed, reaching fever pitch after Heydrich was assassinated by the Czech resistance in June 1942 (see p.89). The "final solution" was meted out on the country's remaining Jews, while the rest of the population were frightened into submission – very few acts of active resistance being undertaken in the Czech Lands for the remaining duration of the war.

In independent Slovakia, Tiso's government met with widespread support until the extremist Hlinka Guards (the Slovak equivalent of the SS) got the upper hand and began the inexorable Nazification of Slovak society, including the deportation of Slovak Jews. The resistance movement was slow to start, but strong enough by August 1944 to attempt an all-out **Slovak National Uprising** in the central mountains (see p.297). When the hoped-for Soviet offensive failed to materialise, the uprising was brutally suppressed and any pretence at Slovak independence abandoned for full-scale Nazi occupation.

By the end of 1944, Czechoslovak and Russian troops had begun to liberate the country, starting with Ruthenia, which Stalin decided to take as war booty despite having guaranteed to maintain Czechoslovakia's pre-Munich borders. On April 4, 1945, under Beneš' leadership, the provisional **Národní fronta** government was set up in Košice, a coalition of Social Democrats, Socialists and Communists. On May 5, the people of Prague finally rose up against the Nazis, many hoping to prompt an American offensive from Plzeň, which General Patton's Third Army had recently captured. In the end, the Americans made the politically disastrous (but militarily wise) decision not to cross the previously agreed upon demarcation line, leaving the Russians to liberate Prague, which they did on May 9.

AFTER THE WAR: THE THIRD REPUBLIC

Reprisals against suspected collaborators and the German-speaking population in general began as soon as the country was liberated. With considerable popular backing and the tacit approval of the Red Army, Beneš began to organise the **forced expulsion of the German-speaking population**, referred to euphemistically by the Czechs as the *odsun* (transfer). Only those Germans who could prove their anti-Fascist credentials were permitted to stay, and by the summer of 1947, nearly 2.5 million Germans had been kicked out or had fled in fear. On this occasion, Sudeten German objections were brushed aside by the Allies who had given Beneš the go-ahead at the postwar Potsdam Conference. Attempts by Beneš to expel the Hungarian-speaking minority in similar fashion, however, proved unsuccessful.

On October 28, 1945, in accordance with the leftist programme thrashed out at Košice, sixty percent of the country's industry was nationalised. Confiscated Sudeten German property was handed out by the largely Communist-controlled police force, and in a spirit of optimism and/or opportunism, people began to join the Communist Party (KSČ) in droves, membership shooting up from 17,000 to over a million in less than a year. In the **May 1946 elections**, the Party reaped the rewards of their enthusiastic support for the *odsun*, of Stalin's vocal opposition to Munich, and of the recent Soviet liberation, emerging as the strongest single party in the Czech Lands, with up to forty percent of the vote (the largest ever for a European Communist Party). In Slovakia, however, they failed to push the Democrats into second place, with just thirty percent. President Beneš appointed the KSČ leader, **Klement Gottwald**, prime minister of another Národní fronta coalition, with just three (strategically important) cabinet portfolios going to Party members: Finance, Information and Interior.

Gottwald assured everyone of the KSČ's commitment to parliamentary democracy, and initially at least even agreed to participate in the Americans' Marshall Plan (the only Eastern Bloc country to do so). Stalin immediately summoned Gottwald to Moscow, and on his return the KSČ denounced the Plan. By the end of 1947, the Communists were beginning to lose support, as the harvest failed, the economy faltered and malpractices within the Communist-controlled Ministry of Interior were uncovered. In response, the KSČ began to up the ante, constantly warning the nation of imminent "counter-revolutionary plots", and arguing for greater nationalisation and land reform as a safeguard.

Then in February 1948 – officially known as **"Victorious February"** – the latest in a series of scandals hit the Ministry of Interior, prompting the twelve non-Communist cabinet ministers to resign *en masse*, thus hoping to force a physically weak President Beneš to dismiss Gottwald. No attempt was made, however, to rally popular support against the Communists. Instead, thanks to the divisions within the Social Democrats, Gottwald was able to maintain his majority in parliament, while the KSČ took to the streets (and the airwaves, given their control of the Ministry of Information), arming "workers' militia" units to defend the country against counter-revolution, calling a general strike and finally, on February 25, organising the country's biggest-ever demonstration in Prague. The same day Gottwald went to an indecisive (and increasingly ill) Beneš with his new cabinet, all Party members or "fellow travellers". Beneš accepted Gottwald's nominees and the most popular Communist coup in Eastern Europe was complete, without bloodshed and without the direct intervention of the Soviets.

THE PEOPLE'S REPUBLIC

Following the February coup, the Party began to consolidate its position, a relatively easy task given its immense popular support and control of the army, police force, workers' militia and trade unions. A **new constitution** confirming the "leading role" of the Communist Party and the "dictatorship of the proletariat" was passed by parliament on May 9, 1948. President Beneš refused to sign it, was ousted by Gottwald, and died (of natural causes) shortly afterwards. Those political parties that were not banned or forcibly merged with the KSČ were prescribed fixed percentage representation within the so-called "multi-party" Národní fronta.

With the Cold War in full swing, the **Stalinisation** of Czechoslovak society was quick to follow. In the Party's first Five Year Plan, ninety percent of industry was nationalised, heavy industry given a massive boost and compulsory collectivisation forced through. "Class conscious" Party cadres were given positions of power, while "class enemies" (and their children) were discriminated against. It wasn't long, too, before the Czechoslovak mining "gulags" began to fill up with the regime's political opponents – "kulaks", priests and "bourgeois oppositionists" – numbering over 100,000 at their peak.

Having incarcerated most of its external opponents, the KSČ, with a little prompting from Stalin, embarked upon a ruthless period of internal bloodletting. As the economy nosedived, calls for intensified "class struggle", rumours of impending "counter-revolution" and reports of economic sabotage by fifth columnists filled the press. An atmosphere of fear and confusion was created to justify **large-scale arrests of Party members** with an "international" background – those with a wartime connection with the West, Spanish Civil War veterans, Jews and Slovak nationalists.

In the early 1950s, the Party organised a series of Stalinist **show-trials**, the most spectacular of which was the trial of Rudolf Slánský, who had been second only to Gottwald in the KSČ before his arrest. He and thirteen other leading Party members were sentenced to death (eleven of them Jewish, including Slánský) as "Trotskyist-Titoist-Zionists". Soon afterwards, Vladimír Clementis, the former KSČ foreign minister, was executed along with other leading Slovak comrades (Gustáv Husák, the post-1968 president, was given life imprisonment).

AFTER STALIN

Thankfully, Gottwald drank himself to death in March 1953, shortly after attending Stalin's funeral in Moscow. The whole nation heaved a sigh of relief, but the regime seemed as unrepentent as ever. The arrests and show-trials continued. Then, on May 30, the new Communist leadership announced a drastic currency devaluation, effectively reducing wages by ten percent, while raising prices. The result was a wave of isolated **workers' demonstrations** and rioting, particularly in Plzeň and the Ostrava mining region. Czechoslovak army units called in to suppress the demonstrations proved unreliable, and it was left to the heavily armed workers' militia and police to disperse the crowds and make the predictable arrests and summary executions.

So complete were the Party purges of the early 1950s, so sycophantic (and scared) the surviving leadership, that Khrushchev's 1956 thaw was virtually ignored by the KSČ. An attempted rebellion in the Writers' Congress was rebuffed and an enquiry into the show-trials made several minor security officials scapegoats for the "malpractices". The genuine mass base of the KSČ remained blindly loyal to the Party for the most part, and the following year, the dull, unreconstructed neo-Stalinist **Antonín Novotný** – later proved to have been a spy for the Gestapo during the war – became First Secretary and President.

THE FAILED REVOLUTION

The first rumblings of protest against Czechoslovakia's hardline leadership appeared in the official press in 1963. At first, the criticisms were confined to the country's worsening economic stagnation, but soon merged with more generalised protests against the KSČ leadership. Novotný responded by ordering the belated release and rehabilitation of victims of the 1950s purges, permitting a slight cultural thaw and easing travel restrictions to the West. In effect, he was simply buying time. The half-hearted reforms of the economy announced in the 1965 **New Economic Model** failed to halt the recession, and the minor political reforms instigated by the KSČ only increased the pressure for greater reforms within the Party.

In 1967, Novotný attempted a pre-emptive strike against his opponents. Several leading writers were imprisoned, Slovak Party leaders were branded as "bourgeois nationalists" and the economists were called on to produce results or else forego their reform programme. Instead of eliminating the opposition, Novotný unwittingly united them. Despite Novotný's plea to the Soviets, Brezhnev refused to back a leader whom he saw as "Khrushchev's man in Prague" and on January 5, 1968, the young Slovak leader **Alexander Dubček** replaced Novotný as First Secretary. On March 22, the war-hero Ludvík Svoboda dislodged Novotný from the Presidency.

1968: THE PRAGUE SPRING

By inclination, Dubček was a moderate, cautious reformer, the perfect compromise candidate – but he was continually swept along by the sheer force of the reform movement. The virtual **abolition of censorship** was probably the single most significant step Dubček took. It transformed what had been until then an internal Party debate into a popular mass movement. Civil society, for years muffled under the paranoia and strictures of Stalinism, suddenly sprang into life in the dynamic optimism of the first few months of 1968, the so-called **"Prague Spring"**. In April, the KSČ published their Action Programme, proposing what became popularly known as "socialism with a human face" – federalisation, freedom of assembly and expression, and democratisation of parliament.

Throughout the spring and summer, the reform movement gathered momentum. The Social Democrat Party (forcibly merged with the KSČ after 1948) re-formed, anti-Soviet polemics appeared in the press and, most famously of all, the writer and lifelong Party member Ludvík Vaculík published his personal manifesto entitled *Two Thousand Words*, calling for radical de-Stalinisation within the Party. Dubček and the moderates denounced the manifesto and reaffirmed the country's support for the Warsaw Pact military alliance. Meanwhile the Soviets and their hardline allies – Gomulka in Poland and Ulbricht in the GDR – viewed the Czechoslovak developments on their doorstep very gravely, and began to call for the suppression of "counter-revolutionary elements" and the reimposition of censorship.

As the summer wore on, it became clear that the Soviets were planning military intervention. Warsaw Pact manoeuvres were held in Czechoslovakia in late June, a Warsaw Pact conference (without Czechoslovak participation) was convened in mid-July and, at the beginning of August, the Soviets and the KSČ leadership met for **emergency bi-lateral talks** at Čierná nad Tisou on the Czechoslovak–Soviet border. Brezhnev's hardline deputy, Alexei Kosygin, made his less than subtle threat that "your border is our border", but did agree to withdraw Soviet troops (stationed in the country since the June manoeuvres) and gave the go-ahead to the KSČ's special Party Congress scheduled for September 9.

On August 20, fearing defeat at the forthcoming Congress, the anti-reformists within the Party leadership called for "fraternal assistance". In the early hours of August 21, the **invasion of Czechoslovakia** by Warsaw Pact forces (with the exception of Romania) took place. Dubček and the KSČ reformists immediately condemned the invasion before being arrested and flown to Moscow for "negotiations". President Svoboda refused to condone the formation of a new government under the hardliner Alois Indra, and the people took to the streets in protest, employing every form of non-violent resistance in the book. Apart from individual acts of martyrdom, like the self-immolation of **Jan Palach** and four other students, casualties were light compared to the Hungarian uprising of 1956, but the cost in terms of the following twenty years was much greater.

NORMALISATION

In April 1969, there were anti-Soviet riots during the celebrations of the country's double ice hockey victory over the Soviets. On this pretext, another Slovak, **Gustáv Husák**, replaced the broken Dubček as First Secretary, and instigated his infamous policy of **"normal-isation"**. Over 150,000 fled the country before the borders closed, around 500,000 were expelled from the Party, and an estimated one million people lost their jobs or were demoted. Inexorably, the KSČ reasserted its absolute control over the state and society. The only part of the reform package to survive the invasion was **federalisation**, which gave the Slovaks greater freedom from Prague (on paper at least), though even this was severely watered down in 1971. Dubček, like countless others, was forced to give up his job, working for the next twenty years as a minor official in the Slovak forestry commission.

An unwritten social contract was struck between rulers and ruled during the 1970s, whereby the country was guaranteed a tolerable standard of living (second only to that of the GDR in Eastern Europe) in return for its passive collaboration. Husák's security apparatus quashed all forms of dissent during the early 1970s, and it wasn't until the beginning of 1977 that an organised opposition was strong enough to show its face. The brainchild of absurdist Czech playwright, **Václav Havel**, **Charter 77** was an unlikely alliance between former KSČ members and liberal intellectuals, set up to monitor human rights abuses in Czechoslovakia. Havel and many others endured relentless persecution (including long prison sentences) over the next decade, in pursuit of its ideals. The initial gathering of 243 signatories increased to over 1000 by 1980 and caused panic in the moral vacuum of the Party

apparatus, but consistently failed to stir a fearful and cynical populace into action.

THE EIGHTIES

In the late 1970s and early 1980s, the inefficiencies of the economy prevented the government from fulfilling its side of the social contract, as living standards began to fall. Cynicism, alcoholism, absenteeism and outright dissent became widespread, especially among the younger (post-1968) generation. The **Jazz Section** of the Musicians' Union, who disseminated "subversive" pop music, highlighted the ludicrously harsh nature of the regime when they were arrested and imprisoned in the mid-1980s. Pop concerts, annual religious pilgrimages and of course the anniversary of the Soviet invasion all caused regular confrontations between the security forces and certain sections of the population. Yet still a mass movement like Poland's Solidarity failed to emerge.

With the advent of **Mikhail Gorbachev**, the KSČ was put in an extremely awkward position, as it tried desperately to separate perestroika from comparisons with the reforms of the Prague Spring. Husák and his cronies had prided themselves on being second only to Honecker's GDR as the most stable and ortho-dox of the Soviet satellites – now the font of orthodoxy, the Soviet Union, was turning against them. In 1987, **Miloš Jakeš** – the hardliner who oversaw Husák's normalisation purges – took over smoothly from Husák as General (First) Secretary and introduced *přestavba* (restructuring), Czechoslovakia's lukewarm version of perestroika.

1989 – THE VELVET REVOLUTION

Everything appeared to be going swimmingly for the KSČ as it entered 1989. Under the surface, however, things were becoming more and more strained. As the country's economic performance worsened, divisions were developing within the KSČ leadership. The protest movement was gathering momentum: even the Catholic Church had begun to voice dissatisfaction, compiling a staggering 500,000 signatures calling for greater freedom of worship. But the 21st anniversary of the Soviet invasion produced a demonstration of only 10,000, which was swiftly and violently dispersed by the regime.

During the summer, however, more serious cracks began to appear in Czechoslovakia's staunch hardline ally, the GDR. The trickle of East Germans fleeing to the West turned into a mass exodus, forcing Honecker to resign and, by the end of October, prompting nightly mass demonstrations on the streets of Leipzig and Dresden. The opening of the Berlin Wall on November 9 left Czechoslovakia, Romania and Albania alone on the Eastern European stage still clinging to the old truths.

All eyes were now turned upon Czechoslovakia. Reformists within the KSČ began plotting an internal coup to overthrow Jakeš, in anticipation of a Soviet denunciation of the 1968 invasion. In the end, events overtook whatever plans they may have had. On Friday, **November 17**, a 50,000-strong peaceful demonstration organised by the official Communist youth organisation was viciously attacked by the riot police. Over 100 arrests, 500 injuries and one death were reported (the fatality was later retracted), in what became known as the *masakr* (massacre). Prague's students immediately began an occupation strike, joined soon after by the city's actors, who together called for an end to the Communist Party's "leading role" and a general strike to be held for two hours on November 27.

CIVIC FORUM AND THE VPN

On Sunday, November 19, on Václav Havel's initiative, the established opposition groups like Charter 77 met and agreed to form Občanské fórum or **Civic Forum**. Their demands were simple: the resignation of the present hardline leadership, including Husák and Jakeš; an enquiry into the police actions of November 17; an amnesty for all political prisoners; and support for the general strike. In Bratislava, a parallel organisation, Veřejnosť proti nasiliu, or **People Against Violence** (VPN), was set up to coordinate protest in Slovakia.

On the Monday evening, the first of the really big **nationwide demonstrations** took place — the biggest since the 1968 invasion — with more than 200,000 people pouring into Prague's Wenceslas Square. This time the police held back and rumours of troop deployments proved false. Every night for a week people poured into the main squares in towns and cities across the country, repeating the calls for democracy, freedom and the end to the

Party's monopoly of power. As the week dragged on, the Communist media tentatively began to report events, and the KSČ leadership started to splinter under the strain, with the prime minister, **Ladislav Adamec**, alone in sticking his neck out and holding talks with the opposition.

THE END OF ONE-PARTY RULE

On Friday evening, Dubček, the ousted 1968 leader, appeared before a crowd of over 300,000 in Prague, and in a matter of hours the entire Jakeš leadership had resigned. The weekend brought the largest demonstrations the country had ever seen — over 750,000 people in Prague alone. At the invitation of Civic Forum, Adamec addressed the crowd, only to get booed off the platform. On Monday, November 27, eighty percent of the country's workforce joined the two-hour **general strike**, including many of the Party's previously stalwart allies, the miners and engineers. The following day, the Party agreed to an end of one-party rule and the formation of a new "coalition government".

A temporary halt to the nightly demonstrations was called and the country waited expectantly for the "broad coalition" cabinet promised by Prime Minister Adamec. On December 3, another Communist-dominated line-up was announced by the Party and immediately denounced by Civic Forum and VPN, who called for a fresh wave of demonstrations and another general strike for December 11. Adamec promptly resigned and was replaced by the Slovak Marián Čalfa. On December 10, one day before the second threatened general strike, Čalfa announced his provisional **"Government of National Understanding"**, with Communists in the minority for the first time since 1948 and multi-party elections planned for June 1990. Having sworn in the new government, President Husák, architect of the post-1968 "normalisation", finally threw in the towel.

By the time the new Čalfa government was announced, the students and actors had been on strike continuously for over three weeks. The pace of change had surprised everyone involved, but there was still one outstanding issue, the election of a new president. Posters shot up all round the capital urging **"HAVEL NA HRAD"** (Havel to the Castle — the seat of the presidency). The students were determined to see his election through, continuing their occupation strike until Havel was officially elected president by a unanimous vote of the Federal Assembly on December 29.

INTO THE NINETIES

Czechoslovakia started the new decade full of optimism for what the future would bring. On the surface, the country had a lot more going for it than its immediate neighbours (with the possible exception of the GDR). The Communist Party had been swept from power without bloodshed, and, unlike the rest of Eastern Europe, Czechoslovakia had a strong, inter-war democratic tradition with which to identify – Masaryk's First Republic. Despite Communist economic mismanagement, the country still had a relatively high standard of living, a skilled workforce and a manageable foreign debt.

The truth, however, was somewhat different. Not only was the country economically in a worse state than most people had envisaged, it was environmentally devastated, and its people were suffering from what Havel described as "post-prison psychosis" – an inability to think or act for themselves. The country had to go through the painful transition "from being a big fish in a small pond to being a sickly adolescent trout in a hatchery". As a result, it came increasingly to rely on its new-found saviour, the humble playwright-President, Václav Havel.

In most people's eyes, "Saint Václav" could do no wrong, though he himself was not out to woo his electorate. His call for the rapid withdrawal of Soviet troops was popular enough, but his apology for the post-war expulsion of Sudeten Germans was deeply resented, as was his generous amnesty which eased the country's overcrowded prisons. The amnesty was blamed by many for the huge **rise in crime** in the first half of 1990. Every vice in the book – from racism to homicide – raised its ugly head in the first year of freedom. In addition, there was still plenty of talk about the possibility of "counter-revolution", given the thousands of unemployed StB (secret police) at large. Inevitably, accusations of previous StB involvement rocked each political party in turn in the run-up to the elections.

1990: THE JUNE ELECTIONS

Despite all the inevitable hiccups and the increasingly vocal Slovak nationalists, Civic Forum/VPN remained high in the opinion polls. The **June 1990 elections** produced a record-breaking 99 percent turnout. With around sixty percent of the vote, Civic Forum/VPN were clear victors (the Communists got just thirteen percent) and Havel immediately set about forming a broad "Coalition of National Sacrifice", including everyone from Christian Democrats to former Communists.

The main concern of the new government was (and still is) how to transform an outdated command-system economy into a **market economy** which can compete with its EC neighbours. The double burden of having to fork out precious hard currency for Soviet oil and the knock-on effects of the Gulf War quickly plunged the country into a dire energy crisis. The argument over the speed of economic reform became more acute and caused the most serious split in Civic Forum/VPN, with the radical free marketeers, headed by the finance minister, **Václav Klaus**, gaining the upper hand within the movement and introducing their shock therapy on the nation from January 1, 1991. The full implications of this economic reform, effectively introducing a market economy in one great leap, are not yet clear. Unemployment, double-figure inflation and widespread strike actions are inevitable. How bad the situation will get before it improves remains to be seen.

One of the most difficult issues to resolve in post-Communist Czechoslovakia has been the **Slovak problem**. Having been the victim of Prague-inspired centralisation from just about every Czech leader from Masaryk to Gottwald, the Slovaks are in no mood to suffer second-class citizenship any longer. During the whole of 1990, feelings were running high in Slovakia, and, more than once, the spectre of a "Slovak UDI" seemed perilously close. It is unlikely that the problem will disappear overnight, but some kind of compromise solution will have to be worked out if the country as a whole is hoping to attract foreign capital to rectify the most important issue of the day – the economy.

MINORITIES IN CZECHO-SLOVAKIA

Czechoslovakia entered the post-Communist era with a relatively strong economy, a skilled workforce, a political leadership whose democratic credentials were beyond doubt, and was expected to manage the transition to democracy with considerably more ease than some of her neighbours. However, inter-ethnic rivalries and nationalist tensions have emerged as major obstacles to the country's future stability. The major clash has been at a federal level, between Czechs and Slovaks, but attacks on the country's Gypsies and discontent among the Hungarian population have also helped thrust the "nationality question" back to the forefront of domestic politics.

THE SLOVAK QUESTION

The existence of the Czechoslovak state has always rested on a central ambiguity, a union between two closely related, yet nevertheless different, peoples – the **Czechs** and the **Slovaks** – who, despite seven decades of co-existence inside one nation, have yet to work out a relationship of sufficient mutual trust. Before World War II this was exacerbated by the additional presence of three million ethnic Germans. With their forced expulsion after the war, it was hoped that the "nationality question" had been solved once and for all. In fact, the removal of the Germans only shifted the focus more keenly onto the country's other minorities, in particular the **"Slovak question"**, a piece of unfinished business which was kept hidden under the Communist straightjacket of the last forty years.

ORIGINS

After an initial period of enthusiasm and mutual goodwill when the new Republic was declared in 1918, Prague's paternalism and centralisation ultimately reduced Slovakia to a state of near-colonial dependence which the post-war Communist regime did little to remedy. Slovakia's only period of independence came

with Tiso's wartime puppet state, for which the Slovaks have been obliged to carry a collective burden of guilt ever since: a guilt which was forced upon them, they believe, precisely in order to keep their nationalist aspirations under control. The collapse of the Communist regime seemed to offer the Slovaks the opportunity to establish a measure of genuine national sovereignty which had previously been denied. As VPN chairman Fedor Gal told *Le Monde* in September 1990, "The Slovak people have always been an appendage of others. Now, we are going through a period of self-discovery".

OTHER MINORITIES WITHIN SLOVAKIA

However, if the Slovaks are going through a process of rediscovering themselves, this is not necessarily good news for the other ethnic groups which inhabit the same territory, many of whom have grievances and aspirations of their own. Over half a million **Hungarians** in the south of Slovakia, along with smaller groups like the **Rusyns** in the east (see Chapter Four), have no desire to find themselves marginalised in a newly resurgent Slovakia, and tend to regard the retention of a strong central authority in Prague as a desirable restraining influence on the jingoistic Slovaks. The Czechs (who likewise have suffered forty years of Communist mismanagement) feel unjustly accused of having exploited their countrymen in the past. Interestingly, an opinion poll conducted in June 1990 revealed that while only 9 percent of Slovaks favoured outright secession, as many as 39 percent of Czechs expressed a willingness to go it alone should fragmentation set in.

Not that the Czechs are entirely united. Since November 1989, regionalist sentiment in Moravia, the eastern half of the Czech-speaking republic, has begun to cause problems. Moravian nationalists demanding more autonomy from Prague and Bohemia won substantial support in the parliamentary elections of June 1990.

RESENTMENTS AFTER COMMUNISM

These niggling resentments have a lot to do with Czechoslovakia's Communist heritage. Expressions of national and regional sentiment were expropriated for propaganda purposes, or developed according to the whims of competing factions within the ruling elite. With Communism's demise, each group suspects the other of having benefited most. The questions raised by economic development form the most common bones of contention. It's common currency in Czech thinking that resources were diverted away from the west of the country in order to industrialise the backward east, thus starving the Czech lands of much needed investment. Slovaks reply that the industrialisation so graciously bestowed upon them by Prague served merely to place them in a position of economic servitude to the Czechs, landing them with an ecological catastrophe at the same time. Moravians argue that their commercial and cultural riches were consistently run down by Prague in order to help subsidise the expense of industrialising Slovakia.

OUTSIDERS? – THE GYPSIES AND THE VIETNAMESE

One minority without territory and without political muscle, largely ignored or abused by their neighbours, are the **Gypsies**. In April 1990, the Czechoslovak media reported a sudden wave of racist attacks in the grim industrial towns of North and West Bohemia. Local skinheads were reputed to be at the centre of things, directing their agression against unfortunate Gypsies and **Vietnamese** guest workers. Rumours that Gypsies in Plzeň were randomly attacking individuals guilty of resembling punks or skinheads provoked an influx of incensed Czech youths from neighbouring towns bent on settling scores. On May 1, no doubt spurred on by press coverage of events in Plzeň, 200 "skinheads" rampaged through central Prague attacking both Gypsies and Vietnamese. Only later did it emerge that it was the murder of a Turkish truck driver by youths who mistook him for one of the local Gypsies that had in fact brought the latter community out onto the streets.

THE VIETNAMESE

The **problems** faced by the Vietnamese are worth an aside. Brought over as "guest workers" in the 1970s to feed the country's chronic labour shortage, they are now seen as an unwanted Communist legacy. Despite being forced to live in single-sex hostels and legally prevented from marrying Czechoslovak nationals, their presence is increasingly resented now that the economic crisis (and attendant threat of mass unemployment) is beginning to bite. In April 1990, Havel's government announced that

all foreign "guest workers" must **leave the country by 1995**. Whether Czechoslovakia will succeed in pushing through this forced repatriation in the face of growing protest by human rights groups is uncertain. A Vietnamese demonstration at Prague airport in August, ostensibly held in order to criticise Hanoi's failure to embark on political reform, was directed as much at the Czechoslovak government's lack of concern for their plight as against the authorities back home.

THE GYPSIES

Unlike the Vietnamese, the Gypsies (known locally as *Romi*) will not fade from public view quite so easily. For a start, they are hardly "outsiders" as such. Originally a low-caste Indian tribe, they made their way into central Europe via Persia during the fifteenth century. A 1988 report estimated that there were roughly 500,000 of them in Czechoslovakia (the second largest community in Europe after Romania), but given the difficulties in collecting accurate data, the figure is likely to be much higher.

Despite a high rate of infant mortality, caused by the unsanitary conditions in which the majority of Gypsies still live, a rapidly rising birth rate (166 percent higher than the Czechs and Slovaks) means that the Gypsy population is likely to mushroom in the future – making the **"Gypsy question"** an increasingly important issue in Czechoslovak politics. The highest concentration of Gypsies is in Slovakia, especially in the east, where they account for up to twenty percent of the population, and where their overcrowded shantytowns, with few if any of the most basic amenities, are a common feature on the outskirts of towns.

Forced Integration

Successive Czechoslovak governments have rarely found it necessary to minister to the needs of this marginalised community. During the Communist era the accent was on **"integration"**; a process which began in the late 1950s with laws restricting the Gypsies' traditional migratory lifestyle, and gathered pace in the 1960s with the bulldozing of unsanitary slums and the resettling of Gypsies in modern housing units. Gypsy communities were dispersed throughout Czechoslovakia, families ending up in an unfamiliar environment hundreds of miles away from their original home.

The drive towards integration had the opposite effect to that which was intended: the confused philanthropy of trying to turn Gypsies into good Czechs or good Slovaks invariably meant that their traditional language and culture were belittled or overlooked. Schools in the Romany language (an ancient tongue, closely related to Sanskrit) were not provided for, and Gypsy kids stayed away from schools in which they were made to feel like outsiders, with the inevitable consequence that they remained illiterate and lost all chance of upward mobility. Forced onto anonymous housing estates which seemed alien, Gypsies were often surrounded by urban populations who, having to struggle with a perennial housing shortage of their own, regarded the Gypsies at best as unwelcome newcomers and, at worst, undeserving parasites.

The industrial towns of Bohemia and Moravia were earmarked for the **resettlement** of the majority of displaced Gypsies. The existing inhabitants of these towns, unused to Gypsies, saw them as an essentially alien culture, contributing to their continuing ghettoisation (thus it came as no surprise that these dour cities played host to much of 1990's ethnic violence). Although the post-war decades have seen an increasing number of Gypsies in settled employment, much of the work is seasonal (in the construction industry, for example), thus forcing many Gypsy breadwinners onto the black economy in order to make ends meet. Certain aspects of a migratory lifestyle still remain, and popular stereotypes of the Gypsy predilection for black-marketeering and crime are still strong.

Political Representation

Gypsies have yet to gain any real **political voice** in Czechoslovakia. A Union of Romanies was formed by Bratislava-based Gypsy intellectuals in 1968, but its calls for the promotion of Gypsy language and culture fell on increasingly deaf ears after the end of the Prague Spring. The new political climate brought about by the 1989 revolution has allowed a certain amount of Gypsy consciousness to come into the open. The emergence of a Gypsy political party, in alliance with the ruling VPN in Slovakia, ensured the community some leverage, however small. In the local council elections of November 1990, the Romany Civic Initiative won a mere 63 seats across the whole of Czechoslovakia, but it was a significant step forward nevertheless.

However, **popular hostility** towards Gypsies remains as widespread as ever: an opinion poll on inter-ethnic relations published in August 1990 revealed that only eleven percent of Czechoslovaks saw no problem in maintaining good relations with Gypsies; while as many as sixty percent said the opposite. It seems that Czechs and Slovaks know as little about the lives of the Gypsies living in their midst as the average visiting Westerner does. The prevailing media image, supplied by intrepid correspondents who tread gingerly through Gypsy-inhabited districts as if penetrating some Middle Eastern refugee camp, continues to portray them as something mysterious, exotic, and essentially alien.

THE HUNGARIANS

Slovak fear of "Pragocentrism" has always been the determining factor in the shaping of national sentiment since 1918, but it was the relationship between Slovakia and its **Hungarian minority** which initially provided for the upsurge in Slovak consciousness. The nineteenth-century Slovak national revival or národné obrodenie was born out of resistance to Magyar domination and fear of Hungarian revanchism. However distant, this threat remains a distinct feature on the Slovak intellectual landscape.

There are over half a million Hungarians in Slovakia, mainly concentrated along Slovakia's southern border. In most of these areas Hungarian and Slovak populations are considerably intermingled; but in some parts, notably in the Danube Basin around Komárno, the Hungarians have a sizeable majority. These territories were awarded to Czechoslovakia by the Treaty of Trianon in 1920, the legitimacy of which Hungarians everywhere have always disputed. With the increasingly open discussion of Trianon brought about by the newly liberalised climate in Hungary proper, and widely-publicised remarks made by Hungary's President Antal (the country's first post-Communist president, elected in 1990) to the effect that all the world's 15 million Hungarians were now in his care, long-dormant Slovak suspicions of Hungarian interference in its domestic policy began to re-emerge.

ELECTORAL SUCCESS

Benefiting from the extensive cross-border links they maintained with opposition groups in Hungary itself, Hungarians in Slovakia were quick to organise themselves in November 1989, seeing the Velvet Revolution as a golden opportunity to improve their lot. In the **elections of June 1990**, the Hungarian community voted virtually en bloc for parties of a specifically Hungarian orientation: Hungarian Christian Democracy, "Coexistence", or the Independent Hungarian Initiative (the latter in alliance with VPN), which are, for the most part, moderate organisations seeking to defend the status of the Hungarian language and improve schooling facilities for Hungarian children. One prominent demand is for the establishment of a Hungarian-language university in Bratislava – something which they believe would prevent the gradual "Slovakisation" of their educated elite.

Resentment for the neglect of Hungarian interests under Communism is very strong. According to a spokesperson for the Independent Hungarian Inititiative, "the past regime had done everything possible to put an end to the life of our minority. Schools were being closed, and neither our political nor cultural life were free". Discontent of this nature came as an unwelcome surprise to Slovaks, who had always assumed that Hungarians had been reasonably well catered for. Slovaks were particularly keen to point out that the Hungarian government had done far less to provide educational facilities for the Slovak minority in Hungary, implying that Hungarians in Slovakia were by contrast lucky and should be grateful. The idea that the Hungarian government was encouraging discontent in southern Slovakia from behind the scenes was taken for granted by a wide section of the Slovak public.

THE SLOVAK CHARGE

The political awakening of Slovakia's Hungarians naturally produced a backlash, which boosted the emotional appeal of right-wing **Slovak nationalism**. From the plethora of groups emerging in the wake of the November revolution, the **Slovak National Party** (SNS) established itself as the leading mouthpiece of the right. Its fortunes fluctuated wildly during the course of 1990, winning ten percent of the vote in June's parliamentary elections, but slumping to three percent in the local council elections in November, by which time Slovakia's ruling VPN/Christian Democrat coalition had successfully demonstrated its own nationalist credentials through its tough negotiating stance on the question of Slovakia's future role in the federation. It's important to note just how successful the right had been in propelling the Slovak question to the forefront of the political agenda, thus forcing the ruling coalition to adopt a fiercely populist stance – which was perhaps not in its original nature.

LANGUAGE PROBLEMS

Right-wing pressure crystallised around the question of the status of the **Slovak language** within the Slovak republic. The ruling coalition, eager to demonstrate its attachment to human rights, drafted a law granting official status to the language of any national minority constituting twenty percent of the population in any given commune. Opponents of the law argued that Slovaks living in Hungarian-dominated areas would be discriminated against, and Slovak culture in the south of the country would be under serious threat. The Slovak parliament prepared to pass the law at the end of October, provoking a spate of **nationalist demonstrations**, and student hunger strikes outside the parliament building.

Main organiser of opposition was the newly reinvigorated **Matica slovenská**, the cultural foundation which had been the main organ of the národné obrodenie during nineteenth-century resistance to Hungarian rule. The Matica's new leadership, elected in August 1990, delivered a proclamation warning that Slovaks were in danger of becoming subservient to the republic's ethnic minorities, of becoming "lodgers in their own home". The legislation was passed without too much trouble, but it all put a severe strain on the ruling coalition, especially the Christian Democrats, who saw their position as the dominant right-of-centre party being challenged by the more extreme SNS. This meant that the coalition had to limit the damage inflicted by the twenty percent law by pursuing a tougher line on the more serious issue of Slovakia's position in the federation.

THE FUTURE

Negotiations between the Czech, Slovak and federal government on the division of authority in a **new Czechoslovak constitution** dragged on throughout the summer and autumn of 1990. The main area of disagreement was **the economy**, with the Slovaks holding out for as much control over Slovakia's commercial life as possible: requesting the right to establish a Slovak central bank capable of minting its own currency was one of their more extreme bargaining positions. Such a hard line is not just motivated by the desire to enforce the principle of republican sovereignty; there is also an underlying desire to protect a comparatively weak Slovak economy from the full force of market reforms. The potential of the Czech-Slovak dispute for applying the brakes to much-needed economic change is one of the prime frustrations of the federal government.

Just as ominously, the seeming pettiness of the division of administrative functions between Czechs and Slovaks threatens to repeat the mistakes of the Communist bureaucracy. Leading Civic Forum politician Jan Urban adequately expressed the distaste of the Prague intelligentsia in a commentary published in the independent daily newspaper *Lidové noviny* on August 13, 1990: "are we going to start counting out locomotives and wagons? Shall we share out all the airlines and naval vessels? Will we in future appoint generals, colonels, and perhaps even majors of our army not on the basis of their capacity to do the job, but on the basis of the nationality of their parents?" Slovaks felt that such an attitude reflected the typical failure of Prague to take their grievances seriously.

For the moment at least, it seems unlikely that Slovak brinkmanship will ultimately bring the federation down. Opinion polls continue to show that only a minority of Slovaks favour outright separation (figures hover around ten percent), but the events of 1990 reveal that the uneasy balance between Czechs, Slovaks and smaller ethnic groups will continue to be the Achilles heel of Czechoslovakia's fledgling democracy. Shouldering the awkward burden of central European history, with its competing national traditions and seemingly unrealisable national aspirations, will be as difficult for the Czechoslovaks as for any of their neighbours. As one ethnic Hungarian schoolteacher in Bratislava remarked: "In the West, the processes of national awakening and democratic awakening often went hand in hand; but in central Europe they are in conflict . . . the psychological state in which we central Europeans have been living makes normal political life impossible."

JONATHAN BOUSFIELD

THE ENVIRONMENT

Andrew Tickle is an environmental scientist and former guest researcher with the Czechoslovak Academy of Sciences. He now works for Greenpeace's East-West project and is currently involved in setting up new campaigns in Czechoslovakia. The article below was originally published in New Ground magazine in summer 1990.

THE ICE CRACKS BUT THE WATER IS STILL POLLUTED

In 1983 the first detailed picture of the state of the Czechoslovak environment emerged. The report, a stunning indictment of the full horrors of pollution in the country, was written by a small group of scientists who had formed themselves into a group called the **Ecological Section**, under the loose auspices of the Party-dominated Academy of Sciences. The report was immediately suppressed, the preparatory material was confiscated and in some cases the authors were harassed by the StB (secret police).

Ecological repression increased when the document was leaked to the Western press by Charter 77. Entirely innocent people, such as the forester who compiled the forest damage statistics for the grossly polluted area of Northern Bohemia, were now singled out and persecuted for having traded "state secrets" to the West.

When, four years later, the Slovak Union of Nature Protectors published their long litany describing the grave ecological situation in Bratislava, the cost of publishing such material had not changed much – confiscation and destruction of the booklet quickly followed and criminal proceedings were begun against the editor. But by this time the environment had become an open enough issue for the article to be condemned in the Slovak Party paper, *Pravda*, as "anti-communist propaganda attempting to use ecological arguments in its struggle against socialism". By 1989, however, several thousand copies of the document were reckoned to be freely circulating in *samizdat* form.

POLLUTION TO REVOLUTION

In reality the issue of environmental protest was indivisible from that of human rights, and as such, anyone daring to engage in the mildest ecological criticism could expect to be treated as a subversive dissident. But you didn't need to be any kind of expert to realise that something was drastically wrong with your living environment in Czechoslovakia. Some four million people live in the most heavily contaminated areas. During the winter, when continuous smog conditions can prevail for weeks, children are forbidden to indulge in strenuous activity, playground time is curtailed and people retreat into their houses with their doors and windows firmly closed. Even having the window open just a fraction during the night would result in a throbbing headache the next day. People described industry – and thereby the government – as "waging chemical war against their own citizens".

Many now believe that it was this state of affairs, with food, water and air becoming progressively more poisoned, that caused life expectancy to drop through the 1970s and 1980s and catalysed the Czechs and Slovaks into the Velvet Revolution of November 1989. Some of the earliest open demonstrations that took place during that period were in fact protests about the ecological situation. Those in Teplice, one of the most heavily polluted towns in North Bohemia, actually preceded the students' beatings at the hands of the police in Prague – the event that is usually perceived as having sparked off the revolution proper. In Slovakia too, the first demonstrations were organised largely by the formerly suppressed ecologists from Bratislava.

REPAIRING THE DAMAGE

The environment now features very strongly on the political agenda of the new government headed by *Občanské fórum* (Civic Form) and its Slovak counterpart, *VPN* (People Against Violence). However the Green Party, despite indications of strong support before the elections, failed to gain representation in either the Federal or Czech assemblies – the few elected now sit in the Slovak Parliament in Bratislava.

The new ministries and commissions are now mainly staffed by former environmental movement dissidents, with the top roles going to the leading activists in the Ecological Section and the Slovak Union of Nature Protectors. Just as the jailed Havel became President, the hardline ecologists are now in charge of righting forty years of environmental abuse.

This is obviously going to be a hard and painfully slow job. The pitfalls are already evident – now that environmental problems are described fully in the new liberated press, people are pressuring for immediate improvements. Everyone is protesting against something, and very often these demands are conflicting. A simple case could be the need for new housing which meets with protests about where it will be built. But more important is the question of future energy supply.

Even the former Communist government realised that the extraction and burning of brown coal (lignite) reserves in North Bohemia to supply the vast demand from heavy industry was one of the country's severest environmental problems. The uncontrolled fumes from industry and power stations were responsible for the winter smogs, the appalling health of the local population and the laying waste of millions of hectares of coniferous forests along the borders with East Germany and Poland – both countries also experiencing severe environmental problems. The former government's answer lay in nuclear power and large hydro-electric power schemes.

FALSE SOLUTIONS – HYDRO-ELECTRIC AND NUCLEAR POWER

These schemes brought problems of their own, such as those associated with the joint Hungarian-Czechoslovak dams project on the Danube (see p.286). Now half-completed with the help of enormous loans from Austria, the full scheme threatened to destroy a large part of the unique Danube floodplain forests, pollute the groundwater reserves from which most of Hungary's drinking water was drawn and flood large areas of productive agricultural land. Despite these heavy sacrifices the electricity generated from the scheme would not even pay back the original Austrian loan – repayment of which was demanded in power supplied onto their grid for the next two years. Hard lobbying by Green activists over the past ten years, principally in Hungary and Bratislava, has now led

to the scheme's cancellation in Hungary, while the Czechoslovak government has imposed a two-year moratorium on further building.

Nuclear power has become an even thornier problem, and one that divides Czechoslovakia both geographically and politically. In the north of Bohemia and Moravia it is supported, even by some of the Greens, as the answer to the problems of burning brown coal; but in the largely unpolluted south it has become a "not in my backyard" issue, with fears that the Soviet-designed (but Czechoslovak-built) reactors could suffer the same design faults that lead to the Chernobyl disaster in 1986.

A test case for the continuation of the Czechoslovak nuclear programme is the complex of four 1000 megawatt pressurised water reactors being built at Temelín in rural South Bohemia, close to the Austrian border (see p.130). A study of the site, written in 1983 but since kept secret by the former regime, showed that there would be insufficient water in the nearby river to cool the reactors, that the steam from the cooling towers would cause a continuous fog over the South Bohemian basin, and worst of all, that the reactors were being located within an active seismological zone. Once again, the new government has declared a moratorium on the final completion of the project. But the new environmental ministry has already pragmatically accepted that nuclear power is a necessary alternative to fossil-fuel combustion, until other sources of energy are developed.

THE FUTURE – AID AND INDEPENDENCE

What are the remaining energy options for Czechoslovakia? The use of gas, now favoured for UK electricity generation because of its minimal polluting emissions, higher thermal efficiency (compared with coal) and hence lower carbon dioxide emissions, has been ruled out – mostly on the grounds that it is only available via the Soviet Union, who could hold the country to ransom by either prices or a blockade – a strategy used to powerful effect in the Baltic States. The Czechs and Slovaks clearly want no repetition of their former dependence on Moscow, particularly with the present unstable and unpredictable situation in the Soviet Union.

The solution being put forward in the new Czechoslovak environmental policy, formulated before the elections, is the same as that now being proposed by policy-makers both East and West: energy conservation and efficiency. In this way, the need for expensive pollution control technology will be minimised, ensuring the best use is made of their own limited funds and whatever may become available through Western loans or credits. And although President Havel has made clear that he does not want Czechoslovakia to take on large quantities of foreign aid, new bodies such as the recently established Bank for Economic Reconstruction and Development in Europe (BERD) and the European Community are likely to make available large sums for clearing up pollution in the former Eastern Bloc.

A final irony is that although rigid and centrally-planned economies were, in the main, responsible for the current ecological catastrophe in Eastern Europe, the introduction of a market economy (after initial recession) may cause energy demand to rise, making matters far worse. It is now time for both East and West to wake up to the fact that as far as energy, transport and environmental planning are concerned, policy decisions made centrally in government could be the best way forward to solving our environmental problems.

BOOKS

The best source of specialist books on Czechoslovakia is *Collets International Bookshop*, 129 Charing Cross Road, London W1 (☎071-734 0782). For out-of-print and most Slovak books, try joining the library of the School of Slavonic and East European Studies (*SSEES*), Malet Street, London WC1. With a reference, non-students pay a £35 deposit to obtain borrowing rights. The library also has a wide selection of magazines and journals about Czechoslovakia and Eastern Europe.

HISTORY, POLITICS AND SOCIETY

R. W. Seton-Watson *The History of the Czechs and Slovaks* (o/p). Seton-Watson's highly informed and balanced account, written during World War II, is hard to beat. The Seton-Watsons were lifelong Slavophiles but managed to maintain a scholarly distance in their writing, rare amongst emigré historians.

Elizabeth Wiskemann *Czechs and Germans* (Macmillan, o/p). Researched and written in the build-up towards Munich, this is the most fascinating and fair treatment of the Sudeten problem. Meticulous in her detail, vast in her scope, Wiskemann nevertheless manages to suffuse the weighty text with enough anecdotes to keep you gripped. Unique.

Jaroslav Krejčí *Czechoslovakia at the Crossroads of European History* (I. B. Tauris £16.95). Fairly breezy, lacklustre account of Czechoslovakia's history by a 1968 Czech emigré. Despite its recent publication, it contains only the briefest summary of the events of November 1989.

Zbyněk Zeman *The Masaryks – The Making of Czechoslovakia* (I. B. Tauris £9.95). Written in the 1970s while Zeman was in exile, this is nevertheless a very readable, none too sentimental biography of the country's founder Tomáš Garrigue Masaryk, and his son Jan Masaryk, the post-war Foreign Minister who died in mysterious circumstances shortly after the 1948 Communist coup.

Hans Renner *A History of Czechoslovakia since 1945* (Routledge £25). General history by one of the 1968 emigré generation, finishing with the accession of Jakeš to General Secretary in December 1987.

Karel Kaplan *Report on the Murder of the General Secretary* (I. B. Tauris £19.95). Detailed study of the most famous of the anti-Semitic Stalinist show trials, that of Rudolf Slánský, number two in the KSČ until his arrest.

Zbyněk Zeman *Prague Spring; A Report on Czechoslovakia 1968* (Penguin, o/p). Short, straightforward, and in many ways the easiest of the books on 1968, including useful background stuff on the country's post-war history.

William Shawcross *Dubček and Czechoslovakia (1918–1990)* (Hogarth £9.99). Biography of the most famous figure of the 1968 Prague Spring, updated to include Dubček's role in the 1989 Velvet Revolution.

Dubček Speaks (I. B. Tauris £14.95). Verbatim account of Dubček's interview with Andras Sugar, one of Hungary's leading political writers, in which Dubček spoke for the first time in public about the events of the 1968 Prague Spring.

Janusz Bugajski *Czechoslovakia – Charter 77's Decade of Dissent* (Praeger £8.55). Informative, comprehensive but rather dry account of Charter 77's background and campaigns as well as information on a host of other dissident activities in the 1980s.

Tim Garton Ash *We The People: The Revolutions of 89* (Granta/Penguin £4.99). A personal, anecdotal, eye-witness account of the Velvet Revolution (and the events in Poland, Berlin and Budapest), and for that reason by far the most compelling of all the post-1989 books.

Misha Glenny *The Rebirth of History: Eastern Europe in the Age of Democracy* (Penguin £4.99). Eight chapters in all, one of which deals with Czechoslovakia, focusing on the events of

1990 and the problems of the future rather than the Velvet Revolution itself. Correspondent for *The Guardian* and *BBC*, Glenny knows his stuff, but don't expect any jokes.

Mark Frankland *The Patriots' Revolution* (Sinclair Stevenson £16.95). Falls somewhere between Tim Garton Ash's eye-witness account and Glenny's more lengthy analysis, but fails to be convincing either way.

ESSAYS AND MEMOIRS

Patrick Leigh Fermor *A Time of Gifts* (Penguin £4.99). The first volume of Leigh Fermor's trilogy based on his epic walk along the Rhine and Danube rivers in 1933–34. In the last quarter of the book he reaches Bratislava, indulging in a quick jaunt to Prague before crossing the border into Hungary. Written forty years later in dense, luscious and highly crafted prose, it's an evocative and poignant insight into the culture of *Mitteleuropa* between the wars.

Heda Margolius Kovaly *Prague Farewell* (Gollancz £3.95). An autobiography that starts in the concentration camps of World War II, ending with the author's flight from Czechoslovakia in 1968. Married to one of the Party hacks executed in the 1952 Slánský trial, she tells her story with simplicity, and without bitterness. The best account there is on the fear and paranoia whipped up during the Stalinist terror.

Václav Havel *Living in Truth; Letters to Olga; Disturbing the Peace* (all Faber & Faber £4.99). The first essay in *Living in Truth* is *Power of the Powerless*, Havel's lucid, damning indictment of the inactivity of the Czechoslovak masses in the face of "normalisation". *Letters to Olga* is a collection of Havel's letters written under great duress (and heavy censorship) from prison in the early 1980s to his wife, Olga – by turns philosophising, nagging, effusing, whingeing. *Disturbing the Peace* is probably Havel's most accessible work yet: a series of autobiographical questions and answers in which he talks interestingly about his childhood, the events of 1968 when he was in Liberec, and the path to Charter 77 and beyond (though not including his reactions to being thrust into the role of President).

Václav Havel et al. *Power of the Powerless* (Hutchinson £8.95). A collection of essays by leading Chartists, kicking off with Havel's semi-

nal title-piece. Other contributors range from the dissident Marxist Petr Uhl to devout Catholics like Václav Benda.

Josef Škvorecký *Talkin' Moscow Blues* (Faber & Faber £9.99). Without doubt the most user-friendly of Škvorecký's works, containing a collection of essays on his wartime childhood, Czech Jazz, literature and contemporary politics, all told in his inimitable, irreverent and infuriating way.

Ludvík Vaculík *A Cup of Coffee with My Interrogator* (Readers International USA). A life-long Party member until 1968, and signatory of Charter 77, Vaculík revived the *feuilleton*, a short political critique and a journalistic literary genre much-loved in central Europe. This collection dates from 1968 onwards. His first novel, *The Axe* (Andre Deutsch, o/p), is *the* definitive account of the forced collectivisation of the 1950s.

Nikolaus Martin *Prague Winter* (Peter Halban £14.95). Brought up in Prague in the 1930s, Martin ended up in Terezín, Czechoslovakia's most notorious ghetto and concentration camp, due to his mother's Jewish background. This autobiography follows his life up to and including the 1948 Communist coup, after which he escaped to Canada.

Phyllis Myrtle Clarke Sisperova *Not Far From Wenceslas Square* (The Book Guild Ltd £12.95). Autobiography of an English woman who married a Czech airman in World War II, and after the war settled in Prague, only to be arrested during the 1950s "terror". She was released and finally returned to England in 1955 to a blaze of publicity in the West.

Miroslav Holub *The Dimension of the Present Moment* (Faber & Faber £4.99). A series of very short musings/essays by this unusual and clever scientist-poet.

Jan Šejna *We Will Bury You* (Sidgwick & Jackson, o/p). The memoirs of Czechoslovkia's highest ranking military defector, Major General Šejna, who fled to the West in February 1968. The memoir part is the most interesting, the sections uncovering the Commies' secret plan to take over the world little short of hysterical.

Stephen Brook *The Double Eagle: Vienna, Budapest and Prague* (Picador £4.99). Taking their shared Habsburg tradition as a starting point, Brook's readable, personal foray gives an illuminating picture of dissident life in Prague in the late 1980s before the neo-Stalinist bubble finally burst.

Tim Garton Ash *Uses of Adversity* (Granta/Penguin £5.99). A collection of Garton Ash's journalistic pieces on Eastern Europe, written mostly in the 1980s, including several informative pieces on Czechoslovakia.

Granta 30: New Europe! (Penguin £5.99). Published at the beginning of 1990, this state-of-the-continent anthology includes Graham Swift's *Looking for Jiří Wolf*, as well as a series of brief reactions to events by a dozen or so European intellectuals.

New Left Review (Number 179 £4.50). Contains a rare interview with leading Charter 77 spokesperson and dissident Marxist Petr Uhl, conducted during the heady first few months of the Velvet Revolution.

CZECH AND SLOVAK FICTION

Václav Havel *The Memorandum* (Methuen o/p); *Three Vaněk Plays* (Faber & Faber £4.99); *Temptation* (Faber & Faber £3.99); *Redevelopment* (Faber & Faber £3.99). Havel's plays are not renowned for being easy to read (or watch). *The Memorandum* is one of his earliest works, a classic absurdist drama which, in many ways, sets the tone for much of his later work, of which the *Three Vaněk Plays,* featuring Ferdinand Vaněk, Havel's *alter ego*, are perhaps the most successful. For a rare sampling of Havel's poetry, see p.383.

Jaroslav Hašek *The Good Soldier Švejk* (Penguin £8.99). The rambling, picaresque tale of Czechoslovakia's most famous fifth columnist, *Švejk*, who wreaks havoc in the Austro-Hungarian army during World War I, written by Bohemia's most bohemian writer.

Bohumil Hrabal *Closely Observed Trains* (Abacus £3.99); *The Death of Mr Baltisberger* (Abacus £3.99); *I Served the King of England* (Picador £5.99). A thoroughly mischievous writer, Hrabal's slim but superb *Closely Observed Trains* is one of the post-war classics, set in the last days of the war and relentlessly unheroic. *I Served the King of England* follows the anti-hero Dítě through the crucial decade after 1938. For an extract of Hrabal's writing, see p.387.

Zdena Tomin *Stalin's Shoe* (Picador £3.99); *The Coast of Bohemia* (Picador £3.99). Tomin writes in English (the language of her exile since 1980), and imbues it with a style and fluency all her own. *Stalin's Shoe* is the compelling and complex story of a girl coming to terms with her Stalinist childhood, while *The Coast of Bohemia* is based on Tomin's experiences of the late 1970s dissident movement.

Josef Škvorecký *The Cowards* (Penguin £5.99); *The Swell Season* (Picador £3.99); *The Bass Saxophone* (Picador £3.50); *Miss Silver's Past* (Picador, o/p); *Dvořák in Love* (Hogarth £5.95); *The Engineer of Human Souls* (Picador £7.99). A relentless anti-Communist, Škvorecký is typically Bohemian in his bawdy sense of humour and irreverence for all high moralising. *The Cowards* (which briefly saw the light of day in 1958) is the tale of a group of irresponsible young men in the last days of the war, an antidote to the lofty prose from official authors at the time. *The Bass Saxophone* is based around Škvorecký's other great love, jazz, while *Dvořák in Love* and *The Engineer of Human Souls* are both set in and around the Czech emigré communities of the "New World" where Škvorecký has lived since 1968.

Josef Škvorecký *The Mournful Demeanor of Lieutenant Boruvka; Sins for Father Knox; The Return of Lieutenant Boruvka* (all Faber & Faber £3.50–4). Less well known (and understandably so) are Škvorecký's detective stories, featuring the podgy, depressive Czech cop, which he wrote in the 1960s at a time when his more serious work was banned. The later book, *The Return of Lieutenant Boruvka*, is set in Škvorecký's new home, Canada.

Milan Kundera *The Joke; Laughable Loves; The Farewell Party; The Book of Laughter and Forgetting* (all Penguin £4.99); *Life is Elsewhere; The Unbearable Lightness of Being; Immortality* (Faber & Faber £4.99–9.95). Milan Kundera is Czechoslovakia's most popular writer – at least with non-Czechs. Certainly, if you can stand his sexual politics, his books are very obviously "political", particularly *The Book of Laughter and Forgetting* which caused the Communists to revoke Kundera's citizenship. *The Joke*, written while he was still living in Czechoslovakia, and in many ways his best work, is set in the very unfunny era of the Stalinist purges. Its clear, humorous style is far removed from the carefully poised posturing of his most famous work, *The Unbearable Lightness of Being*, set in and after 1968, and successfully turned into a film some twenty years later.

Arnošt Lustig *Diamonds of the Night; Darkness Casts No Shadow; Night and Hope; A Prayer for Kateřina Horovitová* (all Quartet £5.95–6.95); *Indecent Dreams* (Northwestern University Press £6.75). A Prague Jew exiled since 1968, Lustig spent World War II in Terezín, Buchenwald and Auschwitz, and his novels and short stories are consistently set in the Terezín camp.

Ladislav Mňačko *The Taste of Power* (Weidenfeld & Nicolson, o/p). Now exiled in Israel, Mňačko is one of the few Slovak writers to have been widely published abroad, most frequently his novel about the corruption of ideals which took place after the Communist takeover.

Franz Kafka *The Collected Novels of Franz Kafka* (Penguin £4.99). A German-speaking Prague Jew, Kafka has drawn the darker side of Central Europe, its claustrophobia, paranoia and unfathomable bureaucracy, better than anyone else, both in a rural setting, as in *The Castle*, and in an urban one, in one of the great novels of the twentieth century, *The Trial*.

Ivan Klíma *A Summer Affair* (Penguin £4.99); *My Merry Mornings* (Readers International £4.95); *First Loves* (Penguin £3.99); *Love and Garbage* (Chatto & Windus £13.99). Klíma is another writer in the Kundera mould as far as sexual politics goes, but his stories are a lot lighter. His latest novel, *Love and Garbage*, is based on his experiences as a street sweeper, while banned from writing in the years of "normalisation".

Jiří Weil *Life With a Star* (Flamingo £4.99). A novel based on Weil's experiences as a Czech Jew in Prague as the Nazis occupied Czechoslovakia, written just after the war.

Karel Čapek *Towards a Radical Centre* (Catbird USA). Čapek was the literary and journalistic spokesperson for Masaryk's First Republic, but he's better known in the West for his plays, some of which (though by no means all) feature in this anthology.

Eva Kantůrková *My Companions in the Bleak House* (Quartet £7.50). Kantůrková spent a year in Prague's Ruzyně prison, and *Companions* is a well-observed novel based around the characters within the prison's women's wing, the measure of their kindness, violence and despair mirroring the outside world.

New Writing in Czechoslovakia (Penguin, o/p). First published in 1969, this is one of the easiest collections of Czech and Slovak writing to get hold of second-hand.

Jozef Cíger-Hronský *Jozef Mak* (Slavica USA). A pro-Tiso Slovak writer, exiled in Argentina after the war. This is the simple, common story of the sufferings of a Slovak villager.

Božena Slančiková-Timrava *An Incipient Feminist: Slovak Stories* (Slavica USA). Not strictly a feminist as such, Slančiková-Timrava tells her Slovak tales from a decidedly female perspective.

POETRY

Miroslav Holub *The Fly* (Bloodaxe £5.95); *Poems Before & After* (Bloodaxe £7.95); *Vanishing Lung Syndrome* (Faber & Faber £4.99). Holub is both a scientist and scholar, and his poetry reflects this unique fusion of master poet and chief immunologist. Alternately banned and unbanned in his own country, he is the Czech poet *par excellence* – classically trained, erudite, liberal and Westward-leaning. *Vanishing Lung Syndrome* is his latest volume; the other two are collections. For two poems from *Poems Before & After*, see p.382.

Sylva Fischerová *The Tremor of Racehorses: Selected Poems* (Bloodaxe £5.95). Poet and novelist, Fischerová is one of the new generation of Czech writers, though in many ways she is continuing in the Holub tradition. By turns powerful, obtuse and personal, as was necessary to escape censorship during the late 1980s (see p.383 for an extract of her work).

Jaroslav Seifert *The Selected Poetry of Jaroslav Seifert* (Andre Deutsch £9.95). Czechoslovakia's one and only Nobel Prize-winning author, Seifert was a founder-member of the Communist Party and the avant-garde arts movement *Devětsil*, later falling from grace and signing the Charter in his old age. His longevity means that his work covers some of the most turbulent times in Czechoslovak history, but his irrepressible lasciviousness has been known to irritate.

Jaroslav Čejka, Michal Černík and Karel Sýs *The New Czech Poetry* (Bloodaxe £5.95). Slim, but interesting volume by three Czech poets all in their late forties, all very different. Čejka is of the Holub school, and comes across simply and strongly; Černík is similarly direct; Sýs the least convincing.

Vladimír Janovic *The House of the Tragic Poet* (Bloodaxe £6.95). A bizarre epic poem set in the last days of Pompeii in 79 AD, and centred around six young men who are rehearsing a satyr play.

Child of Europe – A New Anthology of East European Poetry (Penguin £6.99). This collection contains many hitherto untranslated Czech poets, including Ivo Šmoldas, Ewald Murrer and Jana Štroblová.

LITERATURE BY FOREIGN WRITERS

Bruce Chatwin *Utz* (Picador £3.99). Chatwin is one of the "exotic" school of travel writers, hence this slim, intriguing and mostly true-to-life account of an avid crockery collector from Prague's Jewish quarter.

Ellis Peters *The Piper on the Mountain* (Headline £2.99). Ellis Peters, whose real name is Edith Pargeter, is the author of the popular crime series *The Chronicles of Brother Cadfael*. A woman with strong Czech connections, Peters has chosen Prague and the Slovak Tatra mountains as the setting for this modern-day detective story.

Martha Gellhorn *A Stricken Field* (Virago, o/p). The story of an American journalist who arrives in Prague just as the Nazis march into Sudetenland. Based on the author's own experiences, this is a fascinating, if sentimental, insight into the panic and confusion in "rump" Czecho-Slovakia after the Munich Diktat. First published in 1940.

THE ARTS

Czech Modernism 1900–1945 (Little, Brown & Co £35). Wide-ranging and superbly illustrated, this American publication covers the journey of the Czech modern movement through Cubism and Surrealism to Modernism and the avant-garde. The accompanying essays by leading art and film critics cover fine art, architecture, film, photography and theatre.

Devětsil – Czech Avant-Garde Art, Architecture and Design of the 1920s and 30s (Museum of Modern Art, Oxford, £14.95). Published to accompany the 1990 Devětsil exhibition at Oxford, this is the definitive account of Czechoslovakia's most famous left-wing art movement between the wars, which attracted artists from every discipline.

Miroslav Lamač *Osma a skupina 1907–1917* (Odeon £25). Czech text, but good selection of full-colour reproductions (mostly of paintings) of the Cubist phase in Czech art.

Josef Koudelka (Photo Poche, o/p). Without doubt the most original Czech photographer and purveyor of fine Prague Spring photos. This pocket-size monograph is occasionally available in second-hand art bookshops.

Markéta Luškacová *Pilgrims* (V & A, o/p). A collection of incredible photographs taken in 1967–74 of the religious rituals and pilgrimages of Slovak villagers from eastern Slovakia.

Josef Sudek – A Photographer's Life (John Murray £35). Hauntingly beautiful set of sepia photographs by the old man of Czech photography who died in the 1970s.

Bohemian Glass (Flammarion £45). Five centuries of Bohemia's most lucrative export, taken from the country's own vast collection and exquisitely photographed.

POETRY AND FICTION

Czechoslovak literature has frequently been excluded from the mainstream of Western literature, either through snobbery towards "minor canons" or, during Communism, through political censorship. For the last twenty years the only writers known to the West were the 1968 generation of exiles. The extracts below break a trend in that all the authors – whatever their apparent differences – either lived or still live in Czechoslovakia.

ONDRA ŁYSOHORSKY

ÓNDRA ŁYSOHORSKY (1905–1989) was the ninth son of a coal-mining family in the district of Ostrava in North Moravia. Despite having his education in German, Łysohorsky chose to write most of his life's work in Lachian, the local dialect/language of his father, halfway between Polish and Czech. In the 1930s he was deeply influenced by the poverty and misery of the local miners. On January 22, 1933, Anton Pertille, an unemployed metal-worker, was shot dead on the Czechoslovak–German frontier bridge at Bohumín, trying to smuggle ten pounds of margarine into Czechoslovakia. Łysohorsky wrote the following poem, translated by David Gill.

THE BALLAD OF THE TEN POUNDS OF MARGARINE

To the crematorium they darkly crowded
forward.
On their crimson banners the snowflakes fall.
Suppressed cries of anger blaze in their eyes.
The police hold back like nervous laughter.

He toiled after truth; got the boot for his pains.
For two whole years no work came his way.
They starved to death his wife and daughter.
Turn thief? Not that. There was always the
bridge.

Frontier and bridge at Bohumín.
Border-guards, shots, a scream, a thud.
From his hands had tumbled ten pounds of
margarine.
The snow he lay in was red with blood.

MIROSLAV HOLUB

Born in Plzeň in 1923, **MIROSLAV HOLUB** is Czechoslovakia's most famous living poet. He studied medicine at the Charles University in Prague, but didn't begin writing poetry until the age of thirty. He is now the chief immunologist at the Institute of Clinical and Experimental Medicine in Prague. He has been in and out of favour with the authorities since his first published works in the late 1950s. The following two poems were both written in 1961, and reflect the stifling atmosphere in the country before the Prague Spring of 1968. They are reprinted from *Poems Before & After* (Bloodaxe Books 1990), and translated by Ian Milner.

POLONIUS

Behind every arras
he does his duty
unswervingly.
Walls are his ears,
keyholes his eyes.

He slinks up the stairs,
oozes from the ceiling,
floats through the door
ready to give evidence,
prove what is proven,
stab with a needle
or pin on an order.

His poems always rhyme,
his brush is dipped in honey,
his music flutes
from marzipan and cane.

You buy him
by weight, boneless,
a pound of wax flesh,
a pound of mousy philosophy,
a pound of jellied
flunkey.

And when he's sold out
and the left-overs wrapped
in a tasselled obituary,
a paranoid funeral notice,

and when the spore-creating mould
of memory
covers him over,
when he falls
arse-first to the stars,

the whole continent will be lighter
earth's axis straighten up
and in night's thunderous arena
a bird will chirp in gratitude.

THE DOOR

Go and open the door.
  Maybe outside there's
  a tree, or a wood,
  a garden,
  or a magic city.

Go and open the door.
  Maybe a dog's rummaging.
  Maybe you'll see a face,
or an eye,
or the picture
          of a picture.

Go and open the door.
  If there's a fog
  it will clear.

Go and open the door.
  Even if there's only
  the darkness ticking,
  even if there's only
  the hollow wind,
  even if
    nothing
        is there,
go and open the door.

At least
there'll be
a draught.

SYLVIA FISCHEROVÁ

Born in Prague in 1963, **SYLVA FISCHEROVÁ**
lived for twenty years in the Moravian town of
Olomouc before going to the Charles University
in Prague to study philosophy and physics. The
following poem was written just two days
before the beginning of the Velvet Revolution;
it is reprinted from *The Tremor of Racehorses:
Selected Poems* (Bloodaxe Books 1990).

THE STONES SPEAK CZECH

The stones speak Czech.
Water speaks salt
and remembers the salt
            mines of the Mayas.

The clouds stand
like holes into some other country
that everyone remembers.
Only the Czechs do not remember.
Once they looked round their land
and were saddened
and became stones
which now speak Czech.
Take them in your hand
and go to sleep with them.
On this earth
not one Czech is left
but in a moment
everyone will be speaking Czech.

              Translated by Ian and Jarmila Milner

VÁCLAV HAVEL

Born in Prague in 1936, **VÁCLAV HAVEL** was
one of the prime movers behind the human
rights movement Charter 77, and Civic Forum,
the opposition coalition which toppled the
Communists from power in November 1989.
Since December 1989 Havel has been
President of Czechoslovakia. Better known as a
playwright, the following absurdist poems
were written in the mid-1960s when Havel was
working at the *Divadlo na zábradlí* in Prague.

STALINIST PHILOSOPHY

            !!!!!!!!!!!!!!!!!!!!!!!!
            !!!!!!!!!!!!!!!!!!!!!!!!
            !!!!!!!!!!!!!!!!!!!!!!!!
            !!!!!!!!!!!!!!!!!!!!!!!!
            !!!!!!!!!!!!!!!!!!!!!!!!
            !!!!!!!!!!!!!!!!!?!!!!!!
            !!!!!!!!!!!!!!!!!!!!!!!!

FORWARD

              FORWARD
        FORWARD   FORWARD
        FORWARD   FORWARD
        FORWARD   FORWARD
        FORWARD   FORWARD
      FORWARD   FORWARD
        FORWARD   FORWARD
        FORWARD   FORWARD
        FORWARD   FORWARD
          FORWARD   FORWARD
              FORWARD

HUMOUR UNDER STALINISM

100%	100%	100%	100%	100%	100%	100%
100%	100%	100%	100%	100%	100%	100%
100%	100%	100%	100%	100%	100%	100%
100%	100%	100%	100%	100%	100%	100%
100%	100%	100%	100%	100%	100%	100%
100%	100%	100%	100%	100%	100%	100%
100%	100%	100%	100%	100%	100%	100%
100%	100%	100%	100%	100%	100%	100%
100%	100%	100%	100%	100%	100%	100%
100%	100%	100%	100%	100%	99%	100%
100%	100%	100%	100%	100%	100%	100%
100%	100%	100%	100%	100%	100%	100%

Taken from Václav Havel: ANTIKÓDY
Copyright © 1966 by Václav Havel

MILO URBAN

Born in 1904, **MILO URBAN** is a typically enigmatic Slovak writer; arrested by the Americans after the war on suspicion of involvement in the Tiso Nazi puppet government, he made up for it in the 1950s by acquiring a passion for Socialist Realism. The following extract, set in World War I, was written long before his subsequent trouble with the authorities.

THE LIVING WHIP

In the beginning, the inhabitants of Raztoky did not understand what really happened. They knew the word and they used it in their talks about the past; however, at that time there was nothing dreadful about it. The word flowed freely from their lips and evoked notions of mist and of the turns inherent in folk tales. The fields had not been torn up. The cities were not burning. And the blood, some sort of strange and beautiful blood, gushed painlessly from wounds. Not even death itself seemed awesome. Komar, a veteran of the Austro-Hungarian campaign in Bosnia, smiled whenever he spoke of a comrade who had been hit by a bullet directly in his heart. Komar smiled as if he were narrating a story from the Arabian Nights. People liked his stories and he told them again and again whenever there was an occasion for them, now and then adding something to his narration, now and then abridging it, now and then changing its parts. Komar's stories constituted almost all the Raztokian knowledge of war.

Thus the Raztokians did not know anything specific about war, even when the war was in full swing. Raztoky was situated in the northernmost part of Slovakia as people say — "behind God's back". The news about the war reaching the village seemed to be strained, amorphous, and bland. The villagers heard about the number of Russians drowned in the Masurian Marshes or about the skirmishes between the Serbian national guard and the Austro-Hungarian army or about the soldiers dying of thirst on the distant Plain of Doberda. But all this was far, far away. The inhabitants of Raztoky saw no cannons or machine guns. They confused grenades with shrapnels. The heavy cannons, whose fire cracked windows for a two-mile radius, seemed to the Raztokians to be some kind of supernatural monsters possessed of both free will and intelligence. The Raztokians believed that such cannons killed merely wicked men and demolished sodomite cities. Good men kept winning with the help of these cannons. And whenever it happened that one of the good fell, his death was just a tragic error, a stupid accident, and he — an instant hero — went directly to heaven.

Thus the villagers did not understand, and would not understand, the true meaning of war had war not stricken them with its cruel hand and hit them directly in the heart. The war did not hold back. It found the village of Raztoky and pulled it into the whirlpool of worldwide conflict despite the village's location "behind God's back".

Komar's son Albert was the first link weakly connecting the war and Raztoky. He came home with a wounded hand. Though the bullet drilled a hole through Albert's hands and flew farther, perhaps into someone's heart, the wound attracted unusual attention throughout Raztoky. All the citizens wanted to see Albert's hand again and again and examined the wound as a rarity, discussing it at length. Nevertheless, Albert's wound eventually healed, and he was able to work with his hand as if nothing had happened.

"That was nothing," the people repeated, until the return of Juraj Povala, the father of three children, who had three fingers torn from his left hand by shrapnel. Then, for the first time, the villagers found out that shrapnel explodes in the air. Juraj Povala was as strong as an oak. He came home happy, but he wept when he was recalled to the front. And the Raztokians, seeing tears in the eye of a man who had never cried, resented the war for the first time.

"No question, war is a bad thing," they said, and their resentment grew day after day, for the war began to cut more and more deeply in their own flesh. Flour began to disappear from the stores, while the price of kerosene and vegetables rose. From month to month the number of men in the village decreased. Abandoned fields begged for men's hands; however, only the wailing of women and prematurely matured children replied. Conscriptions of property, collections to support the government war efforts, and forced hauling of military equipment and supplies ensued. Not a single day passed without some exciting event. The death notices from military authorities kept coming and striking entire families like blows from an iron fist. The sorrowing ones bent beneath the blows and twisted like iron hoops under the blacksmith's sledge.

An awesome confusion took hold of everything, compelling a change in their way of thinking. The sun was hidden behind a steel coating. Fields stretched out like corpses and became almost deserted. The people working in the fields were apathetic, not ever feeling the heavy drops of sweat flowing down their bodies and tainting their linen shirts as they toiled. Some sort of beastly and awesome indifference gripped the men, although twisted perceptions stirred their subconsciousness to rebellion against an anomalous life.

The war and its concomitant hardships had already lasted some three years. Yet a strong connection with the front was missing. Everything important in the war took place far away, out of the immediate contact or interest of the Raztokians.

But one day in the spring of the war's fourth year, a soldier came to Raztoky. Clad in a dusty uniform hanging loosely on his prematurely withered body, the soldier was bent over and the wind rushing now and then from the mountains played with the empty right sleeve of his military jacket. A long scar ran aslant across the face of the soldier, from his slightly closed right eye down to the chin, taking away the lower right side of his strong nose and bridging his lips. Although dark with the redness of recent healing, the scar still seemed to be fresh and sharp, as if purposely painted on so that everyone would notice it and remember it for a long time. As it slashed along the soldier's face, the scar seemed to have been caused by a whip. The face under the scar was stretched and stiffened, giving the impression of a curious memorial tablet fastened by a pair of brown eyes to the soldier's head.

The sun's rays glued themselves to the steaming earth, but the water had not had a chance to dry out. Here and there, on the slopes that had evaded the direct sunlight, islands of dirty snow stubbornly retained their positions. The snow was permeated with brownish, unpleasant colours. Muddy water, flowing from under the snow, rippled around in the ditches and carried down the soggy rubbish which, in turn, became entrapped at the tiny dikes. Releasing odours of spring, the water and dikes and rubbish, despite their appearance, awakened fresh and happy sentiments.

The soldier, however, was influenced neither by springlike nature nor by the spring-coloured sentiments. As he entered Raztoky, nothing seemed out of the ordinary to him. Stepping over pools and ditches of water in the unpaved street, he looked now to the left, now to the right, without any special interest, as if walking through a strange village, not knowing anyone and accepting everything apathetically.

Only a few children, seeing the soldier, ran out of their houses and called, "Look, a soldier, a soldier!"

But the soldier, Andrej Koren, paid no attention to the children. He proceeded forward, drawing around himself a strange sort of silence. This silence drifted over the old widow, Ilčička, as she went to buy salt. Noticing him, she hastened her steps and asked him, "Say, who are you?"

Andrej Koren turned around. A numb look of surprise flitted across his face. He opened his mouth; however, as if suddenly coming to his senses, he did not say anything. He only nodded sadly.

"Andrej!" Ilčička cried, with surprise in her voice. "Where have you come from?"

Andrej Koren nodded toward the south. Ilčička looked him over with wide-open eyes. Seeing his empty sleeve, she cried out in horror, "And where is your hand?"

Andrej raised his eyes. His little eyes, as if dried by some strange fire, seemed to emit sparks of anger for a while. Then raising his left hand, he made a large half-circle in the air toward his right shoulder.

"They cut it off!" Ilčička exclaimed in awe.

Koren nodded, assenting to her words.

"What? Are you also mute?"

Koren nodded again.

"Mute!" Ilčička burst out in anger. Her voice broke in dismay at the heaped brutalities committed against this man, her godson. The hardships of life touched her suddenly, cutting her being painfully and searing the deepest reaches of her soul with flaming intensity. Seeing her disabled godson, Ilčička felt the world conflict suddenly close at hand. The war had moved from beyond folk tale glass mountains, from the lands of "solid water and liquid sands" directly to Raztoky. Cruel and dreadful primarily because of its abrupt arrival, the war stabbed into Ilčička's heart and penetrated her completely.

But she was not one of those women who, touched and hurt, retreat somewhere into a dark corner to whimper and mitigate their wounds with tears. No. At the very moment she met and recognised her disabled godson, Ilčička felt both her strength and her awesome rage inflaming her offended rebellious ego. Wrathful as she was, she could have drowned one half of the world and torn the other to pieces.

With a limitless and unforgiving wrath in her heart, she took hold of her godson's only hand and led him like a living personification of her anger directly to Koren's house.

JIŘÍ WOLF

Born in 1952, **JIŘÍ WOLF** spent his childhood in various state orphanages. Eventually he worked as a uranium miner in Příbram and later as a stoker. In 1973, he was sentenced to six months' imprisonment for the alleged theft of typewriters. He was a Charter 77 signatory and in 1978 was sentenced to three years for "subversion". While in prison, he was sentenced to a further six months for complaining about maltreatment by the StB. He was arrested for a third time in May 1983 and sentenced to another six years for "subversion", to be followed by a further three years "protective surveillance" for passing on a report on Czechoslovak prison conditions to the Austrian Embassy. The following was published in a *samizdat* journal while Wolf was serving time in Valdice prison, East Bohemia: it first appeared in translation in *East European Reporter* in November 1987.

I'M JUST FINE (SO IS PAKO)

I've just spent a whole week trying to write a letter home but I've not been able to secure a place to sit, or, rather, the right to sit at a table. There are ten of us in our small cell; there are five bunk beds, ten small lockers for our personal things, ten backless stools but only two tables. These seat only eight prisoners so the remaining "cons" have to find a bit of room somehow to sit down . . .

I try to secure at least a corner of the table so I can eat in a civilised manner but everybody here keeps a watchful eye on his bit of living space so I'm not successful. The situation is at its worst when there's no work during public holidays, otherwise we work like slaves every Saturday and Sunday. When it's a public holiday the cell is full; bad ventilation gives us headaches, we suffer from conjunctivitis and you could cut the smoke with a knife. The stench from the toilet in the corner of the cell serves as a sort of aperitif before meals and the whole claustrophobic atmosphere is complemented by constant rows and fights. . .

We always work, throughout the year, and there's no time off to recover our strength. I reckon after my release I'll have to spend at least six months getting myself together under the supervision of a doctor, a neurologist and maybe even a psychiatrist. I went to see the "doctor" here, the convict Ryjaček, and asked him for a check-up. He threw me out with the words "You're not here for recreation but for liquidation!"

I'm sitting now, there's a white sheet of paper in front of me and I don't know what to write home. The conditions here leave no room for any high-minded pursuits, for study or development of one's personality. Our daily routine is broken only by periods of starvation in the isolation cells of the Third Section, murderous, exhausting labour, harassment, constant conflicts among the prisoners, attempts to secure food, the whole merry-go-round. If only I could eat my fill for once! Our food rations are getting smaller and smaller but there's always more harassment and work for us. What can I write home about? About nothing, in fact. It's forbidden to say all this in a letter. It's even forbidden to write anything about the work we do and the remuneration that we get for it. We're only allowed to send greetings, to write nonsensical stupid clichés and. most importantly, to say that we are fine and that we lack nothing. And in reality, I lack everything. After incessant reductions of my pocket money reaching 75 percent, all I've got left is 15 to 20 crowns a month. It's a festive occasion when I have toothpaste, a razor blade, a stamp, a refill for my pencil; I've gone for a year now without socks and the ones that some kind soul sent me are in storage. To this day I don't know who sent them, apparently somebody from far-away Richmond. How I'd like to wear them, especially in the winter! The person who sent them was thinking of my frozen feet in isolation cells and during pointless marching. I wrap rags around my feet but they don't keep me warm; I also use newspapers which at least absorb the sweat. What kind of a "humane" system is this if it does not allow me to accept the gift of a pair of socks or once a year a food parcel of up to two kilograms in weight? I've not received a single one in all this time. What kind of a system is this? It has not legalised physical and psychic torture or punishment by starvation and yet all this is done here and human dignity is violated by beatings and verbal abuse.

I have read in our press that an international commission of the UN had favourably evaluated the handling of human rights on the part of our regime. Is such a thing possible? Is there any greater cynicism? Why, that commission only made legitimate on a international forum the criminal face of the regime, its power and so-called "socialist humanity"!

What are such commissions for? Has any member of this commission ever been in any labour camp? On what were its evaluations based and what information had our delegation submitted to it?

Oh, those empty phrases! They always start and end with lies. Take Pako, a Gypsy prisoner, can he write home that he's not well? No, he can't! If he wrote that the censor would not post his letter so he can only write: "I'm fine". Of course, he can add to this lie: "I've got everything I need, my health is good, they are

kind to me here, I'm not hungry and the work is good." The censor would be willing to send such a letter registered and at the expense of the camp.

So how exactly is Pako? Terribly, terribly unwell. He is regularly beaten, called a black ape, a bastard, shit, animal, nigger; he is starved in the Third Section. Anyone who wants to will kick him, he is harassed and exploited and yet he has to be fine. A few days ago they beat to death the prisoner Skokan in the Third Section. Not a month passes without someone being beaten to death and any day now it will be Pako's turn. One isn't "fine" yet is forced to write otherwise. It is absurd. This absurdity stems from the working of our act regulating the administration of justice (or, execution of punishment) which states that the conditions in labour camps must be humane, there .must be no violation of human dignity and the prisoner must be well. There must be no possibility of the con – a person destined for liquidation – not being well. That would not be in accordance with the law. . .

Translation copyright © 1988 East European Reporter

BOHUMIL HRABAL

Bohumil Hrabal is often said to be the greatest living writer in Czechoslovakia. He is the author of *I Served the King of England, Closely Observed Trains* and *The Death of Mr Baltisburger*. This short reverie, whose title means "Mad Hour", was published in Prague in 1989 and is a philosophical meditation on Schopenhauer, cats, revolution and incontinence, and pulls into its collage such figures as Shirley Temple, James Joyce, Joseph Stalin and T. S. Eliot. It takes the form of an affectionate letter to a friend in America. It is reprinted here by permission of *Storm Magazine*, a quarterly review of writing from Eastern and Western Europe.

MESHUGE STUNDA

Dear April,
I feel it's my duty, when I read something that moves me, to put it in my letters to you. Mr Rüdiger Safranski says in the preface to his book *Schopenhauer und Die wilden Jahren der Philosophie*: At the end, towards the end of his

life Schopenhauer said, "A philosophy where you do not hear between the pages the tears, the wailing and gnashing of teeth and the fearful, tumult of general mutual murder is no philosophy." And Safranski continues, "In a view of the French Revolution, Kant, midwife of the 'wild years of philosophy', wrote, 'Such a phenomenon in man's history can never be forgotten, for it has disclosed an aptitude and a power within human nature for the better." Mr Safranski observes, "Our events, those which we can never forget, are called Auschwitz, the Gulag Archipelago and Hiroshima." Die wilden Jahren: Kant, Fichte, Hegel, junge Marx. . .

I spoke with a man who lived through the events in Romania, in Bucharest. Those children who were shot, the barefoot kneeling children in Timisoara, he also saw all that. But appalling too was the drained blue swimming pool into which they threw the living soldiers of Ceauçescu's Commando, as the Father of the Nation called them. Ceauçescu's children. Those children, alive and swarming, condemned to death because of their upbringing.

Dear April, it was such a long time ago, but memory makes a second present out of the past. Did you know that maybe half or maybe a quarter of a century ago, Leopold Stokowski the famous conductor stayed at the "Golden Goose", the Hotel Šroubek on Wenceslas Square? He was conducting the Czech Philharmonic, and when the time came for him to take a taxi from the hotel to the station, no taxi came, however hard the porters tried, there was no sign of one. And the Paris Express will not wait. So Stokowski was standing there with his five or more suitcases and bags, when who should come along in a little trolley but a young man who guessed what was up at once, addressed the Master in fluent English and offered him a lift. And so they loaded up the luggage and Mr Leopold Stokowski, a fine, handsome, elegantly dressed man, and the trolley conveyed the lot of them off, slowly but surely, to the station. Leopold Stokowski, who was in the film "One Hundred Men and a Girl". And, April, do you know who else was in that film? The young Shirley Temple, who has an article in today's *Svobodné slovo* newspaper. She writes:

"In August 1968 by some ironic quirk of fate I was in Prague as a delegate, a delegate of the World Health Organisation, and I witnessed the revolution. Last year I returned to your country and by coincidence this was also in August and I was able to follow the progress of the Velvet revolution and the period before it. Your people seemed subdued, even subjugated. On the metro they stared at the floor and avoided one another's gaze. But at the same time their eyes shone with a longing to communicate, to say something. As a private individual I took part in the 28 October demonstration in Wenceslas Square. My sports outfit and training shoes helped me manage the obstacle course of police barriers as I fled with the young people from the actions of the forces of law and order. . . "

This, April, is the account of Mrs Shirley Temple, child heroine of the Leopold Stokowski film "One Hundred Men and a Girl", and she goes on:

"I deny the allegation made at the time by the *Rudé právo* newspaper, that I used a room reserved at the Hotel Yalta with a fine view of the Wenceslas statue as an observation post. I especially admire the decency of the Velvet Revolution and the courage and pride of those young people. I was saddened by the brutal intervention of the security forces on National Avenue. American journalists were among those seriously wounded. . . "

April, it makes a marvellous collage: the memory of the heroine of that film "One Hundred Men and a Girl" and the grown woman, Ambassador of your United States in Prague. . .

April, stay with me, please stay with me. I have just seen the abdication of the President of our unfortunate Republic on television again, the abdication of Mr Husák, how he tiptoed away from the presidential throne as if nothing had happened, as if he had just announced the current meteorological situation, he tiptoed away, from what he'd cooked up himself as first person of state, he went like a blind fox. As for me, I'd like to leave this world just like that Romanian Dracula did, that Maldoror, that loftiest simulacrum of evil. But I know what I'm like. In the end I'll just slink off anyway like a blind old fox. . .

April, Mr Safranski ends the preface to his Schopenhauer biography like this, "The wild years of philosophy ignored this philosopher of the 'wailing and gnashing of teeth' and the age old art of the contemplative life whose aim is Peace and Calm. The wild years ignored this philosopher who, far ahead of his time, had apprehended the three great injurious afflictions of human megalomania. The cosmological affliction: Our world is one of the numberless spheres in endless space on which a mouldy coating of living and cognitive beings vegetates. The biological affliction: Man is an animal in whom intelligence must compensate for lack of instincts and poor organic adaptation to life. The psychological affliction: Our conscious I is not master in its own house. These are the three great afflictions of human megalomania.

But April — now for something more cheerful! When I was in Sofia some years back the man my hotel was named after stood in front of it. Stalin himself. The citizens were considerate, they said, in winter women come in the afternoons to dress Stalin in warm longjohns and a warm shirt, and a fur cap with ear-flaps, so that Stalin won't catch cold here in Bulgaria. April, would that such a fine tradition might be kept up. Moreover, Mr Joyce in his *Ulysses* tells sadly of Mr Leopold Bloom remembering the coffin his little son Rudy lay in, and how Rudy's mother, Mrs Marion Bloom, knitted him a long warm jersey so that her little boy wouldn't get cold in his grave.

Dear April, if in the Bulgarian capital when the weather turns cold the little women dress Stalin in warm clothing as evening falls, imagine that similarly in Prague there is an ancient tradition of dressing the pražské Jesulàtko every day, nuns came down, I fancy from the Roudnice convent, and every day the pražské Jesulàtko was dressed in different clothes, the most precious child mannequin on earth. And so, as I have written elsewhere, and as I heard from the Lady Ambassador, General Necanda's wife, in Bolivia the Indians wear medallions with the image of this Infant Jesus of Prague, and among the Indians legend has it that Prague must be the most beautiful city in the world because, according to the Indians, Prague was where the Infant Jesus went to school. Princess Lobkovitz had a church built and her family after her kept up the trust, so that each and every day the Infant Jesus in Prague could wear different clothes from the day before, and so it went on throughout the year, three hundred and sixty-five different sets

of clothes, embroidered and stitched by the nimble hands of the nuns and their helpers.

But now you ask, April, how can I make a connection between this stuff about the Velvet Revolution and the pražské Jesulàtko? But April, can't you see? The South American Indians have their legend that Prague is the most beautiful city in the world. Why? Because little Jesus went to school there. And who made the Velvet Revolution? Millions of little Jesuses dressed up as students, actors, clowns and young people who, in preference to strict knowledge choose the inclination of the heart. General Šalgovič, however, who supervised the landing of heavy Soviet aircraft at Ruzyně airport, hanged himself yesterday in the laundry. Of course some stains can't be washed out without damaging the nature of the fabric. . .

My dear April, I took the number twelve tram up to town to pay homage to Prague's Infant Jesus, to the pražské Jesulàtko. But how I overestimated myself! I rushed off the number twelve and ran down to the public lavatories. But I knocked in vain. They were open, but the lavatories were engaged, I asked the loo attendant, for the mercy of the Lord Jesus, a cubicle! But the old lady with Sibylline eyes merely gave a wave of the hand. All occupied. And when a lavatory compartment became free, I had to confess what had happened to me. And the loo lady said, "Not to worry sir, it's happened before, something of the sort happens here practically every day, specially if there's a big holiday or some large gathering. The catastrophe comes when you get a rally or a congress or mass excursions to see the beauties of Prague." And the lady gazed at me, she had lovely eyes, just like the loo lady must have had who narrates the tale of Buchmendel, by the tragic Stefan Zweig. "What am I to do?" I say. "Take off your dirty underpants and look here. See? I've got a little tub and a basin, and I've even got a washboard . . . and here you can rinse out your underpants and here's a hair-dryer . . . or pop them on the line . . . once I even got told off by the cops, when the Spartakiad was on, for hanging out ladies' knickers in the arches opposite the Malá Strana Café. . . " and so first disgustedly with bog roll, and then with soap and water, the water ran and I washed and rubbed, customers came and went, and the attendant sat down heavily on her chair, rested her hands on her knees and told me all about it.

. . "I've even seen aristocracy caught short the same as you. A Spanish countess just like you, washing and rubbing away on the washboard with her purple frilly pantaloons. Now if only I could write. . ." And there I washed and rubbed and it felt like a scene from Dante's *La Divina Commedia:* Purification – Purgatory. . . and the loo lady sat and went on talking. . . "You know what happened one day? A tram driver rushed down here just like you did, but he'd hardly done his business and paid and run back upstairs, when he was back again. And so it went on about ten times. And there at the tram stop the tram was jingling away. He was quite pale by then and he told me he was the driver of the number twenty-two. It had come on sudden, mid-route, so he slammed the brakes on and ran down here. In half an hour the result was cataclysmic, the tram company inspector came rushing in, because that tram of his was blocking all the trams almost all the way back to the National Theatre. And so the inspector made up his mind to take the tram himself. By now he was pale, sir, beyond recognition, you could tell he'd shat his guts out. Pity I can't write. We carried on chatting like, there he was just like you washing out his long-johns in the tub and rubbing them on the washboard, he wore them very long, down to his ankles, on strings, just like Franta Hrubín the poet, Artist of the Nation – what also washed his longjohns out here once and went on about what a lovely experience it was for him. . . How this opened up a truer insight into the human race for him. He says, 'Here's the jug if you like' and I hopped off to Schnell's to get Hrubín his beer."

But I still haven't told you, April, about our tomcats and their *meshuge Stunden.* Once a day all of a sudden my cats are seized by an hour of crazy behaviour, out of the blue they go nuts and start flying all over the cottage garden, acting like they've gone off their rockers, everything for them is suddenly alive and living, under every little leaf they find mice and they paw away as if they were seeking out and finding pingpong balls, suddenly they speed off again at a gallop, in their rush they gash their ears with their paws and their claws, they leap on each other, roll over, then three groups of them declare an open revolution, an uprising, hissing and mewing resounds all over the lot, out of the blue they rush out swiftly at those spruces and stubby little oaks and fight

together up there in the tree-tops, and then they let themselves come slowly down again on their hind legs, but some of the toms stay up in the branches, and while those below fight and hiss at each other, those up above flash their eyes at one another and fight on, until they lower themselves again down the branches to the ground, or even fall, but that doesn't stop them, my three gangs carry on playing up like that, flying along the path beside the fence, rushing through the lattices, tearing their ears and flying off again somewhere over by the stream, there they turn and fly back under my windows, one after another, at a gallop, with powerful leaps, if I'm brave enough, I go out and have a look at this cats' *meshuge Stunde,* and find that almost all the tomcats have purposely gone nuts, and are panting away with their little tongues sticking out, harum scarum wide-eyed, haring around those great pines and oaks, in opposite directions, only to collide and claw one another with a terrific yowl, truss themselves up into a ball, tear at one another's ears mercilessly, and again. . . those long leaps, a sudden mad dart up branches and trunks, then again along branches onto twigs, and then lowering themselves down again to the ground, but even while they are in mid-air, before they've reached the ground, they fight, they act as if they're fighting. Sometimes I'm glad when, during this cats' *meshuge Stunde* the Soviet planes come flying low over the woods. Milovice isn't far from here, and Soviet planes take off and land there making an awful racket and din. This has its effect on my cats too. Even in the middle of their *meshuge Stunde.* Those aeroplanes horrify them so, they fall, press their little bellies into the leaves and moss, and absolutely flatten themselves with horror. Some of the tomcats fly up to their nooks among the coal and in the woodpile and don't creep out until the Soviet aircraft have landed over there beyond the woods on the Milovice airstrips. They happen once a day, my cats' *meshuge Stunden,* then they get their breath back and it takes them a long time to calm down, slow down. These are, writes Safranski, the *meshuge Jahren der Philosophie* . . . Kant, Fichte, Hegel and the young Marx. . . But now it's evening, in three days we'll have a full moon. It's got to me too, I've had the flu for three days and fevers, which have stopped, now I'm able to go out and look at the evening, I feel restless, the moon has been out a long time, now it's climbing sharply up over the wood and the garden in front of my garden, now it's almost as if the moon too were having its own *meshuge Stunde*, it climbs so swiftly heavenward. I sit at the window and the moon is so high in the sky I have to turn and twist my head to get a view of it, I sit here for a bit and get the feeling that my house, thanks to its windows, is just like a great big cut diamond, and I know where my cats are now. . . I can see glimpses of them through the window beside the white fence around the beige track, so I go out after them and sure enough, the kits are sitting there by the white laths, just like at midday, when the sunlight warms them and they bake themselves there in the grass. . . but now they sit there solemnly, erect, leaning their backs against the latticed laths and squinting up at the sky, where the moon is shining and they are listening to that silence just like me. I walk past them like the President filing out his castle guard, the kits follow after me, the procession closes up, they escort me wherever I go. . . in the day I get scared of the gamekeepers seeing us, those twelve cats following along behind me, dancing and leaping about, lying joyously on their backs and twirling in the sand and smiling, even now in the moonlit night they smile, because they are happy that I'm alive on this earth. And as always Cassius Clay comes along, the little black tom, he stands up on his hind legs and I have to catch hold of him, and lift him up straightaway and press his fur, his furry tummy to my face. . . that is our ceremony, none of the other cats is brave enough, they would all like to be picked up too, but they don't dare, they show by all their dancing about just within shooting range that they would like to do it too, but they don't yet have the courage. Perhaps it's enough for them that Blacking, as I sometimes call Cassius, does it for them. . . and I close my eyes and the fur sizzles out his scent, and Cassius probably knows, because all day he does nothing but clean himself, clean himself all over, just in case I happen to pick him up in my hand and press my face into his fur and speak tender words like the words I said maybe only to you, April, and then only in spirit, but Cassius knows that I really do speak to him, he closes his eyes, his fuses go, and for a moment he almost looks dead. . . Sometimes

the sooty orphan from my sister-in-law's comes, the one left from that pair who always trotted out together to meet me, pulling after them on invisible threads a little invisible, but so essential truckload of happiness. Sometimes I go to find him. I know where he is, he sits near the gate and waits, just in case the one who died in front of the locked door to the building, his kid brother, comes today. And in the moonlit night he came along, I picked him up in my hand, but it wasn't a comfort to him that day, he rattled, he's probably got pneumonia. And, April, he's altogether neglected, like I was when my Pipsi died. I clean him with a rag, I clean his ears, I take him to the others to please him, but he only stays on for a little while, as I walk through the moonlit night he trots behind me for a while, then goes back again, but he can't settle, he's aged terribly, this tender little tom who always used to look after himself like Cassius. Maybe he'll get over it. Today he comes as usual, mewing softly at the latticing, glancing under my sister-in-law's caravan, standing in front of the locked door. then he lies down under the round table where the newspapers and magazines are kept. And then he can't help it, he goes off to keep watch in case his sooty little brother turns up. So he stands there in the meadow, looking around, waiting, he stands where he can be seen, but it's no good, it would take a miracle, but there are no miracles any more nor is there living water. His little brother is buried out there behind the big oak, where they both liked to lie about in the sunshine, by the roots of the mighty oak tree. . .

And so, April, that's how it ends. The happiness of those two did not last for long, but it was worth it. Just as we have actually seen so little of each other on this earth, and look, I am still the same as if you were beside me. Those invisible threads, those invisible threads, those invisible threads? But where would we be without those invisible threads? Who will bring me three mustard grains from a house where no one has died? So there is nothing for it but Te Deum laudamus.

p.s.

Dear April

Arthur Schopenhauer's mother Johanna got her son to write a diary when he was young. Please let me translate a small entry for you — made when he was twelve:

"Wednesday 16 June. Towards midday we departed from Hamburg and after several hours of gloomy weather we reached the Zollenspieker ferry, where we were to be taken across the Elbe. Then before the ferry boat arrived, we started talking to a poor blind lady who had no idea when it was day and when it was night. When we asked her the reason for her blindness, she told us that during the half-hour journey in the frost to her christening, her eyes had become frost-bitten. Yet although she'd been blind since then, she knew all the roads, and everything she needed she could take care of herself. I felt sorry for this woman, I wondered at the phlegmatic calm with which she bore her suffering. She had paid so dearly for the consolation of becoming a Christian woman! From the Zollenspieker ferry we went on our way after a filling lunch and in the evening we reached Lüneburg, where we saw nothing but Gothic buildings . . . ."

Of course! Dear April, the 150,000 copies of my book, *November Hurricane* have been held up for technical reasons, until March or maybe, dear April, until April. T.S.Eliot . . . "April is the cruellest month . . ." The Waste Land. "breeding/Lilacs out of the dead land . . ."

Translated by James D. Naughton

LANGUAGE

Czechoslovakia's two principal languages, Czech and Slovak, are mutually
intelligible, highly complex Slav tongues.
Whether they are separate languages or
simply diverse dialects of a common one is
still a hotly disputed issue. However, for
the non-Slav, they are sufficiently distinct
to cause serious problems of
understanding.

Unless you're here for some time, it's all
rather academic, since you're not likely to make
any great inroads into either. If you know some
German already, brush up on that, since, among
the older generation in particular, German is the
most widely spoken second language, and as a
visitor you'll be expected to know at least
some. Following the Velvet Revolution, Russian
(once the compulsory second language) has
been wiped off the school curriculum, and the
number of English-speakers has been steadily
increasing. Having said all that, any attempt to
speak Czech or Slovak will be heartily appreciated, if a little difficult to understand for a
people unaccustomed to hearing foreigners
stumble through their language.

PRONUNCIATION

English-speakers often find Czech impossibly
difficult to pronounce (Slovak less so). In fact,
it's not half as daunting as it might first appear
from the traffic jams of consonants which crop
up on the page. Apart from a few special letters,
each letter and syllable is pronounced as it's
written – the trick is always to **stress the first
syllable** of a word, no matter what its length;
otherwise you'll render it unintelligible.

SHORT AND LONG VOWELS

Czech and Slovak have both short and long
vowels (the latter being denoted by a variety of
accents). The trick here is to lengthen the vowel
without affecting the principal stress of the
word, which is invariably on the first syllable.

a like the u in **cup**
á as in f**a**ther
ä closer to the e in l**e**t than an a
e as in p**e**t
é as in f**ai**r
i or y as in p**i**t
í or ý as in s**ea**t
o as in n**o**t
ó as in f**o**rum
ô like the u in l**u**rid
u like the oo in b**oo**k
ů or ú like the oo in f**oo**l

VOWEL COMBINATIONS AND DIPTHONGS

There are very few dipthongs in Czech,
substantially more in Slovak. Combinations of
vowels not mentioned below should be
pronounced as two separate syllables.

au like the ou in f**ou**l
ě or ie like the ye in **ye**s
ia like the ya in **ya**k
iu like the u in fl**u**te
ou like the oe in f**oe**

CONSONANTS AND ACCENTS

There are no silent consonants, but it's worth
remembering that r and l can form a syllable if
standing between two other consonants or at
the end of a word, as in Brno (Br–no) or Vltava
(Vl–ta–va). The consonants listed below are
those which differ substantially from the
English. Accents look daunting, but the only one
which causes a lot of problems is ř (Czech only),
probably the most difficult letter to say in the
entire language.

c like the **ts** in boats
č like the **ch** in chicken
ch like the **ch** in the Scottish loch
ď like the **d** in duped
g always as in goat, never as in general
h always voiced as in have, but more energetic
j like the **y** in yoke
kd pronounced as **gd**

ľ like the **lli** in colliery
mě pronounced as mye
ň like the **n** in nuance
p softer than the English p
r as in rip, but often rolled

ř like the sound of **r** and **ž** combined
š like the **sh** in shop
ť like the **t** in tutor
ž like the **s** in pleasure; at the end of a word
   like the sh in shop

A CZECH–SLOVAK LANGUAGE GUIDE

● There are very few **teach-yourself Czech** courses available – and none for Slovak – and each has drawbacks. *Colloquial Czech* (£7.99 each for the book and tape) is a bit fast and furious for most people. The Czech-produced *Czech for English Speaking Students* (most easily available in Czechoslovakia) is more thorough and wide-ranging, but was designed for foreign students studying Czech under the previous regime. The best portable **dictionaries** are the *kapesní slovník* for Czech and the *vreckový slovník*, most easily purchased in Czechoslovakia. Colletts produce a phrasebook called *Travellers' Czech* (£2.95).

● In many instances the **Czech** and **Slovak words** for things are the same. Where they're different, we've separated them below, giving the Czech word first and the Slovak word second.

BASIC WORDS AND PHRASES

Ano/áno	Yes	Dnes	Today
Ne/nie	No	Včera	Yesterday
Prosím	Excuse me	Zítra/zajtra	Tomorrow
Není zač/nemáte začo	You're welcome	Pozítra/pozajtra	The day after tomorrow
Pardon/pardón	Sorry	Hnet/teraz	Now
Děkuju/ďakujem	Thank you	Pozděje/neskôr	Later
Dobrá/dobre	OK	pusť mě/nechaj ma osamote	Leave me alone
Dobrou chuť	Bon apetit		
Šťastnou cestu	Bon voyage	Jdi pryč/choď preč	Go away
Ahoj	Hello/goodbye (informal)	Pomoc!	Help!
		Tento	This one
Na schledanou/ do videnia	Goodbye (formal)	Trocha	A little
Dobrý den	Good day	Velký–malý	Large–small
Dobré ráno	Good morning	Více–méně/viac–menej	More–less
Dobrý večer	Good evening	Dobrý–špatný	Good–bad
Dobrou noc	Good night (when leaving)	Horký–studený/ horúci–studený	Hot–cold
Jak se máte/ako sa máte?	How are you?	S–bez	With–without

GETTING AROUND

Kde je . . .?	Where is . . .?	Ovně/priamo	Straight on
Jak se dostanu do Zvolena/ ako sa dostanem do Zvolena?	How do I get to Zvolen?	Jízdenka/lístok	Ticket
		Spátečá jízdenka/spiatočný lístok	Return ticket
Jak se dostanu k univerzitě/ ako sa dostanem k univerzite?	How do I get to the university?	Nádraží/železničná stanica	Railway station
		Autobusové nádraží/ autobusová stanica	Bus station
Autobusem/autobusom	By bus	Autobusové zastávka	Bus stop
Lakem/vlakom	By train	Kdy jde . . ./kedy ide najbli žší vlak do Prahy?	When's the next train to Prague?
Autem/autom	By car		
Pěšky/pešo	By foot	Jde to do Brna/ide to do Brna?	Is it going to Brno?
Taxíkem/taxíkom	By taxi		
Tady/tuná	Over here	Musím přestupovat/musím prestupovat?	Do I have to change?
Tam	Over there		
Nalevo/naľavo	Left	Musím mít místenku?	Do I have to have a reservation?
Napravo	Right		

QUESTIONS AND ANSWERS

Mluvíte anglicky/ hovoríte anglicky?	Do you speak English?	Kdy/kedy	When
Nemluvím německy/ nehovorím nemecky	I don't speak German	Proč/prečo	Why
		Kolík stojí/koľko stojí?	How much is it?
Nerozumím/ nerozumiem	I don't understand	Máte volné pokoje/ Máte voľhé izby?	Are there any rooms available?
		Dhtěl bych dvou lůžkovy/	I want a double room
Rozumím/rozumiem	I understand	Chcem dvojposteľovú izbu	
Mluvte pomalu/hovorte pomalšie	Speak slowly	Na jednu noc	For one night
		Se sprchou/se sprchy	With shower
Jak se tohle řekne česky/ako sa to povie slovenský?	How do you say that in Czech/Slovak?	Jsou tyto místa volná/ Sú tieto miesta voľná?	Are these seats free?
		Můžeme/môžme?	May we (sit down)?
Mužete mí to napsat/ mohli by ste mi to napísať?	Could you write it down for me?	Zaplatím prosím	The bill please
		Máte . . .?	Do you have . . .?
		Nemáme	We don't have
Co/čo	What	Máme	We do have
Kde	Where		

SOME SIGNS

Vchod	Entrance	Otevřeno/otvorené	Open
Východ	Exit	Zavřeno/zavreté	Closed
Záchod	Toilets	Pozor!	Danger!
Muži	Men	Nemocnice/ nemocnica	Hospital
Ženy	Women		
Pánové	Ladies	Kouření zakázáno/ zákaz fajčiť	No smoking
Dámy	Gentlemen		

Koupání zakázáno/ zákaz kúpania	No bathing
Vstup zakázáno	No entry
Příjezd/príchod	Arrival
Odjezd/odchod	Departure
VB	Police

DAYS OF THE WEEK

Pondělí/pondelok	Monday	Neděle/nedeľa	Sunday
Úterý/uterok	Tuesday	Den/deň	Day
Středa/streda	Wednesday	Týden/týždeň	Week
Čtvrtek/štvrtok	Thursday	Měsíc/mesiac	Month
Pátek/piatok	Friday	Rok	Year
Sobota	Saturday		

NUMBERS

Jeden	1	Patnáct/pätnásť	15	Sto	100
Dva	2	Šestnáct/šestnásť	16	Sto jedna	101
Tří/tri	3	Sedmnáct/sedemnásť	17	Sto padesát pět/ stodpätdesiatpäť	155
Čtyří/štyri	4	Osumnáct/osemnásť	18		
Pět/päť	5	Devatenáct/devätnásť	19	Dvě stě/dvesto	200
Šest/šesť	6	Dvacet/dvadsať	20	Tří sta/tristo	300
Sedm/sedem	7	Dvacetjedna/dvadsaťjeden	21	Čtyří sta/štyristo	400
Osum/osem	8	Třícet/tridsať	30	Pět set/päťsto	500
Devět/deväť	9	Čtyšícet/štyridsať	40	Šest set/šesto	600
Deset/desať	10	Padesát/päťdesiat	50	Sedm set/sedemsto	700
Jedenáct/jedenásť	11	Šedesát/šesťdesiat	60	Osum set/osemsto	800
Dvanáct/dvanásť	12	Sedmdesát/sedemdesiat	70	Devět set/deväťsto	900
Třináct/trinásť	13	Osumdesát/osemdesiat	80	Tisíc	1000
Čtrnáct/štrnásť	14	Devadesát/deväťdesiat	90		

MONTHS OF THE YEAR

Czechs and Slovaks use completely different words to denote the **months of the year**. Czech has its own highly individual system, translated below, in which the words for the names of the month are descriptive nouns – sometimes beautifully apt for the month in question.

CZECH

January	*Leden* – ice	July	*Červenec* – redder
February	*Únor* – hibernation	August	*Srpen* – sickle
March	*Březen* – pregnancy	September	*Září* – blazing
April	*Duben* – oak	October	*Říjen* – rutting
May	*Květen* – blossom	November	*Listopad* – leaves falling
June	*Červen* – red	December	*Prosinec* – supplication

SLOVAK

January	*Január*	May	*Máj*	September	*September*
February	*Február*	June	*Jún*	October	*Október*
March	*Marec*	July	*Júl*	November	*November*
April	*Apríl*	August	*August*	December	*December*

AN A–Z OF STREET NAMES

Since the Velvet Revolution, many streets named after erstwhile stars of the Communist party disappeared. It's not the first time that the sign writers have had their brushes out either: after World War II, all the Herman-Göring-Strasses were quickly renamed, and a similar process occurred after World War I. The following names currently appear in almost every major town in Czechoslovakia; remember that street names always appear in the genitive or adjectival form, eg Palacký street is Palackého and Hus street is Husova.

29 August. The day the unsuccessful Slovak National Uprising against the Nazis began in 1944.

Beneš, Edvard (1884–1948). President from 1935 until the Munich Crisis and again from 1945 until the Communist coup in 1948. Making a stronger than expected comeback.

Bernolák, Anton (1762–1813). Slovak theologian and pioneer in the Slovak written language. Author of the first Slovak dictionary.

Bezruč, Petr (1867–1958). Pen name of the Czech poet Vladimír Vašek who wrote about the hardships of the Ostrava mining region.

Čapek, Karel (1890–1938). Czech writer, journalist and unofficial spokesperson for the First Republic whose most famous works were *The Insect Play* and *R.U.R.*, which introduced the word *robot* into the English language.

Čech, Svatopluk (1846–1908). Extreme Czech nationalist and poet whose best-known work is *Songs of a Slave*.

Chelčicky, Petr (born c.1390). Extreme pacifist Hussite preacher who disapproved of the violence of Žižka and his Taborite army.

Dobrovský, Josef (1753–1829). Jesuit-taught pioneer in Czech philology. Wrote the seminal text *The History of Czech Language and Literature*.

Duklianské hrdiny (The Dukla Heroes). The name given to the soldiers who died capturing the Dukla Pass in October 1944, the first decisive battle in the liberation of the country from the Nazis.

Dvořák, Antonín (1841–1904). Perhaps the most famous of all Czech composers whose best-known work is his *New World Symphony* inspired by his extensive sojourn in the USA.

Fučik, Julius (1903–1943). Communist journalist murdered by the Nazis whose prison writings, *Notes from the Gallows*, were obligatory reading in the 1950s. Doubts about the authenticity of the work now, and general hostility towards the man could see his name disappear off the streets yet.

Havlíček-Borovský, Karel (1821–56). Satirical poet, journalist and nationalist, exiled to the Tyrol by the Austrian authorities after 1848.

Hurban, Jozef Miroslav (1817–1888). Slovak writer and journalist who edited various pioneering Slovak-language journals.

Hus, Jan (1370–1415). Rector of Prague University and reformist preacher who was burnt at the stake as a heretic by the Council of Constance.

Hviezdoslav, Pavol Orságh (1849–1921). The father of Slovak poetry who lived and worked in the Orava region where he was employed as a court official until his retirement.

Janáček, Leoš (1854–1928). Moravian-born composer, based in Brno for most of his life, whose operas in particular have become quite widely performed in the West.

Jánošík Fabled Slovak folk hero, modelled along the lines of Robin Hood, who operated in the Malá Fatra range (see p.307).

Jesenský, Janko (1874–1945). Slovak poet who accompanied the Czechoslovak Legion in its long trek across the Soviet Union during the Bolshevik Revolution.

Jirásek, Alois (1851–1930). Writer for both children and adults who popularised Czech legends and became a key figure in the národní obrození.

Jungmann, Josef (1773–1847). Prolific Czech translator and author of the seminal *History of Czech Literature* and the first Czech Dictionary.

Kollár, Ján (1793–1852). Professor of Slav archaeology in Vienna and Slovak poet who wrote in Czech and opposed the formation of a separate Slovak written language.

Komenský, Jan Amos (1592–1670). Leader of the Protestant Czech Brethren. Forced to flee the country and settle in England during the Counter-Reformation. Better known to the English as Comenius.

Kráľ Janko (1822–76). A Slovak poet who wrote folk ballads, while **Fraňo** (1903–55) is a Slovak Communist poet and no relation to the former.

5 května (May 5). The day of the Prague Uprising against the Nazis in 1945.

9 května (May 9). The day Czechs and Slovaks (and the Soviets) celebrate as VE Day 1945.

Mácha, Karel Hynek (1810–36). Romantic nationalist poet, great admirer of Byron and Keats who, like them, died young. His most famous poem is *Maj*, published just months before his death.

Masaryk, Tomáš Garrigue (1850–1937). Professor of Philosophy at Prague University, President of the Republic (1918–1935). His name is synonymous with the First Republic and was removed from all street signs after the 1948 coup. Now back with a vengeance.

Nálepka, Ján (1912–1943). Slovak teacher and partisan in World War II who won fame through his daring antics in the Nazi-occupied Ukraine where he eventually died.

Němcová, Božena (1820–1862). Highly popular writer who got involved with the nationalist movement and shocked with her unorthodox behaviour. Her most famous book is *Grandmother*.

Neruda, Jan (1834–1891). Poet and journalist for the *Národní listy*. Wrote some famous short stories describing Prague's Malá Strana.

Palacký, František (1798–1876). Nationalist historian, Czech MP in Vienna and leading figure in the events of 1848.

Purkyně, Jan Evangelista (1787–1869). Czech doctor, natural scientist and pioneer in experimental physiology who became professor of physiology at Prague and then Wrocław University.

Ressel, Josef (1793–1857). Fascinatingly enough, the Czech inventor of the screw-propeller.

Rieger, Ladislav. Nineteenth-century Czech politician and one of the leading figures in the events of 1848 and its aftermath.

Šafárik, Pavol Jozef (1795–1861). Slovak scholar and son of a Slovak Lutheran pastor whose major works were actually written in Czech and German.

Sládkovič, Andrej (1820–1872). Slovak poet who lived and worked in the Detva region, and whose pastoral love poem *Marína* is regarded as a classic.

Smetana, Bedřich (1824–1884). Popular Czech composer and fervent nationalist whose *Ma vlast* ("My Homeland") traditionally opens the Prague Spring Music Festival.

SNP (*Slovenské národné povstanie*). The ill-fated Slovak National Uprising against the Nazis which took place in August/September 1944.

Štúr, Ľudovít (1815–1856). Slovakia's number one nationalist hero, who led the 1848 revolt against the Hungarians and argued for a Slovak language distinct from Czech.

Svoboda, Ludvík. Victorious Czech General from World War II, who acquiesced to the 1948 Communist coup and was Communist President (1968–1975).

Tajovský, Jozef Gregor (1874–1940). Slovak dramatist and short story writer whose moral ethics and identification with the underdog made him a sharp social critic of the times.

Tyl, Josef Kajetán (1808–1856). Czech playwright and composer of the national anthem, *Where is my Home?*.

Vajanský, Svetozár Hurban (1847–1916). Romantic Slovak novelist whose Russophile views were as unpopular then as now.

Wolker, Jiří (1900–1924). Czech Communist who died of tuberculosis at the age of 24, and whose one volume of poetry was lauded by the Communists as the first truly proletarian writing.

Žižka, Jan (died 1424). Brilliant military leader of the Táborites, the radical faction of the Hussites.

GLOSSARIES

CZECH/SLOVAK WORDS

BRÁNA Gate.

ČESKÝ Bohemian.

CHATA Chalet-type bungalow or country cottage.

CHRÁM Large church.

CINTORÍN Cemetery (Slovak).

DIVADLO Theatre.

DOLINA Valley (Slovak).

DÓM Cathedral.

DŮM/DOM House.

DŮM KULTURY/DOM KULTURY Communal arts and social centre; literally "House of Culture".

HRAD Castle.

HRANICE/HRANICA Border.

HŘBITOV Cemetery (Czech).

HORA Mountain.

HOSTINEC Local pub.

JESKYNĚ/JASKYŇA Cave.

JEZERO/JAZERO Lake.

KÁMEN/KAMEŇ Rock.

KAPLE/KAPLNKA Chapel.

KAŠTIEĽ Manor house (Slovak).

KATEDRÁLA Cathedral.

KAVÁRNA/KAVÁRIEŇ Coffee house.

KLÁŠTER/KLÁŠTOR Monastery.

KOSTEL/KOSTOL Church.

KOUPALIŠTĚ/KÚPALISKO Swimming pool.

LABE River Elbe.

LANOVKA Funicular or cable car.

LÁZNĚ Spa (Czech).

LES Forest.

LOGGIA Covered area on the side of a building, often arcaded.

MĚSTO/MESTO Town; *staré město* – Old Town, *nové město* – New Town, *dolní město* – Lower Town, *horní město* – Upper Town.

MORAVSKÝ Moravian.

MOST Bridge.

NÁDRAŽÍ Train station (Czech).

NÁMĚSTÍ/NÁMESTIE Square, as in *náměstí Svobody/námestie Slobody* – Freedom Square.

NÁRODNÍ VÝBOR Town council.

NISA River Neisse.

ODRA River Oder.

OSTROV Island.

PAMÁTNÍK/PAMÄTNÍK Memorial or monument.

PIVNICE/PIVNICA Pub.

PLANINA Valley basin (Slovak).

PLESO Mountain lake (Slovak).

PRAMEN Natural spring.

PROHLÍDKA/PREHLIADKA Viewpoint.

RADNICE/RADNICA Town hall.

RATHAUS Town hall (German).

RESTAURACE/REŠTAURÁCIA Restaurant.

SADY Park.

SÁL Room or hall (in a chateau or castle).

SEDLO Saddle (of a mountain).

SKÁLA/SKALA Crag/rock.

SKANSEN An open-air folk museum, with reconstructed folk art and architecture.

SLOVENSKÝ Slovak.

STANICA Train station (Slovak).

ŠTÍT Peak (Slovak).

STUCCO Plaster used for decorative effects.

SVATÝ/SVÄTÝ Saint, such as svatý Václav – Saint Wenceslas. Abbreviated to sv.

TEPLICE Spa.

TŘÍDA/TRIEDA Avenue.

VĚŽ/VEŽA Tower.

VINÁRNA/VINÁRIEŇ Wine bar or cellar.

VLTAVA River Moldau.

VRCHY Hills.

VÝSTAVA Exhibition.

ZAHRADA/ZÁHRADA Gardens.

ZÁMEK/ZÁMOK Chateau.

ART/ARCHITECTURAL TERMS

AMBULATORY Passage round the back of the altar, in continuation of the aisles.

ART NOUVEAU Sinuous and stylised form of architecture and decorative arts: in Czechoslovakia dating from 1900–10, imported from Vienna and Budapest, and therefore known as the Secession, rather than *Jugendstil*, the German name.

BAROQUE Expansive, exuberant architectural style of the seventeenth and mid-eighteenth centuries, characterised by ornate decoration, complex spatial arrangement and grand vistas.

BEAUTIFUL STYLE Also known as the Soft Style of painting. Developed in Bohemia in the fourteenth century, it became very popular in Germany.

CHANCEL Part of the church where the altar is placed, usually at the east end.

EMPIRE A highly decorative Neoclassical style of architecture and decorative arts, practised in the first part of the nineteenth century.

FRESCO Mural painting applied to wet plaster, so that the colours immediately soak into the wall.

FUNCTIONALISM Plain, boxy, modernist architectural style, prevalent in the late 1920s and 1930s in Czechoslovakia, often using plate-glass curtain walls, and open-plan techniques for the interior.

NAVE Main body of a church, usually the western end.

NEOCLASSICAL Late eighteenth- and early nineteenth-century style of architecture and design returning to classical models as a reaction against Baroque and Rococo excesses.

ORIEL A bay window, usually projecting from an upper floor.

ROMANESQUE Solid architectural style of the late tenth to thirteenth century, characterised by round-headed arches and geometrical precision.

ROCOCO Highly florid, fiddly though (occasionally) graceful style of architecture and interior design, forming the last phase of Baroque.

SECESSION Style of early twentieth-century art and architecture based in Germany and Austria which reacted against the academic establishment.

SGRAFFITO Monochrome plaster decoration effected by means of scraping back the first white layer to reveal the black underneath.

SHINGLE Wooden roof-tiles.

STUCCO Plaster used for decorative effects.

TROMPE L'OEIL Painting designed to fool the onlooker into believing that it is actually three-dimensional.

HISTORICAL AND POLITICAL TERMS

CIVIC FORUM (Občanské fórum). The umbrella coalition which brought down the government in 1989, and won the general election of 1990.

CZECH LANDS A phrase used to denote Bohemia and Moravia.

FIRST REPUBLIC The new Czechoslovak Republic founded by Masaryk after World War II, made up of Bohemia, Moravia, Silesia, Slovakia and Ruthenia, dismantled by the Nazis in 1938–39.

GREAT MORAVIAN EMPIRE The first Slav state covering much of what is now Czechoslovakia, which ended shortly after the Magyar invasion of 896 AD.

HABSBURGS The most powerful family in central Europe, whose power base was Vienna. They held the Bohemian throne from 1526 to 1918, the Hungarian kingdom from 1526 to 1867, and by marriage and diplomacy acquired territories all over Europe.

HISTORIC PROVINCES Land traditionally belonging to the Bohemian crown, including Bohemia, Egerland, Moravia, Silesia and Lusatia.

HOLY ROMAN EMPIRE Name given to the loose confederation of German states (including for a while the Czech Lands) which lasted from 800 until 1806.

HUSSITES Name given to Czech religious reformers who ostensibly followed the teachings of Jan Hus (1370–1415).

JAGIELLONIANS Polish-Lithuanian dynasty who ruled over the Czech Lands from 1471 to 1526.

MAGYARS The people who ruled over the Hungarian Kingdom, and now predominate in modern-day Hungary.

MITTELEUROPA Literally German for central Europe, but it also conveys the idea of a multilingual central European culture, lost after the upheavals in post-1945 Europe.

NÁRODNÍ FRONTA Literally the National Front, the dummy coalition of parties dominated by the Communists which ruled the country until December 1989.

NÁRODNÍ OBROZENÍ/NÁRODNÉ OBRO-DENIE The Czech/Slovak national revival movements of the nineteenth century which sought to rediscover the lost identities of the Czech/Slovak people, particularly their history and language.

PŘEMYSLID The dynasty of Czech princes and kings who ruled over the Historic Lands of Bohemia from the ninth century to 1306.

RUTHENIA Officially Sub-Carpatho-Ruthenia, the easternmost province of the First Republic, annexed by the Soviet Union at the end of World War II.

SUDETENLAND Name given to mostly German-speaking border regions of the Czech Lands, awarded to Nazi Germany in the Munich Diktat of September 1938.

UNIATE CHURCH The Uniate Church was formed from various breakaways from the Eastern (Orthodox) Church in the sixteenth century. It retains many Orthodox practices and rituals but is affiliated to the Roman Catholic Church.

VELVET REVOLUTION The popular protests of November/December 1989 which brought an end to forty-one years of Communist rule. Also known as the Gentle Revolution.

ACRONYMS

CKM (Cestovní kancelář mládeže) Youth Travel Organisation.

ČEDOK State travel and tourist agency.

ČSD (Československé státní dráhy) State Railways.

ČSAD (Československá státní automobilová doprava) State bus company.

KSČ (Komunistická strana Československská) The Czechoslovak Communist Party.

OF (Občanské fórum) Civic Forum.

SdP Abbreviation of the Sudeten German Party (Sudetendeutsche Partei), the main proto-Nazi Party in Czechoslovakia in the late 1930s.

StB (Státní bezpečnost) The Communist secret police.

VB (Veřejná bezpečnost) Police.

VPN (Verejnosť proti nasiliu) People Against Violence. The Slovak partner of Civic Forum, formed during the Velvet Revolution.

INDEX

ROUGH GUIDES – THE FULL LIST

EUROPE
- Amsterdam
- Barcelona and Catalunya
- Berlin
- Brittany and Normandy
- Crete
- Czechoslovakia
- Eastern Europe
- Europe
- France
- Germany
- Greece
- Holland, Belgium and Luxembourg
- Hungary
- Ireland
- Italy
- Paris
- Poland
- Portugal
- Prague
- Provence and the Côte d'Azur
- The Pyrenees
- Scandinavia
- Sicily
- Spain
- Tuscany and Umbria
- Venice
- Yugoslavia

Forthcoming:
- Bulgaria
- Romania
- St Petersburg
- Cyprus
- Albania

NORTH AMERICA
- California and West Coast USA
- Florida
- New York
- San Francisco and the Bay Area
- USA
- Canada

CENTRAL AND SOUTH AMERICA
- Brazil
- Guatemala and Belize
- Mexico
- Peru

AFRICA
- Egypt
- Kenya
- Morocco
- Tunisia
- West Africa
- Zimbabwe and Botswana

ASIA & AUSTRALASIA
- Hong Kong and Macau
- Israel and the Occupied Territories
- Nepal
- Turkey

Forthcoming:
- Thailand
- Australia

ROUGH GUIDE SPECIALS

- Mediterranean Wildlife
- Women Travel: Adventures, Advice and Experience
- Nothing Ventured: Disabled People Travel the World

Forthcoming:

- World Music: the Complete Handbook (large format, fully illustrated)

For mail order enquiries please write to:
Marketing Dept. RG, Penguin Books, 27 Wrights Lane, London W8 5TZ, England

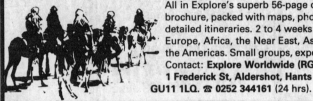

BEFORE YOU TRAVEL THE WORLD, TALK TO AN EXPERIENCED STAMP COLLECTOR.

At STA Travel we're all seasoned travellers so we should know a thing or two about where you're headed. We can offer you the best deals on fares with the flexibility to change your mind as you go – without having to pay over the top for the privilege. We operate from 120 offices worldwide. So call in soon.

74 and 86 Old Brompton Road, SW7, 117 Euston Road, NW1. London.
Manchester. Leeds. Oxford. Cambridge. Bristol.
North America **071-937 9971.** Europe **071-937 9921.** Rest of World **071-937 9962**
(incl. Sundays 10am-2pm). **OR 061-834 0668 (Manchester)**

WHEREVER YOU'RE BOUND, WE'RE BOUND TO HAVE BEEN. ST/

STA TRAVEL

Retail Agents for ATOL Holders.